RECORDS OF WESTERN CIVILIZATION

The See of Peter

RECORDS OF WESTERN CIVILIZATION

A series of Columbia University Press

The Correspondence of Pope Gregory VII: Selected Letters from the Registrum
Translated with an introduction by EPHRAIM EMERTON

Medieval Handbooks of Penance
Translated by JOHN T. McNEILL and HELENA M. GAMER

Macrobius: Commentary on the Dream of Scipio
Translated with an introduction by WILLIAM HARRIS STAHL

Medieval Trade in the Mediterranean World
Translated with introductions by ROBERT S. LOPEZ and IRVING W. RAYMOND

The Cosmographia of Bernardus Silvestris
Translated with an introduction by WINTHROP WETHERBEE

Heresies of the High Middle Ages
Translated and annotated by WALKER L. WAKEFIELD and AUSTIN P. EVANS

The Didascalicon of Hugh of St. Victor: A Medieval Guide to the Arts
Translated with an introduction by JEROME TAYLOR

Martianus Capella and the Seven Liberal Arts, vol. 1
The Quadrivium of Martianus Capella
Translated by WILLIAM HARRIS STAHL and RICHARD JOHNSON with E. L. BURGE

Two Renaissance Book Hunters: The Letters of Poggius Bracciolini to Nicolaus de Niccolis
Translated and annotated by PHYLLIS WALTER GOODHART GORDAN

Guillaume d'Orange: Four Twelfth-Century Epics
Translated with an introduction by JOAN M. FERRANTE

THE SEE OF PETER

BY

JAMES T. SHOTWELL

AND

LOUISE ROPES LOOMIS

COLUMBIA UNIVERSITY PRESS
New York

Columbia University Press
New York Oxford

Library of Congress Cataloging-in-Publication Data

Shotwell, James Thompson, 1874–1965.
The See of Peter / by James T. Shotwell and Louise Ropes Loomis.
p. cm.—(Records of western civilization)
Includes index.
ISBN 0-231-0394-3—ISBN 0-231-09635-6 (pbk.)
1. Papacy—History.
2. Peter, the Apostle, Saint.
3. Church history—Primitive and early church, ca. 30–600.
I. Loomis, Louise Ropes, 1874–
II. Title.
III. Series.
BX955.S5 1991
262′.13—dc20 91-2299
CIP

Casebound editions of Columbia University Press books are Smyth-sewn
and printed on permanent and durable acid-free paper

Printed in the United States of America

c 10 9 8 7 6 5 4 3 2 1
p 10 9 8 7 6 5 4 3 2 1

EDITOR'S PREFACE

The series of which this volume forms a part was planned with reference to a definite need. The growing pressure of the present, which is transforming the outlook of our time by its unprecedented challenge to intelligence, is also making more and more rare in our colleges and universities the adequate training in those implements of research which the historian must use if he is to come into direct contact with the past. It is unnecessary here to discuss the advantages or disadvantages of this drift in education away from the old disciplines. The present age is determined to test the values of its more immediate interests; and certainly the scientist has as good a case for regarding as uneducated the man who does not know the rudiments of the laws of physics, as the historian has for regretting current ignorance on the history of the medieval Papacy. Without entering into this controversy, it may be said that the present series was based upon a recognition of the undoubted fact that something should be done within the field of history to the end that the present tendency toward the study of scientific and contemporary subjects should not result in a complete loss of contact with the original sources from which our knowledge of the past is derived. Therefore it was decided to prepare a number of translations of important documents, not otherwise easily accessible, sometimes *in extenso,* sometimes only as far as they were pertinent to the subject in hand. In other volumes, as in the present one, an anthology of quotations was to trace the documentary outlines of the great historical themes. Then, alongside these translations, a number of guides and studies were to assist the student in fields where the material already exists in greater or less abundance, but where he might still find useful the suggestions of recent scholarship, as in the case of Professor Bewer's *Literature of the Old Testament,* or a richly equipped bibliographical apparatus opening up a field as yet almost undeveloped by historical workers, as in Professor Williams' *Guide to the Printed Material for English Social and Economic History.*

The series was purposely planned to serve as a sort of historical miscellany extending over many fields, on the ground that it would fail of its purpose if it were held strictly within the orthodox lines of history proper. While it still pays most attention to the documentation of subjects included in ordinary historical instruction, it recognizes the legitimacy of historical inquiry in other fields, more especially in those of science itself. It reaches down even to contemporary history, with contributions to the investigation of modern problems for which the vital documents have been hitherto inaccessible.

The place of the present volume in this series needs no explanation. It is a strange, almost an incredible fact, that no such collection has yet been made, in English at least, of the texts on which the historical — as distinguished from the other — claims of the Papacy rest. Indeed there is only one anthology of the originals which is anything like adequate, the collection of the German scholar, Mirbt, *Quellen zur Geschichte des Papsttums*. The fact that this anthology has gone through several editions shows how useful such a volume is for students of Church history. Yet even the Mirbt collection gives but the barest fragments of these original texts, and can be used only by those who can then proceed to work out the setting of the citations by further reading in the literature of the period.

The present volume first took shape along similar lines, but has since become something quite different. It grew out of a seminar in medieval history conducted by the Editor of this series almost twenty years ago. The plan then was to make a guide which, within the compass of somewhat less than the size of the present volume, would cover the entire field of papal history down to Gregory VII, in the eleventh century. It was to have been a book of readings, similar to others already in use in American colleges. A considerable amount of material was prepared with this end in view, and some of the pertinent bibliographical apparatus added thereto, when with the outbreak of the World War all work upon it was interrupted. Fortunately, however, the Editor was able to enlist the interest of Professor Loomis, who had already contributed the translation of the *Liber Pontificalis* to this series, and to her is due the transformation of what was to be little more than an anthology of texts, with short editorial comment, into a volume which covers a more limited period of time but gives a much fuller selection of texts for that period and, in addition to these, discussions which carry the reader some distance beyond the documents into the obscure but vital lines of history which they illustrate. For the latter part of the volume as it stands, the credit should go to Dr. Loomis, and she shares as well the responsibility for much of the earlier part. The translations of texts have been revised by her or else made new. For this coöperation which has made the completion of this volume possible, a coöperation carried through in the face of serious and protracted illness, the present writer would express his grateful recognition. Wherever the volume falls short, the blame may rest upon the shoulders of the Editor who could give to its final form only the fragments of leisure stolen from other occupations. To others who have contributed to make the work possible, in particular to Professor Harold H. Tryon and Professor Preserved Smith who read and criticized portions of the manuscript, and to Harriet J. Church to whom the volume owes its index, the authors are much indebted.

James T. Shotwell

Records of Western Civilization is a new series published under the auspices of the Interdepartmental Committee on Medieval and Renaissance Studies of the Columbia University Graduate School. The Western Records are, in fact, a new incarnation of a venerable series, the Columbia Records of Civilization, which, for more than half a century, published sources and studies concerning great literary and historical landmarks. Many of the volumes of that series retain value, especially for their translations into English of primary sources, and the Medieval and Renaissance Studies Committee is pleased to cooperate with Columbia University Press in reissuing a selection of those works in paperback editions, especially suited for classroom use, and in limited clothbound editions.

CONTENTS

BOOK I THE PETRINE TRADITION

PART I NEW TESTAMENT TEXTS

PART III THE APOCRYPHAL TRADITION

PART III THE SUPREME BISHOPRIC OF THE UNIVERSAL CHURCH

GENERAL INTRODUCTION

The texts upon which the Papacy rests its claims and asserts its great prerogatives, — the vital ones at least, — are so few in number, that it would seem as if they should have been long ago understood and evaluated by every reader of history. But when one examines them in detail, one realizes that the very scarcity of this material but enhances its difficulty. Practically every text has been and still is the object of controversy. For where the texts are few, criticism cannot easily check up one with another and so establish their historical value.

The first problem confronting the historical scholar is to make sure of the genuineness of the document upon which his work depends. This means more than simply to establish the fact that some document similar to that which he has in hand was produced at a certain time and by a certain person. He must identify every part of the text of the document he is using as that of the original, must be certain that the passage upon which he relies is not the addition of some later editor or interpolator; otherwise his problem is not entirely solved and his subsequent conclusion to some extent insecure. Since, however, few genuine texts have come down to us from beyond the Middle Ages, — most documents reaching us in the form of later copies made by scribes in monasteries, — and since these early copies naturally lack the precision of the printing press, modern research is obliged to try to reconstruct the lost original by a comparison of the later texts, noting differences which are due to the peculiarities of individual scribes or of different periods of monastic learning, following clues of similarities which are evidently imposed upon the copyists, and adopting a thousand and one other devices. In this field of textual criticism scholars have in the last century or so achieved remarkable results, of which the reconstruction of biblical texts is perhaps the best known.

The history of the Papacy naturally presents many such problems, and yet so much has been done, partly by polemical writers straining every energy to justify or destroy the texts involved in their controversies, partly by scholars of the judicial temper, weighing the evidence thus adduced, that — outside of the *Liber Pontificalis* which is analyzed in another and parallel volume of this series — there seems little likelihood of serious challenge to the documents at present accepted as genuine. There are some textual problems left, but, upon the whole, textual criticism has apparently almost completed its work. There remain, in addition to the controversies over the New Testament texts, which, of course, are fundamental, some uncertainties over texts for which we are dependent upon a Latin or oriental translation of a lost Greek original, as in the case of Irenaeus, or the *Chronicle* of Eusebius, or upon a quotation by a later writer, like Eusebius, from a document of an earlier day. A few other problems are noted in the following pages. But there seems little likelihood of any very radical change in the present position of textual criticism in this field.

The establishment of a text, however, difficult as it is, is only the preliminary step in the historical reconstruction of the past. It is, upon the whole, an easier task than to estimate the original meaning of the documents in the days when they were first called out or their significance later when they were decisive for policies or institutions. To judge of their original import, one must know the situations which led to their production, the character of the writers or the way in which they wished to be understood. Even when this is satisfactorily established — as is seldom possible — the historian's work is hardly more than begun. For documents, like individuals, have careers in history and their influence sometimes depends less upon their real origin than upon the way in which they coincide with the general outlook and demand of the subsequent age in which they are mainly used. Indeed in some cases an obscure authorship is an asset in the later career, since it permits posterity to attribute a more honorable origin than would be possible if more were known of the production. And to the historian this later, somewhat illegitimate, importance of the document, based upon ignorance, may be as valuable a part of its history as its origin. In any case, the whole history must be kept in mind when dealing with any part.

To illustrate this statement of the importance of viewing documentary history as a whole, let us take a famous document in secular history. Magna Carta offers relatively little difficulty in the line of textual criticism. Its genuineness is established beyond all question; we know when and how it was drawn up and granted, and the readings are not reconstructed from copies made by scribes centuries later. But even so well authenticated a document may be quite misconstrued. For instance, when it called for a trial before one's peers, was it establishing a principle of a national constitution, which, in coming centuries, as trial by jury, should safeguard the liberties of the people, or was it turning back to feudal customs, where justice was rudely dispensed in a suzerain's court? Sceptical scholars, interpreting this and other clauses in the latter sense, have gone so far as to claim that the charter did not become the constitutional landmark it is represented in our school histories, a palladium of liberties and an ideal for government, until the era of the struggle for liberty in the seventeenth century, when it was clothed with retrospective and legendary significance. However that may be, it is clear that subsequent history played its rôle in exalting the original charter to an importance and scope which are hardly justified by the original event. There are, therefore, two charters in English history: the original one and the subsequent one — legendary, perhaps, but more real to history than the mere feudal document.

The only way to understand the historical importance of documents is to know them in their setting at every stage of their history. One must not be blinded to realities by the posthumous glory of those more fortunate ones which have proved valuable to a later age; nor on the other hand leave aside those which have been decisive but once. They must be interpreted by the historical imagination, reproducing both the conditions under which the documents were written and also those under which they were used.

The documents of papal history, in a sense, are singularly like those of the British constitution. The development of the papal monarchy took place in response to inherent forces and under pressure from each successive age. Like the national state, which built ostensibly upon precedent and framed even its revolutions upon pretexts of past models, the Papacy found the justification for its policies and its claims in certain fundamental records. These records are the texts given below.

Most of these texts have been the object of so much theological controversy that it is something of a novelty to bring them to the cold light of historical analysis. And there is perhaps a danger in doing so, if the slightness of the textual evidence is to be accepted thoughtlessly, as sufficient proof in itself that the claims they embody are as slight as they. The fact that there are so few texts cannot be taken by itself to lessen the weight of those we have. Such reasoning would be allowable in modern history, where one would be sure to find numerous references in all kinds of sources to events or documents of any importance whatever. But in the days when the Church was taking shape there were few documents of any kind. If one were to cut out all statements in ancient or medieval history which are unsupported by contemporary evidence, we should have little history left. It is quite possible, to be sure, that much of what we accept as ancient history does rest upon false and wrong data. In the nineteenth century of our era, historians finally rejected such world-old stories as those of the Roman kings and reconstructed the narrative of the Bible, thus branding as unhistorical some of the most fundamental texts in history. The mere fact that documents have been accepted for centuries does not in itself protect them from the tests of historical criticism. Wherever texts are not buttressed up by further contemporary evidence the attitude of that criticism toward them is apt to appear sceptical, or at best reserved, as to their genuineness; and this scepticism is the very soul of scientific work in history. Yet one can go too far, and by failing to realize, through a well-disciplined use of the historical imagination, the conditions which make the existence of corroborating evidence improbable, deny what is really genuine.

For example, the first definite statement which has come down to us that Peter and Paul founded the Roman church, is made by Dionysius of Corinth about 170 A.D. That is a long way from contemporary evidence. We have no lists of the early bishops of Rome until about the same period, and those we have do not quite agree. There is almost a blank, as far as precise documentary evidence goes, for the preceding century; and that was a century of turmoil, persecution and obscurity for the Christians, in which mythical legends of saints and martyrs were springing up. The Christians themselves were, according to pagan critics, rather credulous people and were living under that high emotional pressure in which historic accuracy is of relatively little importance compared with the free life of the spirit. The great growth of what we call spurious apostolic literature in this and the following period points to a continuance of the same unscientific and unhistorical habits of mind. Who, under such circumstances, would be prepared to accept a text a century old as adequate evidence for any historical fact? This is how the case appears to the critic who is predisposed against papal claims. But, on the other hand, whatever other sources there are all point to the existence of some element of fact behind the text. Recent studies in the origins of the Apostles' Creed, for instance, show that there was more than casual reference in the words of Irenaeus, when he intimated that the church at Rome, as was the case with others, preserved "scriptures" which were sufficient to confound the heretics, and which carried the authority of the church back to the apostles. Since Irenaeus, too, wrote in the closing part of the second century, one might perhaps challenge his statement that these scriptures were as valid and genuine evidence as he asserted. But then we come upon the " tradition " of the churches, to which he appealed, and which, at least in his day, was all in favor of the Catholic claims.

Here we strike a problem that can never be solved. What is the value of tradition as a basis for the papal claims? Since, in the nature of things, a tradition is never contemporary evidence, the determination of its value must depend upon verification through other sources. Undoubtedly the tendency to reject tradition went too far in the nineteenth century. It is now generally agreed that tradition, while losing or distorting the details, very commonly embodies some historical elements. This is especially true where varying traditions come back to some essential starting point. If one applies this receptive attitude to the legends of the Church, one is still left with an unsolved problem. For even although this attitude strengthens the probability of the tradition in its general lines, still it by no means excludes the possibility that the details, which tradition by its very nature rearranges or develops at a later time, may in this case be those which are regarded by the critical historian as essential for the claims. Therefore, although it is safe to say that few traditions are more solidly fixed, and few groups of them so readily fuse, as regards their essential facts, as those which support the Petrine claims of the Papacy, this does not finally settle the matter. Indeed it can never be settled, so far as historical evidence is concerned. The Catholic scholar is sure to see more in the argument than the Protestant, because the one is predisposed to accept and the other to refuse.

With reference to the Petrine doctrine, however, the Catholic attitude is much more than a " pre-disposition to believe." That doctrine is the fundamental basis of the whole papal structure. It may be summed up in three main claims. They are: first, that Peter was appointed by Christ to be his chief representative and successor and the head of his Church; second, that Peter went to Rome and founded the bishopric there; third, that his successors succeeded to his prerogatives, and to all the authority implied thereby. In dealing with these claims we are passing along the border line between history and dogmatic theology. The primacy of Peter and his appointment by Christ to succeed Him as head of the Church are accepted by the Catholic Church as the indubitable word of inspired Gospel, in its only possible meaning. That Peter went to Rome and founded there his See, is just as definitely what is termed in Catholic theology a dogmatic fact. This has been defined by an eminent Catholic theologian as " historical fact so intimately connected with some great Catholic truths that it would be believed even if time and accident had destroyed *all* the original evidence therefor." In this sense it may be said that Catholics accept the presence of Peter at Rome, on faith. But they assert at the same time that faith is really not called upon, since the evidence satisfactorily establishes the event as an historical fact.

The following pages present, in the first place, all the texts, as far as the editors have been able to collect them, which form the basis for the Roman belief in Peter's primacy and in his institution of the Roman bishopric. These texts are divided into three groups. The first comprises those in the New Testament which throw light upon the extent of Peter's preëminence among the apostles and the scope of his later labors. The second contains all historical references to Peter's sojourn and death at Rome that can be found in the Greek and Latin Fathers down to the opening of the fifth century, when the Petrine tradition assumed its final shape. These references are, in a few instances, from very early writers, and in every case represent the opinions of sober and conscientious men, derived by them from older authorities now lost or from traditions regarded in their day as genuine. They include little inherently incredible; and many Protestants in these days are willing to concede the plausibility of a part, at least, of the theory built upon them. The third group is made up of a curious and less respectable set of documents, the popular apocryphal literature, which grew up around the figure of Peter almost as soon as reliable records began, literature sprung from misconceptions and confusions or else frankly fictitious. It needs but little attention to distinguish the character of this group of texts from that of the second. Now and then an idea or a picturesque anecdote from this last group is repeated by a serious scholar for its force or illustrative value, but the group as a whole was marked from the first as dubious, untrustworthy or heretical. It played its part, however, in the exaltation of Peter and his See in the general imagination during the centuries when the Papacy was rising to greatness.

After the texts concerned with Peter himself come those which show step by step the development of the institution which he was believed to have founded, texts depicting both the awakening of the popes themselves to a consciousness of their unique position and the gradual recognition by others of their peculiar prerogatives, exegetical arguments drawn from the New Testament, instances of authority actually exercised, disputed or admitted through the first three hundred years after Peter's death.

These texts also are divided into three groups. The first, a collection in the main of random sentences and incidental allusions, comprises every contemporary record that we have of the bishops of Rome to the end of the second century of our era. It is clear toward the close that their position is already one of unusual dignity and prestige. It is not clear, however, that it rests upon more than the accepted fact of the consecration of the Roman church by the two famous missionary apostles, the location of that church in the capital of the Empire, and the number and efficient organization of its members. Our second group of texts carries the chronicle on to the reign of Constantine, at the opening of the fourth century. Through this period again the evidence is intermittent and there are long gaps of years when it fails altogether. But here and there it becomes suddenly comparatively abundant, letters, comments, diatribes, called out for the most part by debatable policies and acts of the Roman See. We cannot always date this material with precision nor tell which pontiff nor what deed of his aroused the agitation. Because we know so little of the circumstances, we cannot organize the material otherwise than loosely, putting together whatever we are fairly sure belongs to the story of one pontificate but leaving much else arranged merely in approximate, chronological order under the name of its author. Yet the light which this spasmodic, controversial literature throws upon the situation is every now and then enough to let us see both the Roman bishop claiming definitely for himself the supremacy over all other bishops as heir in his own person to Peter, the chief of the apostles, and the resentful and hesitant bishops and theologians of the West and the East.

The last group of texts, far exceeding the other two in volume and diversity, portrays the popes of the fourth century, enriched and assisted, save for one short interval, by the friendly emperors, fully accepted as heads and leaders by their colleagues in the West and slowly, by dint of favoring circumstances, convincing even the reluctant East of their right to spiritual predominance. Here we arrive at a time when pontificates can be accurately dated and the character of the man in office read with increasing distinctness in letters of his own writing as well as in the impression he produced upon the religious and secular world of his day. The material, which heretofore it has been impossible to coördinate closely, for lack of exact chronology and information, can now be assembled and grouped more definitely under the head of the particular pope and topic to which it relates. Miltiades, Silvester, Julius, Liberius and Damasus, — the names represent substantial progress in our knowledge of the papal position as well as its own steady advance in power and renown.

If space had permitted, there might have been added here a section devoted to the apocryphal achievements of the early bishops, the spurious acts, miracles and decrees attributed to them, invented apparently, as the apocryphal *Acts of Peter* were invented, to enhance the popular reverence for the supposititious doer. In particular, the legendary *Acts of Silvester* are worthy of consideration, originating, as they probably do, before the period of our study is over, and making bold capital for the Roman See out of the renown of the great Constantine by ascribing that emperor's bodily healing and religious conversion to the agency of the Roman bishop Silvester. Ignored at first by every reputable historian, this fable made its way, gathering volume as it went, reënforced eventually by a forged Donation, until it had imposed upon all Europe the conception of Silvester as the potent influence behind Constantine's most striking measures and of Constantine himself as the dutiful servant of the See of Peter.

Six years before the death of Damasus, our last bishop, in 384, the emperor Valens was defeated and killed by a host of invading Visigoths. Almost unsuspected by men of the day the fall of the Empire in the West had begun and the world in which the Papacy had arisen had started on its swift transformation into the new, strange world of the Goth, the Lombard and the Frank. In the familiar pages of Gibbon, Gregorovius, Hodgkin, Villari and others, that transformation is depicted. Everyone has heard how the dissolution of the imperial fabric in the West opened up fresh vistas of opportunity to the head of the western Church and how the Papacy of Gregory VII and Innocent III grew out of that of Leo I and Gregory I. But the student who has read the records of the Papacy of the Roman Empire is also aware that the famous sermon of Leo on the Petrine supremacy, quoted in so many textbooks, and his assertion of doctrinal authority over the Council of Chalcedon were but repetitions in forcible terms of claims that were first enunciated by his predecessors two hundred years before. Such a student may examine, one by one, all the well-known declarations of papal power from the fifth century to the nineteenth. He will find everywhere the same fundamental theory, propounded and to a considerable extent accepted before the Empire fell, varying only in the details of its working out and of its application to a later age.

BOOK ONE
THE PETRINE TRADITION

PART I

NEW TESTAMENT TEXTS

Introduction

A survey of the evidence of the New Testament for the appointment of Peter by Christ to a position of primacy in the Church and his later exercise of leadership among the apostles raises two distinct problems. In the first place, there is the question of the value of the texts themselves, their authenticity, origin and interrelation, a question which can be answered only by the methods of textual criticism. In the next place, there is the question of the effect of these texts, as they have actually been handed down, upon the doctrines of the Church and the beliefs of mankind.

In this book, it is mainly the second of these problems with which we have to deal, for the New Testament was already formed, or at least the essential portions of it were already compiled, before there was any use of it as documentary proof of the claims of the Roman See. In a general way, the Christian Scriptures and the Church took shape side by side as contemporary and complementary movements. The apostolic and subapostolic ages were not dominated by a great hierarchical system, supported by well regulated archives. They were times of intense, free spirituality, when inspiration was still producing sacred books and apostles and prophets continued to receive and teach " divine oracles." Formal elements were there, but traditions and opinions were not yet fixed and the functions of the local officials, overseers or bishops (ἐπίσκοποι, episcopi) and elders (πρεσβύτεροι, presbyteri) were undefined.[1] Toward the end of

[1] At this primitive stage, the term, elders, or presbyters, seems to have been generally applied to the seniors of the church community and to have included the appointed overseers or bishops, possibly also the deacons. The presbyter does not become a specific official in the clerical hierarchy, *i.e.*, priest, until the latter part of the second century.

the period, one may see both Church and Scriptures[2] emerging from the welter of inspiration and prophecy as solid, visible structures, the preservation of which was thenceforth to be accepted as " orthodox."

This growth of ecclesiastical organization and New Testament canon was at first hindered by the fact that inspiration and prophecy were regarded in the apostolic and sub-apostolic ages as not limited to a definite number of apostles and prophets nor to times in the past. Wandering evangelists still carried the gospel, as Paul had done, " driven by the Spirit," and those who spoke " with tongues " were still likely to interrupt or take over part of the service, even in the presence of bishops and elders.[3] Similarly, inspiration was still producing scriptures, such as *The Shepherd of Hermas*,[4] *The Ascension of Isaiah*,[5] and a whole series of " visions," " parables " and " teachings." This liberty of revelation and lack of any comprehensive system of control led naturally to divergent views of Christian doctrine and disorder in the churches. Paul's epistles display the situation with great distinctness, when he was preaching one form of truth in the north country, Peter another variation, and James and John yet another in the strictly Jewish circles of Palestine.[6] But with the disappearance of the apostles divergences became even more serious and numerous, for the exuberant spirituality, which preserved the prophetic aspects of early days, developed unexpected tendencies toward various kinds of oriental and Greek mysticism and new theologians tried to interpret and adapt it to the speculations of Hellenistic philosophy. Thus arose the first great heresies, in particular the complex and variegated movement known as Gnosticism,[7] which might have swept Christianity entirely away from its early moorings, had it not been held in check, as we have already intimated, by the parallel, conservative development of the institutions of the episcopate and the canon of sacred, Christian Scriptures, upon whose authority the faithful

[2] The word " scriptures " was restricted to the sacred writings of the Jewish synagogue and not used for Christian literature until after the apostolic age.

[3] According to *The Didache* (c. 120–130), it is a sin to interrupt a prophet when in the spirit. However, by this time the local church is cautioned to be sure that the prophet is genuinely inspired.

[4] *Infra*, p. 242.

[5] *Infra*, p. 69.

[6] See especially the Epistle to the Galatians.

[7] *Infra*, p. 77, n. 39.

could rely. At the opening of the second century, Ignatius of Antioch demanded in ringing terms a strong head in the churches to meet the trials of the times and to stand as the representative of Christ.[8] By the middle of the century, the process of the formation of the New Testament was sufficiently advanced for Papias to prepare a book entitled *Interpretation of the Sayings of Our Lord,* in which he described the way in which the gospels had been written.[9] Toward the close of the century, the process was all but complete, as the *Muratorian Fragment,* composed somewhere between 170 and 190 A.D., contains a list of accepted books.[10] By that time the Church had, as well, passed definitely under episcopal control.

This parallel history indicates how, in a general way, the complicated history of the documentary foundation of the Papacy requires two distinct processes. The actual formation of those documents which in the last analysis are the most vital for the claims of the Roman See can be studied only by means of a learned investigation of those parts of the New Testament that reach back to the apostles or to their immediate tradition. In order to arrive at their original significance it is necessary to apply to them the tests of what in theology is called the higher criticism but what is actually nothing more nor less than expert historical criticism. The great history of the Papacy, however, as we have said, did not begin until after the New Testament had acquired practically its present form, so the texts in the shape they had then assumed, familiar to us now and to all Christendom since then, are after all the materials with which the Papacy has always worked and, therefore, of prime importance even as they stand. Reading them as they are, we uncover the bottom foundation on which the Papacy rests; testing them by historical criticism, we probe into the nature of the foundation to ascertain how far it is genuine rock and how far crumbling sand.

This present study, however, contains nothing that can be called textual criticism. The field of New Testament exegetics is a specialist's province and the student must turn elsewhere for a restatement of the texts as they appear after the critic of to-day

8 *Infra,* pp. 71, 239. 9 *Infra,* p. 73. 10 *Infra,* p. 49, n. 60.

has torn them apart and put them together again. The object of the present study is primarily to review, with the addition of a few suggestions and comments, these texts in the form in which they were employed to erect the fabric of a papal monarchy. Therefore the text used is the authorized Catholic translation [11] into English from the Latin Vulgate, which was declared the official text at the Council of Trent (IV Session, April 8, 1546),[12] having been in universal use in the West during the entire Middle Ages, that is, during the long period of practically undisputed realization of the papal claims. Whatever the critic may now think of the origins and meanings of these texts, to Christians of earlier centuries they were indisputably authentic and to the historian of the institution reared upon them they are indispensable as the groundwork underlying the whole structure.

The life of Peter, as recorded in the New Testament, falls naturally into two parts: the first, coeval with the life of Jesus; the second, after Jesus' death and resurrection. In the first part, he appears principally in the relation of a disciple to his master; in the second, as one apostle in the group of apostles. Generally speaking, the sources for the first part lie in the four Gospels, for the second in the Book of Acts and the Epistles. For any connection of Peter with the city of Rome the witness of the New Testament is vague and inconclusive. Such as it is, we give it here, though taken by itself it is insufficient to *prove* anything. Were it not for the tradition that begins to find expression in the writings of the Fathers at a date hardly later than

[11] This version is popularly known as the Douay Version. The translation of the New Testament in this edition was made in 1582 at Rheims, whither the Douay English College was transplanted between the years 1579 and 1593; the completed "Douay" version of the Bible, into which this was incorporated, was published in 1609–1610. The variations in text from editions in use by Protestants are not vital in the case of any citations in question, being for the most part merely slight rearrangement of phrases or the substitution of different synonyms. For the purposes of this history either the King James Edition or the Revised Edition would yield practically the same results. It should be added that while this study does not enter the field of Biblical criticism as such, it deals with some of the chief results of that criticism in so far as it affects the texts relating to the papal claims.

[12] The Council in this session (Session IV) declared, "ut haec ipsa vetus et vulgata editio . . . in publicis lectionibus, disputationibus, praedicationibus et expositionibus pro authentica habeatur," *i.e.*, the Vulgate text may be used for Scriptural proof and is the official text to be used at Catholic services. The Church in adopting the Vulgate as her official version did not maintain that it is a scientifically correct translation of the original texts.

that of the last of the books of the New Testament, Peter's prerogatives, however great, would have lacked their historical relation to the Roman See. This tradition and its outgrowths in legend are traced in the following sections.

1. JESUS AND PETER

THE GOSPEL OF MARK

The prime source for the life of Peter during his discipleship is the Gospel of Mark, if, as seems probable, it was based partly as to substance upon Peter's own recollections. The tradition that this was the case was recorded by Papias toward the middle of the second century.[13] The date for the composition is about 75 A.D., and the place apparently Rome. Mark, listening to Peter's preaching, made note of anecdotes in the life of Jesus, and then, somewhat later, strung these together into a narrative. The narrative displays just the qualities which such an origin presupposes. The gospel is not a biography of Jesus but a collection of striking incidents fitted into a loose scheme. These incidents, therefore, appear to be those upon which Peter placed his emphasis in preaching. If we could be absolutely sure of this and if there were no other elements in the second gospel, we should have here the most direct evidence possible as to Peter's own ideas concerning his relations with Christ. Unfortunately for the historian, the problem is not so simple. For Mark was a companion of Paul as well as of Peter,[14] and his gospel reveals

[13] *Infra,* pp. 73, 80.

[14] The first incident connected with Mark's life is given in Acts XII, 12, where Peter, on his escape from prison, went to "the house of Mary, the mother of John, who was surnamed Mark, where many were gathered together. . . ." The next is an isolated verse (v. 25) attached to the end of the chapter, stating that Barnabas and Saul took Mark with them when they left Jerusalem. In the next chapter, however, Mark leaves them in Pamphylia and returns to Jerusalem (XIII, 13). Paul regarded this as something akin to apostasy and would have nothing more to do with Mark, according to Acts XV, 38, 39, feeling so strongly on the subject that it caused "dissension" between him and Barnabas resulting in a complete rupture. Barnabas took Mark and sailed for Cyprus, while Paul chose another companion, Silas, and went through Syria and Cilicia. With that, Mark disappears from Acts. From the epistles of Paul, however, it is evident that the dissension has been healed. Colossians IV, 10, throws a new light on the incident, from the remark that Mark was a cousin of Barnabas; but Paul now supports his mission. Finally in Philemon, v. 24, Mark is mentioned as a fellow worker by Paul, who is now

sufficient Pauline tendencies to make one hesitate before accepting it as a simple mirror of Peter's point of view. Mark uses his data much as Paul would have done. He is explaining to the Gentiles why Jesus was not recognized by the Jews as the Messiah, and also why the disciples themselves were slow to comprehend. His conception of the significance of Jesus' life is essentially like Paul's. He puts the emphasis upon the death and resurrection and the spiritual Messiahship; and yet the incidents he relates show that that was not the conception of the disciples at the time. It appears almost as though Mark were attempting to write a Pauline gospel with Petrine data. In other words, it would seem as if we have a harmonizer at work, and we can not tell how much of the gospel he wrote reflects the specific attitudes of Peter. One thing, however, does seem clear; and that is that it was at Rome that the first gospel was prepared, and that it was so catholic in temper, so wide in its appeal, and weighted with such apostolic authority as to secure a decided preëminence for itself among the literature of the early Church, and thus to become a mine from which other gospels largely drew.

The part played by Peter in the Gospel of Mark is therefore a question of the first importance for the history of the Papacy; since there, if anywhere, we may look for some account of Peter's own ideas upon his primacy. The results are interesting, if perhaps somewhat disappointing. *For none of the vital texts upon which the Petrine claims rest comes from the Gospel of Mark.* The incidents of Jesus' life are partly grouped around that of Peter, it is true; but there is no assertion of claims nor grant of power. The fact that this gospel was not written to elucidate

---

apparently a prisoner in Rome. Some apply the remark in 2 Timothy IV, 11, where Paul is quoted as charging Timothy to "take Mark and bring him with thee: for he is profitable to me for the ministry," as indicating that Mark was to come from Colossae to Rome expressly to help Paul. So far, all the relations of Mark have been with Paul. But in 1 Peter V, 13, greeting is sent from Rome (Babylon) by the church and "my son, Mark." This little intimate touch, which is generally taken to refer to spiritual parenthood, and more especially to the conversion of Mark by Peter, is to be balanced against the whole Pauline relationship. Mark was apparently a link between the two apostles. The gospel of Mark bears out this impression by its contents. See recent comment on the traditional origin and character of the gospel in F. J. F. Jackson and K. Lake, *The Beginnings of Christianity* (2 vols., London, 1920–1922), Pt. I, vol. I, pp. 267, 316–317.

such matters lessens but does not entirely get rid of the implications of such a silence. For again we must remember that it was written in Rome some years after Peter's death. We shall recur to this point again.

The Call

The story of Mark as to Peter begins with what is generally referred to as " the call." After a short introduction, describing the baptism in the Jordan and the forty days in the wilderness (I, 1–13), we read of Jesus in Galilee preaching and calling to him four fishermen, who follow him as he goes into the synagogues along the seashore and the hills. One of these is Simon, who has a house in Capernaum (Capharnaum), to which Jesus comes when he returns to that town (v. 21). The following texts contain all specific references to Simon in the opening chapters, indeed until we reach the account of the organization of the group of twelve disciples, in the third chapter. The English rendering is that of the Douay Version.

I 16 And passing by the sea of Galilee, he saw Simon and Andrew his brother, casting nets into the sea (for they were fishermen).

17 And Jesus said to them: Come after me; and I will make you to become fishers of men.

18 And immediately leaving their nets, they followed him.

19 And going on from thence a little farther, he saw James the son of Zebedee and John his brother, who also were mending their nets in the ship:

20 And forthwith he called them. And leaving their father Zebedee in the ship with his hired men, they followed him.

21 And they entered into Capharnaum: and forthwith upon the sabbath days going into the synagogue, he taught them.

. . . .

29 And immediately, going out of the synagogue, they came into the house of Simon and Andrew, with James and John.

30 And Simon's wife's mother lay in a fit of a fever . . . [Jesus heals her. By nightfall a great crowd gathers at the door.]

. . . .

35 And rising very early, going out, he went into a desert place: and there he prayed.

36 And Simon and they that were with him followed after him.

The Twelve

In contrast with the informal character of Jesus' preaching in the synagogues and along the countryside in Galilee, and the intimate, personal relationship which exists between him and the little group of fishermen whom he calls first to accompany him, a more formal organization of discipleship is inaugurated with the appointment of "the Twelve," as recorded in the extract from the third chapter quoted below. In the sixteenth verse of this extract, we have as well the only reference in Mark to the definite act of changing Simon's name to that of Peter, which, in the Gospel of Matthew is given in a different setting, — being connected with the incident of Peter's confession.[15] Here the renaming is given no deep significance, but is paralleled by that of James and John. It should be noted, however, that while the name Peter tends from the first to stick to Simon, though Jesus continues to call him Simon up to the last,[16] the characterization of James and John is not treated later as a name at all.

The Twelve are chosen, according to the fourteenth verse of the third chapter, "that twelve should be with him, and that he might send them to preach." The sections of Mark immediately following may be said to deal with this Galilean ministry almost as though these two clauses embodied a program; at first, we are given the story of Jesus in touch with the Twelve, then, a definite

[15] *Vide infra*, p. 25.

[16] *Cf.* XIV, 37, in Gethsemane. "And he saith to Peter: Simon, sleepest thou?"

commission charging them to disperse and, two by two, go about the country preaching the gospel. The instruction of the Twelve is carried on, during this first phase, at times when he can get them by themselves. A crowd generally follows them, but once "when he was alone, the twelve that were with him asked him the parable. And he said to them: To you it is given to know the mystery of the kingdom of God: but to them that are without, all things are done in parables": (IV, 10, 11). A little later in the text, in the passages cited from the sixth chapter, comes the assignment of their mission and the bestowal of the gift of miracle. This is for all the Twelve; nothing is said here as to their mutual relationship. The two passages are as follows:

III 13 And going up into a mountain, he called unto him whom he would himself. And they came to him.

14 And he made that twelve should be with him, and that he might send them to preach,

15 And he gave them power to heal sicknesses and to cast out devils.

16 And to Simon he gave the name Peter;

17 And James the son of Zebedee, and John the brother of James; and them he surnamed Boanerges, which is, The sons of thunder.

18 And Andrew, and Philip, and Bartholomew, and Matthew, and Thomas, and James of Alpheus, and Thaddeus, and Simon the Cananean,

19 And Judas Iscariot, who also betrayed him.

VI 7 And he called the twelve, and began to send them two and two and gave them power over unclean spirits.

8 And he commanded them that they should take nothing for the way, but a staff only: no scrip, no bread, nor money in their purse,

9 But to be shod with sandals, and that they should not put on two coats.

10 And he said to them: Wheresoever you shall enter into an house, there abide till you depart from that place.

11 And whosoever shall not receive you nor hear you:
going forth from thence, shake off the dust from your feet
for a testimony to them.

12 And going forth they preached that men should do
penance.

13 And they cast out many devils and anointed with oil
many that were sick and healed them.

. . . .

30 And the apostles coming together unto Jesus, related
to him all things that they had done, and taught.

31 And he said to them: Come apart into a desert place
and rest a little. For there were many coming and going:
and they had not so much as time to eat.

32 And going up into a ship, they went into a desert
place apart.

33 And they saw them going away: and many knew.
And they ran flocking thither on foot from all the cities,
and were there before them.

Peter's Confession

As he was teaching his gospel and performing miracles in the company of his disciples, Jesus turned upon them one day, on the road from one village to another, with the query: "Whom do men say that I am?" The answer of Peter, "Thou art the Christ," was rebuked and the disciples were charged not to speak so to anyone about him. In Matthew, as we shall see, the passage was rewritten and absolutely reversed. Here, however, the incident is slight and the next follows it as a part of a continuous narrative in which Peter is twice reproved for excessive zeal for his master's glorification.

VIII 27 And Jesus went out, and his disciples, into the
towns of Caesarea Philippi. And in the way, he asked his
disciples, saying to them: Whom do men say that I am?

28 Who answered him, saying, John the Baptist; but some, Elias, and others as one of the prophets.

29 Then he saith to them: But whom do you say that I am? Peter answering said to him: Thou art the Christ.

30 And he strictly charged them that they should not tell any man of him.

31 And he began to teach them that the Son of man must suffer many things and be rejected by the ancients and by the high priests and the scribes: and be killed and after three days rise again.

32 And he spoke the word openly. And Peter taking him, began to rebuke him.

33 Who turning about, and seeing his disciples, threatened Peter, saying: Go behind me, Satan: because thou savourest not the things that are of God, but that are of men.

The Inner Group and the Question of Precedence

Running through the whole gospel is a series of references to the inner group of intimate disciples, Peter, James and John, whom Jesus had first called with Andrew from their fishing boat on the lake of Galilee. For instance, when raising the daughter of Jairus: "he admitted not any man to follow him, but Peter, and James and John the brother of James" (V, 37). They are the ones chosen to witness the scene of the Transfiguration. "And after six days, Jesus taketh with him Peter and James and John and leadeth them up into a high mountain apart by themselves: and was transfigured before them."[17] In this case, as so frequently, Peter is the one who impetuously speaks: "Rabbi, it is good for us to be here" (verse 4 [5]). In the ministry at Jerusalem, to which the remainder of Mark after the eleventh chapter is devoted, it is this inner group of disciples which is at hand on the Mount of Olives, Peter and James and John and Andrew (XIII, 3), and in Gethsemane (XIV, 32, 33). "And he saith to his disciples: Sit you here, while I pray. And he

[17] Mark IX, 1, Douay Version; *cf. ibid.*, IX, 2, King James' Version.

taketh Peter and James and John with him." A study of each of these incidents shows that even in this group Peter occupies a certain personal prominence. The difficulty, however, of coming to a positive conclusion upon the extent of this prominence is increased by the fact that the apostles themselves appear to have had their own disagreements concerning the rank which each was entitled to hold in the future organization of the expected kingdom. The first incident in their controversy occurred in Peter's own house at Capernaum, and is described below in the ninth chapter, verses 32–34 (33–35). The rebuke is plain: "if any man desire to be first, he shall be the last of all and the minister of all." Jesus refused to encourage any ambitions for office or power. The next verses of the same chapter have apparently no bearing upon the dispute; but Matthew connects the two passages. The whole is given here for purposes of comparison.

The question of precedence, however, was not settled by one rebuke. It came up again and again, showing that among the disciples themselves there was still rivalry for honor in the kingdom which they believed Jesus about to establish. Mark records these incidents to show apparently that Jesus himself singled out no one for leadership and forbade his disciples to concern themselves over which one of their number should head them. The replies of Jesus are as insistent as their queries. In the tenth chapter, the question of the rich man entering the kingdom brings out such a response from Jesus as to indicate that his phrase, "the first shall be last," is part of his general outlook on the future and does not apply simply to the one matter of apostolic precedence. The whole extract is of great interest because Matthew employs it later with an additional verse to give it a narrower sense (Matthew XIX, 27–30). The specific problem of the apostles' jealousies is taken up by Mark, however, in verses 35–36 of the same chapter (IX), and is there settled, as far as this gospel is concerned, in the most definite manner.

IX 32 And they came to Capharnaum. And when they were in the house, he asked them: What did you treat of in the way?

33 But they held their peace, for in the way they had disputed among themselves, which of them should be the greatest.

34 And sitting down, he called the twelve and saith to them: If any man desire to be first, he shall be the last of all and the minister of all.

35 And taking a child, he set him in the midst of them. Whom when he had embraced, he saith to them:

36 Whosoever shall receive one such child as this in my name receiveth me. And whosoever shall receive me, receiveth not me but him that sent me.

. . . .

X 26 Who wondered the more,[18] saying among themselves: Who then can be saved?

27 And Jesus looking on them, saith: With men it is impossible; but not with God. For all things are possible with God.

28 Peter began to say unto him: Behold, we have left all things and have followed thee.

29 Jesus answering said: Amen I say to you, there is no man who hath left house, or brethren, or sisters, or father, or mother, or children, or lands, for my sake and for the gospel,

30 Who shall not receive an hundred times as much, now in this time; houses, and brethren, and sisters, and mothers, and children, and lands, with persecutions: and in the world to come life everlasting.

31 But many that are first shall be last: and the last first.

. . . .

35 And James and John, the sons of Zebedee, come to him, saying: Master, we desire that whatsoever we shall

[18] At Jesus' statement that it is easier for a camel to pass through the eye of a needle than for a rich man to enter into the kingdom of God.

ask, thou wouldst do it for us.

36 But he said to them: What would you that I should do for you?

37 And they said: Grant to us that we may sit, one on thy right hand, one on thy left hand, in thy glory.

38 And Jesus said to them: You know not what you ask. Can you drink of the chalice that I drink of or be baptized with the baptism wherewith I am baptized?

39 But they said to him: We can. And Jesus saith to them: You shall indeed drink of the chalice that I drink of; and with the baptism wherewith I am baptized you shall be baptized.

40 But to sit on my right hand or on my left is not mine to give to you, but to them for whom it is prepared.

41 And the ten hearing it, began to be much displeased with James and John.

42 But Jesus calling them, said to them: You know that they who seem to rule over the Gentiles lord it over them: and their princes have power over them.

43 But it is not so among you: but whosoever will be greater, shall be your minister:

44 And whosoever will be first among you, shall be the servant of all.

45 For the Son of man also is not come to be ministered unto: but to minister and to give his life a redemption for many.

Peter's Denial and the Resurrection

The presence of Peter, James and John with Jesus in the garden of Gethsemane has been already noted. The most detailed story that is told of Peter, however, is that of his denial, which bears the marks of personal reminiscence. At the betrayal, "one of them that stood by, drawing a sword, struck a servant of the chief priest . . ." (XIV, 47). Mark, Matthew and Luke leave the incident thus vague. The fourth gospel alone asserts that the assailant was Peter (John XVIII, 10). But when Jesus was led away, "Peter followed him afar off" (XIV, 54) and in the court below denied him repeatedly until a look from Jesus brought him back to shame and bitter repentance. He plays no further part in Mark's gospel; except that at the resurrection, the young man at the tomb said to the women: "But go, tell his disciples and Peter, that he goeth before you into Galilee" (XVI, 7).

The oldest manuscripts of Mark carry the story no farther, stopping with the next verse. The risen Christ is going back to the scene of his ministry, by the sea of Galilee, where lived Peter and James and John. In the text of the New Testament as we now have it, verses 9 to 20 have been added, ending with a charge to all the eleven disciples, "go ye into the whole world and preach the gospel to every creature," with the assurance that they will be accompanied with the power of miracle. "But they going forth preached everywhere, the Lord working withal, and confirming the word with signs that followed" (XVI, 20).

The Gospel of Mark, upon the whole, is singularly lacking in the assertion of claims to special authorization for Peter. The fact that Jesus used Peter's house as the center of his ministry in Galilee is not dwelt upon and there are no especial favors shown Peter. He is mentioned more definitely than the other disciples, but his prominence in the narrative is hardly greater than he as a source of it would be bound to have. Whether one views this absence of specific claims as implying a modest reticence on Peter's part or as an accommodation by Mark to the situation in the Church at the time he wrote, or simply as characterizing a true account of the original situation, the text itself is before us. And it is the most solidly established of the gospels.

THE GOSPEL OF MATTHEW

The Gospel according to Matthew is a still more composite work, much too complex for detailed examination here. But the following points, at least, bear directly upon our problem.

In the first place, its narrative of the "doings" of Jesus is taken literally and almost bodily from Mark. This implies either that in the circles which produced the new gospel no other extensive tradition of the acts of Jesus was available, or that the account of Mark was accepted already as of such authority that it was incorporated inevitably by the compiler. Since the compilation was made undoubtedly in Palestine or Syria, this absence of another tradition or narrative to rival the Petrine Mark is itself of distinct historical significance.

In the second place, the substance of the "sayings" of Jesus, which Matthew adds to Mark, was drawn from another source. Since Luke also used this in blocks, like Matthew, it is relatively easy to distinguish it by picking out what is common to Matthew and Luke but omitted from Mark. This non-Markian source (often referred to as "Q" from the German word *Quelle,* meaning "source"), is mainly composed of "sayings," but it adds a few incidents — such as that of the centurion's child, — and offers some hints of another narrative. Consequently scholars, analyzing the text still further, have concluded that this Q is itself made up of two parts, — the one a Greek narrative and the other a collection of sayings, known as the *Logia,* written in Aramaic (*i.e.* Hebrew). This latter alone is probably what Papias, who is our first informant, writing about a hundred years later, refers to when he says that "Matthew wrote the oracles in the Hebrew language, and everyone interpreted them as he was able."[19] Matthew probably wrote down these first "sayings" about 45–50 A.D., about the time when the church in Rome was being founded. But the whole Gospel of Matthew, as we have it now, is the result of a longer process of development, which was perhaps only completed by the end of the century. Into this tangled problem we cannot enter fully here. The fact remains that from the "doings" of Jesus recorded by Mark, and the composite Q containing mainly the "sayings," the compiler of the Gospel of Matthew drew seven-eighths of his material. Other additions cannot be traced back to any text previous to that of the finished gospel, — that is a text of the closing years of the century, later than Mark by a generation. It is of decided historical interest that it is among these *extra* texts that those are found upon which the Petrine claims rest fundamentally. No inferences are

[19] Eusebius, *Historia Ecclesiastica,* III, 39, 16. *Infra,* pp. 73–74.

here suggested beyond the statement of the results of textual criticism. It is conceivable that the Mark tradition is supplemented by authentic material, reaching back by paths unknown to us to the apostolic age. On the other hand, it must be said that these texts at least lack corroborative evidence enabling us positively to trace them back as far as the rest.

A recent book by authoritative scholars [20] proposes a reasonable hypothesis, that the Gospel of Matthew, as we have it, was compiled at Antioch. This hypothesis is in accord with such evidence as we possess. Peter was the first of the Twelve to go to Antioch and was associated from the first with the Gentile church there. Ancient tradition made him bishop in Antioch before he went to Rome. In the struggle between the Judaistic and Gentile groups in the Church for supremacy, although at first he hesitated, Peter was the one original apostle to take up and champion the broader policy of Paul, both in Samaria and at Antioch, against the conservative Jewish group, headed by James at Jerusalem. The emphasis laid by Matthew's gospel upon the prerogatives of Peter, if its author were an Antiochene, finds therefore a historical explanation. Jerusalem lent its great prestige to any doctrine emanating from it; it had the sacred sites connected with Jesus' life and death, and many apostles who had been his personal disciples. But Antioch had the apostle Peter;

[20] F. J. F. Jackson and K. Lake, *The Beginnings of Christianity,* Pt. I, vol. I, *The Acts of the Apostles,* pp. 329–330. "It is clear that the Matthaean tradition cannot be that of Jerusalem. Two places are suggested by historical probability — Rome and Antioch. At first sight Rome seems natural; but this is due to the impression made by later controversy. There is no trace in the second century that Rome claimed supremacy because of its connection with Peter, nor is there evidence of the special use of Matthew in Rome. The claim of Antioch is less obvious but more probable. The epistles of Ignatius suggest that Matthew was the Antiochene gospel; the tradition that Peter was the first Bishop of Antioch is as old and as probable as that which makes him the first Bishop of Rome. Both reflect his historical connection with these cities, though expressed in the language of later ecclesiastical organization. The hypothesis may therefore be ventured that 'Tu es Petrus' represented originally not Roman but Antiochene thought, and reflects the struggle between Jerusalem and Antioch for supremacy. Jerusalem had James the brother of the Lord, who presided over the flock on Mount Zion. But Antioch claimed that Peter, not James, had been appointed by Jesus; on him, not on James, was the Church founded; and he, not James, had the keys of the Kingdom, to admit or exclude whom he would. This is of course a hypothesis which cannot be demonstrated, but it seems more probable than the suggestion that the passage had originally anything to do with the claims of Rome." In a footnote the author adds: "For the study of Acts, part of the importance of this tentative identification of the Matthaean tradition with Antioch lies in the presumption created against the otherwise probable Antiochene provenance of the editor of Acts."

and the story of his life with the Master, which he had left behind him, — a story in which his own part was often a conspicuously faulty one, — might easily have been interpreted or retouched under these conditions so as to bring out in better perspective the career and work of Peter as locally understood. This would not involve a conscious or deliberate rewriting of history. It would merely call for a change in coloring and the addition of some details necessary to make Peter conspicuous for good and finally the appointed head of the new Church, the Rock on which it was founded.

The Call

The story of Peter according to the gospel of Matthew is obviously based upon the narrative of Mark, — in part, literally. After a somewhat longer introduction, with incidents of the birth and childhood of Jesus, of Herod and John the Baptist, and of the temptation in the wilderness, the first gospel follows the second in its treatment of the ministry in Galilee, but with a variation forced upon it by the other source from which it is drawn, the Q material. The "sayings" of Jesus are naturally quoted here, where they are appropriate. The reader is told what Jesus was teaching as well as when or how he taught. Mark had limited himself more to the latter. The effect, however, is to separate the incidents in Matthew and so to lose some of that sense of intimacy which the Gospel of Mark conveys. This expansion of the narrative in Matthew makes it difficult to quote upon this point; and the fact that whatever narrative there is relating these early events of the ministry is based upon Mark makes quotation unnecessary.

The account of the first call to the fishermen of Galilee, given in Matthew IV, 18–22, is repeated almost verbatim from Mark I, 16–20. But whereas in Mark nothing is said of what was done until the Sabbath, when Jesus taught in the synagogue at Capernaum and then went "immediately" to Peter's house, — which becomes a center to which they return from time to time, — in Matthew, Jesus goes teaching in all the synagogues of Galilee (IV, 23), preaches the Sermon on the Mount (V–VII), and restores the servant of the centurion (VIII, 5–13), before mention is made of his going to Peter's house (VIII, 14; *cf.* Mark I, 30). Moreover, the healing of Peter's wife's mother is to Matthew the main point in the incident; he draws a scriptural proof from it that Jesus was the Messiah. It is not until the seventeenth and eighteenth chapters that Matthew brings in the associations of the group in Peter's house in Capernaum, varying only slightly from Mark as to substance. In studying Matthew, therefore, one must constantly remember that the two sources, Mark and Q, are interwoven so as to furnish one theme.

But the fact that Matthew is somewhat less homely and intimate than Mark does not mean that Peter is treated with less distinction. On the contrary, it is the Gospel of Matthew which contains the prime sources for the historical claims of the Papacy. As we run over these texts in the succeeding sections, constant reference should be made to the corresponding passages from Mark, to note the additions or variations.

The Twelve

As in the case of the first call of Peter, Andrew, James and John and the ministry of Jesus in Galilee, the appointment of the twelve disciples is used by Matthew as an appropriate place in which to insert more of the "sayings," which were to be the gospel taught by the disciples. So instead of a simple statement that Jesus chose twelve disciples "that twelve should be with him and that he might send them to preach," as in Mark III, 14, and that later he sent them forth clothed with authority over unclean spirits, as in Mark VI, 7, the calling of the Twelve becomes in Matthew a formal act, combining the two separate passages of Mark and including a long charge to the disciples, which extends throughout the whole tenth chapter of the gospel. We shall have to refer to this later in connection with Luke's treatment of the event, to which reference should be made. But in the text of Matthew one point must be noted here. That is, that in listing the Twelve, Matthew (X, 2) places Peter first, and in doing so mentions that he is first. It is the view of Catholic theologians that this is a formal statement of Peter's primacy, one of the most definite in the New Testament, a recognition by

Matthew of what was then positively accepted fact.[21] More sceptical views naturally also prevail, according to which there is nothing here but a list of names, beginning perhaps with the most prominent, neither indicating nor implying anything further. The text runs as follows:

X 1 And having called his twelve disciples together, he
gave them power over unclean spirits, to cast them out, and
to heal all manner of diseases and all manner of infirmities.
2 And the names of the twelve apostles are these: The
first, Simon, who is called Peter, and Andrew his brother;
3 James the son of Zebedee and John his brother, Philip
and Bartholomew, Thomas and Matthew the publican,
James the son of Alpheus, and Thaddeus;
4 Simon the Cananean, and Judas Iscariot, who also
betrayed him.
5 These twelve Jesus sent: commanding them, saying:
Go ye not into the way of the Gentiles, and into the city of
the Samaritans enter ye not.
6 But go ye rather to the lost sheep of the house of
Israel.
7 And going, preach, saying: The kingdom of heaven is
at hand.
8 Heal the sick, raise the dead, cleanse the lepers, cast
out devils. Freely have you received, freely give.
9 Do not possess gold, nor silver, nor money in your
purses.
10 Nor scrip for your journey, nor two coats, nor shoes,
nor a staff. For the workman is worthy of his meat.
11 And into whatsoever city or town you shall enter,
inquire who in it is worthy; and there abide till you go
thence.
12 And when you come into the house, salute it, saying: Peace be to this house.

[21] For early use of this, *vide infra*, pp. 94, 163.

13 And if the house be worthy, your peace shall come upon it. But if it be not worthy, your peace shall return to you.

14 And whosoever shall not receive you, nor hear your words, going forth out of that house or city shake off the dust from your feet.

15 Amen I say to you, it shall be more tolerable for the land of Sodom and Gomorrha in the day of judgment, than for that city.

16 Behold I send you as sheep in the midst of wolves. Be ye therefore wise as serpents and simple as doves.

Peter's Confession, — Peter, the Rock

As we have seen, Peter's confession, "Thou art the Christ," as related in Mark is a very simple event, cut short with no specific implications and without further word from Jesus. But in Matthew it becomes something entirely different. It is made the basis for the selection by Jesus of Peter as the foundation for his Church and so gives rise to the strongest text in the arsenal of the Roman See in subsequent ages.

The passage, as indicated below, is an enlargement of the account of Mark, containing in the added material two vital texts: in the eighteenth verse, the doctrinal interpretation of the name which Jesus had given Simon, — mentioned only casually in Mark III, 16; and in the nineteenth, the statement of what is known as "the doctrine of the keys."

The name Peter, by itself, says nothing to the English reader, since the word is not a common noun as well, although we have the root in a few Latinized words like *petrify*. Nor have we actually translated the proper noun, to convey its significance of "rock" or "stone." In the original, as in some modern languages, the implication is apparent. For instance, in Italian Peter is *Pietro* and rock is *pietra*, the two words differing merely in gender. The Italian thereby preserves the Latin *Petrus* and *petra*, which in turn go back to the Greek Πέτρος (*Petros*) and πέτρα (*petra*). But in the Aramaic, the language in which

Peter received his name, even the distinction of gender disappears, *Kepha,* — which the Greek rendered as *κηφᾶς*, *Kephas,* our Cephas, — being exactly the word for a rock,[22] just as in French *Pierre* is the same form and gender for common and proper noun.

The name Peter would have little interest for history, if it had not been linked up with the interpretation given in full in this eighteenth verse of the sixteenth chapter of Matthew just mentioned. That interpretation, which has become the foundation text of the Papacy, has, however, been given varying interpretations itself. The orthodox Catholic view has been the simple and literal one, — that the rock was Peter (Kepha in both cases). But it was also held by some of the Fathers that it was the confession which Peter made — " thou art Christ, the son of the living God " — which was the corner-stone of the Church, since upon that belief the new religion was in reality based. This view was especially seized upon by the Fathers who were disputing with the bishop of Rome or with the heretics who denied the orthodox statement of Christ's divinity. Peter's confession, ratified so emphatically by Jesus, was the strongest text they had.[23] In course of time, however, as the creed was settled, the literal meaning became the common one, exalting the " fisherman's chair " above the other apostolic foundations as the historical embodiment of Christ's promise. This was not seriously challenged until the Protestant theologians found the text, as commonly accepted, a stumbling block in their denial of papal claims. Most of them fell back, then, to the interpretation first discussed, and found support in the fact that some of the Fathers had once so held. Others, however, have maintained that the

[22] Except for this formal naming, Jesus continues, according to the gospels, to call him Simon (except Luke XXII, 34, where the name Peter is added to the text of Mark XIV, 30). When referred to by the writers of the gospels and Acts, however, he is generally spoken of as Peter. In the fourth gospel, he is frequently given both names, Simon Peter, also once in Matthew and once in Luke. Peter is stated to be a surname in Matthew IV, 18.

[23] *Infra*, pp. 317, 589. *Cf.* Epiphanius, *Haereses*, 59. An exhaustive list of such citations is given by P. Ballerini in *De Vi ac Ratione Primatus Romanorum Pontificum* (1770), Chap. XII. There is even a considerable number of papal utterances to the same effect, and when Luther insisted upon this interpretation, Eck, the papal champion, replied (*De Primatu Petri contra Lutherum,* Chap. XIII) that no one denied it.

texts can be so construed as to imply that Jesus was referring to himself as the rock, and not to Peter at all.

The passage runs as follows, bracketing the sections taken from Mark:

XVI 13 [And when Jesus came into the quarters of
Caesarea Philippi: he asked his disciples, saying: Whom
do men say that] the Son of man [is?
14 But they said: Some John the Baptist, and other
some, Elias, and others] Jeremias or [one of the prophets.
15 Jesus saith to them: But whom do you say that I am?
16 Simon Peter answered and said: Thou art Christ]
the son of the living God.
17 And Jesus answering saith to him: Blessed art thou,
Simon Bar-Jona; because flesh and blood hath not revealed
it to thee, but my Father who is in heaven.
18 And I say to thee: That thou art Peter, and upon
this rock I will build my church. And the gates of hell
shall not prevail against it.
19 And I will give to thee the keys of the kingdom of
heaven. And whatsoever thou shalt bind upon earth, it
shall be bound also in heaven: and whatsoever thou shalt
loose on earth, it shall be loosed also in heaven.[24]
20 [Then he commanded his disciples that they should
tell no one that he was Jesus the Christ].

The Question of Precedence and the Apostolic Succession

This central text for the Petrine claims does not stand entirely apart, however, from some others. It should be compared, first of all, with a similar charge to *all* the disciples, two chapters later in the same gospel (XVIII, 15–20). This text, as against the previous one, is a document for the episcopalian theologian, indicating a legitimate succession of *all* the apostles, without

[24] A phrase in use in rabbinical literature in this sense. *Cf.* Isaias XXII, 22.

regard to any special primacy of one. Moreover, if one were to press the interpretation, it might be asserted that these verses in the eighteenth chapter are more suggestive of ecclesiastical institutions and episcopal jurisdiction than those in the sixteenth chapter, the grant of the power of absolution being in a setting that suggests rather definitely the institution of confession.

However that may be, the trend of this text seems to be in line with that which Matthew (XIX, 27–30) adds to the discussion in Mark (X, 23–31) about the rich man entering the kingdom of God. The rebuke to Peter for intimating an interest in the reward for the apostleship of himself and his fellow-disciples is used by Matthew, but with the wording changed to make it more definite. In doing this he inserts the striking clause, "Ye also shall sit on twelve seats judging the twelve tribes of Israel," which, if it presents an implication of equality, yet carries with it no suggestion of ecclesiasticism. Now the significant thing about this clause is that it is from Q, that early source which was also known to Luke. Indeed, this is the only sentence from Q which comes into our survey. The incident itself receives further development from Luke.[25]

The request that James and John be seated on either side of Jesus in his kingdom, which we have already considered in Mark, is repeated in Matthew XX, 17–28, with variations which are relatively unimportant for our purpose. It is their mother who makes the request here; but the reply of Jesus is given in the words of Mark, and the rest of the incident — the indignation of the ten other disciples, with Jesus' further admonition — is also direct quotation. The passage is therefore not repeated here.

Finally, in the very closing words of the gospel, Christ, giving his last charge to the apostles, is quoted as making no distinctions as to their power or mission. The extract seems to contain indications of interpolation, however, as in the reference (XXVIII, 19) to the baptism in the name of the Trinity, which is a formula known to us only in relatively late sources. There is no parallel for it in the other gospels nor in the Acts nor in the Epistles of Paul. So critics are inclined to the conclusion that such an

[25] *Cf.* Luke XXII, 24–32; *infra*, p. 34.

isolated reference as this puts the text later than the early apostolic age; that, in short, it is a product of the time when the doctrine of the Trinity was developing under controversy. The Church of the second century, however, was not provided with sceptical textual critics, and the passage was viewed as containing the divine command. It will be recalled that at the close of Mark there is a passage, likewise suspected of being a late addition, in which in general terms Jesus, after his resurrection and return to Galilee, commits his cause to the apostles and gives them the power of miracle. This incident has become in the closing words of Matthew XXVIII, 16–20, a definite grant of succession.

The three extracts run as follows:

XVIII 15 But if thy brother shall offend against thee, go, and rebuke him between thee and him alone. If he shall hear thee, thou shalt gain thy brother.

16 And if he will not hear thee: take with thee one or two more, that in the mouth of two or three witnesses every word may stand.

17 And if he will not hear them: tell it to the church. And if he will not hear the church: let him be unto thee as the heathen and publican.

18 Amen I say to you, Whatsoever you shall bind upon earth shall be bound also in heaven: and whatsoever you shall loose upon earth shall be loosed also in heaven.

19 Again I say to you, that if two of you shall consent upon earth concerning anything whatsoever they shall ask, it shall be done to them by my Father who is in heaven.

20 For where there are two or three gathered together in my name, there am I in the midst of them.

. . . .

XIX 27 Then Peter answering, said to him: Behold we have left all things and have followed thee: what therefore shall we have?

28 And Jesus said to them: Amen, I say to you that

you, who have followed me, in the regeneration when the
Son of man shall sit on the seat of his majesty, you also
shall sit on twelve seats judging the twelve tribes of Israel.
29 And everyone that hath left house or brethren or
sisters or father or mother or wife or children or lands, for
my name's sake, shall receive an hundredfold and shall
possess life everlasting.
30 And many that are first shall be last: and the last
shall be first.

. . . .

XXVIII 16 And the eleven disciples went into Galilee,
unto the mountain where Jesus had appointed them.
17 And seeing him, they adored him: but some doubted.
18 And Jesus coming, spoke to them, saying: All power
is given to me in heaven and in earth.
19 Going therefore, teach ye all nations: baptizing them
in the name of the Father and of the Son and of the Holy
Ghost,
20 Teaching them to observe all things whatsoever I
commanded you. And behold I am with you all days, even
to the consummation of the world.

THE GOSPEL OF LUKE

The Gospel of Luke was apparently written about the same time as the complete Matthew, the main proof of its date being that, although the author claims to have read many sources, he shows no acquaintance with the first gospel. He uses Mark and the Q text, but adds to them a different set of addenda from Matthew's and gives them different editorial treatment. If, on the other hand, the supposition be true that he used the *Antiquities of the Jews* by the Jewish historian Josephus, he must have written later than 96 A.D.

Internal evidence tends to exclude Judaea as the place of authorship. The gospel of Luke carries with it the note of Hellenistic Judaism, although it preserves in its composite narrative marks of the narrower Jewish conception.[26] Eusebius records a tradition that Luke was an Antiochean by birth,[27] and Antioch has been suggested as the probable place of origin of the completed gospel. But in that case there is difficulty in accepting the theory, referred to above, that the Gospel of Matthew originated in Antioch as well; for even if Luke's ignorance of Matthew might be explained by a prior dating of his text, that would merely transfer the problem to the text of Matthew. The supposition that the Aramaic Christians of Antioch were so much out of touch with the Greek-speaking Christians as to make it possible for each group to produce a gospel of which the other was wholly ignorant is hard to follow. However, it is fortunately no part of the historical problem of this book to trace these texts far into the realm of conjectural origins.

In order to judge what was the attitude toward Peter both in the sources used and in the circles using them which Luke represents, one should not separate the gospel from the book of Acts, which is its continuation. But our plan of analysis involves a division of the two phases of Peter's life, — that of the disciple with Jesus, treated first, and that of the apostle, afterwards. Confining ourselves here, therefore, to the gospel, we are confronted with a relative poverty of references, and such as there are require little comment.[28]

The Call

In the first place, we have the story of the call, told in a different mood from the simple, unembellished tale of Mark. Luke introduces a miracle, rearranging the order of the story slightly.

V 3 And going into one of the ships, that was Simon's, he desired him to draw back a little from the land. And sitting, he taught the multitudes out of the ship.

4 Now when he had ceased to speak, he said to Simon:

[26] The reluctance to allow the Jewish Christians to eat unclean meats, as Paul was wont to do, is more clearly shown in Acts.

[27] Eusebius, *Historia Ecclesiastica,* III, 4, 7.

[28] It is unnecessary to repeat every reference already given by Mark, where Luke simply quotes him.

Launch out into the deep and let down your nets for a draught.

5 And Simon answering said to him: Master, we have laboured all the night, and have taken nothing: but at thy word I will let down the net.

6 And when they had done this they enclosed a very great multitude of fishes: and their net broke.

7 And they beckoned to their partners that were in the other ships, that they should come and help them. And they came, and filled both the ships, so that they were almost sinking.

8 Which when Simon Peter saw, he fell down at Jesus' knees, saying: Depart from me, for I am a sinful man, O Lord.

9 For he was wholly astonished, and all that were with him, at the draught of the fishes which they had taken;

10 And so were also James and John, the sons of Zebedee, who were Simon's partners. And Jesus saith to Simon: Fear not; from henceforth thou shalt catch men.

11 And having brought their ships to land, leaving all things, they followed him.

The Twelve and the Seventy

Similar to the treatment of "the Call" is Luke's narrative of the appointment of the Twelve. Again, with but a slight change in the wording, we are given the incident described by Mark, but there is an added touch of formality, indicating a definite setting apart of the twelve apostles, so that when Jesus appeared in public shortly afterwards he was accompanied by the group as a group, one to be distinguished henceforth from other men.

VI 13 And when day was come, he called unto him his disciples: and he chose twelve of them (whom also he named apostles):

14 Simon, whom he surnamed Peter, and Andrew his
brother, James and John, Philip and Bartholomew,
15 Matthew and Thomas, James the son of Alpheus,
and Simon who is called Zelotes,
16 And Jude the brother of James, and Judas Iscariot,
who was the traitor.
17 And coming down with them, he stood in a plain
place, and the company of his disciples, and a very great
multitude of people from all Judea and Jerusalem, and the
sea-coast both of Tyre and Sidon.

Luke's treatment of the story of the appointment of the disciples by Jesus is important, less for its historical value than for the light it throws upon the way in which Luke handles his sources. Unlike Matthew, when he finds somewhat parallel incidents in Mark and in Q, he does not fuse them together. Since, therefore, Mark and Q had each a passage in which the disciples were sent upon their mission, charged with the gospel teaching and endowed with the power of miracle, Luke treats these as referring to two separate incidents, the one in which twelve were chosen, the other in which seventy were chosen. The text given below indicates by italics the part taken from Mark and by quotation marks that taken from Q. Comparison of these texts with those of Matthew shows that Luke applies to the Seventy whole sections of the Q texts which Matthew applies to the Twelve. With reference to the Seventy, it is interesting to find that Eusebius, in the early fourth century, could find no trace of a list of them,[29] and some modern critics have conjectured that the symbolic number, seventy, was used by Luke as furnishing a

[29] Eusebius, *Historia Ecclesiastica,* I, 12, 1, 3. "The names of the apostles of our Saviour are known to everyone from the gospels. But there exists no catalogue of the seventy disciples." Eusebius goes on to say that Clement of Alexandria called Barnabas one of the Seventy and insisted that the Cephas whom Paul withstood at Antioch was another; Matthias, the successor of Judas, and Thaddeus are also said to belong to the Seventy, — evidently from tradition. But "upon examination you will find that our Saviour had more than seventy disciples, according to the testimony of Paul, who says that after his resurrection from the dead he appeared first to Cephas, then to the Twelve, and after them to five hundred brethren at once. . . ."

proper setting for his text from Q, which would otherwise lack application.[30]

All of this seems to be taking us far from Peter and his apostleship. But the appointment of the whole body of disciples must also be considered as well as the call of Peter himself.

IX 1 Then *calling* together *the twelve apostles* he " gave them " power and *authority* over all devils and to " cure diseases."

2 And *he sent* them to " preach the kingdom " of God, and to heal the sick.

3 And he said to them: *Take nothing for your journey, neither staff, nor scrip, nor bread,* " nor money "; *neither* have *two coats.*

4 And " whatsoever " *house you shall enter into abide there* and *depart* not from *thence.*

5 *And whosoever will not receive you,* " when ye go out of that city," *shake* off even " the dust " of *your feet for a testimony against them.*

6 And going out, they went about through the towns, preaching the gospel, and healing everywhere.

. . . .

X 1 And after these things, the Lord appointed also other seventy-two. And he *sent* them *two and two* before his face into every city and place, whither he himself was to come.

2 And " he said to " them: " The harvest indeed is great, but the labourers are few. Pray ye therefore the Lord of the harvest that he send labourers into his harvest." [31]

3 Go: " behold I send you as lambs in among wolves."

4 Carry neither purse, " nor scrip, nor shoes "; and salute no man by the way.

[30] It should be recalled that there had been, traditionally, seventy translators of the Old Testament from Hebrew into Greek, — the Septuagint, — and that the Jewish Sanhedrim had seventy elders.

[31] *Cf.* Matthew IX, 37, 38, where this text is used as a preface to the call to the Twelve. The following verse curiously enough was used by Matthew to close his narrative. The transposition is obviously not without design.

5 And " into whatsoever " house " ye enter," first say,
" Peace " be to this house.
6 And if a son of peace be there, " your peace " shall
rest " upon him; but if not," it shall " return to you."
7 And in the same house, remain, eating and drinking
such things as they have: for the labourer is worthy of his
hire. Remove not from house to house.
8 And " into what city soever you enter," and they
receive you, eat such things as are set before you.
9 And " heal the sick " that are therein, and say to
them: " The kingdom of God is come nigh " unto you.
10 But " into whatsoever city you enter," and they receive you not, going forth into the streets thereof, say:
11 Even " the very dust " of your city, that cleaveth
to us, we wipe off against you. Yet know this, that " the
kingdom of God is at hand."
12 " I say to you, it shall be more tolerable at that day
for Sodom than for that city."

Peter's Confession

This event is treated by Luke as it came to him from Mark, with none of the additions of Matthew. Only the setting is changed.

IX 18 And it came to pass, as he was alone praying, his
disciples also were with him: and he asked them, saying:
Whom do the people say that I am?
19 But they answered and said: John the Baptist; but
some say, Elias; and others say that one of the former
prophets is risen again.
20 And he said to them: But whom do you say that I
am? Simon Peter answering, said: The Christ of God.
21 But he strictly charging them, commanded they
should tell this to no man.

The Question of Precedence

The text concerning the difficulty of the rich man entering the kingdom of God, which is used by Mark (X, 31) to bring in the text that the first shall be last, and by Matthew as the setting for the statement that the Twelve "shall sit on twelve seats judging the twelve tribes of Israel" (XIX, 28), lacks any such implications in Luke (XVIII, 28–30), where both these texts are omitted, leaving the incident one that does not bear upon our question.

The dispute as to precedence, however, is dealt with at length in the twenty-second chapter, in a variant narrative which brings in the text promising the twelve thrones, which Luke omitted from the earlier passage. More significant, however, is the addition of a new charge to Peter alone, which on the face of it seems to give Peter a distinct place over "the brethren." Who the brethren are, and what the extent of the mission so entrusted to Peter will remain matters of controversy.

XXII 24 And there was also a strife amongst them, which of them should seem to be the greater.

25 And he said to them: The kings of the Gentiles lord it over them; and they that have power over them are called beneficent.

26 But you not so; but he that is the greater among you, let him become as the younger: and he that is the leader, as he that serveth.

27 For which is greater, he that sitteth at table, or he that serveth? Is not he that sitteth at table? But I am in the midst of you, as he that serveth.[32]

28 And you are they who have continued with me in my temptations.

29 And I dispose to you, as my Father has disposed to me, a kingdom;

[32] It should be recalled that beginning with Gregory I the popes regularly took the title "servus servorum Dei," servant of the servants of God.

30 That you may eat and drink at my table, in my
kingdom: and may sit upon thrones, judging the twelve
tribes of Israel.
31 And the Lord said: Simon, Simon, behold, Satan hath
desired to have you, that he may sift you as wheat.
32 But I have prayed for thee, that thy faith fail not;
and thou, being once converted, confirm thy brethren.
33 Who said to him: Lord, I am ready to go with thee
both into prison and to death.
34 And he said: I say to thee, Peter, the cock shall not
crow this day till thou thrice deniest that thou knowest
me. . . .

The Apostles After the Resurrection

Finally, at the close of the gospel, it is intimated that Jesus appeared specially to Simon, — an event which undoubtedly would be regarded as of the greatest significance. The rest of the story is given in Acts, which is the continuation of this gospel.

XXIV 33 And rising up, the same hour, they went back
to Jerusalem: and they found the eleven gathered together,
and those that were with them,
34 Saying, The Lord is risen indeed and hath appeared
to Simon.[33]

THE GOSPEL OF JOHN

The authorship of the fourth gospel is the subject of the most serious controversy in the whole field of New Testament criticism. From early times, at least from the latter part of the second century, until the nineteenth, no one, except a few sceptical English Deists, questioned that it was written by St. John the Divine, that son of Zebedee who belonged, with his brother James and with Peter and Andrew, to the little group of Galilean fishermen whom Jesus first chose, and who formed the most intimate

[33] It is not clear if this refers to the incident on the road to Emmaus, just related, or not.

circle with Jesus. The gospel itself does not state this, but has a method of referring to the author without naming him, as the "disciple whom Jesus loved," a phrase which occurs several times.[34] Twice the indication of authorship by this disciple is definite: in the twenty-sixth and twenty-seventh verses of the nineteenth chapter, after describing how on the cross Jesus "had seen his mother and the disciple standing whom he loved," the writer tells how Mary was committed to the disciple's keeping.[35] Then, after relating how Jesus died before the soldiers had broken his legs, as they did those of the others, and how they pierced his side, the text runs: "And he that saw it hath given testimony: and his testimony is true. And he knoweth that he saith true: that you also may believe."[36] The statement that the author, or his source, was an eye-witness, and the inference that that eye-witness was the beloved disciple, is plain. But the passage continues: "For these things were done that the scripture might be fulfilled: You shall not break a bone of him. And again another scripture saith: They shall look on him whom they pierced." Such an obviously doctrinal treatment of the incident as indicated by this latter part of the passage leaves some room for the sceptical critic to doubt whether the attribution or implication of authorship is not on a par with the use of Messianic prophecy. The other reference to the author comes in the last chapter (XXI, 24), where, after referring to Jesus' last words concerning the beloved disciple, a similar assertion of authenticity occurs. "This is that disciple who giveth testimony of these things and hath written these things; and we know that his testimony is true." Again, as above, the sceptical critic is inclined to feel that this protests somewhat overmuch for an account coming with all of the authority of an intimate disciple. Some one else, — "we," — verifies the narrative with something like an episcopal imprimatur. Indeed the whole of this last chapter reads like an appendix, added later. The gospel proper comes to a close at the end of the twentieth chapter, with which this does not readily connect.

In addition to these two references to the author from the

[34] *Vide* XIII, 23 *sqq.*; XIX, 25–35; XX, 1–10.
[35] XIX, 27.
[36] XIX, 35.

gospel itself, the opening passage of the First Epistle of John should also be cited as contributory evidence.[37]

I 1 That which was from the beginning, which we have
heard, which we have seen with our eyes, which we have
looked upon and our hands have handled, of the word of life,
2 For the life was manifest: and we have seen, and do
bear witness and declare unto you the life, the life eternal,
which was with the Father and hath appeared to us,
3 That which we have seen and heard we declare unto
you: that you also may have fellowship with us . . .

. . . .

5 And this is the declaration which we have heard from
him . . .

For scholars agree that whoever wrote the gospel also wrote the epistles which go by the name of John. On the face of it, the question as to authorship might therefore seem settled; none of the other gospels has so definite a text. And yet the drift of criticism is more and more towards a denial of the apostolic authorship of the whole series, — gospel and epistles, — and also of Revelation, of which we have not spoken here. This is naturally a matter of importance in connection with the Petrine texts, for although there are few of much significance in the fourth gospel, the prominence of another apostle, whom Jesus especially loved and favored, bears upon the question of the primacy of Peter.

When we turn to the evidence of other sources, we find that the earliest to ascribe the gospel to John are from the end of the second century, — Theophilus of Antioch and the *Muratorian Fragment*.[38] This is relatively late, but there is no contrary tradition;[39] and from that time on the testimony of the Fathers is universally in favor of the Johannine authorship. As to John's

[37] First Epistle of John I, 1–3, 5.

[38] *Infra*, p. 49, n. 60.

[39] A small sect in the second century, the Alogi, rejected it on doctrinal grounds, since they objected to its *logos* teaching.

later life, there is a similar unanimity of statement, which runs in harmony with the supposition that he wrote the books. For it was held that he passed this time mainly in Ephesus — that seat of Pauline Christianity, which *all* agree was the city at which the books appeared. Irenaeus records that his former master Polycarp, bishop of the neighboring city of Smyrna, was a personal disciple of the apostle John, — who lived in Ephesus until the reign of Trajan (98–117).[40]

The bishop of Ephesus in Irenaeus' day, Polycrates,[41] adds similar testimony, and so does Clement of Alexandria.[42] All of these sources have been pieced together by Eusebius in the third book of his *Church History,* and have been accepted not merely as a preservation of tradition, but as direct documentary evidence.[43] By the third century, the evidence was embellished with further details.[44] We need not, however, follow it further in its career.

This, at first glance, would seem to make out an unquestionable case for the Johannine authorship. Yet critics who are inclined to reject it, point to the fact that Clement of Rome in his

[40] On Irenaeus *vide infra,* pp. 76, 261. His statements, that he studied under Polycarp and that Polycarp had known John, are in the Epistle to Florinus, written in the pontificate of Victor (see below) and quoted by Eusebius, *Historia Ecclesiastica,* V, 20, 5–6. " For when I was a boy, I saw thee [Florinus] in lower Asia with Polycarp. . . . I remember the events of that time more clearly than those of recent years. For what boys learn, growing with their mind, becomes joined with it; so that I am able to describe the very place in which the blessed Polycarp sat as he discoursed, and his goings out and his comings in, and the manner of his life, and his physical appearance, and his discourses to the people, and the accounts which he gave of his intercourse with John and the others who had seen the Lord." At the opening of the third book of his *Adversus Haereses,* written during the pontificate of Eleutherus, 174–189, A.D., Irenaeus further says that " John, the disciple of the Lord, who leaned upon his breast, published a gospel during his residence at Ephesus in Asia." (III, 1, i; *cf.* also III, 3, iv; II, 22, v.)

[41] The antagonist of Pope Victor in the paschal controversy. *Vide infra,* p. 280. Polycrates was upholding the dignity of the Asian see against Rome, by reference to the apostolic foundation. " Moreover John, who was both a witness [μάρτυς] and a teacher, who reclined upon the bosom of the Lord, and being a priest wore the sacerdotal plate. He also sleeps at Ephesus." (Eusebius, *Historia Ecclesiastica,* III, 31, 3.) Legend (or the needs of a polemic) seems already at work.

[42] In *Quis Dives Salvetur,* XLII; Eusebius, *op. cit.,* III, 23.

[43] *Cf.* A. C. McGiffert, *A History of Christianity in the Apostolic Age* (New York, rev. ed., 1916), p. 606, n. 2, referring to Irenaeus, " Weizsäcker justly remarks that this is not tradition, but documentary evidence. (Eng. Trans., II, p. 168.)"

[44] Tertullian added the miracle of John surviving an immersion in boiling oil. *Infra,* p. 294.

epistle to the Corinthians, written at the close of the first century, refers to the apostles as though they were all dead at that time,[45] and call attention to the silence of Ignatius, who wrote a letter to Ephesus a few years later without a reference to John. They point out how, during the sub-apostolic age, the process of legend-making began at an early date and often by way of apocryphal books attributed to apostles and supported by an ever widening cycle of traditions. They maintain, therefore, that the evidence of Irenaeus, writing over three quarters of a century later, is, after all, not contemporary. But their main reason for the rejection comes from the content of the gospel itself. They assert that the little we know of John through Paul's reference in Galatians (II, 9) and Mark's description (I, 19; IX, 37, 38; X, 35–41) gives no impression of the kind of man who could write a book like the fourth gospel. They see in it a treatise written with the purpose of giving the authority of Christ to an "orthodox" doctrine, — emphasizing his life "according to the flesh" as over against the Docetists, who had carried Paul's insistence upon the Spirit to such an extent as to regard Jesus as a phantom, unsubstantial, merely appearing like a man. The keynote of this gospel is given at the first; it is a story of how "the Word was made *flesh* and dwelt among us" (I, 14). Its purpose is not, say these critics, what Eusebius claimed it was, to supply an account of what the other three evangelists had omitted, — mainly the deeds done by Jesus at the beginning of his ministry,[46] — but to offer an interpretation of the life, — drawn largely from different sources, unknown to us, — which would carry conviction to his readers, but which the critic of today finds less reliable than the narrative of the first three gospels.

The only points upon which there seems to be substantial agreement are that the gospel was written at Ephesus, and that its date is about 105 to 110 A.D.

Obviously the historical value of the texts in the fourth gospel depends upon whether it was written by John or not. If it is a product of an external tradition, compounded of doctrine and

[45] *Vide infra*, pp. 237–238.

[46] Eusebius, *op cit.*, III, 24, 8.

miraculous legend, its evidence as to the relations of Jesus with Peter is of no historical value whatever. But, on the other hand, whether originally valid or not, from the second century it has been accepted as genuinely Johannine, and that belief is itself a historic fact, investing the gospel with the full degree of apostolic authority throughout the Church's history.

The Call

As we have indicated, there are few separate passages bearing upon Peter's life. The fourth gospel has little to say on the apostolic history; it concentrates upon Jesus' teaching and miracles. In fact the entire treatment of the history is different from that of the other three gospels. This is evident at the very outset, where the scene of the call of Peter is transferred from the Sea of Galilee to the Jordan at the time of the baptism of Jesus by John the Baptist. The naming of Simon " Peter " is also brought into the same incident.[47]

I 35 The next day again John stood and two of his disciples;

36 And beholding Jesus walking, he saith: Behold, the Lamb of God.

37 And the two disciples heard him speak; and they followed Jesus.

38 And Jesus turning, and seeing them following him, saith to them: What seek you? Who said to him, Rabbi (which is to say, being interpreted, Master), where dwellest thou?

39 He saith to them: Come, and see. They came and saw where he abode: and they stayed with him that day. Now it was about the tenth hour.

40 And Andrew, the brother of Simon Peter, was one of the two who had heard of John and followed him.

[47] Unless one takes the future tense to mean that Jesus will some day later bestow the name Peter (as in F. Vigouroux, *Dictionnaire de la Bible*, 5 vols., Paris, 1895–1912, Article, " Pierre "), which seems to make the text rather a lame one, especially inasmuch as John has no later reference to it.

41 He findeth first his brother Simon, and saith to him: We have found the Messias, which is, being interpreted, the Christ.

42 And he brought him to Jesus. And Jesus looking upon him, said: Thou art Simon the son of Jona. Thou shalt be called Cephas, which is interpreted Peter.

Peter's Confession

Peter's confession that Jesus was the Christ, which Matthew uses as the basis for the grant of the keys, is entirely lacking in the fourth gospel, the nearest approach to it being in VI, 67–72 (King James' Version, verses 66–71), when the followers of Jesus were leaving him because of his veiled references to his death.[48] Peter, whose name had not been mentioned since the scene at the Jordan, spoke up, but not in exactly the phrase of Mark or Matthew. The passage also contains the first reference to the Twelve. It is typical of the gospel that it is so casual. The author draws no further implication from the incident but turns abruptly to another theme.

VI 67 After this, many of his disciples went back, and walked no more with him.

68 Then Jesus said to the twelve: Will you also go away?

69 And Simon Peter answered him: Lord, to whom shall we go? Thou hast the words of eternal life.

70 And we have believed and have known that thou art the Christ, the Son of God.[49]

71 Jesus answered them: Have not I chosen you twelve? And one of you is a devil.

[48] The reference bears indications of the familiarity on the part of the writer with later church services, as the eucharist is obviously in his mind. "Except ye eat of the flesh of the Son of man and drink his blood, ye have not life in yourselves."

[49] The King James Version has "that Christ, the Son of the living God," as in Matthew. The Revised Version, following a different text, has "thou art the Holy One of God."

72 Now he meant Judas Iscariot, the son of Simon; for this same was about to betray him, whereas he was one of the twelve.

Apostolic Succession

In the body of the fourth gospel, none of the vital texts for the Petrine theory is repeated. The only passages in which Peter plays a distinctive rôle are the feet-washing scene, in which Peter was the only one of the disciples who objected to Jesus' action (XIII, 5–11), the statement that it was Peter who drew his sword and cut off the ear of the servant of the high priest (XVIII, 10–11),[50] and the story of Peter's denial of Christ (XIII, 36–38, XVIII, 15–27). At the last supper (XIII, 23–25), it is not Peter but the "one of his disciples whom Jesus loved" who is closest to Jesus. Peter has to beckon to him to question Jesus about the delicate problem as to who is the traitor, not venturing himself.[51] At the crucifixion, as we have seen,[52] the beloved disciple was alone to support Mary, the mother of Jesus. And finally when Mary Magdalene found the tomb open and ran "to Simon Peter and to the other disciple whom Jesus loved" to tell them, the two ran to the tomb, and the "other disciple did outrun Peter and came first to the sepulchre" (XX, 4), although Peter entered first into the tomb (XX, 6–8). Whether this prominence of John in the narrative was the historic fact, as preserved in John's own memory and recorded by him, — as the orthodox hold, — or was due to the same insistence upon the part of the anonymous author, — as the critics believe, — that the source of this gospel was the most authentic representative of Jesus' teaching, the fact remains that the fourth gospel so far offers no text in which Jesus singles out Peter for primacy.

On the other hand, after the resurrection, Christ bestows the power of the keys upon all the disciples together.

XX 19 Now when it was late, that same day, the first of the week, and when the doors were shut, where the disciples

[50] *Vide supra,* p. 16.

[51] XIII, 23. Now there was leaning on Jesus' bosom one of his disciples, whom Jesus loved. 24. Simon Peter therefore beckoned to him, and said to him: Lord who is it of whom he speaketh?

[52] *Vide supra,* p. 36.

were gathered together, for fear of the Jews, Jesus came and stood in the midst and said to them: Peace be to you.

20 And when he had said this, he shewed them his hands and his side. The disciples therefore were glad, when they saw the Lord.

21 He said therefore to them again: Peace be to you: As the Father hath sent me, I also send you.

22 And when he had said this, he breathed on them, and said to them: Receive ye the Holy Ghost.

23 Whose sins you shall forgive, they are forgiven them: and whose sins you shall retain, they are retained.

The Pastoral Charge

The last chapter of the fourth gospel is regarded by some critics as an appendix, written by another hand. The gospel narrative comes to a fitting close at the end of chapter twenty. The story ends, like Luke's, in Jerusalem; and apostolic succession is given to all the apostles together, as we have just seen. Throughout the whole gospel, Peter plays no preëminent rôle; it is John who is the favorite, the intimate companion. This is the character of the narrative, which ends at the close of the twentieth chapter by a formal statement that this is all there is in this gospel: "Many other signs also did Jesus in the sight of his disciples, which are not written in this book. But these are written, that you may believe that Jesus is the Christ, the Son of God, and that believing you may have life in his name" (XX, 30, 31). The opening words of the next chapter indicate that it was added as a supplement, — whoever wrote it. "After this, Jesus shewed himself again to the disciples at the sea of Tiberias." The use of this name for the Sea of Galilee shows that it was added in the second century. When one turns to the contents of the chapter, the trend is seen to be quite different from that of the rest of the gospel. For here Peter is exalted, both in figurative and in direct language, finally receiving a charge for which the rest of the gospel seems to have furnished little preparation. It is true that "the beloved disciple" is still the discerning one (verse 7), but it is Peter who alone pulls in the net and who is then, after a meal described in terms suggestive of eucharistic ritual (verse 13),[53] singled out by Jesus with the impressively reiterated "Feed my lambs." It has, therefore, been suggested that this appended chapter was written to give a Petrine close to a gospel which, proceeding from a center of Pauline Christianity, Ephesus, had the great name of John as witness of a story of the life of Jesus, rich in novel detail and emphatic in its assertion of authority, treating Peter as a person of secondary importance even among the disciples. The last chapter made more easy accommodation for this gospel alongside the other three, in so far as a consistent catholic, apostolic tradition was sought. Some critics therefore suggest that it was added in Rome.

One need not accept these hypotheses nor follow the speculations based upon them. The fact remains, however, that in the last chapter of the fourth gospel we have a definite Petrine passage. Just how much we should make out of it is a matter of interpretation, in which the doctrinal bias of the interpreter will tend to show itself. The chapter, as will be seen, is divided into three main sections: the first includes the first fourteen verses, dealing with the miraculous draught of fishes which Peter pulls in; the second, verses 15, 16 and 17, contains what is known as the Pastoral Charge; the rest of the chapter contains references to Peter's death and John's old age. A postscript from the author closes the chapter. The main difficulty lies in the meaning of the first section. Taken literally, it hardly seems to have any bearing upon the problem. But was it meant to be taken literally? The literature of that period was so largely symbolical that it seems to some modern critics more easy of interpretation if viewed in the light of an allegory than if taken as a record of historical fact. This seems like a far-fetched explanation until one turns to the comparative study of actual literature of the

[53] The symbol of the fish in early Christianity became one of the commonest emblems in connection with the worship, as evidenced in very early Christian archaeology, although literary reference is not found prior to Clement of Alexandria (*Paedagogus* III, XI). Its adoption was probably largely due to the fact that the Greek word for fish Ichthus (Ἰχθύς) is composed of the initials of the Greek words for Jesus Christ, Son of God, Savior (Ἰησοῦς Χριστὸς Θεοῦ Υἱὸς Σωτήρ).

time, of which the book of Revelation, attributed also to the same author as the gospel, is our best known example. It is not suggested here that the text should be interpreted allegorically, but the student of papal history ought to know that it is so interpreted by highly qualified scholarship. The allegory may be viewed as complete or partial; that is, the incident may be regarded as having been invented by the writer, or may be accepted as based upon fact, with the implications simply stressed by having Peter alone draw in the unbroken net of fishes. Jerome, commenting upon this last, says that the number of fishes, 153, was held by naturalists to be the full number of all species of fish in existence. The miracle was cast in conventional terms, whether it refers to the unity of the Church under Petrine rule or not.

The Pastoral Charge and the last section offer no such obscurities. Peter "is invested by Jesus with the insignia and office of chief under-shepherd of the flock of God, the stain of his threefold denial wiped out by a threefold opportunity to prove his special love by special service, and the ignominy of his previous failure to 'follow' (XIII, 36–38) atoned for by the promise that in old age he shall have opportunity to follow Jesus in martyrdom (XXI, 19). There remains nothing that the most exacting friend of 'Catholic' apostolicity could demand in the way of tribute to its great representative." [54]

XXI 1 After this, Jesus shewed himself again to the disciples at the sea of Tiberias; and he shewed himself after this manner.

2 There were together Simon Peter and Thomas, who is called Didymus, and Nathanael who was of Cana of Galilee, and the sons of Zebedee, and two other of his disciples.

3 Simon Peter saith to them: I go a fishing. They say to him: We also come with thee. And they went forth and entered into the ship: and that night they caught nothing.

[54] B. W. Bacon, *The Making of the New Testament* (New York, 1912), pp. 241–242. The treatment of this chapter is especially full in this little book.

4 But when the morning was come, Jesus stood on the shore: yet the disciples knew not that it was Jesus.

5 Jesus therefore saith to them: Children, have you any meat? They answered him: No.

6 He saith to them: Cast the net on the right side of the ship; and you shall find. They cast therefore: and now they were not able to draw it, for the multitude of fishes.

7 That disciple therefore whom Jesus loved said to Peter: It is the Lord. Simon Peter, when he heard that it was the Lord, girt his coat about him (for he was naked) and cast himself into the sea.

8 But the other disciples came in the ship (for they were not far from the land, but as it were two hundred cubits) dragging the net with fishes.

9 As soon then as they came to land, they saw hot coals lying, and a fish laid thereon, and bread.

10 Jesus saith to them: Bring hither of the fishes which you have now caught.

11 Simon Peter went up, and drew the net to land, full of great fishes, one hundred and fifty-three. And although there were so many, the net was not broken.

12 Jesus saith to them: Come and dine. And none of them who were at meat, durst ask him: Who art thou? knowing that it was the Lord.

13 And Jesus cometh, and taketh bread, and giveth them: and fish in like manner.

14 This is now the third time that Jesus was manifested to his disciples, after he was risen from the dead.

15 When therefore they had dined, Jesus saith to Simon Peter: Simon, son of John, lovest thou me more than these? He saith to him: Yea, Lord, thou knowest that I love thee. He saith to him: Feed my lambs.

16 He saith to him again: Simon, son of John, lovest thou me? He saith to him: Yea, Lord, thou knowest that

I love thee. He saith to him: Feed my lambs.

17 He said to him the third time: Simon, son of John, lovest thou me? Peter was grieved, because he had said to him the third time: Lovest thou me? And he said to him: Lord, thou knowest all things: thou knowest that I love thee. He said to him: Feed my sheep.

18 Amen, amen, I say to thee, when thou wast younger, thou didst gird thyself, and didst walk where thou wouldst. But when thou shalt be old, thou shalt stretch forth thy hands, and another shall gird thee, and lead thee whither thou wouldst not.

19 And this he said, signifying by what death he should glorify God. And when he had said this, he saith to him: Follow me.

2. PETER AND THE OTHER APOSTLES

Over against such texts as these concerning the rôle of Peter during the life of Christ, which, in order to be fully appreciated, should, of course, be taken in their context, the following citations from Acts and the Epistles indicate his activity and leadership after the resurrection, in the earliest days of the Church. While they also should be studied in their setting along with the rest of the documents in which they are embedded, the following summary may help to place them historically and serve as an indication of their value.

The Acts of the Apostles opens with a section which might be termed either the New Gospel of the Holy Spirit, since it is the dominating presence, or the Acts of Peter and the Apostles, since he is the leading personality, as Paul is in the latter part. At the very first, we have the retrospective reference to Jesus "giving commandments by the Holy Ghost to the apostles whom he had chosen," which, apparently, places emphasis upon the body as a whole. But it is Peter who takes the initiative in the first act of the apostles to elect a successor to Judas (Acts I, 15–26). The next great event is Pentecost; Peter is the speaker, although the rest of the Twelve are with him (II, 14), and when the people ask them what they shall do, it is Peter who replies (II, 37–39). Then comes the gift of miracles; this time John is associated with Peter, but somewhat secondarily (III, 1, 5, 11–12; IV, 1, 8, 13, 19). Peter's prominence in this line of activity is, however, clearly indicated in V, 15, where it is Peter's shadow which is especially mentioned as having "virtue" in it. In outward defiance of the Jewish priesthood and bold assertion of their own divine mission Peter is the chief spokesman (IV, 8, 19; V, 29). Meanwhile the community itself is taking shape; its quasi-communal character is described in IV, 32–35, and there is a glimpse of its management in the incident of Ananias and Sapphira. They bring their goods to "the apostles' feet," but it is Peter who rebukes and convicts them (V, 1–11). The extension of Christianity into Samaria, — that "border-land . . . between Judaism and Heathendom," — follows as the next great stage in the history. Peter leads here, but does not act alone. "The mission to Samaria, which gives its sanction to Philip's action, is the mission of the whole apostolate, and here again John is associated with him."[55]

In Samaria, it is Peter who meets and rejects Simon Magus, the "father of the Gnostics"[56] (VIII, 18, 20) and, more important yet, to him is revealed the great fact that Christianity is to be opened to the Gentiles. The significance of this great step can hardly be over-estimated (X and XI). Peter disappears from the narrative of Acts after Herod's persecution except to reappear at the Council in Jerusalem in 51 A.D. (XV, 6 *sqq.*), and then we hear no more of him. But in the passages from Galatians and Second Corinthians quoted below, we have Paul's very clear and emphatic statement as to his conception of the relationship existing among the apostles. He went up to Jerusalem to visit not the apostles but Cephas (Gal. I, 18); yet he acknowledges no pretensions to a position higher than his own (Gal. II, 6 *sqq.*; 2 Cor. XI, 5).

[55] J. B. Lightfoot, *The Apostolic Fathers* (2 vols., 2nd ed., London, 1889–1890), Pt. I, Vol. II, pp. 489–490.

[56] On the legend of Simon Magus and its part in the later conception of Peter as the first great opponent of heresy, *vide infra*, p. 124 and *seq.*

Such are the texts. The interpretation is open to infinite controversy. It is largely a matter of emphasis. For instance, the Episcopalian is struck with the prominence of John along with Peter, Paul's attitude, and the texts which indicate a solidarity of the apostolate.[57] The Catholic sees Peter's figure looming large above the group, and insists on his initiative in the crises of the Church.[58] Those who reject apostolic succession altogether are not so vitally concerned with the interpretation, and may seriously question the historical value of the documents themselves. In this connection, it may be well to recall that possible division of Acts into two parts: Chapters I to XII, " The Acts of Peter," Chapters XIII to XXVIII, "The Acts of Paul." The historical accuracy of the second part is now generally held to be considerably greater than that of the earlier part, where the writer seems to be somewhat away from his material.[59] It is possible, therefore, to reserve judgment on the scheme of the narrative which places Peter at the fore in all the early crises. During the opening chapters at least, the author does not handle his sources with the sure touch of the later part. The tradition he embodies may have already been tinged by the inevitable tendency of traditions to develop the rôle of a hero. Such is the point of view of advanced criticism. But the " eloquent silence " of the latter part of Acts, with reference to Peter, loses some of the force of its argument against the Petrine claims when we recall the Pauline and partial character of its survey of the situation. Because Peter drops out of sight in the Acts it is not necessary to suppose that he dropped out of sight in the work of the Church. The first step in historical criticism is to recognize the inadequacy of one's sources. This is commented upon already in the *Muratorian Fragment* of about 180 A.D. Luke records only those things done in his own presence, " as he plainly shows by leaving out the passion of Peter and also the departure of Paul from town on his journey to Spain."[60]

[57] See the fine summary of Bishop J. B. Lightfoot, *op. cit.*, Pt. I, vol. II, pp. 488–490.

[58] See the decree of the Vatican Council on Infallibility, Chapter I, in H. Denzinger, *Enchiridion Symbolorum et Definitionum* (Freiburg, 1911), pp. 483–484.

[59] It is supposed that these early chapters of Acts rest upon an Aramaic source.

[60] *The Muratorian Fragment* is a small section of a document of unknown

THE EVIDENCE OF THE ACTS OF THE APOSTLES

(a.) *The Final Charge to the Apostles*

(Acts I, 1–8)

I 1 The former treatise[61] I made, O Theophilus, of all that Jesus began to do and to teach,

2 Until the day on which giving commandments by the Holy Ghost to the apostles whom he had chosen, he was taken up.[62]

3 To whom also he shewed himself alive after his passion, by many proofs, for forty days appearing to them and speaking of the kingdom of God:

4 And, eating together with them, he commanded them that they should not depart from Jerusalem, but should wait for the promise of the Father, which you have heard (saith he) by my mouth.

5 For John indeed baptized with water: but you shall be baptized with the Holy Ghost, not many days hence.

6 They therefore who were come together asked him, saying: Lord, wilt thou at this time restore again the kingdom to Israel?

7 But he said to them: It is not for you to know the times or moments, which the Father hath put in his own power.

8 But you shall receive the power of the Holy Ghost coming upon you, and you shall be witnesses unto me in Jerusalem, and in all Judea and Samaria, and even to the uttermost part of the earth.

---

authorship, found by the Italian historian Muratori in Milan, and published by him in the *Antiquitates Italicae* in 1740. It is given in C. Mirbt, *Quellen zur Geschichte des Papsttums* (Tübingen, 1924), p. 12; C. Kirch, *Enchiridion Fontium* in J. C. Ayer, *A Source Book for Ancient Church History* (New York, 1913), pp. 117–120.

[61] The reference is to the Gospel of Luke.

[62] *Cf.* Luke XXIV, 48, 49. "And you are witnesses of these things. And I send the promise of my Father upon you; but stay you in the city, till you be endued with power from on high." The connection between this verse and the opening of Acts is self-evident.

(b.) *The First Initiative*

(Acts I, 15)

I 15 In those days, [when the group of disciples had come together after the resurrection] Peter rising up in the midst of the brethren, said . . .

(c.) *Peter at Pentecost*

(Acts II, 14, 37, 38)

II 14 But Peter, standing up with the eleven, lifted up his voice . . .

37 Now when they [the multitude] had heard these things, they . . . said to Peter and to the rest of the apostles: What shall we do, men and brethren?

38 But Peter said unto them, Do penance: and be baptized. . . .[63]

(d.) *Miracles and Preaching at Jerusalem*

(Acts III, 1–6, 11, 12; IV, 1, 8, 13, 19; V, 12, 15, 17–18, 29)

III 1 Now Peter and John went up into the temple at the ninth hour of prayer. . . .

2 And a certain man that was lame from his mother's womb was carried: whom they laid every day at the gate of the temple . . . that he might ask alms of them that went into the temple;

3 He, when he had seen Peter and John about to go into the temple, asked to receive an alms.

4 But Peter with John, fastening his eyes upon him, said, Look upon us.

5 But he looked earnestly upon them, hoping that he should receive something of them.

[63] The significance of Peter's leadership in this first crisis of the Church, as seen by the writer of Acts, is further shown by his statement, in the forty-first verse, that some 3000 were added to the church that day.

6 But Peter said: Silver and gold I have none; but what I have, I give thee. In the name of Jesus Christ of Nazareth, arise and walk. . . .

11 And as he held Peter and John, all the people ran to them to the porch. . . .

12 But Peter seeing, made answer to the people: Ye men of Israel, why wonder you. . . . [The sermon lasts to the end of the chapter. The opening words of the next chapter, however, indicate that John also preached.]

IV 1 And as they were speaking to the people . . .

8 [Upon an inquiry from the high priest and rulers] Then Peter, filled with the Holy Ghost, said to them: Ye princes of the people . . .

13 Now seeing the constancy of Peter and of John . . . [they attempted to quell the disturbance].

19 But Peter and John answering said to them: If it be just, in the sight of God, to hear you rather than God, judge ye.

V 12 And by the hands of the apostles were many signs and wonders wrought among the people. And they were all with one accord in Solomon's porch . . .

15 . . . they brought forth the sick into the streets, and laid them on beds and couches, that, as Peter came, his shadow at the least might overshadow any of them and they might be delivered from their infirmities.

17–18 . . . the high priest . . . and all they that were with him . . . laid hands on the apostles . . .

29 But Peter and the apostles answering said, We ought to obey God rather than men.

(e.) *The Oversight of the Community*

(Acts V, 1–8)

V 1–2 . . . Ananias . . . laid it at the feet of the apostles.

3 But Peter said: Ananias, why hath Satan tempted thy heart . . .

7 . . . when his wife, not knowing what had happened, came in.

8 And Peter, said to her . . .

(f.) *The Mission to Samaria*[64]

(Acts VIII, 14)

VIII 14 Now when the apostles who were in Jerusalem, heard that Samaria had received the word of God, they sent unto them Peter and John.

(g.) *Simon Magus Overcome*

(Acts VIII, 18, 19)

VIII 18 And when Simon saw that, by the imposition of the hands of the apostles, the Holy Ghost was given, he offered them money, . . .

19 . . . But Peter said to him . . .

(h.) *Acceptance of Gentiles, the Vision of Peter*[65]

(Acts X, 34)

X 34 And Peter opening his mouth said, In very deed I perceive that God is not a respecter of persons.

(i.) *The Council at Jerusalem*

(Acts XV, 6, 7, 8, 12, 13, 19)

XV 6 And the apostles and ancients were assembled to consider of this matter.

7 And when there had been much disputing, Peter rising up, said to them, Men, brethren, you know how that in former days God made choice among us, that by my mouth the Gentiles should hear the word of the gospel and believe.

[64] The details of the mission to Samaria are omitted.

[65] The whole account of Peter's vision and its consequences should be read in this connection.

8 And God, who knoweth the hearts, gave testimony, giving unto them the Holy Ghost, as well as to us.

12 . . . and they heard Barnabas and Paul telling what great signs and wonders God had wrought among the Gentiles by them.

13 And after they had held their peace, James answered, saying: . . .

19 . . . I judge that they[66] . . .

THE EVIDENCE OF THE EPISTLES OF PAUL

Paul and Peter

(Galatians I, 15–19)

I 15 But when it pleased him . . .

16 To reveal his Son in me [Paul] that I might preach him among the Gentiles: immediately I condescended not to flesh and blood:

17 Neither went I to Jerusalem to the apostles who were before me: . . .

18 Then after three years I [Paul] went to Jerusalem to see Peter: and I tarried with him fifteen days.

19 But other of the apostles I saw none, saving James the brother of the Lord.

Peter and Paul in Antioch

(Galatians II, 1, 2, 6, 7, 8, 9, 11, 12, 14)

II 1 Then . . . after fourteen years I went up again to Jerusalem . . .

2 . . . and communicated to them the gospel which I preach among the Gentiles: but apart to them who seemed

[66] Note that James assumes personal responsibility for the decision. The King James Version reads: "Whereupon *my* judgment is that we," etc.

[67] Verse 9 explains who is meant by "them who seemed to be some thing," the three who already held positions of influence and authority in the rising Church.

to be some thing:[67] lest perhaps I should run or had run
in vain. . . .

6 But of them who seemed to be some thing (what they
were some time, it is nothing to me. God accepteth not the
person of man): for to me they that seemed to be some
thing, added nothing.

7 But contrariwise, when they had seen that to me had
been intrusted the gospel of the uncircumcision, as to Peter
was that of the circumcision:

8 (For he who wrought in Peter to the apostleship of the
circumcision wrought in me also among the Gentiles.)

9 And when they had known the grace that was given
to me, James and Cephas [68] and John, who seemed to be
pillars, gave to me and Barnabas the right hands of fellowship: that we should go unto the Gentiles, and they unto
the circumcision. . . .

11 But when Cephas was come to Antioch, I withstood
him to the face, because he was to be blamed.

12 For before that some came from James, he did eat
with the Gentiles: but when they were come, he withdrew
and separated himself, fearing them who were of the circumcision. . . .

14 But when I saw that they walked not uprightly unto
the truth of the gospel, I said to Cephas before them all:
If thou, being a Jew, livest after the manner of the Gentiles
and not as the Jews do, how dost thou compel the Gentiles
to live as do the Jews?

Paul's Estimate

(2 Corinthians XI, 5)

XI 5 For I suppose that I [Paul] have done nothing less
than the great [69] apostles.

[68] It will be remembered that Cephas is the Anglicized form of *Kepha,* the Aramaic equivalent of Peter. *Vide supra,* pp. 23–24.

[69] The King James Version has "chiefest" instead of "great."

THE EVIDENCE OF PROPHETIC LITERATURE

(Revelation XXI, 14)

XXI 14 And the wall of the city had twelve foundations: and in them, the twelve names of the twelve apostles of the Lamb.

3. PETER IN ROME AND THE FOUNDING OF THE ROMAN CHURCH [70]

As seen in the last section, Peter is prominent in the first part of the narrative of Acts. But in the twelfth chapter we come upon the persecution by Herod, and after Peter's escape from prison, we have the simple statement that he said, "Tell these things to James and to the brethren. And going out he went into another place" (Acts XII, 17). This is the last we hear of Peter until he reappears some years later at the so-called Council of Jerusalem, 51 A.D. (Acts XV, 6 *sqq.* and see above), and then we have no further reference to him in Acts, which is more Pauline in its latter part than Petrine in the first. James is president of the council; Paul declares his own equality with the "great apostles"; Peter disappears. Later he is in Antioch (Galatians II, 11). He cannot have been in Rome when Paul wrote his Epistle to the Romans, for he is not mentioned among the brethren to whom greetings are sent. Nor was he there when Paul wrote from Rome during his captivity.

The First Epistle of Peter has been the fundamental text for the contention that Peter was in Rome. Its closing salutation, "The church that is in Babylon . . . saluteth you" (1 Peter V, 13), refers undoubtedly to Rome. Babylon was then in ruins, and there was no tradition for five centuries that Peter had been there, whereas the tradition connecting him with Rome is one of the strongest in the Church. Babylon is used for Rome in the Sibylline Oracles and in Revelation (XIV, 8; XVI, 19; XVII,

[70] In view of the fragmentary nature of the evidence on this question, the texts here have been largely embodied in the discussion.

5; XVIII, 2, 10).[71] The genuineness of the epistle was already established in the second century, after its use by Hermas, Papias, the Second Epistle of Peter (which is not by him), etc., and is still generally accepted.

It is possible that isolated converts may have been living in Rome before a formal organization was made.[72] There had been "strangers of Rome, Jews also and proselytes" at Pentecost in Jerusalem (Acts II, 10–11), some of whom, hearing Peter, may have become Christian. Suetonius, the Roman historian, writing in the first quarter of the second century, refers to an uproar among the Jews in 49 A.D. "He [Claudius] expelled from Rome the Jews, who were making incessant disturbances, one Chrestus being the instigator [*impulsore Chresto*]."[73] The spelling Chrestus was common for Christus, so if Suetonius got this fact right,[74] the Christians were there by 49 A.D. at least.[75] The next evidence we have on the Christians at Rome is Paul's Epistle to the Romans, written 54 or 55 A.D. Although he throws no light on how Christianity had been introduced among them, he states that their "faith is spoken of in the whole world" (Romans I, 8), and the passage in the fifteenth chapter (especially v. 20) may very well be taken to imply that Paul delayed his visit to Rome owing to Peter having preached there before. He is not going to found a church, but merely to pay a visit on his way to Spain. Indeed the Roman Christians are addressed with some deference, and he honors them by his greatest theological treatise, "the public exposition of his gospel."[76] The passage in question is from the nineteenth through the twenty-fifth verse, of the fifteenth chapter of the Epistle to the Romans:

[71] *Cf.* R. H. Charles, *The Ascension of Isaiah* (London, 1900), p. lix; J. B. Lightfoot, *The Apostolic Fathers,* Pt. I, Vol. II, p. 492.

[72] For one traditional account of the origin of the Roman church, see the Pseudo-Clementine Literature, *infra,* p. 166.

[73] *Life of Claudius,* c. 25.

[74] Suetonius was, apparently, not very careful in his handling of the incident. Dio Cassius, at least, says that as they proved too many to be expelled, they were merely brought under the laws against unlicensed societies (*collegia*).

[75] This is the persecution of the Jews referred to in Acts XVIII, 2. The name Christ being a Messianic title, it is possible that the Jewish disturbances were disputes over some other imagined Messiah and that the Christians played no part in them.

[76] R. B. Rackham, *The Acts of the Apostles* (London, 1901), p. 362. (*Cf. Muratorian Fragment.*)

XV 19 . . . from Jerusalem, round about, as far as unto
Illyricum, I have replenished the gospel of Christ.
20 And I have so preached this gospel, not where Christ
was named, lest I should build upon another man's foundation.
21 But, as it is written: They to whom he was not
spoken of shall see: and they that have not heard shall
understand.
22 For which cause also, I was hindered very much from
coming to you, . . .
23 But now, having no more place in these countries
and having a great desire these many years past to come
unto you,
24 When I shall begin to take my journey into Spain,
I hope that, as I pass, I shall see you[77] and be brought
on my way thither by you: if first, in part, I shall have
enjoyed you.
25 But now, I shall go to Jerusalem, to minister to the
saints.

On the other hand, judging from the account in Acts XXVIII, 21, when Paul arrived in Rome (58 A.D.), he found the Jews ignorant of his doings, which seems strange, had Peter (and Mark) been instructing them before, for in that case they would have established direct connections with Jerusalem.

If Peter preceded Paul to Rome, it has been suggested that it was between his disappearance from Palestine in 44 A.D. and his return to Jerusalem in 48 A.D. (Acts XII and XV), the "other place" of Acts XII, 17, being Rome. Jerome, in his life of St. Peter, states that Peter came to Rome "in the second year of Claudius," or 42 A.D.; and although Jerome wrote at the end of the fourth century, he may have relied on earlier sources.[78] Upon the whole, there seems nothing improbable in the tradition and the belief of Catholic writers in St. Peter's early labors in

[77] *Cf.* Acts XIX, 21 . . . I must *see* Rome also.
[78] *Infra,* p. 115.

Rome. His martyrdom there, at a later period, is vouched for by a fairly continuous line of references in the documents from Clement on.

Peter's presence in Rome does not necessarily imply, however, that he founded the Roman church, or again that he was "bishop." The one most telling text in favor of regarding Peter as the founder of the Roman church is the reference of Paul in the fifteenth chapter of Romans (v. 20), when he says that he would not "build upon another man's foundation," which in view of the relations between Peter and Paul has been taken to refer to Peter. From the second century on, there was no doubt of the matter.

Yet here we come upon that most tangled of all questions, the rise of the episcopate.

Was Peter both apostle and bishop? Such a position was somewhat anomalous. In the apostolic age, there was a "ministry of the word," consisting of apostles, prophets, and evangelists, whose business it was to go on missionary journeys and to spread the gospel (*Cf.* Acts VI, 1–8). The business affairs and direction of the local community were turned over to members of the community or residents, the eldest converts (presbyters) and the overseers (bishops). Reference has already been made to the problems involved in this earliest phase of the constitutional history of the Church.[79] When and how did the structure of church administration emerge in solid outline through the fluid enthusiasm which found its chief utterance in the itinerant ministry of "apostles and teachers"? If these questions could be answered, we might be able to reach agreement as to Peter's position in Rome. But unfortunately, the questions are themselves unreal, for they seem to presuppose distinctions in the minds of the members of those early congregations which could hardly have existed, at least in any general way. The powers or prerogatives of a growing executive are seldom questioned when first exercised under the original impulse which brings them into being. It is rather in a second phase of their history that organizations become aware of constitutional questions of this kind,

[79] *Supra*, pp. 3–4.

when criticisms arise upon the part of those who feel that either their rights or the welfare of the organization in question suffers through the exercise of the debated functions. There are echoes of such controversies from the primitive Church, but they are not set forth in formal terms of hierarchical theory or jurisprudence.[80]

When one asks, therefore, what was the position of Peter in Rome, the answer of the texts and of tradition is open to diverse interpretations. On the one hand, his ministry in Rome is held to be merely the continuation and completion of his activities as "apostle"; on the other hand, it is interpreted as being that of the first of the Roman bishops. According to the later tradition, he resided there for a considerable time. This tradition grew, most probably, from the connection with the story of Simon Magus.[81] The claim that Peter was bishop of Rome for twenty-five years is not found before the *Liberian Catalogue* in 354,[82] and is historically inadmissible, as it can not be reconciled with the earlier texts. But however long may have been his stay in Rome, one can readily conceive of him as dominating the little community while he was there. If we limit ourselves to the texts, we do not know what Peter did in Rome nor what function he performed. But it is not well to press distinctions of office in this early period, and one is safe in imagining that Peter played a leading rôle here as elsewhere. It seems, therefore, unnecessary to deny him the title of "overseer" or *episcopus*, although Irenaeus himself, in giving the list of the Roman bishops,[83] does not definitely allude to Peter as bishop, possibly

[80] For an account of the itinerant ministry, see the *Teaching of the Apostles;* for the exaltation of the bishop's position, see *The Epistles of Ignatius.*

[81] *Vide infra,* Part III.

[82] This tradition of the twenty-five year episcopate of Peter has been widely accepted in Catholic books. The regular tradition was that Peter, having gone to Rome to meet Simon Magus in 42 A.D., founded the church there and remained until his martyrdom under Nero in 67 A.D. Lipsius, owing to the large amount of falsehood connected with the tradition, rejected the whole of it, and even went so far as to deny that Peter was ever in Rome (R. A. Lipsius, *Die Quellen der römischen Petrus-sage,* Kiel, 1872). See the discussion in such thorough, controversial studies as R. F. Littledale, *The Petrine Claims* (London, 1889), a Protestant work; C. Guignebert, *La Primauté de Pierre* (Paris, 1911); and L. Rivington, *The Primitive Church and the See of Peter* (London, 1894), standard Catholic statement; or F. U. Puller, *The Primitive Saints and the See of Rome* (London, 1900); J. B. Lightfoot, *The Apostolic Fathers,* Pt. I, Vol. I, pp. 201 *seq.*

[83] *In Haereses,* Book I, Chap. XXVII, 1; Book III, Chap. IV, 3. *Vide infra,* p. 268.

from a sense of the greater glory of the title "apostle." He does state, however, that Peter "committed to the hands of Linus the office of the episcopate." In 252, Cyprian of Carthage speaks of the See of Rome as the See of Peter but not until 354, when the tradition was growing old, do we find Peter definitely and positively styled the first bishop of Rome.[84]

[84] *Infra*, pp. 379, 107.

PART II

THE TRADITION ACCEPTED AS HISTORICAL

Introduction

We have given already [1] a short description of the documents contained in the present section, the "accepted" texts from the early Greek and Latin Fathers, which have been from the first the usual accredited sources for the belief in Peter's labors at Rome and his death there by crucifixion under Nero. By the end of the second century, it was understood that there were both an authentic tradition of Peter and a spurious one, the latter reaching its full development in literature that was palpably apocryphal. Serapion, bishop of Antioch from about 190 to 210, wrote in condemnation of a so-called Gospel of Peter: "For we, brethren, accept both Peter and the other apostles as Christ; but, being persons of intelligence, we reject the writings falsely ascribed to them, knowing that we have not received such traditions." [2] A century later, the historian Eusebius distinguished between genuine works of the apostles and those "which we know have not been generally accepted among Catholics, because no ecclesiastical writer, ancient or modern, has made use of materials drawn from them." [3] These apocryphal legends of the apostle have a place and use of their own and are summarized in the next section, but they were never, until the fourth century, regarded by discriminating scholars as historical and even then seem to have received only a partial endorsement. The texts we have here, on the other hand, are taken mainly from those whom Eusebius calls "ecclesiastical writers," men of authority and weight in the early Church, who though not scientific historians

[1] *Supra*, p. x.

[2] Quoted by Eusebius, *Historia Ecclesiastica*, VI, 12, 3.

[3] Eusebius, *op. cit.*, III, 3, 2. The epithet, "ecclesiastical," applied at this period to a writer, means orthodox as distinguished from doubtful or heretical.

in the modern sense, did not wilfully or recklessly invent, but set down what they soberly believed to be the truth. Among them are also a few scraps of contemporary pagan testimony which throw some light on the prevalence or character of the tradition.

The tradition which these texts record contains nothing at first glance absurd or incredible. It appears to have arisen within thirty years, at latest, after Peter's death, in the region where he died. If it is altogether groundless, how explain its unchallenged circulation at such an early date or the subsequent invariable coupling at Rome of Peter's name and portrait with Paul's? [4] It was never, so far as we know, controverted by a claim from any other place to be the scene of Peter's last days, even when the other prominent apostles had been in course of time definitely consigned to other tombs around the world.[5] It was the " received " tradition, repeated without question by one great writer after another throughout those first centuries.

Not that the tradition, however it first arose, was written down clearly at the outset for the benefit of oncoming generations. One characteristic of primitive Christian literature is that it ex-

[4] The figures of Peter and Paul appear together in Roman art among the first specimens of Christian portraiture, dating from the second and third century. W. Lowrie, *Christian Art and Archaeology* (London, 1901), pp. 251–252; R. A. Lanciani, *Pagan and Christian Rome* (Boston, 1893), pp. 212–213.

[5] A third century Syrian version of the apocryphal letter of Dionysius the Areopagite to Timothy on the deaths of Peter and Paul contains the sentence: " Lo, the bodies of the saints are buried at Rome and there is no portion of them outside Rome." *Analecta Sacra Patrum Antenicaeanorum,* ed. by Martinus, 266; quoted by F. Haase, *Apostel und Evangelisten in den orientalischen Überlieferungen* (Münster, 1922), p. 213. Save for a few episodes of John's old age, preserved by Polycarp and repeated by Eusebius, nothing but dubious and hesitating tradition remains about the later years of any apostle but Peter and Paul. Eusebius was as much in the dark about them as we are today. Whatever records may have once existed had obviously been lost to the general knowledge of the Church by his time. Harnack goes so far as to say: " Probably then it is not too hazardous to affirm that the church really had never more than two apostles in the true sense of the term . . . *viz.* Paul and Peter, — unless perhaps we add John of Ephesus." — A. Harnack, *The Mission and Expansion of Christianity* (trans. by J. Moffatt, 2 vols., 2nd ed., New York, 1908), Vol. I, pp. 351–352. It may be for this reason that the only two proper names taken from the Old or New Testament to be borne by gentile Christians during the first three centuries were Paul and Peter. Dionysius, bishop of Alexandria, wrote in the latter half of the third century that " the children of the faithful are often called after Paul and also after Peter." Quoted by Eusebius, *Historia Ecclesiastica,* VII, 25, 14. After the middle of the Bible became increasingly common. For examples of this see A. Harnack, of the fourth century, the custom of naming children after other saints and heroes *op. cit.,* Vol. I, pp. 422–430; R. A. Lanciani, *op. cit.,* p. 18, n. 2.

plains and defines so little, that it confidently looks for a speedy end of the world, heeds only the immediate emergency, and addresses itself to persons who understand the situation as the author does and for whom a hint will suffice. The tradition of Peter's death is referred to apparently twice in documents of the first century but both times barely in passing, as a thing familiar to everyone. The writers are speaking darkly of trials and persecutions still recent and remembering the example of the good apostles. It is impossible to guess what lies behind the scanty phrases. In the second century, the tradition is still handled as fresh and living, and knowledge of it is taken for granted. At least, if it has been written down, the record soon afterward disappears. We are given, indeed, incidentally another detail or two, namely, that Peter as well as Paul preached at Rome and established the church and that their monuments are to be seen close outside the city walls. The motive for recalling them is now to put the seal of authenticity on the doctrines of the church which they taught. The contest with heresy has begun and the apostles are needed not so much for patterns of martyrdom as for sources of faith. In the third century, comes a more conscious effort to formulate and set down reminiscences in order to preserve them, but by this time the years have dimmed their vividness and many are gone beyond recovery. However, the commission to Peter in Matthew is brought forward and Peter himself is exalted as first of the apostles. The fourth century offers us succinct and formalized biographies, anniversary festivals, memorial basilicas and tombs of bronze. The tradition, amplified and perfected, takes its place and exerts its influence thereafter in history.

The problem which confronts every student of this tradition is, of course, how far the completed version, which Jerome, for instance, gives us in 392, corresponds to the facts which the Church of the first century knew too well to write down. Jerome himself, in all probability, could hardly have said how trustworthy were the documents on which he depended for his additions to Clement's hazy allusions. As matters stand there will always be ground for diversity of opinion. Many Protestant scholars now concede that the " accepted " tradition in its oldest and simplest form is in all likelihood reliable and that Peter preached and died at Rome and, possibly, even chose an overseer, " episcopus " or bishop, to assist him or to serve the church after his death, while they still doubt how far Catholics are justified in believing that Peter himself was the first bishop and, in any strict sense, the founder of the Roman See.[6] The chronology has always presented distracting and seemingly insoluble difficulties. Nevertheless, such as it is, the tradition here recorded, taken in conjunction with the New Testament texts already cited, is the foundation upon which the institution of the Papacy rests.

Without this tradition it is obvious that the New Testament texts would possess little more significance for the bishop of Rome than for any other member of the Church catholic. The power of the keys, the charge to " feed my sheep," bestowed by Christ upon Peter, would, if Peter's recorded activity had ceased with his canonical epistles, have enhanced in our eyes his personal prestige during his lifetime but would have lapsed altogether with his death. A grant of rights, conferred by however competent an authority upon an individual almost two thousand years ago, can have no vital import for anyone today, unless the individual has left behind him a line of successors who have inherited and continuously exercised those rights down to the present time. On the other hand, even without the tradition to build upon, the Roman church would still undeniably have become one of the directing forces of Christendom by virtue of its location in the imperial city and the size and character of its membership. It would also have been an apostolic church and a repository of authentic doctrine, profiting by Paul's teaching and martyrdom and distinguished by his special commendation. But the bishop of Rome would have occupied legally no different rank from that of the bishops of Antioch and Alexandria, who also could boast of apostolic founders.

To raise him to the unique position of heir in his one person to Peter's peculiar powers there must be a link connecting Peter so closely with the Roman bishopric that he, either with or with-

6 *Cf. supra*, pp. ix–x.

out Paul, might be considered to have been its originator and to have bequeathed to it as its particular legacy the authority which his Master had once entrusted to him. The tradition which we are about to trace creates this link, taking up the last years of Peter, when the New Testament falls silent, and laying the scene of them at Rome. It is never, as we have it, more than a meagre tradition. It makes no attempt to explain Peter's own conception of his place in the rising Church nor his attitude toward his followers. For any interpretation or application of the Petrine powers we must wait for the action of his heirs, the popes, as gradually they realize the wider implications of their inheritance. But the tradition supplied the essential connection between Peter and the Roman See and thereby made it possible to inscribe around the central dome of the Vatican cathedral and to chant triumphantly in the train of its pontiff: "Tu es Petrus; et super hanc petram aedificabo ecclesiam meam." [7] "Thou art Peter; and upon this rock I will build my church."

1. PETER THE PREACHER AT ROME

Clement of Rome

(c. 96)

The First Epistle of Clement [8] to the Corinthians is, perhaps, the most famous document of primitive Christianity outside the New Testament. It was written probably about 95 or 96 A.D., in the name of the church of Rome to the church of Corinth, and contains no sign in itself of the identity of the author. The first indication we have that it was composed by Clement is found in a letter sent some eighty-five years later by Dionysius, bishop of Corinth, to the contemporary bishop of Rome.[9] In the early

[7] The wording is, of course, the Latin of the Vulgate.

[8] For the so-called *Second Epistle of Clement, vide infra*, pp. 251–255.

[9] *Infra*, p. 253. In the early fourth century, Eusebius' comment on I Clement was as follows: "There is extant one letter of this Clement, which is accepted as genuine. It is of great length and remarkable character. He wrote it in the name of the church of Rome to the church of Corinth because of a disturbance that had arisen at Corinth. We know also that this letter has been read publicly in many churches in the past and in our own day." *Historia Ecclesiastica*, III, 16.

lists of Roman bishops, Clement stands second after Linus, who is said to have succeeded the apostles.[10] Nothing is known of Clement's history, although there has been much speculation as to his possible relationship with the Clement whom Paul mentions in his letter from Rome to the Philippians [11] and with that Titus Flavius Clemens of the Roman aristocracy, who with his wife Domitilla fell under the displeasure of the emperor Domitian for countenancing a strange religion. Perhaps our Clement was a freedman of the great Flavian household. His familiarity with the ordinances of the Jewish priesthood suggests that he may also have been a Hellenistic Jew. The ancient Roman church of San Clemente was built over the traditional site of his house, between the Caelian and the Esquiline Hills.

The epistle ascribed to him, a long and dignified appeal to the Corinthian church to maintain harmony and order, is, of course, of unparalleled value for the study of ecclesiastical development.[12] Here, however, our business is solely with its significance as the starting point for the Roman tradition of the apostle Peter. In the fifth chapter, is a reference to the deaths of Peter and Paul, closely connected with an allusion in the next chapter to events in the persecution under Nero, which had taken place only thirty years before the author wrote. The reference is utterly vague. The place and manner of their deaths are not specified. More is made of Paul's life and sufferings than of Peter's. The writer evidently supposed that the Corinthians understood all the circumstances and that a bare reminder would be enough. The striking thing is that Peter should be named at all with Paul, as fellow martyr and example, by the spokesman of the Roman community at this early date.

For full discussion of the Clementine literature and problems, *vide* J. B. Lightfoot, *The Apostolic Fathers* (2 vols., London, 1889–1890), Pt. I; also W. Wrede, *Untersuchungen zum ersten Klemensbriefe* (Göttingen, 1891); A. Harnack, *Geschichte der altchristlichen Litteratur bis Eusebius* (2 vols.,

[10] *Infra,* pp. 249, 268.

[11] Philippians, IV, 3.

[12] For further extracts, *vide infra,* pp. 236–239. The first manuscript of this epistle to be known to the West in modern times was sent by the Patriarch of Constantinople to King Charles I. An English translation was printed in 1633. The manuscript, however, was imperfect, lacking Section 5. The whole was printed from a better text in 1875.

Leipzig, 1893–1904), Vol. I, pp. 39 *sqq.*; Vol. II, pp. 240 *sqq.*, pp. 438 *sqq.*; V. H. Stanton, *The Gospels as Historical Documents* (3 vols., Cambridge University Press, 1903–1920), Pt. I; E. Hennecke, *Handbuch zu den neutestamentlichen Apokryphen* (Tübingen, 1904); C. H. Turner, *Studies in Early Church History* (Oxford, 1912), pp. 220 *sqq.*; G. Edmundson, *The Church in Rome in the First Century* (Bampton Lectures for 1913, London, 1913), Chaps. VII–VIII; E. T. Merrill, *Essays in Early Christian History* (London, 1924), Chap. IX.

Clement, *Ad Corinthios,* 5 and 6. Text. *The Apostolic Fathers,* ed. by K. Lake (*The Loeb Classical Library*), I, 16–18.

5 But to pass from the examples of ancient days, let us come to those champions who lived very near to our time. Let us set before us the noble examples of our own generation. Through envy and malice, the greatest and most righteous pillars of the Church were persecuted and contended even unto death. Let us set before our eyes the good apostles. There was Peter, who by reason of unrighteous envy endured not one nor two but many trials, and so, having borne his testimony,[13] he passed to his appointed place of glory. Amid envy and strife, Paul pointed out the way to the prize of patient endurance. After he had been seven times in bonds, been driven into exile, been stoned, been a herald in the East and the West, he won noble renown for his faith, for he taught righteousness unto the whole world and reached the farthest bounds of the West and bore his testimony before the rulers; thus he departed from the world and passed unto the holy place, having set an illustrious pattern of patient endurance.

6 Unto these men of holy lives was gathered a vast multitude of the elect, who through many indignities and tortures endured envy and set a fair example among us.

[13] In Greek μαρτυρήσας, "having been a martyr," that is, a witness. The word was not yet confined exclusively to its later Christian meaning of bearing testimony unto death. After the first two centuries, the term "confessor" gradually came into use for persons who testified to their faith under trial or persecution of any sort and "martyr" denoted those who sealed their profession by death.

Through envy women were persecuted as Danaids and Dircae, suffering cruel and unholy insults; they steadfastly finished the courses of faith and received a noble prize, feeble in body though they were.[14]

The Ascension of Isaiah

(Document of 75–100)

The Ascension of Isaiah is a curious, composite work, thrown together by an unknown editor of the second or third century with no regard for clarity or chronology in the arrangement of the material. The elements of which it is composed are three, each originally a distinct document. The first, the *Martyrdom of Isaiah,* is a Jewish legendary history of the sawing asunder of the prophet and was written, probably, sometime during the first century of our era. The second, the *Testament of Hezekiah,* is an apocalyptic tract of Christian authorship, cast in the guise of a vision seen by King Hezekiah during an illness and related by him afterward to Isaiah and Josab, Isaiah's son. Its date can be more definitely determined than that of the *Martyrdom,* as somewhere between the years 75 and 100. The writer was filled with forebodings over the decline of fervor and purity in the Church and the approaching advent of Antichrist or Beliar, the spirit of evil, who would assume the form of the dead emperor Nero. The belief that Nero was actually still alive and would return to wreak vengeance on his disloyal subjects haunted the common people of the Empire for years after his death. It was natural then for a preacher of doom to conjure up the menace of his figure, the one persecutor whom the Church had yet known, the embodiment of wanton cruelty and impious conceit. Antichrist, when he came, would certainly wear his shape, would, in fact, be Nero Redivivus, Nero returned to earth.[15] In one

[14] This passage has always been taken to refer to the persecution under Nero. No universally accepted interpretation of the phrase, "Danaids and Dircae," has ever been given. It may allude to licentious, theatrical performances, in which condemned Christian women had been compelled to play a part, or to certain famous female criminals, who had previously been put to torture, or the text may be corrupt.

[15] Suetonius, writing at the beginning of the second century, mentions the fear still widespread in his day that Nero would reappear. *Nero,* c. 57. As late

place, the author draws a distinction between the believers still alive who had seen Christ in the flesh and those who had not, a distinction which, of course, became impossible soon after the year 100. From the *Testament* comes the passage which we cite and which is probably the oldest extant statement to the effect that one of the apostles was executed by Nero.

The third document in the compilation, the *Vision of Isaiah,* a rhapsodical description of the seven heavens, the life of the blessed, the coming of Christ and the resurrection, was composed apparently late in the first century or early in the second.

No Greek text of the entire *Ascension* has been preserved. A fragment of a later Greek recension has recently been discovered and published by Grenfell and Hunt; but our knowledge of the work as a whole is based upon a reconstruction from Ethiopic, Slavonic and Latin translations. It played no noticeable part in later orthodox church history. The author of the fictitious *Acts of Peter* [16] and also Origen, Epiphanius and Jerome had some knowledge of it but its principal circulation was among heretical sects of the third and following centuries. In the Middle Ages, it was still read by the Massalides or Bogomils of Eastern Europe and the Cathari of the West. But only within the last few years have scholars realized its value as the most ancient of surviving testimonies as to the manner of Peter's death.

Some recent discussions of the *Ascension* are A. Harnack, *Geschichte der altchristlichen Litteratur bis Eusebius* (2 vols., Leipzig, 1893–1904), Vol. I,[2] pp. 854–856; Vol. II,[1] pp. 573–579, 714; J. V. Bartlett, *The Apostolic Age* (New York, 1899), pp. 521–524; B. C. Grenfell and A. S. Hunt (editors), *The Amherst Papyri* (2 vols., London, 1900–1901), Vol. I; C. Guignebert, *La Primauté de Pierre* (Paris, 1911); R. H. Charles, *The Apocrypha and Pseudepigrapha of the Old Testament in English* (2 vols., Oxford, 1913), Vol. II, pp. 155 *sqq.*; A. L. Davies, *Ascension of Isaiah,* in J. Hastings, *Dictionary of the Apostolic Church* (2 vols., New York, 1916–1918), Vol. I.

---

as the fourth century, Lactantius speaks of a popular superstition that Nero was miraculously alive and would return as the forerunner of Antichrist to lay waste the earth. *De Mortibus Persecutorum,* II. In the year 1113, Pope Paschal II built a chapel near the Porta Flaminia to overawe the ghost of Nero, which pursued and terrified belated travellers coming into Rome at night.

[16] *Infra,* pp. 136–153. Peter, in his apocryphal sermon (*infra,* p. 144), quotes a line from the *Ascension.* Origen, Epiphanius and Jerome simply refer to it as an apocryphal work.

Ascensio Jesaiae, IV. Text. *The Ascension of Isaiah,* ed. by R. H. Charles, 24–28.

IV And now, Hezekiah and Josab my son,[17] these are the days of the consummation of the world; and after it is consummated, Beliar, a great angel, the king of this world, will descend. He has ruled it since it began and he will descend from his firmament in the form of a man, a king without law, the murderer of his mother.[18] He himself, even this king, shall persecute the plant which the twelve apostles of the Beloved shall plant and one of the twelve shall be delivered into his hands.[19] . . . And all that he hath desired he will do in the world; he will do and speak like the Beloved and he will say: " I am God and before me there has been none." [20] And all the people in the world will believe in him and they will sacrifice to him and serve him, saying: " This is God and beside him there is no other." And the greater part of those who have joined together to receive the Beloved he will turn aside after him and there will be the power of his miracles in every city and region and he will set up his image before him in every city.[21]

Ignatius of Antioch

(c. 116)

The letters of Ignatius, second bishop of Antioch, were written during the reign of Trajan, while Ignatius himself was on his way under guard to death at Rome, to be ground like " God's wheat . . . by the teeth of wild beasts " in order to become

17 The preceding five words are probably interpolations of the compiler. The whole passage is presumably spoken by Hezekiah to Isaiah and Josab.

18 An unmistakable description of the emperor Nero.

19 The reference cannot be to Paul, for he was not at this time included among the Twelve.

20 A reminiscence, probably, of the claim of Caligula to be reckoned as a god. Domitian forbade anyone to speak or write of himself under any other title. R. H. Charles, *op. cit.*, p. 27, notes.

21 Statues of the Roman emperors were erected in various cities of the provinces and divine honors paid to them there.

"the pure bread of Christ."[22] At various stopping places on his journey he wrote letters to the churches he was leaving behind in Asia, exhorting them to steadfastness in the face of perils without, and to unity and loyalty to their bishops in view of dissensions within. He also sent ahead a letter of greeting to the Romans, begging them not to attempt intercession nor to bring any influence to bear to prevent his martyrdom. We shall give other extracts from this letter later to show his idea of the generosity to be expected from Roman Christians.[23] We quote here only the three short sentences in which he compares his own admonitions to the Romans to the commandments given them by the apostles Peter and Paul. Whether he has in mind oral commandments, delivered in person, or whether he is thinking merely of the hortatory epistles sent by these same apostles to the churches, no one can be quite sure.

On Ignatius, *vide* J. B. Lightfoot, *The Apostolic Fathers* (2 vols., London, 1889–1890), Pt. II, Vol. II; A. Harnack, *Geschichte der altchristlichen Litteratur bis Eusebius* (Leipzig, 1893–1904), Vol. I,[1] pp. 75 *sqq.*, Vol. II,[1] pp. 381 *sqq.*; A. Harnack, *Entstehung und Entwickelung der Kirchenverfassung und des Kirchenrechts in den zwei ersten Jahrhunderten* (Leipzig, 1910); P. Batiffol, in J. Hastings, *Dictionary of the Apostolic Church* (2 vols., New York, 1916–1918), Vol. I, pp. 594 *sqq.*; S. Dunin-Borkowski, *Die Anfänge des Episkopats* (Freiburg, 1901); R. Knopf, *Nachapostolische Zeitalter* (Tübingen, 1905); A. Lelong, *Ignace d'Antioche et Polycarpe de Smyrne* (Paris, 1910).

Ad Romanos, 4. Text. *Apostolic Fathers*, ed. by K. Lake (Loeb Classical Library), I, 230.

I do not command you as Peter and Paul did. They were apostles; I am a convict. They were free; I am a slave to this very hour.[24]

22 Eusebius has an account of Ignatius. *Historia Ecclesiastica,* III, 36, 31.

23 *Infra,* pp. 241–242.

24 H. Grisar, *History of Rome and the Popes in the Middle Ages* (trans. by L. Cappadelta, 3 vols., London, 1911–1912), Vol. I, p. 283, remarks on this: "In these words he assumes it to be well known to his hearers that Peter and Paul had preached in person to the faithful at Rome. . . . It is evident that great historical weight must be attached to such remarks, when the writer so readily assumes a universal belief in the fact that he is at no pains to enforce it or even express it at all clearly."

Phlegon

(Reign of Hadrian, 117–138)

The following excerpt, derived from the writings of Origen,[25] is trivial enough at first sight but grows in interest as one begins to grasp its implications. Phlegon was a favorite freedman of the emperor Hadrian and the reputed author of historical and other works, most of which have long been lost. Spartianus, who a century and a half later compiled the most valuable life of Hadrian that we have, says that Hadrian himself actually wrote many of the books which passed as Phlegon's and that he preferred to publish under his freedman's name rather than under his own.[26] It is therefore possible that the *Chronicles* mentioned in our quotation were composed by the emperor. In any case, the author, a member of the Roman imperial court, knew some facts or reports about Peter as well as about Christ and found it easy to confuse Peter with the founder of Christianity.

Origen, *Contra Celsum*, II, 14. Text. *Origenes Werke* (*Die griechischen christlichen Schriftsteller der ersten drei Jahrhunderte*), I, 143–144.

Now Phlegon, in the thirteenth or fourteenth book, I think, of his *Chronicles,* ascribed to Christ a power to foretell future events, confusing some incidents which are related of Peter with those related of Jesus. And he testified that the results accorded with Christ's predictions.

Papias of Hierapolis

(fl. c. 120)

Papias, like Clement of Rome and Ignatius of Antioch, belonged to the group which we now call the Apostolic Fathers,

[25] On Origen, *vide infra,* pp. 87, 316.

[26] Spartianus, *Vita Hadriani,* 16, 1. Quoted by A. C. McGiffert, Translation of Eusebius, *Church History,* II, p. 129, n. 7, in *A Select Library of Nicene and Post-Nicene Fathers of the Christian Church* (14 vols., New York, 1890–1903), Second Series, Vol. I.

men who in their youth had come into contact with one or more of the original apostles. He was a citizen of Hierapolis, a city in Phrygia which claimed to possess the sepulchre of Philip the apostle.[27] Papias himself is said to have spoken with Philip's daughters and with a mysterious "John, the presbyter," whom he regarded as high authority. From them and other sources he collected various traditions which threw light on the meaning of the teachings of Christ and the apostles and which he recorded in a book called *Interpretations of the Lord's Sayings.* The book has long since disappeared, but a few references were made to it or quotations taken from it by Greek writers of the first three or four centuries, such as Irenaeus and Eusebius.

From Papias comes indirectly in this way the oldest extant account of the composition of the gospel of Mark. Unfortunately Eusebius does not give us Papias' own words, preferring in this instance to quote the version of a later man, Clement of Alexandria, and using Papias' name merely to confirm Clement's story. The text, therefore, with Eusebius' comment is given under Clement.[28] Here, however, we mark the fact that the story itself is traced back to Papias, together with the view it gives of Peter's activity at Rome. Taken along with Ignatius' allusion to Peter, cited above, it seems to show that at the opening of the second century, Peter was connected with the community at Rome in the minds of prominent Christians of Asia Minor.[29]

An account of Papias with every recoverable fragment of his book is in J. B. Lightfoot, *The Apostolic Fathers* (2 vols., London, 1889–1890). See also the article on Papias in W. Smith and H. Wace, *Dictionary of Christian Biography* (4 vols., Boston, 1877–1887), Vol. IV; and in J. J. Herzog and H. Hauck, *Realencyklopädie für protestantische Theologie und Kirche* (24 vols., Leipzig, 1896–1913), Vol. XIV; B. W. Bacon, *Is Mark a Roman Gospel?* (Harvard University Press, 1919); F. J. F. Jackson and K. Lake, *The Beginnings of Christianity* (2 vols., London, 1920–1922), Vol. I, pp. 316–317; B. J. Kidd, *A History of the Christian Church to A.D. 461* (3 vols., Oxford, 1922–1925), Vol. I, pp. 186–189.

[27] *Infra,* p. 281 and n. 104.

[28] *Infra,* p. 80.

[29] This much may certainly be said, whether one does or does not accept the theory of the Petrine or Roman authorship of the Gospel of Mark.

Dionysius of Corinth

(c. 170)

Dionysius, bishop of the church in the busy seaport of Corinth and a contemporary of Soter, bishop of Rome, wrote letters to various churches in Greece, Asia Minor and Crete, which were later assembled in a collection read by Eusebius in the early fourth century.[30] He wrote also a letter to the Roman community in acknowledgment of a letter which had been previously sent him by Bishop Soter. Eusebius, in his *Church History,* has quoted four short passages from this letter to the Romans.[31] In one, Dionysius recalls the letter sent by Clement to the Corinthians seventy-five years before; in another, he makes the earliest statement we possess to the effect that Peter and Paul actually founded the Roman church.

This is also the earliest text to imply that Peter and Paul met their deaths on the same day, although the Greek wording is perhaps too vague to be much insisted upon. Somewhat later, however, the Roman church is to be found celebrating their martyrdoms or depositions together.[32] At the beginning of the fifth century, Prudentius and Augustine tried to solve the chronological difficulty involved by advancing the theory that the apostles died on the same day of the month but in different years,[33] but the *Index* attributed to Pope Gelasius condemned as heretical any suggestion that they did not die at the same time.[34] Since then until recent times, the prevailing tendency in church history as in legend has been to unite their deaths.[35] Nevertheless it is now usually recognized as impossible to adjust the chronology to fit such a hypothesis. It seems more likely that the Roman church

[30] On Eusebius *vide infra,* pp. 96–102.

[31] For two more of these extracts *vide infra,* pp. 252–253.

[32] *Infra,* p. 108.

[33] Augustine, *Sermones,* 295, 381, "On the anniversary of the apostles Peter and Paul." Prudentius, *Peristephanon,* XII. *Infra,* p. 118.

[34] The so-called decretal, *De Recipiendis et Non Recipiendis Libris,* II.

[35] The *Breviarium Romanum,* in the order for vespers on June 29, contains the following chant: "Today Simon Peter mounted the gibbet of the cross, alleluia; today the keybearer of the kingdom passed rejoicing to Christ; today the apostle Paul, the light of the world, bowed his head and for the name of Christ was crowned with martyrdom, alleluia."

fixed originally upon the single date because of a simultaneous translation of the two bodies sometime during the first few centuries.[36]

On Dionysius of Corinth, *vide* A. Harnack, *Geschichte der altchristlichen Litteratur bis Eusebius* (2 vols., Leipzig, 1893–1904), Vol. I,[1] pp. 235 *sqq.*; G. Krueger, *History* of Early Christian Literature (trans. by C. R. Gillett, New York, 1897), p. 55. On the anniversary of Peter and Paul *vide* C. Erbes, *Die Todestage der Apostel Paulus und Petrus und ihre römischen Denkmäler* in O. Gebhardt, A. Harnack, C. Schmidt (editors), *Texte und Untersuchungen zur Geschichte der altchristlichen Literatur* (Leipzig, 1882–), New Series, Vol. IV.

Eusebius, *Historia Ecclesiastica,* II, 25. Text. *Eusebius Werke* (*Die griechischen christlichen Schriftsteller der ersten drei Jahrhunderte*), II[1], 178.

And Dionysius, bishop of the Corinthians, in the letter he wrote to the Romans, stated in the following words that they [Peter and Paul] both suffered martyrdom at the same time. "You have thus by this admonition bound together the plantings of Peter and Paul at Rome and at Corinth. For they both alike planted in our Corinth and taught us [37] and both alike taught together in Italy and suffered martyrdom at the same time."

Irenaeus of Asia and Gaul

(c. 130–c. 200)

Irenaeus, a native of Asia Minor, who in later life came west to settle in Lyons on the Rhone, was among the first to employ the traditions of the apostles in the churches, in particular the Roman traditions of Peter and Paul, as a systematic defense against innovations of doctrine and heresies. By the middle of the second century, there were springing up various mystical or

[36] *Infra,* p. 106.

[37] Chapter XI of Paul's Second Epistle to the Corinthians contains allusions to another apostle who had been visiting the church at Corinth and preaching a somewhat different form of gospel. Compare also the First Epistle to the Corinthians, III, 22, and IX, 5.

speculative sects, such as the Montanists,[38] who claimed to be the direct recipients of fresh revelations, and the Gnostics,[39] who asserted that they had passed in deeper knowledge beyond the slow-witted, uncomprehending disciples of Jesus. Irenaeus and others like him turned for reassurance to the churches who could be trusted to teach and interpret the Scriptures as the apostles had done. Preëminent among them was the church of Rome with its unbroken records and its twofold apostolic tradition.

Irenaeus' writings had a momentous effect upon the development of ecclesiastical polity and the rise of the papal office. We give fuller extracts from them later.[39a] Here we quote but two sentences to illustrate his conception of the origin of the Roman episcopate.

Irenaeus is in many respects the most important Christian writer of the second century, after Ignatius, whose work has come down to us. He is discussed in every history of the Church or of dogma. A recent biography is that of F. R. M. Hitchcock, *Irenaeus of Lugdunum* (Cambridge University Press, 1914). A translation of his chief book, *Against Heresies,* was published in 1916 by the Society for the Propagation of Christian Knowledge.

[38] The Montanists were a puritanical sect of Phrygian origin that protested against the growing formalism in the Church. Like the Brethren of the Free Spirit or the Quakers of later days, they affirmed the right of every believer to be a priest for himself and follow his own light, and the necessity of a more austere moral discipline. On this heresy, *vide* A. Hilgenfeld, *Die Ketzergeschichte des Urchristenthums* (Leipzig, 1884); J. De Soyres, *Montanism and the Primitive Church* (London), 1878; N. Bonwetsch, *Montanismus* in J. J. Herzog and A. Hauck, *Realencyklopädie für protestantische Theologie und Kirche,* Vol. XIII; H. M. Gwatkin, *Early Church History to A.D. 313* (2 vols., London, 1912), Vol. II, chap. XVI; J. C. Ayer, *Source Book for Ancient Church History,* pp. 106–109.

[39] Gnosticism is a name commonly applied to a fluctuating series of dualistic and syncretistic systems of philosophy, deriving their origin from Persian and Babylonian sources but assimilating features of Greek philosophy and finally of Christianity as they spread into the West. In its early forms, Gnosticism antedates Christianity. In its later shapes, it vexed and divided the Church for several centuries, although its influence gradually waned after the second. In the fourth, its place was taken by Manicheanism. Some Christian Gnostics taught that the God of the Old Testament, the Creator of the material world, was cruel even when he seemed to be just, that Jesus was an emanation from another and spiritual God, that he appeared to be born and die but in reality was subject to no fleshly limitations, and that he had ascended into heaven without feeling pain or death. Hence came the answering orthodox insistence upon God the Father as also the Creator and upon the reality of the incarnation and sufferings of Christ. A. Harnack, *History of Dogma* (trans. by N. Buchanan, 7 vols., Boston, 1897–1901), Vol. I, pp. 222 *sqq.*; E. de Faye, *Introduction à l'Étude de Gnosticisme* (Paris, 1903); W. Bousset, *Gnosticism,* in *Encyclopaedia Britannica* (11th ed., 29 vols., London, 1910–1911), Vol. XII; H. M. Gwatkin, *op. cit.,* Vol. II, chap. XVI; W. Schültz, *Dokumente der Gnosis* (Jena, 1910); J. C. Ayer, *op. cit.,* pp. 76–106.

[39a] *Infra,* pp. 265–272.

Irenaeus, *Contra Haereses*, III, 1, 3. Text. J. P. Migne, *Patrologia Graeca*, VII, 844, 849.

So Matthew among the Hebrews issued a gospel written in their tongue, while Peter and Paul were preaching at Rome and establishing the church. . . . The blessed apostles then founded and reared up this church and afterwards committed unto Linus the office of the episcopate.

Clement of Alexandria

(fl. 190–215)

Clement of Alexandria, for years the light of the Christian training school in Alexandria, had been before his conversion an earnest student of Greek literature and philosophy; in after life, instead of deriding and repudiating pagan learning, as the first apologists had done, he aimed to bring it into a harmonious relation with his new faith. Hence his chief contribution to the development of Christian thought was a conception of Christianity itself as a revelation of philosophy made perfect and of the older discipline as "a schoolmaster to bring the Hellenic mind to Christ, as the law was to bring the Hebrews."[40]

His greatest works were an introduction to Christianity, entitled *Protrepticus,* addressed to Greeks; an account of Christian life and ethics, called *Paedagogus*; and a collection of miscellaneous chapters on true faith as the highest manifestation of philosophy, which he named *Stromata, Tapestries*. He wrote also an important commentary on the Scriptures, known as the *Hypotyposes,* of which only a few fragments, preserved in other men's writings, have come down to us.

The peculiar interest of Clement for us here lies in the fact that he made a point of visiting and talking with the survivors of a more primitive Christian generation than his own and of recording the information and ideas which he gathered from these older sources. The introductory paragraph of his *Stromata*

[40] *Stromata,* I, 5.

runs as follows:[41] "This handbook is not a composition fabricated artistically for display, but notes preserved for my old age as a remedy for forgetfulness, a bald outline and memorandum of those powerful and glowing words which I was privileged to hear, as well as of those blessed and extraordinary men. Of these men one, an Ionian, was in Greece and two in Magna Graecia,[42] one of whom had come from Coele-Syria[43] and the other from Egypt. There were others in the East, one of them an Assyrian, another a Hebrew in Palestine. But when I discovered the last, — although in might he was truly first, — and hunted him out, that Sicilian bee, in his lurking place in Egypt, I found rest. These men, who guard the true tradition of the blessed doctrine, received directly from the holy apostles, Peter and James and John and Paul, the son having heard it from the father, — yet few were like the fathers, — have by God's will continued even unto us to plant in us those inherited and apostolic seeds."

Through Clement, therefore, we catch a few last, disappearing echoes of the age that followed upon the apostolic and that knew the sons of the apostles' disciples. His anecdotes of the apostles have at times the flavor of personal recollections, handed down from actual eyewitnesses. But he never says where he heard any specific story and without such definite corroboration it is impossible to be sure how far he is in any given instance repeating from floating hearsay or legend and how far from direct, reliable tradition. Eusebius tells us that one of the episodes he quotes from Clement, which we give below, was confirmed by Papias.[44] But Clement alone leaves one usually a little uncertain.

On Clement, *vide* O. Bardenhewer, *Patrology* (St. Louis, 1908), § 38; A. Harnack, *History of Dogma* (trans. by N. Buchanan, 7 vols., Boston, 1897–1901), Vol. II, pp. 319–332; A. Harnack, *Geschichte der altchristlichen Litteratur bis Eusebius* (2 vols., Leipzig, 1893–1904), Vol. I,[1] pp. 296–327; V. Pascal, *La Foi et la Raison dans Clement d'Alexandrie* (Montdidier, 1901);

[41] *Stromata*, I, 1. Quoted by Eusebius, *Historia Ecclesiastica*, V, 11, 3–5.

[42] Southern Italy.

[43] Coele-Syria was the name given to the valley lying between the eastern and the western ranges of the Lebanon mountains.

[44] For Papias *vide supra*, p. 73.

W. Wagner, *Der Christ und die Welt nach Clemens von Alexandrien* (Göttingen, 1903); R. B. Tollinton, *Clement of Alexandria, A Study in Christian Liberalism* (2 vols., London, 1914); H. M. Gwatkin, *Early Church History to A.D. 313* (2 vols., London, 1912), Vol. II, chap. XIX.

Clement of Alexandria, *Hypotyposes,* quoted by Eusebius, *Historia Ecclesiastica,* II, 15. Text. *Eusebius Werke* (*Die griechischen christlichen Schriftsteller der ersten drei Jahrhunderte*), II[1], 140.

And so brightly did the splendor of piety illumine the minds of Peter's hearers [at Rome] that they were not satisfied with one audience only nor with the unwritten teaching of the divine gospel, but with all manner of urgency they besought Mark, a follower of Peter and the one whose gospel is extant, that he would leave to them a written record of the doctrine which had been communicated to them by word of mouth. Nor did they cease until they had prevailed with him and had thus become the instigators of the written gospel which is called "according to Mark." And they say that when Peter learned through a revelation of the Spirit of that which had been done, he was pleased with their zeal and sanctioned the book for use in the churches. Clement gives this account in the eighth book of his *Hypotyposes* and the bishop of Hierapolis, named Papias, agrees with him. And they say that Peter makes mention of Mark in his first epistle, which, they say, he wrote also in Rome, as he indicates when he calls the city figuratively Babylon, in the following words: "The church that is at Babylon, elect together with you, saluteth you, and so doth Mark, my son."[45] This Mark, they say, was the first sent to Egypt, and he preached the gospel which he had written down and founded the first church in Alexandria itself.[46]

[45] I Peter V, 13.

[46] This is the traditional origin of the see of Alexandria, which in time ranked with the Petrine sees of Rome and Antioch.

Hypotyposes, quoted by Eusebius, *Historia Ecclesiastica,* VI, 14. Text. *Eusebius Werke* (*Die griechischen christlichen Schriftsteller der ersten drei Jahrhunderte*), II[2], 550.

Again in the same book [*Hypotyposes*] Clement records the tradition of the ancient presbyters regarding the order of the gospels, which is as follows. He says that the gospels which contain the genealogies [47] were written first. The gospel according to Mark had the following origin. When Peter was preaching the word publicly at Rome and proclaiming the gospel in the Spirit, his hearers, who were many, urged upon Mark, who had long been his follower and remembered his sayings, to write them down. And Mark did so and gave his gospel to those who had asked for it. When Peter learned of it, he neither directly forbade nor encouraged it.

Stromata, III, 6; VII, 11, quoted in Eusebius' *Historia Ecclesiastica,* III, 30. Text. *Eusebius Werke* (*Die griechischen christlichen Schriftsteller der ersten drei Jahrhunderte*), II[1], 262, and *Clemens Alexandrinus* (same series), II, 220; III, 46.

Clement,[48] indeed, whose words we have just quoted, after this statement gives an account of the apostles who had wives, aimed against those persons who rejected marriage. "Or will they," says he, "disapprove even of the apostles? For Peter and Philip [49] begat children; and Philip also gave his daughters husbands. And Paul does not hesitate, in one of his epistles, to greet his wife, whom he did not take about with him, that he might not be impeded in

47 *I.e.,* of course, Matthew and Luke.

48 Clement has been arguing against the extreme asceticism advocated and practised by many ardent believers of his day.

49 Matthew VIII, 14; Acts XXI, 8, 9. For the legend of Peter's daughter, Petronilla, *vide infra,* p. 198.

his ministry." [50] Since we have broached this subject, it does no harm to include another anecdote which is given by the same author and which is worth reading. In the seventh book of his *Stromata,* he tells the following incident: [51] "They say, accordingly, that when the blessed Peter saw his own wife led out to die, he rejoiced because of her summons and her return home, and called to her very encouragingly and comfortingly, addressing her by name, 'Oh thou, remember the Lord.' Such was the marriage of the blessed, and their perfect disposition toward those dearest to them."

2. PETER THE ROMAN MARTYR

Caius of Rome

(fl. 199–217)

The next clear allusions to Peter's presence at Rome come from Rome itself in the shape of traditions as to the circumstances of his death or burial. The author of our first quotation is one Caius, a person of whom we know nothing certain except what Eusebius tells us a century later, namely, that he was "a very learned man," a member of the church under Bishop Zephyrinus (c. 199–217) and that he wrote at Rome a polemic in the form of a dialogue against Proclus, a leader of the Montanist faction.[52] Eusebius cites passages from this dialogue on more than one occasion.[53] In the extract below, Caius is apparently maintaining the superior authority of orthodox Roman doctrine over Montanist teaching on the ground that the Roman church was the direct creation of the apostles and is still the repository of their bones. He is elaborating the argument already forged by Irenaeus,[54] which was to prove a potent weapon against all manner of change and dissent.

[50] I Cor. IX, 5. However, the words do not prove conclusively that Paul was married, and I Cor. VII, 7, 8, seems to imply as clearly that he was not. Clement is the only one of the early Fathers to say that he was and others deny it.

[51] There is no other authority for this tradition.

[52] On the Montanists, *vide supra*, p. 77, n. 38.

[53] *Historia Ecclesiastica,* VI, 20, 3; III, 28, 1–2.

[54] *Supra,* p. 76.

On Caius, and the tombs of Peter and Paul, *vide* A. Harnack, *Geschichte der altchristlichen Litteratur bis Eusebius* (2 vols., Leipzig, 1893–1904), Vol. I [2], p. 601; A. Harnack in J. J. Herzog and A. Hauck, *Realencyklopädie für protestantische Theologie und Kirche* (24 vols., Leipzig, 1896–1913), Vol. III, p. 638: Listerer, *Die Apostelgräber nach Gaius,* in *Theologische Quartalschrift* (Tübingen, 1892), pp. 121–132; C. Erbes, *Die Todestage der Apostel Petrus and Paulus und ihre römischen Denkmäler,* in O. Gebhardt, A. Harnack, C. Schmidt (editors), *Texte und Untersuchungen zur Geschichte der altchristlichen Literatur* (Leipzig, 1882–), New Series, Vol. IV; H. Leitzmann, *Petrus und Paulus in Rom*; *Liturgische und archäologische Studien* (Bonn, 1915), pp. 155 *sqq.*; F. Haase, *Apostel und Evangelisten in den orientalischen Überlieferungen* (Münster, 1922), pp. 211–213.

Eusebius, *Historia Ecclesiastica,* II, 25. Text. *Eusebius Werke* (*Die griechischen christlichen Schriftsteller der ersten drei Jahrhunderte*), II[1], 176–178.

Moreover, it is said that Paul was beheaded in Rome and that Peter also was crucified under Nero. And this report is confirmed by the fact that the names of Peter and Paul are preserved in the cemeteries there to this day. It is further confirmed by a member of the church, Caius by name, who lived under Zephyrinus, bishop of Rome. In an argument that he wrote against Proclus, the leader of the Phrygian heresy,[55] he speaks as follows of the places where the sacred bodies of the aforesaid apostles are laid. " But I can show you the trophies [56] of the apostles. For if you will go to the Vatican or to the Ostian Way, you will find the trophies of those who laid the foundation of this church."

[55] Montanus, the first prophet of the Montanist movement, was a Phrygian.

[56] The Greek word τρόπαια, trophies, is vague. To erect a trophy was customarily to mark a victory and some scholars have thought that the " trophies " mentioned here were stones that marked the sites of the apostles' martyrdom. Others have interpreted the word as meaning tombs, containing the apostles' bodies. In either case, these monuments must have been in Caius' day comparatively small and inconspicuous, for Rome was still a pagan city. The tradition that Peter was crucified on the slope of the Janiculum, on the spot now covered by the buildings of the church of San Pietro in Montorio, and that his body was carried down to the Vatican lowland for burial is late and based upon an error. R. A. Lanciani, *Pagan and Christian Rome* (Boston, 1893), pp. 126–128.

Tertullian of Carthage

(c. 160–c. 235)

Tertullian, the most thorough-going theologian of the Latin West before Augustine [57] and, unlike Clement of Alexandria, the uncompromising foe of all Greek philosophy, was a younger contemporary of Clement and of Caius of Rome. He was born at Carthage, where his father was serving a term of office as centurion, and he returned to Africa to spend the latter part of his life, but for some years in his early manhood he led the career of a lawyer and rhetorician at Rome. At about thirty-five years of age, he was converted to Christianity and flung himself thereafter with impetuous ardor into religious pursuits, renouncing scornfully his previous profane interests. Whether or not he was ordained a priest, as Jerome says,[58] he became a man of influence and distinction in the Christian community, until about 202, when he joined the Montanists, a group peculiarly likely to attract one of his fiery temperament.[59] He died, therefore, under the odium of heresy. He wrote many books on religious subjects, some in defense of Christian doctrine against pagan philosophers, Jews and heretics of the Gnostic stamp,[60] for whom he had no sympathy, others on various phases of Christian life and practice, a few, after 207, in contemptuous denunciation of the orthodox Roman church for what seemed to him then its degenerate morality and discipline.

One of his most important dogmatic works, written while he was still a Catholic, was *The Prescription of Heretics*.[61] In it, he enlarged upon the theory enunciated by Irenaeus,[62] that only churches founded by the apostles or by bishops whom the

[57] Tertullian's *Apology* was one of the few early Latin, Christian writings thought worthy of translation into Greek. Cyprian's correspondence shared the distinction.

[58] *De Viris Illustribus*, LVI. Jerome wrote this about 390.

[59] On the Montanists, *vide supra*, p. 77, n. 38.

[60] On the Gnostics, *vide supra*, p. 77, n. 39.

[61] "Praescriptio" under the Roman law was a form of defense which might be employed in civil cases involving claims to real estate. It was based upon the length of the defendant's occupation of the land under dispute. If admitted by the judge, it excluded the plaintiff at once from any further proceedings.

[62] *Supra*, p. 76; *infra*, p. 261.

apostles had appointed could claim to transmit the true, unalloyed doctrine without flaws and that all heresy, being a novelty, was for that reason false. The first passage here quoted is a portion of this argument. Tertullian is dwelling particularly on the authoritative character of the Roman church, which had received the witness not of one apostle only, but of two or even three, and which possessed a record of the ordination of Bishop Clement by Peter.[63] Another example of this same argument is in the excerpt from the treatise against the Gnostic Marcion.[64]

The *Scorpiace* or *Antidote against Scorpions* was an indignant vindication of the value and meritoriousness of Christian martyrdom as against the suggestion of certain Gnostics, that even the most holy martyrs were merely expiating sins committed in a previous state of existence and did not deserve the honors paid them by the Church. It held up Peter as a pattern of suffering and spiritual power.[65] A short essay on Baptism refuted objections to the orthodox doctrine of that sacrament and mentioned by way of illustration Peter's baptisms in the Tiber. From the sum of these scattered references it is plain that Tertullian accepted as unquestioned the belief that Peter had both preached and endured death by crucifixion at Rome[66] and had selected a bishop to succeed him. The allusions are brief and cursory, but slightly more definite than those we have

[63] About this time, appears the tendency in the more popular writers to crowd out Linus and Cletus, who were named by Irenaeus (*infra,* p. 268) as the successors of Peter and Paul, in favor of the better known Clement and to make the latter the recipient of Peter's final charge and blessing. The more accurate historians, as will be noticed, keep Linus and Cletus in their places, although some, like Rufinus (*infra,* p. 162), attempt later to compromise with the legend by calling these two the assistants or coadjutors of Peter during his lifetime and Clement his successor after his death. Such a compromise became easier as the term of Peter's residence at Rome was gradually lengthened. The "register" mentioned here by Tertullian must have contained apocryphal material. An elaborate invention of the sort was the so-called *Letter of Clement* to the Apostle James, from which we quote. *Infra,* pp. 163–165.

[64] On Marcion, *vide infra,* pp. 258, 259, 266, n. 65, 270, 272.

[65] For a quotation from the *Scorpiace* and a fuller discussion of its bearing, *vide infra,* pp. 286–288, 295.

[66] Lengthy accounts of Peter's crucifixion were by this time coming into circulation in the apocryphal Acts. Whether the mode of his execution was originally an apocryphal invention, adopted by the author of John XXI, 18, and after him by Tertullian and Origen, who first among "ecclesiastical writers" refer to it, or whether the authors of the earlier apocryphal literature and of the passage in John, as well as Tertullian and Origen, all took it independently from some trustworthy source or tradition now lost, it is impossible to decide positively. *Vide infra,* pp. 151–152, 177.

found in the older writers. They still deal apparently with facts which every reader was expected to know and no one doubted and which, therefore, it was unnecessary to reënforce by proofs.

On Tertullian, *vide* E. Nöldechen, *Tertullian* (Gotha, 1890); P. Monceaux, *Histoire Litteraire de l'Afrique Chrétienne* (7 vols., Paris, 1901–1923), Vol. I; A. Harnack, *History of Dogma* (trans. by N. Buchanan, 7 vols., Boston, 1897–1901), Vol. V, pp. 14–23; E. Rolffs, *Das Indulgenz-Edict des römischen Bischofs Kallist,* in O. Gebhardt, A. Harnack, C. Schmidt (editors), *Texte und Untersuchungen zur Geschichte der altchristlichen Literatur* (Leipzig, 1882–), Vol. XI; J. B. Lightfoot, *The Apostolic Fathers* (2 vols., London, 1889–1890), Pt. II; T. R. Glover, *The Conflict of Religions in the Early Roman Empire* (London, 3rd ed., 1909), Chap. X; N. Bonwetsch in J. J. Herzog and A. Hauck, *Realencyklopädie für protestantische Theologie und Kirche* (24 vols., Leipzig, 1896–1913), Vol. XIX, pp. 537 *sqq.*; H. M. Gwatkin, *Early Church History to A.D. 313* (2 vols., London, 1912), Vol. II, Chap. XXII.

De Praescriptione Haereticorum, 32, 36. Text. Ed. by P. de Labriolle (*Textes et Documents pour l'Étude Historique du Christianisme*) IV, 68, 78 *sqq.*

32 . . . For in this form [*i.e.,* episcopal lists] the apostolic churches present their registers, such as the church of Smyrna, which shows that Polycarp was appointed thereto by John, and the church of Rome, which states that Clement was ordained by Peter. . . .

36 Come then, you who would better exercise your wits about the business of your own salvation, recall the various apostolic churches, in which the actual chairs of the apostles are still standing in their places, in which their own authentic letters are read, repeating the voice and calling up the face of each of them severally. Achaea is very near you, where you have Corinth. If you are not far from Macedonia, you have Philippi.[67] If you can travel into Asia, you have Ephesus. But if you are near Italy, you have Rome, whence

[67] Some texts add: "You have the Thessalonians."

also our authority is derived close at hand.[68] How happy is that church on which the apostles poured forth all their teaching together with their blood! Where Peter endured a passion like his Lord's! Where Paul won his crown in a death like John's! [69]

Adversus Marcionem, IV, 5. Text. *Corpus Scriptorum Ecclesiasticorum Latinorum,* XLVII, 430.

Let us see what milk the Corinthians drank from Paul, by what rule of faith the Galatians were corrected, what the Philippians, the Thessalonians, the Ephesians [70] are repeating, what also is the utterance of the Romans, who stand so very near [to the apostles], to whom both Peter and Paul bequeathed the gospel and sealed it further with their own blood. We have besides John's foster churches.

De Baptismo, 4. Text. *Corpus Scriptorum Ecclesiasticorum Latinorum,* XX, 204.

Therefore it does not matter whether one is washed in the sea or in a pool, in a river or in a fountain, in a lake or in a tank, nor is there any difference between those whom John baptised in the Jordan and those whom Peter baptised in the Tiber.

Origen of Alexandria

(c. 185–c. 254)

Origen, the most powerful intellect in all that group of church Fathers who were living when the second century passed into the

68 The church of Carthage was founded perhaps by missionaries from Italy. Its nearest apostolic connection was certainly at Rome and it seems to have looked to Rome in the beginning as its model.

69 *I.e.,* John the Baptist, who was beheaded. This passage is given again in its full context, *infra,* pp. 288–295.

70 These are all churches to which Paul wrote epistles.

third, was in boyhood a pupil of Clement of Alexandria [71] in the famous Christian school in that city. In 202, when Clement fled before the persecution of Septimius Severus, the bishop Demetrius chose out Origen, then only eighteen years of age, to succeed Clement as headmaster. He remained at his post with few interruptions for twenty-eight years, lecturing and composing a vast number of works on every aspect of religious thought. It is said that seven amanuenses were kept busy taking down his dictation, and the defective catalogue of his books that still survives contains eight hundred titles.

He developed further the characteristic idea of Clement that Christianity was a form of revealed philosophy and built up a comprehensive Christian philosophic system, which he supported by an exhaustive use of both pagan and Christian literature. The fullest exposition of this system is contained in his *De Principiis,* which has come down in a free Latin translation by Rufinus.[72] He originated the science of Biblical, textual criticism in an immense undertaking known as the *Hexapla,* a collation in parallel columns of the Hebrew text of the Old Testament with the Greek of the Septuagint and three other Greek versions. His purpose in the enterprise was to defend rather than to correct the text of the Septuagint, which he regarded as a work of inspiration as much as its Hebrew prototype, but the method which he devised has been utilized ever since by scholars for purposes of pure criticism. He compiled an elaborate and interminable series of notes and commentaries upon the Scriptures, searching everywhere to detect and explain not the literal or temporary meaning, but the deep, hidden or spiritual meaning, ignoring almost entirely the plain, historical significance, and in this way promoting a method of Biblical exegesis as tortuous and mystifying as his method of textual criticism was clear and exact.[73]

Unfortunately, in his desire to state religion in terms of philosophy and thus win over the educated circles of his day, he

[71] On Clement, *vide supra,* p. 78.

[72] On Rufinus, *vide infra,* p. 160.

[73] A quotation illustrating Origen's use of allegory and symbolism may be found, *infra,* pp. 317–322.

gave philosophical conceptions so prominent a place in his work that the Church began to be suspicious of it. In 231 and 232, synods were called at Alexandria which deposed him from his office as headmaster and expelled him from the city for heterodox teaching and irregular ordination to the priesthood. The sentence was approved by a synod held at Rome about the same time.[74] After vainly endeavoring to obtain reinstatement, he moved to Caesarea and opened a school of theology there, which soon drew many pupils. For nearly twenty years more, he continued to lecture, preach and write, until the outbreak of the bitter persecution under Decius in 250–251. He was then seized, thrown into prison and tortured. In 254 or 255, he died, whether still in prison or not we do not know.

The storms of controversy, however, that were to rage around his name only began in his lifetime. His books were too compelling and too extraordinary to be left alone. They were read everywhere in the East and in the course of time many were translated into Latin, expurgated of the more offensive portions. But they were still repeatedly and virulently attacked for their too philosophical, too broadly figurative treatment of religious topics.[75] As the state of learning declined and men became more literal minded, their distrust of Origen increased. In the year 400, he and his "blasphemous opinions" were condemned by Pope Anastasius. In 553, the Fifth General Council held at Constantinople anathematized him along with Arius and other heretics.[76] In the West, he almost ceased to be read and the stigma of heresy hung around his name through all the Middle Ages. The commentaries on Genesis and Matthew are extant in only a few fragments, quoted in other men's writings. Our references barely suffice to show that Origen shared the general opinion regarding the place and manner of Peter's death.

[74] *Infra*, pp. 312–313. On Origen's attitude toward the Roman theory of the Petrine powers, *vide infra*, p. 316.

[75] See, for example, Jerome's list of Origen's errors; *Epistola* 7, *Ad Pammachium* (trans. in J. C. Ayer, *A Source Book for Ancient Church History*, pp. 486–487) and the decretal attributed to Pope Gelasius, *De Recipiendis et Non Recipiendis Libris*, IV. *Cf.* E. v. Dobschütz, *Das Decretum Gelasianum de Libris recipiendis et non recipiendis* (Leipzig, 1912), p. 10. The translation in Ayer, *op. cit.*, pp. 532–536 (V, 21), follows the numbering in Mansi.

[76] J. C. Ayer, *op. cit.*, pp. 487–488, 542–543, 552–553.

On Origen, *vide* A. Harnack, *Geschichte der altchristlichen Litteratur bis Eusebius* (2 vols., Leipzig, 1893–1904), Vol. I, pp. 332–405, Vol. I,[2] pp. 835–842; A. Harnack, *History of Dogma* (trans. by N. Buchanan, 7 vols., Boston, 1897–1901), Vol. II, pp. 332–378; J. Langen, *Vaticanische Dogma* (4 vols., Bonn, 1871), Vol. I, p. 67; K. J. Neumann, *Der römische Staat und die allgemeine Kirche* (Leipzig, 1900), Vol. I, pp. 265 *sqq.*; W. Fairweather, *Origen and Greek Patristic Theology* (New York, 1901); R. Seeberg, *Lehrbuch der Dogmengeschichte* (Leipzig, 1895–1898), Vol. I, pp. 393 *sqq.*; O. Bardenhewer, *Patrology* (trans. by T. Shahan, St. Louis, 1908), § 39; H. M. Gwatkin, *Early Church History to A.D. 313* (2 vols., London, 1912), Vol. II, chap. XX.

In Genesim, III, summarized by Eusebius, *Historia Ecclesiastica*, III, 1. Text. *Eusebius Werke* (*Die griechischen christlichen Schriftsteller der ersten drei Jahrhunderte*), II[1], 188.

Meanwhile the holy apostles and disciples of our Savior were scattered over the whole world. Parthia, according to tradition, was allotted to Thomas, Scythia to Andrew and Asia to John, who, after he had dwelt there for some time, died at Ephesus. Peter seems to have preached in Pontus, Galatia, Bithynia, Cappadocia and Asia [77] to the Jews of the dispersion. And at last, having come to Rome, he was crucified head downward,[78] for he had asked that he might suffer in this way. What do we need to say of Paul, who fulfilled the gospel of Christ from Jerusalem to Illyricum and afterwards suffered martyrdom in Rome under Nero? These facts are related by Origen in the third volume of his *Commentary on Genesis.*

In Matthaeum, I, quoted by Eusebius, *Historia Ecclesiastica*, VI, 25. Text. *Eusebius Werke* (*Die griechischen christlichen Schriftsteller der ersten drei Jahrhunderte*), II[2], 576.

The second [gospel] is by Mark, who composed it after the instructions of Peter, who in his catholic epistle acknowl-

[77] I Peter I, 1. [78] *Supra*, p. 85, n. 66.

edges him as a son, saying: "The church that is at Babylon, elect together with you, saluteth you and so doth Mark, my son." [79]

Porphyry of Tyre (?)

(c. 230–300)

In the following excerpts we have the only known surviving comment of a pagan on the story of Peter, preserved by the fact of its incorporation in an apologetic Christian work of the early fifth century. The author of this latter was one Macarius Magnes, probably to be identified with Macarius, bishop of Magnesia in Lydia or in Caria, who was a member of the church party hostile to Chrysostom. He wrote in five books an imaginary dialogue between himself and a pagan philosopher, in the course of which the philosopher criticised or ridiculed various passages in the New Testament and he himself defended them. The speeches of the philosopher seem to have been culled mainly from the treatise of the Neoplatonist Porphyry, *Against the Christians,* composed about the year 280 and now lost. Macarius does not expressly say, as he does in other instances, that our quotations are from Porphyry, but they are both like Porphyry in style and scathing sarcasm. Porphyry himself spent much time at Rome about the middle of the third century and came into relations with the Christians there. It is clear that he investigated their writings and traditions with unusual care. He regarded Christ with respect as a noble sage but despised the Church of his own day as crude, inconsistent and steeped in delusion. He was mystified that men like Origen, who had delved into "the old philosophy," could still remain believers.[80] Porphyry's onslaught was answered by Eusebius, Methodius of

[79] I Peter V, 13. Compare the similar extract taken by Eusebius from Clement, *supra,* p. 80.

[80] See Porphyry's scornful references to Origen, quoted by Eusebius, *Historia Ecclesiastica,* VI, 19, 2–3, and to the Christian Gnostics' criticisms of Plato and their use of spurious revelations, in his *Life of Plotinus,* printed as introduction to *Plotinus* (trans. by S. Mackenna, 3 vols., London, 1917–1924), Vol. I, p. 15. A. Harnack, *Porphyrius "Gegen die Christen"* in *Abhandlungen der Königlich Preussischen Akademie der Wissenschaften, Philosophische-Historische Klasse* (Berlin, 1916).

Tyre and other Christian scholars before Macarius, but their books have disappeared.

On Macarius, *vide* A. Harnack, *Miscelle zum Aufenthalt des Petrus in Rom* in *Theologische Literaturzeitung* (Leipzig, 1902), pp. 604–605; T. H. Bernard, *Macarius Magnes* in *Journal of Theological Studies* (London, 1901), pp. 610–611; A. Harnack, *Kritik des Neuen Testaments von einem griechischen Philosophen des 3. Jahrhunderts,* in O. Gebhardt, A. Harnack, C. Schmidt (editors), *Texte und Untersuchungen zur Geschichte der altchristlichen Literatur* (Leipzig, 1882–), Third Series Vol. VII.

Macarius Magnes, *Unigenitus,* III, 22; IV, 4. Text. Ed. by C. Blondel, *Macarii Magnetis Quae Supersunt,* 102, 162.

This leader [Peter] of the band of the disciples, who had been taught by God to despise death, was seized by Herod and escaped and thus brought punishment on his guards. For he escaped by night and when day broke there was consternation among the soldiers as to how Peter had got out. And Herod inquired for him and when he did not find him, questioned the guards and ordered them to be led away, that is, to be executed. So one wonders why Jesus gave the keys of heaven to such a man as Peter and why in such a time of disorder and tumult, beset with such grave dangers, he said: " Feed my lambs," if, in fact, the sheep are the faithful who flock to the mystery of consummation and the lambs are the throng of catechumens who are fed still on the simple milk of doctrine. Furthermore, it is recorded that Peter fed the lambs for several months only before he was crucified,[81] although Jesus had said that the gates of hell should not prevail against him. . . .

Now let us notice what was said to Paul. " Then spake the Lord to Paul in the night by a vision, ' Be not afraid but speak, . . . For I am with thee and no man shall set

[81] The writer, who knew the New Testament so well, cannot mean that Peter's death occurred only a few months after his master's. It is more reasonable to suppose that he is alluding to the length of Peter's activities in Rome before his martyrdom. If so, this is the oldest suggestion that we have as to the duration of Peter's stay there.

on thee to hurt thee.' "[82] Notwithstanding, this fine fellow was overpowered at Rome and beheaded, he who had said that we should judge angels, even as Peter, who had received the right to feed the lambs, was fastened to the cross and crucified.

Peter of Alexandria

(d. 311)

Our next allusion to the martyrdom of Peter comes from a successor of Clement and Origen in the school at Alexandria. Peter of Alexandria was both headmaster and bishop from 300 until his own death as a martyr, in 311. In 306, he wrote a treatise on penance, which has been preserved in both Greek and Syriac. Its fourteen canons prescribed the conditions on which persons who had abjured Christ or lapsed during the persecution of Diocletian might be restored to communion in the church of Egypt. Those who had sacrificed to the pagan gods in sheer panic, without facing the torture, were assigned long periods of probation, whereas those who had broken down only after imprisonment and torment were treated more leniently. Those who had yielded temporarily under suffering and had later repented of their weakness and borne what penalty the magistrates laid upon them were received again into full communion as having already performed an adequate penance. In such connection, it was natural to speak of the great martyr apostles.

On Peter of Alexandria *vide* A. Harnack, *Geschichte der altchristlichen Litteratur bis Eusebius* (2 vols., Leipzig, 1893–1904), Vol. I, pp. 443 *sqq.*; N. Bonwetsch in J. J. Herzog and A. Hauck, *Realencyklopädie für protestantische Theologie und Kirche* (24 vols., Leipzig, 1896–1913), Vol. XV, pp. 215 *sqq.*; W. E. Crum, *Texts Attributed to Peter of Alexandria,* in *Journal of Theological Studies* (London, 1903), Vol. IV, pp. 387 *sqq.*

[82] Acts, XVIII, 9, 10.

Peter of Alexandria, *Epistola Canonica,* canon IX. Text. J. P. Migne, *Patrologia Graeca,* XVIII, 483.

Thus Peter, the first of the apostles,[83] after being frequently arrested and imprisoned and treated with dishonor, was finally crucified at Rome. Likewise, the illustrious Paul, who was often betrayed and imperilled unto death, after enduring greatly and glorying in his many persecutions and afflictions, was beheaded with a sword in the same city.

Lactantius of Africa

(fl. 310)

Lucius Caelius Firmianus Lactantius, a native probably of Africa, was the son of pagan parents, who in mature life became a convert to Christianity. For his wide acquaintance with the classics and the elegance of his literary style he was nominated by Diocletian professor of Latin rhetoric in the new capital city of Nicomedia but, after a few years in office, he was ejected for his faith during the Christian persecution. Thenceforth he seems to have suffered much privation. In or about the year 314, after the accession of Constantine, he wrote an impassioned book, entitled *The Deaths of Persecutors,* in which he described the direful ends of Diocletian, Maximian, Maximin and other enemies of Christianity, both past and contemporary. His longest and most important work was *The Divine Institutes,* a manual of Christian theology, couched in fine, Ciceronian diction. Jerome accused him of failure to comprehend the inner mysteries of Christ's teaching, but in the fifteenth century, when grace of expression was at a higher premium than solidity of thought, his writings were hugely admired and went through many editions.

His references to Peter at Rome contain substantially nothing new, but in *The Deaths of Persecutors* they are so put to-

[83] The first appearance in our ecclesiastical writers of this title, which was soon to become a commonplace. Matthew's list of the Twelve whom Jesus called begins: "The first, Simon, who is called Peter," etc. *Supra,* p. 22. As the prestige of Peter increased, it was natural to interpret the adjective "first," *primus,* or, in Greek, πρῶτος, as meaning first in precedence or rank.The title had been also conferred upon him by Pseudo-Clement, *infra,* p. 163.

gether as to form a clearer and more connected story than any we have met hitherto, giving what is apparently a summary of the tradition in the shape that was then current. We may note that Lactantius does not conceive of Peter's residence at Rome as covering more than a short time during the reign of Nero,[84] and that, although he reckons Peter's missionary years as twenty-five, he distinctly implies that they were spent elsewhere.

On Lactantius, *vide* A. Harnack, *Geschichte der altchristlichen Litteratur bis Eusebius* (2 vols., Leipzig, 1893–1904), Vol. I,[2] pp. 736 *sqq.*; Preuschen in J. J. Herzog and A. Hauck, *Realencyklopädie für protestantische Theologie und Kirche* (24 vols., Leipzig, 1896–1913), Vol. XI, pp. 203–210; R. Pichon, *Lactance, Étude sur le Mouvement Philosophique et Religieux sous le Règne de Constantin* (Paris, 1901).

Lactantius, *Divinae Institutiones,* IV, 21. Text. *Corpus Scriptorum Ecclesiasticorum Latinorum,* XIX, 367.

But the disciples, dispersed through the provinces, laid everywhere the foundations of the Church, doing great and almost incredible miracles in the name of their Lord and Master; for at his departure he had endowed them with power and strength, by which the doctrine of the new gospel might be founded and made firm. But he also unfolded to them all things which were about to happen, which Peter and Paul preached at Rome.[85] And this preaching, being written down for the sake of remembrance, has remained with us.

De Mortibus Persecutorum, 2. Text. *Corpus Scriptorum Ecclesiasticorum Latinorum,* VII, 174–177.

[After Christ's ascension] the disciples, of whom there were eleven at that time, added Matthias and later Paul in place of the traitor Judas and scattered throughout the whole earth to preach the gospel, as their Lord and Master had

[84] In this respect Lactantius' account harmonizes with that of Porphyry, written some thirty years earlier. *Supra,* p. 92 and n. 81.

[85] Compare this with Phlegon's ascription to Jesus, — or Peter, — of power to foretell events. *Supra,* p. 73.

commanded them, and for twenty-five years, until the beginning of the reign of Nero, they were laying the foundations of churches through every province and in every city. And during Nero's reign, Peter came to Rome and, after performing certain miracles by the power of God committed unto him, converted many to the true religion and built up a faithful and steadfast temple to God. When Nero heard of these things and observed that not only in Rome but everywhere and daily a great multitude was abandoning the worship of idols, going over to the new religion and condemning the old, forasmuch as he was an execrable and pernicious tyrant, he set about to raze the heavenly temple and destroy the true faith; and he was the first of all the persecutors of God's servants. He crucified Peter and slew Paul. . . .

3. PETER THE FOUNDER OF THE ROMAN EPISCOPATE

Eusebius of Caesarea

(c. 265–340)

Eusebius, the "Father of Church History," bishop of Caesarea in Syria, was a friend of the emperor Constantine and wrote during his reign and immediately afterwards. His career, whether as bishop or as theologian, was not wholly satisfactory to the orthodox party in the Church of his day. His mind did not run spontaneously along metaphysical channels and he failed to maintain a sound and unequivocal position in the current controversies regarding the first two persons of the Trinity. He thought peace more important than insistence upon difficult points of theology and preferred to make concessions on dogmas, which profounder men thought vital, rather than to perpetuate antagonisms. He signed, to be sure, the militant profession of faith drawn up at Nicaea, but only at the express wish of the emperor. Later, he held communion with members of the Arian party, who denied the eternal, uncreated being of the Son, and took part in synods which deposed bishops of the orthodox persuasion for being too zealous or too contentious.

His fame at the present time rests chiefly upon his achievements as a historian, his *Life of Constantine,* his *Chronicle* and his *History of the Church* from its foundation to the year 323. *The Life of Constantine* [86] contains much invaluable biographical material but it is colored by Eusebius' purpose to depict his friend and patron as the blameless Christian warrior and prince, in opposition to the pagan writers who dwelt heavily upon his faults. *The Chronicle,* based on earlier tables by Julius Africanus,[87] was the most ambitious attempt made thus far to correlate and combine the historical records of the Jewish and the Gentile past. It was in form a tabulated list in parallel columns, synchronizing the principal events from the creation to the year 325, set down in order of their several dates in the various national systems of chronology. It marked an immense advance toward the construction of a world history and a comprehensive survey of the movements of the human race. The Greek text of *The Chronicle* has been lost, except for a few extracts preserved by Syncellus, a historian of the ninth century. The substance survives in Armenian and Syrian versions and in a Latin paraphrase by Jerome, who carried on the tables to the year 379. Eusebius' calculations were revised and corrected from time to time but from the date of their publication they fixed a starting point from which all subsequent work began.

The Church History, from which we have already drawn numerous quotations, was in its way just as unique an accomplishment. Nothing of the sort had been undertaken during the period of Christian obscurity and persecution, which lasted until Eusebius' own day, but in the episcopal library of Caesarea he found stored away a mass of loose documents of varying age and character, which he studied to excellent purpose. Many of them he incorporated in part or entire in his *History.* His narrative,

86 For an extract from *The Life of Constantine, vide infra,* p. 484.

87 Julius Africanus, a Libyan, who saw service in the Orient under Septimius Severus, compiled in 221 a chronography or outline of world history. It was much admired and used by later students but nothing of it in its original form has come down to us. H. Gelzer, *Sextus Julius Africanus und die byzantinische Chronographie* (Leipzig, 2 Pts. in I, 1880–1898).

therefore, though often imperfect in arrangement and uncritical or partisan in viewpoint, has saved for us a quantity of priceless information which otherwise would undoubtedly have perished. In fact, to write a history of the early Church without using the material preserved by Eusebius would be almost as hopeless a task as to write a history of the Jewish race without consulting the Old Testament.

The chief interest of the following excerpts lies in the effort they show on the part of Eusebius as a chronologer to fix the exact dates of Peter's sojourn at Rome. In his *Church History*[88] Eusebius named no years but said merely that Peter came to Rome in the reign of Claudius (41–54). His reason for placing Peter's arrival so surprisingly early is not evident. It may have been simply the influence of the popular legend. Justin Martyr, who wrote of Simon Magus, Peter's deadly adversary in the realm of apocryphal fiction, had said that Simon reached the city at that time[89] and Peter in the common versions of the legend followed hard on Simon's heels. Eusebius himself depicted Peter as coming to destroy Simon.[90] All forms of tradition, however, united in making Nero (54–68) the instrument of Peter's death. The impression, therefore, was growing up that Peter had lived and labored in Rome for many years. The allusions in the New Testament to Peter's later life, which might have discouraged such an impression,[91] seem to have been totally overlooked. But Eusebius felt some uncertainty in the matter, for in *The Chronicle* he set a yet earlier date for Peter's arrival at Rome, namely, the third year of Caligula, 39. He may have possibly recalled for the moment the narrative of Hippolytus, who appears to imply that Peter was already in Rome when Simon Magus presented himself there.[92] Eusebius then put Peter's death in 66 and, by an oversight, assigned the general persecution by Nero to the same year. Thus he actually gave the apostle a residence of twenty-six or twenty-seven years in the capital.

88 *Historia Ecclesiastica,* II, 14, 6. *Infra,* p. 189.

89 *Infra,* p. 130.

90 *Infra,* pp. 188–189. Eusebius is the first of the more serious or "ecclesiastical" writers to countenance any part of the apocryphal legend of Peter. For his method of treating it, *vide infra,* p. 181.

91 *Supra,* pp, 47–56.

92 *Infra,* p. 133.

The excerpts have a value also as betokening some perplexity in Eusebius' mind as to the precise position occupied by Peter in the church organization at Rome. In the *Chronicle* he stated that Peter "presided over" the church, a rather vague phrase, and that after him Linus became bishop.[93] The *History* was hardly more explicit. Eusebius there remarked that "Linus was the first after Peter to hold the bishopric" and went on to speak of Clement, the second from Linus, as "the third bishop of the Roman church." Scholars have argued at length over these ambiguous passages in endeavors to ascertain whether or not Eusebius thought of Peter as a bishop as well as an apostle. He certainly conceived of him as head or leader of the Roman community but nowhere evidently among his ancient documents did he find warrant for bestowing on him the formal title of bishop. It was in Rome itself that Peter's name was put at the head of an episcopal list as the first bishop of the see.[94]

On Eusebius, see A. Harnack, *Geschichte der altchristlichen Litteratur bis Eusebius* (2 vols., Leipzig, 1893–1904), Vol. I,[2] pp. 551 *sqq.*; J. B. Lightfoot in W. Smith and H. Wace, *Dictionary of Christian Biography* (4 vols., Boston, 1877–1887), Vol. II, pp. 308 *sqq.*; J. Van den Gheyn in P. Vigouroux, *Dictionnaire de la Bible* (5 vols., Paris, 1895–1912), Vol. II, pp. 2051 *sqq.*; A. C. McGiffert, *Eusebius*, in *A Select Library of Nicene and Post-Nicene Fathers of the Christian Church* (14 vols., New York, 1890–1903), Second Series, Vol. I, *Introduction*; O. Bardenhewer, *Patrology* (St. Louis, 1908), § 62; C. H. Turner, *The Early Episcopal Lists*, I; *The Chronicle of Eusebius*, in *Journal of Theological Studies* (London, 1900), Vol. I, pp. 181 *sqq.*; J. T. Shotwell, *An Introduction to the History of History* (*Records of Civilization Series*), (New York, 1922), chap. XXVI.

93 See note 95 on the next page. The Greek verbs, προΐσταμαι, προκάθημαι literally "stand before" or "over," "sit before" or "over," are employed in Paul's Epistles and in the writings of the early Fathers in two senses, the first, of directing or acting in general as a leader anywhere, and the second, of presiding over in an official or magisterial capacity, as a bishop presides in a church or a chairman in an assembly. Compare, for example, Ignatius' uses of the second verb, *infra*, p. 241, n. 13, and often elsewhere in his letters. Justin Martyr, *I Apology*, LXV. Eusebius, in his *History*, frequently but not always employs the first verb as the equivalent of "serve as bishop." Yet it does not seem possible to insist dogmatically on such an interpretation here. He may have chosen the word for the very reason that it was not too definite.

94 In the *Liberian Catalogue*. *Infra*, p. 107. In the middle of the third century, Cyprian of Carthage believed that Peter exercised episcopal power at Rome and that from him all subsequent bishops derived their authority and Stephen of Rome declared that he occupied "the chair of Peter." *Infra*, pp. 328, 379, 415. In the West, Peter may have been regarded as bishop much earlier than in the East.

Eusebius, *Chronicon*. Texts. *Eusebius Werke* (*Die griechischen christlichen Schriftsteller der ersten drei Jahrhunderte*), V, 214, 216. Armenian text translated into German. *Eusebii Chronicorum Libri Duo,* ed. by A. Schoene (Berlin, 1866–1875), II, 150, 156. Armenian text translated into Latin.

	Olympiad	*Year from the birth of Abraham*	*Year of Gaius*[96]	*Year of Agrippa*[97] *in Judaea*
Peter the apostle, having first founded the church at Antioch, goes to the city of Rome and there preaches the gospel and abides there as head of the church for twenty years.[95]	204	2055	3	2
.	.	.	.	.
			Year of Nero	*Year of Agrippa*[98]
After Peter, Linus held the bishopric of the Roman church for fourteen years.	211	2082	12	22
To crown all his other crimes Nero instituted the first persecution of the Christians, in the course of which the apostles, Peter and Paul, suffered martyrdom at Rome.	212	2083	13	23

95 Syncellus (*supra*, p. 97) preserves the original Greek of this sentence. "And he presided over the church in Antioch and then over the church in Rome until his death." 'Ο δὲ αὐτ ς μετὰ τῆς ἐν 'Αντιοχείᾳ ἐκκλησίας καὶ τῆς ἐν 'Ρώμῃ προέστη." The phrase, "for twenty years," is the addition of the Armenian translator.

96 The emperor Caligula.

97 Herod Agrippa I, appointed tetrarch by Caligula soon after his accession.

98 Herod Agrippa II. His reign is reckoned as beginning with his father's death in 44, though he was not appointed to any kingdom until 49 and was not transferred to Palestine until 53.

Historia Ecclesiastica, III, 4: 1, 2, 9; 13; 36: 2. Text. *Eusebius Werke* (*Die griechischen christlichen Schriftsteller*), II[1], 192, 194, 228, 274.

III 4: 1 That Paul preached to the gentiles and laid the foundations of the churches " from Jerusalem round about even unto Illyricum " is evident both from his own words and from the account which Luke has given in the Acts.

2 And in how many provinces Peter preached Christ and taught the doctrine of the new covenant to those of the circumcision is clear from his own epistle, which we have said is undisputed,[99] and in which he writes to the Hebrews of the dispersion in Pontus, Galatia, Cappadocia, Asia, and Bithynia. But the number and names of those who became faithful and zealous followers of the apostles and were deemed worthy to tend the churches they had founded, it is not easy to tell, except for those enumerated in the writings of Paul.

. . . .

9 As to the rest of his followers, Paul tells us that Crescens was sent to Gaul. Linus, whom he mentions in the Second Epistle to Timothy as his companion in Rome, was the first after Peter to hold the bishopric of the Roman church,[100] as we have already said. Clement also, who was himself appointed third bishop of the Roman church, was, as Paul testifies, his co-laborer and fellow soldier.

. . . .

13 In the second year of his [Titus'] reign, Linus, who had been bishop of the church of Rome for twelve years,[101] delivered up his office to Anencletus.

. . . .

99 *Supra,* p. 57.

100 A little earlier, Eusebius speaks of Linus as " the first to hold the bishopric of the Roman church after the martyrdom of Paul and Peter." *Historia Ecclesiastica,* III, 2.

101 The figures for the duration of the first pontificates are all as mythical as

36: 2 And at the same time, Papias,[102] who was himself bishop of the parish of Hierapolis, won renown, as did Ignatius,[103] who held the bishopric of Antioch, second in succession to Peter, and whose fame is celebrated by very many to this day.

Liber Pontificalis

(Fourth Century Source)

The *Liber Pontificalis,* the oldest history of the Papacy, was put together by an unknown member of the Roman curia during the sixth or the seventh century. In its final shape, it was a strange composite of authentic record, embellished tradition, and downright fabrication. It comprised a series of lives of individual popes from Peter to the writer's own day and incorporated and blended materials from many earlier sources. The account of Peter was, of course, quite mythical, based upon the apocryphal histories. On the other hand, the life of Silvester, the contemporary of Constantine, contained, beside the fantastic legend of Silvester's part in Constantine's conversion, descriptions of basilicas built by the emperor and of imperial donations to the churches, which rest apparently upon genuine fourth century registers, preserved perhaps in the Roman episcopal archives down to the author's time.

It is no longer possible to doubt that Constantine actually built a basilica in honor of Peter over what he supposed to be

---

those for Peter's own. *Supra,* p. 98. On the origin and value of these figures, see L. R. Loomis, *The Book of the Popes* (*Records of Civilization Series,* New York, 1916), ix–xiv.

102 On Papias, *vide supra,* pp. 73–74.

103 On Ignatius of Antioch, *vide supra,* pp. 71–72. Eusebius refrained from calling Peter the first bishop of Antioch, as Jerome eventually did. *Infra,* p. 115. However, he could not allow that the Peter whom Paul withstood and rebuked there (Galatians, I–II) was the great apostle. He suggested that it was one of the young men whom the disciples sent out from Jerusalem and only a "name brother" of Peter, the apostle. *Historia Ecclesiastica,* I, 12, 1. Jerome also tried to explain away this blemish on Peter's reputation by arguing that the disagreement between the apostles was not real but feigned and that Peter voluntarily assumed the position of wrongdoer in order that Paul might have more ground for insisting vehemently on the truth. Jerome had a warm discussion with Augustine as to the admissibility of such a method of exegesis. Jerome, *Epistolae,* CXII; Augustine, *Epistolae,* XXVIII and XL.

the apostle's tomb. The form of ancient St. Peter's was that of a "tomb church," constructed around and adapted to the requirements of a site already fixed by an older grave. During the fifteenth and sixteenth centuries, this basilica was torn down to make way for the present cathedral, but the bricks taken from it show the Constantinian stamp. In 1594, when the masons were digging to lay the foundations for the modern high altar, they opened up a narrow shaft at the bottom of which they saw by the light of a torch a golden cross lying on a dark floor. Pope Clement VIII, who was summoned to witness the sight, ordered the shaft filled up at once and the spot has never since been disturbed. Whether the cross was Constantine's or not, whether the sarcophagus he enclosed in bronze is still intact as his workmen left it, cannot be told. Where Constantine found the coffin which he encased so solidly we do not know. All that can positively be asserted is that the fourth century did enshrine and venerate upon the traditional site of martyrdom [104] what it believed to be Peter's very bones.

The following passage is part, apparently, of the extracts taken by the compiler of the *Liber Pontificalis* from the records of the Roman church. It may or may not have been written originally by one who saw the work done or who had heard a first-hand report of it. It is probably as old, at least, as the close of the fourth century.

For full text and description of the *Liber Pontificalis,* see L. Duchesne's edition (2 vols., Paris, 1886–1892); also Th. Mommsen's edition of the first part, *Libri Pontificalis Pars Prima* (Berlin, 1898), in *Monumenta Germaniae Historica, Gesta Pontificum Romanorum,* Vol. I; L. R. Loomis, *The Book of the Popes* (*Records of Civilization Series,* New York, 1916). For archaeological studies and plans of old St. Peter's, *vide* A. L. Frothingham, *The Monuments of Christian Rome* (New York, 1908), pp. 25–29; R. A. Lanciani, *The Destruction of Ancient Rome* (New York, 1903), pp. 31–32; R. A. Lanciani, *Pagan and Christian Rome* (Boston, 1893), pp. 132–142, 148–150; H. Leitzmann, *Petrus und Paulus in Rom*; *Liturgische und archäologische Studien* (Bonn, 1915); O. Marucchi, *Élements d'Archéologie Chrétienne* (3 vols., Paris, 1899–1902), Vol. III, *Basiliques et Églises de Rome*; H. Grisar, *History of Rome and the Popes in the Middle Ages* (London, 1911), Vol. I, pp. 266–305.

[104] *Supra,* p. 82.

Liber Pontificalis. Text. Ed. by Th. Mommsen, *Monumenta Germaniae Historica, Gesta Pontificum Romanorum,* I, 56–57.

At the same time, Constantine Augustus built, by request of Silvester the bishop,[105] the basilica of blessed Peter, the apostle, in the shrine of Apollo[106] and laid there the coffin with the body of the holy Peter; the coffin itself he enclosed on all sides with bronze, which is unchangeable; at the head 5 feet, at the feet 5 feet, at the right side 5 feet, at the left side 5 feet, underneath 5 feet, and overhead 5 feet: thus he enclosed the body of blessed Peter, the apostle, and laid it away.

And above he set porphyry columns for adornment and other spiral columns,[107] which he brought from Greece.

He made also a vaulted roof in the basilica, gleaming with polished gold, and over the body of the blessed Peter, above the bronze which enclosed it, he set a cross of purest gold, weighing 150 lbs., in place of a measure.[108]

Chronographer of 354

The name given above is commonly applied to the unknown compiler of a manual or almanac for the city of Rome, drawn up in 354 and designed especially for the convenience of Christian residents or visitors to the city. It contained a miscellaneous collection of documents, chronological lists of Roman consuls and

105 The clause, " by request . . . bishop," is not in all the texts and is probably an interpolation.

106 The spot covered by the basilica lay between the ancient Via Aurelia and the Via Triumphalis, near the edge of the circus built by Caligula and used by Nero for public games, combats and spectacles, close to the temple of Cybele, which by a popular error was later known as a temple of Apollo. For a diagram of the site, see R. A. Lanciani, *Pagan and Christian Rome,* pp. 126–132.

107 These spiral columns formed a row or colonnade in front of the altar, separating it from the nave. Several of them may still be seen filling niches in the piers that support the cupola of the present church, and one is venerated in a side chapel. A legend arose during the Middle Ages that they had been brought from the Gate Beautiful of the Temple in Jerusalem and they appear in Rafael's cartoon of the healing of the impotent man by Peter and John.

108 An unintelligible expression. The text is undoubtedly corrupt.

prefects, an official municipal calendar, a topographical description of the various city districts or wards, and brief topical outlines of general and Roman history. Of particular value to a Christian reader were a table of dates for Easter from the year 312 to the year 411, a calendar of the feast days and anniversaries of martyrdoms observed by the Roman church, and a catalogue of the popes from Peter to Liberius, who was installed bishop in 352. The last named document has been called the *Liberian Catalogue*[109] from the fact that it was compiled during Liberius' pontificate, although there is nothing to prove that he had any part in its preparation or that it ever received official sanction.

Our extracts are taken, one from the Liberian Catalogue, the other from the calendar of Roman feasts. The former includes the explicit assertion that Peter was the founder not only of the Roman church but of the Roman see and occupied it as its first bishop for twenty-five years. The formalizing tendency, which we observed at work in the Asiatic Eusebius, with his interest in offices and dates, has in this anonymous Roman advanced still further. The simple, shadowy tradition, which in the beginning reported simply that Peter had once preached at Rome to the infant church and had shed his blood there under Nero, is here transformed into a precise statement of years, months and days and pontifical function. The imagination calls up no longer a vagrant, missionary apostle, appealing here and there to groups of hearers on inconspicuous street corners or under a sheltering roof, but a stately prelate in his official robe speaking "ex cathedra," from an official throne. The tendency to magnificence had, of course, been accelerated by the increase in the power of the popes after Constantine and the natural desire to justify this power by the oldest and highest sanctions. Our chronographer goes so far in his zeal as to bring Peter to Rome under Tiberius, directly after the Ascension, thus outdoing even Eusebius[110] and contradicting utterly the testimony of the Book of Acts. He also sets his death at an impossibly early date, the year after Nero's accession. Jerome corrected these

[109] For the *Liberian Catalogue* in full, *vide infra*, pp. 710–715.
[110] *Supra*, pp. 98, 100.

glaring errors, while preserving the length of Peter's Roman episcopate.[111]

The excerpt from the calendar of feasts is of considerable archaeological interest but raises some troublesome questions. Why, one hundred and fifty years after Caius pointed to Peter's "trophy" at the Vatican,[112] and twenty-five years after Constantine built a basilica there over his tomb, was his memory venerated by the church at the crypt called "ad catacumbas" on the Appian Way? What is the meaning of the date 258, associated in the calendar with this commemoration? Duchesne,[113] in agreement with many other scholars, offers a plausible solution for the riddle, to the effect that in 258, when the persecution of Valerian was at its height, the bodies of both Peter and Paul were removed for safety from their original tombs on the Vatican and on the Ostian Way, and secreted temporarily in this obscure hiding place, thence to be produced in triumph under the peace of Constantine, and that the church continued to regard as hallowed the place where they had lain for some sixty years. A more iconoclastic critic refuses to accept this explanation. Guignebert,[114] for example, believes that Caius' "trophies" were merely monuments erected by the Christians to mark the sites of martyrdom and that the actual burial places of the apostles were unknown for the first two centuries after their death; that the date 258 was the year of a so-called "discovery" of their bodies in the crypt "ad catacumbas," which adjoined two Jewish cemeteries, and that the translation of these bodies under Constantine to the Vatican and the Ostian Way respectively, coupled with the old tradition of martyrdom on those spots, gave rise to the conviction in the later fourth century that they had been originally interred there.[115]

[111] *Infra,* pp. 114–116. [112] *Supra,* p. 83.

[113] L. Duchesne, *Liber Pontificalis,* I, civ; 151, n. 7. A recent argument for this view is in H. Lietzmann, *Petrus und Paulus in Rom*; *Liturgische und archäologische Studien,* backed by fresh data from investigations into the crypt beneath the church of San Sebastiano.

[114] C. Guignebert, *La Primauté de Pierre,* pp. 377 *sqq.*

[115] See also the confused stories offered by the apocryphal legends of the fourth and fifth centuries to explain the association with the "ad catacumbas." They describe an attempt by Oriental Christians to steal the apostles' bodies from their original tombs and their transfer for safety to the crypt on the Appian Way, until they could be laid in new and stronger sepulchres on the old sites. *Infra,* pp. 178, 180. Gregory I knew of some such legend. *Epistolae,* IV, 30.

Catalogus Liberianus. Text. *Monumenta Germaniae Historia, Auctores Antiquissimi,* IX, *Chronica Minora,* ed. by Th. Mommsen, I, 73.

In the reign of Tiberius Caesar our Lord Jesus Christ suffered under the constellation of the Gemini, March 25, and after his ascension blessed Peter instituted the episcopate. From his time we name in due order of succession every one who has been bishop, how many years he was in office and under what emperor.

Peter, 25 years, 1 month, 9 days, was bishop in the time of Tiberius Caesar and of Gaius and of Tiberius Claudius and of Nero, from the consulship of Minucius and Longinus (A.D. 30) to that of Nero and Verus (A.D. 55). He suffered together with Paul, June 29, under the aforesaid consuls in the reign of Nero.

Feriale Ecclesiae Romanae. Text. *Monumenta Germaniae Historica, Auctores Antiquissimi,* IX, *Chronica Minora,* ed. by Th. Mommsen, I, 71.

December 25 Birth of Christ in Bethlehem of Judaea.

In the month of January

January 20 Fabianus [116] in the cemetery of Callistus and Sebastian [117] in the Catacombs.

January 21 Agnes [118] on the Nomentana.

In the month of February

February 22 Anniversary of the chair of Peter.[119]

In the month of March

116 The festivals at this period consisted mostly of commemoration services in memory of certain third and fourth century martyrs, held usually at their tombs. Pope Fabianus died in 250 and his name may still be seen in the papal crypt of the cemetery of Callistus. *Vide infra,* p. 313.

117 A Roman soldier and martyr, said to have been executed by Diocletian in 288. The church of San Sebastiano over the crypt "ad catacumbas" marks his grave.

118 Another traditional victim of Diocletian's persecution. A basilica was erected during the fourth century in her honor on the Via Nomentana, over the catacomb where she was supposed to lie.

119 A later martyrology, ascribed to Jerome, gave this title more fully.

March 7 — Perpetua and Felicitas [120] in Africa.

In the month of May

May 19 — Parthenus and Calocerus [121] in the cemetery of Callistus, in the 9th consulship of Diocletian and the 8th of Maximian (304).

In the month of June

June 29 — Peter in the Catacombs and Paul on the Ostian Way, in the consulship of Tuscus and Bassus (258).[122]

Damasus of Rome

(Bishop from 366 to 384)

Another record of considerable interest, testifying to the presence of the apostles' bodies in the crypt "ad catacumbas," mentioned in the previous paragraphs, is the inscription erected by Pope Damasus in the chamber presumably once sanctified by their holy relics. Damasus and his secretary Philocalus were the first of the long line of Roman church antiquarians. They lived at a time as far removed from the beginnings of their church as our own time is from that of the sailing of the Mayflower and

"Anniversary of the chair of the holy apostle Peter, in which he sat at Antioch." J. P. Migne, *Patrologiae Cursus Completus, Series Latina* (179 vols., Paris, 1844–1880), Vol. XXX, p. 459. The so-called "chair of Peter," now preserved at the cathedral of St. Peter at Rome, is not older than the third century. The "anniversary of the chair" was probably designed to celebrate Peter's installation as bishop either at Rome or at Antioch. It may have been started early in the fourth century, when the fact of Peter's episcopacy was regarded as established, in order to christianize the pagan festival of Caristia. See, on the significance of the anniversaries of February 22 and June 29, H. Lietzmann, *Petrus und Paulus in Rom*; *Liturgische und archäologische Studien,* pp. 19–74, 81–105.

[120] Perpetua, a young matron, and Felicitas, a slave, were among a group of martyrs thrown to the wild beasts in Africa in 203. Extracts from an account of their death, written by an eyewitness, are in J. C. Ayer's *A Source Book for Ancient Church History,* pp. 145 *sqq.*

[121] Two Roman martyrs, the memory of whose sufferings was still comparatively fresh.

[122] Another fourth century calendar gives this note in a more expanded form. "The anniversary of the holy apostles Peter and Paul, Peter in the Vatican and Paul on the Ostian Way, both in the catacombs; they suffered under Nero; in the consulship of Bassus and Tuscus (258)." The martyrology which passes as Jerome's has it still differently. "At Rome, the anniversary of the holy apostles Peter and Paul and of nine hundred and eighty-seven other martyrs." This last may perhaps be an echo of the tradition that the apostles died in company with many other Christians during Nero's persecution. *Supra,* pp. 67, 68. J. P. Migne, *Patrologiae Cursus Completus, Series Latina,* Vol. XXX, p. 479.

they set themselves the serious task of identifying and rescuing from oblivion the countless sacred graves and sites in and about the city which were already crumbling and overgrown, in danger of being totally lost and forgotten. The observant visitor to the catacombs or the primitive basilicas can still mark the discolored fragments of their memorial inscriptions on the walls, carved in letters which set a new standard of beauty for the Roman alphabet. Many more of their tablets have long ago fallen to pieces and disappeared through fire, neglect or the blows of rude invaders. The memorial verses on them, however, were in some cases copied down by pilgrims, while the tablets were yet in place, and thus have been kept to our day.[123]

The following lines are a translation of the inscription which Damasus set up in the so-called Platonia or tomb chamber of the apostles, which he also decorated with marbles and frescoes. The chamber, now renovated almost beyond recognition, is a part of the crypt beneath the church of San Sebastiano on the Via Appia. It is to be noted that the lines give no clue whatever as to the date or length of time that the bodies rested there.

On Damasus, *vide* O. Marucchi, *Il Pontificato del Papa Damaso* (Rome, 1905); O. Marucchi, *Christian Epigraphy* (trans. by J. A. Willis, Cambridge University Press, 1912); J. Wittig, *Papst Damasus I,* in *Römische Quartalschrift für christliche Altertumskunde und für Kirchengeschichte* (Rome, 1902); H. Lietzmann, *Petrus and Paulus in Rom; Liturgische und archäologische Studien* (Bonn, 1915).

Inscription in the Platonia. Text. M. Ihm, *Damasi Epigrammata,* No. 26.

This place, you should know, was once the abode of saints;
Their names, you may learn, were Peter and likewise Paul.
The East sent hither these disciples, as gladly we confess.
For Christ's sake and the merit of his blood they followed him among the stars
And sought the realms of heaven and the kingdoms of the righteous.

[123] For other inscriptions of Damasus and for an account of his pontificate, *vide infra,* pp. 446, 595.

Rome was deemed worthy to retain them as her citizens.
May Damasus offer them these verses, new stars, in their praise!

Optatus of Mileve

(c. 370)

During the pontificate of Damasus, Optatus, bishop of Mileve, a town in the Roman province of Numidia, wrote a treatise on the Donatist schism, which he dedicated to the Christian emperors. We know practically nothing of the life of Optatus but his book made a lasting impression on the Church and more than sufficed to save his name from oblivion.

The Donatist party [124] had arisen in Numidia during the reign of Constantine and by Optatus' day maintained its own bishops and churches throughout a great part of northern Africa. Its original ground for opposition to the catholic organization was the charge that the bishop of Carthage had been among those who betrayed the faith under the persecution of Diocletian and that he was therefore incompetent to administer the sacraments, on which depended the salvation of his flock, and that his successors, who had received their ordination through him, were equally disqualified. Optatus composed a full and painstaking answer to the Donatist contentions, beginning with a review of events to show the reprehensible and unwarranted character of their schism at the start, passing on to urge the immediate importance of unity under the leadership of Rome and finally refuting in detail the argument that the efficacy of sacraments depended ever in any way upon the worthiness of the administrant. The Roman church had insisted for over a century that baptism in the name of the Trinity was valid, even when bestowed by heretics.[125] Optatus was the first, however, to put into definite and concise form the " opus operatum " theory for all sacraments alike. " The sacraments are holy through themselves, not through men . . . it is God who cleanses, not the man." [126]

[124] For some account of the rise of the Donatist schism, *vide infra*, pp. 450–454, 463–467.
[125] *Infra*, pp. 394, 395, 421, 466.
[126] *De Schismate Donatistarum*, V, 4.

In the second book of this treatise, while pressing his point that the Donatists should admit the superior authority of the catholic Church and the See of Peter, Optatus makes one assertion more sweeping than any we have found upon the subject hitherto. Not only, he says, was Peter "head of the apostles" and the first bishop of Rome, but his bishopric at Rome was the first to be established anywhere in the Church. It was the original episcopate. The claim, however, was excessive even for that credulous age. It violated such widely accepted ideas as those of the bishopric of James the apostle at Jerusalem[127] and of Peter's foundation of the bishopric at Antioch. It was not taken up for repetition[128] and Jerome's version of the offices of Peter was adopted instead.

For Optatus see particularly the histories of dogma, *e.g.*, A. Harnack, *History of Dogma* (trans. by N. Buchanan, 7 vols., Boston, 1897–1901), Vol. V, pp. 42–48. On the Donatist platform, see L. Duchesne, *Le Dossier du Donatisme* in *Melanges d'Archaeologie et d'Histoire* (Paris, 1890), pp. 589–650.

Optatus, *De Schismate Donatistarum,* II, 2–3. Text. Ed. by C. Ziwsa, *Corpus Scriptorum Ecclesiasticorum Latinorum,* XXVI, 36–37.

2 We must note who first established a see and where. If you do not know, admit it. If you do know, feel your shame. I cannot charge you with ignorance, for you plainly know. It is a sin to err knowingly, although an ignorant person may be blind to his error. But you cannot deny that you know that the episcopal seat[129] was established first in the city of Rome by Peter and that in it sat Peter, the

[127] *Infra,* pp. 163, 167, 203.
[128] We have not found this claim repeated. It certainly was not generally used even by ardent papal propagandists. Compare, however, the loose phrase in the *Liberian Catalogue,* "blessed Peter instituted the episcopate," *supra,* p. 107. The implication might be regarded as the same. Cyprian, an African Christian of the third century, had used language about the original unity of the episcopate in Peter which might have given Optatus the suggestion for his idea. *Infra,* pp. 322, 328.
[129] The word in this extract translated "seat" is "cathedra," *i.e.,* the magisterial chair of bishop.

head of all the apostles, wherefore he is called Cephas.[130] So in this one seat unity is maintained by everyone, that the other apostles might not claim separate seats, each for himself. Accordingly, he who erects another seat in opposition to that one is a schismatic and a sinner.

3 Therefore, Peter was the first to sit in that one seat, which is the first gift of the Church.[131] To him succeeded Linus. Clement followed Linus. Then Anacletus Clement. . . .[132] After Damasus, Siricius, who is our contemporary, with whom our whole world is in accord by interchange of letters in one bond of communion. Do you, if you would claim for yourselves a holy church, explain the origin of your seat.[133]

Jerome

(c. 335–420)

With Jerome we come again to one of the outstanding personalities, like Origen or Tertullian, in early church history. Born in Dalmatia, he went for higher education to the provincial capital of Trier and to Rome. After some pleasant years of literary activity in Italy, he undertook, in company with several friends, a tour through Greece and Asia Minor. At Antioch, a sudden illness carried off one of the little party and Jerome, horror-struck, abandoned the expedition and plunged into the Syrian desert to live alone as a hermit for five years. In his retirement, he took up the study of Hebrew and resolved to devote his life thenceforth entirely to the cause of sacred learning.

In 378, he emerged from the desert and began his chosen task of translating the Greek Fathers for the use of the West,

[130] Optatus mistakenly tries to derive the Aramaic name, "Cephas," by which Peter is sometimes called in the New Testament and which also means "rock." (*Vide supra*, pp. 23–24) from the Greek word κεφαλή, "kephale," or "head," thus making it into an equivalent of the Latin "caput." "Omnium apostolorum caput Petrus, unde et Cephas est appellatus."

[131] The Donatists had a list of the "six gifts" or "notes" of the Church, in which the episcopate was the first.

[132] The list of Roman bishops from Peter to Siricius.

[133] Compare this turn of the argument with Tertullian's *De Praescriptione*, 32. *Infra*, p. 293.

where by this time the Greek language had ceased to be generally spoken or understood. He turned more than thirty homilies of Origen into Latin and prepared his version of the *Chronicle* of Eusebius.[134] In 382, he was sent on ecclesiastical business to Rome and remained there for two years as counsellor and friend to Pope Damasus.[135] A scholar of unrivalled reputation, a fiery advocate of the new ideals of monasticism and a favored adviser of the bishop, he at first swept Roman Christian society fairly off its feet. In time, however, his scorching comments on the life of the Roman clergy and his influence over women members of the church stirred up jealousy and bitterness. At one period it seemed inevitable that he would be elected Damasus' successor but when the moment actually arrived, Siricius, a man of cooler temperament, was chosen and Jerome withdrew again to the East.

A monastery was founded for him at Bethlehem, near a convent erected to receive the Roman ladies who followed from Italy. There he spent the rest of his life at work. In Rome, his attention had been called to the corrupt and discordant state of the Latin versions of the Scriptures and he had received a commission from Damasus to revise and purify the text. Before leaving the city he had completed a version of the New Testament and Psalms, based upon the Septuagint. This Psalter was at once adopted into the Roman liturgy and known thenceforth as the *Psalterium Romanum.* It was employed in all the city churches until the sixteenth century and is still used in the recitation of the canonical hours at the Vatican. On his way to Bethlehem, however, Jerome discovered at Caesarea the original manuscript of Origen's *Hexapla,*[136] and recognised in it a grade of scholarship higher than any he had yet attained. On his arrival in Bethlehem, he made a fresh translation of the Psalms on the basis of the *Hexapla* texts. This version was accepted first in Gaul and came therefore to be called the *Psalterium Gallicanum.* Later yet, he undertook an entirely new translation of the whole Old Testament directly from the Hebrew or Aramaic, as far as it was then available, with the aid of such Jewish rabbis as he could find to assist him. A combination of this

134 *Supra,* p. 97. 135 *Infra,* pp. 694–696. 136 *Supra,* p. 88.

edition of the Old Testament, omitting the Psalms, the *Psalterium Gallicanum,* his Roman revision of the New Testament and the remaining Apocryphal books in the older, existing Latin texts make up the Latin Bible, now known as the Vulgate, which has been the authorized version of the Roman church since the seventh century.[137]

Besides carrying further Origen's work of textual restoration, Jerome compiled a series of commentaries on the Scriptures, as Origen had done, and translated more of Origen's writings into Latin. His own books show signs of hasty workmanship and hurried dictation to amanuenses, but they are none the less remarkable for erudition, especially for their profuse citations from earlier authors and from Jewish traditional lore. He composed also argumentative treatises in defense of particular points of doctrine and carried on a wide and animated correspondence with his contemporaries of both sexes and every station in life. He wrote biographies of the hermit saints, of whom he had heard in the Syrian desert, and the first patrology or collection of lives of the Christian Fathers, which he called *Illustrious Men.* This last book, composed at Bethlehem, purported to furnish concise information regarding everyone who had ever taken part in the construction and elucidation of the Christian Scriptures, including Jerome himself. It opened with a life of Peter as the author of the epistles bearing his name and the source of the gospel of Mark. The material for this life, as well as the allusion to Simon Magus, was taken from Eusebius' *History,*[138] a few items, such as the episcopal title, the twenty-five-year residence at Rome and the burial spot, being added. Jerome may have gleaned the first two from the Roman catalogues and he was himself, of course, familiar with the tomb at the Vatican. He was, however, too sharp a scholar to accept the dates proposed by either Eusebius or the Liberian chronologer.[139] He worked out his own calculation to meet the exigencies of the New Testament narrative and the primitive records and with such success that his reckoning

[137] The revision of the Bible text, now in process by the Benedictine Fathers at Rome, is an attempt to recover the authentic phraseology of Jerome and to clear the Vulgate of the accretions and errors that have crept into it since his day.

[138] *Supra,* pp. 97, 101; *infra,* pp. 188–189.

[139] *Supra,* pp. 105, 107.

has been commonly repeated ever since by all who uphold the theory of the twenty-five-year episcopate. In fact, Jerome's life of Peter became the convenient and authoritative epitome for the West of everything that reputable scholarship had preserved or evolved concerning the later career of the apostle. With it, the accepted tradition assumed its final shape.

On Jerome, *vide* O. Bardenhewer, *Patrology* (St. Louis, 1908), § 93; O. Zöckler in J. J. Herzog and A. Hauck, *Realencyklopädie für protestantische Theologie und Kirche* (24 vols., Leipzig, 1896–1913), Vol. VIII, pp. 42 *sqq.* Also, P. Largent, *Saint Jerome* (Paris, 1898); L. Sanders, *Études sur Saint Jerome* (Paris, 1903); G. Grutzmacher, *Hieronymus* (2 vols., Leipzig, 1901, and Berlin, 1906); P. de Labriolle, *History and Literature of Latin Christianity from Tertullian to Boethius* (New York, 1925).

De Viris Illustribus, I and V. Text. *Texte und Untersuchungen,* ed. by O. Gebhardt, A. Harnack, C. Schmidt, XIV, 6–7, 10.

I Simon Peter, son of John, of the province of Galilee, of the village of Bethsaida, brother of Andrew the apostle, and himself chief of the apostles, after his bishopric at Antioch and his preaching to the dispersed of the circumcision who believed, in Pontus, Galatia, Cappadocia, Asia and Bithynia,[140] in the second year of the emperor Claudius, went to Rome to expel Simon Magus [141] and occupied there the sacerdotal seat for twenty-five years until the last year of Nero, that is, the fourteenth.[142] By Nero he was fastened to a cross and crowned with martyrdom, his head downward toward the earth and his feet raised on high, for he maintained that he was unworthy to be crucified in the same manner as his Lord.

He wrote two epistles which are called catholic, the second of which in the opinion of many is not his, since in style it differs from the first. In addition there is ascribed

140 An allusion to 1 Peter, I, 1.
141 A.D. 42. On Simon Magus, *vide supra,* p. 98; *infra,* pp. 124 ff.
142 A.D. 67.

to him the Gospel according to Mark, who was his pupil and interpreter. But the books, of which one is called his Acts, another his Gospel, a third his Preaching, a fourth his Apocalypse and a fifth his Judgment,[143] are rejected along with the apocryphal scriptures.

He was buried at Rome in the Vatican, near the Via Triumphalis,[144] and is celebrated by the veneration of the whole world.

V [Life of Paul.] . . . So in the fourteenth year of Nero on the same day on which Peter was executed, he [Paul] was beheaded at Rome for the sake of Christ and was buried on the Via Ostiensis,[145] in the thirty-seventh year after the Lord's passion.

Chronicon. Text. Jerome's *Chronicle* is published as an appendix to that of Eusebius in *Eusebius Werke* (*Die griechischen christlichen Schriftsteller der ersten drei Jahrhunderte*), VII, 179, 185.

Reign of Claudius[146]

Olympiad

CCV Peter the apostle, having first founded the church of Antioch,[147] is sent to Rome, where he preaches the gospel and remains for 25 years as bishop of the same city.

Mark the evangelist, the interpreter of Peter, proclaims Christ in Egypt and Alexandria.

Evodius is ordained first bishop of Antioch.

. . . .

143 *Infra*, pp. 120, 136, 158.

144 *Supra*, p. 104, n. 106.

145 On the fourth century basilica over the reputed tomb of Paul on the Via Ostiensis, *vide* R. A. Lanciani, *Pagan and Christian Rome*, pp. 150–158.

146 The following extract should be compared with the corresponding passage from Eusebius' *Chronicle* to note Jerome's alterations. *Supra*, p. 100.

147 In his life of Peter on the previous page, Jerome speaks of his "bishopric" at Antioch. Here he calls Peter the founder of the Antiochene church but Evodius the first bishop.

Reign of Nero

Olympiad

CCXI To crown all his other crimes Nero institutes the first persecution against the Christians, in which Peter and Paul perish gloriously at Rome.

Prudentius

(348–c. 410)

To end this survey of the development of the tradition of Peter at Rome we quote a few lines from the Christian poet Prudentius, which picture the Roman church of the year 400, with its adornment of rich tombs and colonnaded courts and ceremonious rituals regularly performed in honor of its two august founders. It is a glimpse of the institution in operation. The tradition is not only definitely fixed and located; it is now finding expression in terms of solemnity and beauty to shed undying lustre over the inheritors of Peter's office and Peter's merits.

There is little to say of Prudentius himself. He was born in 348, in Spain, probably at Saragossa, of a distinguished Christian family. He held various public offices in his own country until at length he was appointed to a high post at the court of Theodosius. The approach of old age decided him to retire from the pomps and distractions of the world in order to pass the rest of his time in religious pursuits and save his soul. Early in the fifth century, he visited Rome and shortly afterward published seven books of poetry on religious topics. The *Peristephanon,* or *Crowns,* from which our excerpt is taken, contains fourteen lyrics in praise of divers Christian martyrs of Rome and Spain.

On Prudentius, *vide* T. R. Glover, *Life and Letters in the Fourth Century* (Cambridge University Press, 1901), Chap. XI; G. Boissier, *La Fin du Paganisme* (2 vols., 3rd ed., Paris, 1898), Vol. II, pp. 105 *sqq.*; A. Ebert, *Allgemeine Geschichte der Litteratur des Mittelalters in Abendlands* (3 vols., Leipzig, 1880–1889), Vol. I (2nd ed.), pp. 251–293; F. Thackeray, *Translations from Prudentius* (London, 1890); F. Maigret, *Le Poète Chrétien Prudence* in *Science Catholique* (Paris, 1903), Vol. XVII, pp. 219 *sqq.*, 303 *sqq.*

Peristephanon, Hymn XII. *On the Passion of Peter and Paul.* Text. J. P. Migne, *Patrologia Latina,* Vol. LX, 556–569. A better edition is V. Lanfranchi's *Aurelii Prudentii Clementis Opera* (2 vols., Turin, 1896 and 1902).

More than their wont men gather and rejoice. Say, friend, why?
All over Rome they hasten and exult in triumph.
To us is returned the day of the victorious feast of the apostles,
Marked with the blood of noble Peter and Paul.
The same day, tho' separated by the space of one full year,[148]
Saw them both crowned with the lofty wreath of death.
The marsh on the Tiber, laved by the bordering river,
Holds earth consecrated by two trophies
And saw both the cross and the sword; twice a bloody stream
Rolled down and flowed over the same grass.
The sentence fell first upon Peter, doomed by the laws of Nero
To hang suspended from the tall beam.
But he feared to emulate the majesty of the supreme death
And to aspire to the glory of the great Master
And asked that they lift his feet above his prostrate head,
That with his eyes he might face the base of his cross.

. . . .[149]

The Tiber, hallowed on either bank, divides their bones,
Flowing between the consecrated sepulchres.
The right shore holds Peter, entombed in a golden shrine,
Musical with olive trees, murmurous with running brooks.

. . . .[150]

148 Prudentius recognized the chronological difficulty of making Peter and Paul meet death at the same time. He, like Augustine, solved the dilemma presented by the single anniversary date by suggesting that the two apostles died on the same day but in different years. *Supra,* p. 75.

149 Account of the death of Paul.

150 Description of the fountain and colonnade before the basilica of St. Peter and of the basilica of St. Paul.

Let us turn where the road leads over Hadrian's bridge.[151]
Then let us cross again to the river's left bank.
The vigilant priest first performs his sacred office beyond the Tiber,
Then returns speedily hither to repeat his vows.[152]

151 The bridge leading to Hadrian's tomb, now usually known as Castel Sant' Angelo. In Prudentius' time, as now, this bridge would be the principal way of approach to the Vatican area.

152 It had evidently become the custom for Roman priests to celebrate the anniversary by saying two masses, one in each of the two basilicas. *Cf.* the quotation from the *Breviarium Romanum, supra*, p. 75, n. 35. About this same time, Jerome was writing a protest against spending the day in conviviality and feasting. *Epistolae*, XXXI, to Eustochium, who had sent him a present in honor of the anniversary.

In Prudentius' hymn to St. Lawrence, he again commemorates together the two apostles of Rome.

> "Here reign now the two
> Princes of the apostles.
> He who summons the gentiles,
> He who, holding the seat [cathedram],
> As chief opes wide the gates
> Of eternity, his trust."
>
> *Peristephanon*, II, ll. 461–466.

PART III

THE APOCRYPHAL TRADITION

Introduction

The "accepted" tradition of Peter's presence at Rome was, as we have already pointed out, at best a meagre one. By itself, it threw no light on the manner of his coming, the extent of his activities, the provision for the transmission of his powers to his successors or the circumstances of his death. Granted the facts of his sojourn and martyrdom there and an enthusiastic and credulous body of believers, it was inevitable that devout imagination should soon set to work around his name, as it did around those of his fellow apostles. By the end of the second century, we find notices in the writings of Clement of Alexandria[1] and of Serapion of Antioch[2] of a strange mass of literature professing to record the last years of the apostolic band. Serapion rejected such works as false on the ground "that we have not received such traditions." Early in the fourth century, Eusebius[3] attempted a classification of these documents, distinguishing between merely doubtful writings and others which he rejected altogether as false, some of these last unobjectionable from the point of view of orthodoxy, others yet distinctly dangerous and heretical. He included under the final category "the gospels of Peter, Thomas, Matthias, and others besides, and the Acts of Andrew and John and the other apostles, which no one belonging to the succession of ecclesiastical writers[4] has ever deemed worthy of mention in his works. Furthermore," he added, "the character of their style is at variance with apostolic usage and both the thoughts and the nature of the incidents they describe are so completely out of accord with true orthodoxy that they plainly convict themselves of being the fabrications of heretics."

[1] *Supra,* p. 78.
[2] Quoted by Eusebius, *Historia Ecclesiastica,* VI, 12, 3.
[3] Eusebius, *op. cit.,* III, 25, 4–7. *Supra,* pp. 96 ff.
[4] *Supra,* p. 62, n. 3.

About 383, Philaster, bishop of Brescia,[5] wrote a disquisition on heresies, enumerating one hundred and fifty-six different varieties. Chapter 88 of his book opens as follows: "There is another heresy which uses only the *Apocrypha,* that is the unrecognized writings of the prophets and apostles, . . . And both the Manicheans and other similar heretics have *Acts* of blessed Andrew and of John, the blessed evangelist, and also of Paul, the blessed apostle. And because in these *Acts* they performed great signs and wonders, so that cattle and dogs and beasts spoke, the perverted heretics declare that the souls of men are like those of dogs and cattle."[6] Epiphanius, bishop of Cyprus,[7] writing on the same topic at about the same time, described a so-called *Journey of Peter,* which had a Gnostic coloring and represented the apostle as abstaining from animal food and receiving baptism every day in order to keep his purity unsullied.[8] Yet both Philaster and Epiphanius quoted as authentic a story of Peter which could have been drawn only from *Acts* like those they condemned.[9]

At Rome, the popes eventually took up the problem of dealing with this increasing literature, that sheltered itself behind the names of the apostles or of their disciples but which the abler critics in the Church had once and again pronounced unreliable invention. Innocent I (401–417), in a letter intended for general circulation, banned as unfit for use the uncanonical works ascribed to Matthew, James the Less, Peter, John, Andrew and Thomas.[10] The sixth century *Index* attributed to Gelasius I (492–496) positively anathematized both them and their authors.[11] Yet the popes did not repudiate material borrowed from such works by borrowers who themselves were orthodox and who turned it to commendable account.

It is clear, nevertheless, both from these definite statements

5 *Infra,* pp. 184, 185.
6 *Diversarum Hereseon Liber* or *De Heresibus,* 88.
7 *Infra,* p. 185.
8 *Adversus Haereses,* XXX, 15.
9 Compare Eusebius and Jerome, who both reject the apocryphal Acts of Peter and yet say that Peter came to Rome to contend with Simon Magus. *Supra,* p. 115; *infra,* p. 189.
10 *Epistolae,* VI, 13, *Ad Exuperium.*
11 *Epistola de Recipiendis et Non Recipiendis Libris,* V (ed. Dobschütz).

and from the failure of the earliest scholars to draw largely from these documents that they were at first placed in a different class from the scanty fragments we have already reviewed, which recorded the "received" tradition of Peter's life and death at Rome. As one turns the pages of these apocryphal *Acts, Gospels, Apocalypses* and didactic tracts, one is struck with the justice of Eusebius' strictures. Their character, even when not heretical, is indeed "at variance with apostolic usage." The "received" or, as it may be called, the legitimate tradition, although in time it annexed various inconsistent and improbable details, never descended to the level of the utterly preposterous and fantastic. The apocryphal accounts, on the other hand, of Peter's deeds at Rome leaped at once beyond all bounds of sober credibility. They may have concealed a modicum of fact beneath the fiction, but the fiction so far exceeded and distorted the fact that it is hopeless now to try to disentangle one from the other. They are simply an expression of naïve faith and an ambition either to glorify the great apostle personally by attributing to him a showy and inconsequent series of magical tricks and marvels, or to justify an unorthodox sect like the Gnostic by representing him as an advocate of its doctrines, or to exalt the episcopal office by depicting him as the fountainhead of its authority.

None the less, this literature cannot be overlooked by one who aims to comprehend the growth of papal prestige. Conceptions founded upon it and incidents borrowed from it were in time accepted by most of the influential writers of Roman Christendom, even by those who like Eusebius or Jerome fully realized that the literature as a whole was a web of falsehood. In particular, the figure of Simon Magus, once installed at Rome, could never be entirely exorcised, nor could Peter be deprived of the renown of being the first mighty victor over heresy as embodied in Simon's person. In fact, it is difficult to name one of the Fathers after the third century who does not sometime allude to that famous story. Ambrose, Jerome, Augustine and others, whom we cite below, could none of them rid themselves altogether of the impression it made upon them. It did not contradict the "accepted" tradition but, rather, supplemented and illumined it. It lit up splendidly the obscurity of Peter's last days and raised him to a magnificent position as deliverer as well as teacher of the Church. It appeared to find support in the unimpeachable testimony of Justin Martyr and Irenaeus. How could anyone help admitting that some features of it might be true, although so much was unquestionably erroneous? Popular opinion never saw an objection to any part and rapidly elevated Peter to a place high above Paul, who, in spite of all his merits, had never led in so spectacular a combat with sorcery.[12] The protests of the few older historians went unregarded. Even after the popes forbade the use of spurious Scriptures, the story of Peter and Simon continued to circulate in varying forms and to heighten the universal esteem for the prince of the apostles. The so-called *Letter of Clement to James*[13] was not blacklisted. In the ninth century, it stood at the head of an ostensibly official collection of papal decretals.[14] In the fourteenth century, an enlightened scholar like Petrarch pointed out the stone stained with Simon's wicked brains.[15] In our own day, we find ourselves loath to discard the *Quo Vadis* story[16] and a bit of the Clementine romance survives, perhaps, in curiously altered guise as the germ of the legend of Faust.[17] All this could not fail to invest with additional glamour the scene of Peter's triumph and the person of his successor.

The origins of this branch of apocryphal literature are singularly complex. To begin with, there existed, as we have said, throughout the early, uncritical Christian community a natural tendency to supplement the scanty information furnished by the

[12] For examples of familiar allusion to Peter as conqueror over Simon Magus, one by a fourth century papal envoy, the other, a little later, by a writer on the practice of fasting at Rome, *vide infra*, pp. 563, 195.

[13] *Infra*, pp. 163–165.

[14] The so-called *Pseudo-Isidorian Decretals*.

[15] *Epistola ad Philippum de Vitriaco*. Francesco Vanni's painting of Simon's fall is now in St. Peter's cathedral.

[16] Sienkiewycz' novel *Quo Vadis* is one modern version which has had a wide circulation in several languages. In May, 1924, an opera entitled *Nerone*, by the composer Boito, was produced at Milan, the theme of which was the struggle of Simon Magus to obtain ascendancy over the emperor and destroy the Christians.

[17] Faustus, Clement's father, is described as one who abandoned everything, his family included, to devote himself to astrological science. Peter cures him of this over-weening passion for knowledge.

New Testament and authentic tradition with imaginative and detailed descriptions of the apostles' latter days and miracles in various regions of the world. Local pride in many instances demanded an apostolic founder for a particular church. The well-known tale of James of Compostella is an illustration of how far an apostle might be made to wander before he was finally allowed to sink into his tomb. As early as the beginning of the second century, such legends were springing up. Peter himself was duly credited with a *Gospel,* a *Preaching,* an *Apocalypse* and a *Journey,* all treating of his career before his arrival in Rome. These, accordingly, we shall now pass over without more consideration.

The name of one man, however, already associated with Peter in the Acts of the Apostles, became before the end of the second century the starting-point of a special legend. Simon, the sorcerer of Samaria, or Simon Magus, figures in the eighth chapter of the Acts as one who had persuaded his own people that he was "the great power of God," but who was converted by the preaching of Philip and later rebuked sternly by Peter for offering to buy with money the power of conferring the Holy Ghost.[18] In the New Testament narrative, Simon is overcome by the rebuke, asks the apostles' prayers that he may escape punishment and thenceforth disappears from the history. But the mysterious sorcerer convicted of sin by the superior might of an apostle was a tempting subject for speculation, especially when other writings of the period furnished hints of a possible after-career. Josephus, speaking of the procurator Felix, mentions a magician called Simon, who helped Felix entice Drusilla, the wife of Azizeis, away from her husband.[19] Josephus' Simon was a Jew, a native of Cyprus, not a Samaritan, and was in the field some years after Peter had his encounter with Simon of Samaria. Simon was a common name and the profession of magic not rare in those days and in that region, but one man was soon confused with the other.

[18] Acts, VIII, 9–24. The offense of trying to buy spiritual gifts with money has since been called simony. As the first simoniac, Simon Magus was placed by Dante in the eighth circle of the *Inferno.* Canto XIX.

[19] Josephus, *Antiquitates,* XX, 7, 2.

The next step brought Simon to Rome. Justin Martyr, who wrote his *First Apology* about 140, described therein a statue erected in the city to one Simon, a Samaritan from a village called Gitta, the founder of a new religion, who, he said, had come to the capital in the reign of Claudius Caesar and received the honors of a god.[20] Irenaeus, forty years later, repeated Justin's story with the added touch that this was the Simon who had been abashed by Peter and had "set himself eagerly to contend against the apostles."[21] He proceeded to identify this Simon of Samaria with a Simon reputed to be the founder of a primitive form of Hellenistic or Gnostic theosophy, which was actually introduced into Rome at the close of the first century, and was for a time a formidable rival to the young church. The Simonian heresy was confounded with the teaching of Simon Magus as reported in the book of Acts. Finally, the historian Suetonius, in his account of the reign of Nero, mentioned a charlatan who had attempted during the celebration of games in Nero's amphitheatre to fly into the air and had fallen and been dashed to pieces near the imperial box.[22] To someone now came the ingenious idea that the unknown charlatan and the sorcerer of Samaria were the same person. The elements of a telling story were by this time at hand. A wizard, famous and powerful at home, comes to Rome propagating a pernicious heresy and enthralling the inhabitants until they set up his statue as that of a divinity, but finally perishes in a feat of impious audacity. It only remained to bring Peter, the author of the wizard's first discomfiture in Samaria, upon the scene of his fatal catastrophe at Rome and to ascribe that catastrophe to Peter's agency. The outlines of the great romance were then complete.

A legend like this would make, of course, an instant appeal as pure story. In addition, a motive less obvious than any we have yet suggested may at first have played some part in its composition and wide circulation. As the Tübingen school of New Testament criticism has pointed out, traces of an antagonism on the part of Jewish Christians and the more conservative apostles toward Paul and the liberal type of gentile Chris-

20 *Infra*, pp. 128, 130, for text and explanation of Justin's error.
21 *Infra*, p. 131. 22 *Infra*, p. 130.

tianity which he fathered are manifest in the New Testament and here and there in the writings of the primitive age of the Church.[23] Even Irenaeus could say that in his day there were Christians who would not call Paul an apostle.[24] Whether our legend was once meant to portray Paul himself under the cloak of Simon Magus as the enemy of the Church, whom Peter had pursued and overthrown, or whether Peter was merely celebrated as outrivalling Paul in good works, accomplishing in Paul's absence more than he had ever done, the oldest version which we possess does actually show Peter standing as a solitary hero, facing unaided the assaults of the powers of darkness and saving the Roman church from destruction. The same Jewish or Ebionitic coloring may be discerned again in the Clementine documents, in the deference which Peter is made to pay to James, the head of the church at Jerusalem.[25] In time, however, the Jewish party in the Church became negligible or disappeared and the old jealousies and differences which had centered around it were forgotten. The simple impulse to magnify the Roman See could have free rein and inasmuch as two apostolic deliverers are more glorious than one, a fresh version of the legend was composed which brought Paul to Peter's side, though keeping him distinctly in the second place.[26]

Other versions of the legend, embellished with new features or combined with elements from other apocryphal tales, arose from time to time in different parts of the Empire, written in the different tongues of the provinces. The few from which we give extracts are samples of a multitude that have been lost. The heretical versions most obnoxious to orthodox authority have naturally vanished altogether, but here and there a stray touch of Gnostic dualism may be observed in a document that happened to survive. Peter, for example, preaches asceticism to the noble Roman ladies and betrays no sign of suffering under

[23] Paul did not receive all the support and comfort he had expected to find at Rome. *Philippians,* I, 15–17; 2 *Timothy,* IV, 16. The Jewish community was very large, probably 10,000 under Tiberius, and the first Roman Christians may have been mostly Jews.

[24] Irenaeus, *Contra Haereses,* III, 15, 1.

[25] *Infra,* pp. 159, 165. In the Clementines, Peter is also made to utter remarks which undeniably are meant as slurs upon Paul. *Vide* J. V. Bartlet, *Clementine Literature,* in *Encyclopaedia Britannica,* 11th ed.

[26] *Infra,* p. 168.

the torture of crucifixion.[27] One of our texts goes so far as to ascribe his death to his interference with the marital relations of Roman society.[28] Others take the more orthodox course of attributing it to the emperor's wrath at the loss of Simon.[29]

This apocryphal literature is, as we have intimated, diffuse in style and voluminous in bulk, in striking contrast to the scattered crumbs that make up the "received" tradition. We cannot here reproduce in full even one of the more important compositions. We have attempted only to indicate the character and trend of a few representative narratives and thus to show how the figure of Peter was made grandiose and inspiring to the popular imagination and the gaps in the "received" tradition were filled up. The Simon Magus legends and the Clementine letter taken together made invaluable propaganda for the rising Papacy, at first appealing mainly to the uncritical and unlearned believer but subsequently admitted, as a part of history, by the gravest Fathers of the Church.

For fuller discussion and bibliographies on these topics consult St. G. Stock, *Simon Magus,* in *Encyclopaedia Britannica* (11th ed., 29 vols., London, 1910–1911); J. V. Bartlet, *Clementine Literature,* in *Encyclopaedia Britannica* 11th ed.); G. Krueger, *History of Early Christian Literature* (trans. by C. R. Gillet, New York, 1897), *passim*; A. Harnack, *Geschichte der altchristlichen Litteratur bis Eusebius* (2 vols., Leipzig, 1893–1904), *passim*; E. Hennecke, *Handbuch zur den neutestamentlichen Apokryphen* (Tübingen, 1904); R. A. Lipsius and M. Bonnet (editors), *Acta Apostolorum Apocrypha* (2 vols. in 3, Leipzig, 1891–1903); F. J. A. Hort, *Notes Introductory to the Study of the Clementine Recognitions* (London, 1901); C. Guignebert, *La Primauté de Pierre* (Paris, 1911); A. C. Headlam, *Simon Magus,* in J. Hastings, *Dictionary of the Bible* (5 vols., New York, 1901–1904); B. Pick, *Paralipomena* (London, 1908); E. A. W. Budge, *Gadla Hawâryât, The Contendings of the Apostles* (Ethiopic versions of the lives and deaths of the apostles), (London, 1899), Vol. II, pp. 7–41, 382–436.

1. BEGINNINGS OF THE SIMON MAGUS LEGEND

The following group of extracts from the pagan historian Suetonius and from four church writers of the second and early third centuries comprises all the material extant on the Roman Simon, whoever or whatever he or they may have been, before

[27] *Infra,* pp. 150, 152, 170, 177, 203, 204.
[28] *Infra,* p. 150.
[29] *Infra,* pp. 177, 180.

the emergence of the full-fledged Simon Magus legend. The passage from Suetonius refers to an episode of which we have no other report than what he gives us. A second-century Christian, searching through the history of Nero's reign for light, perhaps, on the circumstances of Peter's death, might conceivably have seized upon this suggestion for the story of Simon's fate. At least, we have no other source for the bizarre idea of the aerial flight.[30]

The quotation from the Christian philosopher, Justin Martyr, however, is part of an account of a genuine Simon, a Samaritan, whom Justin believed to be the founder of one of the curious, syncretistic forms of belief, characteristic of the age, which were fervently denounced by the Christians. His disciple Menander performed feats of magic of which Justin had heard, and taught his converts that they would never die. Justin did not identify this Simon with the Simon of the Acts but he dated his coming to Rome so early that there was no incompatibility of time. In point of fact, the heresiarch Simon must have lived a full generation later than Justin placed him. Justin gave a short description of Simon's peculiar doctrines and inserted a surprising statement to the effect that the Romans were so impressed by his teaching as to erect a statue to him as a god. Justin himself spent many years in Rome and spoke as if he knew the statue in question. For centuries after him there seemed no possible way of contraverting his statement. But in 1574, a stone pedestal was dug up on the island of the Tiber, bearing the inscription SEMONI DEO SANCIO SACRUM, which offered a clue to the mystery. Semo Sancius, otherwise known as Dius Fidius, was an ancient Sabine divinity who guarded the sanctity of oaths and treaties.[31] It seems now beyond doubt that Justin, like many other citizens of the Hellenized Empire, was unacquainted with the cults of the old-fashioned, local deities and simply misinterpreted the inscription. A comparison with the reading which he gives will show that the mistake would not have been difficult for a mind historically so uncritical.

[30] *Infra*, p. 149.
[31] This pedestal, probably the very one seen by Justin, is now in the Vatican Museum. *Vide* R. A. Lanciani, *Pagan and Christian Rome*, pp. 104–106.

Some forty years later, Irenaeus,[32] in his analysis and refutation of the heresies of his time, made a more careful study of the Simonian philosophy, drawing evidently from some treatise on the subject which he had read. The woman Helen, whom Justin had mentioned, Irenaeus explained more fully as the embodiment of the Divine Thought, even as Simon was of the Supreme Power, both having been incarnate from time to time in varying guises on the earth. As Simon's philosophical propositions, however, played no real part in the popular legend that was developing about him, we omit the discussions of them. Irenaeus also alluded to the statue, but as an object of hearsay. Though he wrote his book in Rome, he apparently took the statue on Justin's word without any verification of his own eyes. The chief contribution he made to the legend was his positive assurance that the wandering heretic Simon and the New Testament Simon were the same, with the corollary that the latter after his rebuke by Peter applied himself afresh to magic in order to resist the apostles.

Tertullian[33] added nothing to the portrait of Simon's character but made frequent and scathing references to him in his writings, basing his judgment on Justin, Irenaeus and the unknown source which Irenaeus had used. Bishop Hippolytus,[34] who, about Tertullian's time, wrote a compendium of heresies, described in still greater detail Simon's philosophic system, drawing partly from the source just mentioned and partly from a book called *The Declaration,* which purported to be the work of Simon himself. At the close, he added that Simon and Peter had met and withstood each other on several occasions at Rome, and that Simon had finally left the city and died elsewhere. It is possible that his account of Simon's death represents a bit of actual Roman tradition as to the heresiarch's end.

Other writings of this same general period give further information on the course of the Simonian heresy. The Clementine romances describe Simon's earlier preaching in Syria and his argumentative encounters with Peter there.[35] Origen re-

[32] For further account of Irenaeus, *vide infra,* pp. 261 ff.
[33] For Tertullian, *vide supra,* p. 84; *infra,* p. 261.
[34] For Hippolytus, *vide infra,* pp. 297–299. [35] *Infra,* p. 167 and n. 104.

marks upon the decline of Simonian influence in his own day.[36] But the germs of the legend of the conflict of Simon and Peter at Rome, as far as they are now discoverable at all, lie in the excerpts given below.

SUETONIUS
(fl. c. 95–120)

De Vita Caesarum, Nero, c. 12. Text. Ed. by J. C. Rolfe (*The Loeb Classical Library*), II, 104.

[A description of spectacles performed in Nero's amphitheatre, near the Campus Martius.] An Icarus at his first attempt fell instantly, close to his [Nero's] box, and spattered him with his blood.

JUSTIN MARTYR
(d. c. 165)

Apologia Prima, c. 26. Text. J. P. Migne, *Patrologia Graeca,* VI, 368. A better text is in *Apologies,* ed. by L. Pantigny (*Textes et Documents pour l'Étude Historique du Christianisme,* I.

There was a Samaritan, Simon, a native of the village called Gitta, who in the reign of Claudius Caesar and in your royal city of Rome did mighty acts of magic by virtue of the craft of the demons operating through him. He was regarded as a god and was honored by you as a god with a statue, which statue was erected on the river Tiber, between the two bridges, and bore this inscription in the Roman language:

SIMONI DEO SANCTO [To Simon, the holy God].

And almost all Samaritans and even a few from other nations worship him and acknowledge him as the first god. A woman named Helen, who went about with him at that time

36 Origen, *Contra Celsum,* I, 57.

and had previously had a stand in a brothel, they call the First Thought conceived by him.[37]

IRENAEUS

(c. 130–c. 200)

Adversus Haereses, I, 23, 1 and 4. Text. J. P. Migne, *Patrologia Graeca*, VII, 670 *sqq*.

Simon the Samaritan was that magician of whom Luke, the disciple and follower of the apostles, says: " But there was a certain man, Simon by name," . . . [Quotation from Acts, VIII, 9–23.] He then, not putting his faith in God one whit the more, set himself eagerly to contend against the apostles in order that he himself might appear to be a wonderful being and he applied himself with still more zeal to the study of every magic art that he might the better dazzle the masses of mankind. Such was his course in the reign of Claudius Caesar, by whom furthermore he is said to have been honored with a statue on account of his magic. . . . (Résumé of Simon's teachings.)

They also have an image of Simon fashioned after the likeness of Jupiter and another of Helen in the style of Athene and they worship them.[38] Finally they have a name derived from Simon, the author of their sacrilegious doctrines, and are called Simonians.

TERTULLIAN

(c. 160–c. 235)

Apologeticus adversus Gentes, c. 13. Text. J. P. Migne, *Patrologia Latina*, I, 402.

But when you adore Larentina, a public prostitute, — I could wish that it might at least have been Lais or Phryne,

[37] Justin speaks of Simon again in the same *Apology*, c. 56, and in his *Dialogue with Trypho*, c. 120, but gives no more particulars of his life.

[38] *Cf.* Hippolytus, *infra*, p. 133.

— among your Junos and Ceres and Dianas, when you install in your Pantheon Simon Magus and bestow on him a statue and the title of Holy God,[39] when you make a notorious court page a god of the sacred assembly,[40] your ancient deities, although they are themselves in reality no better, will indeed consider themselves insulted by you.

De Praescriptione Haereticorum, c. 33. Text. Ed. by P. de Labriolle (*Textes et Documents pour l'Étude Historique du Christianisme*), IV, 72.

And the doctrines of Simon's sorcery, which inculcated a worship of angels, were themselves reckoned among the idolatries and condemned by the apostle Peter in Simon's own person.

Hippolytus

(d. 236)

Refutatio Omnium Haeresium, VI, 2 and 15. Text. J. P. Migne, *Patrologia Graeca*, XVI, Pt. 3, 3206–3208, 3226.

It now seems fitting to explain the theories of Simon, a native of Gitta, a village of Samaria, and we shall likewise prove that his successors, taking their pattern from him, have endeavored to promulgate similar views under a change of name. This Simon was an adept in sorcery and after making a mockery of many and perpetrating his villainy, partly by means of the art of Thrasymedes, in the way we have already described, and partly through the assistance of demons, he tried to set himself up as a god. But the man was a fraud and full of folly and the apostles rebuked him in the Acts. . . . [A lengthy account of Simon's philosophy.]

So the disciples of this Magus celebrate magical rites and employ incantations and resort to love spells and charms

39 Sancti Dei, words taken from Justin's inscription.
40 A reference probably to Antinöus.

and demons, said to be "dream senders," in order to drive distracted whomever they choose. And they also call upon beings named Paredroi.[41] They have an image of Simon fashioned in the likeness of Zeus and one of Helen in the form of Athene, and they worship them. And they call the one Lord and the other Lady. But if any one, on seeing the images of either Simon or Helen, calls them by their own names, he is cast out as ignorant of the mysteries.[42] This Simon deceived many in Samaria by his wizardry and was rebuked by the apostles and laid under a curse, as it is written in the Acts. But he afterwards abjured the faith and resumed his aforesaid practices, until he arrived at Rome and fell in with the apostles. And although he was deceiving many by his sorceries, Peter repeatedly withstood him. At last he betook himself to . . .[43] and continued to teach, sitting under a plane tree. Finally, when he was on the point of being exposed, he said, in order to gain time, that if he were buried alive he would rise again the third day. Accordingly he ordered a grave to be dug by his disciples and directed that he should be laid therein. Then they obeyed his command, but he remained in his grave until this day, for he was not the Christ.

2. THE LEGEND OF PETER AND SIMON

(180–220)

The last sentences of Hippolytus' story of Simon Magus would show us, if we had no other evidence, that there were tales already current of contests between Simon and the apostle Peter at Rome, concluding with Simon's discomfiture and retirement. How early these tales had begun to circulate we have no means of learning, nor how far they included reminiscences of actual

[41] Familiar spirits.

[42] This sentence shows that the Simonians denied that they worshipped their founders.

[43] Some words are missing here from the original manuscript.

occurrences. The central idea of an encounter between Peter and Simon was, of course, absolutely fictitious. The Simon Magus of the Acts was never in Rome, so far as we are aware. The Simon of Gitta, whom Justin Martyr had in mind, may or may not have been the same as the founder of the Simonian sect. The latter, however, certainly belonged to the close of the first century rather than to the middle and probably did not see Rome until twenty-five years, at least, after the apostle's death. The romantic conception of the master of black art pitted against the disciple of Christ sprang entirely from such chance suggestions as have already been noted in the literature of the time.[44] But once started, the romance was bound to grow with speed and gather color and episode, jumbling in one extraordinary medley scraps of remembered incident or detail and flights of ingenuous fancy. The facts of Simon the heretic's death away from Rome and of the expectation of his followers that he would rise again were soon woven into it. The fact of Peter's crucifixion was worked up to form a moving close, although the connection of his martyrdom with the preceding incidents was at first a little lame. It was not until considerably later that a clever remodelling of the legend brought Peter's death into organic relation with the central plot by representing it as a consequence of his victory over Simon.[45] The whole story was given a religious tone by Peter's addresses and prayers, which had sometimes a touch of rude eloquence. It made an instant appeal to simple-minded, uncritical folk, such as composed the bulk of the Church.

The date of the first appearance of the completed story cannot be fixed with any precision. The document which we give here in abridged form is the earliest version of it known to be in existence. Lipsius, who edited the text from which we translate, put the date of its composition about the year 165, but Harnack, Erbes and other scholars incline to the opinion that it belongs between 180 and 220. There must, to begin with, have been shorter and simpler versions, older by some years. One, at least, was definitely Gnostic in character and supplied the ascetic features noticeable in ours. The place of composition is also a

44 On this subject *vide supra*, pp. 124, 125; 128, 129.
45 *Infra*, p. 177.

matter of doubt. Our author displays an acquaintance with the apocryphal *Acts* of John and of Paul, which were both probably composed in Asia Minor during the second century. He shows also some slight knowledge of the city of Rome, though whether it is more than might be expected of any well informed citizen of the Empire it is hard to say. Hippolytus' words are proof that stories of this sort were going about in Rome soon after the year 200. If our version was first written in Greek in Asia, it was speedily brought to Rome and translated into Latin and the clumsy play upon the words "Petrus" and "paratus," possible only in a Latin text, was introduced.

The most complete text now extant is the crude Latin one called *Actus Petri cum Simone* or *Codex Vercellensis* from the Library at Vercellae where it was discovered. Two fragments of Greek texts have been found and portions of translations into Coptic, Slavonic, Arabic and Ethiopic, testifying to the story's wide popularity. Our translation is from the Latin, collated toward the end with the Greek fragment which covers the account of Peter's crucifixion.

For further information on this subject, see F. H. Chase, *Simon Peter*, in J. Hastings, *Dictionary of the Bible* (5 vols., New York, 1901–1904), Vol. III. Other important discussions are contained in the Prolegomena to the edition of the text of R. A. Lipsius and M. Bonnet; C. Schmidt, *Die Alten Petrusakten in Zusammenhang der apokryphen Apostellitteratur* in O. Gebhardt, A. Harnack, C. Schmidt (editors), *Texte und Untersuchungen zur Geschichte der altchristlichen Literatur* (Leipzig, 1882–), New Series, Vol. IX; *Geschichte der altchristlichen Litteratur bis Eusebius*, Vol. II [1], pp. 450 *sqq.*; Th. Zahn, *Forsuchungen zur Geschichte des neutestamentlichen Kanons* (2 vols., Erlangen, 1881–1883), Vol. II, 841 *sqq.*; C. Erbes, *Petrus nicht in Rom sondern in Jerusalem gestorben*, in *Zeitschrift für Kirchengeschichte* (Gotha, 1901), Vol. XXII, pp. 1–147, 161–232; M. R. James, *Apocrypha Anecdota*, 2nd Series, Vol. XXIV, *sqq.*; F. Legge, *Forerunners and Rivals of Christianity* (Cambridge, 1916). An English translation of the entire Acts is in B. Pick, *Apocryphal Acts of Paul, Peter, John, Andrew and Thomas* (Chicago, 1909), and in M. R. James, edition of the *Apocryphal New Testament* (Oxford, 1924). For a recent account of other Oriental apocryphal Acts and Martyrdoms of Peter, see F. Haase, *Apostel und Evangelisten in den orientalischen Überlieferungen* (Münster, 1922), pp. 202 *sqq.*

The Acts of Peter with Simon

Actus Petri cum Simone; also called *Actus Vercellenses.* Text. *Acta Apostolorum Apocrypha,* ed. by R. A. Lipsius and M. Bonnet, I, 45–103.

[Paul in Rome has a vision bidding him go to Spain. During his absence, Simon Magus enters the city, flying over the gate.]

4 . . . And the brethren in turn were greatly perturbed because Paul was not at Rome, nor Timothy nor Barnabas,[46] for they had been sent by Paul into Macedonia, and there was no one to hearten them save such as had recently been catechumens. And Simon vaunted himself increasingly with his deeds and some men in their daily talk called Paul a sorcerer, some even openly. And all the vast multitude which had been grounded in the faith abandoned it, except Narcissus,[47] the presbyter, and two women in the hospice of the Bithynians and four who were no longer able to leave their homes but remained shut up day and night, giving themselves to prayer and beseeching the Lord that Paul might quickly return or that some other one might visit his servants, seeing that the devil with his wickedness had destroyed them.

5 And while they mourned and fasted, God instructed Peter in Jerusalem. For twelve years being now fulfilled since the Lord had called him,[48] Christ revealed to him a vision, saying to him: " Peter, that Simon whom thou didst

[46] Paul at one time sent Timothy on a mission from Rome. Philippians, II, 19. He never speaks of Barnabas as at Rome but one tradition connected Barnabas with the first preaching of Christianity in the city. *Infra,* p. 166.

[47] The name may be taken from Romans, XVI, 11. The Narcissus mentioned by Paul was probably the secretary and influential friend of the emperor Claudius.

[48] An early tradition existed to the effect that the apostles had been commanded by Christ to wait twelve years in Jerusalem before setting out to preach abroad. Clement of Alexandria quotes it from the apocryphal *Preaching* (Κήρυγμα) *of Peter,* which was composed about the beginning of the second century. *Stromata,* V, 4. A. Harnack, *The Mission and Expansion of Christianity,* Vol. I, p. 45, n. 1.

proclaim a sorcerer and didst drive out from Judaea has again forestalled thee at Rome. And shortly thou shalt hear of it, for Satan, whose power Simon claims to be, has by his craft and energy destroyed all who believed in me. But do not delay; tomorrow go [to Caesarea] and there thou shalt find a ship in readiness, sailing to Italy; and within a few days I shall impart to thee my grace, which has no bitterness." Then Peter, admonished by this vision, related it straightway to the brethren, saying: "It is needful for me to journey to Rome to expel the foe and adversary of the Lord and of our brethren." And he went down to Caesarea and immediately embarked upon a ship. . . .

7 And the rumour spread through the city to the dispersed brethren that it was reported that Peter had come to Rome on account of Simon, that he might prove him a seducer and persecutor of the good. Then the whole multitude gathered together, that they might see the apostle of the Lord laying the foundation in Christ.[49] And on the first Sabbath, when the multitude had assembled to see Peter, Peter began to speak in a loud voice: . . . [Exhortation to repent.]

8 And the brethren repented and implored Peter to drive out Simon, who said he was the power of God and who was staying in the house of Marcellus, the senator,[50] whom he had beguiled with his enchantments. And they said: "Believe us, brother Peter; no man was nobler among men than this Marcellus. All the widows who hoped in Christ had him for refuge; all the orphans were fed by him. Nay more, brother, all the poor called Marcellus their patron and his house was named the house of the strangers and the poor. . . . Now this Marcellus is enraged and repents of his charity, saying: 'So much wealth wasted for so long a

[49] *Vide* I Corinthians III, 11.

[50] Harnack thinks that this "Senator Marcellus," who plays such a prominent part, may have been an historical character. A. Harnack, *op. cit.*, Vol. II, p. 43, n. 4.

time and I in my folly believed that God knew of it and so I spent it!' Thus if any stranger comes to the door of his house he will beat him with a lash and order him driven away, saying: 'Would I had never spent so much money on the impostors!' And he utters other blasphemies. . . ."

9 . . . And the brethren asked Peter to contend with Simon and not to suffer him longer to delude the people. And Peter without delay left the synagogue and went to the house of Marcellus, where Simon was staying. And great throngs followed him. When he came to the house, he called the porter and said to him: "Go, say to Simon: 'Peter, through whom you fled from Judaea, awaits you at the door.'" And the porter answered and said to Peter: "Whether you are Peter, I know not, my lord. But I am under instruction, for he saw you yesterday enter the city and said to me: 'Whether by day or by night, at whatever hour he comes, say that I am not in the house!'" And Peter replied to the young man: "You have spoken aright, because you were compelled by him to say this." And Peter turned to the people who followed him and said: "You shall now behold a great and wonderful portent." And observing a large dog fastened with a heavy chain, Peter drew near and released him. And the dog, being released, assumed the voice of a man and said to Peter: "What will you bid me do, servant of the ineffable and living God?" And Peter said to him: "Go in and say to Simon, in the midst of his companions: 'Peter says to you: "Come out into an open place, since for your sake have I come to Rome, you wicked man and deceiver of simple souls."'" And the dog bounded from the spot and into the house and sprang into the midst of those who were with Simon and lifting up his forepaws, said with a loud voice: "Simon! Peter, the servant of Christ, who stands at the door, says to you, 'Come out into an open place, for on your account have I come to Rome, most wicked of men and seducer of simple souls.'" And when Simon

heard this and saw the incredible sight, he paused in the words with which he was seducing his companions and they were all amazed.

10 But Marcellus at the sight came out of the door and cast himself at Peter's feet and said: " Peter, I embrace your feet, holy servant of the holy God. I have sinned exceedingly; punish not my sins, if you have the true faith of Christ whom you preach, if you are mindful of his commands, to hate no one, to be cruel to no one, as I have heard them from Paul, your fellow apostle; . . . He [Simon] but now prevailed upon me to erect to him a statue with the inscription: 'To Simon, the youthful god.'[51] . . . And this Simon has said that you, Peter, were faithless and doubted on the water.[52] And I have heard that he [Christ] also said: 'They who are with me have not understood me.'[53] Therefore, if you, upon whom he laid his hands, whom he chose, in whose presence he wrought his miracles, doubted, I have your example for my penitence and seek refuge in your prayers. . . ."[54] Then Peter said in a loud voice: " Thine, our Lord, is the glory and the honor, God omnipotent, Father of our Lord Jesus Christ! To thee be praise and glory and blessing forever and ever. Amen! Since now thou hast strengthened and established us fully in the sight of all who see, holy Lord confirm Marcellus and send thy peace on him and on his house this day. . . ."

11 With these words Peter embraced Marcellus and turned to the throng who stood by and saw one in the throng who smiled and in whom was an evil demon. And Peter said to him: " Whoever you are who laughed, show yourself

[51] Simoni Iuveni Deo. A garbled version of the inscription mentioned by Justin Martyr. *Supra*, p. 130.

[52] Matthew, XIV, 28–31.

[53] *Cf.* Matthew XV, 15–17; XVI, 8–11; Mark VII, 18; VIII, 17–21. These exact words are in an extra-canonical saying mentioned by B. Pick, *Paralipomena*, 66.

[54] The appeal made here for a merciful treatment of one who had lapsed from faith and Peter's compassionate response are reasons in favor of dating this version of the story at the end of the second century, when the harshness of primitive discipline was being mitigated. *Infra*, pp. 243, 299, 310.

openly before us all!" And hearing this, the young man rushed into the atrium of the house and shouted aloud and cast himself against the wall and said: " Peter, there is a great struggle between Simon and the dog that you sent to him, for Simon is saying to the dog: 'Tell him that I am not here.' And the dog is saying to him more than you charged him and after he has performed the mystery with which you charged him, he will die at your feet." Then Peter said: " Demon, whoever thou art, in the name of our Lord Jesus Christ come out of the youth and do him no harm; show thyself to all who stand here." And hearing this, the young man rushed forward and, laying hold of a great marble statue that stood in the atrium of the house, shattered it with kicks. And it was a statue of Caesar. At that sight Marcellus beat his forehead and said to Peter: " A great crime has been committed and if it be reported to Caesar by a spy, he will punish us heavily." But Peter said to him: " I see you are not in the state in which you were a short time since, for you said you were ready to spend the whole of your substance to save your soul. But if you are truly penitent and believe in Christ with all your heart, take flowing water in your hands and pray the Lord and in his name sprinkle the fragments of the statue and it will be restored as before." Then Marcellus, nothing doubting but believing with all his heart, before he took the water lifted up his hands and said: " I believe in thee, Lord Jesus Christ, . . ." And he sprinkled water upon the stones and the statue became whole. . . .

12 But Simon in the house said to the dog: " Tell Peter that I am not in the house." And the dog in the presence of Marcellus said to him: " Most wicked and impudent of men, the enemy of all who live and believe in Jesus Christ, a dumb animal has been given a human voice and sent to you to convict you and openly prove you an impostor. . . ." And when the dog had said this, it turned from him and the

crowd followed after it, leaving Simon alone. The dog returned to Peter, who was seated with the multitude that they might look upon his face, and the dog told what it had done with Simon. And the dog said to the messenger and apostle of the true God: "Peter, you shall have a great struggle against Simon, the enemy of Christ, and of his servants; but many whom he has seduced you shall restore to the faith. Therefore you shall receive from God the recompense of your labor." And when the dog had said this, it fell down at the feet of the apostle Peter and gave up the ghost.[55] And the throng beheld with great amazement the dog speaking and some threw themselves at Peter's feet, but others said: "Show us another sign that we may believe in you as a minister of the living God; for Simon did many signs in our presence and for that reason we followed after him."

13 . . . [Peter makes a smoked fish swim like one alive.[56]] Then many followed him for that sight and believed on the Lord and they met day and night in the house of Narcissus, the presbyter. And Peter expounded to them the writings of the prophets and the words and deeds of our Lord Jesus Christ.

14 And Marcellus was daily established through the signs which he saw done by Peter with the grace of Jesus Christ granted unto him. And Marcellus repaired to his own house, to Simon, who was sitting in the dining-hall. And he cursed him and said to him: "[Denunciation of Simon]." Then Simon was severely beaten and driven from the house and he went quickly to the house whither Peter was returned. And he stood before the house of Narcissus, the presbyter, at the door, and called out: "Lo, here am I,

[55] In the *Acts of Thomas,* c. 41, the episode of the speaking ass ends in the same way, with the animal's death. B. Pick, *Apocryphal Acts of Paul, Peter, John . . . ,* pp. 260–262.

[56] The reader will observe the unethical character of many of these signs and miracles, mere exhibitions of wizard magic superior to its rival.

Simon! Come down, therefore, Peter, and I will prove that you have put faith in a Jew and the son of a carpenter."

15 Thereupon it was reported to Peter that Simon had said this. And Peter sent out to him a woman with a sucking child, saying to her: "Go down quickly and you shall see a man asking for me. But it is not for you to answer him; keep silence and hear what the babe whom you hold will say to him." So the woman went down. And the child whom she suckled was seven months old. And it received the voice of a man and spoke to Simon: "O hateful to God and men, O destroyer of truth and baneful seed of corruption! . . . But against your will on the coming Sabbath another shall bring you to the forum of Julius [57] that it may be proved upon you what you are. . . . And now I speak my last word: Jesus Christ says to you: 'Keep silence under the power of my name and go out from Rome until the coming Sabbath.'" Then he immediately fell speechless and was constrained to go out from Rome until the Sabbath and abode in a stable. And the woman returned with her infant to Peter and related to him and the other brethren what it had said to Simon. And they magnified the Lord who had revealed these things to men.

16 [Peter has a vision of Christ encouraging him for the contest.]

17 and 18 [Peter tells the brethren how in Judaea he recovered the jewels of a woman named Eubola, stolen from her by the arts of Simon.]

19 [Marcellus purifies his house for a gathering place.]

20 Then Peter entered the house [of Marcellus] and saw one of the older women blind in her sight and her daughter holding her hand and leading her into the house of Marcellus. And Peter said to her: "Come hither, mother! Yesterday Jesus gave you his right hand and through him

[57] Appian, *De Bello Civili,* II, 102, says that the Forum of Julius was especially reserved for hearing disputes and was closed to trade.

we have light unapproachable, which darkness does not obscure. He says to you through me: 'Open your eyes and see and walk alone!'" And straightway the blind woman saw Peter laying his hand upon her. And Peter went into the dining-hall and saw the gospel being read. And rolling it up, he said: "Men who believe and hope in Christ, . . ."

21 [Other blind women ask to have their sight restored. A dazzling light appears filling the place and some see an old man, some a young man, some a boy touching their eyes and their sight returns.]

22 [All spend the night together in preparation for the Sabbath.]

23 Then there gathered together the brethren [in the forum], all who were in Rome, each with a gold piece occupying a seat.[58] And there were assembled also the senators and the prefects and the magistrates. And Peter came and stood in the midst. They all cried out: "Show us, Peter, who is your god or what is the majesty that has given you your confidence! Be not unkind to the Romans; they are lovers of the gods. We have the feats of Simon; let us have yours also! Convince us now, both of you, whom we ought to believe!" And as they said this, Simon appeared. He stood confused beside Peter and for the first time looked upon him. Then, after a long silence, Peter said: "Men of Rome, be true judges between us. For I say I have believed in the living and true God. . . . [He relates Simon's discomfiture in Judaea.] Peter is my name, because the Lord Christ deigned to call me to be on patrol [59]

[58] The gold for the seats had been furnished by Marcellus, who was generous again in his repentance.

[59] A feeble attempt to give a new meaning to the name of Peter. "My name is 'Petrus,' because I was called to be 'paratus,'" that is, ready or prepared. We have used the phrase "on patrol" in the text in an effort to reproduce in English the rough similarity in sound, but there is, of course, no more genuine connection between one pair of words than between the other. This play on a chance phonetic resemblance would be impossible in Greek and must therefore have been the invention of the Latin translator. It is significant chiefly as suggesting that he was not acquainted with or saw no significance in the explanation given in our Gospel of Matthew for the same name, XVI, 18. *Supra*, pp. 23–25. Yet the

in every way. For I believe in the living God, through whom I shall overthrow your sorceries. Now let him do in your presence the marvels which he has been doing. And then will you refuse to believe what I said of him?" Simon said: "Have you the audacity to speak of Jesus, the Nazarene, the son of a carpenter and himself a carpenter, whose family is in Judaea?[60] Listen, Peter, the Romans have understanding; they are not fools." And turning to the people, he said: "Men of Rome, is a god born? Is he crucified? He who has a lord is not a god."[61] And when he spoke thus, many answered: "You say well, Simon."

24 But Peter said: "Anathema upon what you have said of Christ! . . . [He quotes from the prophets and apocryphal literature on the mystery of Christ's birth.[62]] But these things shall be unfolded to you afterwards. Now for you, Simon; do some one of the marvels with which you have hitherto seduced them and I will undo it through my Lord Jesus Christ." And Simon gathered boldness and said: "If the prefect will permit it, I will offer you a long contest."

25 Then the prefect agreed to give permission, provided no impiety were committed.[63] And the prefect led out one of his attendants and said to Simon: "Take this man and put him to death." And he said to Peter: "And do you revive him." And the prefect said to the people: "It is for you now to judge which of them is accepted of God, he who kills or he who makes alive." . . .

26 [Simon speaks to the youth and he dies. Peter

---

incident of Peter's failure to walk upon the water, to which reference is made, *supra*, p. 139, is found in no other Scripture text but Matthew. It, however, may have been contained in the Greek original of our story.

[60] Matthew, XIII, 55, 56; Mark VI, 3.

[61] These and other speeches on the part of Simon are illustrations of what were presumably ordinary pagan comments on Christian preaching. Celsus also called Christ derisively a carpenter. Origen, *Contra Celsum,* VI, 34; cited by B. Pick, *Apocryphal Acts,* p. 95, n. 5.

[62] One quotation is from *The Ascension of Isaiah,* chap. XI, v. 14. *Supra,* pp. 69–71.

[63] *I.e.,* no sacrilege in the pagan sense.

restores him to life. A believing widow prays to Peter to bring her son also back to life.]

27 [The body of the widow's son is brought in on a bier. Peter says:] ". . . And I hear the voice of Christ my Lord and say unto you: 'Young man, arise and walk with your mother as long as you are useful to her. And afterwards you shall serve me and minister at the altars in the office of deacon and of bishop.' "[64] And immediately the dead man arose and the crowds who saw it were astounded and the people shouted: "Thou God the Savior, thou the God of Peter, God the invisible and the Savior!"

28 [The mother of the wealthy senator Nicostratus, who has just died, begs that her son also be raised to life. The body, escorted by a great retinue, is carried into the forum and set down before Peter.] And Peter demanded silence and said in a loud voice: "Men of Rome, now let there be a just judgment between me and Simon and do you determine which of us believes in the living God, he or I. Let him revive the body lying here and you may trust him as a messenger of God. But if he cannot, I will call upon my God; I will return the son alive to his mother and you shall believe that he is a sorcerer and a deceiver, who is dwelling among you." And all who heard this thought that Peter's words were fair. And they urged on Simon, saying: "Now show openly what is in you; either convict or be convicted. Why stand still? Up, begin!" Then Simon, when he saw everyone turning toward him, stood silent. But after he saw the people were hushed and watching him, he cried out and said: "Men of Rome, if you see the dead man raised, will you expel Peter from the city?" And all the people answered: "We will not only expel him but we will burn him that very hour with fire." And Simon went to the dead man's head and thrice bent down to him and thrice lifted himself up and he showed

[64] According to the legend, this was Linus. *Vide supra*, p. 77.

to the people that the man had raised his head and was moving and opening his eyes and bowing a little toward Simon. Forthwith they caught up wood and kindlings to burn Peter with fire. But Peter, receiving the power of Christ, lifted up his voice and said to them as they clamored against him: "Now I see, people of Rome, that I may not [65] call you foolish and vain, while your eyes and your ears and your hearts are darkened. How is your understanding obscured that you do not see that you have been bewitched, so as to imagine that a dead man has come to life who has not stood up? [66] I might easily, men of Rome, say nothing but die in silence and leave you to the delusions of this world. But I have before my eyes the penalty of inextinguishable fire. So, if you wish, let the dead man speak; let him arise, if he is alive; let him loosen with his hands the band about his chin; let him call his mother and say to you, when you shout: 'Why do you shout?' Let him beckon you with his hand. . . ." Then Agrippa, the prefect,[67] no longer restraining himself, stood up and struck Simon away with his hands. And from that moment the dead man lay still as he was before. And the people, turning in fury from the witchcraft of Simon, began to cry: "Hear, Caesar, if the dead man does not now arise, let Simon burn in place of Peter, since truly he has blinded us!" But Peter stretched out his hand and said: "O men of Rome, now be patient! I do not say to you that Simon should burn when the youth is revived, for if I say it to you, you will do it." The people cried out: "Even against your

[65] Thus the text. The sense seems to require the omission of the "not."

[66] Stories of corpses which moved in obedience to the words of a miracle worker or magician were common in both pagan and Christian literature during the second century. Tertullian (*De Anima,* 51) tells of a dead woman, who to his own knowledge raised her hands in the posture of devotion while the priest was reading the prayers at her burial service. Peter surpasses other thaumaturgists by bringing the deceased back to the full activity of life. See Lucian's dialogue, *The Lover of Falsehood.*

[67] The name may have been taken from the inscription over the portico of the Pantheon or from some other of the public buildings erected by Marcus Agrippa, the friend of Augustus.

will, Peter, we will do it." And Peter said to them: "If you persist in this course, the youth will not arise. For we have not learned to render evil for evil [68] but to love our enemies and to pray for our persecutors.[69] And if even Simon can repent, it will be better. For God will not remember his sins. Let him come, therefore, into the light of Christ. And if he cannot, let him possess the portion of his father, the devil.[70] But your hands will not be stained." And when he had said this to the people, he went up to the youth and before reviving him he said to the mother: "These young men, whom you have freed in honor of your son, may still be free and serve their living master? For I know that some of them will be cut to the heart when they see your son raised from the dead, because they will again become his slaves. But let them all remain free and receive their food as they have done heretofore, for your son shall rise again, and let them be with him." [71] And Peter looked upon her for a while to see what she thought. And the mother of the youth said: "What else can I do? So here before the prefect I say that whatever I had to spend upon the body of my son they may have." And Peter answered her: "Let the rest be divided among the widows." Then Peter, rejoicing in his heart, said in the spirit: "Lord, who art pitiful, Jesus Christ, . . . let Nicostratus now arise!" And Peter touched the youth upon his side and said: "Arise!" And the youth arose and threw off his cerements and sat up and loosed the band about his chin and asking for other garments, came down from the bier and said to Peter: "I entreat you, man of God, let us go

[68] Romans XII, 17; 1 Peter III, 9.

[69] Matthew V, 44; Luke VI, 27, 28.

[70] John VIII, 44.

[71] The attitude of the apostles and the early Church toward slavery was to accept it, like the institutions of the State, but to practice it with mercy. Slaves were to serve their masters dutifully and masters to be considerate of their slaves, for in the eyes of God there was neither bond nor free. 1 Peter II, 18 *sqq*. A. J. Carlyle, *History of Mediaeval Political Theory in the West* (4 vols., London, 1903), Vol. I, chaps. VIII, X.

to our Lord Jesus Christ, whom I saw talking with you and who said to you, pointing you to me: 'Bring him hither to me, for he is mine.' " . . .

29 From that same hour they adored him as a god, falling at his feet and bringing to him all whom they had diseased at home, that he might heal them. But the prefect, seeing the great multitude waiting upon Peter, commanded Peter to depart. And Peter bade the people come to the house of Marcellus. . . . [Nicostratus and his mother bring money for distribution to the widows.]

30 [72] [Chryses, a harlot, brings Peter money for the poor.]

31 . . . And Simon Magus after a few days promised the multitude to convict Peter of believing not on a true god but on a false. Therefore he performed many feats of magic, but the disciples, who were now steadfast, laughed at him. For in the dining-halls he made spirits return to their bodies, yet only in a fantasy, for in reality they did not.[73] And what more is there to tell? He was extolled by many for his sorcery and he made the lame appear whole for a short time and the blind likewise and the dead he seemed to bring to life and awaken for a moment, even as he did Stratonicus.[74] And Peter followed him everywhere and exposed him to those who looked on. So, when he was continually shamed and ridiculed by the Roman crowd and disbelieved for not achieving what he promised to do, he said to them: " Men of Rome, do you now think that Peter has vanquished me by his superior power and are you following after him? You have been deceived. Tomorrow I will leave you, godless and irreligious people, and fly to God, whose power I am even in my affliction. Though you have fallen,

72 Thus far these Acts of Peter are extant only in a Latin version. From this point on we have a Greek version as well. Lipsius prints both texts. *Op. cit.*, 78 *sqq*.

73 *Supra*, p. 146, n. 66.

74 Another form of the name Nicostratus, the two roots of which it is composed being transposed.

lo, I am the Standing One;[75] and I shall ascend to my Father and say to him: ' Even me, the Standing One, thy son, they have endeavored to overthrow; but I did not yield to them and escaped to myself.' "

32 And the next day a vast multitude gathered in the Via Sacra, that they might behold his flight. And Peter came thither to see the spectacle, that he might expose him even in this, since, when Simon entered Rome, he had amazed the people by flying. For Peter, who exposed him, was not then at Rome and he had deluded the city with his wiles, so that some clave to him. And now, taking his stand upon a high place[76] and seeing Peter, he began to speak: " Peter, now that I am about to ascend in the sight of all these people, I say to you: ' If your god has power, whom the Jews slew, stoning you whom he had chosen, let him show that his faith is of God and let it appear forthwith if it is worthy of God. For I shall ascend and reveal myself to all this multitude as I am.' " And lo, he rose on high over all Rome, while everyone beheld him soaring even over the temples and the hills, and the faithful bent their eyes upon Peter. And Peter, perceiving the marvel of the sight, cried to the Lord Jesus Christ: " If thou sufferest him to accomplish what he has begun, now all who have trusted in thee will be put to shame and the signs and wonders which thou gavest them through me will be vain. Hasten thy grace, Lord, I pray, and let him fall from high and be wounded but not killed; let him be made impotent and let his leg be broken in three places." And he fell from high and broke his leg in three places. Then they stoned him and went every man to his own house and everyone thereafter believed upon Peter. . . . [Gemellus, Simon's friend,

[75] The accounts of Simon, the heretic, in Irenaeus, Hippolytus, the Clementine documents and later writers, all mention this epithet which he is said to have applied to himself.

[76] In a later *Passion of Peter and Paul* the " high place " above the Via Sacra is named as the Capitoline Hill. R. A. Lipsius and M. Bonnet, *Acta Apostolorum Apocrypha*, Vol. I, p. 23.

abandons him and joins Peter. Simon escapes from Rome, is carried to Aricia and finally dies at Terracina.]

33 And Peter abode in Rome, being glorified with the brethren in the Lord and giving thanks night and day for the multitude who daily were gathered to the holy name by the grace of the Lord. And the concubines of the prefect Agrippa came to Peter, four in number, Agrippina, Nicaria, Euphemia and Doris.[77] And hearing the doctrine of chastity and all the teachings of the Lord, they were smitten to the heart and agreed together to abstain from intercourse with Agrippa; and they were persecuted by him. Then Agrippa, being at a loss and greatly disturbed about them, for he loved them much, set a watch secretly to see where they went and ascertained that it was to Peter. And on their return, he said to them: " That Christian has taught you to have no intercourse with me; understand that I will kill you and burn him alive." But they endured all abuses from Agrippa and would no longer be inflamed by him, being strengthened by the might of Jesus.

34 [Xantippe, wife of Albinus, a friend of Caesar, and other women hear Peter and withdraw from their husbands. Husbands also leave their wives, "because they desire to serve God in holiness and chastity." A tumult arises and Albinus complains to Agrippa, urging him to put Peter to death.]

35 And while they considered the matter, Xantippe heard that her husband was taking counsel with Agrippa and she sent and informed Peter, that he might leave Rome. And the other brethren, together with Marcellus, besought him to go away. But Peter said to them: " Shall we be put to flight, brethren? " And they said to him: " Nay, but

[77] There are some indications that Christianity spread more rapidly among high-born women than among men of the same class. Whether these and the subsequent names are those of traditional first century converts it is impossible to say. On the ascetic character assigned here to Peter's teaching, *vide supra*, p. 126.

that you may be able still to serve the Lord." And he was persuaded by the brethren and went forth alone, saying: "Let no one of you depart with me, but I will go out alone, for I have changed my purpose." And when he was passing out through the city gate, he saw the Lord coming into Rome. And when he saw him, he said: "Lord, whither goest thou?" And the Lord said to him: "I am coming to Rome to be crucified." And Peter said to him: "Lord, art thou crucified again?" He answered him: "Yea, Peter, I am crucified again." And Peter came to himself and saw the Lord ascending into heaven; and he turned back into Rome, glorifying and praising the Lord, because he said: "I am crucified." For that selfsame death was to befall Peter.[78]

36 So returning again to the brethren, he related to them what he had seen. And they were sorrowful in heart and mourned and said: "We beseech you, Peter, take thought for us who are young." And Peter said: "If it is the Lord's will, it will come to pass, even though it be not ours. And the Lord is able to establish you in his faith. . . ." And while Peter thus spoke and all the brethren lamented, behold, four soldiers seized him and led him away to Agrippa. And he in his frenzy gave command that Peter be crucified on the charge of impiety. Then all the company of the brethren gathered together, both rich and poor, orphans and widows, weak and strong, eager to see and deliver Peter; and the people clamored incessantly with one voice: "What wrong has Peter done, Agrippa? How has he harmed you? Tell the Romans!" And others said: "[We ought to fear] lest, if he be put to death, his Lord may destroy us all." And Peter, reaching the spot, calmed the multitude and

[78] One may note that in this oldest version of the *Quo Vadis* story the words of Jesus to Peter are not understood as a rebuke but as an assurance. He is not to suffer in Peter's stead, because Peter is too weak to face death, but is to die with Peter, the master with the disciple. The "Domine Quo Vadis" chapel outside the Porta San Sebastiano still marks the spot where Peter is supposed to have turned back.

said: "Men who are soldiers for Christ, men who hope in Christ, remember the signs and wonders which you have seen through me; remember the compassion of God, what works of healing he has wrought for you. Endure patiently until he come and render to every man according to his works. And be not angry now against Agrippa, for he is a minister of inherited power. And it is altogether come to pass as the Lord showed me it would. But why do I delay and come not to the cross?"

37 And when he had come and was standing by the cross, he began to say: "O name of the cross, a hidden mystery, O grace inexpressible, called by the name of the cross, O race of man, that cannot be parted from God, O unspeakable and unescapable love, that cannot be declared by polluted lips, . . . And I ask you, executioners, to crucify me head downward and not otherwise; and the reason I will unfold to those who hear."

38 and 39 And when they had suspended him in the manner which he desired, he began to speak again: "Men who are ready to hear, listen to what I, hanging from the cross, shall now disclose unto you. . . . [He expounds the mysteries of up and down, right and left, quoting the saying of the Lord: 'Unless you make your right as your left and your left as your right and your up as your down and your back as your front, you will not know the kingdom.'[79]]"

40 And the multitude standing by said: "Amen," with a loud voice, and at the "Amen," Peter yielded up his spirit to the Lord. . . . [Marcellus takes down Peter's body, wraps it in spices and lays it in his own tomb. Shortly afterward, he sees Peter in a dream and is admonished to cease mourning and let the dead bury their dead.] And Marcellus, waking from sleep, described the vision of Peter

[79] A saying contained probably in the lost *Gospel of the Egyptians*. B. Pick, *Paralipomena*, p. 65. For two other such sayings *vide infra*, pp. 253, 254.

to the brethren and was himself confirmed the more, as were also those who had been confirmed by Peter in the faith of Christ, until the return of Paul to Rome.

41 And Nero, hearing later of the death of Peter, blamed the prefect Agrippa, because he had put him to death without Nero's knowledge. For he had intended to inflict more punishment on him and crueler torture. For Peter had made disciples of some of Nero's household[80] and had caused them to leave him; on that account he was angry that Agrippa had not spoken at the time. And he set about to destroy all the brethren who had been disciples of Peter. . . . [But he has a dream warning him not to persecute the Christians for the time being.]

The Acts of the Apostle Peter with Simon are ended in peace. Amen.

3. REFERENCES TO THE PETRINE LEGEND IN THIRD CENTURY LITERATURE

The four extracts which follow, taken two from Greek and two from Latin literature, give some idea of the impression produced by the legend of Peter and Simon and the uses to which it was put in various circles during the century after its appearance. The more serious third century scholars and theologians for the most part ignored it but popular writers were caught by its glamour. The first reference to it that can be dated with any degree of certainty is in a poem written by one Commodian, about the year 250. Commodian, a resident of the Western Empire, was converted from paganism by reading the Scriptures and some time later composed what is usually called the first distinctively Christian poetry, two didactic works in Latin verse, intended to warn and convince his Jewish and pagan readers and to instruct and hearten his fellow Christians. In the course of an argument addressed particularly to the Jews, he likened the miracle of the

80 *Vide* Philippians, IV, 22. The conclusion here leaves room for the historic persecution of the Christians by Nero and the death of Paul to happen later.

dog that summoned Simon to the Old Testament portent of Balaam's ass that spoke.[81]

The second reference comes also from the writings of a convert with a taste for polite letters. Arnobius, like his contemporary Lactantius,[82] was a rhetorician in the province of Africa during the closing years of the third century. He was persuaded of the truth of Christianity by a vision seen in a dream and in order to prove to the local bishop the sincerity of his conversion, he wrote a treatise, *Against the Pagans,* containing a warm defense of his new faith and a denunciation of pagan mythology and ritual. The paragraph we quote forms the climax of an effort to prove the authenticity of the Christian religion by the rapidity of its expansion.

The Teaching of the Apostles, from which we take our third set of extracts, belongs to quite a different type of document. It is itself an apocryphal work, ostensibly a general letter of instruction sent out by the twelve apostles, after the meeting in Jerusalem described in the Acts.[83] As a matter of fact, the book was composed during the earlier half of the third century as a manual of Christian discipline for the use of Syrian and Arabic communities. The author enumerates the qualifications and functions of the various church officials, emphasizing particularly the authority possessed by bishops as the chief instrument of government. The power to bind and loose belongs to them as representatives of the apostles, on whom collectively Christ conferred it.[84] Peter is not here mentioned as wielding that power to any superior degree, but as the illustrious victor over heresy embodied in Simon Magus. The author depicts observances customary in the Syrian church of his day but draws the material for his exhortations and his literary allusions from an earlier and shorter *Teaching* or *Didache,* dating from the end of the first century, and also from the letters of Ignatius of Antioch, Justin Martyr's *Dialogue,* the *Acts of Peter,* and other more primitive writings. He wrote originally in Greek but the first text has disappeared and the book survives only in a Syriac and in fragments of a Latin translation.

81 Numbers, XXII, 23–31.
82 *Supra,* p. 27.
83 Acts, XV, 1–29.
84 Matthew XVIII, 18.

Our last selection is from still another branch of Christian literature, the Greek religious novel, and is interesting principally as showing how the story of Peter and Simon was utilized and adapted by fiction-mongers, as well as by propagandists with earnest purposes. *Xanthippe and Polyxena* is an historical romance of the fearful adventures of certain converts to Paul's preaching during his tour in Spain. The Christian heroine suffers abduction to the farther end of the Mediterranean and every sort of appalling peril and is saved from one unbelievable situation after another by a series of equally unbelievable interpositions of Providence. The whole is the product of a trite and sentimental imagination and resembles the works of Tatius and Heliodorus.[85] Peter on his way to meet Simon at Rome is introduced as one more figure in the scene of turmoil.

On these various authors *vide* G. Krueger, *History of Early Christian Literature* (trans. by C. R. Gillett, New York, 1897); O. Bardenhewer, *Patrology* (trans. by T. Shahan, St. Louis, 1908), *passim*; A. Harnack, *Geschichte der altchristlichen Litteratur bis Eusebius* (2 vols., Leipzig, 1893–1904); E. Freppel, *Commodien, Arnobe, Lactance* (Paris, 1893); F. X. Funk, *Didascalia et Constitutiones Apostolorum* (2 vols., Paderborn, 1905); P. de Labriolle, *History and Literature of Latin Christianity from Tertullian to Boethius* (New York, 1925).

Commodian

(fl. c. 250)

Carmen Apologeticum, lines 623–626. Text. Ed. by B. Dombart. *Corpus Scriptorum Ecclesiasticorum Latinorum*, XV, 155–156.

He is God, yet he often has made himself man,
And will perform what he will, making dumb creatures speak.
He made the ass address Balaam, who sat on its back,
And the dog say to Simon: "Peter is calling for thee!"

85 An example of this style of romance, well known to every English reader, is Shakespeare's play of Pericles, Prince of Tyre. The source of its plot is this late Greek fiction.

Arnobius
(fl. 284–305)

Adversus Gentes or *Adversus Nationes,* II, 12. Text. Ed. by A. Reifferscheid, *Corpus Scriptorum Ecclesiasticorum Latinorum,* IV, 57.

For there can be reckoned up and set down in a catalogue the deeds accomplished in India, among the Seres, Persians and Medes, in Arabia and Egypt, in Asia and Syria, among the Galatians, Parthians and Phrygians, in Achaia, Macedonia and Epirus, in all the islands and provinces lighted by the rising and the setting sun, and finally in Rome, the mistress city itself. There, although the inhabitants were infatuated with the arts of King Numa and with ancient superstitions, yet they did not hesitate to abandon their ancestral customs and gather to the Christian truth. For they saw the fiery chariot and horses of Simon Magus disperse at the word of Peter and vanish with the name of Christ;[86] they saw, I say, the believer in false gods betrayed by them in their fear, fallen by his own weight and lying prostrate with broken legs, then carried to Brunda,[87] overwhelmed by pain and humiliation, and casting himself down again from the roof of a high house.

The Teachings of the Apostles
(Third Century)

Didascalia Apostolorum, cc. V, IX, XXIV. Text. Ed. and trans. by M. D. Gibson, *Horae Semiticae,* No. II, 27–28, 51, 106–107.

V . . . Because of this, O Bishop, strive to be pure in

[86] Whether Arnobius had read another version of the Simon Magus legend, which made him fly in a fiery chariot, or whether Arnobius was making fanciful use of a figure drawn from the Scriptural account of the translation of Elijah (4 Kings, II, 1; in the King James Version, 2 Kings II, 1), it is hard to say.

[87] Or Brundisium, the modern Brindisi. The scene of Simon's death was always a matter for variation.

thy works and know thy place, that thou art appointed in the semblance of God Almighty and that thou holdest the place of God Almighty; thus sit in the church and teach, as one who hath power to judge, in the place of Almighty God, those that sin; for to you bishops it is said in the Gospel that what ye bind on earth shall be bound in heaven.

IX . . . What more can we say? For the king, who wears the crown, reigns only over the body and binds and looses only in this world, but the bishop reigns over both soul and body, that he may loosen on the earth and bind in heaven by heavenly power.[88]

XXIV [Peter speaks of the rise of heresies.] . . . " When he [Simon] was in Rome, he greatly troubled the church and perverted many and showed himself as if he were ready to ascend to Heaven; and he captivated the gentiles, exciting them by the power of the energy of his sorceries. One day, I went out and saw him in the market deceiving the people; we disputed with one another about the Resurrection and about the life of the dead. And when he was conquered, he pretended to fly in the air and began to give a sign to his attendants to raise him. And when he had risen to a great distance, then I stood and said to him: ' By the power of the name of Christ, I cut off thy powers, that they depart from thee.' Then the demons departed from him and he fell and was broken from the heel of his foot and he died. And many turned from him; but others, who were worthy of him, remained with him. Thus first his heresies were fixed."

[88] The oldest explicit statement, as far as we are aware, of the superiority of the ecclesiastical to the civil power. For fourth century protests against the intrusion of the State into church affairs, *vide infra*, pp. 541, n. 173; 579.

The Acts of Xanthippe and Polyxena
(Third Century)

Acta Xanthippis et Polyxenae, XXIV. Text. Ed. by M. James, *Texts and Studies,* II, No. 3.

XXIV While she [Polyxena] was saying these words, those who were dragging her away walked in haste and reaching the shore, they hired a ship and sailed for Babylonia, for he that carried her off had a brother there, a ruler of a district. But the wind blew against them, so that they could not proceed by reason of it. And as they were rowing on the sea, behold, the great apostle of the Lord, Peter, was sailing past in a ship, having been urged in a dream to go to Rome, because when Paul departed for Spain, there had entered into Rome a certain charlatan and magician, Simon by name, who had broken up the church which Paul had established. And behold, as he sailed, he heard a voice from heaven saying to him: "Peter, tomorrow there will meet thee a ship coming from Spain; arise, therefore, and pray for the soul that is troubled in it." . . .

4. DEVELOPMENT OF THE PETRINE LEGEND DURING THE THIRD CENTURY

Side by side with the legends of Peter at Rome was rising, as we have said, a network of fabrication woven about his career before his journey to Rome.[88a] Some of this originated in Egypt, some in Syria, where faint memories of his presence may still have persisted. At the beginning of the third century, there was, it appears, already in existence a book of *Preachings* (κήρυγμα) *of Peter,* in which Peter was portrayed as the mainstay of the Church, expounding the principles of a Gnostic form of Judaistic Christianity, opposed both to the freer gentile Christianity of Paul and to the more thoroughly Hellenized Gnostic philosophies

[88a] *Supra,* p. 124.

of the Samaritans and other non-Christian inhabitants of Syria. Prefixed to the *Preachings* was a fictitious letter from Peter to James, the apostolic head of the church at Jerusalem, in which Peter reported to James, as his official chief, on the progress of his mission and made a bitter allusion to "converts from the gentiles," who were being taught by an enemy to disobey "the law of God as spoken through Moses," a clear thrust at Paul.[88b]

During the latter half of the third century, the *Preachings* seem to have fallen into the hands of some resident of one of the cities on the Syrian coast, who knew the legend of Peter and Simon at Rome and perhaps the letter of Clement of Rome to the Corinthians.[88c] To this man occurred the fruitful idea of rewriting and expanding the *Preachings* and enclosing them in the framework of a new romance which should bring them into connection with Peter's later adventures at Rome. A connecting link was supplied in the person of Clement, who was made the narrator of an imaginary autobiography, describing, first, his youth at Rome, the singular loss of his parents and brother and the first appearance of a Christian missionary in the city, then, his own voyage in search of an apostle who could teach more of the new doctrine, his attendance upon Peter during his travels along the Syrian seacoast and his public discussions with Simon Magus, with Apion, the grammarian, and with Faustus, the devotee of astrological science, finally, the happy reunion of all Clement's family under Peter's benevolent auspices and Peter's determination to go on to Rome to meet Simon Magus again.

This newer book was called the *Journeys* or *Circuits* (περίοδοι) *of Peter* and was furnished with an introduction in the shape of a fictitious letter from Clement to James after Peter's martyrdom. In this letter, Clement related his own ordination by Peter to succeed him in his chair and authority and Peter's request that he should send a report of his death to James. The two aims conspicuous in the *Preachings*, namely, the exaltation of Peter at the expense of Paul and, at the same time, the acknowledgment by Peter of the headship of the church at Jerusalem,

88b *Epistola Petri ad Jacobum*, printed in Migne with the later *Epistola Clementis*. *Supra*, pp. 125–126.

88c *Supra*, pp. 66 ff.

were perceptible here but not so marked. As compared with the *Preachings*, the later book expressed a milder Jewish, national sentiment, already half reconciled to the more metaphysical viewpoint of the Hellenized gentile church of the East in that period. In Clement's letter, the deference paid to James was of negligible importance in comparison with the sanction bestowed upon the office of the episcopate, above all the Roman episcopate, by Peter's delegation of absolute powers to Clement. Indeed, Harnack and Waitz regard the Roman bias as strong enough here to justify the theory that the *Journeys* and its introductory letter were written not by a Syrian but by a catholic of Rome.[89]

The *Journeys of Peter* in its original form, save for Clement's letter, has perished, as has its predecessor, the *Preachings*. We deduce the nature of their contents from two paraphrases or summaries of the *Journeys*, which were composed during the fourth century and have since been known, the one as the *Recognitions*, the other as the *Homilies*. The former was written like the rest in Greek, but, at the end of the fourth century, was translated by Jerome's friend, Rufinus, into Latin, along with the letter of Clement to James. Called *Recognitions* from the denouement of the story, namely, Clement's discovery of his long lost relatives, it reproduced all the romantic episodes of the *Journeys*, abridged the discussions and eliminated most of the remaining Jewish characteristics.[90] In particular, the discourses of Peter were pruned of any intention other than the refutation of paganism. The book could be read without offense by any Christian who took a speculative interest in current philosophical problems. The *Homilies*, on the other hand, as the title suggests, omitted portions of the romance and repeated the discussions at length, retaining the semi-Judaistic flavor of the *Journeys*.[91] Hort hazards the opinion that the *Recognitions* certainly, if not

[89] See Tertullian's statement, about 200 A.D., that the Roman church could produce a record of Clement's appointment as bishop by Peter. *Supra*, p. 86. Origen knew some account of the teaching of Clement by Peter. *Commentary on Genesis* and *on Matthew*, XXVI, 6, quoted by J. P. Migne, *Patrologia Graeca*, vol. I, 1158. Earlier yet, Irenaeus had spoken of Clement as one who had heard the apostles preach. *Infra*, p. 268.

[90] It is considerably less Jewish than the *Teachings* or *Didascalia of the Apostles*, from which we have quoted. *Supra*, p. 156.

[91] For example, in *Homilies*, XVII, 5, 14, Peter is made to deride Simon Magus for claiming that he obtained a real knowledge of Jesus through seeing him once

the *Journeys,* are Roman handiwork. Lightfoot, however, seems assured that both *Recognitions* and *Journeys,* as well as *Homilies,* were compiled in Syria, though in different circles and under different influences.

Translated into Latin, the *Recognitions* soon gained a wide popularity in the West. The dramatic incidents of the story appealed to public taste and Clement became the patron saint of countless churches all over Christendom. Faith in the greatness of Peter was given more food for growth. The eastern form of his legend, that brought him to Rome under Claudius, was now commonly accepted, even though it did violence to the New Testament and to the oldest tradition at Rome itself. The letter of Clement to James, that drew so plain a picture of Peter's transfer of his full authority to his successor, was in time valued at its strategic worth. It was cited as genuine by the Synod of Vaison in 442 and excepted from the apocryphal literature condemned by Pope Innocent I and by the *Index* attributed to Gelasius. In an enlarged form, it was set at the head of the ninth century collection of pontifical letters and decretals that went under the name of pseudo-Isidore, where it remained unchallenged until the Renaissance.

The complicated problems presented by the Clementine literature have been the subject of much conjecture and argument. We have stated the case here in barest outline. For more adequate consideration, see A. Harnack, *Geschichte der altchristlichen Litteratur bis Eusebius* (2 vols., Leipzig, 1897–1904), Vol. II (*Der Chronologie der altchristlichen Litteratur*), pp. 518 *sqq.*; H. Waitz, *Die Pseudo-Clementinen Homilien und Rekognitionen* (Leipzig, 1904) in *Texte und Untersuchungen zur Geschichte der altchristlichen Literatur,* Vol. XXV[4]; J. B. Lightfoot, *The Apostolic Fathers* (2 vols., London, 1889–1890), Pt. I (*Clement of Rome*); F. J. A. Hort, *Notes Introductory to the Study of the Clementine Recognitions* (London, 1901); A. C. Headlam, *The Clementine Literature* in *Journal of Theological Studies* (London, 1901), Vol. III, pp. 41–58; J. V. Bartlet, *Clementine Literature* in *Encyclopaedia Britannica* (11th ed., 29 vols., London, 1910–1911); F. H. Chase, *Peter* in J. Hastings, *Dictionary of the Bible* (5 vols., New York, 1901–1904); H. U. Meyboom, *Die Clemens-Roman* (Groningen, 1902–1904), Pts. I–II.

---

in a vision. A slight on Paul is obviously intended there. But such passages are exceptional. Most of the discussion turns on matters that have nothing to do with Paul's peculiarities.

Rufinus' Preface to His Translation of the *Recognitions*

(c. 395)

Rufinus, *Praefatio ad Recognitiones.* Text. J. P. Migne, *Patrologia Graeca,* I, 1207.

. . . There is a letter[92] in which this same Clement, writing to James, the Lord's brother, gives an account of the death of Peter and says that he has left himself as his successor to be ruler and teacher of the Church, and which furthermore includes a complete picture of ecclesiastical government. This I have not prefixed to the work [*Recognitions*], both because it deals with a later time and because it has already been translated and published by me. Nevertheless, there is a point in it, which perhaps seems inconsistent to some people, and which I believe I can properly explain here. For some ask how, since Linus and Cletus were bishops of the city of Rome before Clement,[93] Clement himself when writing to James can say that Peter committed to him his chair of instruction. The explanation of this difficulty, as we have received it, is as follows. Linus and Cletus were, no doubt, bishops in the city of Rome before Clement but that was during Peter's lifetime; that is, they performed the episcopal duties while he filled the office of the apostolate.[94] He is known to have done the same at Caesarea, for there, although he was himself on the spot, yet he had with him Zacchaeus, whom he had ordained as bishop.[95] Thus we see that both things may be true, namely,

[92] This whole extract from Rufinus shows how seriously the letter to James was being taken.

[93] Linus and Cletus stand before Clement in the oldest episcopal lists. *Infra,* pp. 249, 268. But from the beginning of the third century there was a popular tendency to disregard them and to make the more famous Clement Peter's direct successor. *Supra,* p. 85, n. 63.

[94] Rufinus draws a distinction between the position of an apostle and that of a bishop. Not all of the Fathers were so exact. Many of them, as we notice, speak as if the bishops succeeded to the apostolic office and carried on the same functions.

[95] *Recognitions,* III, 65 *sqq.*; *infra,* p. 167.

that the two are counted before Clement in the list of bishops and yet that Clement after Peter's death became his successor in the seat of instruction.

PSEUDO-CLEMENT, *LETTER TO JAMES*
(Third Century)

Epistola Clementis ad Jacobum, 1–19. Text. J. P. Migne, *Patrologia Graeca,* I, 463–472.

Clement to James, the brother of the Lord and bishop of the bishops,[96] who governs at Jerusalem the holy church of the Hebrews and all the churches that have been everywhere founded by the providence of God, with the priests and deacons and all the other brethren, peace always.

1 Be it known unto you, my lord, that Simon Peter, who for his true faith and sure foundation of doctrine was set apart to be the foundation of the Church and for this cause was renamed Peter by the Lord's divine lips, the first fruit of our Lord's choosing, the first of the apostles, to whom first God the Father revealed the Son, whom Christ with good reason pronounced blessed,[97] the called and elect, the Lord's companion and follower, the good and most approved disciple, who as mightiest of them all was commanded to enlighten the dark realms of the world, that is, the West, and was able to accomplish it well,[98] — but how I am prolonging my words out of reluctance to tell sad tidings, which yet I must, indeed, though sorrowfully, give you! This Peter then, impelled by his vast love for all mankind, in full confidence, even though the tyrant of the whole earth withstood him,[99] preached publicly that there was a good King

96 A title which in the third century was also applied to the bishop of Rome. *Infra,* pp. 231, 301, 396.

97 Matthew, IV, 18–20; X, 2; XVI, 17–18.

98 This eulogy of Peter as the chief missionary to the West completely ignores Paul.

99 Probably Simon Magus is meant, though the allusion may be to the emperor.

forever over all the world, and he came as far as Rome so as to save the city. But he, I say, consented to suffer for his fidelity and has now ended this life.

2 But during those days when he felt the end of his life approaching he was in a gathering of the brethren and he took my hand and stood up suddenly and said in the presence of the entire church: "Hear me, brethren and fellow servants! Forasmuch as I have been warned by him who sent me, my Lord and Master Jesus Christ, that the day of my death is nigh, I ordain this Clement to be your bishop and to him alone I entrust my chair [100] of preaching and instruction. For he has been my comrade in all things from the beginning to the end and so has learned the truth of all my preaching. He has shared in all my trials and proved himself steadfast. I have found him above the rest devout, charitable, pure, industrious in study, grave, kindly, just, patient, with understanding to bear some ingratitude, even from those whom he is training in the word of God. Therefore, I bestow on him the power of binding and loosing, which the Lord bestowed on me, so that whatever he shall decree on earth shall be decreed in the heavens.[101] For he shall bind what ought to be bound and loose what ought to be loosed, knowing the clear rule of the Church. Therefore, do you hear him and understand that he who grieves the teacher of the truth sins against Christ and offends God the Father of all, so that he shall not live. Likewise, he who presides ought to play the part of a physician and not yield to the temper of an unreasoning beast."

3 As he thus spoke, I fell at his feet and entreated him, excusing myself and refusing the honor and authority of the

100 *Cathedram.*

101 *I.e.*, the power to bind and loose gives the power to legislate as absolute ruler. In § 17 the people are told to be "obedient in all things." Peter says nowhere that the power he gives to Clement is more than that which belongs to any bishop, but the gift is made as a personal transfer of his own peculiar authority to the man he has selected to follow him in the Church. It would be easy to understand from this that Clement was privileged above other bishops.

chair. But he answered. ". . . [Clement should be willing to undertake the care and responsibility, in order to help the church.]

4 . . . Therefore, accept gladly the office of the bishopric and all the more that you have learned from me how to administer the church, that the welfare of the brethren who have taken refuge in God through us be not shaken.

5–16 [Instructions on the duty of bishops, to refrain from secular concerns and teach; also on the duties of priests, deacons, catechists and lay members, on the need of brotherly love, etc.] . . . ."

17 And having said this and more than this, he looked again upon the people and said: " And you also, my beloved brethren and fellow servants, be obedient in all things to him who presides over you to teach you the truth and rest assured of this, that he who grieves him has not received Christ, who entrusted to him the chair of teaching, and he who has not received Christ shall not, as we believe, receive the Father and shall not therefore be received in the kingdom of heaven. . . ."

19 With these words he laid his hands upon me in the presence of them all and compelled me, overcome by my great reverence, to sit in his own chair. And when I was seated, he again said to me: " I beseech you, O Clement, before all who are here, that whensoever I depart this life, as depart I must by nature, you send to James, the Lord's brother, a brief story of your experiences from the beginning of your faith.[102] . . . And then at the end do not fail to inform him briefly, as I said, of the death I have met in this city. And do not fear that he will grieve much, when he knows that I endured it for the faith. . . ."

[102] It will be remembered that this letter was composed as an introduction to the *Journeys*. *Supra*, p. 159.

PSEUDO-CLEMENT, *THE RECOGNITIONS*

(Third Century)

Recognitiones, I, *passim*; III, *passim.* Text. J. P. Migne, *Patrologia Graeca,* I, 1209–1210, 1214, 1232, 1246, 1309–1310.

I 6 . . . A certain rumor, which first arose in the regions of the East, in the reign of Tiberius Caesar, gradually reached us [in Rome]; and gaining strength as it passed through every place, like some good message sent from God, it spread through the whole world. . . . For it was related everywhere that there was a man in Judaea, who, beginning in the spring, was preaching the kingdom of God. . . . This report and more like it were confirmed in process of time not only by repeated rumors but by the positive declarations of persons who came from that country; and day by day the truth of it was more fully made clear.

7 At length, meetings began to be held in various places in the city and the subject to be discussed in conversations, . . . until, during the same year, a man stood up in a crowded spot in the city and made a proclamation to the people, saying: "Hear me, O citizens of Rome![103] . . . [He tells of the coming of Christ.]" Now the man who spoke thus to the people was from the regions of the East, by nation a Hebrew, by name Barnabas, and he said that he himself was one of his disciples. . . .

[Clement sets sail for the East and finds Peter in Caesarea.]

13 [Peter speaks to Clement.] ". . . If there is nothing to prevent you, come with us and hear the word of truth,

[103] This passage possesses some interest as the earliest attempt, even though an apocryphal one, to describe the first coming of a Christian messenger to Rome. The *Homilies* have a similar passage but leave the first preacher nameless. In them, Clement finds Barnabas in Alexandria. Barnabas was the one chosen to preach first to the Greeks at Antioch. Acts, XI, 22.

which we are going to preach in every place until we come even to the city of Rome. . . .

43 . . . The church of the Lord which was established in Jerusalem was most plentifully multiplied and grew, being governed with most righteous ordinances by James, who was ordained bishop in it by the Lord. . . .

72 While, therefore, we abode in Jericho and gave ourselves to prayer and fasting, James, the bishop, summoned me and sent me here to Caesarea, saying that Zacchaeus had written to him from Caesarea that one Simon, a magician of Samaria, was subverting many of our people. . . ."

III 63 [Simon Magus has been outdone in a long debate with Peter on the nature of God, origin of evil, inconsistencies of the Old Testament, idolatry, etc. One of his followers turns against him and comes to Peter and gives him an account of Simon's doings.] "Then he [Simon] asked me [the follower] to accompany him, saying that he was going to Rome and that he would please the people there so much that he would be counted among the gods and publicly offered divine honors. . . . And after this he set out for Rome, as he said." . . .

65 [Peter speaks.] ". . . Since therefore, as you have heard, Simon has set out to engage the minds of the gentiles who are called to salvation, it is needful that I also follow upon his track, so as to refute whatever arguments he presents. . . ."

[Peter appoints Zacchaeus as ruler of the church in Caesarea, giving him directions as to the duties of a bishop and other officers, discipline, etc., more concise than those he is represented as giving to Clement in the latter's letter to James but not dissimilar.][104]

[104] In the *Homilies,* Simon after his defeat flees before Peter into Judaea, and Peter goes on to Antioch without mention of any immediate purpose to go to Rome. *Homilies,* XX. Peter says only once at the beginning that he expects ultimately to arrive at Rome. *Homilies,* I, 16. In the *Recognitions,* Rome is spoken of several times. *Vide,* beside the passages quoted, I, 74.

5. DEVELOPMENT OF THE LEGEND DURING THE FOURTH AND FIFTH CENTURIES

Martyrdom of the Holy Apostles Peter and Paul — Acts of Peter and Paul

The two following documents, the *Martyrdom* and the *Acts of Peter and Paul,* represent the orthodox response to the first Judaistic or Gnostic accounts of the labors and death of the apostle Peter. In their present form, both these narratives date perhaps no farther back than the fifth century but they are unquestionably expansions and revisions of legends that may have originated by the end of the second century, soon after the rise of the crop of primitive tales that showed Peter working and dying in solitary grandeur.

The purpose of these is obviously, in the first place, to offset the Jewish campaign against Paul and to put him in his rightful position by Peter's side as fellow hero and martyr. The depth of the impression created by the earlier Petrine legend is indicated, however, by the fact that even here, at the hands of his friends and contrary to what the New Testament would lead us to expect, Paul is set distinctly second to Peter and leaves to Peter the initiative both in speech and action. This Paul is a subdued and colorless creature, a sharp contrast to the man whose genius and ardor burn in the Epistles. Peter rules the church, shoulders the responsibility and is far the sturdier and more spirited character throughout. But Paul has a kind of formal justice done him, and the Roman church is enriched by the recognition of its other patron saint.

The second purpose is to provide a chronicle of the apostles' last days free from the taint of Gnostic dualism and asceticism. Accordingly, Nero is portrayed as condemning them on the ground of sacrilege or murder, and less is made of the female converts to celibacy. The stock features of the Simon Magus story are preserved, the statue, the conjuring tricks, the flight and fall, but the figure of the spiteful Simon himself has shrunk somehow to smaller proportions. The more dreadful antagonist is the loquacious and ruthless Nero. Perhaps in the minds of the authors the solid, crushing weight of the civil power seemed a more formidable thing to face than the puny tricks of a sorcerer and his demons. Perhaps they had themselves some knowledge of long-drawn trials before magistrates.

It is not possible at present to decide which is the older, our first document, which opens with both apostles at Rome, covers only the events resulting directly in their deaths and goes by the title of the *Martyrdom* or *Passion,* or the second, more comprehensive account, known as the *Acts.* The *Martyrdom* is contained in a sixteenth century Greek manuscript, called the *Codex Marcianus,* and in an old Latin version which bears the name *Passio Sanctorum Apostolorum Petri et Pauli.* It has also been found in Slavonic and Old Italian translations. The Greek and Latin are both printed by Lipsius and Bonnet. The second narrative is somewhat less diffuse in style but includes the story of Paul's journey from the island of Melita to Rome, where he finds the church already organized by Peter. It is extant in a number of Greek texts. We give an abridged version of the *Martyrdom* and a few extracts from the *Acts* to illustrate the differences between the two.

There has been less study of these *Acts* than of the *Acts of Peter* or of the Clementine literature. For further discussion and bibliography see F. H. Chase, *Peter* in J. Hastings, *Dictionary of the Bible* (5 vols., New York, 1901–1904); A. Harnack, *Geschichte der altchristlichen Litteratur bis Eusebius* (2 vols., Leipzig, 1897–1904), Vol. II (*Die Chronologie der altchristlichen Litteratur*); R. A. Lipsius and M. Bonnet, *Acta Apostolorum Apocrypha, Prolegomena* (Leipzig, 1891–1903); O. Bardenhewer, *Patrology* (trans. by T. Shahan, St. Louis, 1908), § 30, 4.

Martyrdom of the Holy Apostles Peter and Paul

Martyrium Sanctorum Apostolorum Petri et Pauli. Text. *Acta Apostolorum Apocrypha,* ed. by R. A. Lipsius and M. Bonnet, 118–177.

1–3 [Paul comes from Spain to Rome and is appealed to by the Jews, who say that Peter has overthrown the law and does not observe the Sabbaths or the feastdays.[105] Paul sends word to Peter asking him to come to his lodging, since he himself is not allowed to go about, being held to appear before Caesar.][106] And hearing this, Peter rejoiced with great joy and arose immediately and went to him. And when they saw each other, they wept for gladness and embraced each other for a long time and bathed each other with their tears.

4 And Paul gave to Peter a report of all his deeds and of how he had come through the shipwreck [107] and Peter in turn related to Paul the wiles he was enduring on the part of Simon Magus. And when evening came, Peter departed to his own dwelling.

5–9 [Paul and Peter each address discordant Jewish and gentile factions.]

10 And while Peter and Paul said this and other things like this, they were everyone silent and listened to them as they taught and preached to all the faithful the word of the Lord; and daily there were added a countless number of those who believed on the Lord Jesus Christ. And when the chiefs of the Jewish synagogue and the priests of the Greeks saw that through the preaching of these men all Rome would soon believe on our Lord Jesus Christ, they began themselves to excite a tumult and an uproar among the people and to laud Simon Magus before the multitude whom the apostles had gathered together; and they endeavored to have him acclaimed in the presence of King Nero and to malign the apostles of the Lord. . . . [As a result of Peter's exhortations Livia, the wife of Nero,[108] and

105 A simple form of retort to the Jewish attacks on Paul for subverting the law. Peter becomes here the one criticized for disregard of Mosaic observances, whereas Paul is expected to uphold them.

106 Acts, XXVIII, 16.

107 Acts, XXVII, 14–44.

108 The social rank of the persons with whom the apostles come in contact grows more exalted, the further the narrative is from being contemporary record. Compare the position of these women with that of those mentioned in the *Acts of Peter, supra,* pp. 148, 150.

Agrippina, wife of the prefect Agrippa, resolve to have no more intercourse with their husbands. At the preaching of Paul, many of the emperor's soldiers become soldiers of Christ and abandon the army and the palace.]

11 Then the people started a seditious uprising and Simon was aroused to envy and began to bring accusations against Peter, declaring that he was a sorcerer and a cheat. And the people wondered at his signs and believed on him, for he caused a bronze serpent to move and statues of stone to laugh and move, and himself to appear suddenly soaring in the air.

12 And to rival these feats Peter healed the sick with a word and gave sight to the blind by prayer and put demons to flight at command and even raised the dead. . . .

13 And thus it came to pass that all devout men denounced Simon Magus and called him impious; and the followers of Simon contended that Peter was a sorcerer and witnessed falsely against him, for many clave to Simon Magus. So the report came to Nero Caesar and he ordered Simon Magus to be brought before him.

14–15 [Simon changes shape before Nero and astounds him, " so that he believes him to be the son of God." Simon also tells Nero that his kingdom will be destroyed if he fails to put the apostles to death.]

16 Then Nero, full of concern, ordered that they should be brought speedily before him.[109] And on the following day, Simon Magus and Peter and Paul, the apostles of Christ, appeared before Nero and Simon said: " These are the disciples of the Nazarene, who, unfortunately, are of the Jewish nation." Nero said: " What is the Nazarene? " Simon answered: " There is a city of Judaea which has always been rebellious against you; it is called Nazareth and the teacher of these men came from there."

109 The apostles here face the emperor himself, instead of the prefect as in the *Acts of Peter*. *Supra,* p. 151.

17 Nero said: "God enjoins us to love every man;[110] why then do you persecute them?" Simon said: "The race of these men has prevailed upon all Judaea not to believe in me. . . ."

18 Nero said: "Who is Christ?" Peter said: "He is the one whom this Simon Magus professes to be. . . . But, noble King, if you wish to learn what was done with Christ in Judaea, take this letter of Pontius Pilate, which he sent to Claudius, and then you will know it all." And Nero commanded it to be brought. . . . [Text of the letter.][111]. . .

24 Nero said: "Are you not in fear of Simon, who confirms his divinity with his deeds?" Peter replied: "Divinity abides with him who reveals the secrets of the heart. Let him, therefore, tell me what I am thinking or what I am doing. I will impart to your ears some thought of mine, before he falsely invents it, so that he may not dare to invent my thought." Nero said: "Come forward, then, and tell me what you are thinking!" Peter said: "Command that a barley loaf be brought and given to me secretly!" And when he had commanded the bread to be brought and delivered to Peter secretly, Peter said: "Let Simon tell now what was thought, what was said, and what was done!"

25 Nero said: "Do you wish me to believe that Simon does not know this, when he has raised the dead and been himself beheaded and arisen the third day[112] and accomplished whatever he said he would do?" Peter answered: "But he did not do it before me." Nero said: "But he did it all before me; and he bade angels come to him and they came." Peter said: "If he did the greatest thing, why does he not do the smallest? Let him tell what I thought and what I did!" . . .

[110] It was certainly a simple soul who put such words into the mouth of Nero.

[111] A fabrication, but an early one. Justin Martyr knew what purported to be an official report by Pilate on the trial of Christ (*I Apology*, XXXV) and Tertullian a letter written by Pilate to the Emperor Tiberius (*Apology*, V and XXI).

[112] Compare the tradition mentioned by Hippolytus, *supra*, p. 133.

26 Simon said: "Hear this, noble King; no one knows the thoughts of men but one, who is God. Is not Peter beguiling you?" Peter said: "But you say that you are the son of God. Tell me, then, what I have in my thoughts and reveal, if you can, what I have done in secret!" For Peter had blessed the barley loaf which he had received and broken it with his right and left hands and gathered it up in his sleeves.

27 Then Simon was angry because he could not tell the secret of the apostle and cried out and said: "Let great dogs come forth and devour him before the face of Caesar!" And suddenly great dogs appeared and sprang upon Peter. And Peter, stretching out his hands in prayer, showed to the dogs the bread which he had blessed; and at that sight, the dogs disappeared from their view.[113] . . .

28 Then Nero said to Simon: "What of it, Simon? I think we have been worsted." Simon replied: "This man did these same things to me in Judaea and in all Palestine and in Caesarea."[114] . . .

29 Then Nero turned to Paul and said: "Why do you say nothing, Paul?" Paul answered and said: ". . . [Profession of faith in Christ.]" . . . Nero said [to Simon]: "Now then, why do you delay and do not prove yourself God, that these two may be punished?"

30 Simon said: "Command that a high tower of wood be built for me and I will mount upon it and summon my angels and bid them bear me in the sight of everyone up to my Father in heaven. And those who cannot do it will be exposed in their folly." . . .

31–32 [Description of a trick with a slaughtered ram by which Simon had previously persuaded Nero that he had been beheaded and come to life again the third day.

33 And when Nero had spoken, . . . he turned to Paul

113 An instance of magical power attached to the sacramental element.

114 A reference to the Clementine story. *Supra,* p. 167.

and said: " As for you, Paul, why do you make no sound? Who taught you or what teacher did you have? . . ."

34–38 [Paul answers at length, refuting Simon and recounting his own labors and ethical teachings.]

39 Nero said: " What say you, Peter? " He answered and said: " All that Paul has said is true. For during many years I have received letters from our bishops, who are in all the Roman world, and the bishops of almost every city have written me of his deeds and words.[115]. . ."

41 Nero said: " Paul, what say you? " Paul answered: " What you have heard from Peter believe that I too have said; for we are of the same mind, because we have one Lord, Jesus the Christ." . . .

42 Simon said: " I am sparing you until I display to you my power." Paul said: " See to it that you emerge hence in safety!" Peter said: " Unless, Simon, you see the power of our Lord Jesus Christ, you will not believe you yourself are not Christ." Simon said: " Most sacred King, do not believe them, for they are circumcised knaves." Paul said: " Before we knew the truth, we had circumcision of the flesh; but since the truth was revealed, we are circumcised and do circumcise in the circumcision of the heart." Peter said: " If circumcision is evil, why were you circumcised, Simon? "

43 Nero said: " Was Simon also circumcised? " Peter said: " By no other means could he deceive souls, except he feigned himself to be a Jew and appeared to teach the law of God." Nero said: " Simon, I perceive you are driven by envy to persecute these men. For there seems to me to be a great rivalry between you and their Christ and I am uneasy lest you be vanquished by them and consumed in utter destruction." . . .

115 This sentence is in the Latin version but not in the Greek. The Roman translator aims to make Peter out as already the head and center of an established system of bishoprics, covering " all the Roman world." As the head, he vouches for Paul.

44 Simon said: " Christ did not teach Paul." Paul said: " Yes, through a vision he taught me also." . . .

47 . . . Nero said: ". . . But why do I say more? You three have shown me that your minds are all unstable and thus you have made me a doubter among you all, so that I find no one whom I may believe."

48 Peter said: " We preach one God the Father, in Christ the Savior, with the Holy Spirit, Creator of all things, who made heaven and earth and the sea and all that is therein, who is verily King and of whose kingdom there shall be no end." Nero said: " Who is this lord King? " Paul said: " The Savior of all nations." Simon said: " I am he of whom you speak." Peter and Paul said: " May it never be well with you, Simon Magus, full of bitterness!"

49 Simon said: " Hear, Caesar Nero, that you may know these men are impostors and I have been sent from heaven; for tomorrow I shall ascend to heaven and shall make blessed those who believe on me and show my wrath on those who have denied me." Peter and Paul said: " God has called us to his own glory; you are called by the devil and hasten to punishment." . . .

51 Then Nero ordered that a tower be erected on the Campus Martius and that all the people and the dignitaries be present at the spectacle. And on the next day, when the multitude had assembled, Nero commanded Peter and Paul to appear before him and said to them: " Now the truth has to be made clear!" Peter and Paul said: " We do not reveal it, but our Lord Jesus Christ, the Son of God, whom Simon has pretended to be."

52 And Paul turned to Peter and said: " It is my part to bow the knee and supplicate God and yours to do the deed, because you were the first to be chosen by the Lord!"[116] And, falling on his knees, Paul prayed. And Peter, fixing his gaze upon Simon, said: " Perform what you

116 An explicit acknowledgment on Paul's part of Peter's right to leadership.

have begun; for your exposure is at hand and our summons; for I see Christ calling both me and Paul."

53 Nero said: "And whither will you depart against my will?" Peter said: "Wherever our Lord may summon us." Nero said: "And who is your lord?" Peter said: "Jesus Christ, whom I see summoning us." Nero said: "And will you also go away into heaven?" Peter said: "Whenever it seems good to him who calls us." . . .

54 Then Simon ascended the tower before them all and stretched forth his hands, with a laurel crown upon his head, and began to fly. And Nero, when he saw him flying, said to Peter: "This Simon is true, but you and Paul are false." And Peter said to him: "Straightway you shall see that we are true disciples of Christ and he is no Christ but a sorcerer and evildoer." Nero said: "Do you still resist? Lo, behold him ascending into heaven!"

55 Then Peter, looking toward Paul, said: "Paul, look up and see!" And Paul looked up, full of tears, and seeing Simon flying said: "Peter, why delay? Perform what you have in mind; for already our Lord Jesus Christ summons us." And Nero, hearing this, smiled and said: "They see themselves defeated and talk wildly." Peter said: "Soon you shall see that we are not wild." And Paul turned and said to Peter: "Perform what you have in mind!"

56 And Peter, looking upon Simon, said: "I adjure ye, angels of Satan, who bear him in the air to deceive the hearts of the faithless, by God, the Creator of all things, and by Jesus Christ, whom he raised from the dead on the third day, from this hour forth support him no longer but let him go!" And immediately he was released and fell upon the place called Via Sacra, which is to say Sacred Way, and was broken into four pieces, perishing miserably.[117]

[117] The Latin says, "was broken into four pieces and knit together four stones, which remain for a testimony of the victory of the apostles unto this day." This is our first reference to any relic or visible memorial of the Simon Magus episode. Others were exhibited during the following centuries. *Vide infra,* pp. 200, 206.

57 Then Nero commanded that Peter and Paul should be put in chains but that the body of Simon should be closely watched for three days in the expectation that he would rise on the third day.[118]. . .

58 Then Nero called Agrippa, the prefect,[119] and said to him: "It is right that worshippers of strange gods should be put to death. Wherefore, I am giving commandment that they be executed in torment in the Naumachium."[120] Agrippa, the prefect, said: "Most sacred King, your commandment is not suited to them both, for Paul seems innocent beside Peter." Nero said: "How then shall they be put to death?" Agrippa answered and said: "It seems just to me that Paul should be beheaded and Peter hung on a cross, for he is guilty of murder." Nero said: "Your judgment is best."

59 Then Peter and Paul were led away from the presence of Nero. And Paul was beheaded on the Via Ostiensis.

60 And Peter came to his cross and said: "Since our Lord Jesus Christ, who descended from heaven to earth, was lifted erect upon his cross and deigns to call me, who am of the earth, to heaven, my cross should be set with head to the earth that it may direct my feet to heaven; for I am not worthy to be crucified like my Lord." Then they turned his cross about and nailed his feet upward.

61 And the multitude gathered together and reviled Caesar and were eager to slay him. But Peter prevented them, saying: "Be not angry against him! . . . For a few days since, when Agrippa prepared to attack me, I was prevailed upon by the brethren and left the city and my Lord Jesus Christ met me. And I worshipped him and said to him: 'Lord, whither goest thou?' And he answered and

118 *Supra*, p. 172.

119 *Supra*, p. 146.

120 A name for the circus of Caligula across the Tiber, at the edge of which was later built the church of St. Peter. *Supra*, p. 104, n. 106. It was often the scene of mock naval battles, a highly popular form of public entertainment.

said to me: 'I am going to Rome to be crucified.' And I said to him: 'Lord, wast thou not crucified once?' And the Lord answered and said: 'I saw that thou wert fleeing from death and I am willing to be crucified in thy stead.'[121] And I said: 'Lord, I will go; I will fulfil thy behest.' And he said to me: 'Fear not, for I am with thee.'

62 . . ." And with these words he gave up his spirit to the Lord.

63 And straightway there appeared noble men, strange in aspect, and said to one and another: "We have come from Jerusalem for the sake of the holy and chief apostle." And together with the illustrious Marcellus . . . they removed his body secretly and laid it by the terebinth[122] near the Naumachia, in a place called the Vatican.

65 [A popular uprising takes place against Nero, who escapes into the desert and dies of hunger and thirst. His body is eaten by wild beasts.][122a]

66 And some devout men from the East attempted to carry off the relics of the saints and at once there was a great earthquake in the city and the inhabitants of the city perceived it and ran and seized them; and the men fled.[123] Then the Romans took the bodies and laid them in a place three miles from the city; and they were kept there under guard one year and seven months, until the place

[121] Jesus' words are reproachful in this version of the story. *Cf. supra,* p. 151 and n. 78.

[122] The medieval guidebooks or *Mirabilia* of the city of Rome applied the name Terebinth to a great mausoleum, similar in shape to Hadrian's tomb, which stood beside the Via Triumphalis, near the circus of Caligula, here called the Naumachia, and which was demolished during the Renaissance in order that its marbles might be used to build the steps and court of the new St. Peter's. For a Renaissance representation of Peter's crucifixion with the Terebinth in the foreground see R. A. Lanciani, *Pagan and Christian Rome,* p. 272.

[122a] This is the Greek version. The Latin version is tempered by more regard for history, for at Rome it would hardly have done to perpetrate such outrageous fiction. According to it, Nero was condemned to death by the Romans and fled, and some persons said he was eaten by beasts.

[123] Pope Gregory I speaks of an attempt on the part of Oriental Christians to steal away the bodies of the apostles from the chamber "ad catacumbas," where they had been lying. *Epistolae,* IV, 30. *Supra,* pp. 106, 108. The Latin version of the next sentence reads: "and laid them in a place which is called Catacumba on the Via Appia, at the third milestone."

was built in which they were to be buried. And afterwards they all assembled with glory and hymns and buried them in the place built for them.[123a]

Acts of Peter and Paul

Acta Petri et Pauli. Text. *Acta Apostolorum Apocrypha,* ed. by R. A. Lipsius and M. Bonnet, I, 178–222.

[The Jews in Rome hear that Paul is on his way thither to be tried before Caesar and appeal to Nero to forbid it. Paul, they say, has done enough harm already among their people in Judaea and Samaria, and Peter is a disturbance now at Rome. Nero promises to write to all the magistrates in the provinces to seize Paul before he can reach Italy.]

And while this was taking place, some converts from the gentiles, who had been baptized through the preaching of Peter, sent priests to Paul with a letter which ran as follows: "To Paul, the noble servant of our master Jesus Christ and brother of Peter, the first of the apostles. We have heard from the leaders of the Jews who are here in Rome, the capital city, that they have requested Nero to send word into all his provinces to have you put to death, wherever you are found. But we have trusted and do trust that as God does not divide the two great lights which he created, so he may not permit you to be separated from each other, that is Peter from Paul, or Paul from Peter. . . ."

[Paul sets out from the island of Melita and journeys by slow stages, with sundry adventures, to Rome. He is entertained on the way by bishops and deacons ordained by Peter and is met at the Three Taverns by disciples sent from Peter to greet him. The Jews, hearing that he has arrived, are much perturbed and come to urge him to oppose the

123a Latin version: "and the body of the holy Peter was laid in the Vatican by the Naumachia and that of the holy Paul on the Via Ostiensis, at the second milestone."

teaching of Peter and his disparagement of the law. Peter and Paul meet with rejoicing and both make addresses to the Jews.[124] The wives of Nero and Agrippa are converted by Peter and many soldiers and courtiers by Paul. Even the emperor's tutor becomes Paul's friend.[125]

Simon Magus appears, and he and Peter work miracles in competition. Simon goes before Nero and by changing shapes convinces Nero that he is truly "the son of God." Peter, Paul and Simon hold their argument in Nero's presence. Simon starts to fly in the air but falls and is dashed to pieces at the apostles' prayers. Nero proposes to Agrippa to put all men like Peter and Paul to death also.]

They beheaded Paul at the spot called Aquae Salviae,[126] near the pine tree.

[Story of Perpetua. Peter is taken to be crucified. He tells of leaving Rome and meeting Christ coming into the city.] And I worshipped him and said: "Lord, whither goest thou?" And he said to me: "Follow me, for I go to Rome to be crucified again." And while I followed him, I returned again into Rome. And he said to me: "Fear not, for I am with thee until I lead thee to my Father's house."

[Martyrdom of Perpetua after the burial of Peter. Men from the East steal away the apostles' bodies. The Romans, aroused by an earthquake, overtake them] in a place called Catacumbae,[127] on the Via Appia, at the third milestone

124 The narrative from this point is similar to the preceding but briefer. Here and there a few new details are added.

125 An apocryphal correspondence between Paul and Seneca was the invention of the early fourth century.

126 The ancient name of the springs, now called Tre Fontane, which lie an hour's walk beyond the Porta San Paolo and are the traditional scene of Paul's execution. A memorial chapel was built there during the fifth century, the foundations of which have been descried beneath the present seventeenth century edifice. In 1875, the Trappist monks excavating behind the chapel found a mass of coins of the reign of Nero, lying together with some fossilized pine cones. R. A. Lanciani, *Pagan and Christian Rome*, pp. 156–157.

127 On the association of the apostles' bodies with the crypt Ad Catacumbas, *vide supra*, pp. 106, 108, 109.

from the city; and the bodies of the saints were kept there under guard for one year and six months, until the places were constructed where they were to be buried. And the body of the holy Peter was interred with glory and hymns in the place of the Vatican, near the Naumachium, and the body of the holy Paul on the Via Ostiensis, two miles from the city.

6. REFERENCES TO THE PETRINE LEGEND BY THE FATHERS OF THE FOURTH AND FIFTH CENTURIES

The following group of nine selections, taken from the writings of the most respected leaders in the Church of the fourth and fifth centuries, in widely separated regions of the Roman Empire, is evidence of the final acceptance of the main features of the apocryphal legend of Peter and Simon Magus and of the seriousness with which it was generally treated thenceforth until the revival of the more critical scholarship of the later Middle Ages.[128] Even here, however, one may remark some difference in the attitude of the Fathers toward it. No one actually disputes it, but Eusebius, with a discriminating sense sharpened by much comparing and weighing of documents for his *History*, cannot bring himself to repeat the improbable literal details. He knows that the *Acts of Peter* are spurious;[129] still he cannot disregard the contributions of Justin Martyr and Irenaeus to the making of the story. He supposes there is something at the bottom of it but cannot decide precisely what. So he compromises by shrouding the whole affair in a veil of highsounding, mixed metaphor. Peter is the victorious general of God, bearing the rich merchandise of light to the West, to overcome Simon, the "base destroyer of life," but the nature of the victory won by the merchandise is not explained.[130] Augustine also gives one the im-

128 See also Jerome's allusion to Simon Magus in his brief life of Peter. *Supra*, p. 115.

129 *Supra*, p. 120.

130 Both before and after his handling of this special topic Eusebius relates clearly and definitely what he has been able to ascertain of the later careers of the other apostles. It is only when he reaches Peter and Simon Magus that he plunges into a cloud of mystifying language, to emerge as he passes to the next subject.

pression of not committing himself. He describes the Simonian heresy as outlined by Irenaeus and Hippolytus but dispenses with the sensational incidents of the legend. Perhaps they struck his acute mind as too crude and incongruous. At any rate he limits himself to the mere statement that Simon was destroyed by Peter at Rome. But these two men are the exceptions. Otherwise, the most learned, like Theodoret, and the most lofty-minded, like Ambrose, repeat the legend as genuine history and confidently draw from it their morals and conclusions.

There is a difference to be observed also in the versions of the legend adopted by the several Fathers. Cyril of Jerusalem is the first to bring Paul distinctly into his narrative and prove thereby an acquaintance with the *Acts* of the two apostles. Sulpicius Severus, the Gaul, is another who relies upon some recension of the double legend and credits Paul with a share in Simon's defeat. The rest mention only Peter. They may, of course, have known only the *Acts of Peter* or they may have preferred it to the version that included Paul. The most influential of our authors are among the six who omit Paul altogether.

Eusebius' *Church History,* the first book from which we quote, is already familiar.[131] Cyril was priest, in the year 348, in the church at Jerusalem, which, after the favor shown it under Constantine and the rise of the custom of making pilgrimages to holy places, had rapidly increased in size and wealth. In Lent of that year, Cyril delivered a series of twenty-three addresses to the catechumens who were being prepared for baptism at Easter. The addresses dealt with the elements of Christian faith and refuted the most dangerous theories of paganism and the leading heretical sects. They were composed with such pains and care, in so clear and orderly a style, that they have ever since been looked upon as models of religious exposition and throw much light on third-century liturgy and dogma in the East. The passage given below is from Cyril's survey of the original rise of heresy in the Church. It has a hortatory tone, appropriate to the audience for which it was meant.

131 *Supra,* pp. 96–98.

Our first western writer is Ambrose, bishop of Milan, the protagonist of his generation in the struggle of the ecclesiastical organization against domination by the State. Ambrose, as the reader may remember, was chosen in 374, in an outburst of popular relief and enthusiasm, to fill the chair of Auxentius, the Arian [132] bishop of Milan, although until that time he had held nothing but civil office under the government and was actually no more than an unbaptized catechumen in the Church. One week after his baptism, he was consecrated bishop and found himself contending against discord and weakness within his flock and a capricious imperial power without. Gratian, who was western emperor from 375 to 383 and for whom Ambrose wrote two books to explain the orthodox dogma of the Trinity, was devoted to him. But after Gratian's assassination, the youthful Valentinian II was at first influenced by his mother to support the Arian faction, who thereupon set up a rival bishop and demanded that Ambrose be deposed. In 386, Valentinian issued something in the way of an ultimatum, ordering Ambrose either to appear at court to defend his right to the bishopric or to surrender the church property without more ado and retire from Milan. Ambrose refused to make either move, maintaining that it was his duty to stay by his church and that no earthly force could override it. The sermon which he preached in his cathedral during the crisis to make clear his position and encourage his terrified people has been preserved, and from it we quote one of the examples which he gives of frailty made strong to endure

[132] We shall hear much of the Arian party later in our book. Suffice it here to say that it arose during the period when the attention of the Church was intensely occupied with the effort to define the nature of Christ and his relation to the Father. The twofold problem invariably confronting the disputants was how to keep Christ human and yet exalt him above other teachers of humanity to the height of complete divinity and, on the other hand, how to make him uncreated God, distinct in person from the Father, and yet preserve the monotheistic principle; or, in other words, how to avoid the Gnostic or Docetic or Monarchian position, which deprived Christ of human personality and interpreted the historic Jesus as a phantom or as pure deity in disguise, without lapsing either into a denial of his perfect godhead or into polytheism. The orthodox dogma of the Trinity, as embodied in creeds like the Athanasian, still in common use, was an attempt to reconcile these apparently irreconcilable phases of the dilemma. The Arian party took the ground that to call the Son, as the orthodox did, " very God of very God, . . . not created, of one substance with the Father," was tantamount to setting up two gods. They insisted that Christ, though of divine substance, was a created being and essentially subordinate to the eternal Father. On the rise of the Arian controversy under Constantine, *vide infra,* p. 467.

peril, the *Quo Vadis* story of the Petrine legend.[133] Ambrose's steadfastness saved his cause. Valentinian gave way and shortly afterward accepted Ambrose's advice on the stand to be taken against those members of the Roman Senate who were agitating for the restoration of the altar of Victory, which Gratian had removed from its ancient place in the Senate House. When he felt his personal safety threatened by conspiracies in Gaul, Valentinian sent for Ambrose to come to him but sent too late, for midway on his journey Ambrose was intercepted by the news of the emperor's murder.

About this same time, Ambrose came into contact with Theodosius the Great, the governor for a few years of the whole Roman world. In 388, he persuaded him to withdraw a harsh edict for the punishment of some Mesopotamian Christians who had destroyed a Jewish synagogue, and in 390, he compelled him to do solemn penance before the church at Milan for the hasty massacre of his riotous subjects at Thessalonica. In the difficult situation in which the church then found herself, alternately spoiled and badgered by rulers who came and went, Ambrose set a stimulating precedent of spiritual independence and fearlessness, which was not forgotten, even when it was not followed. In the intervals of his busy life, he found time to compose a number of hymns and works on moral and religious subjects for his people's use. His most famous set of commentaries on a Biblical text were the nine homilies on the six days of creation that were called the *Hexaemeron,* written in the allegorical, imaginative style of Origen.[134] From them we cite a few lines on the prowess of Peter and Paul, in which an episode from the New Testament is put beside one from the apocryphal *Acts,* with no distinction of authenticity drawn between one and the other.

Of the life of Philaster, bishop of Brescia, one of Ambrose's colleagues in northern Italy, nothing is known but the fact that about 383, he produced a manual of one hundred and fifty-six different kinds of heresies, past and current, with a concise

[133] The same sermon contains some telling passages on the relation of civil authority to ecclesiastical.

[134] *Supra,* p. 87; *infra,* p. 317.

description of the most conspicuous tenets of each. The subject was timely in an age when theological controversies rent the air more vociferously than ever, and the task of expressing the gospel in a series of accurate, metaphysical terms, which might serve as a permanent standard of correct belief, seemed occasionally hopeless. Philaster appears to have taken his idea from the *Syntagma,* a smaller compilation by Hippolytus,[134a] now lost, of which his own was an enlargement and continuation. The first heresy, in his catalogue, to arise after the death of Christ, was that of Simon Magus, exposed and vanquished like its founder by "the blessed apostle."

At almost the same time, another manual of heresies was drawn up in the East by Epiphanius, the metropolitan bishop of Cyprus, who concentrated the fervor of his life on the practice and preaching of asceticism and the ceaseless combat with heterodoxy. His particular detestations were Arianism and the broad, philosophic Christianity of Origen.[135] To him also Simon Magus was the first heretic of the Christian era, the first to misuse the name of Christ.

Sulpicius Severus, our next author, was a noble Aquitanian, educated in the law, who renounced his wealth and profession at the death of his wife and the preaching of St. Martin of Tours and chose a life of monastic solitude and poverty. Beside his famous *Life of St. Martin,* he composed a *Chronicle* of religious history, beginning with an outline of the events of the Old Testament and going on to narrate briefly the development of the Church to the year 400. He wrote in a grave and tempered style, modelled upon the histories of Sallust and Tacitus. The conflict of Peter and Paul with Simon seemed to him an affair of sufficient importance to be included in his sketch of the rise of Christianity at Rome.

We cannot stop here long enough to attempt a characterization of the great Augustine, the pupil of Ambrose, who became bishop of the city of Hippo in the province of Africa, the man whose thought and experience shaped the outlook and moulded the faith of the western Church down to our own day. Here we

[134a] On Hippolytus *vide infra,* pp. 297 ff.

[135] *Supra,* pp. 88–89.

are concerned only with one of his controversial letters and with a minor treatise, written about 428, near the end of his life, in response to a request from a Carthaginian deacon, named Quodvultdeus, that he should prepare a textbook on the vexed subject of heresies. Augustine referred the inquirer to the existing treatises of Epiphanius and Philaster but Quodvultdeus replied that he desired something more concise and definite. Augustine thereupon goodhumoredly prepared a summary of eighty-eight heresies, not much unlike the despised manuals of his predecessors, save for its greater brevity, and opening, as theirs did, with Simon Magus. He intended to conclude the summary with a discussion of the fundamental nature of heresy and of the question, what made a man a heretic, but this latter part he never finished. Our citations are of interest chiefly because they show that Augustine, like his contemporaries, endorsed the Petrine legend, though in distinctly guarded terms.

Theodoret, bishop of Cyrus, a small town in Northern Syria, two days' travel from Antioch, is now remembered principally for the *Church History* he wrote about 450, to carry on the work of Eusebius. In his own day, however, he was better known for his indefatigable exertions on behalf of harmony and orthodoxy in the Church. In 449, he wrote to Pope Leo: "with the aid of divine grace I have cleansed more than one thousand souls from the poison of Marcion and from the sectarianism of Arius and Eunomius.[136] I have led back many others to Christ the Lord." In the struggles of the fifth century to perfect a creed that would sufficiently refute one error without falling backward into its opposite, in the wranglings of bishops, synods and councils, he took an active part and was even forced at one time to spend a year in exile for opposing too stoutly the Monophysite faction,[137] headed by the patriarchs of Alexandria and Constantinople. No wonder that after his return from exile he too felt called upon

136 On Marcion *vide infra*, pp. 258; 266, n. 65; 272. On Arius and Eunomius *supra*, p. 183, n. 132; *infra*, pp. 467–468.

137 The Monophysites occupied a position midway between the Gnostics and the orthodox. They held that Christ was truly God incarnate in the flesh but that his nature was always and solely divine. The orthodox insisted that he had taken on himself a human nature as well as the human garment of flesh. Between Monophysites on one side and Arians on the other, the orthodox of the period were hard pressed.

to compile a *Compendium of Heretical Tales*, beginning as usual with the arch heretic Simon Magus and closing with a sketch of what he regarded as the true faith of the Church. He wrote with a touch of Eusebius' figurative imagination. Simon was the symbol of the darkness of evil teachings in the Church, and his overthrow by Peter was the scattering of that darkness by the radiance of truth.

Extracts like these are given, as we have said, mainly in order to show the way in which the legend of Peter was eventually accepted by the influential spokesmen, even of the orthodox circles. During this same period, the claim of the Papacy to superlative rights was for the first time being urged with persistency and to an increasing extent formally acknowledged. The part which the legend, as distinct from the legitimate tradition, played in fortifying this claim or in bringing about its acknowledgment is indeed quite impossible to estimate. One may form a vague conjecture from the few hints which will appear now and then in those sections of our book that trace the growth of papal power, as far as that process is revealed in surviving documents.[138] The effect, however, of so widespread a legend, repeated and confirmed by leading theologians, on the mind of the ordinary priest and lay member in making him ready to acquiesce in a claim based upon Peter's exceptional achievements and authority is the sort of thing that is never fully disclosed in records such as these. None the less some allowance should reasonably be made for it in an attempt to account for the rise of the Petrine See to its final preëminence.

On these authors, see the standard dictionaries and histories of Christian literature and biography already cited; also J. Mader, *Der heilige Cyrillus, Bischof von Jerusalem in seinem Leben und seinen Schriften* (Einsiedeln, 1891); E., Duc de Broglie, *St. Ambroise* (4th ed., Paris, 1901); A. Largent, *St. Ambroise* in *Dictionnaire de Théologie Catholique* (8 vols., Paris, 1909–1910), Vol. I, 942–951; F. van Ortroy, *St. Ambroise et l'empereur Théodose, Analecta Bollandiana* (Paris, 1904), Vol. XXIII, pp. 417, 426; R. A. Lipsius, *Die Quellen der ältesten Ketzergeschichte* (Leipzig, 1875); Th. Zahn, *Geschichte des neutestamentlichen Kanons* (3 pts. in 2, Erlangen, 1881–1884), Pt. II, 1, 233–239; H. Gelzer, *Sextus Julius Africanus* (2 pts. in 1, Leipzig,

138 *Infra*, pp. 235 ff.

1880–1898), Pt. II, pp. 107–121 (on Sulpicius Severus); J. McCabe, *St. Augustine and his Age* (London, 1903); J. Martin, *St. Augustin* (Paris, 1901); A. Hatzfeld, *St. Augustin* (6th ed., Paris, 1901); Th. Specht, *Die Lehre von der Kirche nach dem heilige Augustin* (Paderborn, 1892); G. Boissier, *La Fin du Paganisme* (3rd ed., 2 vols., Paris, 1908), Vol. II, pp. 291 *sqq.* and *passim.*

Eusebius

(c. 265–c. 340)

Historia Ecclesiastica, II, 13: 1, 2, 6; 14: 1–6. Text. *Eusebius Werke* (*Die griechischen christlichen Schriftsteller der ersten drei Jahrhunderte*), II[1], 132–134, 136–138.

II 13 But faith in our Savior and Lord Jesus Christ being now spread abroad among all men, the enemy of man's salvation devised a plot for seizing the imperial city for himself. He brought thither the aforesaid Simon, assisted him in his crafty wiles and led many of the inhabitants of Rome astray and into his own power. This is related by Justin, one of the distinguished writers among us, who lived not long after the time of the apostles. . . . [Quotation from Justin Martyr.[139] Reference to Irenaeus.[140]] Indeed we ourselves have understood that Simon was the original author of all heresy. . . . [Description of the Simonian heresy.]

14 The evil power that hates what is good and plots against man's salvation produced at that time Simon, the father and author of this great wickedness, as if to oppose him as a mighty antagonist against the noble and inspired apostles of our Savior. But that divine and heavenly grace which works with its ministers, by their arrival and strength extinguished speedily the rising flame of evil and humbled and cast down through them "every high thing that exalted itself against the knowledge of God." [141] Wherefore, neither

139 This quotation is given *supra*, p. 130.
140 The reference is to the passage cited *supra*, p. 131.
141 II Corinthians, X, 5.

the conspiracy of Simon nor that of any other man who arose in that age could avail anything in the lifetime of the apostles. For everything was conquered and subdued by the splendor of the truth and the divine Word, which had lately come to shine from God upon men and was potent then in the earth and dwelling in those same apostles. The said impostor was early smitten in the eyes of his mind by a divine and miraculous flash and after his malice had been once detected by the apostle Peter in Judaea, he fled and journeyed a long way across the sea from the East to the West, thinking that by such a course he could live according to his will. And he came to the city of Rome by the strong aid of that power which was lying there in wait for him and shortly he succeeded so well in his enterprise that the inhabitants honored him as a god by the erection of a statue. But this situation did not continue long, for straightway, during the reign of the same Claudius, the all good and benevolent Providence, that watches over all things, led Peter, the strongest and greatest of the apostles,[142] who on account of his valor was spokesman for all the rest, to Rome against this base destroyer of life. He, like a noble general of God, clad in divine armor, carried the rich merchandise of spiritual light from the East to the dwellers in the West, heralding the same light and the Word, which is the salvation of souls, and the tidings of the kingdom of heaven.

Cyril of Jerusalem

(c. 315–c. 386)

Catecheses, VI, 14, 15. Text. J. P. Migne, *Patrologia Graeca*, XXXIII, 561–564.

14 And the inventor of all heresy was Simon Magus, the Simon who in the Acts of the Apostles thought to buy with

[142] Peter of Alexandria had already called Peter "the first of the apostles." *Supra*, p. 94.

his silver the unpurchasable grace of the Spirit and heard the words: "Thou hast neither part nor lot in this matter,"[143] and so on. Of him it was written: "They went out from us but they were not of us; for if they had been of us they would have remained with us."[144] And he, after he had been rejected by the apostles, went to Rome, taking with him one Helena, a harlot, and he was the first who dared say with blasphemous tongue that it was himself that appeared upon Mount Sinai as the Father, that afterward showed himself among the Jews not in flesh but in outward shape as Christ Jesus and that still later came as the Holy Ghost, whom Christ had promised to send to be a comforter. And he deluded the city of Rome so completely that Claudius erected a statue of him and inscribed under it in the Roman tongue: "Simoni Deo Sancto," which, being interpreted, means: "To Simon, the holy God."

15 And as the delusion was spreading far and wide, Peter and Paul, a noble pair, the leaders of the Church, arrived and corrected the error and when the supposititious god was displaying himself, they quickly displayed him as a corpse. For Simon proclaimed that he would ascend into heaven and on a chariot of demons he was rising into the air. But the servants of God fell upon their knees, practicing the harmony of which Jesus spoke: "If two of you shall agree as touching anything that they shall ask, it shall be done for them."[145] They launched the weapon of their agreement in prayer against Magus and brought him down to earth. And marvellous though it was, it was no marvel. For it was Peter, who carries the keys of heaven.[146] And again no marvel, for it was Paul, who was "caught up to the third heaven and heard unspeakable words, which it is not lawful for a man to utter."[147]

[143] Acts, VIII, 18–21. [144] I John, II, 19. [145] Matthew, XVIII, 19.

[146] In another address, Cyril speaks of Peter as "prince of the apostles and chief herald of the Church." *Catecheses.* XI, 3.

[147] II Corinthians, XII, 2, 4.

Ambrose

(c. 340–397)

Sermo contra Auxentium: De Basilicis Tradendis, 13. Text. J. P. Migne, *Patrologia Latina,* XVI, 1053.

13 The same Peter afterwards, when he had overcome Simon and was planting the seeds of the word of God among the people and preaching chastity, stirred the minds of the gentiles to resentment. And when they sought to seize him, the Christians besought him to leave them for a little while. And although he was eager for his passion, yet the spectacle of the people entreating him prevailed upon him, for they begged him to save himself in order to establish and strengthen them. What then? By night he set forth to pass outside the walls and saw Christ coming to meet him in the gate and entering the city. He said: "Lord, whither goest thou?" Christ replied: "I am come to be crucified a second time." Peter understood that the Lord's answer had reference to his own cross, for Christ could not be crucified a second time, since in undergoing his passion and death he had put off the flesh. "For in that he dies unto sin, he died once; in that he liveth, he liveth unto God." [148] Therefore Peter understood that Christ must be crucified a second time in his poor servant. So willingly he returned again and made answer to the Christians who questioned him and being apprehended shortly afterward, he honored the Lord Jesus in his cross.

In Hexaemeron, IV, 8. Text. *Corpus Scriptorum Ecclesiasticorum Latinorum,* XXXII, 139.

Thus Paul blinded Elymas, the sorcerer, not only through the weakening of his art of prophecy but also by the dark-

[148] Romans, VI. 10.

ening of his eyes.[149] Thus Peter brought down Simon, who was soaring in magic flight to the heights of the sky, and undid the strength of his incantations and destroyed him.

Philaster of Brescia

(d. before 397)

Diversarum Hereseon Liber, 29. Text. *Corpus Scriptorum Ecclesiasticorum Latinorum,* XXXVIII, 14–15.

Then after the passion of our Lord Christ and his ascent into heaven, there appeared one Simon Magus, a Samaritan by birth, from Githo, a village in Samaria that bears this name. And he applied himself to magic arts and deceived many, saying that he was the power of God, which, he asserted, was superior to all other powers. And the Samaritans revere him as their father and extol him as the founder of their pernicious heresy and seek to glorify him with highsounding praise. Although he was baptized by the blessed apostles, he abandoned their faith and taught an abominable and dangerous heresy, declaring that he had undergone a presumptive transformation, that is, in form, and thus had suffered, although he said he was not suffering.[150] . . . [Brief account of the Simonian heresy.] And after he had fled from the city of Jerusalem before the blessed apostle Peter and was come to Rome, he was vanquished entirely by the prayer of the blessed apostle and let fall by his angel and thus he perished as he deserved, so that his sorcery and lies were openly manifest to all men.

149 Acts, XIII, 6–12.

150 An allusion to the Gnostic theory that Christ felt no physical pain upon the cross. *Supra,* p. 77, n. 39.

Epiphanius of Cyprus

(c. 315–403)

Adversus Haereses (*Panarion*), XXI, 1, 5. Text. Ed. by K. Holl (*Die griechischen christlichen Schriftsteller der ersten drei Jahrhunderte*, I, 238, 244.

1 Beginning with the time of Christ and coming down to the present day, the first heresy is that of Simon Magus. It is one of those which has a wrong and sacrilegious faith in the name of Christ and which is adroit to devise corruption. This Simon was a sorcerer and came from the town of Githo in Samaria, which now is but a village. And he deceived the Samaritan nation with his magic arts, hoodwinking and ensnaring them. For he said that he was the mighty power of God and had descended from heaven. And to the Samaritans he said he was the Father and to the Jews he said he was the Son and had suffered and not suffered, but suffered in appearance only. . . . [The Simonian philosophy. The encounter with the apostles in Judaea.]

5 . . . But why after a season is he to be seen submitting in his turn to fate at Rome, when in a concourse of the Roman people he fell down wretchedly and died? With what words did Peter convict him of having no part or share in the lot of the godly?

Sulpicius Severus

(c. 363–c. 425)

Chronica, II, 28, 4–5; 29, 3–4. Text. *Corpus Scriptorum Ecclesiasticorum Latinorum*, I, 83.

28 . . . For at that time [the reign of Nero] the religion of God was gathering strength at Rome. Peter was holding the office of bishop there and Paul, after he had appealed

to Caesar from the unjust judgment of the governor, was brought to Rome. And many assembled to hear him and comprehended the truth and were moved by the powers of the apostles, which they then frequently displayed, and joined in the worship of God. For then took place that famous contest of Peter and Paul with Simon. He with the aid of his magic arts had been flying in the air, supported by two demons, in order to prove himself God. But the demons were put to flight by the prayers of the apostles and he fell to the ground in the sight of the people and was broken to pieces.

29 . . . Then Peter and Paul were condemned to death. The former was beheaded with the sword and Peter was lifted up upon a cross.

Augustine of Hippo

(354–430)

De Haeresibus, I, 1. Text. J. P. Migne, *Patrologia Latina,* XLII, 25–26.

The Simonians were disciples of Simon Magus, who was baptized by the deacon Philip, as we read in the Acts of the Apostles,[151]. . . and, in addition, he tried to make himself accepted as Jupiter and one Helen, a harlot, whom he had associated with him in his crimes, as Minerva. And he presented images of himself and of this harlot to his disciples for adoration and by public permission set them up at Rome as images of the gods. And in that city the apostle Peter overthrew him by the true power of omnipotent God.

Epistolae, XXXVI,[152] ix, 21–22. Text. *Corpus Scriptorum Ecclesiasticorum Latinorum,* XXXIV[2], 2, 50–51.

151 Acts, VIII, 9–13.

152 This letter was written in reply to a polemical treatise, advocating the custom peculiar to Rome and a few other western communities of keeping fast on Saturday. The treatise itself we know only by this rebuttal of it.

"Peter," he says, "the head of the apostles, the doorkeeper of heaven and the foundation of the Church, after he had destroyed Simon, who, being the image of the devil, was only to be overcome by fasting, taught this very custom to the Romans, whose faith is proclaimed to all the world." Then did the rest of the apostles teach the Christians in all the world to dine [on that day] in opposition to Peter? Peter and his fellow disciples lived together in harmony and in harmony do the Saturday fasters, instituted by Peter, and the Saturday diners, instituted by his fellow disciples, live together now. There is, indeed, a very common opinion, although many Romans consider it false, that when the apostle Peter was expecting to contend with Simon Magus on the Lord's day, he fasted the day before in company with the church of the city because of the danger of that great trial and after he had achieved that happy and glorious victory, maintained the same custom and that some of the churches of the West copied it. But if, as this author says, Simon Magus was an image of the devil, then he is certainly not a Saturday nor a Sunday but a daily tempter. . . .

But if he replies that James at Jerusalem and John at Ephesus and the others in other places did teach the same practice that Peter taught at Rome, namely, of keeping fast on Saturday, but that the other countries have strayed from this teaching and that Rome had persisted steadfastly in it, and if again we answer that some places in the West, where Rome is, have not preserved it as a tradition from the apostles and that the countries of the East, where the gospel itself was first preached, have continued without any divergence in the belief that all the apostles, including Peter himself, taught that fast was not to be kept on Saturday, then the argument becomes endless and stirs up antagonism and opens countless questions.

Theodoret of Cyrus

(c. 393–458)

Haereticarum Fabularum Compendium, I. Text. J. P. Migne, *Patrologia Graeca,* LXXXIII, 341–344.

First of all, Simon Magus, the Samaritan, appeared as a minister of the devil's machinations. . . . [Account of Simon's origin and activities in Palestine.] But the grace of God armed great Peter against his mad spirit. For he followed him about and scattered his evil doctrine like a cloud of darkness and revealed the radiance of the light of truth. Nevertheless, though openly convicted of falsehood, the wretch did not cease to struggle against the truth and went to Rome in the reign of Claudius Caesar. And he so amazed the Romans by his tricks that they honored him with a statue of bronze. But the divine Peter in turn arrived also and stripped him of his plumes of deceit. At length, he challenged him to a contest of miraculous power and exhibited the difference between divine grace and wizardry. In the sight of all the Romans, he brought him down by prayer from a great height and won to salvation the spectators of the prodigy.

7. LATER ELABORATIONS OF THE LEGEND

In concluding this brief survey of the appearance and rise of the apocryphal legend of Peter at Rome, first to a dubious notoriety and eventually to the respectable rank of genuine history, it seems desirable to add a few words on the later amplifications of this legend after the fourth century and on the material evidences of it that were from time to time produced within the locality, some of which are pointed out to this day, although they probably no longer excite the same simple-minded awe.

Our first document is the *Apostolic Constitutions,* a lineal descendant of the third century *Didascalia* or *Teachings of the Apostles,* from which we have already quoted,[153] and framed upon the same general model. Like the *Teachings,* it was written in Syria and in Greek, but at the end of the fourth century or at the beginning of the fifth. Like the *Teachings* also, it describes the contemporary beliefs and practices of the eastern church, while purporting to be a report of the deliberations of the first apostles, met together for counsel in Jerusalem. It informs us that Clement of Rome was attending in the name of the apostles to the distribution of the report among the bishops and priests of the Church. The last book of the *Constitutions,* which has no counterpart in the *Teachings,* contains miscellaneous material, such as formulae for ordinations to ecclesiastical offices, explanations of the liturgy of the mass, closing with eighty-five "ecclesiastical canons of the holy apostles." Of these the first fifty were translated by Dionysius Exiguus early in the sixth century and placed at the head of his collection of ancient church canons, whence they were taken over by the author of the pseudo-Isidorean *Decretals* of the ninth century. In the twelfth century, they were incorporated by Gratian in his *Decretum,* where they still stand among the organic law of the Church. The body of the *Constitutions,* however, from which these canons were plucked, was condemned by the Council of 692 as tainted with heretical opinion and soon disappeared from general notice and circulation. Our principal extract is from the description given by Peter to his fellow apostles of his own triumph over heresy.

Our second document, the *Martyrdom of Peter,* is an enlarged and florid version of the latter part of the *Acts of Peter,*[154] covering the events at Rome after the destruction of Simon Magus. A Gnostic or ascetic feeling betrays itself more plainly than in any other recension we have seen. Peter preaches chastity far more vehemently than he preaches Christianity and is denounced in the Senate for separating wives from husbands. Suspended from the cross, head downward, he maintains his complete superiority to fleshly weakness. He delivers calmly two long,

[153] *Supra,* pp. 154, 156.

[154] *Supra,* pp. 133, 150.

mystical harangues and two rhetorical prayers and does not die until he has wound up his discourse. Lipsius, who edits this work along with the other apocryphal *Acts,* puts its date in the third or fourth century. Other scholars, however, set it later. Guignebert suggests the fifth century and Harnack the sixth. The enthusiasm for a monastic or celibate life, which mounted rapidly after the fourth century, may partly account for the extraordinary emphasis laid upon contempt of the body. To invest this new *Martyrdom* at once with an authority comparable to that of the works ascribed to Clement, it was foisted upon Linus, Clement's traditional predecessor in the Roman church. It is therefore often called the *Pseudo-Linus.* We subjoin merely a summary of its contents.

In the late fifth or early sixth century, a legend of somewhat different type was composed around the names of two historical persons, Nereus and Achilleus, which contributed incidentally new features to the story of Peter. Nereus and Achilleus in life were body servants of the noble lady Flavia Domitilla, who was banished from Rome about the year 95, by her kinsman, the emperor Domitian, on the ground of her religion. Her two retainers were executed and buried in the catacomb which Domitilla had constructed for the use of Christians on land belonging to her outside the city. A relief commemorating the death of Nereus may be seen there today. In an arcosolium of the same catacomb, are also the tomb and portrait of another martyr, a woman, Petronilla, of whom nothing whatever is known. Her name is the regular feminine form of the masculine Petronius and she may perhaps have been a relative of Domitilla.[155] By the time, however, that the legend of which we speak was written down, Latin scholarship had long been on the wane and some visitor to the disused catacomb imagined that he had discovered in her tomb the resting-place of a forgotten daughter of the apostle Peter.[156] The bare hint was enough. A shrine was dedicated to St. Petronilla by the side of that erected to Nereus and Achilleus, and the legend was enlarged to embrace all three. An element of pathos was brought into the apostle's masterful career. Pet-

155 The wording of the inscription is simply, "Aurelia Petronilla filia dulcissima."

156 The feminine form of Peter or Petrus is Petrilla.

ronilla became his virgin, paralytic daughter, borne about on a litter beside him, whom he could not heal. Nereus and Achilleus were converts to his later preaching at Rome and after his death, the comrades and guardians of Petronilla until their martyrdom. A lively version of the battle with Simon Magus came in as part of a letter from Marcellus, Peter's earlier friend,[157] to the more recent converts, describing the apostle's former miracles to which he had been witness. Petronilla herself enjoyed, in time, considerable personal popularity. In the eighth century, King Pepin expressly requested Pope Stephen II to move her remains for better protection from the catacomb to the shelter of her father's great basilica. They were carried to the imperial mausoleum at the south end of the transept of St. Peter's which was thereupon christened the chapel of Santa Petronilla, a title which it kept until its destruction in the sixteenth century. The huge painting of Guercino, in which Petronilla is the central figure, is now a conspicuous ornament of the Palazzo dei Conservatori on the Capitoline Hill.

Our last specimen of apocryphal composition, the *Passion of Peter and Paul,* coming on top of so many others, when a reader has become a trifle sated with thaumaturgy, proves what fresh and startling ideas might yet be evolved by an ingenious mind working with the rich materials of the legend and the monuments of the city and unhampered by any historical scruples. This *Passion* was written probably near the end of the sixth century or the opening of the seventh, when classical Rome had already sunk so far out of memory that a man wandering among her neglected statues and temples could interpret them as his fancy chose. Only on such an hypothesis can one account for the amazing explanation of the statue of Janus, that still stood in its famous shrine near the Curia or Senatehouse on the edge of the Forum. The notion here propounded did not for some reason commend itself to popular favor and the *Passion* as a whole never attained the reputation of its forerunners. We confine ourselves to a summary of its most striking novelties. It is palpably the most medieval of the documents we have handled.

157 *Supra,* p. 137.

As, in course of time, every important event of Christian history was substantiated by concrete and tangible evidence in the shape of relics, such as drops of Mary's milk and wine of Cana, crowns of thorns and winding cloths from the holy sepulchre, so also the legend of Peter was confirmed by solid memorials, a few of which are exhibited to pilgrims to this day. We have met already an allusion to the four stones united into one by the impact of Simon's fall.[158] The four stones have disappeared but the gigantic print left upon the pavement by the foot of Christ, when he parted from Peter at the city gate, is still displayed in a chapel of the church of San Sebastiano. The chains which Peter wore in prison have been, since the fifth century, in the keeping of the church of San Pietro ad Vincula, founded by the Empress Eudoxia to receive them. We append to the last of our apocrypha some random notices of other relics which were pointed out in the Rome of the Middle Ages. The first, the slab on which wide grooves were worn by the knees of Peter and Paul, as they knelt in prayer, is now preserved in the church called San Francesca Romana, which stands on the site of the ancient temple of Venus and Rome, to one side of the Via Sacra. The earliest basilica erected on this spot was dedicated to Peter. Simon Magus, it will be remembered, crashed to his destruction on the Via Sacra.[159] The slab whereon he fell is mentioned by Gregory, bishop of Tours, who visited Rome about 590, and again by Anastasius, the papal librarian, who recorded the building of the church of St. Peter by Paul I, about 765. Another relic, a stone stained by Simon's gore, perhaps a block of porphyry, has also vanished, but in the twelfth century it was listed among the memorable objects passed by a pope in his progress from the Vatican to the Lateran and in the fourteenth century, Petrarch spoke of it to a friend as one of the notable sights of Rome.[160]

[158] *Supra,* p. 176, n. 117.

[159] *Supra,* pp. 149, 176.

[160] A psalter, painted in Byzantium in the late ninth century and containing a picture of the defeat of Simon by Peter as symbolic of the overthrow of the iconoclasts by the orthodox forces at the Seventh Council of Nicaea in 843, is now in the Vatican Library and known as the Barberini Psalter. J. B. Bury, *A History of the Eastern Roman Empire* (London, 1912), pp. 431–432.

Our subject has dropped to the level of folk lore and superstition and for that reason may be held no longer worthy the attention of the serious investigator. The connection between the rise of the majestic institution of the Papacy and the appearance in the Forum of the trumpery relics of Simon's downfall may indeed be impossible to establish. Yet if any powerful and far-reaching authority, in order to prove enduring, has had always to construct for itself a foothold of faith and reverence in the people over whom its power was exerted, these childish legends and relics had their uses. They told the multitude in simple language wonderful things of Peter, the reported founder of the Roman See, and, more than the writings of a hundred scholars, instilled into their minds an awe and admiration for what he had accomplished and suffered.[161]

F. X. Funk, *Die apostolischen Konstitutionem* (Rothenburg, 1891); ibid. in *Die Kirchengeschichtliche Abhandlungen und Untersuchungen* (2 vols., Paderborn, 1887–1889), Vol. II, pp. 359–372; F. Nau, *Constitutions Apostoliques, Dictionnaire de Théologie Catholique* (7 vols., Paris, 1909–1924, pp. 1520 *sqq.*); A. Harnack, *Geschichte der altchristlichen Litteratur bis Eusebius* (2 vols., Leipzig, 1897–1904), Vol. II (*Die Chronologie der altchristlichen Litteratur*); C. Guignebert, *La Primauté de Pierre* (Paris, 1909); *passim*; R. A. Lanciani, *Pagan and Christian Rome* (Boston, 1893), pp. 335–342.

The Constitutions of the Apostles

(Fourth or Fifth Century)

Constitutiones Apostolorum, VI, 9; VII, 46. Text. *Didascalia et Constitutiones Apostolorum,* ed. by F. X. Funk.

VI 9 ". . . And Simon, meeting me, Peter, first at Caesarea Stratonis, where the faithful Cornelius, a gentile, believed on the Lord Jesus through me,[162] tried to pervert the word of God. There were with me there the holy youths,

[161] On the effect of increasing public acquaintance with the personality of a ruler or an official, in order to stimulate affection and loyalty to him, see Graham Wallas, *Human Nature in Politics* (Boston, 1919), 30–34.

[162] Acts, X.

Zacchaeus, who was once a publican,[163] and Barnabas, Nicetas and Aquila, brothers of Clement,[164] the bishop and citizen of Rome, the disciple of Paul, our fellow apostle and co-worker in the gospel. I thrice in their presence reasoned with Simon concerning the true Prophet and concerning the kingdom of God and when I had vanquished him by the power of the Lord and put him to silence, I drove him away into Italy.

Then when he was in Rome, he distressed the church mightily and seduced many and won them over to himself and astounded the gentiles with his skill in magic, insomuch that once, in the middle of the day, he went into their theatre and bade the people to bring me also by force into the theatre and promised that he would fly in the air. And when all the people stood in suspense at this, I prayed by myself. And he was truly carried up into the air by demons and flew aloft in the air, saying that he was returning to heaven and that thence he would bestow benefits upon them. And while the people acclaimed him as a god, I stretched out my hands to heaven and with my soul besought God through the Lord Jesus to overthrow this pest, destroy the power of those demons that made use of him for the seduction and ruin of men, dash him to the ground and bruise him but not kill him. Then, fixing my eyes on Simon, I said to him: ' If I be a man of God and true apostle of Jesus Christ and teacher of piety and not of falsehood, as you are, Simon, I command the wicked powers of the rebel against good, by whom Simon, the wizard, is upborne, to loose their hold, that he may fall headlong from his height and be exposed to the mockery of those who have been deluded by him.' When I had said this, Simon was bereft of his might and fell headlong with a great noise and was dashed violently upon the ground and his hip and ankle bones were broken.

[163] *Supra*, p. 167.

[164] These brothers figure in the Clementine *Recognitions*. *Supra*, p. 160.

And the people shouted, saying: 'There is but one God, whom Peter preaches rightly and in truth!' Then many forsook him, but some, who deserved perdition, continued in his evil doctrines. . . ."

VII 46 ". . . As regarding these bishops who have been ordained in our lifetime, we now write unto you that they are these: James, bishop of Jerusalem, . . .; at Antioch, Euodius,[165] ordained by me, Peter, and Ignatius [166] by Paul; . . . in the church at Rome, Linus, son of Claudia, was the first, ordained by Paul, and Clement, after Linus' death, the second, ordained by me, Peter,[167]. . ."

The Martyrdom of the Blessed Apostle Peter as Recorded by Linus, the Bishop

(Fourth or Fifth Century)

Martyrium beati Petri apostoli a Lino episcopo conscriptum. Text. *Acta Apostolorum Apocrypha,* ed. by R. A. Lipsius and M. Bonnet, I, 1–22.

[The four concubines of the prefect Agrippa, and Xandipe, the wife of Albinus, friend of Caesar, are all converted to a life of chastity by Peter's preaching. Xandipe warns Peter and his disciple Marcellus, son of the prefect Marcus, of the danger threatening Peter. He is denounced in the Senate for separating wives from husbands and some of the senators, "enlightened [168] by the Lord through Peter," also send him warning.

His converts implore him to flee the city. Processus and Martinianus, "keepers of the prison," advise him to leave while he can. "For since you called the fountain from the

165 *Supra,* p. 116.

166 Ignatius was bishop of Antioch fifty years after Paul's death. *Supra,* pp. 71–72.

167 Another attempt to account for Clement's ordination by Peter. *Supra,* pp. 85, 86, 162.

168 The Latin word is "illuminati."

rock by your prayers and by the wondrous sign of the cross and baptized us, who believed, in the Mamertime prison hard by, you have gone freely whither you pleased and no one has opposed you."[169] Peter sets out and meets the vision of the Lord at the gate. He returns rejoicing, saying that the Lord will be crucified in him again.

Hieros with four "apparitores" and ten other guards arrests him and brings him before the prefect Agrippa for trial. After sentence, he is crucified "at the place which is called the Naumachia, near the obelisk of Nero,[170] on the hill." Before his death, he makes a long address and prayer from the cross. Marcellus takes down the body and lays it in his own tomb. Nero hears of it and is angry, because he had intended himself to punish Peter for depriving him of Simon Magus.]

Acts of Nereus and Achilleus

(Fifth or Sixth Century)

Acta Nerei et Achillei, IV, 14. Text. Ed. by H. Achelis in *Texte und Untersuchungen zur Geschichte der altchristlichen Literatur,* XI, no. 2.

[Marcellus, the disciple of Peter, sends a letter to Nereus and Achilleus, containing an account of the contest with Simon Magus. He describes how Peter raised a dead man to life and tamed the fierce dog that Simon set to attack him and how the dog tore Simon's clothes, so that the boys jeered at him and drove him out of the city.]

169 This passage proves the previous existence of a form of the legend which we have not met, according to which Peter had passed some time in confinement in the Mamertine prison and was still, nominally at least, in custody. Since the fifteenth century, there has been a shrine over the Mamertine vault known as San Pietro in Carcere and the trickling spring which Peter summoned from the rock has been pointed out to visitors.

170 The obelisk which now stands in the center of the Piazza di San Pietro was brought from Heliopolis in Egypt to Rome by Caligula and set up in the center of his circus or Naumachia. It was moved on rollers to its present position by Pope Sixtus V, in 1586. It is the only obelisk in Rome that has never been thrown down.

IV 14 After this he could not endure the shameful disgrace and for a year never showed himself. But then he found someone who brought him to the favorable notice of Nero Caesar; and thus it came to pass that a malignant man acquired a malignant friend, nay, one more wicked than himself. And afterwards the Lord appeared to the apostle Peter in a vision and said: "Simon and Nero, being filled with demons, are plotting against you. Fear not, for I am with you and I will give you the solace of my servant, the apostle Paul, who tomorrow will arrive in Rome. With him you shall make war together upon Simon for seven months and when you have cast him out and overcome him and driven him down to hell, you shall both come together victorious to me." And this came to pass, for Paul arrived on the next day. And how in turn they saw one another and contended with Simon for seven months, I have thought needless to tell you, as you know it, for you were here and beheld it with your eyes and Saint Linus wrote the whole story of their passion in the Greek tongue for the churches of the East.[171]

The Passion of the Apostles Peter and Paul

(Sixth or Seventh Century)

Passio Apostolorum Petri et Pauli. Text. *Acta Apostolorum Apocrypha,* ed. by R. A. Lipsius and M. Bonnet, I, 223–234.

[The usual narrative is varied with several new incidents. Simon Magus professes to be Christ, who was rejected and crucified by the Jews but has returned to earth at Rome. The imposture is detected by relatives of Pontius Pilate, who had been in Judaea during Christ's lifetime and who knew that his personal appearance differed from Simon's.

Nero has a statue erected to Simon, and later, after

[171] *Supra,* pp. 198, 203.

Simon has spoken at one and the same time to the emperor in the Senate and to the people standing outside, he has another statue set up "with two faces, one looking toward the Senate and one toward the people."][172]

8. RELICS IN EVIDENCE OF THE LEGEND[173]

Gregory of Tours

(Late Sixth Century)

De Gloria Martyrum, I, 28.

There may be seen today in the city of Rome two grooves in the rock, on which the blessed apostles with bended knees poured out their prayer to the Lord against Simon Magus. The water which collects in these grooves after a rain is sought for by sick persons and, when drunk, speedily restores the health.

Anastasius

(757–767)

Vita Pauli Papae I.

He [Paul I] built recently a church within this city of Rome, on the Via Sacra, near the temple of Romulus,[174] in honor of the holy apostles Peter and Paul, where the same most blessed princes of the apostles, at the time when they were crowned with martyrdom, poured out their prayers to

[172] The celebrated temple of Janus, the doors of which always stood open except in time of peace, was situated to one side of the Senate House, between it and the Basilica Emilia. The great bronze statue of the two-faced god was seen still in its place by the historian Procopius, when he visited the Forum about the middle of the sixth century. *De Bello Gothico,* IV, 22.

[173] For further information on this subject see G. B. de Rossi, *Della memoria topografica del sito ove cadde Simone il mago sulla Via Sacra* in *Bullettino di archeologia cristiana* (Rome, 1867), Vol. V, pp. 70 *sqq.*; P. Lugano, *Le memorie leggendarie di Simon Mago e della sua volata* in *Nuovo bullettino di archeologia cristiana* (Rome, 1900), pp. 60 *sqq.*

[174] The circular shrine or Heroön erected by the emperor Maxentius in memory of his son Romulus. It now forms the vestibule of the church of Santi Cosma e Damiano, at the end toward the Via Sacra.

our Redeemer and were seen kneeling with bended knees. In this spot even to this day their knees may be seen impressed upon the solid rock for a witness to all future generations.

Benedict, Canon of St. Peter
(1130–1143)

Ordo Romanus, V.

He [the pope] passes by the rock where Simon Magus fell, near the temple of Romulus.

Petrarch
(1304–1374)

Epistola ad Philippum de Vitriaco.

You will see the stone stained with the wicked brains of Simon.

BOOK TWO

THE RISE OF THE SEE

THE RISE OF THE SEE

Introduction

Having traced through our documentary chronicle the growth of the tradition of Peter's presence at Rome and of his foundation of the Roman episcopate, we may now attempt a similar review of the history of the see itself during the three hundred years after Peter's death. We begin, as before, with the period of shadowy origins in an obscure cult that had recently struck root in the byways of the capital and follow down to the time of that see's recognition as the chief authority in a triumphant and expanding state religion, whose power was felt throughout the Mediterranean world.

In this second part of our book, we print, entire or abridged, most of the documents and passages that throw light of any kind upon the popes of the first three hundred and eighty years of our era. Up to the reign of Constantine, these documents are so sparse and fragmentary and, when all is said, leave such wide intervals wholly untouched and blank that it has seemed desirable to give everything that could be found, even such scraps of personal biography and anecdote as do not strictly belong in the history of an institution. Our imaginations need every discoverable aid if they are to frame any conception whatever of the men and events that were slowly preparing the Papacy of Julius I and Damasus. During this primitive period, we hear but two bishops speaking unmistakably and at any length in their own words, Clement, about 96, and Cornelius, between 250 and 254. The letter here attributed doubtfully to Soter and the sermon ascribed on slender grounds to Victor may be genuine but both are couched in such general terms that they are of little help toward the understanding of a specific age. We read, of course, of momentous letters and declarations issued by Eleutherus, Victor, Callistus, Stephen and Felix but no remnants of their papers are now to be discovered in any archives. Eusebius preserves a few excerpts from the manuscripts he handled at Caesarea, where copies of the correspondence of many famous bishops, Roman, Alexandrian, Greek and Asiatic, were kept in the library of the church, but the documents he cites are insignificant in number when compared with those he merely lists. Indeed to read Eusebius on papal history is a painful pleasure in spite of his priceless excerpts. One is so constantly tantalized by his allusions to what else he might have quoted. If it were not for the writings of the early theologians, Irenaeus, Tertullian, Hippolytus and Cyprian, who in one capacity or another had relations with contemporary Roman bishops, it would not be possible to form any connected outline of this period at all.

From the time of Constantine onward, the records are considerably fuller and more diversified in character. There is more visible effort to save material that may be of value for the future. Eusebius recounts at length the benevolent activities of the first Christian emperor and inserts the text of many imperial letters and decrees. He is followed by other ecclesiastical historians, Athanasius, Hilary, Jerome, Socrates, Sozomen and Theodoret, as well as by some whose names have disappeared, who not only narrate events but also begin systematic collections of documents, edicts, petitions, letters and acts of councils. Here we find more than one illuminating letter from the Roman bishops Julius, Liberius and Damasus. The correspondence of such distinguished persons as Athanasius, Basil and Ambrose, the pagan history of Ammianus Marcellinus, the statutes of the Theodosian Code, all these and other things contain references to the position or policies of the Roman See. For our last fifty years, therefore, it becomes necessary to make some selection, if our chronicle is not to outrun its limits. We still, however, try to include everything that possesses genuine importance or suggestive association, omitting only what is repetitious or less significant for the purpose we have in mind.

At this juncture, we should perhaps remind ourselves that we are not following the rise of the general institution of the episcopacy nor the evolution of the functions of the bishop as such. We have, as we have said, assembled first and last much miscellaneous information on the Roman bishops, but our main intention throughout is to watch the progress of the office from a simple bishopric to a primacy. We make no effort to account for the appearance within the church of Rome, as elsewhere, of the single, autocratic bishop, presiding over the collegiate body of presbyters, bishops and deacons which the apostles knew. Discussions of the episcopal form of government are to be found in any history of the Church or of church law.[1] Here we try to observe chiefly in the Roman See not the features which it shared in common with other sees all over the Empire but its unique aspects, whatever was exceptional in its domestic or foreign affairs, its relations with other bishoprics and branches of the Church outside its diocesan jurisdiction and ultimately its assumption of superiority over all other churches, East and West. Our object of study is not the bishop of Rome *per se* but the bishop of Rome on his way to becoming the supreme pontiff of the universal Church.

Certain broad questions which naturally arise at the commencement of such a study should find some answer in our series of extracts and documents. What, first of all, were the outstanding reasons for the rise of the Papacy to hegemony in the Church? What were the character and extent of that hegemony before the period of the barbarian invasions? Some of these answers stand out in our texts, conspicuous on the surface. Others must be reached, if at all, by a painstaking process of inference. Different readers will have different views as to how the emphasis should be distributed. We shall devote the remainder of this introduction to demonstrating how readily answers do build themselves up out of our material and what aspects they tend to assume as the chronicle progresses. We shall ourselves make no exhaustive examination but merely try to suggest the constructive ends such a study may be made to serve.

In the first place, it is evident that the Roman church had advantages of location that would have ensured for it a measure

[1] See, for example, A. Harnack, *Expansion of Christianity* (2nd ed.), Vol. I, pp. 334–482; A. Harnack, *Entstehung und Entwickelung der Kirchenverfassung und des Kirchenrechts in den zwei ersten Jahrhunderten*; J. Reville, *Origines de l'Épiscopat* (Paris, 1895).

of prominence, even if no apostle had crossed the Mediterranean. It was planted in the city of Rome, the capital of the world.[2] Among the Jews and Greeks of the foreign quarter and the slaves and freedmen attached to noble households the gospel spread so quickly that when Paul wrote his Epistle to the Romans he could refer to several congregations, " ecclesiolae," already in existence among them.[3] The passage in Clement's letter on the persecutions of Nero implies that the body of Christians was really considerable.[4] A few years later, Ignatius of Antioch wrote to beg the Roman church not to interfere to prevent the execution of his sentence of martyrdom.[5] If the letter usually known as II Clement be actually the composition of Bishop Soter or of some other Roman between the years 120 and 170, as Harnack supposes, the statement contained in it, that the Christians of that day outnumbered the Jews,[6] must have been meant for Rome and Southern Italy. Not long afterward, Irenaeus could remark that the faithful from everywhere habitually met at Rome.[7] As a matter of fact, not only the orthodox faithful but also the innovators and champions of every kind of doctrine made their appearance sooner or later at the great capital. Simon, the reputed author of the first heresy,[8] Valentinus,[9]

[2] Athanasius speaks of the respect due to the Roman church not alone because of its apostolic foundation but also because of its situation in the " metropolis " of the Empire. *Infra,* p. 569.

[3] Romans, XVI, 1–16. Aristobulus and Narcissus are known to have been nobles high in official life. A little later, Paul mentions the saints " that are of Caesar's household." Philippians, IV, 22. On the subterranean chapel, discovered in 1776 near the church of Santa Prisca, which may have marked the site of the house of Prisca and Aquila but which has since been buried again, see R. A. Lanciani, *Pagan and Christian Rome,* pp. 110–111.

[4] *Supra,* p. 68. Tacitus, describing the persecution, speaks of the Christians as " a vast number." *Annales,* XV, 44. His phrase, however, is somewhat to be discounted as a rhetorical exaggeration. But by the end of the first century, the construction of Christian catacombs, similar to the Jewish but ere long surpassing them in size, had begun outside the city walls. J. Wilpert, *Die Malereien der Katakomben Roms* (2 vols., Freiburg, 1903). One or two members of the inner group at court, Titus Flavius Clemens and Domitilla, had joined the new sect.

[5] *Infra,* p. 241.

[6] It was natural to compare the Christian community with the Jewish, both because of the connection between the two faiths and also because their members were drawn mostly from the same foreign populations at Rome. Of the first sixteen traditional popes only four, Linus, Clement, Pius and Victor, had Latin names; Victor, the thirteenth, was the first apparently to conduct his correspondence in Latin. The first recorded church building was put up in the Jewish district beyond the Tiber. *Infra,* p. 300. [7] *Infra,* p. 267. [8] *Supra,* pp. 128, 131.

[9] On the following names, *vide infra,* pp. 258, 272, 278, 279. Plutarch, in his panegyric on the Roman Fortuna, says that the city has become the sacred shrine of

Cerdon, Marcion, Tatian, Theodotus, Artemon, and other well-known teachers of heterodoxy, all were heard there. Marcion brought with him a gift of two hundred thousand sesterces to the Roman church. By the opening of the third century, four or five different Christian sects or schools had quarters at Rome, each professing its particular type of discipline or dogma, a situation which lasted on even after the government had begun to maintain orthodoxy in the fourth century.

The letter of Bishop Cornelius, written between 251 and 254, gives us authoritative data as to the size and resources of the orthodox church in his time.[10] His figures seem to indicate a membership of at least thirty thousand, a widespread system of domestic poor relief and an elaborately graded hierarchy of clergy. A century later, Optatus of Mileve wrote that there were more than forty basilicas in the city.[11] During a vacancy in the Roman See, caused by the severity of persecution, the emperor Decius is said to have remarked that he would rather hear of the appearance of a rival claimant to the throne than of a new bishop at Rome.[12] The emperor Aurelian appointed a Roman bishop to act as arbitrator in a heated controversy that had arisen in the freshly conquered province of Syria over the see of Antioch.[13] The period just preceding the reign of Diocletian saw a rapid increase in the church's numbers and worldly influence. When Eusebius wrote his *History,* he thought it at least plausible to say that Maxentius proclaimed himself a Christian in Rome " in order to please the Roman people." [14]

The Christian emperors of the fourth century preferred Milan to Rome as a western seat of government but they still regarded Rome and its institutions with dutiful feelings of respect and honor. Constantine himself exhibited no marked deference toward the Roman bishopric, although he sanctioned the gift of

---

every man's faith. *De Romanorum Fortuna,* 316; quoted by H. M. Gwatkin, *Early Church History,* Vol. II, p. 215, n. 1.

[10] *Infra,* pp. 352–353, 384–385.

[11] *Supra,* p. 110. *De Schismate Donatistarum,* II, 4.

[12] *Infra,* p. 372.

[13] *Infra,* pp. 439–441.

[14] *Historia Ecclesiastica,* VIII, 14, 1. Rome was, of course, more pagan than Eusebius imagined.

a palace to Miltiades as an episcopal residence and enriched the Roman church in his customary, lavish manner with handsome basilicas over the tombs of its patron apostles.[15] His son Constans, however, gave Julius I a substantial and steady backing that no bishop had ever before received, going even as far as to threaten his brother Constantius with war if he failed to reinstate Julius' candidate in the see of Alexandria.[16] In fact, the eastern Arians once taunted Julius with the material basis of his authority, which came, they implied, from the greatness of his city, not from any spiritual superiority.[17] The Arian Constantius took special pains to win over Bishop Liberius, although in the end he sent him into exile as he had the obstinate bishops of Milan and Vercellae and ordered an Arian consecrated in the Lateran.[18] But under the orthodox rulers who succeeded Constantius in the West the Roman pontiff was again assured of favor and support. Damasus was many times protected from his enemies by the magistrates and an imperial edict confirmed him in his jurisdiction over all other bishops.[19]

Items like these enumerated seem to show that the Roman church was bound by the bare fact of its strategic position in the mother city of the Empire to fill a notable place in the Christian organization. Because of a similar position in the "royal city" of "New Rome" the bishopric of Constantinople was in time recognised as the foremost see of the East, devoid though it was of any pretension whatever to age or to an apostolic tradition. Furthermore, the Roman Christians, who were, as we have said, from the beginning men of varied races, habitats and sympathies, were in these first centuries peculiarly generous in the use of their wealth and influence. Clement, in his letter to the Corinthians, lays great stress on the duty of hospitality to strangers and cites examples of members of his church who were selling their property and themselves into slavery to ransom prisoners in the mines.[20] Ignatius of Antioch calls the Romans

[15] *Supra,* p. 104; *Infra,* p. 449.

[16] *Infra,* p. 530.

[17] *Infra,* p. 506.

[18] *Infra,* pp. 568–577.

[19] *Infra,* pp. 671–672.

[20] *Infra,* pp. 236–239. "We know that many of our number have surrendered themselves to captivity so as to ransom others; many have sold themselves into slavery and used the price of their own bodies to feed others." I Clement, LV, 2.

"foremost in love."[21] Dionysius of Corinth, writing about the year 170, refers admiringly to the Roman practice of sending assistance to weaker churches in every city.[22] The Roman Victor procured the release of prisoners in Sardinia and Dionysius forwarded money to Cappadocia to redeem Christian slaves.[23] Stephen sent aid to Arabians in distress.[24] Basil of Cappadocia pleads for the charity of Rome to be continued to the East as it had been in generations past.[25] Unquestionably the Roman church very early developed something like a sense of obligation to the oppressed all over Christendom. The very eastern bishops who, in the third century, firmly repudiated the claims of a Roman bishop to ecclesiastical domination admitted willingly enough the reputation of the same bishop for benevolence to distant and needy brethren.[26]

The political status of Rome in the peninsula of Italy also gave the bishopric in that city a noteworthy advantage over those eastern sees that vied with it for precedence. Everywhere, as Christianity spread through the Empire, we know that the framework of ecclesiastical administration tended to pattern itself upon the civil. Each local capital or seat of a provincial governor eventually possessed a metropolitan or archbishop with rights of general presidency over the bishops of the cities within his province. The countries lying about the eastern end of the Mediterranean were divided into many provinces. There were many capitals, each nominally of the same rank as every other and none so indisputably superior as to be able to impose its supremacy upon the rest, before the rise of Constantinople in the fourth century. In Italy, circumstances were different. Italy itself, for purposes of government, was treated as a unit until the reign of Diocletian. All its primitive tribal divisions had been abolished under the Republic. The peninsula was regarded as the

[21] *Infra,* p. 241.
[22] *Infra,* p. 252.
[23] *Infra,* pp. 308, 642.
[24] *Infra,* p. 420.
[25] *Infra,* pp. 641–642. In his account of the eastern persecutions under Diocletian, Eusebius says that the Roman custom of dispensing succor had lasted to his own day. *Historia Ecclesiastica,* VII, 5, 2. A Roman deacon accompanied the Alexandrian bishop to his trial during Valerian's persecution. *Infra,* p. 422.
[26] *Infra,* p. 420.

setting or background of the city Rome and was ruled from Rome. Consequently there was but one focus of authority. By the year 252, there seem to have been one hundred bishops in central and southern Italy [27] but outside Rome there was nothing to set one bishop above another. All were on a level together, citizens of Italy, accustomed to look to Rome for direction in every detail of public life. The Roman bishop had the right not only to ordain but even, on occasion, to select bishops for Italian churches. Not until the late fourth century, did the exceptional position of the bishop of Milan at the courts of Valentinian and Gratian and the personal gifts of Ambrose himself result in the establishment at Milan [28] of a second center of ecclesiastical influence in Italy and by that time the primacy of Rome was too firmly grounded to be shaken.

Beyond Italy there was no city in the West to approach Rome in dignity or grandeur. Carthage, the greatest commercial port on the African coast west of Egypt, seems to have received her Christianity first through Roman missionaries [29] and although the Carthaginian bishop acted later as metropolitan of the provinces of Africa, Numidia and Mauretania, he expressed habitually for the Roman bishop the deference due to an older brother.[30] With painful reluctance and distress of mind did Cyprian bring himself to oppose Stephen on what he deemed a fundamental principle of church constitution.[31] Caecilian had the emperor's command to carry his quarrel with the Donatists to Rome for judgment.[32] In Spain and Gaul, there was apparently no thorough organization of the church by provinces until after the time of Constantine. A Spanish or Gallic dispute was regularly referred to Rome for settlement.[33] A Spanish metro-

[27] *Infra,* pp. 353, 382. Christianity made its way more slowly in northern Italy. There the bishoprics known to have existed in the year 300 are only Ravenna, Milan, Aquileia, Brescia, Verona, Bologna, and Imola. A. Harnack, *The Mission and Expansion of Christianity* (2nd ed.), Vol. II, pp. 258–260.

[28] The church of Milan, like the churches of Ravenna and Aquileia, may have been founded by missionaries from Illyricum or Dalmatia during the third century. In time, it invented a legend of foundation by the apostle Barnabas.

[29] *Infra,* p. 294.

[30] *Infra,* pp. 363, 377–379.

[31] *Infra,* pp. 395–398, 404 ff.

[32] *Infra,* p. 457.

[33] *Infra,* pp. 399, 402. Hosius, bishop of Cordova, was a favorite of the emperor Constantine and much employed by him in the transaction of church

politan of the fourth century wrote to Damasus for instruction how to deal with an ungovernable band of ascetics and a Spanish synod took his reply as its rule for guidance.[34] Throughout the West it seemed quite natural to turn to the source of political authority for religious leadership also.

The reasons thus far adduced for the rise of the Roman church to eminence may be called the material or adventitious reasons, due to its special advantages of location and resources. As long as the city Rome continued to be the resplendent mistress of the world, these reasons alone would give the church within her walls what might be described as an aristocratic place among other churches. Whether they would have sufficed to keep it in that place when imperial Rome declined and fell is another matter. At any rate, other factors of an ecclesiastical and religious nature also entered soon into the situation, one set of factors continually reënforcing the other. With all the religious support in the world the Papacy, as we find it, could hardly have arisen in a petty, country town. On the other hand, material advantages alone could not have given it the hold it gradually came to possess over men's minds and spirits. A consciousness of owning both material and moral forces, an ability to wield the weapons of power and to justify them by spiritual sanctions are traits perceptible even in the earliest Roman bishops. They soon became fixed characteristics of the office, endowing the incumbents one after another with extraordinary positiveness and assurance.

As, by the end of the first century, the expectation of Christ's speedy return began to wane and it became increasingly clear that the Church must adapt itself to an indefinite career of struggle on earth, the looseness of organization and the simplicity of belief, which had been tolerable when all Christians lived in daily anticipation of the end, grew more and more impossible. The apostles and eye-witnesses of the truth had disappeared. It became necessary then to formulate traditions and

---

business, but his prominence was purely personal and accidental. After his death the see of Cordova slips back into obscurity.

[34] *Infra*, pp. 609, 692–693.

decide upon rules to keep the faithful in the straight path. The Church of the second and third centuries was, as we have said elsewhere, a church in process of crystallizing into a permanent institution, equipping itself, bit by bit, with ritual for its services, creeds for its neophytes and a specialized body of officials for its administration. Several congregations put forth particular claims to be regarded as the spokesmen for the vanished apostles, those, of course, which were known to have had close relations with the apostolic leaders in their lifetime and which, therefore, might be supposed to have kept the fullest memories of their teaching. In the East, the most prominent of these congregations were Smyrna and Ephesus in Asia Minor, Antioch in Syria and Alexandria in Egypt. Each had its venerable set of traditions and its line of bishops running back to the apostolic age.[35] The result, however, of the juxtaposition of four such churches was that no one of them was able to assert its tradition above the others. The church at Jerusalem, which might reasonably have demanded a more exalted reverence, was dispersed at the destruction of the city and the congregation which gathered later in Roman Aelia counted for less abroad than Antioch or Alexandria.[36] No one was indisputably first and from time to time they broke up into hostile and jealous factions. Each in its own region developed its own calendar of feasts, its own variety of liturgy and creed, and priests suspended in one circle for infraction of rules or heterodoxy of opinion might find support and shelter in another.[37]

In the West, as in other ways, the situation was different. There was but one apostolic church and that a singularly illustrious one, consecrated by the labors of the two most famous missionary apostles. To Christians of the Occident the Roman church was their sole, direct link with the age of the New Testament and its bishop was the one prelate in their part of the world

[35] *Supra*, pp. 80, 102, 116; *infra*, 269, 270, 281, 485.

[36] Once, in the middle of the third century, we find the Romans blamed for departing from the customs of Jerusalem. *Infra*, p. 413. With the growth of the cult of relics and holy places in the fourth century Jerusalem comes again into something like importance, but it never plays the part in ecclesiastical politics that is taken by Antioch or Alexandria. *Infra*, p. 486, n. 95.

[37] *Infra*, pp. 312, 467–468.

in whose voice they discerned echoes of the apostles' speech. The Roman bishop spoke always as the guardian of an authoritative tradition, second to none. Even when the eastern churches insisted that their traditions were older and quite as sacred, if not more so,[38] the voice in the West, unaccustomed to rivalry at home, spoke on regardless of protest or denunciation at a distance. The first authentic utterance of a Roman bishop, the letter of Clement, is an admonition from Rome to the Pauline church at Corinth.[39] The first authentic incident related of a Roman bishop has to do with a visit paid by the revered Polycarp of Smyrna to Anicetus. Polycarp informs Anicetus that the Roman mode of fixing the date of Easter is not that which he himself once learned from the practice of the apostle John.[40] There could be, one would imagine, no more impressive testimony but it does not affect the Roman. His church has its own tradition and he will not change that which he has received from his predecessors.

A few years later, Hegesippus, travelling from place to place to ascertain what is the genuine teaching of the apostles, finds at Rome a satisfactory line of episcopal succession reaching back to apostolic days, which ensures to his mind an unbroken continuity of doctrine.[41] Irenaeus of Asia Minor, who in his youth had heard Polycarp preach, is sent to Rome to obtain the endorsement of Eleutherus on the action taken by the Asiatics in the Montanist dispute. He is so struck by the positiveness and confidence of the Roman attitude and the representative, cosmopolitan character of the Roman membership that he writes his extraordinary glorification of the Roman church.[42] "It is necessary," he says, "that every church . . . should resort to this church on account of its commanding position; and in it the apostolic tradition has been preserved continuously by persons from every land." In Irenaeus' old age, he expostulates with the Roman Victor for his harshness in passing sentence of excom-

[38] *Infra*, pp. 281, 416, 506.

[39] *Infra*, p. 236. Hermas says that letters may be sent to all the churches through Clement. *Infra*, p. 245.

[40] *Infra*, p. 247.

[41] *Infra*, pp. 249–251.

[42] *Infra*, p. 267.

munication on the Asiatic churches, because they clung to Polycarp's tradition in the matter of Easter observance, but, so far as our extracts show, he does not challenge Victor's right to insist upon conformity to Roman usage.[43] In the middle of the third century, the Roman clergy as a body still pride themselves upon the faith that had won Paul's commendation and maintain their responsibility to keep "watch over all who call on the name of the Lord."[44]

To the close of the second century, indeed, the religious prestige of Rome seems to have attached to the church as a whole and to have been based upon its primitive connection with both Paul and Peter and its legacy of a double apostolic tradition. Upon this as its distinctive, inalienable possession the church had by this time erected a remarkable working apparatus for efficient, ecclesiastical life, including a brief and practical statement of the essentials of belief, a paraphrase of which passes today as the Apostles' Creed, a canon of sacred books, enumerated in the so-called *Muratorian Fragment*,[45] and a code of discipline for the regulation of Christian behavior. Toward the middle of the second century, the Roman Hermas proposed a modification of the rigorous moral standard of the earlier generation[46] and at the end of that century, Bishop Callistus was scandalizing the Puritans in the community with his further innovation in rules.[47] Step by step, however, congregations everywhere followed the Roman lead in the direction of greater leniency in the punishment of sins and more implicit faith in the efficacy of sacraments. The first system of graded clergy of which we happen to hear is the Roman. Under Cornelius, it already embraced a complete hierarchy, from bishop to doorkeeper.[48] There was some element of statesmanship in a body that found its way so successfully along every road that led to corporate solidarity. How far its bishops were responsible for these early achievements, how far the inspiration was borrowed from the huge organ of civil government functioning in the same city, it is now impossible to tell.

43 *Infra*, pp. 282–284.
44 *Infra*, p. 337.
45 *Supra*, p. 49, n. 60.
46 *Infra*, pp. 243–244.
47 *Infra*, pp. 301, 310–312.
48 *Infra*, p. 384.

Until the third century, as we have said, one can hardly separate the policy and prestige of the Roman church from those of the bishopric. Even when Victor refused fellowship to the churches of the East, there is nothing to prove that he acted other than as the head and mouthpiece of the Roman community in an effort to compel universal acceptance of the well-known Roman tradition. But in the first quarter of the third century, an outcry is suddenly raised against the Roman bishop individually, not on the ground of his moral shortcomings, such as prompted a great part of Hippolytus' attack upon Callistus,[49] but for his novel and subversive view of the constitution of the Church catholic. The name of the bishop is not mentioned nor the form in which he first enunciated his momentous idea. There is merely the flare of resentment against one who is not content with his honor as president of his great see but who is grasping after the office of "bishop of the bishops."[50] Tertullian and Origen write full and elaborate explanations of the Matthew passage, "Thou art Peter," etc., to show that the blessing and promise bestowed by Christ on Peter are not confined to Peter's lineal successors in the Roman See but belong of right to every Christian who makes Peter's confession.[51]

Somewhat later, a group of distinguished ecclesiastics of the South and East, led by Cyprian of Carthage, Firmilian of Cappadocia and Dionysius of Alexandria, join in resolute opposition to a set of propositions advanced by the Roman Stephen. Stephen's own statements have disappeared but Firmilian's letter to Cyprian and Cyprian's speech at the council of African bishops give us a fair notion of the issues at stake.[52] In Stephen's eyes, the Church was not as the other bishops conceived it to be, a loose federation of autonomous units, each unit governed by its bishop, each bishop legally equal to every other bishop, supreme over his own flock and answerable only to God or, in cases of flagrant misdeed, to a provincial council of his fellows. The theory of Stephen, that kindled his contemporaries to such utter exasperation, was rather that the Church was a monarchy, a congeries in-

[49] *Infra*, pp. 306 ff.
[50] *Infra*, p. 301.
[51] *Infra*, pp, 302, 317.
[52] *Infra*, pp. 410, 411.

deed of bishoprics but all of them subject to the superior authority of the one bishop who sat upon the throne of the prince of the apostles. The Roman See, as distinct from the Roman church, was and ought to be predominant, not for its situation or other worldly advantages, not even for its treasure of doctrine, bequeathed by its two founders, but, primarily and fundamentally, because its bishop was heir in his own person to the unique prerogative conferred upon Peter. To Peter had been granted a primacy among the apostles, so to the Roman bishop was assigned a leadership over the bishops.

Roman and Carthaginian perished alike during the season of persecution that set in soon after these words were written. Whether the question was raised again so acutely during that century we do not know. About ten years later, certain disaffected persons reported to Bishop Dionysius at Rome some heretical opinions on the nature of Christ which were being attributed to Bishop Dionysius of Alexandria. The Roman wrote to his eminent namesake "to inform him of what they had said about him." The Alexandrian replied with a refutation of the slander and the matter rested there. Dionysius of Rome, however, called "a great synod" to define for the Church the relation of the Son to the Father.[53] In the fourth century, these acts were recalled as arguments to show that a Roman bishop had already approved the dogma of Nicaea and had passed judgment on an accusation against the metropolitan of Alexandria.[54] The appointment by the emperor Aurelian of the Roman Felix to arbitrate the contest over the see of Antioch must have seemed a little bitter to those Asiatics who not long before had resisted the imperiousness of Stephen, but this time the Roman does not seem to have antagonized his eastern brethren.[55]

We have almost no information regarding the bishops from Felix to Miltiades and are quite in the dark as to their policies, except in local affairs. It is significant, however, that during these years both the accepted tradition and the popular legends of Peter's labors at Rome were expanded and embellished to fit the

[53] *Infra,* pp. 434, 436. [54] *Infra,* pp. 472, 515, 607. [55] *Infra,* pp. 440–441.

new papal theory, and that when the bishops emerged again from obscurity they had seemingly lost no ground but continued to act upon the assumptions previously expressed. The language of the Council of Arles shows that the western episcopates were generally convinced of the superiority of Silvester's office to their own. They practically apologize for doing anything without him.[56] At Nicaea, a predominantly eastern assemblage, the example of the Roman bishops was cited for guidance in the wording of the creed.[57]

But the direful war of doctrine that followed the dispersal of the Nicene Council gave Rome her real opportunity to display her virtue as a leader in religion. As long as the churches everywhere were living at ease, in general peace and harmony, there was little chance for one to be accepted by the rest as first, in any real or positive sense of the word. But now the eastern communities were torn with dissension over their new definitions of the Godhead and the eastern emperors were aggravating the disorder by their free use of force to intimidate, torment or banish all who were not of their own sect. With a few negligible respites this condition lasted for more than forty years, until the inner morale of eastern Christianity, as well as its outer organization, was corroded through and through by chicanery, rancor and fear. No one of the groups into which the church divided could trust or coöperate with the others and all were at the mercy of Constantius or Julian or Valens, to be rewarded or punished as the emperor saw fit. From such turmoil and trial the western church was exempt, save for the short term of Constantius' reign in the West. As a whole, it remained satisfied with the definition of Nicaea,[58] which it soon came to regard as a repetition in fuller phraseology of Peter's original confession, and which it was, therefore, peculiarly incumbent upon Rome to guard against every assault. The contending factions in the East all desired the support and approbation of the unperturbed bishop of Rome. The Arians, who had ousted Athanasius from Alexandria, offered to submit the case to Julius for his judgment.[58a] Athanasius himself and other orthodox refugees from

[56] *Infra*, p. 480. Compare the language of the Council of Aquileia, *infra*, p. 607. [57] *Infra*, p. 472. [58] *Infra*, p. 517. [58a] *Infra*, pp. 503, 504, 509.

eastern sees went directly to Rome as to a court of appeal. Only as the Arians lost hope of Julius' favor, did they revive the old complaint of western arrogance and presumption.[59] At the general Council of Sardica, their deputation seceded to issue a heated proclamation of eastern independence, but the orthodox Easterners and Westerners stayed behind to issue another, in which they claimed for the Roman bishop an appellate jurisdiction over all the Church in honor of "the memory of Peter, the apostle."[60]

For one brief period, while the Arian Constantius ruled both East and West, did the western church have its constancy tested by persecution. Many yielded and apostatized and even the Roman Liberius succumbed to the weariness of exile and purchased his release by recantation. But after Constantius' death, Liberius contrived to return unostentatiously to his old profession, ignoring his own lapse and hoping by scrupulous insistence on proofs of orthodoxy from others to prevail upon the Church to ignore it too. There had been no parade about his fall and there was none about his recovery. The nobler spirits of the West had meanwhile been rallying their brothers to repentance and loyalty to the faith of Peter. The East, engrossed by its own persistent misfortunes, for the most part failed to realize that any blot whatever had stained the Roman record.

Neither this little advertised misstep of Liberius nor the local ferment that followed it in some few western churches lowered the growing prestige of Rome in the eyes of Oriental catholics. The Romans, they were ready to admit, had received from God through Peter the priceless gift which the eastern prelates as a body seemed to lack, namely, the power to hold fast to the truth and to transmit it undefiled to posterity.[61] As a consequence, the western church was blessed by God above the eastern, being free, by comparison, both from tyrants and from heretics.

In the East, the conflict went on shifting from one phase to another. The very sects were in a continual state of flux, unable to maintain any clean-cut or permanent lines of division. Antioch reached the pass of possessing five different claim-

[59] *Infra*, pp. 505–506. [60] *Infra*, pp. 518, 520, 522.
[61] *Infra*, pp. 592, n. 235; 645, 652, 680.

ants for the episcopal chair, each representing some different shade of belief. In desperation, men like Basil and Gregory Nazianzen, whose hearts were sore over the wretched state of Christ's flock, appealed to Damasus and the western brotherhood to revive the ancient bonds of communion and send envoys to show them how to reëstablish orthodoxy and peace.[62] One group after another professed its assent to the Roman creed. If Damasus had been more far-sighted or more generous-hearted, he might have made himself a true shepherd for all the sheep. But he wasted his opportunity in tedious and irritating negotiations. When the death of Valens in 378 delivered the East from Arian coercion, it proceeded to hold its own councils and make its own adjustments and decisions. The representatives of Rome arrived too late and their attempts then to dictate only stirred the long-suffering eastern bishops to exasperation. They passed, to be sure, a canon raising the see of Constantinople to the first rank in the East, second only to Rome, an acknowledgment indirectly of the primacy of Rome.[63] But they implied also by their wording of the canon, whether intentionally or not, that that primacy was due to Rome's position as an imperial capital. For that reason Damasus and his successors refused to confirm it. Yet there can be no doubt that large numbers of eastern Christians had by this time become convinced of the genuine superiority of the Roman See in faith and religious insight. The eastern emperor Theodosius published an edict requiring his subjects to accept the doctrine which Peter had committed to the Romans.[64] More than one eastern writer expressed the western view, that the confession of Peter was in essence synonymous with the Nicene creed and described the bishop apostle as the rock upon which the Church had been established against false doctrine.[65] But it was the trustworthy authority of Peter to which the East paid its homage in the fourth century, not the wealth nor the power of Rome.

Such in general outline were the causes which we find making for the early development of the papal office. As for the form

[62] *Infra*, pp. 641, 644, 651, 681.
[63] *Infra*, p. 686.
[64] *Infra*, pp. 619, 675.
[65] *Infra*, pp. 644, 666.

which that office assumed, the functions which the Roman bishop exercised as leader of the Church, they have been largely indicated in the preceding paragraphs. The first was that of defining doctrine. From the time when Eleutherus was asked to condemn the Montanists, through the period when Callistus, Stephen and Dionysius revised and interpreted dogma, down to the days when the Nicene creed was defended on the ground of its Roman origin and Liberius and Damasus endorsed or rejected eastern declarations of faith according as they did or did not measure up to their own standards, the Roman bishops asserted their right to speak for the tradition of Peter. In the fourth century, when the eastern churches had for the time being lost confidence in their own ability to maintain truth, the only authority that could be weighed against Rome was a great council, in which, as Constantine once said,[66] the Spirit of God must certainly be present enlightening his wise bishops. But the veneration which the orthodox multitude felt for Nicaea did not in itself militate against an equal or even greater veneration for Rome. Were they not both agreed upon the creed? Was not the source of that creed Roman, its wider promulgation Nicene? There was no need to decide whether its binding force came more from Rome or from the council. An Italian synod later repudiated the creed of the great Council of Rimini on the ground that it had never been ratified by the bishop of Rome.[67]

The second prerogative claimed by the Roman bishops, a natural corollary to the first, was that of excluding from their communion all who disagreed with them on what they considered essentials in faith or practice. Victor and Stephen made the first sweeping uses of this power with sensational effect.[68] In the fourth century, the situation was inevitably complicated by the entrance of the emperors upon the stage of ecclesiastical politics and their frequent resorts to physical violence to suppress the parties in the Church of which they disapproved. But the Roman bishops continued independently to prescribe the terms on which they themselves would receive their fellows into communion. Julius and Liberius examined and passed upon the

[66] *Infra*, p. 488. [67] *Infra*, p. 635. [68] *Infra*, pp. 282, 417.

professions of their eastern visitors.[69] In one case, at least, an Asiatic church received back, at Liberius' bidding, a bishop whom it had previously deposed for his errors. Damasus laid down a creed which the eastern bishops must endorse without the alteration of a word, if they were to be taken into his fellowship.[70] The power to bind and loose meant first of all the right to open and close the haven of the orthodox church of Peter to those who believed or failed to believe its authentic doctrine.

Almost immediately a third prerogative grew out of the other two, the right to give final judgment in cases of episcopal controversy. Whether Origen's defense to Fabianus [71] was a case in point may be considered doubtful, but later in the third century, appeals from the bishops of Gaul and Spain were sent to Stephen [72] and a charge against Dionysius of Alexandria was carried to Dionysius of Rome.[73] Aurelian's appointment of Felix to judge the contest at Antioch [74] gave an impetus to the development of this custom. Constantine turned over to Miltiades the Donatist difficulty at Carthage.[75] Julius asked the bishops at Antioch if they were not aware that their accusations against Athanasius ought to have been brought before him.[76] The western contingent at Sardica formally conferred upon the bishop of Rome the right to try in person or through his appointees any case of dispute involving a bishop anywhere that might be appealed to him.[77] When Damasus had difficulty in executing his verdicts on the malcontent bishops in Italy and could get no response whatever to his communications to Restitutus of Carthage, a Roman synod addressed a petition to the emperors, asking them to confirm by civil statute the power of their bishop to judge all metropolitans and all appeals regarding bishops and to instruct the officials of the government to see that his power was enforced. The emperors obligingly complied, stipulating merely that the penalty imposed by the Roman bishop should not go beyond the exclusion of the offender from his see.[78] Yet Damasus sometimes hesitated to exert this prerogative, as

[69] *Infra,* pp. 505, 513, 592.
[70] *Infra,* pp. 655, 646, 647, 673.
[71] *Infra,* p. 315.
[72] *Infra,* pp. 399, 402.
[73] *Infra,* p. 434.
[74] *Infra,* p. 441.
[75] *Infra,* p. 457.
[76] *Infra,* p. 515.
[77] *Infra,* p. 520.
[78] *Infra,* pp. 669, 672.

witness his refusal to proceed further in the affair of the Priscillianists.[79] He was also unable to get the case of Constantinople brought before him in 381 and 382.[80] After all, when the emperor had once intervened in a situation, it became delicate ground for any subject to tread upon, no matter what his legal privileges.

The Roman bishops of the late fourth century added to their exercise of these three established prerogatives some measures that can only be described as experiments in the field of general administrative control. Liberius issued letters of instruction to the bishops of the West on the methods they should use in restoring Arian apostates.[81] Damasus sent directions to the Spanish bishops how to treat the Priscillianists.[82] Both Liberius' and Damasus' letters on these topics have been lost, but a similar and longer letter from their successor Siricius to another bishop of Spain is usually regarded as opening the series of the so-called Papal Decretals or executive regulations put forth for the guidance of bishops at large by their head, the bishop of Rome.[82a] Julius and Damasus convoked councils of greater size than ordinary metropolitan synods. They summoned bishops from Gaul and from Greece and, with the emperor's sanction, even called upon the bishops of the East to meet at Rome.[82b] A beginning was being made at the creation of a centralized system of supervision over all the churches.

Besides the powers that taken together made up the substance of the hegemony exercised by the Roman bishop, a few special marks of dignity had come to be associated with his office. He had his dwelling in an imperial palace and he rarely left his see, except when compelled to do so by a persecuting government. He may, of course, have made journeys that are not reported but, as far as we hear, all business that required his attention was uniformly carried to him. The bishops of Alexandria and Antioch went hither and thither, to Nicaea or to Constantinople, but the bishop of Rome sent a deputy, if he wished to be represented at any assembly held outside Rome. The Councils of Arles and Sardica understood that he could not leave

79 *Infra*, p. 609.
80 *Infra*, pp. 625, 626.
81 *Infra*, p 690.
82 *Infra*, p. 692.
82a *Infra*, pp. 699–708.
82b *Infra*, pp. 505, 604, 608.

his apostolic seat.[83] The eastern bishops asked Damasus to send commissioners to visit them.[84] One dignity, however, to which he aspired in the fourth century he did not attain. The fact that an accusation against Silvester had been investigated by Constantine and that the suit against Damasus had been transferred by Gratian from the Roman prefect's court to his own, emboldened Damasus and his clergy to ask for a decree formally exempting the bishop of Rome thenceforth from any civil jurisdiction but the emperor's. It was the first step on the path that would lead ultimately to the declaration that the Pope could be tried by no man. But the emperors demurred at that request and the Roman bishop, like his colleagues, remained for a while longer as a citizen under the authority of the magistrates.

In sum, these powers and privileges amounted to the working out in practice of the theory that the Roman bishop held the post of "bishop of the bishops," "*episcopus episcoporum.*"[85] As yet he was hardly more than that, head of the widespread college of bishops, defining for them what they were to profess and teach their flocks, imposing uniformity and discipline upon them, calling them to account if they disobeyed. As yet he was making no attempt to reach past them to the lower clergy or to the laity or to build up any direct relation with the mass of the people of God. Each bishop was still sole head within the local church and his word therein was final. The Pope had scarcely begun to realize the possibilities implied in the later title *servus servorum Dei.*[85a]

It is clear from all this also how far his authority had come to be accepted by the orthodox churches of the fourth century, and where such resistance as it met was chiefly centered. In the West, as we have pointed out, a combination of causes had from the first set the Roman bishop on an eminence above his fellows. One has only to read the language of the councils of Arles and Sardica or of Damasus' later synods or of men like Hosius and Hilary to realize that the Roman supremacy was to them an accomplished and unassailable fact. The East, on the other hand, had heard with a shock of indignation and

[83] *Infra,* pp. 480, 527. [84] *Infra,* pp. 639, 641. [85] *Infra,* pp. 301, 411.
[85a] But note the change already showing in Siricius' Decretal, *infra,* pp. 697 ff.

amazement the claim of Stephen to set his single prerogative over all their ancient traditions and institutions. Was not Christianity itself an eastern faith? In one form or another that resentful query was made again and again, by Firmilian, by the eastern episcopate at Antioch, at Sardica and at Constantinople. But the exigencies of the fourth century drove the orthodox leaders of the eastern churches to take refuge at Rome or to look to Rome for help against their heretical emperors and compatriots. The bishop of Rome was the one free and steadfast religious power in the whole world. The slow and grudging change in the attitude of the eastern bishops found expression in that canon of the Council of Constantinople which we have already described. The canons of Chalcedon in the next century show how much further that change was yet to go.

For Damasus, so far as one may judge, there was no earthly authority comparable to his own but that of the emperors. Actually their authority had not been so much felt within the Church during the period that they were pagan. They were then an external and material force, destructive on occasion, like an earthquake or a pestilence, and as such to be patiently endured along with other mundane afflictions. They could not touch the internal springs of the ecclesiastical organism. Inwardly the Church was free. Not until the emperors themselves entered the Church could they affect it continually and profoundly from within, at times laying violent hands upon its politics and its creeds, at other times standing more reserved in the background but ready always to assist and give the deciding word, watching what the councils said and did, retaining the right to allow or to prohibit every act. For the most part, the Roman bishop availed himself unhesitatingly of all the support and favor the emperors would give him. As long as their might was on his side he invoked it to crush opposition and to increase his own splendor and prestige. Even when the Arian Constantius demanded his apostasy and he refused and went into exile in consequence, he made no complaint against imperial intrusion, as such, into religious affairs.[86] The few protests that came from

[86] *Infra*, pp. 572–576.

the West in the name of ecclesiastical liberty were the work of heretics, like the Donatists,[87] or of provincial bishops, like Hosius and Hilary.[88] Not until the fifth century, when the system of imperial government in the West had broken down, did the popes enunciate the principle of the two powers and solemnly declare the right of the Church and its officers to religious independence.

But although the popes of the fourth century had not yet ventured to contest the privilege of the emperor to treat the Church as he did his other departments of state, they possessed in the Petrine theory, as it had by that time been worked out and generally accepted, a charter that could easily be extended in the future to cover whatever powers they might choose to wield. Thirty-four years after Damasus' death, a clear statement of it was sent by Bishop Zosimus to a synod at Carthage.[89] A quotation from his letter puts the Roman position before us finally in its essentials, as the fourth century understood it. "The tradition of the Fathers ascribed such authority to the Apostolic See that no one dared to dispute its judgment but by canons and rules they always preserved it. And passing down to the present day, the constitution of the Church still pays through its laws the reverence it owes to the name of Peter, from which it is itself derived.[90] For canonical antiquity, it is universally reported, attributed to this apostle such might from the promise of Christ our God himself that he could loose what was bound and bind what was loosed. And an equal position of power has been committed to those who by his permission have obtained the inheritance of his see. For Peter has the care of all the churches but especially of this one, where he himself had his see. He suffers no prerogative to be withheld from it

[87] *Infra,* pp. 458, 541, n. 173.

[88] *Infra,* pp. 541, n. 173; 577. It is curious to see so ardent a religious enthusiast as Gregory Nazianzen, who had known, too, the wretchedness produced by imperial persecution, appealing to Theodosius to compel the bishops at Constantinople to come to terms, if their own sense of duty to the Church does not bring them to it. *Infra,* p. 685.

[89] Letter of March 21, 418. *Collectio Avellana,* 50, *Corpus Scriptorum Ecclesiasticorum Latinorum,* Vol. XXXV, pp. 115–116. *Cf.* the statements of Siricius and Innocent I, bishops between Damasus and Zosimus, given *infra,* pp. 699, 707, and in C. Mirbt, *Quellen zur Geschichte des Papsttums* (4th ed., Tübingen, 1924), pp. 62–64.

[90] Compare this with the ascription to Peter of the founding of the institution of the episcopacy, *supra,* p. 111; *infra,* pp. 328, 348.

nor any wind of opinion to shake it, for he himself has established for it the firm and unassailable foundation of his own name, which no one may rashly impugn without peril to himself. Since then Peter is the source of its great authority and the statutes of all the Fathers since his time have confirmed it, now by every human and divine law and constitution it is ordained that the church of Rome, where he once held sway, still possesses the power of his name. You are not ignorant but well aware of this, dearest brothers, and as bishops you must comprehend it."

PART I

THE BISHOPRIC OF THE ROMAN APOSTOLIC CHURCH

1. THE BENEVOLENCE OF THE ROMAN CHURCH

CLEMENT
(fl. c. 96)

The fifth chapter of this epistle has been quoted in an earlier section for the evidence it contains as to the death of the apostle Peter.[1] The extracts which follow are chosen to show the tone and bearing of the first Roman bishop who wrote a letter that was preserved by posterity. The letter, as we said before, was sent in the name of the Roman church and keeps throughout the form of the first person plural. It makes no allusion whatever to Clement, the individual, or to his position. It was addressed to another apostolic church, where Peter and Paul had both labored before they came to Rome,[2] and it opens with a half apology for delay, as if under the circumstances the Corinthians might have expected to hear from the Romans more promptly. It proceeds to discuss gravely and at considerable length the anarchical state into which the Corinthian brethren had fallen, reminding them of their solemn faith and duty and urging them to display more self-control and forbearance and to support loyally the officers whom they themselves had elected. The Roman church assumes the right to remonstrate, apparently because of its own past record and present standing, as a body that had itself received apostolic traditions, passed through fiery ordeals and sufferings and emerged with its unity and charity unimpaired. Its spirit is one of concern for the welfare and good name of the Christian brotherhood, which the Christians in Corinth had perversely imperilled. Its words, it knows, are the words of God speaking through it. For that reason the Corin-

[1] *Supra*, pp. 68–69. [2] *Supra*, p. 76.

thians must beware of disobedience; at any rate, even if some refuse to heed, the Roman conscience is henceforward clear.

Already all bishops and deacons are regarded as clothed with authority derived by the apostles from Christ and transmitted by them in turn to the men whom they selected to fill the offices in the churches. No one bishop is mentioned as greater than another. The episcopate and diaconate, that serve the "flock of Christ" and offer its sacrifices, are the objects of defence. The plea is above all for harmony and order.[3]

Ad Corinthios, 1, 42, 44, 57, 59, 63. Text. *Apostolic Fathers,* ed. by K. Lake (*The Loeb Classical Library*), I, 8–10, 78–80, 82–84, 106–108, 110–112, 118, 119.

The church of God that is at Rome to the church of God that is at Corinth, to those who are called and sanctified by the will of God through our Lord Jesus Christ. Grace to you and peace from God Almighty be multiplied through Jesus Christ.

1 Owing to the sudden and repeated calamities and afflictions which have befallen us,[4] we think that we have been somewhat slow in turning our attention to the divisions that have arisen among you, beloved, and to the abhorrent and unholy sedition, so foreign and strange to God's elect, that a few headstrong and wayward persons have stirred up to such a frenzy as greatly to vilify your name, once venerable, renowned and lovely in the eyes of all men. For who that has tarried among you has not approved your virtuous and steadfast faith? Who has not admired your sober and patient devotion in Christ? Who has not spread abroad the munificent character of your hospitality? Who has not congratulated you on your sound and perfect knowledge? For you did everything without respect of persons and

[3] For bibliography on Clement, *vide supra,* p. 67.

[4] This reference may be to the persecution under Domitian.

walked in the ordinances of God, submitting yourselves to your rulers and rendering due honor to the elders among you. On the young too you enjoined temperate and modest thought. The women you charged to fulfil all their duties with a blameless, seemly and pure conscience and to be content with their own husbands, as is meet; you taught them also to observe the rule of obedience and to manage the affairs of their households in decorum and all discretion. . . .

42 The apostles received the gospel for us from the Lord Jesus Christ; Jesus Christ was sent from God. Christ, therefore, is from God and the apostles from Christ. In each case, then, they were in the appointed order of the will of God. So, having received their instructions and being completely assured by the resurrection of our Lord Jesus Christ and confident in the word of God, they went forth in full assurance of the Holy Ghost, proclaiming that the kingdom of God was at hand. Thus they preached from place to place and city to city and ordained those who were their first fruits, when they had tested them by the Spirit, to be bishops and deacons of those who should afterwards believe.[5] Nor was this a new thing, for many years earlier there had been written word of bishops and deacons; for thus saith the Scripture in a certain place: "I will establish their bishops in righteousness and their deacons in faith."[6] . . .

44 Our apostles also knew through our Lord Jesus Christ that there would be strife over the title of bishop. For this reason, therefore, inasmuch as they had received perfect foreknowledge, they appointed to office those whom

[5] Philippians I, 1.

[6] This is a loose quotation from the Septuagint version of Isaias LX, 17, which is correctly translated in the Douay Version: "And I will make thy visitation peace and thy overseers justice." The King James Version translates: "I will also make thy officers [in the sense of magistrates] peace and thine exactors [in the sense of taskmasters] righteousness." *Cf.* the J. B. Lightfoot text of this epistle of Clement, Chap. XLII, n. 12 (*The Apostolic Fathers,* Pt. I, Vol. II, p. 129). Lightfoot calls attention to the fact that Irenaeus in applying the passage to the Christian ministry (*Haereses* IV, 26, 5) quotes the Septuagint text correctly.

we have mentioned and afterwards made provision that when they should fall asleep, other approved men should succeed to their ministry. We, accordingly, believe that it is not right to dismiss from their ministry those who were appointed by them or afterwards by other eminent men with the consent of the whole church and who have served the flock of Christ without fault, humbly, peaceably and disinterestedly, and received for a long time the good testimony of everyone. For our sin will not be small if we remove from the episcopate those who have blamelessly and holily offered its sacrifices. Blessed are the presbyters[7] who have finished ere now their journey and obtained a fruitful and perfect release, for they have no dread that anyone shall remove them from their appointed place. . . .

57 You, therefore, that laid the foundation of sedition, submit yourselves unto the presbyters and receive correction unto repentance, bending the knees of your hearts. Learn to be submissive and lay aside the proud and boastful stubbornness of your tongues. . . .

59 But if some be disobedient unto the words spoken by him [God] through us, let them see that they will involve themselves in grave transgression and danger, but we shall be guiltless of their sin and shall pray with instant entreaty and supplication, that the Creator of all things may guard unhurt unto the end the number of his elect that have been numbered in all the world through his beloved Son Jesus Christ, through whom he has called us from darkness to light, from ignorance to the full knowledge of the glory of his name. . . .

63 . . . For you will give us joy and gladness if you

[7] The word "presbyters" or "elders" seems to be used here in its first sense, as a general title for the leaders and officers in the Church, the "*seniores,*" bishops and deacons. Not until the second century does it appear to denote a special group of ministers, the priests, and even then it may still keep its inclusive meaning. See, for instance, the use of it by Irenaeus, *infra,* pp. 266, 283. J. F. J. Jackson and K. Lake, *The Beginnings of Christianity,* I, Prolegomena, p. 332; A. Harnack, Appendix to edition of *Didache* (*Texte und Untersuchungen zur Geschichte der altchristlichen Literatur,* Vol. II[1-2], 1884).

are obedient to the things which we have written through the Holy Spirit and root out the wicked passions of your jealousy in compliance with the request we have made in this letter for peace and harmony. And we have sent you faithful and prudent men that have walked among us blamelessly from youth to old age and they shall be witnesses between you and us. This we have done that you may know that all our care has been and still is that you should be speedily at peace.

Ignatius of Antioch

(c. 116)

The letters of Ignatius of Antioch follow naturally upon Clement's in a sequence both of time and of ideas.[8] Written twenty years later, they show first of all the quick enhancement of the position of the bishop in the Church. Clement argues, of course, for an orderly church, obedient to the admonitions of its bishops and its deacons. Though the bishop is named first, as first in dignity, allegiance is required equally to the whole body of officers. Though there is distinction of function, there is as yet no conspicuous distinction of rank. By the time of Ignatius, the bishop looms up high above all the rest as the peculiar embodiment of heavenly authority and grace. Without the bishop no sacrament is valid; without him there is indeed no church.[9]

To Ignatius too, Asiatic though he is and head of one of the oldest and most distinguished of gentile churches, the Roman community seems to stand upon a level somewhat above that of the others to whom he writes. To no other does he address quite such ardent phrases of praise for its unwavering steadfastness

[8] For previous reference to Ignatius and bibliography, *vide supra,* pp. 71–72.

[9] The question naturally arises how far Ignatius' views of the episcopacy may have been peculiar to himself or how far they may have represented a sentiment confined to Antioch, created there perhaps by his own magnetic and forceful personality. For discussion of these intricacies see the books mentioned in the bibliography.

and faith. One of the most significant of these phrases we have translated here as "foremost in love." Catholic scholars have been apt to interpret it rather as "presiding over the society of love," that is the Christian fellowship, and have taken it as an acknowledgment of a genuine Roman supremacy at this early date. To others it has seemed merely a reference to the brotherly interest shown by the Romans in members of other churches, the generous quality of which Clement speaks, of which his letter is an example, and for which the Roman Christians were already renowned abroad.[10] Ignatius writes to them now as sure of their concern not only for himself but also for the other humbler martyrs from Syria, who are due to reach Rome before him, and for the church he has left behind at Antioch, which is for the moment bishopless. He begs only that they will not in their loving kindness hinder his martyrdom.

Ad Smyrnaeos, 8. Text. *The Apostolic Fathers*, ed. by K. Lake (*The Loeb Classical Library*), I, 260.

8 . . . Do ye all follow your bishop, as Jesus Christ followed the Father, and the presbyters, as if they were the apostles, and pay heed to the deacons, as to the commandment of God. Let no man perform any churchly act apart from the bishop. Let that eucharist be regarded as valid which is celebrated by the bishop or by one whom he appoints. Wheresoever the bishop appears, there let the people be, even as where Jesus Christ is, there is the catholic Church.[11] It is not lawful either to baptize or to hold a love-feast [12] without the bishop, but whatever he approves this is well-pleasing also to God.

[10] For special articles on Ignatius' attitude toward the Roman church, see A. Harnack, *Das Zeugniss des Ignatius über das Ansehen der römischen Gemeindes* in *Sitzungsberichte der Königlichen Preussische Akademie der Wissenschaften* (Berlin, 1896), pp. 111–131; J. Chapman, *St. Ignace d'Antioch et l'Église Romaine*, in *Revue Benédictine* (Maredsous, 1896), Vol. XIII, pp. 385–400.

[11] Ignatius is the first to use the phrase "catholic Church," in the sense of the whole body of believers.

[12] ἀγαπή. The word means "love" and was so used by Paul and other primitive Christians. It was also used to designate the eucharistic meal, at which all members of the church sat together around a common table.

Ad Romanos, 1, 3, 4, 9, 10. Text. *Apostolic Fathers,* ed. by K. Lake (*The Loeb Classical Library*), I, 224 *sqq.*

1 Ignatius, who is also Theophorus, to her that has found mercy in the bounty of the Father most high and of Jesus Christ, his only Son, to the church that is beloved and enlightened through the will of him who has willed all things that are, according to the love of Jesus Christ our God, even to her that is preëminent in the land of the Romans, worthy of God, worthy of honor, worthy of blessing, worthy of praise, worthy of prosperity, worthy in her purity and foremost in love,[13] upholding the name of Christ and upholding the name of the Father, to them that are united in flesh and spirit with his every commandment, filled with the grace of God without wavering and cleansed from alien stain, abundant greeting in Jesus Christ our God. . . .

3 You have never been grudging to any one; you have been teachers of others. And my desire is that the instruction which you give when you teach shall hold fast. Only pray that I may have strength within and without, so that I may find not only the speech but also the impulse, that I may not only be called a Christian but also be proved one. For if I be proved one, then can I also be called one and then be esteemed faithful, when I am no more visible on the earth. Nothing visible is good. For our Lord Jesus Christ, now that he is in the Father, is the more plainly visible.[14] . . .

4 I write to all the churches and I bid all men know that of my own free will I die for God, unless you prevent

[13] προκαθημένη τῆς ἀγαπῆς. The first word is the same as that translated just above, "that is preëminent," etc. It is also employed by Ignatius to denote the presidency of bishop or presbyter over the community of believers. *Ad Magnesios,* 6. *Vide supra,* pp. 239, 240. The last word is the one described in the preceding note. This is the first of several obscure and vague passages in the early Fathers that testify to a prominence or leadership of the Roman church but leave one uncertain as to the exact nature or extent of the distinction. *Vide supra,* p. 221.

[14] One of Ignatius' enigmatic passages. Apparently he means to say: "Nothing visible to the material eye is truly good and Jesus Christ, now that he is no longer visible in the flesh, is the more clearly manifest as God."

me. . . . Supplicate Christ for me that through these instruments [15] I may be made a sacrifice to God. . . .

9 Remember in your prayers that church in Syria that has God for its shepherd in my stead. Its sole bishop is Jesus Christ and your love. . . . My spirit greets you, as does the love of the churches, which have received me in the name of Jesus Christ, not as a mere wayfarer. For even those that did not lie on my road according to the flesh went ahead of me from city to city.

10 I write you this from Smyrna by the blessed Ephesians. And Crocus, one dear to me, is also with me and many others. As for those who preceded me from Syria to Rome to the glory of God, I trust you have seen them. Tell them that I am near at hand. They all are worthy of God and of you and it is right that you should refresh them in every way. I have written this to you on the twenty-fourth of August. Farewell unto the end, in the steadfastness of Jesus Christ.

Hermas of Rome

(c. 150)

The *Shepherd of Hermas* is a Roman apocalyptic work of the second century, a series of visions recorded by one who claims to be simply the vehicle for the spirit that has visited him.[16] In form, it reminds the reader of the *Ascension of Isaiah*.[17] It contains a commission to one Clement, who is described as the spokesman of the Roman church, and for that reason it has been sometimes assigned to the period of Clement I, that is, to the opening of the second century. On the other hand, the author of the *Muratorian Fragment*, composed about 170–180, says positively: " But the *Shepherd* was written quite recently in our

[15] *I.e.*, the wild beasts of the arena.

[16] It is probably connected with other cryptic writings of the time, such as the *Corpus Hermeticum*.

[17] *Supra*, pp. 69–71.

own time by Hermas, while his brother Pius, the bishop, was filling the chair of the church of the city of Rome."[18] Pius was bishop probably somewhere between 140 and 155. The tone of Hermas seems more suited to this later date. The Church which he visualizes has weathered persecutions in the past but is now growing lax in its security and losing its oldtime ardor and spirituality. The description suggests a period of outward quiet, like that under Antoninus Pius, 138–161. In case the later date is correct, the allusion to Clement may have been introduced to give the book an appearance of greater age and therefore more authority. That its message was widely received as opportune and helpful in the solution of second-century difficulties is proved by the high regard in which it soon came to be held in distant places. Irenaeus of Lyons, Tertullian of Carthage, Clement and Origen of Alexandria, the ablest leaders of the late second and early third century, speak of it with profound respect and it seems to have been read frequently in the churches. A little later, however, it lost its timeliness and dropped gradually out of use. Jerome says that in his day it was almost unknown among the Latins.[19]

Parts of the *Shepherd* are elliptical and obscure, probably intentionally so, as is apt to be the case in apocalyptic writings. But the hard problem with which the author is struggling stands out plainly enough. It is that of the question of the forgiveness of sins committed after baptism. The primitive, austere belief had been that Christians, who had been once washed from sin, were capable of living thereafter without further serious lapse and that those who after baptism were so weak as to commit a mortal offense, such as adultery or apostasy, were irremediably lost and could hope for no second chance of salvation.[20] In Hermas' time, it was becoming obvious that few under that theory would be saved. Were the erring multitudes inevitably doomed? What had become of the mercy of God? Hermas through a long course of revelations arrives at the con-

[18] The text of the *Muratorian Fragment* is printed in C. Mirbt, *Quellen zur Geschichte des Papsttums* (4th ed.), No. 31. Translation in J. C. Ayer, *Source Book for Ancient Church History*, pp. 117–120.

[19] *De Viris Illustribus*, 10.

[20] See, for example, Hebrews, VI, 4–6.

clusion that perfect uprightness is not demanded of human frailty and that one fall after baptism will be forgiven to those who repent. He explains carefully the methods and efficacy of repentance and fasting. It is the first stage in the slow development of doctrine that is to arrive ultimately at the theory of the long-suffering and forgiving patience of the Church and the sacrament and code of penance.[21]

Our excerpt consists merely of the sentences which contain the reference to Clement. As the use of Clement's name is perhaps a deliberate anachronism, the reference is valuable only for the suggestion it gives as to a Roman bishop's relations with churches beyond Rome. Hermas proposes to have his book set in circulation among "the cities abroad" by means of Clement, "for that is his duty." It seems unlikely that he would have said this if he had not known of some correspondence between a Roman bishop and other branches of the Church. We are led to wonder if Bishop Pius had a hand in the subsequent rapid circulation of the *Shepherd* through the churches of Christendom.

On Hermas see A. Mitchell, *Shepherd of Hermas,* in J. Hastings, *Dictionary of the Apostolic Church* (2 vols., New York, 1916–1918); J. Réville, *La Valeur du Témoignage Historique du Pasteur d'Hermas* (Paris, 1900); P. Batiffol, *Hermas et le Problème Moral au Second Siècle* in *Revue Biblique* (Paris, 1901), Vol. X, pp. 337–351; P. Batiffol, *Études d'Histoire et de Théologie Positive* (Paris, 1902), pp. 45–68; A. Stahl, *Patristiche Untersuchungen* (3 pts., Leipzig, 1901), Pt. III, *Der Hirt des Hermas*; L. Duchesne, *Early History of the Christian Church* (trans. from 4th ed., by C. Jenkins, 3 vols., London, 1910–1924), Vol. I, pp. 165–171.

Pastor, Vision II, 4. Text and translation. *The Apostolic Fathers,* ed. by K. Lake (*The Loeb Classical Library*), II, 24.

4, 1 And a revelation, brethren, was made to me, as I slept, by a beautiful young man, who said to me: "Who, do you think, is the ancient lady from whom you received

21 *Infra,* pp. 296, 310, 332, 351, 370.

the little book?" I said: "The Sibyl." "You are wrong," he said; "it is not she." "Who then is it?" I said. "The Church," he said. I replied to him: "Why then is she old?" "Because," he said, "she was established the first of all things; for this reason she is old and for her sake the world was framed."

2 And afterwards I saw a vision in my house. The ancient lady came and asked me if I had already given the book to the presbyters. I said that I had not given it. And she said: "You have done well, for I have some words to add. But when I finish all the words, they shall be made known to all the elect through you.

3 For you will write two little books and you will send one to Clement and the other to Grapte.[22] And Clement will send his to the cities abroad, for that is his duty. And Grapte will instruct the widows and orphans. And you will read it yourself in this city in company with the presbyters [23] who will preside over the church.

2. THE TRADITION OF THE ROMAN CHURCH

Anicetus

(c. 154–c. 165)

Anicetus was the successor of Bishop Pius, who according to tradition was the brother of Hermas, who wrote the *Shepherd*.[24] With him we step for a short instant out of the foggy atmosphere of vague and baffling hints and conjectures into something that by contrast looks almost like daylight. For we have a real story about Anicetus, told by someone who was either an eyewitness himself or who got it from eyewitnesses within ten years of its occurrence. The incident is small but concrete and significant not only as to the character of Anicetus but also as to the

22 Grapte was perhaps a deaconess.
23 On the use of this word *vide supra*, p. 238, n. 7.
24 *Supra*, p. 243.

tenacity that already marked the Roman tradition even in matters of detail.

The story is told by Irenaeus, bishop of Lyons, who must have passed through Rome somewhere between the years 155 and 165, on his way from the home of his youth in Asia Minor to settle in Gaul.[25] It relates to a visit paid to Rome about 154 or 155 by the aged Polycarp, the last notable survivor of the generation that heard the preaching of the apostles, who himself was to die the next year as a martyr in Smyrna. Irenaeus had previously in Asia listened to his recollections of John, the beloved disciple of the Lord.[26]

Already petty differences in practice were springing up in the churches dotted here and there about the Empire. One of the most serious in their own estimation was the variation in the method of fixing each year the date of the Easter festival. In Asia Minor, the churches had generally kept in mind the original connection of the Lord's resurrection with the Jewish Passover and had commemorated it yearly at the Passover season, that is, on the fourteenth day of the Jewish month Nisan, regardless of the day of the week on which it might fall. This had been the habit of the group of apostolic teachers in Asia. On the other hand, both at Rome and elsewhere, in Syria, Greece and Egypt, the churches had considered it more important to keep the exact day of the week and had held their celebration on the Sunday after the first full moon following the vernal equinox, thus severing the connection with the Passover and creating a new and distinctively Christian feast. Apparently this had become the custom wherever the influences of Peter and Paul had predominated. As a result, the most solemn anniversary of the Christian year was observed on different days by different branches of the Church. The divergence was felt to be deplorable but so far no decided measures had been taken to end it.

At this time, Polycarp, nearly ninety years of age, made the

[25] This story is part of a long letter written by Irenaeus to Bishop Victor about 198. For the context *vide supra*, pp. 282–284.

[26] Eusebius repeats some of Polycarp's beautiful reminiscences of the apostle John. *Historia Ecclesiastica*, III, 23.

long journey by sea and land from Smyrna to Rome. Why he chose to go at all, whether to confer with the Roman Christians in an effort to knit closer the bonds between the brethren in the face of rising heresies or not, we are not told. That he and Bishop Anicetus discussed the points of variance, especially the question of the date of Easter, Irenaeus says positively and also that neither could persuade the other to accept his own view. Polycarp certainly could not be expected to abandon the practice he had learned directly from John's own example. The curious thing is that Anicetus, the younger man, second or third removed from any contact with apostolic authority, was equally sure that he could not alter the custom of his predecessors even out of deference to his venerable guest. He entertained Polycarp with honor and invited him to perform the eucharistic service in his church. Polycarp preached there against the Gnostics, pointing out that in all essential things the Roman tradition harmonized with that which he had himself received from the apostles in Asia.[27] The two bishops parted as friends at peace but the irritating little difference between the churches was not healed. A few years later a Roman bishop, less tolerant than Anicetus, attempted to compel uniformity by outlawing the followers of Polycarp and John.[28]

Quotation from Irenaeus, given by Eusebius, *Historia Ecclesiastica,* V, 24. Text. *Eusebius Werke* (*Die griechischen christlichen Schriftsteller der ersten drei Jahrhunderte*), II[1], 496.

And when the blessed Polycarp was in Rome, in the time of Anicetus, they held views differing slightly about various points but they immediately made peace with one another and would not quarrel even over this, their chief disagreement. For neither could Anicetus persuade Poly-

[27] This last piece of information is given by Irenaeus in another connection. *Infra,* pp. 269–270.

[28] The communities that clung to the Asiatic custom were in time denounced as heretics under the name of Quartodecimanians. The Easter controversy in one form or another dragged on for several centuries. *Infra,* pp. 469, 472, 482, 487.

carp not to observe [29] what he had always observed in company with John, the disciple of our Lord, and the other apostles whom he had known. Nor could Polycarp prevail upon Anicetus to adopt that observance, since he said that he ought to adhere to the custom of the presbyters [30] who had preceded him. But in spite of all this they communed together and in the church Anicetus yielded the administration of the eucharist to Polycarp, plainly as a mark of respect. And they parted from one another in peace, both those who kept the observance and those who did not, maintaining the peace of the whole Church.

Hegesippus of Syria

(fl. c. 160–c. 175)

While Anicetus was still presiding as bishop over the weekly gatherings of Roman Christians, another traveller came from the East to visit the community, one Hegesippus, a Syrian by birth, on a tour to discover from the various sources of apostolic tradition just what was the true and original Christian doctrine.[30a] The questions that troubled Hegesippus were not so much details of procedure, like the determination of the date of Easter, but more fundamental problems of faith. Gnostic teachers,[31] who claimed to dignify the new religion by providing it with a background of cosmic philosophy and denying the humanity of its Founder, were attracting many adherents and Hegesippus set out to refute them by making a round of the apostolic churches and collecting from their bishops such reminiscences as they could give him of the apostles' own preachings. The authenticity of these reminiscences in each case was guaranteed by the continuous line of episcopal succession in each church reaching back to the apostles' days.

[29] The " observance " is that of the fourteenth day of Nisan.

[30] On the use here of the word " presbyters," *vide supra*, p. 238, n. 7.

[30a] On Abercius, bishop of Hierapolis in Phrygia, who visited Rome about 170 and " saw the people who hold aloft the glorious seal," *vide*, Lightfoot, *Apostolic Fathers*, Pt. 2, Vol. I, pp. 476 ff.

[31] On the Gnostics *vide supra*, p. 77, n. 38.

The *Memorabilia* which Hegesippus composed after his return to his native land contained an account of what he had seen and learned. That his trip was satisfactory, as far as establishing the existence of a body of essentially harmonious tradition accepted by all the leading churches, we may infer from his statement that he had met many bishops and received the same doctrine from them all. The precious *Memorabilia* itself was long ago lost and all we have of its contents are the three or four sentences that struck Eusebius as notable enough to repeat.

In the course of these few sentences, Hegesippus speaks first of a pleasant sojourn at Corinth and then of his arrival at Rome during the episcopate of Anicetus. The phrase which he uses in connection with his stay at Rome, if taken in the generally accepted sense, indicates that, as a security for the genuineness of the Roman tradition, he compiled a list of the Roman bishops through whom the tradition had been transmitted during the hundred years from the apostles Peter and Paul to Anicetus. There must still have been old men at Rome who could furnish reminiscences reaching back to the time of Clement. The names of Linus and Cletus, the two leaders of the community before Clement, both perhaps more or less connected with the heroic memories of the apostles, would still be treasured as part of the church's heritage. Later, Hegesippus added to his list the names of Soter and Eleutherus, who succeeded Anicetus. Whether he obtained similar episcopal lists from other churches on his tour, our tantalizing sentences do not say nor do they include the Roman list itself. We gather, however, from our other sources that a catalogue of the first Roman bishops was early in circulation and generally regarded as a sanction for the validity of Roman doctrine and practice.[32] Hegesippus' record may have been used as the basis for the list of Roman bishops drawn up by the Syrian Epiphanius in the fourth century, which opened as follows: Peter and Paul, Linus, Cletus, Clement, Evaristus, Alexander, Xystus, Telesphorus, Hyginus, Pius and Anicetus. During the bishopric of Eleutherus, Irenaeus of Gaul

[32] Irenaeus and Tertullian, *vide infra*, pp. 267, 293.

also made out a line of the Roman bishops to his own day but his record differed in one particular from that preserved by Epiphanius. The form of the name of Linus' successor was given as Anacletus instead of as the shorter Cletus. In the middle of the fourth century, the author of the expanded *Liberian Catalogue* of the popes, comparing these two primitive lists, mistook the different forms of the same name for two names and put both Cletus and Anacletus into his chronology.[33]

On Hegesippus and his papal catalogue see: J. B. Lightfoot, *The Apostolic Fathers*, Pt. I, Vol. I, p. 201; Th. Zahn, *Der griechische Irenaeus und der ganze Hegesippus im 16. und 17. Jahrhundert* in *Theologische Literaturblatt* (Leipzig, 1893), Vols. XIV–XV, pp. 495–497; Th. Zahn, *Forschungen zur Geschichte der neutestamentlichen Kanons* (6 vols., Erlangen, 1881–1900), VI, pp. 228–273; J. Chapman, *La Chronologie des Premières Listes Episcopales de Rome* in *Revue Benédictine* (Maredsous, 1901), Vol. XVIII, pp. 399–417; (1902), Vol. XIX, pp. 13–30, 144–170.

Eusebius, *Historia Ecclesiastica*, IV, 22, 1–3. Text. *Eusebius Werke* (*Die griechischen christlichen Schriftsteller der ersten drei Jahrhunderte*), II[1], 368–370.

After certain statements regarding the letter of Clement to the Corinthians he [Hegesippus] continues as follows: " And the church of the Corinthians abode in the right faith until Primus was bishop. Their acquaintance I made on my voyage to Rome and I stayed with the Corinthians many days, while we refreshed one another with the right faith. And when I arrived at Rome, I drew up a list of succession as far as Anicetus.[34] Eleutherus was his deacon and after

[33] *Infra*, pp. 709, 711.

[34] The text of Hegesippus quoted by Eusebius, as we have it, is διαδοχὴν ἐποιησάμην μέχρις Ἀνίκητου. The word διαδοχήν, translated here, " list of succession," is the same as that which is used again two lines later and is translated there, " line of succession." Its use in the former sense of " list " or " catalogue " is without precedent elsewhere but the context seems to warrant the interpretation. Rufinus, however, translating this passage into Latin at the end of the fifth century, rendered it: " *permansi ibi usque ad Anicetum*," *i.e.*, " I remained there until the time of Anicetus," *i.e.*, literally, " I made a stay there." Evidently a different word appeared in his Greek manuscript. Later editors and scholars have in some instances followed Rufinus and suggested that the original text read διατριβήν or διαγωγήν instead of διαδοχήν. But Eusebius himself apparently did not under-

Anicetus, Soter succeeded, and after Soter, Eleutherus. And in every line of succession [35] and in every city they adhered to the ordinances of the law and the prophets and the Lord."

SOTER

(c. 166–c. 174)

Bishop Soter was also a continuator of Roman tradition, the benevolent tradition established in the days of Clement,[36] as one may gather from a letter of acknowledgment written to him and to the Roman church by Bishop Dionysius of Corinth.[37] All we have of this letter are the few sentences quoted by Eusebius but fortunately these are informative. They speak appreciatively not only of the customary charity of the Romans but also of Soter's own part in enlarging this bounty and of his graciousness to visiting brethren at Rome, like that of a loving father to his children. Soter had, moreover, written a pastoral letter to the Corinthians, which had just been read aloud in their church and would be preserved to be read again in the future, as had been done with the letter from Clement.

At this point Eusebius halts his quotation and we are left in the dark as to the purpose or substance of Soter's letter to Corinth. A second-century homily, with neither address nor name in the text, was in Eusebius' time circulated with the well known letter of Clement to the Corinthians as a second letter of Clement. Eusebius expressed some doubt as to its authenticity but it continued to be coupled in both Greek and Syriac manuscripts with

---

stand the passage as Rufinus did, for when speaking of Anicetus in another connection, he remarks: "In his time, Hegesippus says that he came to Rome and remained there until Eleutherus was bishop." *Historia Ecclesiastica,* IV, 11, 7. This is not enough to make one positive that he took the clause to mean what we do but it does prove that his reading was not that of Rufinus. For a concise summary of the arguments for the divergent interpretations of this important passage, see the note by A. C. McGiffert in his translation of Eusebius, *A Select Library of Nicene and Post-Nicene Fathers of the Christian Church,* Second Series, Vol. I, p. 198, n. 3.

35 ἐν ἑκάστῃ δὲ διαδοχῇ.

36 *Vide supra,* pp. 216, 235.

37 For Dionysius of Corinth and another extract from this same letter, *supra,* pp. 75–76.

I Clement. A few years ago Harnack propounded the theory that Soter had sent to the Corinthians an old homily of his own or of some one else, which had then been laid up in the archives at Corinth side by side with the older letter from Clement, also, of course, of Roman origin. Dionysius, as we have seen, alludes to the two letters together. In the course of time the distinction between the authors was forgotten and both were copied as letters of Clement. Lightfoot and other scholars disagree with this proposition and regard the so-called *II Clement* as the work of a Corinthian or perhaps an Alexandrian Christian, but on this hypothesis they are unable to account for its association with *I Clement*. On the chance that it is the message Soter sent to Corinth we give some extracts here.[38]

On the so-called *II Clement* see J. V. Bartlet, *Clementine Literature* (*Encyclopaedia Britannica,* 11th ed.); A. Harnack, *Geschichte der altchristlichen Litteratur bis Eusebius,* Vol. II¹, pp. 438–450; J. B. Lightfoot, *The Apostolic Fathers,* Pt. II, Vol. II, pp. 191–316; F. X. Funk, *Der sogen. zweite Clemensbrief,* in *Theologische Quartalschrift* (Münich, 1902), Vol. LXXXIV, pp. 349–364.

Eusebius, *Historia Ecclesiastica,* IV, 23: 9–11. Text. *Eusebius Werke* (*Die griechischen christlichen Schriftsteller der ersten drei Jahrhunderte*), II¹, 376.

23: 9 There is in existence also a letter written by Dionysius[39] to the Romans, addressed to Soter, who was bishop at the time. We cannot do better than insert some extracts from this letter, in which he commends the custom of the Romans that they have followed even down to the persecution in our own days.[40] His words are as follows:

10 "For from the beginning it has been your habit to assist all the brotherhood in various ways and to send contributions to divers churches in every city. Thus you have

[38] Eusebius says also that Soter wrote against the Montanists but tells us nothing of the occasion nor of what he said.

[39] Dionysius, bishop of Corinth.

[40] *I.e.*, to the fourth century persecution under Diocletian and his successors, in Eusebius' own day.

relieved the poverty of the needy and provided for the brethren in the mines. By these gifts, which you have sent from the beginning, you Romans do preserve the hereditary Roman custom and your blessed bishop Soter not only maintains but even enlarges upon it, furnishing abundant supplies to the saints and encouraging the brethren who come from abroad with benignant words as a loving father his children."

11 In this same letter he mentions also the letter of Clement to the Corinthians, indicating that it had been the practice from the beginning to read it aloud in the church. His words are as follows: "Today we have passed the Lord's holy day, in the course of which we have read your [Soter's] letter. From it, whenever we read it, we shall always be able to draw instruction, as we do also from the earlier letter which was written us by Clement."

Ad Corinthios, I, V, XII, XVIII, XIX. Text. *The Apostolic Fathers*, ed. by K. Lake (*The Loeb Classical Library*), I, 128, 134–136, 146–148, 158–160.

I Brethren, we must think of Jesus Christ as God, as judge of quick and dead, and we must not think lightly of our salvation. . . .

V Wherefore, brethren, let us leave our sojourning in this world and do the will of him who called us and be not afraid to depart from this world. For the Lord said: "Ye shall be as lambs in the midst of wolves." And Peter answered and said to him: "What if the wolves tear the lambs?"[41] Jesus said to Peter: "Let not the lambs fear the wolves after their death; and do you have no fear of them that kill you and can do no more to you, but rather fear him who after your death hath power over your soul

[41] The source of this quotation is unknown. It may be the lost *Gospel of the Egyptians*.

and body to cast them into hell fire." And know, brethren, that the dwelling of our flesh in this world is short and lasts but a little time but the promise of Christ is great and wonderful and so is the rest in the kingdom which is to come and life everlasting. . . .

XII Let us then wait hourly for the kingdom of God in love and righteousness, since we know not the day of the appearing of God. For when the Lord himself was asked by a man when his kingdom should come, he said: "When two shall be one and the outside as the inside and the male with the female as neither male nor female."[42] And the two are one when we speak truth to one another and there is one spirit in two bodies without hypocrisy. And by "the outside as the inside" he means this: by the inside he means the spirit and by the outside the body. So, just as your body is visible, let your spirit be apparent in your good works. And by "the male with the female as neither male nor female" he means this: that when a brother sees a sister he should not think of her as female nor she of him as male. When you do these things, he says, the kingdom of my Father shall come. . . .

XVIII Let us also then be of those who give thanks, the servants of God, and not of the ungodly who are judged. For I myself too am altogether sinful and have not yet escaped from temptation but am still beset by the wiles of the devil. Nevertheless I strive to follow after righteousness, that I may have strength at least to approach it, fearing the judgment that is to come.

XIX Therefore, brethren and sisters, in obedience to the God of truth I read you a warning to heed the things that are written, that you may save both yourselves and him who is reader among you. For in return I ask you

[42] This saying may also have been taken from the *Gospel of the Egyptians*. In its cryptic character it reminds one of the similar saying quoted in the apocryphal *Acts of Peter*. *Supra*, p. 152.

to repent with all your hearts and secure for yourselves safety and life. . . . Blessed are they who obey these commandments; though they suffer pain for a short space in this world, they shall reap the deathless fruit of the resurrection.

Eleutherus

(c. 175–c. 188)

The Church of the second century was a church in a trying stage of development. Weak as yet in numbers, unpopular with the pagan public, persecuted intermittently by the State, unprovided with any uniform canon of authority or system of organization, shaken by the rise of parties that interpreted the personality and intention of Jesus in radically opposite ways, she must often have seemed to her leaders on the verge of breaking apart into impotent, small groups, doomed speedily to perish altogether. Practically all the information we have about the Roman bishops of the latter half of the century concerns their relation to one or another of these early schisms and the measures that were being gradually devised to consolidate the Church against them.

Eleutherus was confronted by at least two dilemmas, one created by the presence of the able Gnostic, Marcion, as a wealthy and influential member of his Roman congregation,[43] and the other by the growth of the new puritan Montanist faction everywhere.[44] Marcion, in spite of his generosity to the church, was plainly a case for discipline. No body that felt the call to consistency and order as the Romans did could tolerate long his philosophic vagaries. His money was returned and he was expelled from communion, received back on trial and again expelled. The Montanists required more consideration. Montanus himself and Priscilla and Maximilla, the women who first joined him, were Phrygian Christians, who about the middle of the century had begun to have trances and ecstasies and, under divine prompting, to utter revelations, — a sort of phenomenon that had been common in the first days of the Church, when prophecy and

[43] For more about Marcion and his theories *vide infra*, pp. 266, n. 65; 270, 272.
[44] On the Montanists see also *supra*, p. 77, n. 38.

vision had been reckoned among the peculiar gifts of the Spirit. Now, however, these unregulated and inspirational preachers and revivalists came as troublesome interruptions to the establishment of a decorous liturgy. Their insistence on the right and capacity of every Christian to receive in his own soul his own message of truth directly from God threatened the increasing ascendency of the bishops and priests, who could trace their offices back to the apostles and by virtue of that fact were claiming to be the only reliable mouthpieces of the faith. The Montanists did not agitate themselves over cosmic theories, as the Gnostics did, but they were much concerned with practical questions of spiritual life and morals. In course of time, the Asiatic bishops held a council to determine the attitude to be adopted toward these unruly brethren and ended by condemning them and forbidding further outbursts of such unauthorized zeal.

The problem, however, was not finally settled by the action in Asia. Sometime, not long afterward, the case of the Montanists was carried on to Rome, at first, apparently, by sympathizers with the movement, who hoped to bring about some kind of reconciliation between the parties in Asia through the mediation of the Roman bishop, Eleutherus. At least, that seems to be the implication of the third sentence in the following extract from Tertullian's polemic *Against Praxeas.*[45] Tertullian himself had become a Montanist by the time he wrote this and is indignantly recalling the fact that after Eleutherus had expressed his confidence in Montanus and his gifts and had set about using his influence to persuade the Asiatics to readmit him to communion, the conservative Praxeas had come to Rome and talked Eleutherus into reconsidering his opinion by laying particular stress upon the necessity of loyalty in every respect to the Roman tradition and the danger of countenancing strange inspirations. According to Tertullian, it was the memory of his predecessors, the bishops before him, that finally decided Eleutherus. He could not, after all, support any movement that set up novel standards of authority to supersede them. We ourselves know that Eleutherus had been deacon under Anicetus,

[45] For Tertullian *vide supra,* p. 84; *infra,* p. 286.

who had refused to modify Roman tradition in a comparatively small matter, even for Polycarp.[46]

In addition to Tertullian's bitter resumé of this incident, we have an allusion to it, from the opposite point of view, in Eusebius. He mentions it casually in connection with his account of the persecution of the churches of Lyons and Vienne under Marcus Aurelius, in 177. He had before him, when he wrote, a series of letters sent out by these churches in Gaul, several of them being addressed to the churches in Asia and Phrygia and one to Eleutherus, bishop of Rome. The letters to Asia are long and detailed and seem to presuppose close, personal ties of friendship between members of the Gallic and Asiatic communities. It is likely that other young men had emigrated from the thickly populated cities of Asia Minor, as Irenaeus had done,[47] to seek their fortunes along the valley of the Rhone. The letter in which Eusebius takes most interest and which he quotes at length is one describing the events of the Gallic persecution and the hardships endured by the martyrs, who were confined for a long while in prison before their execution. He adds that he has also copies of letters discussing the Montanist problem, one written in the name of the church as a whole, others in that of the imprisoned martyrs. Obviously the Asiatic churches had sent to Gaul a report of their troubles with Montanus and his followers and their correspondents had replied with expressions of sympathy and approval of the stand which the Asiatics had taken. More than this, the prisoners of Lyons had determined to go farther and, as a body of men about to suffer for the faith, to bring what pressure they could to bear upon the bishop of Rome to induce him to take their view of the situation.[48]

Salmon, indeed, understands from the passage "that the Montanists had appealed to Rome, that the church party (in Asia) solicited the good offices of their countrymen settled in Gaul, who wrote to Eleutherus representing the disturbance of the peace of the churches (a phrase probably preserved by Eusebius from the letter itself) which would ensue if the Roman

[46] *Supra*, pp. 247, 250.

[47] On Irenaeus *vide supra*, p. 76; *infra*, p. 261.

[48] For another instance of the display of authority by martyrs *vide infra*, pp. 332 and n. 107, 339, 340, 345.

church should approve what the church on the spot condemned." [49] Both Tertullian and the Gallic Christians desired "the peace of the churches," though their ideas as to how that peace might be attained were diametrically opposed.

Irenaeus, now an ordained priest at Lyons, was actually sent to Rome as spokesman for the martyrs. Eusebius gives us the opening phrases of the letter of introduction which he carried with him. Clearly much hope was staked upon his eloquence to bring Eleutherus around to the right attitude, but how far he really contributed to Eleutherus' final decision we do not know. Tertullian puts all the blame upon Praxeas but he may have had special reasons for doing so. On the other hand, Irenaeus may not have reached Rome until after the question was settled. His satisfaction at the outcome and the impression which the attendant circumstances made upon him may be inferred from some portions of his great work, *Against Heresies,* which he wrote during his stay at this time in Rome.[50]

See on this affair J. Langen, *Geschichte der römischen Kirche* (4 vols., Bonn, 1881–1893), Vol. I, pp. 179 *sqq.*; G. N. Bonwetsch, *Die Geschichte der Montanismus* (Berlin, 1881); Th. Zahn, *Forschungen zur Geschichte des neutestamentlichen Kanons* (2 vols., Erlangen, 1881–1893), V, 1 *sqq.*; P. de Labriolle, *Les Sources de l'Histoire du Montanisme*; *La Crise Montaniste* (Paris, 1913).

Tertullian, *De Praescriptione Haereticorum,* c. 30. Text. Ed. by P. de Labriolle, *Textes et Documents pour l'Étude Historique du Christianisme,* IV, 62.

30 Where then [during the apostolic age] was Marcion, the ship's pilot from Pontus, the devotee of Stoicism? Where was Valentinus,[51] the disciple of Platonism? Everyone knows that they were not of that ancient time but lived in recent days, during the reign of Antoninus. And they

[49] G. Salmon, *Montanus,* in *Dictionary of Christian Biography,* Vol. III.

[50] Extracts from this work are given on pp. 265–272. Book III, at least, must have been finished before Eleutherus' death, for the list of the bishops of Rome closes with his name.

[51] Valentinus was really of an older generation than Marcion.

first accepted the catholic doctrine in the church at Rome, during the bishopric of the blessed Eleutherus,[52] until on account of their continual restless speculations, with which they were also corrupting the brethren, they were twice expelled, Marcion with the 200,000 sesterces which he had presented to the church. Then, condemned to perpetual separation, they spread far and wide their poisonous teachings. But afterwards Marcion confessed his repentance and submitted to the condition imposed upon him for obtaining peace, namely, that he should restore to the church those persons whom he had led to perdition by his teaching, but death too soon overtook him.

Tertullian, *Adversus Praxeam*, 1. Text. *Corpus Scriptorum Ecclesiasticorum Latinorum*, XLVII, 227–228.

He [Praxeas] came from Asia and was the first to import this kind of perversity into Roman soil. He was a turbulent man in various ways, especially conceited over his boasted martyrdom, because he had suffered one simple, short confinement in prison, although, even if he had given his body to be burned, it would have profited him nothing, since he had not the love of God and repudiated his gifts.[53] For after the bishop of Rome[54] had admitted the genuineness of the prophecies of Montanus, Priscilla and Maximilla and through his acknowledgment had brought peace to the churches of Asia and Phrygia, he [Praxeas] by importu-

52 Tertullian is employing here the argument formulated before him by Irenaeus, that the orthodox teaching of the Church can be traced directly back to the apostles and is therefore older and more authentic than heresies whose origin was comparatively modern. *Infra,* pp. 266, 272.

53 *Charismata.* This is the name given by Paul to the "gifts of the Spirit," prophesying, speaking with tongues, etc., characteristic of the apostolic Church.

54 Tertullian does not mention the name of the Roman bishop of whom he is speaking. Some scholars have taken it to be Victor. See C. Mirbt, *Quellen zur Geschichte des Papsttums* (4th ed.), p. 16, and references given there. We are following the opinion of P. Jaffé, *Regesta Pontificum Romanorum* (2 vols., Leipzig, 1885–1888), Vol. I, p. 10, and H. M. Gwatkin, *Early Church History,* Vol. II, pp. 187, 221. It is impossible to be quite positive.

nately urging false charges against those prophets and their churches and insisting upon the authority that belonged to the bishop's predecessors in the see forced him to recall the conciliatory letter which he had sent out and also to desist from his purpose of accepting those gifts. So Praxeas accomplished two works of the devil at Rome: he shut out prophecy and brought in heresy, put to flight the Holy Spirit and crucified the Father.[55]

Eusebius, *Historia Ecclesiastica,* V, 3, 4; 4, 1–2. Text. *Eusebius Werke* (*Die griechischen christlichen Schriftsteller der ersten drei Jahrhunderte*), II[1], 432–434.

The followers of Montanus, Alcibiades and Theodotus,[56] now began promulgating widely in Phrygia their views on prophecy, and numerous miracles also were at this time by the grace of God taking place in different churches, causing many people to believe in their prophesying. So dissensions arose about these manifestations. The brethren in Gaul promptly expressed their own pious and orthodox judgment in the matter and dispatched also several letters from the martyrs who had been slain among them, which they had written, while still in prison, to the brethren in Asia and Phrygia and also to Eleutherus, at that time the bishop of Rome, to plead for the peace of the churches.

The same martyrs also recommended Irenaeus, who was then a priest of the parish of Lyons, to the said bishop of Rome, testifying highly of him, as the following words show: "We pray, father Eleutherus, for your rejoicing in God again and always. We have committed this letter to our brother and comrade Irenaeus to carry to you and we com-

[55] Praxeas belonged to the Monarchian or Patripassian party in the Church, that denied any distinction in person between Christ and God, and taught that the Father himself had endured birth, suffering and death in the flesh. At the beginning of the third century, the Roman bishops Zephyrinus and Callistus were Monarchians. *Infra,* pp. 304, 309.

[56] On Theodotus *vide infra,* p. 279.

mend him to your esteem as a zealous adherent of the covenant of Christ." [57]

Irenaeus

(c. 130–c. 200)

We have mentioned already more than once the name of Irenaeus,[58] a son of Asia Minor, who emigrated soon after the middle of the second century by way of Italy to Lyons on the Rhone and there became prominent as a priest in the local church and, in his latter years, its bishop. As a youth he lived in or near the Christian community at Smyrna and listened to Bishop Polycarp, who remembered the apostle John. "I recall." [59] he wrote in 189, "the events of that time more clearly than those of recent years. For what we observe in boyhood grows into the mind and becomes part of it. Thus I can describe the exact spot where the blessed Polycarp sat when he talked and his goings and comings and habits of life and physical appearance and discourses to the people and the accounts he gave of his conversations with John and the others who had seen the Lord. And as Polycarp repeated their words and what he had heard from them about the Lord and his miracles, having received it all from eyewitnesses of the Word of Life, everything that he related was in harmony with the Scriptures. And while he told us all this, by the mercy of God I listened to it intently and noted it down not on paper but in my heart."

Thus as a lad Irenaeus learned reverence and loyalty to the tradition of the apostles from the lips of one who had it at first hand. Whether he was still in Rome when Polycarp came to confer with Anicetus,[60] we do not know. At any rate he heard of that visit and was impressed by the fact that Polycarp had met there a tradition derived from other apostles than John, which in some minor points was at variance with his but which accorded with it on the fundamentals of the faith.

57 Eusebius pursues the subject no further but passes immediately to another.
58 See particularly *supra*, p. 76.
59 Fragment quoted by Eusebius, *Historia Ecclesiastica*, V, 20, 4–7.
60 *Supra*, p. 247.

As the years passed and the last of the older generation disappeared and new men of different antecedents and training proceeded to put their explanations and estimates upon the Christian faith, the question of what must still be accepted unchanged as the essential historic facts and what beside as the legitimate interpretation of them became, as we have said, continually more pressing and difficult. Justin Martyr, Dionysius of Corinth and others wrote against what seemed to them perverted misrepresentations of the gospel story. Hegesippus made his pilgrimage to collect authentic reminiscences of the apostles.[61] To Irenaeus, bred as he had been in the line of a direct, simple, oral tradition, all the labored, fanciful philosophies that now passed as higher developments of Christian teaching seemed utterly repugnant and alien to the spirit of Jesus and his disciples. The mystic Montanist party from Asia Minor was almost equally distasteful. The trend toward unbridled ratiocination must be withstood, of course, but not by wayward ascetics, falling into trances and setting up new revelations and communions. Error could be exposed only by getting back to the first, clear sources of truth, which were to Irenaeus the words of the Lord and his appointed messengers. In 177, the report of the Montanist disturbance in Asia reached the church at Lyons, and Irenaeus, as a priest in the church, was dispatched to Rome to lay the views of himself and his fellow-members before Eleutherus and save him from being deluded by the Montanist prophets.[62]

Eleutherus may have wavered for a while but in the end he seems to have realized that his duty lay in following the example of Anicetus, resisting the spirit of innovation and adhering steadfastly to the tradition that was the heritage of his church. To the Asiatics who had condemned the Montanists he sent the approval of Rome. Irenaeus, who saw in the temptation to " despise the companions of the Lord " the supreme peril of the age and who took pride in his earnest Gallic converts, prevented by their ignorance from knowing either the Greek Scriptures or the newfangled heresies, felt the reassurance of this conservative and powerful support.

[61] *Supra*, pp. 248, 250. [62] *Supra*, p. 260.

During the remaining years of Eleutherus' pontificate, Irenaeus spent much time at Rome, whether in any ecclesiastical capacity or not we do not know. He used the opportunity for study and writing to grapple seriously with the menace of heresy and to lay down for the use of the Church certain broad principles by which it might henceforth be tested and resisted. Other writers had disproved particular errors, point by point. Irenaeus' book was directed especially against the Gnostic schools of Valentinus and of Marcion, the latter of whom had been freshly excommunicated. He patiently described their doctrines in order fairly to refute them, but his method of refutation was general and applicable to any pernicious novelty. What, after all, had the disciples of John or Peter or Paul to do with aeons or the demiurge? Had Christ taught dualism or distinguished between the inferior creator god and his own spiritual Father? Christianity was the doctrine of the Lord and of his apostles, uncontaminated by spurious, later inventions.

As to what was genuine doctrine, the Church possessed two authentic sources of knowledge, the four gospels and the tradition bequeathed by the apostles to their successors. Irenaeus describes briefly the origin of the gospels, using information drawn largely from Papias. Then for those who object that the gospels are incomplete and demand interpretation and supplement he adds that the apostles left their own interpretations and instructions with the men whom they appointed bishops of the churches which they had founded and he challenges the Gnostics to show any such authority for their theories or any break in the Christian line of inheritance. Every apostolic church, he says, has its own legacy of tradition, handed on, since its first reception, as a sacred charge from bishop to bishop. It would take too long to trace back the episcopal genealogy in every case. Let one suffice as an example, to wit, that of the "very great and ancient and illustrious church founded and organized at Rome by the two glorious apostles Peter and Paul." This church because of its commanding position at Rome is necessarily visited by everyone and the tradition which it derives from the apostles is confirmed by everyone who comes to it. Did Irenaeus have Polycarp in mind, as he wrote this passage? One is tempted to think it in view of his references further on to Polycarp's preaching against the Roman Gnostics. He goes on to give a list of Roman bishops [63] from Peter down to Eleutherus and a summary of the baptismal creed in use at Roman services.

From Rome he passes to Asia and cites the testimony of Polycarp, his own closest link with the apostolic age, who had abhorred heretics and had always taught the same faith in one God, Creator and Father, and one Son of God, who lived and suffered in the flesh. But his reliance upon Polycarp is apparently no greater than his reliance upon Rome. He has added to his allegiance to the revered teacher of his youth another allegiance, to the church whose weighty influence has been cast also on the side of staunch fidelity to the past. He writes in Greek and he knows that his book will be read in the East. He intends, possibly, to remind his readers, orthodox as well as Gnostic, that the church of the great metropolis has not only wealth and numbers but also a faith, founded upon a continuous tradition, that no one can despise, not even those who live nearer to the birthplace of their religion. Polycarp himself once preached at Rome and helped to confirm that faith. Rome is the champion of all Christians against those who pervert or belittle the apostles' message. Let them recognize her trustworthiness! Let them accept as a test of orthodox belief its harmony either with the written gospel or with the oral tradition preserved in such a church! One feels, of course, that to Irenaeus the real desideratum was loyalty to apostolic Christianity and that he had become a partisan of Rome because her record in regard to that special virtue stood so clear. If Eleutherus had compromised with Marcion or decided differently in the matter of the Montanists, Irenaeus would hardly have selected his church as a standard by which to try heretics. How the eastern brethren received his argument at the time we have no means of telling. The next step in the development of Roman ecclesiastical leadership, taken by Bishop Victor, the successor of Eleutherus, brought out an urgent protest, even from Irenaeus.

[63] For a comparison of Irenaeus' list with one which perhaps represents the list drawn up by Hegesippus *vide supra*, pp. 249–250.

The Greek text of Irenaeus' work against heresy was lost during the period of neglect that fell upon second century writers. We possess the original of only a portion of the first book and some disconnected passages quoted by Hippolytus or Eusebius. The substance, however, of the whole has been preserved in a rude, literal, Latin translation, used by Tertullian and, therefore, almost as old as the original itself.

Contra Haereses, III, 1–4. Text. J. P. Migne, *Patrologia Graeca,* VII, 844–857.

1 Now we have learned the plan of our salvation entirely from the men through whom the gospel came to us. For at first they proclaimed it abroad and afterwards, by the will of God, they set it down for us in the Scriptures to be the foundation and pillar of our faith. It is wicked to say, as some venture to do, who boast that they improve upon the apostles, that the latter preached before they had attained to "perfect knowledge."[64] For after our Lord arose from the dead and they were filled with the power of the Holy Ghost descending from on high, they were complete every whit and had perfect knowledge; they went forth to the ends of the earth, bearing the glad tidings of the good things bestowed by God upon us and declaring the peace of heaven to men, each one equally and individually possessing the gospel of God. So Matthew among the Hebrews issued a gospel written in their language, while Peter and Paul were preaching at Rome and establishing the church. And after their death, Mark, the disciple and interpreter of Peter, himself wrote down the teachings of Peter and bequeathed them to us. Luke also, the follower of Paul, recorded in a book the gospel he had preached. Finally,

[64] A reference to those Gnostics who taught that Christianity, like the religions of the pagan mysteries, had its esoteric philosophy, not comprehended even by all the apostles. Marcion, for example, repudiated all the books of the New Testament except a modified form of the Gospel of Luke and the Epistles of Paul.

John, the disciple of the Lord, who also had leaned upon his breast, did himself publish his gospel during his sojourn at Ephesus in Asia.

These have all made plain to us that there is one God, the Creator of heaven and earth, proclaimed by the law and the prophets, and one Christ, the Son of God.[65] Whoever does not accept this, despises the companions of the Lord; despises also Christ himself, the Lord; yea, he despises the Father also and stands self-condemned, resisting and opposing his own salvation, as do all the heretics.

2 But when these people are refuted out of the Scriptures, they turn and accuse the Scriptures themselves, on the ground that they are mistaken or not authoritative or not consistent in their wording, and they say that the truth cannot be learned from them by persons who do not know the tradition, for that was not transmitted in writing but by word of mouth. . . .

Then when we challenge them again with the tradition which comes from the apostles and is preserved in the churches by the presbyters in their successions, they attack the tradition and insist that they are wiser not only than the presbyters but even than the apostles and that they have discovered the unalloyed truth. . . .

3 Now it is within the power of anyone, who cares, to find out the truth and to know the tradition of the apostles, professed throughout the world in every church. We are also able to name those who were appointed bishops by the apostles in the churches and their successors down to our own times. They neither taught nor knew of any such thing

[65] Cerdon and his pupil Marcion explained the conflict between the moral standards of the Old and New Testaments by declaring that the God of creation and of the Old Testament was a cruel demiurge, a different being from the merciful Father of Jesus, and that Jesus himself, the Son of God, was not to be identified with the Messiah whom the prophets had predicted. In short, they aimed to eradicate all national, Jewish elements from Christianity in order to free it from the accompanying taints and limitations. Marcion, however, did not feel that his position was incompatible with remaining in the Church and left it only under compulsion. A. Harnack, *History of Dogma,* trans. by N. Buchanan, Vol. I, chap. V; also *Marcion; das Evangelium von fremden Gott* (Leipzig, 1921).

as these hallucinations. Yet, if the apostles had been aware of any hidden mysteries, which were disclosed to "the perfect"[66] apart and secretly from the rest, they would have delivered them first of all to the men to whom they committed the churches.[67] For they desired above all that these men should be perfect and blameless in everything, since they were leaving them behind as their successors and entrusting their own office of government to them, so that if they walked uprightly, it would be of great benefit, and if they fell away, a dire calamity.

But inasmuch as it would be very tedious in a book such as this to rehearse the lines of succession in every church, we will put to confusion all persons who, whether from waywardness or vainglory or blindness or perversity of mind, combine wrongfully together in any way, by pointing to the tradition, derived from the apostles, of that great and illustrious church founded and organized at Rome by the two glorious apostles, Peter and Paul, and to the faith declared to mankind and handed down to our own time through its bishops in their succession. For unto this church, on account of its commanding position, every church, that is to say, the faithful from everywhere, must needs resort and in it the tradition that comes from the apostles has been continuously preserved by those who are from everywhere.[68]

66 A phrase applied in the mysteries to the inner circle of initiates.

67 In another place, Irenaeus says: "They [the heretics] all are much later than the bishops to whom the apostles committed the churches." V, 20, 1.

68 The Greek of this all important passage is lost. The Latin version runs: "Ad hanc enim ecclesiam propter potentiorem [or potiorem] principalitatem necesse est omnem convenire ecclesiam, hoc est, eos qui sunt undique fideles, in qua semper ab his qui sunt undique conservata est ea quae est ab apostolis traditio." The translation ordinarily adopted hitherto by Catholic scholars, *e.g.*, Tillemont, Bossuet, Rivington, *etc.*, is: "With this church, on account of its preëminent authority, every church must be in agreement, that is, the faithful everywhere, among whom the tradition of the apostles has been continuously preserved by those everywhere." The antecedent of "qua" is here "omnem ecclesiam." Harnack gives substantially the same interpretation. *History of Dogma,* trans. by N. Buchanan, Vol. II, p. 157, n. 3. Bardenhewer, however, understands "qua" to refer to "hanc ecclesiam," as we do, and reads also into the preposition "in" the meaning, "in communion with." *Patrology,* p. 121. Everything really hangs upon the rendering

The blessed apostles then founded and reared up this church and afterwards committed unto Linus the office of the episcopate. This same Linus is mentioned by Paul in his epistles to Timothy.[69] His successor was Anacletus, after whom, in the third place from the apostles, Clement was elected to the bishopric. He was one who had seen the blessed apostles and had intercourse with them, in whose ears the apostles' preaching still lingered and who kept their instructions before his eyes. Nor was he unique in this regard, for many were still living in his time who had been taught by the apostles. In the days of this Clement,[70] a grave dissension arose among the brethren at Corinth and the church at Rome sent a compelling letter to the Corinthians, urging them to peace, refreshing their faith and repeating the tradition which they had so recently received from the apostles, of the one God Almighty, Maker of heaven and earth, Creator of mankind, who ordained the deluge, called forth Abraham, led his people from the land of Egypt, spake with Moses, proclaimed the law, sent out the prophets and has prepared fire for the devil and his angels. From this letter whoever chooses may see that this God is the Father of our Lord Jesus Christ, who is preached by the churches, and may comprehend the apostolic tradition of the Church, for this letter is older than the men who

---

of "convenire ad," as to whether the sentence means that every church, through its members who are obliged to visit the capital, has relations with the Roman church and so helps to support its faith, or that every church which has an orthodox tradition must agree with the Roman See. The word "principalitas" is also ambiguous and may contain an allusion to age as well as to dignity of situation. If the Greek original were ever recovered, the obscurity would probably be cleared up. For detailed arguments see L. Rivington, *The Primitive Church and the See of Peter, passim;* F. W. Puller, *The Primitive Saints and the See of Rome,* Lect. I and Appendix; W. Bright, *The Roman See in the Early Church* (London, 1896), pp. 29–36; J. Langen, *Geschichte der römischen Kirche,* Vol. I, p. 171; F. R. M. Hitchcock, *Irenaeus of Lugdunum,* pp. 251–255.

69 II Timothy, IV, 21.

70 On Clement of Rome *vide supra,* pp. 66, 235. His letter does in fact bring out the very point that Irenaeus is trying to establish against the Marcionites, *viz.,* the belief of Christians from the first in the identity of the God of the Old Testament and of the New.

now disseminate falsehood and erroneously insist upon a second God, superior to the demiurge and maker of all things that are.

To this Clement succeeded Evaristus and Evaristus was followed by Alexander. Then, sixth after the apostles, Sixtus held office; after him Telesphorus, who was a glorious martyr;[71] next Hyginus,[72] then Pius, and after Pius, Anicetus. Soter succeeded Anicetus and now, in the twelfth place from the apostles, Eleutherus has the office of the episcopate. In this order and by this succession[73] the tradition of the apostles in the Church and the preaching of the truth have passed down to us. And herein is abundant proof that the lifegiving faith is one and the same which has been preserved in the Church from the apostles until now and handed on in truth.

Likewise Polycarp not only received his training from the apostles and conversed with many who had seen Christ but was appointed bishop of the church in Smyrna by the apostles in Asia. We ourselves saw him in our early youth, for he tarried on earth a long while and when a very old man gloriously and nobly suffered martyrdom and departed this life.[74] He taught always the things which he had learned from the apostles and which the Church is handing down and which alone are true. To this all the churches in Asia bear testimony, as do also those men who until now have succeeded Polycarp, a far more trustworthy and steadfast witness to the truth than Valentinus or Marcion or the other heretics. Polycarp was also at Rome in the time of Anicetus

71 The word "martyr" at this early date means witness for the faith under persecution but not necessarily one who suffered death.

72 A little later Irenaeus speaks of Hyginus as the ninth bishop. *Infra*, p. 272. He may then have been counting the apostles as the first heads of the church, though he nowhere calls one a bishop.

73 διαδοχῇ. It is the word used by Hegesippus. *Supra*, p. 250, n. 34. We have the Greek of this paragraph.

74 Polycarp was burned as a martyr at Smyrna about 150 A.D. His death is described in a letter written by the church of Smyrna soon after the event and quoted by Eusebius. *Historia Ecclesiastica*, IV, 15. He was then at least eighty-six years old.

and converted many from the aforesaid heresies to the Church of God by declaring that there was but one and only truth, which he had received from the apostles, namely, that which is handed down by the Church. There are some who heard him tell how John, the disciple of the Lord, on his way to the bath at Ephesus saw Cerinthus [75] in the bath-house and rushed out without washing, exclaiming: "Let us fly or the bath-house may fall upon us, for Cerinthus, the enemy of the truth, is within!" [76] And Polycarp himself, when Marcion once came into his presence and asked: "Do you know me?" replied: "I know you, the first-born of Satan!" Such was the dread felt by the apostles and their disciples of holding even verbal communication with the corrupters of the truth; as Paul also said: "A man that is an heretic after a first and second admonition reject; knowing that such a one is perverted and a sinner, being condemned of himself." [77] We have likewise an able letter written by Polycarp to the Philippians,[78] from which those who choose and are concerned for their own salvation may gather the nature of his faith and his statement of the truth. Furthermore the church in Ephesus, founded by Paul, where John dwelt until the time of Trajan, is another true witness of the apostles' tradition.

4 Seeing, therefore, that we have such testimony, we do not need to seek elsewhere the truth which it is easy to find in the Church. For the apostles, like a rich man at a

[75] Cerinthus, Menander and Simon, mentioned on this and the following pages, were all prominent members of sects which the primitive Church pronounced heretical. Almost nothing has been preserved of their literature and we are dependent for any knowledge of them upon the denunciations of their heated opponents. See on the subject F. Legge, *Forerunners and Rivals of Christianity* (2 vols., Cambridge, 1915).

[76] It is impossible to decide upon the authenticity of this story, which Irenaeus did not himself hear from Polycarp. Cerinthus was a contemporary of the author of the Gospel of John, which, according to Irenaeus, was composed on purpose to refute him. Readers of Browning will remember Cerinthus in *The Death in the Desert.*

[77] Titus, III, 10, 11.

[78] This letter, which was written soon after the death of Ignatius of Antioch, is the only one of Polycarp's writings that has survived. The text is given by Lightfoot, *The Apostolic Fathers,* Pt. II, Vol. III, pp. 321–350.

bank, deposited lavishly with her all aspects of the truth, so that everyone, whoever will, may draw from her the water of life. For she is the door to life and all others are thieves and robbers. For this reason we ought to shun them and love the things of the Church with utmost diligence and lay hold of the tradition of the truth. What more? Suppose that a disagreement on some important question arises among us, must we not then have recourse to the most ancient churches, with whom the apostles lived, and ascertain from them what is positive and clear in regard to the question in dispute? What if the apostles had left us no Scriptures, would it not then be required of us to follow the course of the tradition which they bequeathed to the men to whom they committed the churches?

This course is followed by the barbarian peoples who believe in Christ and have salvation written in their hearts by the Spirit without paper or ink and who guard carefully the ancient tradition.[79] For they believe in one God,[80] the Creator of heaven and earth and all things therein through Christ Jesus, the Son of God, who for his surpassing love toward his creation underwent birth from a virgin, uniting man through himself to God, and who suffered under Pontius Pilate and rose again and was received up in splendor and shall come in glory, the Savior of those who are saved and the Judge of those who are judged, to send into eternal fire those who pervert the truth and despise his Father and his coming. They who without written books have believed this faith are barbarians as regards language, but as regards doctrine, practice and way of life they are wise indeed

[79] *E.g.*, the Gallic provincials, among whom Irenaeus lived.

[80] The ensuing passage is probably a summary of the creed taught in Irenaeus' day to catechumens before their baptism. Its similarity to the first part of the so-called Apostles' Creed, known to have been in use at Rome in the second century, is striking. On the Roman statement of faith as the archetype of all later creeds, both eastern and western, *vide* F. Kaltenbusch, *Das Apostolische Symbol* (2 vols., 1894–1900); A. C. McGiffert, *The Apostles' Creed* (New York, 1902); W. W. Bishop, *The Eastern Creeds and the Old Roman Symbol* in *American Journal of Theology* (Chicago, 1902), pp. 518–528; B. J. Kidd, *A History of the Church to A.D. 461* (3 vols., Oxford, 1922–1925), Vol. I, pp. 259–268.

through their faith and do please God, abiding in all righteousness, purity and wisdom. If anyone should preach to them the fabrications of the heretics in their own tongue, they would instantly stop their ears and flee away as far as possible, refusing even to hear the blasphemous words. Thus they keep the ancient tradition from the apostles and do not allow their minds to conceive any such monstrous ideas as those of these teachers, among whom neither church nor doctrine has ever yet become established.

Now before the time of Valentinus there were no disciples of Valentinus, nor did the disciples of Marcion exist before Marcion, nor, in short, did any other of those malignant persons whom I have just named live before the founders and inventors of their errors. Valentinus came to Rome in the days of Hyginus, was active under Pius and lived on there until Anicetus. As for Cerdon, Marcion's predecessor, he came into the church and made public confession in the time of Hyginus, who was the ninth bishop.[81] And so he continued, at one time secretly teaching and then again making confession, then being denounced for wrong doctrine and withdrawing from the assembly of the brethren. Marcion, who came after him, was most active under Anicetus, who was the tenth bishop. The others who are called Gnostics had their origin in Menander, the disciple of Simon, as I have shown, although each of them appeared to be both father and high priest of the doctrine into which he was initiated. All of them broke out into apostasy very late, that is, during the intermediate period [82] of the Church.

[81] " Eighth " in the old Latin version, but Eusebius, who has preserved this extract in the Greek, gives " ninth." *Historia Ecclesiastica,* IV, 11. Elsewhere Irenaeus himself makes Hyginus the eighth bishop. *Supra,* p. 269. The difference, as we have said, may be due to the fact that the list of bishops sometimes commenced with Peter and sometimes with Linus.

[82] To Irenaeus this was the period after the apostolic age, extending through the middle of the second century. The times in which he was writing were " late."

Clement of Alexandria

(c. 190–c. 215)

The following sentences from the *Hypotyposes* of Clement of Alexandria,[83] if read in connection with the passage from his *Stromata* already quoted,[84] will show how the search for a canon of apostolic authority was going on all over Christendom. Clement furnishes a salutary corrective for those of us who might feel after reading Hegesippus and Irenaeus that all roads in that search inevitably brought one to Rome. He was a greater scholar and a subtler thinker than either of the other two. He travelled widely and visited southern Italy in his journeys but he felt evidently no impulse to consult the Roman oracles and remained always outside the Roman orbit. The fragments of his writings that we have prove the existence of a number of centers of tradition, especially toward the Southeast, individuals or groups of individuals, that preserved each its own hoard of memories reaching back to apostolic days and lived by them, looking for no other leadership or sanction.

Eusebius, *Historia Ecclesiastica,* II, 1, 3–4. Text. *Eusebius Werke* (*Die griechischen christlichen Schriftsteller der ersten drei Jahrhunderte*), II[1], 104.

3 Clement, in the sixth book of his *Hypotyposes,* writes as follows: " For Peter [85] and James and John, even though they had been highly preferred by the Savior, did not contend with one another for honor but chose James the Just bishop of Jerusalem."

4 And the same writer in the seventh book of the same work tells us this besides about him [James]: " The Lord after his resurrection imparted knowledge to James the Just

[83] On Clement of Alexandria *vide supra,* p. 78.

[84] *Supra,* p. 79.

[85] Peter, to Clement, was merely one of the two or three principal apostles, a member of the small inner circle mentioned in the gospels.

and to John and Peter,[86] and they imparted it to the other apostles and the other apostles to the Seventy, of whom Barnabas was one."

3. THE AUTHORITY OF THE ROMAN CHURCH

VICTOR

(c. 188–c. 198)

Victor,[87] who succeeded Eleutherus, required no urging to take a firm stand against heretics and nonconformists. He was the first man, as far as our knowledge goes, to be pope in anything resembling the modern sense of the term and to regard his position as not only one of councillor and benefactor to the sister churches but also, if need arose, of commander. His pontificate, in fact, marks the passing of the primitive, unostentatious stage in the history of the Roman See and the opening of a new and infinitely more ambitious era.

We know several facts about the militant Victor. The first illustrates his policy toward heterodoxy of opinion in the local church and is given in an anonymous Roman pamphlet of the early third century, quoted by Eusebius. This pamphlet was aimed against an heretical party which found sanction for its views in certain passages of the New Testament and in a work as early and as reputable as *The Shepherd* of Hermas.[88] The party was known later as the Adoptionist. It held the belief that Christ was after all not a god but a man like other men, though qualified peculiarly by divine grace to perform his lofty mission for the world. In the time of Hermas, forty or fifty years before

[86] There is no meeting of Jesus with these three mentioned in our New Testament. Jesus was seen by Peter, by the women, by the two going to Emmaus, then by the Eleven and other larger groups. The extract here shows the influence upon Clement of the Gnostic idea of Christianity, as a knowledge of hidden mysteries, a superior philosophy.

[87] Victor was the fourth Roman bishop to bear a Latin name. The *Liber Pontificalis,* which in his case may be recording a real tradition, says that he was a provincial from Africa. L. R. Loomis, *The Book of the Popes,* 17. The province of Africa had probably received Christianity from Rome and the African church appears to have regarded the Roman with special deference, and to have had an exalted idea of the respect due to its bishop. *Supra,* p. 218. Jerome tells us that Victor wrote several books " of minor importance " in Latin. *De Viris Illustribus,* c. 34.

[88] *Supra,* p. 242.

Victor, when dogma was still hazy and ill-defined, such a view as this might be vaguely suggested in the course of a lengthy treatise, otherwise regarded as useful, and might escape notice or denunciation. *The Shepherd* was read constantly in the churches without apparently giving offense. But when later one Theodotus from Byzantium came to Rome and taught what seems to have been a genuine attempt at a rationalistic form of Christianity and a simple method of textual criticism,[89] Victor detected the heresy lurking in such teaching and excommunicated Theodotus, as Eleutherus had expelled Marcion. Theodotus seems to have accepted his excommunication without a struggle and to have set about founding an independent sect, with its own organization and salaried bishops. A few years later, at the time that this pamphlet was written, Artemon was the leader of the Adoptionists and they were evidently maintaining not only that their doctrine was based upon the New Testament and the traditions of the earliest believers but even that the bishops of Rome down to Victor himself had countenanced or approved it.

Victor was the first bishop whom we know to have had entrée and influence at the court of the emperor, at least during the period when Marcia was the favorite mistress of Commodus. She herself may have had Christian relatives or have grown up in a Christian environment. She is called a " devout woman " and, perhaps, was anxious to propitiate her friends by using her power over Commodus to some laudable end. At any rate, she procured from him his consent to the release of the Christian prisoners who had been sentenced to labor in the mines of Sardinia and got from Victor the list of such prisoners to be sent to the officials in Sardinia. It is possible that Victor prompted her to the whole enterprise. We mention the episode here, though it is found in an account of the early adventures of Callistus, some pages further on.[90]

But the most famous act of Victor is yet to be related. During the ten or twelve years of his pontificate, the difference

89 Eusebius, *Historia Ecclesiastica*, V, 28, 2, 8, 13–19. A. Harnack, *History of Dogma*, trans. by N. Buchanan, Vol. III, pp. 1–77.

90 *Infra*, p. 308.

between the churches over the date of holding the Easter celebration, which we have already described,[91] assumed suddenly the proportions of a grave controversy. The systematization of Christian ideas and practice was proceeding apace and any obstacle to outward uniformity in a conspicuous matter like the date of keeping Easter seemed now more serious than it had ever done before. Synods of all the bishops in each province were meeting to unite upon the policy to be adopted by the churches in that province and to exchange opinions with similar synods representing other provinces. In such an assembly the bishops of Asia Minor had voted to suppress the Montanists.[92] Each synod was as yet, however, supreme in its own province. It was desirable that the various synods should reach the same conclusion on any given question, but there was no way of compelling them to do so. Harmony must be the voluntary fruit of the spirit of brotherhood. About the year 190, these provincial synods up and down the Mediterranean at Victor's suggestion discussed the importance of a general agreement upon the date for commemorating the Lord's resurrection. A concerted effort was made to come to a conclusion that should be accepted by everyone. Clement, as head of the school at Alexandria, published a summary of the traditions he had collected in favor of the Sunday observance. The great majority resolved upon the celebration of the proper day of the week, namely, Sunday, rather than of the exact day of the Jewish month. Synods in Palestine, Pontus, Mesopotamia, Rome, Gaul and elsewhere issued statements to that effect and despatched them to one another. But the church in Asia Minor, of which Polycarp had been a member and which possessed its own memories of the apostle John and the evangelist Philip, protested that it could not in loyalty to its tradition, preserved by its bishops, forsake its ancient custom but must continue to celebrate the fourteenth day of Nisam.

The effect of this disappointing news upon Victor seems to have startled all his contemporaries. With perfect assurance he

[91] *Supra*, p. 246. The trouble seems to have been brought to a head by one Blastus, a Quartodecimanian, who visited Rome and tactlessly insisted on arguing the question.

[92] *Supra*, p. 256.

"immediately undertook to cut off from the common unity the parishes of all Asia and such churches as agreed with them and wrote letters pronouncing all the brethren there totally excommunicate." Assemblies of bishops, acting in concert, had expelled heretical groups from churches in their respective provinces, and a single bishop, such as Eleutherus or Victor himself, had excommunicated individual heretics in his own diocese, but for one bishop singlehanded to excommunicate the whole church of another province was as yet unprecedented. The act called forth instant expostulation, even from bishops in full sympathy with Rome upon the Easter question. Irenaeus, who ten years before had urged Eleutherus to express his disapproval of the Montanists and had extolled the Roman church as the sure guardian of authentic tradition and who now took its side on the Easter question against the teachers of his youth, sent a plea to Victor to remember the relative insignificance of the matter in dispute and the profound need of peace between the branches of the same Church.

As far as we know, Victor remained imperious and obdurate and the ban against the Asiatic church was not withdrawn during his lifetime. His successors may have allowed the contention to drop. At least, we hear no more about it, although there was still an Easter problem to vex the Council of Nicaea [93] and Jerome, at the end of the fourth century, remarks that in his day many bishops of Asia and other districts of the Orient adhered to the Jewish calendar.[94] Nor do we know anything as to the grounds on which Victor based his right to exclude the eastern church. Eusebius, who had all the correspondence before him, says not a word to enlighten us. One can only suppose that Victor gave no reason for his display of authority strikingly different from that already given by Irenaeus for the prestige of the Roman church, namely, the full and well-authenticated, apostolic tradition of Rome, which could not be in error, confirmed, as it had been, by members of other apostolic communions over the Empire. If this supposition be correct, — and we have no warrant for any other, — Victor, like

[93] *Infra*, pp. 469, 472, 487. [94] *De Viris Illustribus*, c. 35.

Clement a hundred years earlier, acted as one vested not so much with a personal as with a corporate dignity. His right to coerce, such as it was, lay not in any power residing in himself individually to take into his hands the government of the Church catholic, but in the strength of the particular church body of which he was the appointed spokesman, the greatest church in Christendom, the most eminent and efficient embodiment of the orthodox tradition of the apostles. There was as yet no distinction between authority derived from one apostle or from another and Paul's name was still equal to Peter's.

There has been much discussion of the significance of Victor's action in the Easter controversy. The following references will show the contrasting points of view. E. Schürer, *Die Paschastreitigkeiten des zweiten Jahrhunderts* in *Zeitschrift für katholische Theologie* (Innsbrück, 1870), pp. 180–184; J. Langen, *Geschichte der römischen Kirche* (4 vols., Bonn, 1881–1893), Vol. I, pp. 182 *sqq.*; F. W. Puller, *The Primitive Saints and the See of Rome* (London, 1900), pp. 15–19 and Appendix; L. Duchesne, *Early History of the Christian Church* (trans. from 4th ed. by C. Jenkins, 3 vols., London, 1910–1924), Vol. I, chap. XVI; J. Turmel, *Histoire du dogme de la Papauté des Origines à la Fin du Quatrième Siècle* (Paris, 1908), pp. 65 *sqq.*

Pamphlet quoted by Eusebius, *Historia Ecclesiastica,* V, 28, 3–6. Text. *Eusebius Werke* (*Die griechischen christlichen Schriftsteller der ersten drei Jahrhunderte*), II[1], 500–502.

For they [the disciples of Artemon] assert that all the first believers and the apostles themselves received and taught what they now say and that the truth of the gospel was preserved until the time of Victor, who was the thirteenth bishop of Rome after Peter, but that from the time of his successor, Zephyrinus,[95] the truth has been corrupted. And their argument might be plausible if, first of all, the divine Scripture did not contradict them. In addition, there are the writings of certain brethren who lived before the

[95] The successors of Victor, Zephyrinus and Callistus, in whose day this pamphlet was evidently written, seem, in fact, to have carried the reaction against the Adoptionist theory to an extreme in the opposite direction and to have denied any distinction in person between the Father and the Son. *Infra,* pp. 304, 309.

time of Victor, framed in defense of the truth against the gentiles and against the heresies that then existed. I refer to Justin [96] and Miltiades and Tatian and Clement and many others, all of whom speak of Christ as God. Who does not know the treatises of Irenaeus [97] and Melito and others that describe Christ as God and man? And how many psalms and hymns there are, composed by faithful brethren from the beginning, which sing of Christ, the Word of God, and proclaim him divine! How then, if the doctrine held by the Church has been taught for so many years, can the preaching of it have been delayed, as they say, until the time of Victor? And why are they not ashamed to utter such calumnies of Victor, when they know well that he expelled from communion Theodotus, the cobbler, the founder and father of this blasphemous apostasy and the first to assert that Christ was a mere man? For if Victor was of their opinion, as their sacrilegious story relates, how could he have excommunicated Theodotus, the inventor of the heresy? [98]

Eusebius, *Historia Ecclesiastica,* V, 23–25. Text. *Eusebius Werke* (*Die griechischen christlichen Schriftsteller der ersten drei Jahrhunderte*), II[1], 488–498.

23 A question of considerable importance arose at that time. For the parishes [99] of all Asia, on the ground that theirs was an older tradition, held that the fourteenth day of the moon, the day on which the Jews were commanded

[96] Justin Martyr, *supra,* pp. 125, 128. Miltiades and Tatian wrote apologies on behalf of Christianity against pagan philosophy in the latter half of the second century. On Clement of Alexandria *vide supra,* pp. 78, 273. It is inaccurate to say that he lived before the time of Victor.

[97] Irenaeus, *supra,* pp. 76, 261. Melito, bishop of Sardis, addressed a defense of Christianity to Marcus Aurelius. He is mentioned as one of the revered saints of Asia Minor. *Infra,* p. 281.

[98] The followers of Artemon seem to have drawn some line between their belief and that taught by Theodotus, although we know too little about either one to tell what it was.

[99] *I.e.,* dioceses in later terminology. Asia is the Roman, proconsular province of that name in Asia Minor.

to sacrifice the lamb, ought to be observed as the feast of the Savior's Passover. They were, therefore, obliged to end their fasting on that day, whatever day of the week it might chance to be. But it was not the custom of the churches in the rest of the world to end it in that way, for they maintained the practice that has come down from apostolic tradition of ending their fast only on the day of our Savior's resurrection.[100]

Synods and assemblies of bishops were held on the subject and all with one consent, after some correspondence, drew up an ecclesiastical decree for persons everywhere, that the mystery of the Lord's resurrection from the dead should be celebrated only on the Lord's Day and that on that day alone should be observed the close of the paschal fast. We have still a resolution[101] of those who then assembled in Palestine under the presidency of Theophilus, bishop of the parish at Caesarea, and of Narcissus, bishop of that at Jerusalem. We have also another resolution of those who assembled at Rome to debate the same question. This bears the name of Bishop Victor. There is also one from the bishops in Pontus, over whom Palmas, as the eldest, presided, and one from the parishes in Gaul of which Irenaeus was bishop, and one from those in Osrhoene[102] and the cities in that district, and a personal letter from Bacchylus, bishop of the church at Corinth, and letters from many others who expressed the same opinion and judgment and cast the same vote. And the view which has been described above was accepted by them all.

24 But the bishops of Asia, led by Polycrates,[103] insisted

100 *I.e.*, they commemorated the death of Christ on the Friday and the Easter feast or termination of the Lenten fast on the Sunday after the first full moon following the vernal equinox.

101 The documents here enumerated by Eusebius had disappeared by Jerome's day, although he says that the memory of them still survived, "quarum memoria ad nos usque perdurat." *Chronicon.*

102 A region in northwestern Mesopotamia.

103 Polycrates was bishop of Ephesus. We know nothing more of him than what we have here.

that they must abide by the custom handed down to them long before. Polycrates himself, in a letter which he addressed to Victor and the church of Rome, explained in the following words the tradition that had come down to him.

"We keep the exact day, neither a later nor an earlier one. For in Asia also great lights have fallen asleep, which shall rise again on the day of the Lord's coming, when he comes with glory from heaven and searches out all the saints. Among these are Philip, one of the twelve apostles,[104] who fell asleep in Hierapolis, as did his two aged virgin daughters; and another daughter of his, who lived in the Holy Spirit, now rests at Ephesus.[105] In addition there is John, who leaned upon the bosom of the Lord, who as a priest wore the sacerdotal plate [106] and was both martyr [107] and teacher. He fell asleep at Ephesus. In Smyrna, there is Polycarp,[108] who was both bishop and martyr, likewise Thraseas, bishop and martyr from Eumenia, who fell asleep in Smyrna. What need of mentioning Sagaris, bishop and martyr, who sleeps in Laodicea, or the blessed Papirius or Melito, the eunuch, who lived altogether in the Holy Spirit and lies in Sardis awaiting the episcopate from heaven, when he shall rise from the dead? All these kept the fourteenth day of the Passover according to the gospel, never departing from it but obeying the rule of faith.

And I also, Polycrates, who am less than you all, observe the tradition of my own kinsmen, to some of whom I have

[104] Probably Philip the evangelist, not Philip the apostle. The two were sometimes confounded. Eusebius, *Church History*, ed. by A. C. McGiffert, *A Select Library of Nicene and Post-Nicene Fathers of the Christian Church*, p. 162, n. 6.

[105] *Cf.* Acts, XXI, 8, 9.

[106] John was not a Jewish priest. The words are either metaphorical or allude to a late and now forgotten legend.

[107] On the meaning of this word at this date *vide supra*, p. 269, n. 71.

[108] On Polycarp *vide supra*, pp. 261, 269. We know little of Thraseas, Sagaris, Papirius, or Melito. They all died, apparently, toward the middle of the second century and had had some acquaintance with the apostles or with their immediate disciples.

succeeded. For seven of my kinsmen were bishops and I am the eighth. And my kinsmen always kept the day when the people put away the leaven.[109] I, therefore, brethren, who have lived sixty-five years in the Lord and have communed with brethren from all the world and have examined every sacred scripture, am not daunted by terrifying words. For those greater than I have said: 'We ought to obey God rather than man.'"[110]

He then alludes to the bishops who were gathered with him when he wrote and who thought as he did. He says: "I could name the bishops who are here assembled, whom you requested me to summon and I did summon. Their names, should I write them down, are a great multitude. And they, though they know me to be of little worth, have bestowed their approval on this letter, for they know that I have not carried my grey hairs in vain and have always lived in Christ Jesus."

Thereupon Victor, who was head of the church at Rome, immediately undertook to cut off from the common unity the parishes of all Asia and such churches as agreed with them as heterodox and he wrote letters pronouncing all the brethren there totally excommunicate. But this did not please all the bishops and they exhorted him to have some consideration for peace and neighborly unity and love. Remonstrances from them have been preserved in sharp rebuke of Victor. Among these was Irenaeus,[111] who sent a letter in the name of the brethren in Gaul over whom he presided, agreeing that the mystery of the Lord's resurrection should be celebrated only on the Lord's Day but

[109] On the first day of the Passover, the Jews began the seven days' feast of unleavened bread.

[110] The tenor of this spirited passage proves that Victor had already written to Polycrates in a tone that he resented and had threatened him with some sort of penalty if he failed to come into conformity with the rest of the Church; also that he had bidden him call an assembly of his provincial bishops to discuss as a body the course they would take.

[111] On Irenaeus *vide supra*, pp. 76, 261. His letter to Victor has been lost except for the extracts given here and one or two other doubtful quotations.

properly admonishing Victor that he ought not to cut off whole churches of God for holding to the tradition of an ancient custom.

After considerable argument, he proceeds as follows: "For there is dispute not only over the day but also over the character of the fast. For there are some who think that they ought to fast one day, others two and others more. Some, moreover, count their day as consisting of forty hours, day and night.[112] And this variation in observance did not originate in our time but long before, in that of our ancestors. Apparently they did not insist upon strict accuracy and thus in their own simplicity and with their own individual differences they formed more than one custom for their posterity. Yet they all none the less lived in peace, and we also live in peace with one another and our disagreement over the fast but strengthens our agreement in the faith."

To this he adds the following account, which I may fittingly insert here: "Among them were the presbyters [113] before Soter, who presided over the church of which you are now the head. We mean Anicetus and Pius and Hyginus and Telesphorus and Xystus.[114] They neither observed it [the fourteenth day] themselves nor did they permit their associates to do so. Yet, although they did not observe it, they were nevertheless at peace with those who visited them from the parishes where it was observed, even though their observance conflicted sharply with the customs of those who were not observing it. But no one was ever excommunicated for this nonconformity and the presbyters before you,

112 The fast before the celebration of the paschal supper was gradually lengthened during the third century until it generally covered the forty days of our Lent or in some quarters even more. It was evidently meant at first to mark the period during which Jesus lay dead, which was early computed as forty hours.

113 The word "presbyter" is used even as late as this in the general sense to mean persons of authority or officials in a church, whether bishops, deacons, or priests in the more restricted sense.

114 This sounds as if Irenaeus had amassed information about the Roman bishops as far back as Xystus I, who died about 126.

who did not observe, sent the eucharist to persons from other parishes, who observed.[115]

And when the blessed Polycarp was at Rome,[116] in the time of Anicetus, they held views slightly differing about various points but immediately made peace with each other and would not quarrel even over this, their chief difference. For neither could Anicetus persuade Polycarp not to observe what he had always observed in company with John, the disciple of our Lord, and the other apostles whom he had known. Nor could Polycarp prevail upon Anicetus to adopt that observance, since he said that he ought to adhere to the custom of the presbyters who had preceded him. But, in spite of all this, they communed together and in the church Anicetus yielded the administration of the eucharist to Polycarp, plainly as a mark of respect. And they parted from each other in peace, both those who kept the observance and those who did not, maintaining the peace of the whole Church."

Thus Irenaeus, who was rightly named,[117] acted as peacemaker in this way, exhorting and negotiating, as aforesaid, on behalf of the peace of the churches. And not only with Victor but also with most of the other heads of the churches he discussed this mooted question by letter.[118]

25 The bishops in Palestine whom we have just mentioned, Narcissus and Theophilus, and beside them Cassius, bishop of the church of Tyre, and Clarus of the church of

[115] *I.e.*, probably to visitors from these other churches who happened to be in Rome during the paschal feast and were prevented by illness or other cause from attending the services. The practice of sending the host to communicants unable to attend is mentioned before this by Justin Martyr. *Apologia,* I, 65.

[116] For comment on this story, *vide supra,* pp. 246–247.

[117] The name Irenaeus is derived from the Greek, *εἰρήνη*, *i.e.*, peace. To Irenaeus, with his ties to both the eastern and the western churches, this harsh sundering of unity must have been a deep grief. He apparently made every effort in his power to bring back the peace.

[118] These letters are lost in their entirety but a fragment or two more from the letter to Victor or from one of those to another bishop may be found in Pseudo-Justinian, *Quaestiones et Responsa ad Orthodoxos,* and in Maximus of Turin's Sermon VII, *De Eleemosynis. Cf.* W. W. Harvey, *Sancti Irenaei Libri Quinque Adversus Haereses* (2 vols., Cambridge, 1857), Vol. II, pp. 477, 478, where the text of these short fragments is given.

Ptolemais and others who joined them,[119] expounded at length the tradition regarding the Passover which had come down to them in succession from the apostles and at the close of their letter added these words: "Do you[120] endeavor to send copies of our letter to every parish, that we may not be blamable for those who carelessly deceive their own souls. And we assure you that in Alexandria also they keep the same day that we do. For letters are carried from us to them and from them to us, so that with one accord and at the same time we keep the sacred day."

119 *I.e.*, the synod held in Palestine, *vide supra*, p. 280. It took the Roman position, that Easter should be celebrated on Sunday, regardless of the day of the month.

120 Eusebius omits to tell us whether this letter was addressed particularly to Victor or whether it was meant for the general fellowship of bishops everywhere.

PART II

THE CLAIM TO THE POWER OF PETER

1. THE ASSERTION OF THE CLAIM

Tertullian of Carthage

(c. 160–235)

About the time of Victor's death, Tertullian,[1] the African lawyer with the caustic pen, wrote his book *De Praescriptione Haereticorum,* in which he repeated and vehemently developed the line of argument laid down by Irenaeus, that heresy was false because it rested on no sure foundation of Scripture or authentic tradition. To Tertullian the argument from tradition was even more decisive than that from Scripture, for there might be dispute about the meaning of Scripture and there could be none about that of local tradition, inasmuch as the transmitter of tradition possessed *ipso facto* the right to interpret it. In the course of his book Tertullian worked out far more definitely than had yet been done the conception of "catholicism" as a characteristic of either church or faith.[2] The "catholic" Church was the Church planted by the apostles in city after city throughout the world,[3] preserving everywhere through its episcopal succession the pure faith which the apostles taught. Thus universality was a sign of authenticity or orthodoxy and the term "catholic" denoted henceforth both universality in extent and orthodoxy in doctrine.

The chief depositaries of trustworthy tradition were, of course, the apostolic churches and Tertullian dwelt glowingly

1 On Tertullian *vide supra,* p. 84.

2 The word "catholic" had been previously applied to the Church by Ignatius of Antioch and the author of the *Muratorian Fragment. Supra,* p. 240 and n. 11. It was also used about this time by Clement of Alexandria and Hippolytus, but Tertullian was the first to define its significance.

3 The belief that the original apostles preached the gospel to every nation in the world goes back to the end of the first century. Matthew XXVIII, 19, may be a later interpolation; but there is Acts I, 8.

upon the wealth of such tradition concentrated at Rome. Not content with Peter and Paul, he robbed Asia of the sole glory of John and brought him too to enrich the capital with his sufferings. Like Irenaeus, he proclaimed the Roman creed and scouted the Gnostic notion that there had been progress in knowledge since the apostles' day. But although in the main framework of his thesis he followed Irenaeus, he argued his points in greater detail, often introducing citations from the New Testament to support his contention. In such a way he quoted among others the momentous passage which was to open a new destiny to the Roman See and change the course of history. In order to prove that the apostles possessed knowledge adequate for the guidance of the churches Tertullian cited the lines contained in the gospel of Matthew in which Peter is called the Rock and is awarded the keys of heaven and the right to bind and loose.[4] It is the first extant, clear reference by any writer of the Church to that passage.[5] Tertullian, at this time, treated it simply as

[4] An ingenious, recent, Protestant explanation of the Matthew verses is the suggestion of F. J. F. Jackson and K. Lake, to the effect that they were composed at Antioch, during the struggle for church domination between Antioch and Jerusalem, and were part of an attempt to elevate Peter, the apostolic founder of the Antiochene community, above James, the head at Jerusalem and the Lord's brother. *The Beginnings of Christianity,* Pt. I, Vol. I, *Prolegomena,* pp. 328–330. If this be true, the Antiochenes certainly saw their handiwork return as a boomerang against them during their later struggles with Rome. For other literary traces of the jealousy between the gentile Christianity that derived from Peter and Paul, and the conservative Jewish elements, centred at Jerusalem, *vide supra,* pp. 125–126.

[5] We have already noted that the author of the Latin, second-century *Acts of Peter,* does not seem to have known this passage, although he apparently had some acquaintance, at first or second hand, with Matthew's gospel. *Supra,* p. 143, n. 59. That the words were, however, to be found in manuscripts of that gospel current in Rome after the middle of the century seems to be established by the fact of their appearance in the *Diatessaron* or *Harmony of the Four Gospels,* compiled between 170 and 180 by Tatian, an Assyrian pupil of Justin Martyr at Rome. Tatian wrote the *Diatessaron* in Syriac on his return to his own country after Justin's death, but he based his work undoubtedly on western texts which he brought back with him. The book itself in its original form has long been lost, but St. Ephraim Syrus, who lived in the middle of the fourth century, and some of whose commentaries, sermons and poems have come down to us, wrote a commentary on it and used it as a source for his quotations elsewhere from the gospels. Two of these quotations, translated into English, run as follows: "The word of our Lord, that of his Church he spake, that the gate-bars of Sheol shall not be able to conquer it." "He said to Simon, 'To thee I will give the keys of the doors.'" F. C. Burkitt, *St. Ephraim's Quotations from the Gospels, in Texts and Studies,* edited by J. A. Robinson (Cambridge, 1901), Vol. VI, 2. For an Arabic quotation, which may also represent the text of Tatian, *vide* F. Haase, *Apostel und Evangelisten in den orientalischen Überlieferungen.* Why the Matthew passage was not earlier adduced to exalt the authority of Peter is not clear, unless it was that the Roman church until the close of the second century rested

a striking confirmation of one apostle's power to found and instruct churches. The idea that it could be regarded as anything more than a record of a special gift bestowed upon a single individual or as creating a perpetual endowment of privilege for an institution does not seem to have occurred to him.

But now that attention had been called to it, the passage began within a surprisingly short time to excite surmise and discussion. A sweeping charter of authority had been brought to light, conferred by the Lord himself on one of the two patron apostles of Rome. How far did that authority extend? Could any man claim it now and if so, who? Tertullian himself revolved these questions further in his mind and referred to them at least twice within the next few years. In the *Scorpiace*, written about 205, he reached a conclusion. Every one who confesses Christ, as Peter did, carries the keys of heaven as did he. How, later yet, Tertullian, grown heterodox and Montanist, perceived the use to which the Roman See might put the passage and attacked it with bitter rage and scorn, will be shown a few pages farther on.

De Praescriptione Haereticorum, cc. 17, 19–23, 32, 36.

Text. Ed. by P. de Labriolle (*Textes et Documents pour l'Étude Historique du Christianisme*), IV, 36–78.

17 These heretics reject some Scriptures and alter what they accept with additions and omissions to suit their own notions. The portions that they do accept they do not accept entire or, if they do keep some almost entire, they none the less corrupt them by devising various interpretations. A false explanation is as much an abuse to the truth as a spurious text. Their reckless assumptions compel them to

upon a double foundation and a twofold tradition and had not begun to enhance one half at the expense of the other. Also, the gospel of Matthew may not have had the circulation at Rome that the others had and may not have been so frequently read by the gentile Christians. It was, as the Fathers of the period almost all remark, addressed to the Hebrews. Still its authenticity was undisputed and it was included in the first known list of canonical books of the New Testament, contained in the *Muratorian Fragment*, a Roman composition of about the age of the *Diatessaron*.

reject the passages that condemn them, but they rely upon those which they have manipulated by forgery and upon those which they have selected for their ambiguity. What headway can you make, you who are wise in the Scriptures, if every passage that supports you they repudiate and if, on the other hand, every passage you repudiate they defend? You yourself will only lose your voice in the argument and will gain nothing but exasperation at their blasphemy.

. . . .

19 For this reason we should not appeal merely to the Scriptures nor fight our battle on ground where victory is either impossible or uncertain or improbable. For a resort to the Scriptures would but result in placing both parties on an equal footing, whereas the natural order of procedure requires one question to be asked first, which is the only one now that should be discussed. "Who are the guardians of the real faith? To whom do the Scriptures belong? By whom and through whom and when and to whom was committed the doctrine that makes us Christians?" For wherever the truth of Christian doctrine and faith clearly abide, there will be also the true Scriptures and the true interpretations and all the true Christian traditions.

20 Christ Jesus our Lord (May he suffer me a moment to speak of him!), whoever he is, of whatever God he is the Son, of whatever substance he is made man and God, of whatever faith he is the teacher, whatever be the reward he promises, did while he was living on earth himself declare what he was, what he had been, what was the Father's will that he fulfilled, what was the duty of man that he ordained; and he declared this either openly to the people or privately to his disciples. Of the latter he had chosen twelve leaders to be with him and had destined them to become the teachers of the nations. Accordingly, after one of them had been cast out, he commanded the eleven others,

on his departure to his Father after his resurrection, to " go and teach the nations " and to " baptize them into the Father and into the Son and into the Holy Ghost."[6]

Immediately, therefore, the apostles, whom their title shows to be " the sent,"[7] in fulfilment of a prophecy contained in a psalm of David,[8] selected by lot Matthias as the twelfth in the place of Judas and received the promised power of the Holy Ghost for the gift of miracles and utterance. After first bearing witness to the faith in Jesus Christ and establishing churches throughout Judaea, they then went forth into the world and preached the same doctrine and the same faith to the nations. Thus in every city they founded churches, from which other churches in turn derived the tradition of faith and the seeds of doctrine and are every day deriving them, in order that they may really become churches. Indeed, for this reason they too may be regarded as apostolic, because they are the offspring of apostolic churches. Every kind of thing must needs be classified according to its origin. Therefore, these many great churches are but the one primitive Church and are all apostolic, while they one and all maintain their unity by peaceful communion and terms of brotherhood and association in hospitality, relations governed by one consideration, which is, the one tradition of the one mystery.[9]

21 Hence, accordingly, we deduce our rule. Inasmuch as the Lord Jesus Christ sent the apostles out to preach, none should be received as preachers but those whom Christ appointed, for " no man knoweth the Father save the Son and he to whomsoever the Son will reveal him."[10] Nor has the Son appeared to reveal him to any but the apostles,

6 Matthew, XXVIII, 19.

7 The Greek word ἀπόστολος, apostolos, is derived from the verb ἀποστέλλω, to send.

8 Psalm CVIII, 8. (In King James Version, Psalm CIX, 8.) *Cf.* Acts, I, 15–20.

9 The Latin word is *sacramenti.*

10 Matthew, XI, 27.

whom he sent forth to preach the message which he revealed to them. Now what was the message which they preached? In other words, what was that which Christ revealed to them? Here I must maintain that this can be rightfully attested only by such churches as the apostles founded in person, preaching the gospel to them directly, both *viva voce,* as the phrase is, and subsequently by letter. If this be so, it is also plain that all doctrine which is in accord with these apostolic churches, these moulds and sources of the faith, must be regarded as true, as comprising undoubtedly that which the churches received from the apostles, the apostles from Christ and Christ from God, but that all doctrine must be branded as false which controverts the truth of the churches and of the apostles and of Christ and of God.

Finally, we must show whether this our doctrine, the rule for which we have just given, is indeed derived from the tradition of the apostles and whether all other doctrines, by the same evidence, originate in falsehood. We are in communion with the apostolic churches, for our doctrine differs in no respect from theirs. This is the sign of our truth.

22 Our proof is, actually, so close at hand that when it is once produced, there is no room left for argument. Let us, therefore, just as if we had no proof to offer, give our opponents opportunity for a while, if they think that they can discover some method of invalidating our rule. They often tell us that the apostles did not know everything. Then, possessed by the spirit of folly, they veer about to the opposite position and declare that the apostles undoubtedly knew everything but that they did not entrust all their knowledge to everyone. In either case they expose Christ to blame for having sent forth apostles who had either too little instruction or else too little honesty.

For what man of sane mind can suppose that those

whom the Lord ordained to be teachers, who were kept by him as his inseparable companions, disciples and intimate friends and to whom, "when they were alone, he did expound"[11] everything obscure, telling them that to them "it was given to know these mysteries"[12] which the people were not permitted to understand, were ignorant of anything? Was anything withheld from Peter, who was called "the rock on which the church should be built," who also obtained "the keys of the kingdom of heaven" with the power of loosing and binding in heaven and on earth?[13] Or was anything hidden from John, the most beloved disciple of the Lord, who used to lean upon his breast, to whom alone the Lord pointed out Judas as the traitor[14] and whom he commended to Mary as a son in his own stead?[15] How far was he aiming to keep them in ignorance, to whom he manifested his glory and Moses and Elias and, above all, the voice of his Father in heaven?[16] . . .

23 But then, in order to stamp the apostles as ignorant, the heretics advance the case of Peter and his companions, who were reproved by Paul.[17] "These did very wrong," they say, so as to build upon this assertion their other argument, that it has been possible since the apostles to reach a fuller knowledge, such as Paul had attained when he rebuked his predecessors. . . . They have yet to prove from the fact which they allege, namely, that Peter was rebuked by Paul, that Paul introduced a different form of gospel from that which Peter and the rest had previously preached. The truth is that after Paul's conversion from persecutor to preacher, he was brought as one of the brethren to the brethren by the brethren,[18] that is, to them by men who had received their faith from the apostles' hands. Afterwards, as he himself relates, he "went up to Jerusalem to

11 Mark, IV, 34.
12 Matthew, XIII, 11; Luke, VIII, 10.
13 Matthew, XVI, 18, 19.
14 John, XIII, 23–26.
15 John, XIX, 25–27.
16 Mark, IX, 1–6.
17 Galatians, II, 11.
18 Acts, IX, 27.

visit Peter "[19] because of his office and by right, undoubtedly, of their common belief and preaching. For the brethren would not have marvelled at his transformation from persecutor to preacher, if he had preached a doctrine at variance with theirs, nor would they have magnified the Lord, because his enemy Paul had submitted to him.[20] . . .

24 I am not so lofty, or rather so low, that I should set apostles against one another. But inasmuch as our perverse cavillers enlarge upon the rebuke in question for the purpose of bringing the earlier form of doctrine into suspicion, I will offer a defense on behalf of Peter, to the effect that Paul himself said that he was "made all things to all men, to the Jews a Jew, to those who were not Jews as one who was not a Jew, that he might win all."[21] . . . Let those beware who pass sentence on the apostles! It is fortunate that Peter is on a level with Paul in martyrdom.[22]

. . . .

32 But if there be any heretics bold enough to claim a foundation during the apostolic age, so that they may seem thereby to be derived from the apostles, because they existed in the apostles' time, we can say to them: "Let them produce the original records of their churches! Let them unfold the roll of their bishops, running down in due succession from the beginning, so that their bishop may show as his ordainer and predecessor one of the apostles or one of the apostles' disciples!" For in this form the apostolic churches do present their registers, such as the church of Smyrna, which shows that Polycarp was appointed thereto by John, and the church of Rome, which states that Clement

[19] Galatians, I, 18.

[20] Galatians, I, 24; Acts, IX, 21.

[21] I Corinthians, IX, 20 *sqq.* Tertullian goes on to remark that Peter might have upbraided Paul for circumcising Timothy after forbidding circumcision. Acts, XVI, 3.

[22] This passage amounts to an argument that Peter is not to be considered inferior to Paul.

was ordained by Peter.[23] In the same way other churches likewise point back to men ordained to the episcopate by the apostles, whom they regard as transmitters of the apostolic seed. . . .

36 Come then, you who would better exercise your wits about the business of your own salvation, recall the various apostolic churches in which the actual chairs of the apostles are still standing in their places, in which their own authentic letters are read, repeating the voice and calling up the face of each of them severally. Achaia is very near you, where you have Corinth. If you are not far from Macedonia, you have Philippi. If you can travel into Asia, you have Ephesus. But if you are near Italy, you have Rome, whence also our authority is derived close at hand.[24] How happy is that church on which the apostles poured forth all their teaching, together with their blood! Where Peter endured a passion like his Lord's! Where Paul won his crown in a death like John's![25] Where the apostle John was first plunged unhurt into boiling oil and then banished to an island![26] See what she has learned, what she has taught, what fellowship she has had with our churches too in Africa! One God does she acknowledge, the Creator of the universe, and Christ Jesus born of the Virgin Mary, Son of God the Creator, and the resurrection of the flesh.[27] To the writings of the evangelists and the apostles she adds the law and the prophets and therefrom she imbibes her faith.

23 This clause proves the existence at the end of the second century of some kind of documentary record intended to show that the Roman bishopric had been formally established in the person of Clement by an apostle. Peter, as the leading member of the Twelve, had been selected for founder rather than Paul. His authority served better to set off against John's in the Easter controversy. Clement, already famous as the author of the *Epistle* and mentioned as one who had known the apostles, had been chosen to receive the apostolic ordination, to the neglect of Linus and Cletus. *Supra*, pp. 85, n. 63, 162 ff.

24 *Supra*, p. 218.

25 *I.e.*, John the Baptist.

26 *Supra*, p. 287.

27 Compare this with Irenaeus' summary of the Roman creed. *Supra*, p. 271. Also *supra*, p. 268.

This faith she seals with water, arrays with the Holy Ghost, feeds with the eucharist, strengthens with martyrdom and against this faith and practice she admits no gainsayer.

Adversus Marcionem, IV, 13. Text. *Corpus Scriptorum Ecclesiasticorum Latinorum,* XLVII, 458.

He [Christ] changes Simon's name to Peter, just as also the Creator changed the names of Abram and Sarai and Ausea, calling the last Jesus [Joshua] and adding a syllable to each of the former. But why " Peter "? If it was for the vigor of his faith, there are many solid materials that might have furnished a name for their strength. Or was it because Christ is both a rock and a stone? As we read that he was set " for a stone of stumbling and for a rock of offense." [28] I omit the remainder of the passage. It was his pleasure then to bestow upon the dearest of his disciples a name drawn especially from the figures applied to himself, and it was, I think, more peculiarly fit than one unassociated with himself.

Scorpiace, X. Text. *Corpus Scriptorum Ecclesiasticorum Latinorum,* XX^1, 167.

. . . For although you think heaven still closed, remember that the Lord left the keys of it here to Peter and through him to the Church; and everyone who has been put to the trial [29] and made confession will carry them with him.

Zephyrinus (198–217) and Callistus I (217–222)

Bishop Victor had been prominent in the movement about the year 190 to bring into closer working harmony the scattered

[28] Isaias, VIII, 14; 1 Peter, II, 8.

[29] The Latin word *quaestionem* was used for judicial examination, often accompanied by torture. On the motive of the tract *Scorpiace, vide supra,* p. 85.

branches of the Christian Church and, as spokesman and head of the community at Rome, had attempted to assume the executive leadership of the loose federation of provincial synods. Under his two successors a formal claim to personal supremacy was put forward, based upon a commission from the Lord to the founder of the Roman bishopric. By the year 222, when Callistus died, the Petrine theory had, in effect, been formulated and at least one application of it had been made in practice. Here again, however, the documents, though fuller than heretofore, are barely sufficient to give us an inkling of what took place. We have no pronunciamento from either bishop concerned. As in the case of Victor, we must surmise what they did from the antagonism and indignation which they aroused.

There is some uncertainty as to which of these two bishops was the first to assert that his position, by virtue of the commission to Peter, differed in kind from that of other bishops, or that he was in point of rank "bishop of the bishops," as Tertullian wrathfully styles him. Tertullian lived through both pontificates and he gives no name nor any circumstance by which we can date his allusion. According to Hippolytus, Callistus dominated episcopal policy for years before his own election to the office, so that we may here for brevity's sake speak of the author of this step as Callistus, although Zephyrinus may at the time have been his mouthpiece. Nor have we any account of the occasion when the passage from Matthew was first used as a warrant for papal authority.[30] From Hippolytus we may infer that it was brought forward to justify a departure from precedent in the matter of church discipline and the introduction by Callistus of new views as to the efficacy of penance. As a matter of fact, the earliest penitential codes, with penalties graded to punish various sins, date from this period. The first modification in the austerity of the primitive Church had, as we have observed, been made about the time of Hermas.[31] The further relaxation of the moral standard by Callistus was bound to meet with bitter resistance from earnest-minded Christians

30 In the apocryphal letter of Clement to James, it is put into the mouth of Peter, as a warrant of his authority which he is transferring to Clement. *Supra*, p. 164. This letter, however, was probably composed after the beginning of the third century.

31 *Supra*, p. 243.

everywhere. He seems to have wasted no breath in defending his policy by the authority of the Roman church. The canon of the New Testament was now pretty generally accepted as the final word, as far as it went, on all questions of faith and practice and already someone in the Roman congregation had perceived the possibilities latent in the passage to which Tertullian had drawn attention a few years previously.[32] Whatever innovations, therefore, Callistus proposed he now backed by his individual power, as successor of the apostle Peter, to open and close the kingdom of heaven.

Tertullian, who had magnified the Roman church under Victor and defended it against pagans, Jews and heretics, found Callistus too much for him, as Irenaeus before him had found Victor.[33] He was one who grew more strenuous, more impatient of change and compromise as he grew older. In protest against the new policy of broader inclusiveness he joined the Montanist party and produced pamphlets denouncing fiercely the betrayal of the older, purer Christianity. Among these was a sarcastic invective on the subject of clerical pretension, entitled *De Pudicitia, On Modesty,* from which we quote two extracts for the light they throw on the situation. Vainly he tried to undo the effect of the fateful quotation from Matthew, by pointing out that the gift of authority to Peter was a special reward for an individual act of loyalty, not the perquisite of an office, and that if it were of such a nature as to be transmitted to anyone, it must be to those who merited it spiritually, as Peter did.

More specific information as to the character and careers of Zephyrinus and Callistus is contained in a long diatribe against them, written by another conservative, Hippolytus, bishop apparently of a group that had broken away temporarily, at least, from the orthodox community and set up an independent organization in or near Rome. Hippolytus was a scholar with scientific tastes, who wrote on chronology, magic and astrology, as well as on Christian doctrine and exegesis.[34] Between 220 and

32 *Supra,* pp. 292, 295.

33 *Supra,* pp. 277, 282.

34 A statue of Hippolytus, with the names of many of his books and his chronological tables engraved upon the back, was unearthed in 1551 and is now in the Lateran Museum.

230 he published a *Refutation of all Heresies,* known also as the *Philosophumena,* in ten books, of which Books I and V–X are still extant. After reviewing the fallacious philosophies and superstitions of the pagans and the errors that had beset the early Christians, he reached in Book IX the heresies of his own day, among which he classed the novel doctrines of Callistus. Callistus himself he regarded as the evil genius of the Church, a profane and low-lived trifler with sacred things. In order utterly to discredit both him and his ideas, he inserted into his theological disquisition an account of Callistus' early adventurous life. This account we give for the picture it affords of the local situation as well as of the making of a bishop. The reader must, however, be on his guard all through against the animus of the writer, which leads him to put a dark interpretation upon every incident of the story. Callistus seems to have been a man of vivid fancy and a dramatic temperament. In his youth, as the slave of an imperial official, he mismanaged the affairs of a bank that his master had entrusted to him and fled in panic to a ship about to sail from the harbor of Porto. When pursued by his master he leapt overboard to drown himself and was with difficulty rescued by the sailors. Later, a thirst for martyrdom led him to interrupt the Sabbath services in a Jewish synagogue by rising to denounce the law of Moses. In the riot that naturally ensued he almost perished and was sentenced by the prefect of the city to the Sardinian mines as a disturber of the peace. He was released in the general pardon that Marcia procured from Commodus, at the instigation, perhaps, of Bishop Victor, and was granted by Victor a small position in connection with the church at Antium.

Upon the accession of Zephyrinus, a dull man according to Hippolytus, Callistus gradually established an ascendency over him and obtained his own return to Rome, where eventually he was much in evidence as Zephyrinus' adviser and assistant. Officially he was in charge of one of the suburban cemeteries. During these years and during the five that followed of his own pontificate, he was responsible for the initiation of various policies that marked the beginning of radical changes in the constitution of the Church. We have already alluded to his extension of the privilege of repentance and his emphasis upon the forgiving grace of God and the all-embracing charity of the Church. He seems to have condoned second marriages among the clergy and to have countenanced relations between Christian noblewomen and their freedmen or slaves, which the Roman civil law attempted to discourage. Perhaps the memories of his own scapegrace youth made him more lenient toward the temptations of others. Some lowering of the bars was probably inevitable, as the Church increased in numbers and prosperity under the Severi. All these departures from the old, rigid rules, so shocking to the soberer minded, he sanctioned by his fullness of power as the successor of Peter. Hippolytus' scorn was as futile as Tertullian's. Before Zephyrinus' death, Origen visited Rome and some years afterward wrote a careful exposition of the Matthew passage, calculated to refute entirely the Roman interpretation,[35] but his labor also was as good as lost, except as it furnished support for the opposition of a later generation to Roman domination. One by one the churches of the Empire adopted in modified form the new penitential system, by which atonement might be made for any carnal sin.[35a] After Callistus' death, even Hippolytus became reconciled. We know almost nothing about the next bishops as far as Pontianus. They may have been less irritatingly self-assertive, and less inclined to experiment with points of theology. But we do know that Hippolytus died in exile as a companion of Pontianus and that his name was enrolled as a martyr in the calendar of the orthodox church.

We can barely mention Callistus' other activities. Like his forerunners, he investigated and expelled heretics. Gnosticism, as a movement, was dying out and the cosmological theories of Valentinus and Marcion attracted few believers. The dogmatic battles of the third and fourth centuries were fought upon narrower issues, the problem of the nature of Christ and his relation to God the Father. We have spoken of Theodotus, the

[35] *Infra*, pp. 317 ff.

[35a] But at the end of the next century, Siricius thinks it impossible to do penance more than once for such a sin. *Infra*, p. 701.

Adoptionist, who was excommunicated by Victor, and the sect which he founded.[36] Under Zephyrinus and Callistus, other teachers came into vogue, Noetus and Sabellius, who preached the opposite sort of Unitarianism and elevated Christ to complete divinity, calling him a manifestation of God. To them the Son was the Father in the guise of flesh, with no distinction of person. New disputes broke out dividing the Church afresh; yet the dignity of the faith seemed to require a satisfactory characterization of its Master. Zephyrinus and Callistus inclined toward the so-called Monarchian party of Noetus, with some slight qualifications, which are difficult for us to appreciate. Hippolytus, who remained a consistent Trinitarian, says that they actually upheld Noetus and that Callistus dubbed himself and the other Trinitarians "ditheists," [37] but also that Callistus drew a line of some kind at Sabellius and at length excommunicated him.

By posterity Callistus was remembered as the builder of a church edifice, the first, perhaps, to be erected within the city for the express purpose of Christian services. It stood on the site of the present Santa Maria in Trastevere, in the quarter beyond the Tiber populated by Jews and other foreigners.[38] His name was perpetuated a second time by a new catacomb or cemetery, which he had constructed near the Appian Way, where many of the bishops who came immediately after him were buried.

After Callistus the Papacy was never quite what it had been before him. Apart from the corporate prestige attaching to the church over which he presided, the Roman bishop thenceforth had his own unique and personal warrant of authority as heir of Peter. Peter was now officially on record as founder of the Roman episcopate and new and richer legends were coming into circulation of the miracles he had performed at Rome.[39] The bishops themselves as we shall see, began to assume a tone of greater finality in dealing with whatever questions of doctrine or discipline arose anywhere in the Church. Callistus had also

[36] *Supra*, pp. 274–275, 279.

[37] *I.e.*, of course, worshippers of two gods. If the Christians made Christ a god and a separate person from the Father Creator, were they not setting up two gods?

[38] L. R. Loomis, *The Book of the Popes*, pp. 20–21.

[39] *Supra*, pp. 133 ff., 158 ff.

set them an example of immortalizing himself by building. Thus he stands as the predecessor not only of Leo I and Gregory VII but also of Damasus and Leo X.

On the men and movements mentioned above, see J. B. Lightfoot, *The Apostolic Fathers* (2 vols., 2nd ed., London, 1889–1890), Pt. I, Vol. II, pp. 317–477; R. L. Ottley, *The Doctrine of the Incarnation* (2 vols., London, 1896); A. Harnack, *Geschichte der altchristlichen Litteratur bis Eusebius* (2 vols., Leipzig, 1893–1904), Vol I², pp. 605–646; A. Harnack, *Monarchianismus* in J. J. Herzog and A. Hauck, *Realencyklopädie für protestantische Theologie und Kirche* (24 vols., Leipzig, 1896–1913), Vol. XIII; E. Rolffs, *Indulgenzedict des römischen Bischofs Kallist,* in O. Gebhardt, A. Harnack, C. Schmidt (editors), *Texte und Untersuchungen zur Geschichte der altchristlichen Literatur* (45 vols., Leipzig, 1883–1924), Vol. XI; L. Duchesne, *Early History of the Christian Church* (trans. from the 4th ed. by C. Jenkins, 3 vols., London, 1910–1924), Vol. I, chap. XVII; H. M. Gwatkin, *Early Church History to A.D. 313* (2 vols., London, 1912), Vol. II, pp. 223–231; K. J. Neumann, *Hippolytus von Rom in seiner Stellung zu Staat und Welt* (Leipzig, 1902), Pt. I; A. d'Alès, *La Théologie de Saint Hippolyte* (Paris, 1906); A. d'Alès, *L'Edit de Calliste* (Paris, 1914).

Tertullian, *De Pudicitia,* cc. 1, 21. Text. *Corpus Scriptorum Ecclesiasticorum Latinorum,* XX¹, 220, 269 *sqq.*

1 . . . I hear also that there has been published an edict and a peremptory one too. The Pontifex Maximus,[40] that is, the bishop of the bishops, has issued a decree. "I remit to such as have done penance[41] the sins of adultery and fornication."[42] O edict that cannot be called "approved"! Where shall this liberality be posted up? On the spot, I should suppose; directly on the gates of lust, beneath the roofs dedicated to it! That is the place for publishing such a penance, where the sin itself makes its home. That is the place for reading the pardon, where men enter confidently expecting it. But this edict is read in church and proclaimed

[40] The title, of course, of the head of the Roman state religion, used ironically here for the head of the Roman church. Jaffé (*Regesta Pontificum Romanorum,* Vol. I, p. 12) thinks that the reference is to Zephyrinus and that Tertullian wrote this passage before 205. The majority of scholars take it to mean Callistus.

[41] *Paenitentia functis.*

[42] These sins of unchastity had previously been considered unpardonable. *Supra,* p. 243.

aloud in church, although the Church is virgin. Away, away, with such displays from the bride of Christ.

. . . .

21 So produce anew for me, O successor of the apostles, your examples from the prophets and I will admit the right divine. But you arrogate to yourself the vast power of forgiveness of sins, although what you have is only the duty of maintaining discipline, not the headship of an empire but of a ministry. Who and what are you to show mercy, who conduct yourself neither as prophet nor as apostle and are destitute of the virtue that is necessary for one who is merciful? "But," you say, "the Church has the power of forgiving sins." If, because the Lord said to Peter: "Upon this rock I will build my Church, . . . to thee have I given the keys of the kingdom of heaven," or: "Whatsoever thou shalt bind or loose on earth shall be bound or loosed in heaven," you therefore assume that the power of binding and loosing has descended to you or to any church related to Peter, what sort of man are you, overthrowing and transforming the manifest intention of the Lord, who conferred the gift personally upon Peter? "On thee," he says, "will I build my Church," and "I will give unto thee the keys," not "unto the Church"; and "whatsoever thou shalt loose or bind," not "whatsoever they shall loose or bind."

This is proved indeed by subsequent events. On Peter in person the Church was reared, that is, through him. He it was who first employed the key. See: "Men of Israel, let what I say sink into your ears! Jesus of Nazareth, a man destined by God for you,"[43] and so on. He, likewise, was the first to unbar in baptism through Christ the entrance to the heavenly kingdom, where the sins that were aforetime bound are loosed and those that are not loosed are bound, according to true salvation. Ananias he bound

[43] Acts, II, 22.

with the chain of death and the weak in the feet he loosed from his infirmity.[44] Moreover, in the dispute as to the observance or non-observance of the law, Peter was first of all to be imbued with the Spirit and to proclaim the calling of the gentiles, saying: "Why do ye tempt the Lord to lay upon the brethren a yoke which neither we nor our fathers were able to bear? Nevertheless through the grace of Jesus we believe that we shall be saved even as they."[45] These words both loosed the parts of the law which they then disregarded and bound those which they kept.

Furthermore, the power of loosing and binding delivered to Peter had naught to do with the mortal sins of believers. If the Lord bade him be merciful to a brother who had sinned against him seventy times seven,[46] surely he would have commanded him to bind, that is retain, no sin committed still later, except only such as the man committed against the Lord, not against a brother. For the very right to forgive sins committed against a man is itself a sentence against the forgiveness of sins against God.

What now has this to do with the Church and in particular your church, O follower of the Spirit?[47] As this power was conferred upon Peter personally, so it belongs to spiritual men, whether apostle or prophet. For the true Church is by nature and origin the Spirit himself, in whom is the Trinity of the one Godhead, Father, Son and Holy Spirit. He unites together that Church which the Lord made to consist of three. So ever since then, any number of persons who join together in faith is accounted a church by its Author and Consecrator. The Church, indeed, will forgive sins but only the Church of the Spirit, through the voice of a spiritual man, not the Church which is merely a collec-

44 Acts, III, 7.
45 Acts, XV, 10, 11.
46 Matthew, XVIII, 22.
47 "Psychic." The Montanists called themselves men of the Spirit in contrast to the orthodox, governed by tradition and a clerical hierarchy.

tion of bishops. For justice and judgment belong to the Lord, not to a servant; to God alone, not to a priest.

Hippolytus, *Refutatio Omnium Haeresium*, IX, 2, 5–7. Text. J. P. Migne, *Patrologia Graeca*, XVI, Pt. 3, 3369–3372, 3377–3388.[48]

2 There appeared a man, Noetus by name, a native of Smyrna, who introduced a heresy based upon the theories of Heraclitus. And a man called Epigonus became his assistant and pupil and during a sojourn at Rome disseminated there his impious opinions. Then Cleomenes, an alien from the church in way of life and conduct, became his disciple and confirmed his doctrines. At that time Zephyrinus, a dull and disgracefully corrupt person, imagined that he was governing the church. He was induced by bribes to connive at those who met to be taught by Cleomenes and he himself, in course of time, was enticed away and fell headlong into the same error, with Callistus as his adviser and champion in these wicked ideas. As for the life of Callistus and the heresy invented by him, I shall describe them a little later. During the successive terms of these bishops, the heretical school grew stronger and increased in numbers, because Zephyrinus and Callistus helped them. Yet never have we joined with them but have often opposed and reasoned with them and forced them to acknowledge reluctantly the truth. And they, abashed and constrained by the truth, have for the moment confessed their errors but soon wallowed again in the same mire.

5 . . . Now everyone knows that he [Noetus] says that the Son and the Father are the same. For he uses the following words: " So even when the Father had not been born, he yet was rightfully called Father; and when it

[48] The authorship of the *Refutatio* has been only recently established. The book is printed in Migne among the works of Origen. In that text, the numbering of the chapters here translated is 7, 10–12.

pleased him to undergo birth, he was born and was born his own Son, not another's." And thus he thinks to establish the undivided sovereignty [49] of God by maintaining that the Father and Son so-called are one and the same, not one person produced from another, but himself from himself, and that God is called by the name of Father or Son with the changes of time, but that he is the one who was made manifest and endured birth from a virgin and dwelt as a man among men. By reason of the birth by which he was born he declared himself a Son to those who saw him; yet to those who comprehended him he made no secret of his being the Father. He was nailed to a tree and suffered and he commended his spirit unto himself and died, yet he did not die. And on the third day he raised himself up. . . .

6 Callistus supported this heresy, for he was a man fertile in wickedness and subtle in deceit, scheming to secure the episcopal chair. Zephyrinus was a dull and uneducated man, ignorant of ecclesiastical terminology, whom Callistus was able to seduce by gifts and illicit pressure to take whatever course of action he pleased, for he was open to bribery and loved money. In this way Callistus continually worked upon him to create disturbances among the brethren, while he himself then took care by crafty words to attach both factions to himself. . . . [Callistus contaminates Sabellius with the heresy of Cleomenes.]

And Callistus brought forward Zephyrinus himself and persuaded him to say in public: " I know that there is one God, Christ Jesus, and I know that there is no other but him, who was born and suffered." And again he said: " The Father did not die but the Son." In this way Callistus stirred up ceaseless controversy among the people. But we, who understood his motives, did not yield to him but reproved and withstood him for the truth's sake. And he

49 μοναρχίαν. This is known as the Monarchian doctrine.

sank deep into folly because everyone acquiesced in his hypocrisy, although we did not, and he called us ditheists,[50] venting fiercely upon us the venom concealed within him. It seems advisable to us now to give some account of his life, inasmuch as he was born about the same time as ourselves, so that, when we have exposed the man's character, the heresy which he attempted to establish may be plainly recognized and perhaps seen to be senseless by persons of intelligence. He became a martyr[51] during the time when Fuscianus was prefect of Rome and the manner of his martyrdom was as follows.

7 Callistus was a slave of one Carpophorus, a man of the faith, belonging to Caesar's household.[52] To him, as a member of the faith, Carpophorus entrusted a considerable sum of money with directions to invest it in the business of banking. On receipt of the money, Callistus attempted to start a bank in the quarter known as Piscina Publica[53] and eventually many deposits were committed to him, as Carpophorus' representative, by widows and brethren. However, he made away with everything and fell into great difficulties. And after he had reached that condition, someone informed Carpophorus, who told him that he would require an account from him. Then Callistus, realizing all

[50] That is to say, that the orthodox in acknowledging two persons in the Godhead were acknowledging two gods.

[51] Another instance of the use of the word "martyr" in its early sense of witness for the faith. Fuscianus did not put Callistus to death, only sent him to the mines, as we shall see. Tradition, however, in time made Callistus a martyr again in his death and his name is venerated on October the 14th. *Vide Acta Sanctorum* under the date.

[52] During the reign of Commodus, there was an influx of new members into the church from the higher social circles. Eusebius, writing of the period, says: "A large number of people in Rome, distinguished for wealth or birth, turned unto salvation, together with all their households and families." *Historia Ecclesiastica,* V, 21, 1. This Carpophorus may be the one who about this time erected a funeral monument at Rome to himself, his family, including his brother, nephews, foster son and their freedmen, and his own freed slaves and their children. The inscription, while not Christian, contains no sign of paganism. A. Harnack, *The Mission and Expansion of Christianity,* Vol. II, p. 47, n. 2.

[53] Πισκινῇ πουβλικῇ. The Latin name is written out by Hippolytus in Greek letters. The Piscina or Fishmarket was one of the fourteen districts of Rome and a resort of money-lenders.

this and anticipating danger from his master, fled in haste and made for the sea. And finding a ship at Portus ready to sail he went aboard, expecting to sail to whatever place she happened to be bound. But he could not escape detection in that way, for someone sent word to Carpophorus of what had happened. On hearing the news Carpophorus went immediately to Portus and tried to reach the ship, which was anchored in the middle of the harbor. But as the boatman was a slow rower, Callistus in the ship saw his master from afar off and, realizing that he was overtaken, became reckless of life and in despair threw himself into the sea. But the sailors jumped into their boats and pulled him out against his will, while the people on shore raised loud shouts. Thus he was handed back to his master and brought to Rome and lodged by his master in the Pistrinum.[54]

But after some time had passed, brethren came to Carpophorus, as they are wont to do, and urged him to release the fugitive from punishment, telling him that Callistus claimed to have funds on deposit with certain parties. Then Carpophorus, who was a devout man, said that he cared nothing for his own property but that he was concerned for the moneys entrusted to Callistus; for many had wept, as they told him that they had committed their money to Callistus in the belief that he was Carpophorus' representative. But Carpophorus yielded to the persuasion and ordered that Callistus be set free. The latter, however, being obliged to pay back and unable to abscond again because he was watched, planned a scheme to bring about his own death. On a Sabbath, he pretended that he was going to his creditors and he broke into the synagogue of the assembled Jews and standing there provoked them to a tumult. Then they, under his provocation, insulted and beat him and haled him before Fuscianus, who was prefect of the city.

[54] Πίστρινον, the domestic treadmill of Roman slaveholders.

And they entered the following complaint: "The Romans have allowed us to read in public the laws of our fathers, but this man came in and tried to hinder us and provoked a disturbance among us, declaring that he was a Christian." Fuscianus happened to be at that hour upon the judgment seat and he was indignant with Callistus on account of the Jews' accusation. Then someone told Carpophorus what was taking place and he hastened to the prefect's judgment seat and exclaimed: "I beg you, my lord Fuscianus, do not believe this fellow; for he is not a Christian but is looking for a chance to die, because he has squandered a quantity of my money, as I will prove." The Jews, however, imagined that this was a stratagem and that Carpophorus was trying under this pretext to save Callistus, so with the more bitterness they clamored against him before the prefect. And Fuscianus was moved by the Jews and after scourging Callistus he sent him to a mine in Sardinia.[55]

But, after a time, Marcia,[56] a concubine of Commodus, a devout woman, was desirous of performing some good deed and she summoned before her the blessed Victor, who was then bishop of the church, and inquired of him what martyrs were in Sardinia, for there were other martyrs there. And he gave her the names of them all but did not include Callistus, for he knew the wrong he had done. Then Marcia obtained her petition from Commodus and delivered the order of release to Hyacinthus, a eunuch of great age. And he took it and sailed to Sardinia and presented it to the man who was then governor of the region and set free the martyrs, all but Callistus. Then Callistus fell upon his knees and with tears implored that he also be released. So Hyacinthus, overcome by his importunity, requested the governor for him and said that it was an oversight of Marcia

[55] The air of Sardinia was considered unwholesome and for that reason the island was often selected as a place of exile for criminals. Hippolytus himself in his old age was banished thither with Bishop Pontianus.

[56] On Marcia and Victor, *vide supra*, p. 275.

and promised the governor that he should run no risk. In this way the latter was persuaded and liberated Callistus also. When Callistus returned, Victor was much displeased at what had happened but since he was a compassionate man, he let it go. But in order to protect himself from numerous reproaches, for the escapades of Callistus were not yet long past, and because Carpophorus was still indignant with him, Victor sent Callistus to live in Antium, assigning him a monthly sum for food. And after Victor's death, Zephyrinus had Callistus as assistant in the management of the clergy and showed him honor to his own hurt. He also transferred him from Antium and put him in charge of a cemetery.

Callistus, who was constantly in the company of Zephyrinus and, as I have already said, paid him false service, represented him abroad as a man able neither to form a judgment upon what was told him nor to comprehend Callistus' own purposes, but all his conversation with Zephyrinus was planned to flatter him. Then, after the death of Zephyrinus, when he saw he had secured the position for which he was struggling,[57] he expelled Sabellius, on the ground that he held unorthodox views, doing this in fear of me and fancying that by this act he could avert an accusation before the churches and prove that his own opinions were not heterodox. Thus he was an impostor and a knave and in course of time carried many away with him. . . . [Description of Callistus' heretical theology.] He asserts that the same Logos is both Son and Father and though called by a different name, is the one, indivisible Spirit; that the Father is not one person and the Son another, but they are one and the same; that all things are full of the divine Spirit, things above and things below, and that the Spirit that became incarnate in the Virgin is not other than the Father but one and the same. . . . "For,"

[57] *I.e.*, the bishopric.

he says, "I shall not profess two gods, Father and Son, but one." . . . At one moment he lapsed into the doctrine of Sabellius, at another into that of Theodore,[58] and was not ashamed.

Having embraced these errors, the impostor established a school to teach the aforesaid doctrine in opposition to the church. And he was the first to devise the idea of indulging men in their pleasures by declaring that he would forgive everyone's sins. So if a man who attends some other congregation and is considered a Christian commits a transgression, his sin, they say, is not reckoned against him, provided he promptly joins the school of Callistus. And numerous persons who had been stricken in conscience and some who had left various heresies and some who had, in accordance with our rule, been expelled by us from the church, were relieved at his declaration and united with the rest and crowded his school. He also propounded the view that if a bishop commits sin, even a sin unto death, he need not be deposed. In his time, bishops, priests, and deacons who had been twice or thrice married began to be installed among the clergy and if one of the clergy married, he continued in the clergy as if he had not sinned,[59] for Callistus maintained that with regard to such a man the words of the apostle had been spoken: "Who art thou that judgest another man's servant?"[60] He insisted further that the parable of the tares was intended for such a case. "Let the tares grow together with the wheat!"[61] That is, let the sinners remain in the Church! He likewise said that the ark of Noah was a symbol of the Church, for in it were dogs, wolves, ravens and everything clean and unclean; and

[58] These stood at the two opposite wings of Unitarianism. *Supra,* pp. 279, 300.

[59] By Canon XVII of the Apostolic Constitutions, a man twice married after baptism could not be admitted to the clergy; by Canon XXVI, a man after admission to the clergy could not marry at all. *Vide* Bishop Siricius on this subject, at the end of the next century. *Infra,* pp. 702–706.

[60] Romans, XIV, 4.

[61] Matthew, XIII, 30.

so, he declared, it must also be in the Church. Whatever passages he could collect bearing on this subject he interpreted in this way.[62]

His hearers delight in his teachings and cling to him, deluding themselves, and crowds pour into his school. So they increase in numbers and boast of the multitudes that come in search of pleasures that Christ forbade. In disdain of him they prohibit no sin, proclaiming that Callistus pardons everyone who believes with him. He has even permitted women who were unmarried and were inflamed by passion unfitting to their age or who were unwilling to forfeit their rank by a legal marriage, to have whatever man they chose as concubine, whether he were slave or free, and to regard him as their husband, although they were not legally married to him.[63] . . . [Further details as to such irregular relations.] After such brazen conduct these shameless people dare to call themselves a catholic [64] church. And other persons, supposing that they will benefit themselves, join with them. During Callistus' episcopate, they have for the first time presumptuously administered second baptism.[65]

[62] The frequency with which Peter's denial of Christ was portrayed on Roman Christian sarcophagi and other monuments of the third and fourth centuries may be due to the fact that the incident seemed to justify the Roman practice of re-admitting sinners. W. Lowrie, *Christian Art and Archaeology*, pp. 260 *sqq*. *Cf.* the use of Peter's doubt on the water in a plea for pardon in the late second century. *Acts of Peter*. *Supra*, p. 139.

[63] Women of high birth apparently outnumbered men of the same rank in the Church at this time and there seems to have been a danger that they would either marry pagans or form secret, illicit connections to avoid losing caste by openly marrying Christians of a rank beneath them. Callistus proposed to recognize in the Church such irregular unions, even without legal marriage. Tertullian was already advising Christian girls of wealth to marry poor young men. *Ad Uxores*, II, 8. Canon XV of the synod of Elvira, held about 303, ran: " Christian girls are not, because they are very numerous, to be married off to pagans, lest their youth and hot blood make them relax into adultery of the soul." A. Harnack, *The Mission and Expansion of Christianity*, Vol. II, pp. 82–83.

[64] On this word *vide supra*, pp. 240, n. 11, 286.

[65] The problem had now presented itself as to whether converts from an heretical sect should be baptized afresh upon their admission into the Church or whether the baptism which they had received from a heretic should be accepted by the Church as valid. Did the efficacy of the sacrament depend upon the hand that administered it? Except at this time, the Roman bishops took the position that a second baptism was not only unnecessary but actually sacrilegious. *Vide infra*, pp. 395 ff.

Such then is the system instituted by the astounding Callistus. And his school still persists and preserves its customs and traditions, not distinguishing the persons with whom one should communicate but offering communion indiscriminately to everyone. From him also they have derived their name, for, since Callistus was the author of their practices, they are called Callistians.

2. THE CASE OF ORIGEN

Pontianus

(230–235)

Again, at a critical time, the documents disappear and we have almost no authentic information about the bishops who succeeded Callistus. The brief epitaph of Urban I (c. 222–230) is in the episcopal crypt of the cemetery of Callistus.[66] Pontianus, as we have already said, died in banishment in Sardinia, according to a statement found in the fourth century Liberian Catalogue of Roman bishops,[67] and his body was brought back to Rome for interment in the same crypt. The only act ascribed to him is mentioned by Jerome, who toward the end of the following century looked up the records connected with the life of his hero, Origen. In 231 or 232, Origen was tried and condemned for ecclesiastical insubordination, self-mutilation, and heterodoxy by a synod of eastern bishops under the presidency of Demetrius of Alexandria.[68] He was by this time famous far and wide as the greatest Christian teacher and scholar of the day and his condemnation was a matter of more than local importance. Other bishops in Asia and Greece protested against it and made him welcome in their own communions. Jerome says that the bishop of Rome called a synod of his own to review the case and that he ratified the sentence passed at Alexandria. It was, technically speaking, an assumption of jurisdiction over a member of another venerable and independent diocese but the

66 L. Duchesne, *Liber Pontificalis,* Vol. I, p. 143, n. 5.

67 *Infra*, p. 712.

68 *Supra*, pp. 88–89.

Asiatic bishops had, perhaps, given ground for it by their refusal to accept the judgment of Alexandria. As Pontianus only confirmed the verdict of the local tribunal, his action aroused no resentment in that quarter. To Jerome's mind the motive behind all this hostility to Origen was chiefly envy of his genius.

Jerome, *Epistolae,* XXXIII, *Ad Paulam.* Text. J. P. Migne, *Patrologia Latina,* XXII, 447.

. . . Who could ever read as much as he [Origen] wrote? For his toil what recompense did he receive? He was condemned by Bishop Demetrius, in spite of the dissent of the prelates of Palestine, Arabia, Phoenicia and Achaea. The city of Rome confirmed his condemnation; there too a synod was summoned to act against him, not because of the novelty of his doctrine nor because of his heresy, as some yelping hounds now pretend, in order to disparage him, but because they could not tolerate the splendor of his eloquence and learning and because, when he spoke, everyone else seemed dumb.

FABIANUS

(236–250)

After the banishment of Pontianus and the six weeks pontificate of Anteros came the fourteen years of the bishop Fabianus. Eusebius, seventy-five years later, had a pleasant story of Fabianus' election, which we repeat chiefly because Eusebius thought it worth telling. Under the tolerant protection of the emperors Gordian and Philip the Roman church multiplied at so rapid a rate and its membership was scattered so widely up and down the seven hills that Fabianus, during his term of office, found it advisable to divide the city into seven ecclesiastical districts for purposes of administration and to put the executive affairs of each district under the supervision of a deacon.[69] The church by this time had considerable funds at

[69] *Vide The Liberian Catalogue, infra,* p. 712.

its disposal and its affairs included relief of the poor, care of widows, orphans and sick, and the construction and management of cemeteries.[70]

Outside of Rome, the question of Origen's standing in the Church was still a matter of heated dispute. Whether he wrote to Fabianus in an effort to procure from him a reversal of the verdict passed upon himself by Pontianus [71] or whether, as seems more likely, his enemies had started some new agitation over some fresh piece of his writing, which he feared might stir up Fabianus to undertake more judicial proceedings on his own account, we do not know. Both Eusebius and Jerome seem to have read Origen's letter but neither one tells us much about its content. However, the bare fact that he thought it important to make an apology and defense to this remote see, as well as to those in his own neighborhood, is significant enough.

Fabianus died a martyr, January 20, 250, one of the first victims of the sudden outbreak of systematic persecution under Decius.[72] A feature of this persecution was the imperial order to strike at the leaders of the Christians. Who, therefore, so sure to be taken at the start as the bishop of the church of Rome? The place that he filled in Decius' estimation may be gauged by the remark attributed to the emperor a little later that he would rather hear of the appearance of a rival prince than of a new bishop in the capital.[73] For over a year the Romans did not dare to choose another. But the persecution itself and its effects upon the Church will be discussed more fully in connection with the letters of Cyprian.[74]

On the ecclesiastical districts of Fabianus see L. Duchesne, *Melanges d'Archéologie et d'Histoire,* Vol. I, p. 126; F. Gregorovius, *History of the City of Rome in the Middle Ages* (trans. by A. Hamilton, 8 vols., London, 1894–1912), Vol. I, pp. 80–82.

[70] See Cornelius' description of the Roman church in 251, *infra,* p. 384.
[71] *Supra,* p. 313.
[72] For more about his martyrdom, *infra,* pp. 331, 337 and n. 118.
[73] *Infra,* p. 372.
[74] *Infra,* pp. 329 ff.

Eusebius, *Historia Ecclesiastica,* VI, Chap. 29, 2–4. Text. *Eusebius Werke* (*Die griechischen christlichen Schriftsteller der ersten drei Jahrhunderte*), II², 582–584.

They say that Fabianus, after the death of Anteros, had come from the country to meet with the rest and was stopping at Rome and was there elected to the office through a marvel of divine and celestial grace. For when all the brethren were assembled to elect the one who should succeed to the bishopric, the majority were considering various distinguished and honorable men, and Fabianus, though present, was in no one's mind. But suddenly, they say, a dove flew in from the sky and alighted on his head, thus reproducing the descent of the Holy Spirit in the form of a dove upon the Savior. Thereupon the people, all as if impelled by one divine spirit, with one united and eager voice cried out that he was worthy and immediately they took and set him upon the episcopal seat.

Eusebius, *op. cit.,* VI, 36, 4. Text. *Op. cit.,* II², 590–592.

He [Origen] wrote also to Fabianus, bishop at Rome, and to many other rulers of the churches regarding his own orthodoxy.

Jerome, *Epistolae,* LXXXIV, *Ad Pammachium et Oceanum.* Text. J. P. Migne, *Patrologia Latina,* XXII, 751.

Origen himself, in the letter which he writes to Fabianus, bishop of the city of Rome, professes his penitence for writing such things and lays the blame of indiscretion on Ambrosius [75] because he had published a private composition.

[75] A wealthy friend of Origen, who provided him with means to write and supplied the copyists.

Origen of Alexandria

(c. 185–c. 254)

The following excerpts show something of the attitude of Origen [76] toward the church of Rome and the wider authority claimed during his lifetime by the Roman bishop. While he was still a young man and teaching undisturbed at Alexandria, amassing the vast knowledge that displayed itself later in his writings, he took a journey to Italy expressly in order to see "the ancient church of Rome." His master Clement, as we have noted, had failed to visit Rome in his wanderjähre [77] and Origen may have wanted to find out what it had to give. He went during the pontificate of Zephyrinus, probably between 211 and 217.[78] It is hard that whatever comments he made on what he saw have long ago been lost. If only we had them to set beside Hippolytus!

Fifteen or twenty years later, Origen was compelled by high-handed procedure on the part of his bishop Demetrius to leave Alexandria under a sentence of excommunication. The bishops of Syria, Arabia, and Greece, who understood the situation, resented the manner in which he had been dealt with and refused to recognize the ban. The Roman bishop Pontianus, who must have known less about the circumstances, took, as we have seen, the side of the regularly constituted government and added the weight of Roman condemnation to the verdict of Egypt.[79] The result was a temporary division in the Church. When, a few years afterward, a new accusation of heterodoxy was brought against Origen by his enemies, which seemed likely to offer excuse for more action at Rome, Origen wrote to Fabianus, Pontianus' successor, as well as to other prominent bishops, to explain that his offending book had not been intended for publication and that he repented having written it.[80] A letter of that kind, from a man already excommunicated by his own

[76] On Origen *vide supra*, pp. 87, 312, 314.

[77] *Supra*, p. 273.

[78] Eusebius mentions this visit among the events of the reign of Caracalla.

[79] *Supra*, p. 313.

[80] *Supra*, p. 315.

bishop, was in effect an appeal to the other governors of the Church to refrain from concurrence with their colleague's judgment. What response it awakened in Fabianus we do not know.

Between 246 and 248, Origen wrote an exposition of the Matthew passage, in the course of which he rejected emphatically the Roman legalistic theory of the keys bestowed upon Peter to be bequeathed to the Roman bishops and developed with characteristic elaborateness the mystic idea of Tertullian [81] that they were given as a reward of faith to Peter and to all who were faithful like him. Whether he wrote this commentary before or after his letter to Fabianus, we would give much to hear. The commentary is our last word from Origen on the subject. We shall soon have opportunity to observe the attitude of his pupils.[82]

Eusebius, *Historia Ecclesiastica,* VI, 14, 10. Text. *Eusebius Werke (Die griechischen christlichen Schriftsteller der ersten drei Jahrhunderte),* II^2, 552.

Now Adamantius, for Origen was known also by that name, visited Rome, as he himself somewhere says, while Zephyrinus was head of the Roman church, because he desired, he says, " to see the ancient church of the Romans." After a short stay there, he returned to Alexandria.

Origen, *In Matthaeum,* XII, 10, 11, 14. Text. J. P. Migne, *Patrologia Graeca,* XIII, 995 *sqq.*

10 And, perhaps, if we make like Peter the answer that Simon Peter made: " Thou art the Christ, the Son of the living God," [83] not through revelation of flesh and blood to us but by a light from the Father in heaven illuminating our hearts, we too become like Peter and are blessed as he was, because the reason for his blessing has become ours, since

[81] Compare Tertullian's exposition with Origen's. *Supra,* pp. 302–304.
[82] *Infra,* pp. 398, 411, 419.
[83] Matthew, XVI, 16.

flesh and blood have not revealed to us that Jesus is Christ, the Son of the living God, but the Father in heaven from the very heavens, so that our citizenship may be in heaven, has revealed to us the revelation that exalts to heaven those who tear away every veil from the heart and receive the spirit of the wisdom and revelation of God. And if we too say like Peter: " Thou art the Christ, the Son of the living God," not as if flesh and blood had revealed it to us but as if a light from the Father in heaven had shone in our hearts, we become a Peter and to us the Word might say: " Thou art Peter," etc. For every disciple of Christ, from whom those drank who drank of the spiritual rock that followed them,[84] is also himself a rock. And upon all these rocks is built every word of the Church and its harmonious polity, for upon each of the perfect, who combine words and deeds and thoughts to fill up blessedness, is the Church built by God.

11 But if you imagine that the whole Church is built by God upon that one Peter alone, what will you do with John, the son of thunder,[85] or any other of the apostles? Or shall we go yet further and dare to say that against Peter alone the gates of hell shall not prevail but that they shall prevail against the other apostles and the perfect? Does not the promise: " The gates of hell shall not prevail against it," hold with regard to everyone and to each one of them? As also the saying: " Upon this rock I will build my Church "? Are the keys of the kingdom of heaven given by the Lord to Peter only and shall no other of the blessed receive them? But if the promise: " I will give unto thee the keys of the kingdom of heaven," belongs also to the rest, why do not all the promises just mentioned and the words that are subjoined as addressed to Peter, belong to them? For although in this passage the following words seem to be addressed to Peter alone: " Whatsoever thou shalt bind on earth shall

[84] I Corinthians, X, 4. [85] Mark, III, 17.

be bound in heaven," etc., in the Gospel of John the Savior, after giving the Holy Spirit to the disciples and breathing upon them, says: " Receive ye the Holy Ghost," etc.[86]

Therefore, many will say to the Savior: " Thou art the Christ, the Son of the living God "; but not all who say it will say it to him by revelation not from flesh and blood but from the Father in heaven, who takes away the veil that has lain upon their hearts, in order that henceforth, " with unveiled face reflecting as in a glass the glory of the Lord," [87] they may speak through the Spirit of God and say of him: " Lord Jesus," and to him: " Thou art the Christ, the Son of the living God." And if anyone says this to him, not through revelation of flesh and blood but through the Father in heaven, he will obtain the promises that were spoken in the letter of the gospel to Peter only, but in the spirit of the gospel to everyone who becomes what Peter was. For all have the surname of " rock " who are imitators of Christ, that is, of the spiritual rock that follows those who are saved,[88] that they may drink from it the spiritual draught. They have the surname of " rock," as Christ has. Furthermore, as members of Christ, they derive a surname from him and are called Christians, while from the rock they are called Peters. So, reasoning on from this, you may say that the righteous have the surname of Christ, who is Righteousness, and the wise of Christ, who is Wisdom, and thus with all his other names you may apply them as surnames to the saints. To all such persons the words of the Savior might be spoken: " Thou art Peter," etc., down to the words: " prevail against it."

But what is the " it "? Is it the rock upon which Christ builds the Church or is it the Church? The phrase is am-

[86] John, XX, 22, 23. " Receive ye the Holy Ghost; whose sins you shall forgive, they are forgiven them, and whose sins you shall retain, they are retained." It is curious that Origen does not use Matthew XVIII, 18.

[87] II Corinthians, III, 18.

[88] I Corinthians, X, 4.

biguous. Or are the rock and the Church one and the same? The last, I think, is the truth, for the gates of hell shall not prevail either against the rock upon which Christ builds the Church or against the Church itself, even as the way of a serpent on a rock, according to the word in Proverbs, cannot be found.[89] Now if the gates of hell prevail against anyone, he cannot be a rock upon which Christ builds his Church nor the Church built by Jesus on a rock, for the rock is inaccessible to the serpent. It is stronger than the gates of hell that are opposed to it, so that by reason of its strength the gates of hell do not prevail against it. As the building of Christ, who built his own house wisely on a rock,[90] the Church cannot be opened to the gates of hell, which prevail against everyone who is outside the rock and the Church, but which have no might against it.

12 [Origen considers what is meant by a "gate of hell" and decides that it is every sin and every false doctrine.[91]]

13 [He draws a contrast with the "gates of Zion," which are the virtues.]

14 Next let us see in what sense it is said to Peter and to every Peter: "I will give unto thee the keys of the kingdom of heaven." [The remainder of the paragraph describes the virtues that enable one to open the heavenly gates.]

But consider how great is the might of the rock upon which the Church was built by Christ and how great is the might of everyone who says: "Thou art the Christ, the Son of the Living God." His judgments abide sure as if God were judging through him, so that in his act the gates of hell shall not prevail against him. But when anyone judges unrighteously and does not bind on earth according to the word of God nor loose on earth according to his will,

89 Proverbs, XXX, 18–19.
90 Matthew, VII, 24–25.
91 *I.e.*, according to Erasmus, every sin on account of which Christ was about to descend to Hades.

the gates of hell prevail against him. Wherever the gates of hell do not prevail against a man, he is judging righteously. Therefore, he has the keys of the kingdom of heaven, opening to those who have been loosed on earth, that they may also be loosed and free in heaven, and shutting to those who by his just judgment have been bound on earth, that they may also be bound and condemned in heaven.

But when those who fill the office of bishop [92] make use of this saying, as if they were Peter, and teach that they have received the keys of the kingdom from the Savior and that whatever is bound, that is, condemned by them, is also bound in heaven, and whatever is allowed by them is loosed in heaven, we must reply that they are right, if they pursue the way of life for which that other Peter was told: "Thou art Peter." If they are men such that upon them Christ might build the Church, the saying may be applied to them with good reason and the gates of hell should not prevail against them, when they wish to bind and loose. But if a bishop is tightly bound with the cords of his own sins,[93] he binds and looses to no avail. You may, perhaps, say that in the heaven which is within the wise man, that is, the virtues, the evil man is bound, and also that through these virtues he may be loosed and receive pardon for the sins that he committed before his virtues. But as not even God can bind a man unless he wears the cords of sin or iniquity like a "long rope or the strap of the yoke of a heifer," [94] no more can any Peter, whoever he may be, bind him. And if anyone who is not a Peter and does not possess what we have here described imagines that, as Peter, he will so bind on earth that whatever he binds is bound in heaven and so loose on earth that whatever he looses is

92 Other bishops, beside the Roman, were by this time claiming the power to bind and loose, as successors also of Peter and of the Twelve. See the third century *Didascalia*, *supra*, p. 157. Also Cyprian, *infra*, pp. 328, 406. Origen may be thinking of Demetrius as well as of Pontianus.

93 Proverbs, V, 22.

94 Isaias, V, 18.

loosed in heaven, he is puffed up, not understanding the meaning of the Scriptures, and being puffed up, has fallen into the destruction of the devil.

3. THE COÖPERATION OF ROME AND CARTHAGE

Cyprian of Carthage

(c. 200–258)

While Tertullian was living out his exacerbated old age in Carthage, there was growing up in the same city one Thascius Cyprianus, a young man of well-to-do parentage, a good education and the gifts of a clear mind and much practical energy. We know nothing of the character of his early years but by 246, when he had reached middle life, he was a lawyer, as Tertullian had been, with a name for eloquence and ability, an owner of landed property and a person of consequence generally in provincial circles. What was his religious belief we do not know nor how his attention came to be caught by Christianity. We are told merely that at this point in his career he became converted and that he sold most of his farms and gardens for the benefit of the poor. He also set himself with ardor to master the sacred books, the code of his new faith, and studied industriously the Scriptures and the writings of Tertullian. In 248, when the bishop of Carthage died, Cyprian, although only two years a Christian and still a novice in the church, was already so prominent in the eyes of the community that public opinion demanded his consecration to fill the empty place. In spite of his own resistance, he was set forthwith in the episcopal chair. A group of priests, who felt, perhaps, that men longer in the service were being unfairly slighted, remained dissatisfied, ready to foment trouble, but for the first year Cyprian met no serious opposition.

The treatises and correspondence of Cyprian during the eight years that follow, 250–258, illumine for us, as nothing else begins to do, the western church of the third century. The letters we shall utilize hereafter in so far as they throw light on the situation at Rome during that period. We quote here some extracts from his writings that show his conception of the office of bishop and the government of the Church. His clear and telling method of statement made his works popular as those of no other Christian author of the age and his thought was to influence church polity more than that of many profounder men for centuries afterward.

One must remember in reading Cyprian that most of his life had been spent as a pagan and a lawyer. To him the Church is a visible society, supernaturally ordained, of course, but at the same time political in type, with fixed laws and government and privileges for its members according to their rank, as orderly as any state. All outside it are outside the grace of God, as barbarians outside the Empire are outside the emperor's protection. Within the Church are the laity and clergy, the latter constituting the officialdom, possessing authority by direct transmission from the apostles and acting as guardians of doctrine and dispensers of salvation, even as civil magistrates guard the law and administer the imperial will. Whoever is estranged from his bishop is estranged also from the Church and from its divine sovereign. Cyprian does not employ this secular language, but strip his thought of its Christian nomenclature and it amounts to this. As for the power of the keys, his view is a variation on the Roman theory of a grant of authority for an office. To him it is clear that under God, the supreme Ruler, the government of the Church is in the hands of an aristocracy of equal bishops, each a successor of the apostles and responsible only to God, each with an equal share of the right to bind and loose. The Matthew passage is broadened by bringing in the text from John and applying them both to all bishops. Yet the keys were bestowed at first on Peter alone and he alone was made the foundation of the Church. The interpretation here ceases to be purely legalistic and takes a mystical turn. One man, indeed, was chosen for honor at the outset, in order that through him might be symbolized the unity of the episcopate and the Church. Peter and after him his successors at Rome stand as corporeal reminders of the unity of the organization that underlies the diversity of its members, somewhat as the modern British king typifies the unity of the British Empire. But neither Peter nor the Roman bishops have any longer superiority of power over the other apostles or the other bishops.

Cyprian, therefore, parts company here with the later Tertullian.[95] His theory, like the Roman, is one of sacerdotal function. He differs from the Romans merely in safeguarding the independence of the whole apostolic episcopate. Yet he concedes a special significance to Peter; and a few trifling alterations in his statements, a small interpolation here and there, would transform his acknowledgment of Peter's significance into one of Peter's preponderance. Such alterations had been made by an unknown hand before the close of the sixth century in the text of the most widely read of all Cyprian's works, the *De Catholicae Ecclesiae Unitate,* which thenceforth was employed through the Middle Ages as one of the strong supports for the theory of the papal autocracy.

Much has always been written about Cyprian. Some of the more recent discussions are E. W. Benson, *Cyprian, his Life, his Times, his Work* (London, 1897); J. Langen, *Geschichte der römischen Kirche* (4 vols., Bonn, 1881–1893), Vol. I, pp. 275 *sqq.,* Vol. II, p. 408; R. Sohm, *Kirchenrecht* (Leipzig, 1892), pp. 15 *sqq.*; P. Monceau, *Histoire Litteraire de l'Afrique Chrétienne, depuis les Origines jusqu'à l'Invasion Arabe* (3 vols., Paris, 1901–1905), Vol. II, *St. Cyprien et son Temps*; J. Chapman, *Les Interpolations dans le Traité de St. Cyprien sur l'Unité de l'Église* in *Revue Benedictine* (Maredsous, 1902), Vol. XIX, pp. 246 *sqq.,* 357 *sqq.*; Vol. XX, pp. 26 *sqq.*; J. Chapman, *The Interpolations in St. Cyprian's De Unitate Ecclesiae* in *Journal of Theological Studies* (London, 1904), Vol. V, pp. 634 *sqq.*; J. Chapman, *Cyprian* in *Catholic Encyclopaedia* (15 vols., New York, 1907–1912), Vol. IV; H. Koch, *Cyprian und der römische Primat* (Leipzig, 1910); H. M. Gwatkin, *Early Church History to A.D. 313* (2 vols., London, 1912), Vol. II, chap. XXIV; O. Bardenhewer, *Patrology* (St. Louis, 1908), § 51; P. Batiffol, *Primitive Catholicism* (trans. by H. L. Brianceau, New York, 1911), Excursus E; B. J. Kidd, *History of the Church to A.D. 461* (3 vols., Oxford, 1922–1925), Vol. I, pp. 436 *ff.* The life of Cyprian by his follower and contemporary has been edited by A. Harnack, *Das Leben Cyprians von Pontius, die erste christliche Biographie* (Leipzig, 1913).

[95] *Supra,* pp. 302–304.

Cyprian, *De Catholicae Ecclesiae Unitate*, 4–6, 17. Text. Ed. by W. Hartel, *Corpus Scriptorum Ecclesiasticorum Latinorum*, III[1], 212–214, 226.

4 Whoever reflects upon and examines into these things will feel no need of lengthy discussion and argument. There is easy support for faith in a brief review of the truth. The Lord speaks to Peter in these words: "I say unto thee that thou art Peter; and upon this rock I will build my church and the gates of hell shall not prevail against it. And I will give unto thee the keys of the kingdom of heaven; and whatsoever thou shalt bind on earth shall be bound also in heaven, and whatsoever thou shalt loose on earth shall be loosed also in heaven." And again after his resurrection he says to him: "Feed my sheep." [96] Upon one man he builds the Church and although he grants to all the apostles after his resurrection an equal power and says: "As the Father hath sent me, even so send I you. Receive ye the Holy Ghost; whosesoever sins ye remit, they shall be remitted unto them; and whosesoever sins ye retain, they shall be retained," [97] yet, that he might make clear their unity, he established by his authority that unity at the beginning as if it originated in one man. Assuredly the rest of the apostles were equal to Peter, endowed with the same partnership in honor and power, but the beginning was made in unity, that the Church of Christ might be manifested to be one. This one Church the Holy Spirit in the person of the Lord describes in the Song of Songs, saying: "My dove, my undefiled is but one. She is the only one of her mother, the choice one of her that bare her." [98] Does he who fails to uphold this unity of the

[96] John, XXI, 16, 17. This sentence is often regarded as one of the later interpolations. But Cyprian elsewhere couples the same two incidents in the story of Peter. "Even Peter, to whom the Lord committed the feeding and guarding of his sheep and upon whom he built and founded his Church, said that he had neither silver nor gold," *etc. De Habitu Virginum*, 10.

[97] John, XX, 21–23.

[98] Canticles, VI, 8.

Church believe that he upholds the faith? [99] Does he who opposes and resists the Church trust that he is in the Church? When, moreover, the blessed apostle Paul teaches the same thing and expounds the mystery of unity, saying: "There is one body and one spirit, one hope of your calling, one Lord, one faith, one baptism, one God."

5 This unity then we should strenuously uphold and maintain, especially we who are bishops and preside in the Church, that we may prove that the episcopate also is one and undivided. Let no one by falsehood deceive the brotherhood; let no one by crafty prevarication corrupt the truth of the faith! The episcopate is one and each bishop holds his portion of it for the whole. The Church also is one, although spread far and wide abroad into a multitude by her increasing fruitfulness, even as there are many rays of the sun and but one light and many branches of a tree and but one trunk, based upon the tenacious root. . . .

6 . . . Whoever is separated from the Church and joined to an adulteress is separated from the promises of the Church, nor shall he who forsakes Christ's Church attain to Christ's rewards. He is a stranger, a blasphemer, an enemy. He who has not the Church for his mother has God no more for his Father. If a man could escape who was outside the ark of Noah, then he also may escape who is

[99] Ephesians, IV, 4–6. This whole passage was sometime later worked over with interpolations to fit it for papal use. In a letter of Pelagius II to the Istrian bishops, written about 585, he quotes it in the following form: "Upon one he builds the Church and commits to him the feeding of his sheep, and although to all the apostles he gives an equal power, yet he establishes one See and institutes by his own authority the beginning and characteristic of unity. Assuredly the rest also were the same as Peter, but the primacy was given to Peter that it might be shown that there was one Church and one See. And all are shepherds but only one flock is mentioned, which is fed by all the apostles in unanimous accord. Then does he who fails to uphold the unity of Paul believe that he upholds the faith? Does he who deserts the See of Peter, upon which the Church was founded, believe that he is in the Church?" Cited in *Corpus Scriptorum Ecclesiasticorum Latinorum,* III, 212. The interpolation contains the word "cathedra," seat or see, which in the original does not appear at all. Cyprian does, however, use the phrase "See of Peter" in one of his letters to Cornelius. *Infra,* p. 379. *Cf.* also "the post of Fabianus, that is, the post of Peter." *Infra,* p. 372.

outside the Church. . . .

17 . . . Does he think he is with Christ who opposes the priests of Christ? who separates himself from the fellowship of his clergy and his people? Such an one takes arms against the Church; he fights against the ordinance of God, a foe to the altar, a rebel against the sacrifice of Christ, faithless in the faith, sacrilegious in religion, a disobedient servant, an undutiful son, an enemy brother. He despises the bishops and forsakes the priests of God and dares to erect another altar, with unsanctified lips to offer another prayer, with false sacrifices to profane the true host of the Lord.

Epistolae, III, 3.[100] Text. *Op. cit.,* III[2], 471.

Cyprian to his brother Rogatianus:[101]

. . . [Answer to a complaint of insubordination on the part of a deacon.]

3 Deacons ought to remember that the Lord chose the apostles, that is, the bishops and rulers,[101a] but that after the Lord's ascension into heaven, the apostles appointed deacons as servants of the bishopric and the Church. So, if we may dare to oppose God who makes the bishops, then the deacons may dare to oppose us who make them.

100 The letters of Cyprian have been published at different times from different manuscripts, in which they were arranged in different order. The numbering, therefore, varies in the various editions. The Migne version follows an old French edition, in which by a printer's oversight the number 23 was omitted altogether. The English translation in the Ante-Nicene Fathers corrects the Migne error but otherwise uses the Migne numbering. The text edited by Hartel is based upon a seventeenth century Oxford edition, which was taken from a manuscript with an entirely different principle of arrangement. We give here Hartel's numbering.

101 Rogatianus was one of the bishops in Cyprian's province of Africa.

101a From this and the following extract it seems clear that Cyprian thought of the power to bind and loose as the episcopal power, possessed in his time by all bishops. The Lord had given it first to Peter but later to all the apostles, who after the Resurrection had all exercised it. Also *infra,* p. 406.

Epistolae, XXXIII, 1. Text. *Op. cit.,* 566.

[The letter opens with no address. It was undoubtedly intended for the lapsed.[102]]

1 Our Lord, whose commandment we must fear and obey, establishes the honorable rank of bishop and the constitution of his Church when in the gospel he speaks and says to Peter: "I say unto thee that thou art Peter and on this rock I will build my church and the gates of hell shall not prevail against it; and I will give unto thee the keys of the kingdom of heaven, and whatsoever thou shalt bind on earth shall be bound also in heaven, and whatsoever thou shalt loose on earth shall be loosed also in heaven." Thence have come down to us in course of time and by due succession the ordained office of the bishop and the constitution of the Church, forasmuch as the Church is founded upon the bishops and every act of the Church is subject to these rulers.[103] Since then this order has been so established by divine decree, I am amazed that some individuals have had the bold effrontery to write to me and send letters in the name of the Church, seeing that the Church is composed of the bishop and the clergy and all who are steadfast. It shall not be, nor will the mercy and unconquerable power of the Lord suffer it, that the multitude of the lapsed should be called the Church, for it is written: "God is not the God of the dead but of the living."[104]

Epistolae, LXVI, 8, 10. Text. *Op. cit.,* 732–734.

Cyprian, called also Thascius, to his brother Florentius, called also Puppianus, greeting: [A sarcastic and indignant letter to a former member of Cyprian's church, who has

102 *I.e.,* those who had tacitly or expressly denied their faith during the persecution of Decius and who were in consequence excluded from the Church. *Infra,* pp. 330–331.

103 Compare this statement of the theory of apostolic succession with those of Irenaeus and Tertullian and note the growing legalism.

104 Matthew, XXII, 32.

believed scandalous accusations against him and has written to charge him with breaking up the church.]

8 . . . And the Lord also in the gospel, when the disciples forsook him because of his words, turned to the Twelve and said: "Will ye also go away?" Peter answered him, saying: "Lord, to whom shall we go? Thou hast the word of eternal life; and we believe and are sure that thou art the Son of the living God." There speaks Peter, on whom the Church was to be built, teaching and declaring in the name of the Church that even though a proud and wayward multitude of the disobedient may depart, yet the Church does not forsake Christ. And they are the Church that are a people united to their priest and a flock cleaving to their shepherd. Wherefore you should understand that the bishop is in the Church and the Church in the bishop and that whoever is not with the bishop is not in the Church, and that they flatter themselves in vain who have no peace with the priests of God and yet creep about and imagine they are in secret communion with someone else. For the Church, which is catholic [105] and one, is not split asunder nor divided but is truly bound and joined together by the cement of its priests, who hold fast one to another. . . .

10 . . . I have written to you in the purity of my mind and conscience, confident in my Lord and God. You have my letter and I yours. In the day of judgment, before the tribunal of Christ, both shall be read aloud.

The Vacancy in the Roman Bishopric

(Spring of 250–Spring of 251)

Cyprian had been bishop for hardly a year when a storm burst over the Church out of a quiet sky. For over fifty years, since the reign of Commodus, there had been no concerted or

[105] Cyprian took the word "catholic" from Tertullian and made even more frequent use of it. *Supra,* p. 286.

persistent effort to suppress Christianity by force. It was still, as it had been since Trajan's time, a *religio illicita* and it was always open to a magistrate or a mob in a season of excitement to call down the law to bring about the banishment or death of guilty individuals. But under the Syrian emperors of the first half of the third century, with their liberal eclecticism in matters of belief, the tendency was toward toleration or even protection. Christians pervaded every rank of society and every profession. It became more and more difficult to credit the old, horrible whispers of promiscuous sexuality and child murder, or to stir up popular tumults against them.

But in the autumn of 249, a new emperor, Trajanus Decius, a Roman of the old-fashioned type, began his reign. The outlook over the Empire was disturbing. The Goths were pressing down upon the Danube frontier and no general seemed able to hold them back for long. In the East, the Parthians and the Persians took turns in breaking through the borders. At home, the long, fatal struggle was going on between the army and the Senate as to which should control the government of the State. To Decius' mind the situation was a result of the universal apostasy from the ways of the Fathers and he did his best to turn back the tide. He treated the Senate with respect and deference, set about to restore discipline in the army and within a few weeks after his accession, issued an edict intended to stamp out the unpatriotic sect that had been allowed to spread itself everywhere and was a constant hindrance to the recruiting of soldiers and the proper cultivation of loyalty to the state religion. The edict itself has not been preserved. It apparently required every citizen of the Empire to sacrifice, pour libation, burn incense, or perform some similar act of homage at one of the public altars. Bishops who refused should be put to death, in order that the disobedient might be deprived at once of their leaders. Other Christians might be tortured or imprisoned, even starved for a while, to break down their resolution. Those who satisfied the magistrates by the required act of worship might receive a certificate of loyalty (*libellus*) to shield them from further inquisition.

The edict was sent out broadcast and in many places the most prominent Christians were quickly arrested. Decius was especially determined to be rid of the Roman bishop and Fabianus was executed in January, 250.[106] Soon afterwards, Bishop Dionysius of Alexandria was rescued from the soldiers by a crowd of his own people. The bishop of Antioch died in prison. Origen was held for slow torture. In Carthage, Cyprian had warning of what was coming and fled from the city into concealment. Meanwhile, throngs of church members, men and women, small and great, were haled before the magistrates to be put to the test. Thousands were unable to meet it. Some avoided the actual commission of idolatry by procuring the magistrates' certificates by underhand means, perhaps through pagan friends who vouched for them. Some came forward with no great reluctance, others pale and trembling, visibly terrified of the consequences, whichever course they chose. Others still gave way only under pressure of persuasion, imprisonment or pain. All of these henceforth the Church regarded as lapsed, shut out by their treachery from its salvation. The magistrates were, however, far from capturing every Christian. In each community, there were clergy and lay members who remained undetected and met in secret, carrying on as best they could the life of the Church amid the general panic and demoralization.

In a month or two, the first severity of the persecution was past. It was still unsafe for bishops to appear openly. At Rome, it would be foolhardy even to elect one. Cyprian could not venture back to Carthage, where he was known. But the mass of common Christians was no longer so harried and the renegades, now that the worst of the terror was over, began to bombard the churches with demands and entreaties for pardon. Some in their contrition voluntarily faced the magistrates again and atoned for their weakness by death. Others undertook heavy penance in the uncertain hope that some day the Church's door might be open for them. Others beset the confessors in their prisons begging them to intercede for them. It had long been the custom in the churches to grant special weight

106 *Supra*, pp. 313–314.

to the wishes and opinions, written or spoken, of those who had suffered for the faith. The martyrs of Lyons had believed that they had a right to be heard on the Montanist question by such a personage as the bishop of Rome.[107] Some confessors now gave letters to a few of the fallen who were personally known to them, recommending them to the bishop's clemency when peace should be restored. Others were less cautious. One Lucian, in prison at Rome, issued in the name of one Paul, who had died, what amounted to wholesale pardons, available to anyone, with no prerequisite of penance.[108] The church organizations were in grave difficulties, for there was no rule in existence that seemed applicable to the situation. The primitive practice had been to deny the possibility of forgiveness for mortal sins, such as adultery, idolatry or apostasy, but during the preceding fifty years this habit had been generally modified so as to admit of repentance and absolution for unchastity.[109] What then could be done with those who had denied the Lord? Was there to be mercy also for them?

To Cyprian in hiding the whole problem was peculiarly vexatious. The discontented faction in his own church had been quick to make capital out of his flight and had at once represented him to Rome as a cowardly, hireling shepherd, in disgraceful contrast to Fabianus, who had died at his post. The clergy at Rome, within a short time after the loss of their head, had taken up the task not only of conducting the local church but also of carrying on the usual correspondence with the

[107] *Supra,* pp. 257, 260. It was widely admitted that confessors and martyrs won special spiritual grace by their pains, in particular, the power to plead for weaker brethren before the Church and before God. See the correspondence of the Carthaginian Celerinus with the Roman Lucian on behalf of his fallen sisters and the general certificate of pardon sent out to Cyprian and other bishops by the Roman confessors dying of starvation. Cyprian, *Epistolae,* XXI–XXIII. See, likewise, the action of the confessors of Alexandria and the influence of it upon Bishop Dionysius. *Infra,* p. 354, n. 150. That the appearance of this privileged class alongside the regular clergy, sometimes interfering with church management, sometimes quarreling among themselves and refusing to live by ordinary rules, presented a problem to orderly-minded bishops, may be inferred from Cyprian's discussion of the subject in *De Catholicae Ecclesiae Unitate,* cc. 20–22. Compare also his *Epistolae,* XIII and XIV, 2–3, where he suggests that clothing and money be allowed the confessors on condition that they show themselves amenable to church discipline. The satirist Lucian ridiculed the devotion of the Christians to their members in prison. *Peregrinus,* 11–13.

[108] *Infra,* p. 345, n. 126.

[109] *Supra,* pp. 243, 296, 311.

churches abroad. As a body, they still kept "watch over all who call on the name of the Lord." At first, then, they wrote to Cyprian in half-concealed contempt, doubtful if he were really to be still regarded as a bishop, sending separate letters of advice and encouragement to the Carthaginian community. Presently Cyprian was able to convince them that he was alive to his duty and their tone to him became one of comradeship, especially after he had adopted for his own guidance the temporary rule which they had already promulgated to meet the emergency at Rome, namely, that penitents at the point of death should be permitted the consolation of communion but that all others should be required to wait until the return of peace, when their status might be settled in proper form by an assembly of bishops in council.

But, athough Cyprian and the Roman clergy worked through the winter of 250–251 in harmony, there was still rebellion in the ranks both at Carthage and at Rome. The dissatisfied priests at Carthage, led by one Novatus and a deacon, Felicissimus, offered to restore the apostates to communion without more delay and set up a rival church organization. Their party formed a connection with some refractory elements at Rome and messengers passed between them, bringing letters from the confessors who favored indulgent treatment and an easy absolution for all the lapsed who asked to be forgiven. Cyprian was at length compelled to appoint a commission to represent him at the seat of his diocese, and Novatus, Felicissimus and their adherents were excommunicated for sedition. At the same time, as the effects of the strain and suspense and moral breakdown became more and more manifest, there arose yet another party to increase the discord. In Rome, the leader of this new schism was Novatian, one of the most serious and learned of the priests. He had at first acquiesced in the temporizing method of dealing with the lapsed, but now he and others with him could see only the mischief wrought to the fabric of the Church through the fault of these sinners and reverted to the position of the earliest Fathers, that those who had forsaken Christ in time of trial had put themselves forever outside the Church's mercy. When finally, some months after Decius had left Rome to fight the Goths along the Danube, it seemed possible to hold an election in the city again and to ordain a new bishop, the church was still rent with the divisions between its sinners and its saints.

A minor detail, worth noticing in the correspondence between Cyprian and the Roman clergy, is the title with which the priests address a bishop, such as Cyprian, namely, *papa,* the Latin equivalent of the Greek πάππας or " father," the word which in English has since become " pope." Tertullian had employed the same term, as if it were a common epithet of reverence, in one of his sarcastic references to a contemporary bishop of Rome, " good shepherd and blessed pope." [110] The fact that Roman priests here apply it to a bishop of Carthage, as also that Jerome in the next century uses it indifferently for Damasus of Rome, Augustine of Hippo, Athanasius of Alexandria and the bishops of Jerusalem, seems to prove that it was originally in the West,[111] as it is to this day in eastern Europe, a title for any bishop. Not until the pontificate of Gregory VII was it formally reserved as the exclusive designation of the bishop of Rome.

On this period, see the references under Cyprian; also G. Schönach, *Die Christenverfolgung des Kaisers Decius* (Jauer, 1907); A. Harnack, *The Letters of the Roman Clergy during the Period of the Papal Vacancy* (volume dedicated to K. H. Weizsäcker, Freiburg, 1892); P. M. Meyer, *Die Libelli der decianischen Christenverfolgung* (Berlin, 1910); C. H. Turner, *Studies in Early Church History* (London, 1912), pp. 97–131; L. Duchesne, *Early History of the Christian Church* (trans. from the 4th ed. by C. Jenkins, 3 vols., London, 1910–1924), Vol. I, pp. 267–272, 288–295.

Cyprian, *Epistolae,* VIII. Text. Ed. by W. Hartel (*Corpus Scriptorum Ecclesiasticorum Latinorum*), III[2], 485–488.

[This letter had no title nor address but was sent from members of the clergy at Rome to the church in Carthage.]

110 *De Pudicitia,* 13. The same treatise contains the allusion to " bishop of the bishops." *Supra,* p. 301.

111 Benson in his life of Cyprian, pp. 29–31, tries to prove that the Roman church adopted the title from Africa. For early instances of its use see C. de F. Ducange, *Glossarium Mediae et Infimae Latinitatis* (10 vols., Paris, 1883–1887), *Papa.*

1 We have been told by Crementius, the subdeacon, who came to us on a particular errand from you, that the blessed father Cyprian has left you and that in doing this he has acted rightly, because he is a prominent person and a struggle is impending, which God has allowed in the world in order to fight with his servants against the adversary. He wills also to show to angels and men by this conflict that the victor shall be crowned but that the vanquished shall receive for himself the doom that he has pronounced upon us. Whereas, then, it devolves upon us, who are clearly set in charge in place of the shepherd, to keep watch over the flock, it will be said to us if we prove neglectful, as it was said to our predecessors, who also had been set in charge and were negligent, that we have not sought that which was lost nor restored the wanderer nor bound up that which was broken, but have drunk their milk and clothed ourselves with their wool.[112] Moreover, the Lord himself, fulfilling what was written in the law and the prophets, instructs us, saying: "I am the good shepherd, who lay down my life for the sheep. But the hireling, whose own the sheep are not, when he seeth the wolf coming, leaveth the sheep and fleeth and the wolf scattered them."[113] To Simon too he says: "Lovest thou me?" He answered: "I love thee." He saith unto him: "Feed my sheep!"[114] We know that these words were occasioned by the fact that he himself was leaving them, and the other disciples did as Simon did.

2 We are anxious, therefore, beloved brethren, that you should not prove hirelings but good shepherds, for you know that if you do not urge our brethren to stand steadfast in the faith there is grave and threatening danger that the brotherhood may rush headlong into idolatry and so be

[112] Ezekiel, XXXIV, 3, 4.

[113] John, X, 11–12, 15. Here and again later there seems to be some reflection intended upon the conduct of Cyprian in going into hiding.

[114] John, XXI, 15–17.

absolutely destroyed. Nor is it by words only that we exhort you to such a course but, as you will be able to ascertain from the many who go to you from us, we ourselves both have so acted and still do, by God's help, in the face of grave uncertainty and worldly peril. For we keep before our eyes the fear of God and eternal punishment rather than the fear of men and shortlived pain and do not abandon the brethren but encourage them to stand firmly in the faith and be ready to depart with the Lord. We have even called back some who were stepping up to perform the deed which they were ordered to do.[115] The church stands strong in the faith, notwithstanding that some have been driven by pure terror to fall, some persons of eminence, others overwhelmed by dread of man. Even these, however, we have not deserted, although they have separated themselves from us, but have admonished them and do admonish them to repent, if in any way they may obtain pardon from him who is able to grant it, for fear that if we should forsake them they might become worse.

3 You see then, brethren, that you also ought to act in the same way, so that even those who have fallen may recover themselves through your exhortations and if they are again arrested, may confess and so make amends for their previous failure. And there are other duties incumbent on you, of which likewise we must make mention. For example, if any who have fallen during this time of trial are taken with illness and repent of what they have done and desire communion, you should by all means grant it them. Or if you have widows or bedridden sick who are unable to maintain themselves, or members in prison or excluded from their own houses, these ought everyone to have some person to care for them. Furthermore, catechumens who are ill ought not to find themselves deluded and left without help. And, — most important of all, — if the bodies of the martyrs

[115] *I.e.*, going up to perform the required deed of worship at a pagan altar.

and others be not buried, those whose business it is to perform this office are running into serious danger. Whoever of you fulfils this duty on any occasion we are sure that he is counted a good servant, one who has been faithful in least and will be appointed ruler over ten cities.[116] May God who gives all things to them that hope in him, grant us that we may all be found doing these works!

The brethren who are in chains greet you, as do the priests and the whole church, which also with deepest concern keeps watch itself over all who call on the name of the Lord.[117] And we beseech you too in your turn to have us in remembrance. We wish also to tell you that Bassianus has reached us. We ask you, who have the zeal of God, to forward a copy of this letter to whomever you can, as opportunity may arise, or to make your own occasion and send a messenger, that they may stand firm and immovable in the faith. We bid you, beloved brethren, ever heartily farewell.

Ibid., *Epistolae,* IX. Text. *Op. cit.,* 488–489.

1 Cyprian to his brethren, the priests and deacons at Rome, greeting.[118]

While the report of the death of my excellent colleague was still unconfirmed among us, my beloved brethren, and our minds were perplexed and doubtful, I received the letter sent to me from you by Crementius, the subdeacon, in which his glorious end was fully described, and I rejoiced greatly that so noble a consummation had suitably closed his up-

[116] Luke, XIX, 17.

[117] The Roman church had not yet, apparently, lost its corporate sense of responsibility for the welfare of the whole Christian brotherhood. That responsibility had not yet become the monopoly of the bishop.

[118] This letter was written by Cyprian to acknowledge the formal notification that had reached him from the Roman clergy of the death by martyrdom of their bishop, Fabianus, January, 250. The text of the notification has not been preserved. He also returned in this letter a copy of Letter VIII, which had fallen into his hands and which had evidently never been intended for his eyes. He disposes of this by presuming it to be a forgery.

right administration. In this connection also I warmly congratulate you for honoring his memory with a testimony so public and distinguished that by means of it we are informed not only of what is splendid for you in the memory of your bishop but also of what affords us a pattern of faith and virtue. For just as a bishop's fall is something that precipitates the fall of his followers, so, on the other hand, it is serviceable and helpful when a bishop by the strength of his faith stands forth to the brethren as a pattern for their imitation.

2 I have read another letter in which neither the persons who wrote it nor the persons to whom it was written were clearly named. Inasmuch as in that letter both the handwriting and the contents and even the paper itself suggested to me that something had been cut out or altered from the original, I am sending you back the actual document, that you may determine whether it is the very same that you gave to the subdeacon Crementius to bring. For it is a solemn matter if the true text of a letter of the clergy has been corrupted by any forgery or trick. In order, then, that we may be sure, do you ascertain whether the writing and subscription are yours and send me word what is the truth.

I bid you, dearest brethren, ever heartily farewell.

Ibid., *Epistolae,* XX. Text. *Op. cit.,* 527–529.

1 Cyprian to his brethren, the priests and deacons at Rome, greeting.[119]

I have discovered, beloved brethren, that what we have done and are doing here has been reported to you in a somewhat distorted and untruthful fashion and have, therefore, thought it essential to write this letter to you, in order to furnish you with an account of our activities and rulings

[119] This letter was written by Cyprian in an effort to get recognition from Rome as being still bishop of Carthage, even *in absentia.*

and watchful care. For, as the commands of the Lord bid us do, at the first outbreak of the disturbance, after my people had repeatedly demanded it with violence and clamor, I left them for a while, thinking less of my own safety than of the public peace of the brethren and fearing that my unintimidated presence with them would aggravate the trouble that had begun. But though absent in body, I have not failed them in spirit or deed or counsel but have obeyed the precepts of the Lord and guided our brethren, as far as lay within my poor powers.

2 And what I have done these thirteen letters which I have sent out at various times and which I am forwarding to you will reveal to you. In them I have not spared advice to the clergy nor encouragement to the confessors nor rebuke, when it was needed, to the outcasts nor appeals and exhortations to the whole brotherhood that they should entreat the mercy of God, as far as with the Lord's help my poor abilities could reach them, in accordance with the law of faith and the fear of God. . . .

3 But afterwards, when some of the lapsed, whether of their own accord or at the suggestion of someone else, burst out with a daring demand, as if trying to extort by violent onslaught the peace that had been promised them by the martyrs and confessors, I wrote two letters to my clergy on this subject as well and gave orders to have them read to them, so as to moderate by some means for a while the turbulence of those people. I said that persons who had obtained a letter from the martyrs and were on the point of death might make confession and receive the laying on of hands for repentance and so be committed to the Lord in the peace which the martyrs had promised them. Nor in this was I issuing a new law or rashly constituting myself a lawgiver. But it seemed to me desirable both that respect should be paid to the martyrs and that the vehemence of those who were aiming to overturn everything should be

restrained. And, besides, I had read your letter which you lately wrote to my clergy by the subdeacon Crementius, to the effect that consideration might be shown to those who after their fall were taken with an illness and penitently asked for communion.[120] I thought that I ought to stand by your judgment, lest our proceedings, which should be alike and harmonious in everything, might in some respect betray disagreement. The cases of the others, even of those who had secured letters from martyrs, I ordered postponed entirely and reserved until my return, so that when the Lord has given us peace, a number of us bishops may meet together and arrange and reorganize everything, informing you likewise of our deliberations.

I bid you, beloved brethren, ever heartily farewell.

Ibid., *Epistolae,* XXVII. *Op. cit,* 540–544.

Cyprian to his brethren, the priests and deacons at Rome, greeting.

[A letter of remonstrance against the conduct of Lucian [121] and other imprisoned Roman confessors, who have sent out broad, general pardons to the lapsed in their own names as also in the name of Paul, a recent martyr, pointing out the impossibility of maintaining order in Africa, when bishops are everywhere besieged by lapsed who insist upon instant restoration to full membership on the ground of pardons from these confessors. The correspondence which Cyprian and members of his church have had on the subject is enclosed. Confessors forget that "martyrs do not make the gospel but martyrs themselves are made by the gospel."]

120 The Roman clergy had perhaps written a third letter, now lost, in which they still ignored Cyprian and advised the Carthaginian clergy again of the policy they had adopted in their treatment of the lapsed who were in peril of dying unreconciled and unforgiven. Can Cyprian be alluding to this letter when he suggests in the first sentences of this paragraph that outside influences might have stirred up the lapsed at Carthage?

121 *Infra,* p. 345, n. 126.

4 . . . But at the opportune moment arrived your letter written to my clergy, which I received, as also that which the blessed confessors, Moyses, Maximus, Nicostratus and the rest,[122] sent to Saturninus, Aurelius and the others, which contained the full vigor of the gospel and the robust discipline of the law of the Lord. Your words have so much assisted us in our struggle here and in our efforts to resist with all the power of our faith the onslaught of discontent that, by God's help, the end will soon arrive. For even before the letter which I last sent you had reached you, you informed me that your judgment in accordance with the gospel law firmly and unanimously concurred with mine.

I bid you, brethren, beloved and longed for, ever heartily farewell.

Ibid., *Epistolae,* XXX. Text. *Op. cit.,* 549–556.

The priests and deacons at Rome to Pope Cyprian, greeting.

1 A soul conscious of its own rectitude, supported by the strength of the gospel rule and a truthful witness to itself of the laws of heaven is ofttime content to have God as its only judge and neither craves the praise nor dreads the censure of anyone beside. Yet they who know that their consciences submit to God as their judge, but who long to have their deeds approved also by their brethren deserve to receive this double commendation. Such, brother Cyprian, has, not unnaturally, been your attitude, for you have wished to make us not your judges so much as participants in your piety and your many industrious counsels, that we ourselves might, as we approve your acts, win praise

122 The party of Moyses, Maximus and others among the Roman confessors seems to have tried to counteract the influence of Lucian and his friends and to have urged that confessors and martyrs should not interfere with the discipline of the regular church organization. Cyprian wrote a letter of gratitude to them. *Epistolae,* XXVIII.

for them along with you and become coheirs of your good counsels through being supporters of them. . . .

2 . . . [Approval of Cyprian's policy of maintaining discipline and a steady hand on the helm.] Nor has this decision been a result of recent reflection on our part nor has the help we have just furnished against wrongdoers been unprecedented, but from of old this strictness has been recorded of us, from of old this faith and from of old this discipline. For the apostle would not have pronounced his great eulogy upon us in the words, "for your faith is proclaimed in all the world,"[123] if even at that time our vigor had not put strength into the roots of faith. After that eulogy and that glory, for us to degenerate would be the worst of crimes. . . .

4 Moreover, you have also received letters of the same tenor as ours from those confessors who are still for the steadfastness of their confession confined here in prison and have been once already gloriously crowned by faith in confession during the gospel conflict. In their letters they have upheld the severity of the gospel rule and for shame of the church have denounced that unwarranted petition,[124] fearing that if they took the easy course they would not find it easy to restore the ruins of the gospel rule. . . .

5 In this connection, we must and do express to you our deep and heartfelt gratitude, because by your letters you have lightened the gloom of their prison,[125] because, as far as you could have access to them, you have visited them, because with your encouraging messages you have put new life into their hearts, strong as they were through their own faith and confession, because by dwelling upon their felicity in admiring words you have kindled them to yearn far more ardently for the glory of heaven, because

[123] Romans, I, 8.

[124] *I.e.*, of course, for quick and easy restoration of the lapsed.

[125] See, for an example, Cyprian's letter to the Roman confessors on their completion of one year of imprisonment. Letter XXXVII.

you have given fresh impulse to their fervor, because, as we believe and hope, by the power of your speech you have fortified them for future victory, so that, even though this might all perhaps have come about from their own faith in confessing, and from the goodness of God, they are still to some extent your debtors in their martyrdom. But, — to return to the subject from which we seem to have digressed, — you will find appended the letters we have sent to Sicily also. However, it is peculiarly necessary for us to postpone action, because since the death of Fabianus of most noble memory no bishop has yet, owing to the perils of the situation and the times, been ordained to bring order into all these matters and to treat the problem of the lapsed with authority and good counsel. Yet, as regards this weighty business, we have reached the conclusion that you yourself have advocated, namely, that first the peace of the Church must be restored and then a council assembled of bishops, priests, deacons, and confessors, as well as the steadfast laity, and in this way the question of the lapsed be taken up for settlement. For it seems to us wrong and invidious and unfair not to investigate in a general gathering the offense that has been so generally committed nor to pronounce sentence together, when so grave a guilt is known to be so widely spread. For an ordinance cannot have force which has not openly received the general assent. The whole world is now almost everywhere laid waste and the remnants and ruins of what has been overthrown lie all about us. For that reason it seems to us that there should be as thorough a searching out of counsel as the sin itself is widespread. . . .

6 and 7 [They urge the whole Church to prayer and the lapsed to patience, repentance and humility, while waiting for relief.]

8 We here have long been trying to preserve this moderation of attitude, both we ourselves, who are many, and some of the bishops who are near neighbors to us, and others

whom the heat of the persecution has driven here from distant provinces, but we have thought that we ought not to initiate any new measures until our bishop is appointed. We have, however, felt it needful to temper a little our treatment of the lapsed. For although, during this interval of expectation and waiting for a bishop to be given us by God, the cases of those who can endure the delay should be kept in suspense, those whose lives are fast approaching their end and who cannot bear delay, provided they repent and declare often their detestation of their sins and grieve with tears and sobs and weeping and display the signs of a heart truly contrite, if humanly speaking there is no likelihood that they will live, then at the last, carefully and mercifully, they should receive relief. God himself knows what he will do with such as these and how he will determine the weight of his judgment. We are anxious both that the unscrupulous should not praise us for weakness and leniency and that true penitents should not accuse us of obdurate cruelty. We bid you, most blessed and glorious pope, ever farewell in the Lord and do you remember us.

Ibid., *Epistolae,* XXXI. Text. *Op. cit.,* 557–564.

Moyses and Maximus, priests, and Nicostratus, Rufinus and the other confessors with them to Pope Cyprian, greeting.

[Fervent thanks for Cyprian's letters and encouragement and a request for his prayers. Approval of his care for his bishopric, especially his treatment of the lapsed.]

Ibid., *Epistolae,* XXXII. Text. *Op. cit.,* 565.

[Cyprian sends copies of both preceding letters to the priests and deacons of his own church, with instructions that they be generally read and that copies be made for bishops, priests or deacons of other churches who may visit

Carthage and that free opportunity be afforded to anyone else who wishes to make a copy.]

Ibid., *Epistolae,* XXXV. Text. *Op. cit.,* 571–572.

Cyprian to his brethren, the priests and deacons at Rome, greeting.

Both our mutual love and our intelligence demand, beloved brethren, that I should conceal from your knowledge nothing which occurs among us, in order that we may plan in common for the salutary administration of the Church. . . . And after I had written you the letter which I sent by our brothers, Saturus, the reader, and Optatus, the subdeacon, some of the lapsed, who balk at penance and at making atonement to God, wrote me a letter in an audacious conspiracy, not to beg for peace to be given them but to claim it, as if it had already been given. For they insist that Paul gave peace to everyone,[126] as you will read in their letter, of which I forward you a copy and with it the brief reply I promptly wrote them. Also, that you may know what sort of letter I then wrote to my clergy, I send you a copy of it as well. And if, after all, this effrontery is not subdued either by my letters or by yours and does not yield to proper methods, we shall take such proceedings as the Lord in his gospel bade us take. I bid you, beloved brethren, ever heartily farewell. Farewell.

Ibid., *Epistolae,* XXXVI. Text. *Op. cit.,* 572–575.

The priests and deacons at Rome to Pope Cyprian, greeting.

1 When, beloved brother, we had read your letter which

[126] For previous mention of Paul *vide supra,* p. 340. Lucian's story was to the effect that Paul, just before his death, had said to him: "Lucian, in the presence of Christ I bid you, if after my departure anyone asks you for peace, give it in my name." *Corpus Scriptorum Ecclesiasticorum Latinorum,* Vol. III, p. 534.

you sent by Fortunatus, the subdeacon,[127] we were smitten with a double sorrow and distressed with a twofold grief, because there has been no respite granted you in the heavy stress of persecution and because the unreasonable dissatisfaction of the lapsed brethren has evidently been pushed to dangerous recklessness of expression. But although these things which we have mentioned are a severe affliction to us and to our spirit, yet the vigor and severity that you have displayed, in accordance with the gospel rule, lighten the oppressive burden of our grief, inasmuch as you are righteously restraining these persons' wickedness and by exhortations to repentance are pointing out the lawful way of salvation. . . . [The inconsistency of those martyrs who believe that they themselves would forfeit salvation by sacrificing and so will die rather than yield and who yet promise salvation to others who have sacrificed. Most martyrs refer these sinners to their bishop and the gospel law. Encouragement to Cyprian to continue his efforts.]

3 . . . For we do not think that without the instigation of certain persons [128] they would all have dared to assert so rudely their claim to peace. We know the faith of the Carthaginian church, we know her training, we know her humility. Wherefore we have wondered to hear some rather harsh reports of you by letter,[129] since we have often witnessed your mutual love and charity in numerous instances of reciprocal affection toward each other. Now, certainly, it is time that the sinners repent, that they prove their remorse for their fall, that they show reverence and exhibit humility. . . .

4 As for Privatus of Lambaesis,[130] you have acted as

[127] *I.e.*, probably, Letter XXXV.

[128] A cautious reference undoubtedly to the party of lenient confessors at Rome, represented by Lucian and his friends. *Supra*, pp. 340, 345.

[129] The reading here is corrupt, and the meaning is obviously not that of the original. The Roman clergy were not finding fault with Cyprian at this juncture.

[130] Lambaesis was the military capital of the province of Numidia. Privatus apparently headed a recalcitrant party there.

you usually do in endeavoring to inform us of the situation as a cause for anxiety. For it becomes us all to keep watch over the body of the whole Church, whose members are scattered through all the various provinces. But even before your letter came, the fraud of that crafty man had been brought to our attention. For already one Futurus, a standard bearer for Privatus, had arrived among us from the same cohort of iniquity and had attempted by guile to procure a letter from us, but we did not fail to discover who he was nor did he obtain the letter that he wanted. We bid you ever farewell.

Ibid., *Epistolae,* XLIII. Text. *Op. cit.,* 590–597.

Cyprian to all his people, greeting.[131]

[A warning against dealings of any kind with Felicissimus and five other priests, who have communicated with the lapsed.]

3 . . . Now again is the same ruinous idea being spread about by the five priests who have joined Felicissimus to the destruction of salvation, namely, that God should not be entreated, that he who has denied Christ should not implore the Christ whom he has denied, that penance after the guilt of sin may be dispensed with and no atonement made to the Lord through the Lord's bishops and priests, but that the Lord's priests should be forsaken and a new tradition of sacrilegious institution be set up in violation of the gospel rule. And although it has once been decided both by us and by the confessors and clergy in the city [132] as well as by all the bishops in our province and across the sea [133] that no new measures should be taken in the matter of the lapsed until we all assemble together and compare judg-

131 This letter was written in March, 251, just before Cyprian emerged from exile, when persecution had, for the time being, almost ceased.

132 *I.e.,* those who remained in Carthage.

133 At Rome.

ments and fix upon a sentence suited to discipline and mercy, they would rebel against this our conclusion and overthrow by faction and conspiracy all the authority and power of the priesthood. . . .

5 . . . They now offer peace who themselves have no peace. They who themselves have deserted the Church are preventing the Church from bringing back and recalling the lapsed. There is one God and one Christ and one Church and one seat of office,[134] established upon Peter by the word of the Lord. Another altar cannot be erected nor a new priesthood created beside the one altar and the one priesthood. . . .

7 . . . This is the last and final temptation of this persecution and this too, with the Lord's aid, will quickly pass, so that I may be present with you and my colleagues after Easter. In the assemblage we shall be able to arrange and make clear what is to be done in accordance with your will and the general judgment of us all, as we once decided. . . .

Cornelius

(251–253)

In the spring of 251, while Decius was engrossed in the campaign against the Goths among the Balkans, the Roman community ventured to elect a new bishop. The election was a signal for all parties to put out their strength. The group that stood for quick and easy restoration of the renegades seems, however, to have become by this time discredited at Rome and was speedily quelled. The real issue lay between the middle party, that favored restoration to communion, though not to office, after a considerable period of penance and satisfactory evidences of contrition, and the austerer party, known as Cathari or Puritans, who insisted upon absolute adherence to the primitive rule, that those who had denied Christ, whether explicitly or

[134] The Latin word is "cathedra." It seems clear from the context that Cyprian is referring to the episcopal office. *Cf. supra,* pp. 326 and n. 99, 329.

tacitly, before the world could never again be counted among his flock. A majority of the clergy, touched by the wretchedness of many of the outcasts, voted finally for Cornelius, a priest who had not hitherto made himself conspicuous [135] but who was known as a pious man of moderate views who had shown some sympathy for the lapsed and would support a policy of prudent reintegration. To the Puritans such a compromise seemed to mark the Roman church as apostate. It was unthinkable that they should remain members of a body that offered Christ again to those faithless and cowardly disciples who had once forsaken him for demons. They solemnly withdrew from the assembly, declared themselves the only true and apostolic church and elected Novatian, a man of far greater learning and distinction than Cornelius,[136] as their bishop. Among their number were some of the confessors to whom Cyprian had written the previous year, praising them for upholding the strictness of the gospel law.[137]

Each organization at once dispatched notice of its action to the other churches of the Empire, asking for recognition and for the establishment of customary relations with its own candidate. To Cyprian in Carthage came from Cornelius merely a formal letter of notification of election, but from the Novatianists a personal delegation, headed by the priest Maximus, with full accounts of the whole affair and a multitude of reasons to justify their secession. They probably hoped that Cyprian's well-known respect for tradition would range him on their side against Cornelius and the threatened relaxation of discipline. If he and the church of Carthage would acknowledge Novatian, it would be a serious blow to Cornelius' standing and prospects. The letters and the messengers reached Cyprian in the midst of the council of African bishops and clergy which he had convened upon his reappearance in Carthage. Cornelius' letter was regular in form and reported what professed to be a perfectly regular election. Therefore, Cyprian read it to his council. The lengthy

[135] Cyprian finds it necessary, in writing of the Roman situation, to explain who Cornelius is and what is his reputation. *Infra*, p. 371.

[136] An English translation of Novatian's extant works is in *Ante Nicene Fathers*, Vol. V, pp. 611 *sqq*. He was probably the most scholarly theologian of his generation.

[137] *Supra*, p. 341 and n. 122.

communication from Novatian reported an admitted irregularity and was polemic in style. It offended Cyprian's taste for legal and proper procedure. He did not read it to his clergy but merely stated the fact of the second election and tried in vain to prevent the Novatianist deputation from gaining entrance to the council hall and arguing their case in person before the interested African bishops. However, their charges against Cornelius of contaminating intercourse with apostates and against the methods by which his election had been secured sounded too grave to be dismissed without investigation. The council at last decided to delay recognition of either bishop until two of its number, Caldonius and Fortunatus, could visit Rome and collect reliable and unbiassed information, and also exert their utmost influence to heal the division and bring the opposing parties together again. Bishop Dionysius of Alexandria was writing directly to Novatian, urging him to endure everything rather than incur the guilt of creating a breach in the unity of the Church.[138]

But before Caldonius and Fortunatus could return, came letters from other clergy who had been in Rome during the election and who confirmed the legitimacy of Cornelius' position. Not long afterwards, two African eyewitnesses, Pompey and Stephen, arrived in Carthage. Their report, to the effect that the priest Novatus and others of Cyprian's troublesome opponents among the Carthaginian clergy during the previous year were now in Rome and figuring prominently among the Novatianists, doubtless helped Cyprian to classify the whole movement as an indefensible outbreak of wilful insubordination. Moreover, in his own case humanity and practical sense had already prevailed over zeal for traditional discipline. Under his presidency, the

[138] Eusebius gives the text of Dionysius' cogent letter. "Dionysius to his brother Novatus [*sic*] greeting. If, as you say, you have been elevated against your will, you will prove it by voluntarily retiring. For it were better to suffer anything than to divide asunder the Church of God. Indeed, martyrdom for resisting division would be no less glorious than martyrdom for refusing to worship idols. Nay, to me it seems even more glorious. For in one case, a man is a martyr for the sake of his own individual soul; in the other, for the sake of the whole Church. If now you induce or compel the brethren to return to harmony, your merit will be greater than your error and the latter will be condoned while the former is applauded. But if you cannot prevail upon the unruly, at least save your own soul! I bid you farewell, and keep the peace in the Lord." *Historia Ecclesiastica,* VI, 45.

Carthaginian council, without waiting for definite action to be taken elsewhere, had agreed upon a concession to mercy for the fallen in Africa and had planned out a scheme of penance and gradual restitution to communion. Such being the situation, Cyprian hesitated no longer but wrote to Cornelius, explaining fully the causes of his own delay and that of his African colleagues and protesting his abhorrence for the schismatics. He wrote also to his friends among the Roman confessors, urgently advising them to make their peace with the lawful episcopate,[139] and to the bishops in Africa who still remained unconvinced. Cornelius, on his part, called a council of the bishops of Italy to excommunicate Novatian, Novatus and their adherents and to adopt a plan of penance similar to that drawn up at Carthage. The church of Egypt was following the same course in a synod at Alexandria. No single general council of the Church was held but three of the great metropolitan sees were thus in substantial accord.[140]

The process of modifying the early austere theories regarding church membership and the purpose of the rite of baptism, as also the compensatory process of increasing the scope of the sacrament of penance, had been begun, as we have seen, at Rome in the second century and carried further by Bishop Callistus' decree that Christians might have forgiveness for sins of the flesh.[141] They both were now pushed to their logical outcome by the legislation of these three provincial councils, that atonement might be made in the Church for the deadly spiritual sin of apostasy. Nevertheless, Novatian, who like Hippolytus before him headed a serious minority bent upon unfaltering observance of the stricter tradition, found groups of conscientious conservatives all over the Empire. Fabius, the patriarch of Antioch, was inclined to take his side and other bishops in Asia wavered.

Cornelius' brief pontificate marks, therefore, one of the crises in the history of ecclesiastical practice and dogma. It is mem-

139 Dionysius of Alexandria wrote also to the Roman confessors, both before and after their reconciliation with Cornelius, and to the whole Roman church. Eusebius, *op. cit.*, VI. 46. *Infra*, p. 386, n. 192.

140 On the need of councils that would be representative of the Church at large, *vide supra*, p. 343.

141 *Supra*, pp. 243, 310. *Cf. infra*, p. 701.

orable also to the hard-pressed historian because of the comparative wealth of our information about it, derived not only from the letters written to or about Cornelius by Cyprian but also from three letters from Cornelius' own pen, the first indubitable utterances of a Roman bishop to be preserved since the letter of Clement. His two letters to Cyprian relate the outcome of the Novatianist movement among the Roman confessors. His long one to Fabius of Antioch, from which Eusebius takes extracts, is an argument against the recognition of Novatian, based upon the latter's alleged scandalous misbehavior, the fraud and irregularity of his election and the size and strength of the organization behind Cornelius. A reading of these letters does not enhance one's impression of Cornelius' own mentality. They have neither the calm assurance and dignity of the letters sent out by the college of Roman priests before his election nor the clarity and honest vigor of Cyprian's. Cornelius seems hot-headed and excitable, easily cast down or elated or made sharp and suspicious. He argues by personalities rather than by principles. Cyprian is presently obliged to urge him not to be upset by fears of misrepresentation nor to believe too readily false calumnies against his friends.[142] He could indeed summon the courage to assume the dangerous post of the bishopric and, again, to make his Christian confession before the magistrates but he had neither the nervous balance nor the intellectual calibre to be the inspiration of his church. Men still kept and read the letters of Cyprian and Dionysius for their steady guidance and authoritative voice.[143]

The priceless passages in Cornelius' letters are those in which he describes to Fabius the contest with Novatian and gives the single piece of exact statistics we possess for the church in Rome before the fourth century. From his account of the part played by Italian bishops in installing Novatian and of his own measures of retaliation we gather that the Roman bishop claimed by this time the right as metropolitan to ordain other Italian bishops, at least in the neighboring districts of the peninsula, to depose

142 *Infra,* pp. 374 ff.

143 Cornelius himself read aloud to his church the letters he received from Cyprian. *Infra,* p. 381.

for breach of order and even to fill single-handed the places of any so deposed. On the other hand, it had become customary for the nearest Italian bishops to meet at Rome to confirm the election of a new Roman bishop and to consecrate him by the laying on of hands. Sixteen helped to ordain Cornelius.[144] Sixty bishops from all over Italy assembled for his synod, a number which, when absentees and Novatianists are taken into calculation, indicates something like one hundred bishops altogether in central and southern Italy.

As for the church in the capital, we now hear that its clergy has become divided into a hierarchy of seven ranks, five inferior orders having been created below the diaconate. With the bishop they form a body of one hundred and fifty-five men. The forty-six priests denote, perhaps, an equal number of churches or separate congregations.[145] The fifteen hundred widows and other dependents imply a normal supporting membership of from thirty to forty thousand, that is from three to four per cent of the total population of the city.[146] The Novatianists, who had withdrawn, probably took their own poor with them. Before their secession the church must have been larger by, at least, several thousands or their going would never have occasioned so much disturbance. Modern scholars, calculating from the known cost of keeping a slave and the price of a bushel of wheat in the third century, have reckoned that the Roman church was spending for the maintenance of its clergy and needy between $25,000 and $50,000 yearly.[147] With that in mind one can appreciate better the

[144] This number is given in Cyprian's letter, LV. *Infra*, p. 374.

[145] Optatus of Mileve writes, sometime about the year 370, that there are over forty basilicas at Rome. *De Schismate Donatistarum*, II, 4.

[146] Chrysostom says, about 380, that at Antioch three thousand Christians are receiving relief out of a church membership of over one hundred thousand. *Opp.* VII, 658, 810. Quoted by Harnack, in his discussion of this passage. *The Expansion of Christianity*, 2nd ed., Vol. II, p. 248. See also Vol. I, p. 157. If that proportion held good for Rome in 252, it would argue a membership of about fifty thousand. It seems reasonable, however, to suppose that third century Rome was more generous than fourth century Antioch and also that the relief roll was especially long just after a persecution. Gibbon, Döllinger, Friedlander, *etc.*, put the church at fifty thousand. Harnack reduces it to thirty. The population of the city is estimated at about nine hundred thousand.

[147] The Carthaginian church, during the same year, raised 100,000 sesterces, $5,000, as a special fund for the ransom of Christians in Numidia, carried off by bandit raiders, and then offered to send more if it were needed. Cyprian, *Epistolae*, LXII.

sentiment that Cyprian attributes to Decius, that he would rather hear of a new rival for the throne than a new bishop in Rome.

By the end of 251, Decius was dead, killed by the Goths in the Dobrudja. Gallus, his successor, had no strong religious convictions and at first forbore to press the edicts against the Christians. The year of 252 was, therefore, one of temporary respite. But towards autumn, an epidemic broke out and spread through the provinces, causing much illness and death. Many were convinced that the gods were taking vengeance for the slackness with which their honor was being upheld and there were in some places sharp outbursts of popular prejudice and panic. Cyprian speaks of a day when the crowd in the circus at Carthage suddenly clamored a second time for him to be thrown to the lions.[148] Early in 253, Gallus was prevailed upon to set the magistrates again at crushing out disloyalty.

Meanwhile, the leading bishops had been spending their energies on efforts to rally and unite the Christian forces everywhere, as far as they could be reached, had been filling the positions of local clergy who had apostatized or had refused to accept the new rules for restoration of the lapsed and had been directing the course of penitential discipline in their own churches. The attitude of Fabius of Antioch and other Asiatic prelates continued to produce uneasiness. Cornelius wrote to Fabius at least three times,[149] feverishly accusing Novatian of cowardice, trickery, greed and unscrupulousness of every description. As far as we can tell from the extracts, he merely attempted persuasion and assumed no tone of threatening or command. He could not display the Petrine authority to one who questioned his right to possess it and, in any case, Cornelius was no second Victor. Both Cyprian and Dionysius of Alexandria wrote also to Fabius.[150] At the beginning of 253, Dionysius informed

148 *Infra*, p. 377.

149 Eusebius mentions three letters that he had seen and one from Cornelius to Dionysius on the same subject. *Infra*, pp. 382, 386. *Historia Ecclesiastica*, VI, 46, 1–3.

150 The difference in temper between Dionysius and Cornelius is striking. The former refrains from becoming violently controversial, but makes a moving appeal to Fabius' veneration for the martyrs. "These saintly martyrs from our midst, who now sit with Christ, share in his kingdom, participate in his counsel and judge together with him, received some of the brethren who had fallen and

Cornelius that he had been invited by the bishops of several eastern provinces, headed by Helenus of Tarsus, Firmilian of Caesarea in Cappadocia and Theoctistus of Caesarea in Palestine, to meet at a synod at Antioch, to decide finally whether or not to ratify Novatian. He added that Fabius himself had just died and that the bishop of Jerusalem was likewise dead in prison. We know nothing further of the Antiochene synod. It concluded probably not to break with the majority organizations in Rome and Alexandria, especially in face of the impending renewal of persecution.[151] But the lack of hearty Asiatic approval of the Roman policy showed itself when the next critical problem with regard to the treatment of Christians outside the orthodox fold came up for settlement a few years later.[152]

In Africa, a formidable faction, led by the deacon Felicissimus, still maintained congregations where the lapsed were admitted to full communion without a previous period of probation and penance. These congregations elected their own bishop, Fortunatus, and then sent Felicissimus and a few companions to Rome to denounce Cyprian there for undue severity and for failure to keep Cornelius completely informed of the trend of African events. That they succeeded in thoroughly agitating Cornelius is shown by Cyprian's anxious and indignant letter, written just before the end of 252, to remind Cornelius of his own unimpeachable record and to express his surprise that Cornelius should be so perturbed by rebels under sentence of excommunication or that he should so infringe upon another man's episcopal jurisdiction as to entertain complaints from members of the

---

been guilty of the sin of offering sacrifice. For when they had ascertained by tests that their remorse and contrition were sufficient to be accepted by him who desires not the death of the sinner but his repentance, they received and gathered them together and met and united with them in their feasts. What advice then, brethren, do you give us regarding these persons? What are we to do? Shall we follow the same course and principle as they and observe their rule and their charity and show mercy to those on whom they had compassion? Or shall we call their decision wrong and set ourselves up as judges of their principle and grieve mercy and overturn order?" Eusebius, *op. cit.*, VI, 42, 5. Cyprian's letter to Fabius has not been preserved. *Infra*, p. 382.

151 Three years later, Dionysius writes to Pope Stephen that the eastern churches have all rejected Novatianism and are at peace. *Infra*, p. 419.

152 The letter written by a synod at Antioch ninety years later to Bishop Julius at Rome expresses what must often have been in the minds of the Asiatic churchmen. *Infra*, p. 506.

African diocese, who ought properly to be referred for judgment to the African church. Either Cyprian's letter, which he asked Cornelius to read aloud to the Roman church, or the representations of cooler heads at Rome seem to have stiffened Cornelius into disregarding Felicissimus. At all events, when we hear again from Cyprian, early in 253, Felicissimus has dropped from view. A council of African bishops under Cyprian's leadership notifies Cornelius of their intention to bring into the church straightway all the lapsed who seem genuinely repentant, that arms may be given " to men about to face the battle." Then Cyprian himself writes in a high key of exaltation He has heard that Cornelius has made a brave confession and rejoices that the church of Rome has such a head. Whichever of them meets death first, let him remember the other in the house of the Lord.

From all this one can make fairly clear the position that Cornelius occupied, at least in the eyes of some of his most prominent associates. To the ecclesiastical statesmen of the day, such as Cyprian and Dionysius, each metropolitan was sovereign in his own territory and each provincial group of bishops competent to solve independently all religious problems, taking care only to preserve harmony and a fair understanding with the rest of the brethren. The See of Rome, deriving from Peter, symbolized in a somewhat special way the unity and authority that characterized the entire episcopate.[153] The power to bind and loose had been bestowed upon Peter first before its extension to the other apostles. To the Roman bishop then, as an elder brother, the younger members of the episcopal family owed a punctilious respect. As bishop also of the church in the imperial capital he was charged with the duty of acting as liaison officer to keep in touch with the Christian organizations everywhere, and he had a right to expect from other bishops reports of important occurrences in their localities. But Christians who differed from him were adjured not to yield their opinions in deference to his prerogative but simply to maintain the peace in concern for the unity of the Lord's Church.[154] Cornelius himself seems to have preferred to take action in company and to

[153] *Supra,* p. 325; *infra,* p. 406. [154] *Supra,* p. 350, n. 138; *infra,* pp. 362, 374.

have fortified himself by the contemplation not of his own unique and solitary authority but of the strength of his backing in the Roman community.[155]

Cornelius' confession was not followed by execution but merely by banishment to Civita Vecchia. Gallus' persecution was, after all, less wholehearted than that of Decius. Nevertheless, Cornelius did not long survive his trial and died in Civita Vecchia before the summer was over. His body was brought back and buried in a private crypt near the cemetery of Callistus, outside the city walls, and popular tradition soon invented a story of a bloody death by the sword. His relations with Cyprian had, as we have seen, been neither intimate nor always sympathetic but the fact that there had been considerable correspondence between them and that Cyprian's own death as a martyr took place five years later on the same day of the year as that of Cornelius' burial, so that their names stood together in the Western martyrologies and liturgical calendars, caused them to become indissolubly linked in the public mind as brother saints and heroes.[156] Frescoes of the sixth century in Cornelius' crypt show the two standing side by side in their episcopal robes and their portraits are repeated in the same posture in many old Roman churches. At last, in the ninth century, emissaries of Charles the Bald disinterred the body of Cornelius from its crypt on the Via Appia and the body of Cyprian from its vault in Carthage and carried them both away to make sacred the church of Compiègne and join their ashes in that last exile.

Every ecclesiastical history contains accounts of the Novatianist controversy and the organization of the Roman church as depicted by Cornelius. See among others J. Langen, *Geschichte der römischen Kirche* (4 vols., Bonn, 1881–1893), Vol. I, pp. 290 *sqq.*; K. Laimbach, *Cornelius,* in J. J. Herzog and A. Hauck, *Realencyklopädie für protestantische Theologie und Kirche* (24 vols., Leipzig, 1896–1913), Vol. IV; G. Hodges, *The Early Church from Ignatius to Augustine* (New York, 1915), pp. 101 *sqq.*; L. Duchesne, *Early History of the Christian Church* (trans. from the 4th ed. by C. Jenkins,

[155] *Infra,* pp. 384–385.

[156] For an abbreviated version of the legend of Cornelius' passion see L. R. Loomis, *The Book of the Popes,* 27–28. Cornelius and Cyprian are venerated on September 16.

3 vols., London, 1910–1924), Vol. I, pp. 295–303; B. J. Kidd, *History of the Church to A.D. 461* (3 vols., Oxford, 1922–1925), Vol. I, pp. 442–454.

Cyprian, *Epistolae*, XLIV. Text. Ed. by W. Hartel, *Corpus Scriptorum Ecclesiasticorum Latinorum*, III^2, 597–599.

Cyprian to his brother Cornelius, greeting.[157]

1 There have come to us from Novatian, beloved brother, Maximus, a priest, Augendus, a deacon, and one Machaeus and one Longinus. But when we discovered, both from the letter which they brought with them and from their own conversation and report, that Novatian had been made a bishop, we were distressed by the wickedness of an unlawful ordination, performed in opposition to the catholic Church, and decided at once to prohibit them from communion with us. Then, while we were peremptorily denying and refuting the assertions they tried obstinately and insistently to make, I and a number of my colleagues who had gathered with me watched for the return of our colleagues, Caldonius and Fortunatus, whom we had shortly before dispatched as envoys to you, and for that of our fellow bishops who attended your ordination. For we thought that on their arrival they would report with full authority the truth of what had happened and by their plain testimony expose the dishonesty of your rival. But, in the meantime, Pompey and Stephen, our colleagues, arrived and themselves brought proofs and statements, convincing to us by their weight and trustworthiness, to enlighten us here, so that there was no need of listening further to the emissaries from Novatian.

2 But they broke in upon our solemn assembly with spiteful abuse and indecent clamor and demanded that the

157 This letter and the next were obviously written within a short time of each other. This may have been the later of the two.

accusations, which they said they had brought and would prove, be publicly investigated by us and the people. Then we said that it was not consistent with our dignity to suffer the honor of our colleague, who had already been elected and ordained and approved and commended by many, to be called in question any longer by the voice of slanderous rivals. And, because it would be tedious to relate in a letter the means by which they were refuted, subdued and thwarted in their unruly efforts to create a heresy, Primitivus, our fellow priest, will tell you everything in full when he reaches you.

3 But, since their wild presumption allows them no rest, they are endeavoring here too to divide the members of Christ into schismatical parties and to break and tear asunder the body of the catholic Church and are hurrying about from door to door, through many houses, and from town to town, through divers cities, searching for companions in their stubbornness and error. We have once already replied to them and we continue to command them to abandon their dangerous dissension and plotting and to recognize that it is impiety to desert their mother and to realize and admit that once a bishop has been appointed and confirmed by the testimony and judgment of his colleagues and the people it is altogether impossible to appoint another. Hence, if they profess to have peaceful and loyal intentions and to be champions of the gospel and of Christ, they ought first to return to the Church. I bid you, dearly beloved brother, ever farewell.

Ibid., *Epistolae,* XLV. Text. *Op. cit.*, 599–603.

Cyprian to his brother Cornelius, greeting.

1 We have recently, dearly beloved brother, in accordance with our duty as servants of God and, more especially, as just and peaceloving priests, sent our colleagues, Cal-

donius and Fortunatus, not so much to persuade you with our letter as to make every possible effort and exertion themselves during their stay, with the help of you all, to restore the members of the rent body to the unity of the catholic Church and knit together the bond of Christian charity. . . .

2 But our own attitude and purpose have already been made clear to all the brethren and people here. For letters have been lately received here from both parties, but we read your letter aloud and announced to every ear your ordination to the episcopate. We were mindful of our common honor and had respect for the dignity and sanctity of the priesthood and we abhorred the bitter accusations massed together in the document put out by your opponents and took into careful consideration what it was fitting to read and to hear in a great religious assembly of the brethren, with the priests of God sitting beside us and the altar standing in its place. For words should not be indifferently spoken nor thoughtlessly and heedlessly repeated abroad which scandalize the hearers by their rancorous tone and create confusion of opinion in the minds of brethren far distant from you, across the sea. . . . And so, dearest brother, although charges of this sort against you came to me from your fellow priest, who held office with you,[158] I gave directions that only those communications that expressed harmoniously the single-mindedness of religion and were not blatant with the loud complaints of malicious wrongdoers should be read to our clergy and people.

3 Nor are we forgetful of the old customs and intent upon innovation, because we have wished to receive the reports of our own colleagues, who were present there at your ordination. For your announcement by letter of your election to the bishopric would have been sufficient, were there not the opposing faction against you, which is confusing the minds and disturbing the sentiments of many of my

158 *I.e.*, Novatian.

colleagues as well as of the brethren by its criminal and slanderous accusations. To allay this mischief we have considered it necessary to procure the solid and indisputable authority of our colleagues, who are writing to us from Rome and who in their letters have furnished adequate testimony as to the character of your life and discipline and have thus removed every pretext for doubt and controversy from those disaffected persons who enjoy either the novelty or the perversity of the situation. . . . For this most of all, my brother, is and should be the object of our endeavor, to maintain, as far as in us lies, the unity committed by the Lord through the apostles to us, their successors. . . .

4 As regards the case of the priests and Felicissimus here, our colleagues have sent you a letter, written in their own hand, to inform you what they have done.[159] When you read it, you will know from their own letter what they decided and what verdict they pronounced. You will be acting wisely, brother, if you have read to your brethren there a copy of the letter which I lately sent by our colleagues, Caldonius and Fortunatus, to be read to you as a sign of mutual affection, that is, the letter I wrote on the subject of the same Felicissimus and priests to the clergy here, not to the people. It treats also of ordination and the course of events. In that way the brotherhood both here and there will have instruction from us. I am now forwarding another copy of the same letter by Mettius, the subdeacon, and Nicephorus, the acolyte, whom I am sending to you. I bid you, dearly beloved brother, ever farewell.

Ibid., *Epistolae,* XLVI. Text. *Op. cit.,* 604–605.

Cyprian to Maximus, Nicostratus and the other confessors,[160] greeting.

159 An allusion to the clerical commission that had passed sentence on Felicissimus, Novatus and their companions before Cyprian's return to Carthage. *Supra,* p. 333.

160 For these Roman confessors, *vide supra,* pp. 341, 342, 344.

[A short letter, expressing pain and grief at hearing that they had taken part in creating a new bishop and setting up a new church. They are urged to return to their mother and to remember their confession.]

Ibid., *Epistolae,* XLVII. Text. *Op. cit.,* 605–606.

Cyprian to his brother Cornelius, greeting.

It has seemed incumbent upon me, dearest brother, and a duty I owe to you that I should write a short letter to the confessors in your city who have been beguiled by the obstinate errors of Novatian and Novatus and have left the church, to plead with them in the name of our mutual affection to return to their mother, the Church catholic. I have told the subdeacon Mettius to read this letter first to you, for fear that someone may report falsely that I have written something beside what is in it. Moreover, I have also told Mettius, whom I am sending to you, to do with it as you wish and to deliver the letter to the confessors only in case you think they will heed it. I bid you, dearest brother, ever farewell.

Ibid., *Epistolae,* XLVIII. Text. *Op. cit.,* 606–608.

Cyprian to his brother Cornelius, greeting.

1 I have read the letter, dearest brother, which you sent by Primitivus, our fellow priest.[161] and I observe in it that you are annoyed, because letters from the colony of Adrumetum in the name of Polycarp had been addressed to you until Liberalis and I went there, when the letters from there began to be addressed to your priests and deacons.[162]

[161] Primitivus had been the bearer of a previous letter from Cyprian to Cornelius. *Supra,* p. 359.

[162] *I.e.,* "to the priests and deacons at Rome," as Cyprian had addressed his own letters during the vacancy in the Roman See.

2 But I wish you to understand and thoroughly believe that this action was not the result of carelessness nor of contempt. For we and a number of our colleagues, who had met together, had previously determined that during the interval while our fellow bishops, Caldonius and Fortunatus, were being sent as envoys to you, all our judgments should be held in suspense as they were, until these same colleagues of ours, on the restoration of concord at Rome or on their own discovery of the truth, should return to us. But since our fellow bishop Polycarp was not with us, the priests and deacons at Adrumetum were ignorant of what we had decided in our meeting. When we went to them in person and they learned of our intention, they also began to follow the example of the rest, so that the harmony of the churches here was in no respect broken.

3 There are persons, however, who at times upset men's minds and spirits by their words, telling things contrary to the truth. Now we, who supply everyone who sails from here with advice, so that they may travel without offence, know that we have exhorted everyone to acknowledge and uphold the root and matrix of the catholic Church.[163] But since our province is widely extended and has Numidia and Mauretania attached to it, and since the schism which has arisen at Rome perplexes with doubt the minds of people at a distance, we likewise decided to ascertain through these bishops the facts of the situation and to obtain authoritative proofs of your ordination and then at last, after banishing every scruple from every breast, to send letters to you from all the inhabitants everywhere in the province. This in fact we have done, so that all our colleagues may heartily approve and support both you and your communion, that is, both the unity and the charity of the catholic Church. We

[163] *I.e.,* the Roman episcopate. Even during the period of waiting Cyprian has not failed to inculcate reverence for the Roman See as "the root and matrix" from which the rest of the Church had sprung.

are rejoiced that all this has, by God's help, come about and that our design has under Providence been successful.

4 For, in this way, both the genuineness and the dignity of your episcopate have been established in the clearest light with the most open and well grounded approval. From the accounts of our colleagues who have written to us from Rome and from the report and testimony of our fellow bishops, Pompey and Stephen, Caldonius and Fortunatus, both the essential grounds and the correct procedure, as well as the glorious spotlessness of your ordination are known to us all. The divine power guard us, that we and our other colleagues may steadfastly and firmly administer our office and preserve it in the peaceful concord of the catholic Church. So may the Lord, who deigns to choose and appoint for himself priests in his Church, protect them, when chosen and appointed, by his favor and bounty, inspiring them to govern and supplying strength to check the forwardness of the wicked and gentleness to foster the repentance of the fallen! I bid you, dearest brother, ever heartily farewell.

Ibid., *Epistolae,* XLIX. Text. *Op. cit.,* 608–612.

Cornelius to his brother Cyprian, greeting.

1 The care and anxiety that we have endured over those confessors who were deluded and almost blinded and estranged from the Church by the guile and malice of an unscrupulous deceiver have been great but the joy which now relieves us is equally great and we give thanks to Almighty God and Christ our Lord that they have perceived their error and recognized the poisonous, serpentine wiles of the evildoer and by their own clear choice, as they themselves declare from their hearts, have returned to the Church which they had left. In the beginning, some of our brethren, tried in the faith, lovers of peace and desirous of unity, told us of

the rebellious obstinacy of one group and of the softening of the others but we had not sufficient confidence to be able to believe readily that they had changed with such suddenness. But afterwards, the confessors Urbanus and Sidonius came to our fellowpriests and asserted that the confessor and priest Maximus . . .[164] were likewise eager to return with them to the Church. However, since many statements had already issued from them, as you also have learned from our fellowship and my own letters, it seemed best not to trust them too hastily but to hear from the confession of their own lips the sentiments which they had transmitted by messengers. So after they had come and had been questioned by the priests as to their behavior and finally as to the fact that numerous letters, crammed with abuse and imprecations, had been sent out in their names to all the churches and had alarmed almost all of them, they stated that they had been deceived and that they had not known what was in those letters but had merely signed them, that they had been misled by his craft and had committed themselves to the schism and been founders of the heresy, so far as to consent to his receiving the laying on of hands like a bishop. And when they had expressed their reprobation of these and other acts, they begged that they might be blotted out and expunged from memory.

2 When the whole affair had been reported to me, I decided that the presbytery should be called together. There were present also five bishops, who were with us on that day. For I wished that after thorough consultation it might be determined by general agreement what should be done with regard to these men. And in order that you may know the feeling of us all and each person's opinion, I have thought best to notify you of our various judgments, which you may read enclosed with this. Then Maximus, Urbanus, Sidonius and many brothers who had agreed with them came into

164 A few words are missing here from the Latin text.

the presbytery and begged earnestly that the events now past might be forgotten and never again mentioned and that henceforth all their sins might be obliterated, whether of deed or word, and that they might now keep their hearts clean and pure before God in obedience to the gospel words: "Blessed are the pure in heart for they shall see God."[165] The next step was to bring the entire performance to the knowledge of the people, so that they too might see them standing within the church, after they had so long sorrowfully beheld them wandering and astray. When this intention was made known, there was a huge gathering of the brotherhood. With one voice they all gave thanks to God and showed by tears the joy in their bosoms, embracing the confessors as if it had been the day of their liberation from the pains of prison. I will give you the confessors' own declaration. "We," they said, "recognize Cornelius as bishop of the most holy catholic Church, chosen by Almighty God and Christ our Lord. We confess our error; we have been victims of imposture; we have been deceived by wily perfidy and loquacity. Yet even though we seemed to hold a kind of communion with one who was a schismatic and a heretic, our heart was always in the Church. And we know that there is one God and one Christ the Lord, whom we have confessed, and one Holy Spirit and that in a catholic church there ought to be one bishop."[166] Who would not have been moved by this profession, seeing them standing in the church and reaffirming what they had once confessed before the powers of the world? So we bade the priest Maximus resume his office. All the past errors of

[165] Matthew, V, 8.

[166] The point on which stress is laid is not the error of Novatian's dogmatic contention but the crime of erecting a second bishopric. The principle that there should be but one bishop of the Church in any city had been formulated, probably as a matter of practical expediency, by the time of Ignatius of Antioch. *Supra,* p. 239. In the third century, it had become an accepted article of faith and men like Cyprian saw in it a mystical significance. The Council of Nicaea put it into law.

the others we committed by an overwhelming vote of the people to Almighty God, to whose power all things are reserved.

3 These events, dearest brother, we are reporting to you by letter the same hour and the same moment and are at once sending back to you Nicephorus, the acolyte, who is hurrying from the assembly down to the ship, so that without delay you may give thanks along with us to Almighty God and Christ our Lord, as if you were here in person among this clergy and in this gathering of the people. We believe, nay, we are confident, that the rest also who have been involved in this error will promptly return to the Church when they see the leaders on our side. I think, dearest brother, that you should send this letter to the other churches as well, so that they all may know that the intrigue and falsity of this schismatic and heretic are unavailing from this day forth. Farewell, dearest brother.

Ibid., *Epistolae,* L. Text. *Op. cit.*, 613–614.

Cornelius to his brother Cyprian, greeting.[167]

Nothing shall diminish the future punishment of this wretch or his overthrow by the powers of God, for after Maximus, Longinus and Machaeus had been rejected by you,[168] he revived again and, as I have told you in the earlier letter which I sent by the confessor Augendus, I believe that Nicostratus, Novatus, Evaristus, Primus and Dionysius have now joined him. So take pains to inform all our fellow-bishops and brethren that Nicostratus is accused of many crimes and not only has committed fraud and robbery against the secular patroness whose affairs he was managing but also has stolen largely from the funds of the church, a sin which has ensured for him eternal punishment, and

[167] This letter, probably, was written before the preceding.
[168] On these men *vide supra,* p. 358.

that Evaristus has been appointed in his place for the people over whom he formerly presided. Novatus has displayed here his malice and insatiable avarice throughout, just as he invariably did with you. So you may realize what sort of leaders and champions this schismatic and heretic keeps always close to his side. Farewell, dearest brother.

Ibid., *Epistolae,* LII. Text. *Op. cit.,* 616–620.

Cyprian to his brother Cornelius, greeting.

[He regrets to hear that Nicostratus and Evaristus have joined the heretical party. As for Novatus, he was always a troublesome character in Africa, a torch to inflame sedition, etc.]

2 . . . He is the one who as an ambitious upstart installed Felicissimus, his satellite, as deacon without my sanction or knowledge and when in due course he journeyed to Rome to overturn that church also, he took similar and equally grave steps there. For he separated a part of the people from their clergy and destroyed the harmony of the brotherhood, which at that time was closely knit together and in charity with one another. And inasmuch as Rome by its greatness is obviously superior to Carthage, he committed there still greater and more serious offenses. For here he had created a deacon in opposition to the church but there he created a bishop. . . .

Ibid., *Epistolae,* LIII. Text. *Op. cit.,* 620.

Maximus, Urbanus, Sidonius and Macarius to their brother Cyprian, greeting.

We are sure, dearest brother, that your joy will be as deep as ours, that we after deliberation and in growing concern for the welfare and concord of the Church have made peace with Cornelius, our bishop, and all the clergy, and that all the past has been wiped out and committed to the judgment of God. We thought that you should be informed by a letter from us that this has taken place, in the midst of rejoicing on the part of the whole church and ready charity from everyone. We bid you, brother, dearest for many years, farewell.

Ibid., *Epistolae,* LIV. Text. *Op. cit.,* 621–624.

[Cyprian replies to the preceding, expressing his joy and congratulations. He sends the confessors a copy of his new treatise, *De Lapsis,* for them to read.]

Ibid., *Epistolae,* LV. Text. *Op. cit.,* 624–628.

Cyprian to his brother Antonianus,[169] greeting.

1 I have received, dearest brother, your first letter, in which you stoutly defended the unity of the sacerdotal fellowship and supported the catholic Church and declared that you held no communion with Novatian but accepted our advice and were one with our fellow bishop, Cornelius. You wrote also that I should send a copy of that same letter of yours to our colleague Cornelius, that he might have no anxiety but be assured that you were in communion with him, that is, with the Church catholic.

2 But since then your second letter has arrived, sent by Quintus, our fellow priest, in which I notice that your mind has begun to vacillate under the influence of a letter from Novatian. For whereas you had before stated positively your opinion and your agreement with us, in this letter you ask me to explain to you what was the heresy introduced by Novatian and on what ground Cornelius is holding communion with Trofimus and persons who offered incense. . . .

169 A bishop in the province of Africa.

3 . . . And first of all, since you seem to be disturbed about my own conduct as well, I must exonerate myself and my course in your eyes, so that no one may fancy that I weakly abandoned my position and after maintaining in the beginning the rigor of the gospel, changed later my original ideas of discipline and censure. . . .

4 For while the battle was still going forward and the conflict of glorious warfare in persecution was at its height, I believed that the energy of the soldiers must be kept up with every kind of encouragement and with all my ardor. In particular, the spirit of the lapsed must be awakened by the trumpet of our voice, that they might not only seek with prayers and mourning the way of penitence but, whenever an opportunity offered of renewing the combat, might be fired and stimulated by our words to bold confession and glorious martyrdom. . . .

5 In addition, I wrote at great length to Rome, to the clergy there, at that time without a bishop, and to the confessors, the priest Maximus and others in prison, now united with Cornelius in the church. What I wrote you can infer from their replies. . . .

6 Then, in accordance with our previous determination, when the persecution was relaxed and there was chance for us to meet together, a numerous concourse of us bishops, who were still preserved, by our own faith and the Lord's protection, safe and unharmed, assembled together. After reading the statements on both sides, we meted out a moderate and wholesome sentence, in order that, on the one hand, the lapsed should not be deprived of all hope of communion and peace, for fear lest in their despair they might fall away still more and seek after the world, because the Church was shut against them, and live as the gentiles do, and also that, on the other hand, the gospel penalty should not be ignored in favor of a hasty rush to communion but a lengthy

penance should be performed and the Father's mercy be implored in grief and the circumstances, motives and compulsions of each person be investigated, as I have described in the treatise[170] which I trust has reached you and which contains every article of our decision. And if the number of the bishops in Africa should not seem to you sufficiently weighty, we wrote also to Rome on this subject, to Cornelius, our colleague. He too held a council of many of his fellow bishops and with equal gravity and wholesome moderation adopted the same policy as we have done.

. . . .

8 I come now, dearest brother, to the question of our colleague Cornelius, that you may know Cornelius more truly, as we do, not through the lies of malignant detractors but through the judgment of God, who created him bishop, and through the testimony of his fellow bishops, all of whom throughout the world uphold him in harmonious unity. One praiseworthy mark of our dearly beloved Cornelius, which commends him to God and Christ and his Church, that is, all his fellow priests, is that he did not attain the episcopate unprepared but was promoted through all the offices of the Church and often won the favor of the Lord by his holy ministrations and thus ascended through all the ranks of religion to the lofty crown of priesthood. Furthermore, he neither requested nor desired the bishopric nor did he attempt to grasp it, as others have done, who are puffed up with swelling arrogance and conceit. But he was always quiet and unassuming and like those whom God selects for this office. In the modesty of his virgin continence and the humility of his inborn, safeguarded piety he employed no force, as some do, to be made bishop but himself suffered force and accepted the bishopric under compulsion. He was ordained by many of our colleagues, who were then in the

[170] The treatise, *De Lapsis, supra,* p. 369.

city of Rome and who sent us letters about his ordination, full of esteem and praise and glowing with accounts of his words. So Cornelius was created bishop through the judgment of God and his Christ, with the testimony of almost all the clergy and the assent of the people who were then present, by the college of aged and saintly bishops. For no one had been bishop before him since the post of Fabianus, that is, the post of Peter and the office of the sacerdotal episcopate, had been left empty. But now that he has assumed it and has been confirmed by God's will and the consent of us all, whoever else tries to become bishop must become one outside the Church and lack the Church's ordination, because he does not preserve the unity of the Church. Whoever that man may be and however much he boasts and claims for himself, he is sacrilegious, he is a stranger, he is an outsider. And since after the first there can be no second, whoever becomes bishop after the one who should be the only one, is not the second but nothing at all.

9 In the next place, after Cornelius had received the bishopric, not by intrigue or violence but by the will of God who creates priests, he displayed such courage in undertaking his bishopric, such fortitude of mind, such constancy of faith, that we are fain to acknowledge and applaud him highly with undivided heart. He assumed his place fearlessly in the sacerdotal see at Rome, at the very time when the hateful tyrant was threatening God's priest with every describable and indescribable penalty and would have considered it far less irksome and intolerable to hear that a rival prince had arisen to attack him than that a priest of God had been installed at Rome.[171] Should he not, dearest brother, be celebrated with the highest awards of courage and faith, should he not be numbered among the glorious

[171] Harnack takes this last clause to be a quotation from Decius' own lips, a remark that he was reported to have made. The Latin seems to us to leave this in doubt. Cyprian may have been expressing in his own language a feeling attributed to Decius.

confessors and martyrs, who accepted the see at such a time, expecting the butchers of the body and the executioners from the ferocious tyrant to murder him with the sword or to crucify him or to burn him with fire or to lacerate his limbs and vitals with some new device of torture, but who disregarded the cruel edicts and despised threats, sufferings and torments by the power of faith? For even if the majesty and goodness of the protecting Lord have kept watch over the appointed bishop whom he has chosen, nevertheless Cornelius in his devotion and his fears endured all that he could endure and by his priestly sanctity overcame the tyrant before that tyrant's defeat by arms in battle. . . .

11 . . . He deliberated with many of his colleagues there before he admitted Trofimus, who atoned for himself by bringing back many brethren and restoring them to salvation. . . .

12 But the rumor that reached you, that Cornelius was holding communion from time to time with persons who had offered sacrifice, originated also in one of the tales invented by the apostates. . . . Therefore, be slow to heed or credit all the stories that go about regarding Cornelius and ourselves, dearest brother. . . . [Need of wisdom and mercy in dealing with the fallen.]

21 Some, indeed, of the bishops among our predecessors here in our province believed that peace should not be given to harlots and excluded adulterers entirely from penance.[172] But they did not on this account withdraw from fellowship with other bishops nor did they by the obstinacy of their severity and discipline destroy the unity of the catholic Church. Because others granted peace to adulterers, he who refused it did not cut himself off from the Church. The bond of harmony stood firm and the indivisible sacrament of the catholic Church continued and each separate bishop gov-

[172] *I.e.*, held the Puritan views of Tertullian. *Supra*, pp. 297, 301.

erned and determined his own conduct, in the knowledge that he would render account of his deeds to the Lord. . . .

24 As to the character of Novatian, dearest brother, about whom you requested that I should write you what heresy he has introduced, remember in the first place that we ought not even to be inquisitive as to what he teaches, so long as he teaches outside the Church. Whoever he is and whatever he is, he who is not in the Church of Christ is not a Christian.[173] However he may boast and proclaim his philosophy and eloquence in lofty words, he who has failed to preserve either brotherly love or ecclesiastical unity has lost even what he once was. Unless, indeed, you deem him bishop, who, after a bishop has been ordained by sixteen fellow bishops in a church, contrives by bribery to be ordained by deserters an adulterous and alien bishop and although there is but one Church, divided by Christ into many members throughout the whole world, and likewise one episcopate, extended far and wide through a harmonious multitude of many bishops, in spite of divine tradition, in spite of the combined and universally compacted unity of the catholic Church, sets about to create a human church and sends his own apostles through many cities, to establish some fresh foundations of his own institution. And although for a long time past, in all the provinces and in every city, men have been ordained bishops who are advanced in years, perfect in faith, tried in adversity, proscribed in persecution, yet he dares to appoint other men, false bishops, over them. . . .

Ibid., *Epistolae,* LIX. Text. *Op. cit.,* 666–691.

Cyprian to his brother Cornelius, greeting.

1 I have read, dearest brother, the letter which you

[173] Here again one notes that it is easier to condemn Novatian as schismatic than to prove him heretic. *Supra,* p. 366, n. 166. Cyprian, however, does not descend to such depths of personal abuse as Cornelius does. *Infra,* pp. 383 ff.

sent by our brother, the acolyte Saturus, so full of fraternal affection and churchly discipline and priestly austerity. In it you told me that Felicissimus, no new enemy of Christ but one whom I expelled long ago for his numerous grave offenses and who was condemned not only by my sentence but by that of many of my fellow bishops also,[174] had been excluded by you at Rome and although he came escorted by a troop from the violent faction, had been shut out from the church with that unhesitating energy with which bishops ought to take action. From that church he was long ago debarred by the majesty of God and the severity of Christ, our Lord and Judge. . . .

2 But when I read your second letter, brother, which you appended to the first, I was much astonished to observe that you had been somewhat perturbed by the threats and menaces of the persons who came and, as you wrote, assaulted you and recklessly declared that if you did not accept the letter which they presented, they would read it in public and who added many disgraceful and abusive accusations, suitable to their lips. But if it is the case, dearest brother, that the audacity of evildoers is to terrify us and that what wicked men cannot accomplish by just and lawful means they can do by desperate daring, there is an end of the strength of the episcopacy and the lofty and divine authority to govern the Church. Nor can we continue any longer nor, in fact, can we now be Christians, if it is come to the point that we are frightened at the threats and snares of outcasts. For the gentiles and the Jews also threaten us, and the heretics and all whose hearts and minds are obsessed by the devil give vent daily to their venomous anger in malignant words. But one should not quail before them, because they threaten, nor is the adversary and enemy mightier than Christ, because he makes so many boasts and claims in this world. Our faith, dearest brother, should stand immovable

174 *Supra*, pp. 333, 347, 361.

and steadfast and our courage stalwart against every onset and attack of the noisy flood and should oppose them with the massive force of the unshaken rock. Nor does it matter from what quarter fear or danger assails a bishop, since he lives exposed to fears and dangers, yet out of these very fears and dangers is made glorious. Nor should we anticipate and expect menaces from gentiles and Jews alone, for we see that the Lord himself was hindered by his brethren and betrayed by one whom he had chosen to be among his apostles. . . .

3 But, dearest brother, ecclesiastical discipline is not on that account to be abandoned nor priestly rules relaxed, because we are beset with reproaches or unnerved with terrors, for divine Scripture foretells and warns us against that. . . .

5 In view of such great and numerous examples, that confirm by divine warrant the priestly authority and power, what sort of persons, do you think, are those enemies of priests and rebels against the catholic Church who are not deterred by the solemn warnings of the Lord nor by the vengeance of future judgment? This has been the very cause why heresies and schisms have arisen, that men do not obey the priest of God nor realize that there is one priest at a time in the Church and one judge at a time in Christ's stead, and that if the whole brotherhood would obey him according to divine command, no one would stir up opposition to the priestly organization, for no one, in the face of God's judgment, the assent of the people and the approbation of other bishops, would constitute himself a judge not of the bishops but of God, no one would rend the unity and tear asunder the Church of Christ and no one, to please himself and his swollen pride, would start a new heresy, separate and apart, — unless there be a man of such blasphemous indifference and erroneous opinions as to suppose that a priest is created without the will of God, whereas the Lord says in

the gospel: "Are not two sparrows sold for a farthing? And one of them does not fall to the ground without the will of the Father."[175]. . .

6 Because I myself am challenged I say more. I say it reluctantly. I say it under compulsion. When a bishop has been set in the place of one who is dead,[176] elected in peace by the love of the whole people, when he is protected by God's help in persecution, supported faithfully by all his colleagues, approved still by his people through four years of episcopacy, when in time of quiet he maintains discipline, in time of storm is proscribed specifically by the name of his bishopric and also on several occasions searched for to be given to the lion, honored by the testimony of divine favor in the circus and amphitheatre, summoned by popular clamor a second time, during the very days in which I am writing this letter to you, to fight the lion in the circus for the sake of the sacrifices which the proclamation requires the people to make, when such a man, dearest brother, is attacked by reckless, unscrupulous persons outside the Church, it is obvious who is his assailant. Not Christ, who appoints and guards his priests, but he who is the enemy of Christ and the foe of his Church, who harasses with hatred the ruler of the Church, so that after he has removed the pilot he may proceed more ferociously and violently to make shipwreck of the Church. . . .

9 As for the election of that false bishop Fortunatus[177] by a few hardened heretics, I did not write you of it at once, dearest brother, for it was not a matter of enough importance or gravity to be reported to you in great haste, especially since you already knew Fortunatus by name. For he is one of the five priests who long ago deserted the church and

[175] Matthew, X, 29.

[176] The following is a summary of Cyprian's own episcopate. He begins by contrasting his election with that of a schismatic bishop, chosen while the lawful bishop is still living.

[177] *Supra*, p. 355.

were later excommunicated by decision of many of our fellow bishops and influential men, who last year wrote a letter to you on the subject.[178] I also thought you would recognize the name of Felicissimus, the standard bearer of sedition, who was mentioned in the same letter written to you at the time by our fellow bishops. The latter was not only excommunicated by these men here but has just now been expelled by you from the church in Rome. Since I supposed that you were aware of these facts and believed that you would certainly be guided by your memory and sense of discipline, I did not consider it necessary to notify you immediately and hurriedly of the heretics' antics. . . . And I did not write you of their performance because we despise all these doings and because I was soon to send you the names of the bishops here who govern the brethren soundly and correctly in the catholic Church. It was the judgment of us all in this region that I should send these names to you, so as to forward the enterprise of exposing error and revealing truth, that you and our colleagues might know to whom you should write and from whom you should receive letters in your turn. Then, if anyone besides these men enumerated in our letter should venture to write to you, you might be sure that he had either been polluted by sacrifice or certificate or that he was one of the heretics, that is, a wrongheaded, blasphemous person.[179] But when I found a chance to send by one of the clergy well known to me, I wrote you an account of this Fortunatus, along with the other news that I thought should be reported to you from here, and dispatched it by the acolyte Felicianus, whom you sent over with our colleague, Perseus. However, while our brother Felicianus was delayed here by the wind or detained in order to take other letters from us, Felicissimus, who started promptly, reached you first. For thus evil always

[178] *Supra*, pp. 347, 361.
[179] *I.e.*, he would be either one of the lapsed or a Novatianist.

makes haste, as if by haste it might prevail over innocence. . . . [The heretics claim a much larger following than they actually possess. They are communicating with the lapsed, etc.]

14 . . . After all this, with a pseudo-bishop besides, ordained for them by heretics, they dare to set sail and carry letters from schismatic and blasphemous persons to the See of Peter, to the leading church, whence the unity of the priesthood took its rise,[180] forgetting that those are the same Romans whose faith was publicly commended by the apostle[181] and whom perfidy cannot touch. And what is the cause of their going to you and informing you that they have set up a false bishop in opposition to the genuine bishops? Either they are satisfied with what they have done and persist in their offense or else they regret and renounce it, in which case they know to what place they should return. For it has been decreed by us all and it is furthermore right and just, that every case should be tried in the place where the wrong was committed. Since to each separate shepherd has been assigned one portion of the flock for him to direct and govern and give hereafter an account of his ministry to the Lord, so those over whom we are set ought not to wander about from place to place nor shatter the harmonious accord of bishops by sly and deceitful impertinence, but they should present their case in the place where they can confront their accusers and the witnesses of their evil doing. Unless, perhaps, the authority of the bishops in Africa seems too slight, in view of the fact that they have already passed sentence upon these men. . . . Their case has already been investigated, the verdict already pronounced, and it is not consistent with priestly discipline that we should be open to the charge of levity and a change-

[180] The Latin is: "ad Petri cathedram atque ad ecclesiam principalem unde unitas sacerdotalis exorta est." *Cf. supra,* pp. 325, 348. This is the first appearance in our literature of the phrase, "See of Peter." Bishop Stephen employed it, a little later. *Infra,* p. 415.

[181] Romans, I, 8.

able and inconstant mind, for the Lord instructs us in his words: "Let your communication be, 'Yea, yea, nay, nay.'" . . .

16 In what language shall I speak of these men, who have now gone to you along with Felicissimus, the author of all this ill, sent as envoys by Fortunatus, their pseudo-bishop, bearing a letter to you as false as he is false whose letter it is, or as their own consciences are deep laden with crime or as their lives are reprehensible and base. Although they are in the Church, yet for such guilt they should have been cast out of the Church. In short, because of their bad consciences they do not dare to approach us or to draw near to the threshold of the church here, but they wander abroad through the province, deluding and defrauding the brethren. And now, because they have become known to everyone here and are everywhere refused entrance for their sins, they take ship from here to you. For they have not the face to come to us or to stand up in our midst, since there are extremely grave and serious accusations brought against them by the brethren. If they wish to test our justice, let them come. Then, if they have any excuse or defense, we shall see what is their notion of reparation and what fruit they show of repentance. The church here is closed to no one and the bishop denies himself to no one. Our patience and consideration and mercy are ready for all comers. . . .

18 Or must, dearest brother, the dignity of the catholic Church and the honor of the faithful and undefiled people within it and the authority and power of its priests be disregarded, so that heretics outside the Church may say that they can sit in judgment on an officer of the Church? . . . Why then should not the Church submit to the Capitol, the priests retire and remove the Lord's altar to make room for images and idols and their shrines in the holy and venerable meeting-places of our clergy and still more ground be afforded to Novatian for upbraiding and denouncing us,

since those who offered sacrifice and openly denied Christ not only are invited to enter without act of penance but have actually begun to terrorize and lord it over us? If they want peace, let them lay down their arms; if they are making atonement, why do they utter threats? If they threaten, let them discover that the priests of God are not afraid! . . .

19 And, inasmuch as I know, dearest brother, that for the mutual love we owe and feel for one another you are always accustomed to read our letters aloud to the distinguished clergy who share your office with you and to your great and holy people, I adjure and entreat you now to do at my request what at other times you do of your own accord in my honor, so that whatever contagion may be working among you from his poisonous words and malicious insinuations may be wholly dispelled from our brothers' ears and hearts by the reading of my letter and the perfect and sincere charity of good men be cleansed from all the vileness of heretical slander.

20 . . . And although I know that our brethren at Rome have been armed by your foresight and are so alert in their own vigilance that the poisons of the heretics can neither hurt nor deceive them and that the laws and precepts of God have weight with them, even as the fear of God is in them, nevertheless our concern and love for you have impelled us to write this out of a full heart, that you may cease from intercourse with such men. . . . For there can be no fellowship between faith and perfidy. He who is not with Christ, who is a foe to Christ, who is an enemy to his unity and his peace, cannot be our associate. If they come to you with prayers and promises and amendment, hear them. If they flaunt threats and curses, spurn them. I bid you, dearest brother, ever farewell.

Eusebius, *Historia Ecclesiastica,* VI, 43, 1–12, 21; 46, 1–4. Text. *Eusebius Werke* (*Die griechischen christlichen Schriftsteller der ersten drei Jahrhunderte*), II², 612–618, 622–624, 626–628.

43 At this time, Novatus,[182] a priest of the Roman church, full of arrogant contempt for the lapsed, on the ground that there was no longer any hope of their salvation, not even if they displayed every sign of a genuine and pure repentance, became leader of the heresy of those who in pride of imagination call themselves Cathari.[183] Whereupon a great synod met at Rome of bishops, sixty in number, and many more priests and deacons, while in other provinces the pastors deliberated separately in their places as to what should be done. A resolution was adopted by them all, that Novatus and his adherents and those who supported his unbrotherly and inhuman attitude should be pronounced aliens to the Church and that it should heal the brethren who had lapsed in the persecution and minister to them with the remedies of penance.

There has come down to us a letter from Cornelius, bishop of the Romans, to Fabius of the church at Antioch, which relates what was done at the synod in Rome and what was the decision of those in Italy and Africa and the regions roundabout. Also other letters, written in the Roman tongue by Cyprian and his party in Africa, which show that they agreed as to the need of succoring those who had been tempted and of expelling utterly from the catholic Church the leader of the heresy and all his followers. Appended to these is another letter from Cornelius, describing the resolutions of the synod, and still another on the conduct of Novatus, from which we must not fail to make quotations, so that the readers of this book may under-

[182] The name all through here, of course, should be Novatian. Eusebius does not distinguish between the two men, the Carthaginian Novatus, and the Roman Novatian.

[183] The Greek word means "pure."

stand about him. In the course of informing Fabius what sort of man Novatus was, Cornelius writes:

"My aim in saying this is to have you see that this fellow has wanted the episcopate for a long time but has kept his ambitious craving secret to himself and has used as a cloak for his rebellion the fact that he had the confessors in agreement with him at the beginning. But Maximus, one of our priests, and Urbanus, both of whom won twice the great glory of confession, and Sidonius and Celerinus, a man who by God's mercy mightily endured every torture and by the power of his faith overcame the weakness of the flesh and by strength conquered the adversary, these men discovered his character and detected the craft and duplicity in him, the perjury and falsehood, the harsh exclusiveness and treachery.[184] And they returned to the holy Church and in a large gathering of bishops, priests and many of the laity declared all his guile and wickedness, which he had kept concealed. And they mourned and repented because through the persuasions of that wily and malicious beast they had forsaken the Church for a little time."

A little further on he writes: "How extraordinary, beloved brother, are the change and transformation that we have seen take place in him in a short while! For this high and mighty person, who bound himself with terrific oaths to make no effort after the bishopric, suddenly appears amongst us as a bishop, as if shot out by some machine.[185] For this believer in dogma, this champion of churchly doctrine, in his endeavor to grasp and seize the episcopate, which had not been bestowed upon him from above, selected two

[184] Compare this with the confessors' own statement of their reasons for wishing to rejoin the regular organization. *Supra*, p. 366.

[185] This account of Novatian's election is obviously libelous and untrustworthy. Cornelius was a credulous person when it came to ugly stories, as even Cyprian had reason to know. *Supra*, pp. 377, 380. He was at special pains here to blacken Novatian's character to Fabius. As a matter of fact, Novatian seems to have been disinterested and thoroughly high-minded and conscientious in his action.

of his companions, who had forfeited their own salvation, and sent them to a small and insignificant corner of Italy to hoodwink by some fictitious argument three bishops there, who were rustic and simple-minded men. They positively and insistently asserted that these bishops must go quickly to Rome in order to allay by their mediation, in common with other bishops, all the strife that had arisen there. Then, when they had come, being, as we have already said, very inexperienced in wicked schemes and devices, they were locked up with some corrupt persons of the same stripe as himself. At the tenth hour, when they were drunk and sick, he compelled them by violence to confer the bishopric on him with some counterfeit and invalid imposition of hands. Thus, because the office had not come to him, he avenged himself by craft and treachery. One of these bishops shortly afterwards returned to the church, grieving and confessing his transgression, and we gave him communion as a layman, for all the people present interceded for him. To the other bishops we ordained successors and sent them to the places where they live. So this avenger of the gospel did not know that there should be one bishop in a catholic church![186] Yet he was not ignorant — for how could he be? — that in our church are forty-six priests,[187] seven deacons, seven subdeacons, forty-two acolytes, fifty-two exorcists, readers and doorkeepers,[188] and fifteen hun-

[186] *Supra,* p. 366.

[187] Cornelius' point seems to be that Novatian had against him the whole organization of the great Roman church.

[188] This is the famous passage containing the first extant enumeration of the seven ranks in the Catholic hierarchy of the order. The titles, priest and deacon, had, of course, been used from the beginning, though with shifting significance. The limitation of the Roman diaconate to seven, which still holds, is due to the statement in Acts, VI, that the apostles first appointed seven to that service. The offices of subdeacon and acolyte are mentioned first here and in the writings of Cyprian. The incumbents were meant to assist at the altar in the liturgy, prepare vessels, lights, wine and bread for the Eucharist, go as messengers to other churches, etc. Exorcists appear in the second century but rather as random, inspired volunteers, not, as here, regular officials in a systematic organization. The reader, who read from the Scripture in public meetings, was employed in Tertullian's day. *De Praescriptione,* 41. The doorkeeper or janitor is named here for the first time.

dred widows and needy persons,[189] all of whom are fed through the Master's grace and loving kindness. Yet not even this large multitude, so essential to the church, nor the number who through God's will are rich and powerful, nor the vast, uncounted mass of our people could deter him from his rash presumption and recall him to the church."

And further on he adds the following: "Well, now, let us say outright for what deeds or conduct he dared to lay claim to the bishopric. Was it because he was brought up within the Church and endured many conflicts on her behalf and was involved in many dire perils for his religion? Not at all. For the instigator of his faith was Satan, who entered into and dwelt within him for a long time. Then, when he was delivered[190] by the exorcists, he fell into a bad illness and expected certainly to die, and he received baptism on the very bed where he was lying, if indeed one must say that such a person did receive it. At any rate, after he had recovered from his illness, he received none of the other rites that according to the rule of the Church are required after baptism, namely, the confirmation by the bishop. Since he failed to receive that, how could he have received the Holy Spirit?"

And again, a little later, he says: "In his cowardice and passion for life he denied that he was a priest during the time of persecution. For when he was asked and entreated by the deacons to come out of the chamber in which he had immured himself, to give aid to the brethren, as far as was lawful and possible for a priest to aid the brethren who were in danger and needed help, he was so far from responding to

---

See A. C. McGiffert's notes on this passage in his translation of Eusebius, *Nicene and Post-Nicene Fathers*, Second Series, Vol. I, p. 288; also *supra*, p. 353.

[189] On the use that is made of this statement of the number of dependents supported by the Roman church to calculate the total membership of the church at this juncture, *vide supra*, p. 353, n. 146.

[190] *I.e.*, from his demoniac possession.

the deacons' entreaties that he went away in irritation and left them. He said that he meant to be a priest no longer and that he was a devotee of another philosophy." . . .

Then he crowns all this with the worst of the man's offenses, as follows: "After he has finished the oblation and is distributing to each person his portion and giving it to him, he compels the wretched people to swear instead of repeating the blessing. He holds the hands of the recipient in both of his own and does not release him until he has taken the following oath (I shall give the man's very words): "Swear to me, by the blood and body of our Lord Jesus Christ, never to desert me and turn to Cornelius." And the unhappy person gets not a taste until he takes the vow and, instead of receiving the bread with the word, "Amen," says: "I will not join Cornelius."[191] . . .

At the close of his letter he gives a list of the bishops who came to Rome and condemned Novatian's folly, their names and the parish over which each of them presided. He enumerates also those who did not come to Rome but who signified by letter their assent to the vote of these bishops and he records their names and the cities from which they each wrote. All this Cornelius says in his letter to Fabius, bishop of Antioch. . . .

46 . . . [Eusebius gives a list of the letters he has found written by Dionysius, bishop of Alexandria, among which is one to Cornelius of Rome in reply to one on the subject of Novatian.[192]] He says in this that he has been

[191] The reader will appreciate this accusation better if he reads in connection with it the third century *Canons of Hippolytus*, which prescribe the liturgy for the Lord's Supper. Canon XIX gives the form to be followed in the distribution. "And when the bishop has now broken the bread, let him give a fragment to everyone of them, saying: 'This is the bread of heaven, the body of Jesus Christ.' And let him that receives say, 'Amen.'" Quoted in G. Hodges, *The Early Church from Ignatius to Augustine*, p. 115. It is impossible, however, to credit these outrageous charges against a man like Novatian.

[192] Eusebius mentions six letters of Dionysius addressed at this time to groups of Roman Christians, one so-called "diaconal letter," one to the Roman church on peace, another to the same on penance, one to the confessors who sided with Novatian and two more to the confessors after their restoration to the church.

invited by Helenus, bishop of Tarsus in Cilicia, and others of his party, Firmilian, bishop in Cappadocia, and Theoctistus of Palestine, to meet them at the synod in Antioch, where some persons are attempting to ratify the schism of Novatian.[193] In addition, he writes that he has heard that Fabius has fallen asleep and that Demetrianus has been elected his successor in the see of Antioch.

Cyprian, *Epistolae*, LVII. Text. *Corpus Scriptorum Ecclesiasticorum Latinorum*, III[2], 650–656.

Cyprian, Liberalis, Caldonius, Nicomedes, . . .[193a] to their brother Cornelius, greeting.

[A new persecution is impending and in the opinion of the writers all the repentant lapsed should have absolution.]

5 . . . At the bidding of the Holy Spirit and the direction of the Lord in numerous clear visions, we have determined that, inasmuch as the enemy is reported and proved to be on the verge of attacking us, we should collect the soldiers of Christ within the camp and after an investigation into each case give peace to the lapsed or rather, furnish arms to men about to face the battle. This resolution we believe will commend itself to you also, for you are touched with fatherly compassion. But if any of our colleagues maintains that peace should not be given to our brothers and sisters at the approach of conflict, he shall render to the Lord an account in the day of judgment for his harsh sentence and inhuman severity. We, as our faith, love and anxiety demanded, have made known the burden on our minds, namely, that the day of struggle is drawing near, that a fierce enemy will soon assail us, that the battle which

193 This synod of Antioch seems to have resulted in the general condemnation of Novatian by the eastern churches. *Vide infra*, pp. 420, 506, 526. Note that the action was recalled by eastern bishops in the next century to prove that the West should confirm their sentence on Athanasius.

193a Forty-two persons in all are named as the senders of this letter, being the bishops present at the council held at Carthage in the spring of 253.

impends will not be as the one before it but much more stern and desperate, that this has been often divinely foretold to us and that by the providence and mercy of God we are being frequently forewarned. Through his power and goodness we who trust in him may be safe, for he who in season of peace tells his soldiers of the coming contest will, when they fight the battle, give them victory. We bid you, dearest brother, ever farewell.

Ibid., *Epistolae,* LX. Text. *Op. cit.,* 691–695.

Cyprian to his brother Cornelius, greeting.

1 We have been told, dearest brother, of the glorious testimonies of your faith and courage and have heard with exultation of your noble confession and count ourselves also sharers and companions in your merits and renown. For since we have one Church, a united mind and indestructible harmony, what priest does not rejoice at the praises of his fellow priest as if at his own or what brotherhood is not glad in the joy of its brethren? I cannot describe to you how keen was the happiness here nor how deep the gladness, when we learned of your triumph and fortitude and knew that you had been the leader in confession there for your brethren's loyalty, so that while you precede them to glory, you make many your comrades in glory and while you are ready to confess first for them all, you incite them to be a people of confessors. We cannot determine what most to commend among you, whether your own quick and steadfast faith or the devoted love of the brethren. You have publicly displayed there the courage of the leader bishop; they have shown the unity of the follower brethren. There has been one spirit, one voice among you. The whole church of Rome has confessed. . . .

5 We beseech you, dearest brother, with all our power, for the mutual love by which we are knit together, that

since, through the provident warning of the Lord and the saving counsel of divine compassion, we are admonished that the day of our own struggle and conflict is drawing nigh, we and all our people cease not from fasting, watching and prayer. . . . Let us be mindful of one another, of one heart and soul! Let us in every place pray for one another! Let us relieve suffering and distress in love for one another! And whichever among us, by the speedy favor of God, first departs hence, let him be constant in love for us in the house of the Lord. Let his prayer for our brethren and sisters cease not in the presence of the pitiful Father! I bid you, dearest brother, ever farewell.

Lucius

(253–254)

Lucius, who succeeded Cornelius, was a priest who had confessed and been banished with him to Civita Vecchia and was ordained bishop in banishment to fill Cornelius' place. Not long after his election, the emperor Gallus was murdered by a band of insurgent soldiers and there came another pause in the persecution. It had certainly not fulfilled its object of putting an end to the plague, which continued unabated to ravage one district after another. The presence of the new emperor, Valerian, was urgently demanded in the East, where the Persians were capturing Antioch and the Goths roaming through Asia Minor. The edicts against the Christians were not revoked but for four years there was no further attempt to enforce them. The clergy who had been banished under Gallus were even allowed to return and pursue their usual vocations without interference. Among the exiles to come back to Rome was the new bishop Lucius. We know, however, nothing more about him, except that he carried on the general policy of Cornelius toward those who had apostatized.[193b] In the summer of 254, without waiting for the answer to Cyprian's enthusiastic prayer for his martyrdom, he

[193b] *Cf. infra,* p. 400.

died and was buried in the cemetery of Callistus. Cyprian's letter is the only document that has reached us from his pontificate.

There are no special references for Lucius.

Cyprian, *Epistolae,* LXI. Text. *Corpus Scriptorum Ecclesiasticorum Latinorum,* III[2], 695–698.

Cyprian and his colleagues to their brother Lucius, greeting.

1 A short time since, dearest brother, we were glad for you, because the favor of God had bestowed upon you a double honor, making you both confessor and bishop in the government of his Church. And now again we rejoice for you and your companions and all the brethren, because the benign and gracious protection of the Lord has brought you back once more to them in full glory and honor. . . .

4 Would that there were some way, dearest brother, that we who are bound to you by mutual love might be present there at your return, so that we too might enjoy with the rest the happy fruit of your coming! . . . But I and my colleagues and all the brethren send this letter to you in our stead, dearest brother, to express our gladness to you by letter and to offer the faithful services of love. Here also we shall not cease in our sacrifices and prayers to give thanks to God the Father and Christ his Son, our Lord, and to implore and beseech him, who is perfect and perfecting, to perfect in you the glorious crown of your confession. Mayhap for this he has brought you back, that your glory might not be concealed nor your confession crowned with martyrdom outside the city. For the victim who supplies an example of courage and faith to the brethren should be slain in the presence of the brethren. We bid you, dearest brother, ever farewell.

4. THE REASSERTION OF THE CLAIM

Stephen

(254–257)

The three years of Stephen's pontificate passed without a renewal of imperial persecution but not on that account without a cloud. The two allied problems of the treatment to be allotted to the apostates and of the efficacy of priestly absolution to pardon mortal sin were, to be sure, regarded as settled in the great majority of churches and one synod after another ratified the rules for penitential discipline drawn up at Rome, Carthage or Alexandria. The Novatianists organized separate minority communions of Puritans in various places but only here and there, as at Arles, was a bishop of a regular church persuaded to join them. If Stephen had been a man of the type of Cornelius, there might have been nothing to make his term of office noteworthy in papal history. The question that did presently arise of the validity of the heretical ceremonies of baptism affected only a comparatively insignificant number in the Church and was in itself far less fraught with tragedy than that of the permanent damnation of the multitudes of lapsed.

But Stephen was not content to fill the peaceful rôle of applying the principles worked out by his predecessors and of coöperating fraternally with the heads of other provincial churches in handling new problems as they appeared. Stephen was a bishop of the stamp of Victor and Callistus. To his mind Cornelius and Lucius had erred in following where they should have led and in acting as members of the common, coördinate apostolate of all the bishops, instead of as the unique heirs of the chief apostolate of Peter. We have, unfortunately, nothing entire of his own writing but we have a few quotations from his letters and a few allusions to his conduct and evidence in plenty of the quick reaction in the provinces to his autocratic and centralizing policy. As Dionysius of Alexandria said, the Church was at peace until he disturbed it.

We have no record of his election nor of events just after it.

We can only surmise that then or previously he became acquainted with some literature that had been composed earlier in the century in support of the new Petrine theory.[194] For a while, he found no conspicuous opportunity to assert the prerogative that he felt to be inherent in his office and that Cornelius and Lucius had allowed to lie unregarded. He could hardly undo the settlement of the problem of the lapsed, much as he might disapprove of the method by which the settlement had been achieved. Such a step would have meant the disruption of the church over which he himself presided and possibly his own deposition at the hands of his Romans. But he evinced no interest in efforts abroad to complete that settlement in the few districts where it was not already in force. Marcian, bishop of Arles in the province of Narbonne, had joined the Novatianists and carried many of his people with him and his provincial colleagues had taken no decisive action. Faustinus, bishop of the city of Lyons, and other bishops in the province of Lyons wrote to Stephen reporting the fact and asking for direction. They believed apparently that they themselves had no jurisdiction over a bishop in another province and that there was no one in his own province likely to cope with him. They turned to the Roman See for advice. Stephen either ignored their letters or sent unsatisfactory and indifferent replies. The invitation to exert his influence in Gaul did not attract him if his influence must go to support the measures of Cornelius.

Faustinus and his friends finally appealed to Cyprian of Carthage, whose personal reputation set him on a high eminence and whose see stood second to Rome in the West. Would he give them his counsel or would he himself stir up Stephen to some suitable response? Cyprian's letter to Stephen is polite but emphatic and scarcely veils his surprise that Stephen should be so remiss in his care for the Church and in loyalty to his predecessors. He outlines for him the correct course of procedure, so that ignorance or inexperience may be no excuse for further delay. Stephen should write three letters at once, one to the bishops of the associated provinces of Gaul, pointing out to them

194 *Supra*, pp. 296–297.

the necessity of excluding Marcian from their synods, the second to the Christians of the province of Narbonne and the third to those of the city of Arles, admonishing them to shut out Marcian from their churches and to set about the process of electing another bishop. In a case like this, where the local machinery had come to a temporary standstill, the head of the leading apostolic church had exercised from of old the elder brother's duty of reminding the local churches how to start it functioning again. Jealous as Cyprian was for the independence of the whole episcopate, he understood that when bishops themselves were at a loss they had a right to expect a word of guidance from the one who had behind him the greatest store of prestige and influence. If the situation had arisen in Africa or Numidia or Mauretania, he himself might have handled it as metropolitan of the principal church in that region, but a difficulty in Gaul should certainly be straightened out by Rome.

It seems unlikely that Stephen complied with Cyprian's suggestions and more probable that he showed some resentment at what he inevitably regarded as an officious attempt by an inferior to dictate to a superior. That his unwillingness to pronounce against Marcian was not due to any actual sympathy with the Novatianist position is proved by his reception of another bishop, who had transgressed the regulations of 251 in the direction of over-laxity instead of over-rigor. In 255 or 256, we find Cyprian, who had evidently come to be looked upon as the refuge of brethren in perplexity, sending a letter in his own name and that of thirty-six African bishops to the priest and people of Leon and the deacon and people of Merida in Spain. Basilides, bishop of Leon, and Martial, priest of Merida, had, it appears, apostatized during the persecution and had accordingly been deposed and excommunicated by the local churches and a new bishop and priest had been regularly elected and installed in their places. Since then, both Basilides and Martial had done the required penance and been readmitted to communion. Neither one, however, had been satisfied with simple readmission. They had demanded also full restoration to office, contrary to the provisions of the rules adopted by the churches.[195] Basilides had even gone to Rome

195 *Supra*, p. 384; *infra*, p. 402.

and asked for Stephen's recognition of himself as lawful bishop of Leon. This recognition Stephen had proceeded to give on the strength of Basilides' representations without waiting for a report from the churches concerned and heedless of the fact that such a step on his part constituted a flagrant reversal of the recent regulations and created an impasse of rival bishops and factions in Spain. Basilides thenceforth would be on the Roman list of accredited bishops, with whom communication was kept up and from whom travellers' credentials were accepted. It was as if the ruler of a great nation had refused to recognize the legally established prince of a tiny nation and had insisted upon treating as sovereign a disorderly pretender whom his own people had rejected. The Spanish Christians protested fruitlessly to Stephen and now turned to Cyprian. This time Cyprian does not hint at any possibility of persuading Stephen to take more suitable action. He speaks of him civilly but distantly, as if there were an estrangement between them that permitted no approaches. He scrupulously reminds the Spaniards that they should not blame him "who carelessly allowed himself to be deceived" so hardly as the one who deceived him. On the other hand, he advises them not to be moved by Stephen's decision nor to eject the bishop they had chosen in obedience to the rules promulgated by Cornelius and "all other bishops everywhere in the whole world." For the first time this law-abiding advocate of episcopal solidarity counsels a small provincial community to ignore the bishop of its venerable mother church. But he appeals from a living bishop, whose arbitrariness threatens the unity of the brethren, to his dead predecessor and to the fellowship of the Church everywhere. He matches one Roman against the other.

With this, the Spanish complication also disappears from our pages and we are faced instead with the major issues of Stephen's pontificate, the two questions of the efficacy of the sacrament of baptism when administered by heretics and of the power of the Roman bishop to compel the Church at large to submit to his solitary decree in such a matter,[196] regardless of inherited tradi-

[196] It is interesting to observe in the third century apocryphal letter of Clement to James, which, in the opinion of many scholars, was the work of a Roman, that the power to bind and loose is interpreted by Peter as meaning the power of *decree*. *Supra*, p. 164.

tions and of previous legislation by local episcopal councils. The Novatianist schism brought the question of heretical baptism to the fore during the year 255. Since the beginning there had been converts to orthodoxy from sects regarded as heretical and in the loose state of early ecclesiastical organization there had grown up diverse ways of receiving them. In Asia and Egypt, it was the custom to rebaptize the convert on the ground that the baptism he had received as a heretic would not avail to cleanse from sin. At Rome, on the contrary, except during the pontificate of Callistus,[197] it had been generally maintained that the sacrament, when performed in the name of the Trinity, contained in itself the miraculous, revivifying efficacy, no matter whose hand sprinkled the water or whose lips uttered the words, and that to repeat it was sacrilege. It was sufficient, therefore, to receive the convert with the simple ceremony of imposition of hands. In Africa, the practice seems to have varied, following sometimes the eastern precedent and sometimes the Roman. One synod in the past had pronounced definitely in favor of the eastern habit[198] but there was still no uniformity.

It is, of course, possible that Stephen himself first started the dispute with a peremptory demand that the Asiatic church bring its methods into line with those countenanced by Rome,[198a] but it soon came to be a question of more than Asia. Cyprian, in answer to several inquiries, took the whole subject under deliberate consideration and concluded that the custom of Rome was wrong and that one could not logically persist in classing schismatics and heretics as outsiders from the Church and at the same time concede that in them lay the power of the Holy Ghost to remit sins. He brought the matter up before a synod of thirty bishops from the province of Africa and in their company went over the baptismal formula and its underlying assumptions. The assembly voted, in agreement with him, that heretics must hereafter be rebaptized. Stephen's tone may have antagonized them and the eastern position was certainly more consistent with the orthodox standpoint toward heretics in general. Before dissolv-

197 *Supra,* p. 311 and n. 65; *infra,* p. 407.
198 *Infra,* p. 403.
198a *Vide* the passage from the letter of Dionysius of Alexandria, *infra,* p. 422.

ing, the synod sent notice of its resolution to the bishops of the adjacent province of Numidia. Cyprian himself wrote to Quintus, a bishop of Mauretania, explaining what had been done. He refrained from mentioning Stephen by name but recalled, in phrases that were plainly intended to be significant, the reasonableness of the apostle Peter, his willingness to accept instruction and his abstention from arrogance. As a matter of fact, Cyprian and his bishops had acted freely as a self-governing branch of the Church, precisely as they had done in adopting their regulations for the lapsed.[199] But this time their right to self-government had been threatened and they were on the defensive.

The bishops of Numidia may have indicated a wish to meet and share also in the debate. At all events, Cyprian was soon afterwards presiding over a second synod of seventy-one members, comprising bishops from Africa and Numidia. Again they scanned the gospel pages and reasoned from theory and tradition and arrived at the conclusion that heretical baptism was futile and worthless but that each bishop should be left to do what he thought right in his own flock. Their letter to Stephen was couched in the customary, respectful terms but ended on a note that clearly meant defiance. The Africans were not so addicted to old opinions that they could not change for the better nor did they lay down laws for anyone else. Every bishop was at liberty to choose his own course and was responsible only to the Lord. Stephen's response to all this was a positive statement of his power, as supreme lawgiver or "bishop of the bishops,"[200] to prohibit all innovations in dogma or practice and to command the churches on pain of his excommunication to admit converts from heresy with the simple laying on of hands. The question of the value of heretical baptism became forthwith entangled with the sharper question of the nature of the constitution of the Church and the location of sovereignty within it. Stephen had thrown down the gauntlet to the whole system of federated, coördinate episcopacy.

199 *Supra,* p. 370.

200 This title had been applied earlier by Tertullian in irony to Callistus or Zephyrinus. *Supra,* p. 301. It is impossible to tell whether or not any of these bishops claimed it seriously for himself.

Cyprian replied by summoning on the first of September, 256, a third synod of eighty-seven bishops from all three provinces of the northwest coast, Numidia, Africa and Mauretania. They met, fully aware that their vote for or against the baptism of converted heretics would be in reality a vote for or against a breach with Rome. Luckily a memorandum of this council, with a short résumé of Cyprian's leading speech and of the remarks of each bishop as he cast his vote, has by some rare chance been preserved. They went unanimously against Stephen. He, on his part, refused to meet the delegates sent as usual to carry him the report of the meeting and forbade members of the Roman community to receive them into their houses or to offer them the ancient Christian services of hospitality. He then formally excommunicated the churches of the African provinces and summoned the bishops of the East [201] to abstain henceforth from rebaptism and from intercourse with the "false apostle," Cyprian. Certain bishops from Cilicia, Galatia and Cappadocia, those same regions of Asia Minor which had resisted Victor's effort to interfere with their Easter tradition and impose an undesired uniformity,[202] sent a definite refusal and were excommunicated also. In dismay, Dionysius of Alexandria tried to expostulate, as Irenaeus had done sixty years before. He wrote both to Stephen and to several of the prominent priests in Rome to explain that second baptism was no innovation to the East but rather its inveterate custom, that it was possible to differ as to the necessity of the rite and still to preserve the Church's peace and that to destroy the harmony that had just been attained after the Novatianist disturbances meant nothing but disaster. But Stephen was not to be shaken. He would isolate himself until, as Firmilian said, it seemed as if he were the outcast and not they, but he would maintain the supreme authority of Peter.

To Cyprian, the champion of unity, the situation must have been unspeakably painful. To find himself after these years of confident, unassailable regularity thrust into the position of leader of an outlawed faction! His distress and exasperation appear in

201 The letter to the church in Arabia, of which Dionysius had heard, may have been in the style of a pastoral. The Arabian church was apparently dependent on Roman help. *Infra*, p. 420.

202 *Supra*, p. 280.

the few letters that survive from this period. He would have kept the peace with Stephen, regardless of the latter's personal delinquencies or of his discordant opinions on baptism. But Stephen would have no such easy-going peace and Cyprian could not submit himself and the African church to Stephen's dictatorship without violating what were in his eyes the fundamental principles of his episcopate and betraying his God-given responsibilities. Cut off from the apostolic church with which Carthaginian intercourse had always been the closest, he turned for comfort and justification to the ancient churches of the East who were also in opposition to Rome. We have none of his letters to the eastern bishops but we have a reply that came to him in the spring, perhaps, of 257, from Firmilian, bishop of Caesarea in Cappadocia.

Firmilian was one of the influential bishops of Asia, a promoter of the synod of Antioch in 253, which had settled the Novatianist question for that part of the Empire.[203] Like Dionysius of Alexandria and others of his colleagues, he had been a pupil of Origen, who had expressly repudiated the theory that the keys of Peter could ever become the personal insignia of any single pontiff.[204] In Firmilian's letter, the pent-up irritation of the venerable East at the overweening attitude of Rome seems for once to find vent.[205] The Roman church, he says, claims the direct sanction of the apostles for everything that it does, but it undoubtedly has departed from original tradition in the celebration of Easter, as well as in other particulars. Its observances are not those of Jerusalem. In this instance, it has contravened the written teachings of its boasted authorities, Peter and Paul, as contained in their Epistles. As for Stephen, who brags so loudly of his succession to the chair of Peter, the rock on which the Church is built, what is he doing in his irascible conceit but setting up other rocks on which the Church may split and founder? The power to bind and loose, bestowed by Christ upon Peter and all the apostles, has come down to all bishops and

[203] *Supra*, p. 387. For more information about Firmilian, see Eusebius, *Historia Ecclesiastica*, VII, 30, 3–5.

[204] *Supra*, pp. 317–322.

[205] It is interesting to compare his vexation with that of the Asiatic bishops who wrote to Pope Julius from Antioch in 342.

remains in the one true Church. It is neither to be monopolized by one bishop nor to be diffused abroad among the heretics. Firmilian's interpretation of the commission to Peter is not, one perceives, the subtle, spiritual explanation of his master Origen but the simple, institutional idea, common to Cyprian and other independent bishops of the day. As Firmilian remarks, Stephen did himself and Cyprian one service when he brought them together.

Whether Stephen would ever have gone on to excommunicate the apostolic sees of Alexandria, Antioch or Jerusalem for non-compliance with his decree we do not know. Dionysius' tactful and conciliatory remonstrances made an impression upon the Roman priests, to whom he wrote a second time at greater length. Disquieting rumors arose of Valerian's intention to revive the persecution and once more an impulse ran through the Church to forget dissension and strengthen itself to endure. Stephen himself may have been too ill to push his aggressive tactics further, for at the end of July he died. His time was too short to fight out the battle to which he addressed himself but he, at least, set squarely before the Church of the Empire the Petrine claims of the Roman bishopric and demanded their acceptance as a price of salvation.

On Stephen, see the discussion in E. W. Benson, *Cyprian, his Life and his Times* (London, 1897); O. Bardenhewer, *Patrology* (trans. by T. Shahan, St. Louis, 1908), § 56, 6; L. Duchesne, *Early History of the Christian Church* (trans. from the 4th ed. by C. Jenkins, 3 vols., London, 1910–1924), Vol. I, pp. 303 *sqq.*; B. J. Kidd, *History of the Church to A.D. 461* (3 vols., Oxford, 1922–1925), Vol. I, pp. 464–474.

Cyprian, *Epistolae*, LXVIII. Text. *Corpus Scriptorum Ecclesiasticorum Latinorum*, III², 744–749.

Cyprian to his brother Stephen, greeting.

1 Faustinus, our colleague who is at Lyons, has once and again written to me, dearest brother, to inform me of what I know he has certainly told you also, as have the rest of our fellow bishops too in that province, namely,

that Marcian at Arles has joined Novatian and has withdrawn from the unity of the catholic Church and from the harmony of our priestly body and has adopted the wicked and cruel heretical doctrine, that servants of God, who are penitent and grief-stricken and who entreat the Church with tears and mourning and sorrow, should be excluded from consolation and help, that the wounded should be refused admission to heal their wounds and left without hope of peace and communion and cast out to become the prey of wolves and victims of the devil.

2 Wherefore, you ought to write full directions to our fellow bishops in Gaul, not to permit any longer the wayward and insolent Marcian, the foe of divine mercy and our brothers' salvation, to insult our assembly. . . .

3 Do you also send letters to the province and to the people of Arles, to the effect that they excommunicate Marcian and appoint another in his place, so that Christ's flock, which today is scattered, wounded and despised by him, may be gathered together. Let it be reason sufficient that many of our brethren have died there in these past years without peace. So let aid be sent to the rest who still survive and who grieve day and night, imploring the compassion of God and their father and begging for comfort from our abundance. . . .

5 The glorious honor of our predecessors, the blessed martyrs,[206] Cornelius and Lucius, should be upheld and while we all revere their memory, much more, dearest brother, ought you, who were chosen their vicar and successor, to revere and uphold it with the weight of your authority. Now they, who were filled with the Lord's spirit and glorious in martyrdom, decided that peace should be given to the lapsed and said in their letters that after due penance the fruits of communion and peace should not be

[206] The word "martyr" is used here apparently of a "confessor" who had died. Cornelius and Lucius were not martyrs in our sense. *Supra*, p. 269, n. 71.

withholden from them. This has also been always and everywhere the opinion of us all. . . . Inform us exactly who is appointed at Arles in place of Marcian, so that we may know to whom to direct our brethren and to whom to write ourselves. I bid you, dearest brother, ever farewell.

Ibid., *Epistolae,* LXVII. Text. *Op. cit.,* 735–743.

Cyprian, . . .[207] to the priest Felix and the people of Leon and Astorga and to the deacon Elius and the people of Merida, their brethren in the Lord, greeting.

[Acknowledgment of a letter of complaint against Basilides, bishop of Leon and Astorga, and Martial, priest of Merida, who persist in exercising their respective offices, though guilty of compromise with idolatry and betrayal of the faith. The people can certainly get no benefit from wicked priests and may even be contaminated by them.]

5 Therefore, the practice derived from divine tradition and apostolic custom must be strictly upheld and preserved, as it is indeed by us and almost all the provinces, namely, that for the correct solemnization of an ordination all the neighboring bishops of the same province shall assemble with the people for whom the prelate is to be ordained and that the bishop shall be chosen in the presence of the people, since they know most thoroughly the life of every man and have learned each one's character from his conversation. This practice, we observe, was followed among you in the ordination of our colleague, Sabinus, so that the bishopric was conferred upon him with the assent of the whole brotherhood and by the judgment of the bishops who met together in person or wrote to you about him, and hands were laid upon him to take the place of Basilides.[208] The ordination,

[207] This letter was sent in the name of Cyprian and thirty-six others. *Vide supra*, p. 393.

[208] *I.e.*, the local church or brotherhood approved the bishop who was elected and "ordained" (*i.e.*, consecrated) by the other bishops of the province. The Council of Nicea required the ratification of the metropolitan also. *Infra*, p. 486.

being rightly performed, cannot be rescinded by the fact that Basilides, after his sins had been detected and further revealed by the confession of his own conscience, went to Rome and deceived Stephen, our colleague, who was a long way off and ignorant of what had happened and of the truth, and intrigued to be unjustly reinstated in the episcopate, from which he had been justly deposed. This means merely that the sins of Basilides have been multiplied rather than absolved, for to his previous wrongdoing he has added the crime of deception and fraud. Nor is the one who carelessly allowed himself to be beguiled so blameworthy as the unspeakable impostor who beguiled him. . . .

6 . . . It is vain for such men to attempt to seize the bishopric, for it is obvious that persons of that sort cannot govern the Church of Christ and are unfit to offer sacrifices to God. In addition, our colleague Cornelius, a just and peace-loving priest, honored with martyrdom by the favor of the Lord, ordained some time ago in company with us and all other bishops everywhere in the whole world, that such men might be admitted to do penance but that they were excluded from clerical ordination and the office of priest. . . .

Ibid., *Epistolae,* LXX. Text. *Op. cit.,* 766–770.

Cyprian, . . . [and thirty others] to Januarius, . . . [and seventeen others[209]], greeting.

[A discussion of the problem whether or not converted heretics should be baptized on their entrance into the true Church.]

2 But even the question which is put during baptism is witness of the truth. For when we say: "Do you believe in eternal life and the forgiveness of sins through the holy Church?" we mean that forgiveness of sins is not

209 *I.e.,* members of a synod of thirty bishops of the province of Africa to the bishops of Numidia. *Vide supra,* pp. 395–396.

granted except in the Church and that among heretics, where there is no Church, sins are not forgiven. . . .

3 . . . Now it cannot be partly invalid and partly valid. If he can baptize, he can also give the Holy Spirit. But if he cannot give the Holy Spirit, because standing without the pale he is not with the Holy Spirit, neither can he baptize a person who comes to him, because there is one baptism and one Holy Spirit and one Church, founded by our Lord Christ upon Peter for the beginning and principle of unity. . . .

Ibid., *Epistolae,* LXXI. Text. *Op. cit.,* 771–774.

Cyprian to his brother Quintus,[210] greeting.

[He has been holding a council of bishops, who have agreed with him on the subject of heretical baptism.]

3 Furthermore, precedent should not be the controlling consideration but reason should prevail. For even Peter, whom the Lord first chose and upon whom he built his Church, when Paul later disputed with him over circumcision, did not claim insolently any prerogative for himself nor make any arrogant assumptions nor say that he had the primacy and ought to be obeyed, especially by novices and latecomers. Nor did he despise Paul on the ground that he had once been a persecutor of the Church. But he admitted the truth of Paul's judgment and accepted his lawful reasoning, setting us thus an example of concord and patience, that we should not obstinately love our own opinions but should instead adopt as our own whatever useful and wholesome suggestions are made at any time by our brethren and colleagues, provided they are lawful and right. . . .

[Under Agrippinus, one of his predecessors, an African council ruled against accepting the baptism of heretics.]

210 Quintus was a bishop in Mauretania.

Ibid., *Epistolae,* LXXII. Text. *Op. cit.,* 775–778.

Cyprian and the others [210a] to their brother Stephen, greeting.

1 We have found it necessary, dearest brother, to assemble and hold a council of many bishops, meeting together in order to arrange and pass upon certain matters by common debate and deliberation, and during this council we have proposed and settled many questions. But the principal decision to be reported from it to you and referred to your dignity and wisdom is that which has most bearing on priestly authority and on the unity and grandeur which by divine ordinance belong to the catholic Church, namely, that persons who have been washed elsewhere, outside the Church, and polluted by the stain of holy water at the hands of heretics and schismatics must be baptized when they come to us and to the Church, which is one. For it is of trifling value to lay hands upon them for the receiving of the Holy Spirit, unless they receive also the Church's baptism. . . . For example, when in the house of Cornelius, the centurion, the Holy Spirit had descended upon the gentiles who were there, fervent in the glow of faith and believing on the Lord with all their hearts, so that filled with the Spirit they blessed God in divers tongues, none the less, the blessed apostle Peter, mindful of the divine command and gospel, gave orders that even they, who were already full of the Holy Spirit, should be baptized, so that nothing should be omitted and apostolic authority should uphold in every respect the law of the divine command and gospel. That the act of the heretics is not baptism and that no advantage can be taken of the grace of Christ by the enemies of Christ, I have recently and carefully explained in a letter which I have written on the subject to our colleague Quintus in Mauretania.[211] The same is made

210a A synod of seventy-one bishops from Africa and Numidia.

211 *I.e.,* the letter just preceding.

plain in a letter which our colleagues sent earlier to their fellow bishops in charge in Numidia. I append hereto copies of both letters.

2 In addition, we have definitely ruled, dearest brother, by general consent and authority, that all priests and deacons who were first ordained in the catholic Church and afterwards turned faithless and rebellious against the Church, and who have been promoted to office among the heretics by profane ordination at the hands of pseudo-bishops and antichrists in disobedience to Christ's commandment and have undertaken to offer false and blasphemous sacrifices outside, in opposition to the one divine altar, these men, when they return to us, are to be readmitted only on this condition, that they receive communion as laymen and think it sufficient to be restored to peace after having been enemies of peace. . . .

3 We have informed you, dearest brother, of these resolutions for the general honor and our sincere love, in the confidence that, since they are both devout and right, they will commend themselves to your true faith and devotion. We are, moreover, aware that there are some who refuse to abandon a position once taken or to alter a policy without difficulty but who still preserve the bond of peace and concord with their colleagues, while retaining certain convictions of their own at which they have already arrived. Therefore, we coerce no one and lay down the law to no one, for every bishop has freedom of decision according to his own will in the conduct of his church and will give an account of his behavior to the Lord. We bid you, dearest brother, ever farewell.

Ibid., *Epistolae,* LXXIII. Text. *Op. cit.,* 778–799.

Cyprian to his brother Jubaianus, greeting.

[He has held a second council of seventy-one bishops

from the provinces of Africa and Numidia, which also has voted against the recognition of heretical baptism.]

7 But it is plain where and by whom remission of sins can be granted, that is to say, the remission granted in baptism. First of all, the Lord bestowed that power upon Peter, on whom he built the Church and whom he appointed and pronounced the source of unity, that whatsoever he loosed should be loosed on earth. And after his resurrection, he spoke to the apostles also, saying: "As the Father hath sent me, even so send I you."[212] And when he had said this, he breathed on them and said unto them: "Receive ye the Holy Ghost; whose soever sins ye remit, they are remitted unto them and whose soever sins ye retain, they are retained." Whereby we understand that only they who are placed over the Church and established by gospel law and the Lord's ordinance are permitted to baptize and to grant remission of sins and that outside the Church nothing can be either bound or loosed, for there is no one there who can either bind or loose anything. . . .

21 . . . [Heretics cannot be saved even by martyrdom.] . . . So there can be no common baptism for us and the heretics, since we have no common God the Father nor Christ the Son nor Holy Spirit nor faith nor even Church, and for that reason persons must be baptized who come out of heresy into the Church. . . .

26 We have written these few words to you, dearest brother, to the best of our poor ability, laying no command on anyone nor passing hasty judgment to prevent any bishop from doing what he thinks right, for each one has free control over his own decision. So far as in us lies, we start no quarrel with our colleagues and fellow bishops over heretics but we keep in divine harmony with them and in the peace of the Lord. . . . [He has been writing a treatise on patience.]

212 John, XX, 21–23.

Ibid., *Epistolae,* LXXIV. Text. *Op. cit.,* 799–809.

Cyprian to his brother Pompey,[213] greeting.

1 Although in the letters of which we sent you copies, dearest brother, we have fully expressed all that is to be said on the baptism of heretics, yet, since you have asked me to notify you what answer our brother Stephen returned to our letter, I am sending you a copy of his reply. On reading it you will more and more appreciate his error in endeavoring to defend the cause of heretics against Christians and the Church of God. For among the other arrogant or irrelevant or inconsistent statements which he has made, without proper instruction and caution, he has inserted this: "If then any persons come to you from any heresy whatsoever, let there be no innovation beyond the rule that has been bequeathed to us, which is, that hands be laid on them to repentance; for the heretics themselves do not baptize persons who come to them from another of their own sects but simply admit them to communion."

2 He has forbidden us to baptize in the Church a person coming from any heresy whatsoever; that is, he has pronounced the baptisms of all the heretics to be right and lawful. And inasmuch as the separate heresies have separate baptisms and different sins, he, holding communion with the baptisms of them all, has heaped up all their sins in one mass into his own bosom. He has issued orders that "there be no innovation beyond the rule that has been bequeathed to us," as if he who maintains unity and insists upon one baptism for the one Church were committing an innovation and not rather he who is oblivious of unity and accepts the false pollution of profane washing. Whence comes the rule that is bequeathed to us? Is it not based upon the authority of the Lord and the gospel and does it not come from the instructions and epistles of the apostles? . . . No one

213 Pompey was an African bishop who had been in Rome. *Supra,* p. 358.

ought to defame the apostles by saying that they approved of heretics' baptisms or held communion with them without the Church's baptism, when the apostles wrote such bitter condemnation of heretics, even before the more flagrant heretical sects had broken out and before Marcion, the Pontian, had emerged from Pontus, whose master Cerdon came to Rome under Hyginus, who was the ninth bishop of the city.[214] . . .

4 An excellent and legitimate rule evidently is the one proposed by our brother Stephen, supplying us with a fine authority! For to this passage in his letter he adds the words: "for the heretics themselves do not baptize persons who come to them from another of their own sects but simply admit them to communion." To this depth of calamity the Church of God and the spouse of Christ has sunk, that she is to follow the example of heretics, that in celebrating the heavenly sacraments the light is to take pattern from the darkness and Christians are to act as do the antichrists! What blindness of mind is this, what wickedness, to refuse to recognize the unity of the faith which proceeds from God the Father and from the rule of Jesus Christ our Lord and God! . . .

7 . . . But as the birth of Christians takes place in baptism and as the generation and sanctification of baptism belong solely to the spouse of Christ, who is able to conceive and bear sons spiritually to God, where and of whom and to whom is he born who is not a son of the Church? How shall he have God as his father before he has the Church as his mother? Yet, although no heresy whatsoever nor even a schism can possess the sanctification of saving baptism outside of the Church, the unshakable obstinacy of our brother Stephen has reached such a pitch that he insists that sons are born to God even from the baptisms of Marcion

214 This information about Marcion and Cerdon Cyprian took probably from Tertullian, who got it from Irenaeus. *Supra*, pp. 258, 272.

or Valentinus or Apelles or other blasphemers against God the Father,[215] and that remission of sins is granted in the name of Jesus Christ in the very spot where blasphemies are uttered against the Father and against our Lord God Christ!

8 Under such circumstances, dearest brother, we ought, on behalf of the faith and the sanctity of our priestly office, to consider whether the account of a priest of God who upholds and approves and accepts the baptism of blasphemers can stand in the day of judgment. . . . Does he give honor to God, who is a friend of heretics, an enemy to Christians, and who maintains that priests of God who guard the truth of Christ and the unity of the Church should be excommunicated? . . .

10 It happens, however, that a man of presumptuous and stubborn zeal will defend his own wrong and false views rather than yield to another's that are right and true. Foreseeing this, the blessed apostle Paul writes to Timothy and admonishes him that a bishop shall not strive nor be contentious but gentle and teachable.[216] And he is teachable who is mild and gentle and has patience to learn. Bishops need not only to teach but also to learn, for he teaches better who daily increases and advances and learns better. . . . If we return to the Master and Source of the divine rule, human error disappears, the nature of the heavenly sacraments is understood and whatever has lain obscure in the shadowy cloud of darkness is made clear in the light of truth. Even so, if a conduit carrying water, which has always before flowed freely and abundantly, suddenly fails, do we not go to the spring to discover there the reason for the failure? . . . This same thing the priests of God who follow the divine commands ought now to do and if in any wise a truth has wavered or faltered, we ought to return

[215] These three were prominent in Gnostic sects that denounced the Jehovah of the Old Testament as cruel and unjust. *Supra,* p. 266, n. 65.

[216] II Timothy, II, 24.

to its source in the Lord and to the gospel and the apostolic rule and find there the guide for our conduct, where the command originated and had its source.

11 . . . Peter himself, when explaining and urging us to unity, taught us that we could be saved only through one baptism in the one Church. "There were few," he said, "in the ark of Noah, to wit, eight souls who were saved by water, as ye also are saved likewise by baptism." [217] . . .

12 This, dearest brother, is our practice and belief after examination and scrutiny of the truth, that all who turn to the Church from any heresy should be baptized by the one lawful baptism, except those who were earlier baptized in the Church before they joined the heretics. The latter on their return, after doing penance, should be received by imposition of hands alone and restored to the fold whence they have wandered from their shepherd. I bid you, dearest brother, ever farewell.

Third Council of Carthage, *Acta*. Text. *Opera Cypriani*, ed. by W. Hartel, *Corpus Scriptorum Ecclesiasticorum Latinorum*, III[1], 435–444.

When, on the first of September, many bishops, as well as priests and deacons, had assembled together at Carthage from the provinces of Africa, Numidia and Mauretania, in the presence of a great number of the people, . . . Cyprian said: "You have heard, dearly beloved colleagues, the letter which our fellow bishop Jubaianus has written me, asking our poor opinion of the irregular and profane baptism of the heretics, and also my reply to him,[218] to the effect that once and again and invariably we have decided that heretics who come into the Church must be baptized and sanctified by the Church's baptism. . . . It is now proper that we, each one, state our opinion on this subject, judging no man

[217] I Peter, III, 20–21.

[218] *Supra*, p. 405.

and denying no man the right of communion if he differ from us. For no one among us sets himself up as a bishop of the bishops,[219] or by tyranny and terror forces his colleagues to compulsory obedience, seeing that every bishop in the freedom of his liberty and power possesses the right to his own mind and can no more be judged by another than he himself can judge another. We must all await the judgment of our Lord Jesus Christ, who singly and alone has power both to appoint us to the government of his Church and to judge our acts therein." . . .

[There follow the names of eighty-six bishops, with a brief summary of each man's speech. We give one illustration, number 17.]

. . . Fortunatus of Thuccabor said:

"Jesus Christ, our Lord and God, son of God the Father and Creator, built his Church upon Peter, not upon heresy, and gave to the bishops, not to the heretics, the power to baptize. Wherefore, persons outside the Church, who oppose Christ and scatter abroad his sheep and his flock, cannot apart from us administer baptism."

[The sentiment was unanimous in favor of rebaptism.]

Cyprian, *Epistolae,* LXXV. Text. *Op. cit.,* III[2], 810–827.

Firmilian[220] to Cyprian, his brother in the Lord, greeting.

1 We have received, dearest brother, by the deacon whom you sent, our beloved Rogatian, the letter which you addressed to us, and have rendered most hearty thanks to God that it has come to pass that we, who are distant from one another in body, are as united in spirit as if we were not only living in one country but even dwelling side by side in the selfsame house. . . .

219 On this phrase *vide supra,* pp. 223, 231, 301.
220 On Firmilian *vide supra,* p. 398; *infra,* pp. 420, 437–438.

2 . . . For this we may thank Stephen, because his cruelty has brought it about that we receive this proof of your faith and wisdom. However, although it is through Stephen that we have obtained the grace of this favor, Stephen has done nothing to deserve favor or grace. No more can Judas be esteemed as the author of a vast good, because of the perfidy and treachery whereby he wrought evil to the Savior, even though through him the world and the gentile peoples were delivered by the passion of the Lord.

3 But let us disregard for the moment the action of Stephen, lest while recalling his effrontery and insolence, we consume too much time in mourning over his offense. . . . [He is happy to find Cyprian in perfect accord with himself on the subjects of the lapsed and of heretical baptism. He himself has held local councils to discuss all these important topics and has committed Cyprian's letter to memory.]

5 And now, as this messenger you sent is in haste to return to you and winter is threatening, we write such answer as we can to your letter. As regards what Stephen has said, that the apostles forbade the administration of baptism to persons who were converted from heresy and transmitted this rule to be observed by posterity, you have made the perfect rejoinder, that no one can be so foolish as to believe that the apostles transmitted such a rule, since it is well known that these accursed and detestable heresies arose after their time. For Marcion, the pupil of Cerdon, we know introduced his sacrilegious ideas against God at a period later than the apostles and many years after them. . . .[221]

6 But anyone may see that the Romans do not adhere in all respects to the rule handed down from the beginning and that their claim to the authority of the apostles is un-

[221] Firmilian enumerates the prominent Gnostics whom Cyprian mentioned in his letter to Pompey and probably cited again in his lost letter to Firmilian, to which this is a reply.

warranted. For in the celebration of Easter and many other divine and sacramental ordinances one may notice certain divergences among them and also that all customs are not observed by them as they are observed at Jerusalem. As in most other provinces, there are many differences, corresponding to the differences in places and men. Yet there has never on this account been a departure from the peace and unity of the catholic Church. Such a departure Stephen has now presumed to make, by breaking the peace with you, which his predecessors always maintained with you in mutual love and honor. Furthermore, he defames hereby the blessed apostles Peter and Paul, saying that they themselves handed down his rule, whereas in their epistles they execrated heretics and warned us to shun them. It is obvious that this rule of his is human, for it upholds heretics and declares that they have the baptism which belongs to the Church alone.

7 Your reply was excellent on the point which Stephen made in his letter of argument, that the heretics themselves were agreed on baptism and did not baptize those who came to them from another sect but simply held communion with them, as we likewise ought to do. On this point, although you have shown conclusively enough that it is preposterous for anyone to imitate the misguided, we might say in addition, — out of the much there is to be said, — that it is not strange if the heretics do this, for even when they differ on various minor details, they are of one and the same mind on the most important matter, which is blasphemy of their Creator. . . .

8 And when Stephen and those who side with him argue that remission of sins and the second birth can follow upon baptism by heretics, with whom even they themselves admit there is no Holy Ghost, they should reflect and realize that spiritual birth cannot take place without the Spirit. For which reason the blessed apostle Paul baptized anew with

spiritual baptism those whom John had baptized before the Lord sent the Holy Ghost.[222] When we find Paul, after John's baptism, baptizing his disciples a second time, why do we hesitate to baptize those who come from heresy into the Church after their unlawful and profane washing? Unless perhaps Paul was inferior to the bishops of these days and they can give the Holy Ghost to the heretics who come to them by imposition of hands merely, but Paul was not competent to give the Holy Ghost by imposition of hands to those whom John had baptized, until he had first baptized them with the Church's baptism!

. . . .

16 But how deep is the error, how profound the blindness of him who says that remission of sins may be granted by the synagogue of heretics and who remains not on the foundation of the single Church, which was set once by Christ upon a rock, we may perceive from the fact that Christ said to Peter alone: "Whatsoever thou shalt bind on earth shall be bound in heaven and whatsoever thou shalt loose on earth shall be loosed in heaven." Again in the gospel Christ breathed on the apostles alone and said: "Receive ye the Holy Ghost; whosoever sins ye remit, they are remitted unto them and whosoever sins ye retain, they are retained." Thus the power of remitting sins was granted to the apostles and to the churches which they established, when sent forth by Christ, and to the bishops who succeeded them by ordination in their stead.[223] But the enemies of the one catholic Church, in which we are members, and the foes of us, who have succeeded to the apostles, lay claim against us to unlawful priesthoods and erect profane altars. . . .

17 In view of this I am right to be indignant with

[222] Acts, XIX, 1–6.

[223] This passage shows that Firmilian in Asia held the same theory as Cyprian, regarding the power to bind and loose as something shared equally by the whole episcopate. *Vide supra,* p. 406.

Stephen for his open and conspicuous folly, since he who brags so loudly of the seat of his episcopate and who insists that he holds his succession from Peter, on whom the foundations of the Church were laid, is introducing many other rocks and building many new churches, as long as he supports their baptism by his authority. For the baptized unquestionably compose the number of the Church. And whoever approves their baptism, must needs also agree that the Church is there with those of them who are baptized. He does not comprehend that one who thus betrays and abandons unity disparages and in a way effaces the truth of the Christian rock. Even the Jews, though blind in their ignorance and enchained by their most dreadful sin, have yet, as the apostle declares, a zeal for God. Stephen, who asserts that he occupies by due succession the See of Peter, feels no stir of ardor against heretics and concedes to them no slight power of grace but the very highest, saying positively that with their sacrament of baptism they wash away the defilement of the old man, pardon previous deadly sins, create sons of God by heavenly regeneration and renew them to eternal life by the sanctification of the divine cleansing. To concede and attribute to heretics such great and celestial privileges of the Church, what is it but to hold communion with them, when one claims for them so much grace? It is foolish for him to hesitate any longer at uniting and sharing with them in everything else, joining in their congregations, mingling his prayers with theirs and setting up a common altar and sacrifice.

18 " But," he says, " the name of Christ avails so much for faith and baptismal sanctification that whoever is anywhere baptized in the name of Christ receives immediately the grace of Christ." This argument, however, may be shortly met and answered. For if baptism in Christ's name outside the Church can avail to cleanse a man, then the laying on of hands in the name of the same Christ in the

same place can avail to bring the Holy Ghost. And the other rites as well which are performed by heretics will come to seem correct and lawful, when performed in Christ's name, whereas you have demonstrated in your letter that the name of Christ can avail only within the Church, on which alone Christ has bestowed the power of heavenly grace. . . .

20 Then, — to refute the argument from custom which they oppose to the truth, — who is so inane as to prefer custom to truth or not to quit the darkness when he beholds the light? Unless, of course, we accept as excuse for them the ancient conduct of the Jews, who when Christ, that is the truth, came, ignored the new way of truth and abode by what was old. You Africans can make the reply to Stephen that you have abandoned a wrong custom on discovering the truth. We, however, combine custom with truth and oppose to the custom of the Romans a custom based upon truth, for from the beginning we have followed the rule delivered by Christ and his apostles. And we do not recollect that this was ever a new rule with us, since we have always here observed it, namely, to recognize but the one Church of God and to count only that a holy baptism which is administered by the holy Church. For some of us were exceedingly doubtful about the baptism of those persons who accept the new prophets, while still acknowledging the same Father and Son as we do,[224] and a great many of us gathered together in Iconium and thoroughly debated the question and concluded once more that every baptism must be absolutely rejected which is performed outside the Church. . . .

22 . . . And Stephen is not ashamed to announce that remission of sins can be granted by those who are themselves immersed in all kinds of sin, as if the laver of salvation could stand in the house of death.

[224] *I.e.*, the Montanists. *Supra*, pp. 77, n. 38, 255.

23 . . . Yea, thou [Stephen] art worse than all the heretics! For when the multitude discovers its error and comes to thee to obtain the true light of the Church, thou abettest their errors at their coming and increasest the darkness of the night of heresy by obscuring the light of the Church's truth. And although they confess that they are in sin and have no grace and therefore are come to the Church, thou deniest them the remission of their sin which is granted in baptism, for thou sayest that they have been already baptized and have received the grace of the Church without the Church. Thou considerest not that their souls will be required at thine hand at the appearance of the day of judgment and thou refusest the water of the Church to those who are athirst and art the occasion of death to those who long to live. And withal thou art angry!

24 See how ignorant thou art, presuming to upbraid those who are contending against falsehood for the truth! For which might the more justly be angry with the other, he who upholds the enemies of God or he who stands for the truth of the Church against God's enemies? However, it is noticeable that the ignorant are also the irascible and angry, because through their lack of discretion and knowledge they are easily swayed to wrath. Of thee as surely as of anyone the Holy Scripture saith: "An angry man stirreth up strife and a furious man heapeth up sins." [225] For what great strifes and dissensions thou has stirred up throughout the churches of the whole world! And what dire sin thou hast heaped up for thyself, when thou didst divide thyself from so many flocks! For thou didst divide thyself; be not deceived! And he is the true schismatic who makes himself an apostate from the communion of the united Church. So, while thou thinkest that thou canst excommunicate them all, thou hast excommunicated thyself in solitude from them all! . . .

[225] Proverbs, XXIX, 22.

25 How faithfully has Stephen obeyed the saving commands and warnings of the apostle, preserving, in the first place, "lowliness of mind and meekness!" [226] What can be more lowly and meek than to quarrel with so many bishops throughout the whole world, breaking the peace with them in turn by various modes of severity, now with the eastern churches, as we believe you have heard, and now with yourselves in the South? From you he received bishop envoys with such "long-suffering" and "meekness" that he did not admit them even to the common intercourse of speech and so mindful was he of "love" and "charity" that he instructed the entire brotherhood that no one should take them into his house, with the result that on their arrival not only peace and communion but even shelter and hospitality were denied them! This is to "keep the unity of the Spirit in the bond of peace," to cut himself off from the unity of love, to alienate himself in everything from the brethren and to rebel in furious bitterness against the sacrament and "bond of peace"! Can there be "one body and one spirit" with such a man, when he himself has, perhaps, not one mind, so slippery it is, so shifting, so unstable? But let us say no more of him! . . .

. . . Then, since we and the heretics have not one God nor one Lord nor one Church nor one faith nor yet one spirit nor one body, it is plain that neither can we and the heretics have a common baptism, for we have nothing at all in common. Nevertheless Stephen is not ashamed to lend his protection to such men against the Church nor to divide the brotherhood in order to endorse heretics nor, above all, to call even Cyprian "false Christ" and "false apostle" and "deceitful workman." He is conscious that all these offenses are in himself and has been beforehand with his lies, bringing against another the accusations he himself richly deserves to hear. We all bid you and all the bishops

226 The references in this paragraph are to Ephesians, IV, 1–4.

who are in Africa and all the clergy and all the brotherhood farewell. May we always have you united with us, of one mind and heart, even though afar off!

Eusebius, *Historia Ecclesiastica,* VII, 2–5. Text. *Eusebius Werke* (*Die griechischen christlichen Schriftsteller der ersten drei Jahrhunderte*), II², 636–640.

2 After Cornelius had held the bishopric in the city of Rome for about three years, he was succeeded by Lucius. He filled the office less than eight months, then died and bequeathed his place to Stephen. To Stephen, Dionysius [227] wrote the first of his letters on baptism, since much controversy had arisen as to whether it was necessary to cleanse by baptism those who had been converted from a heresy. For the ancient custom had prevailed, that such persons should receive simply the laying on of hands with prayer.[228]

3 Cyprian, shepherd of the parish of Carthage, was the first in that generation to maintain that they should not be accepted until they had been purified by baptism from their error. But Stephen considered it wrong to introduce any innovation contrary to the tradition which had obtained from the beginning and he was exceedingly angry at it.

4 So Dionysius discussed the subject at length with him by letter and finally argued that since the persecution had abated and the churches everywhere had rejected the novel teaching of Novatus,[229] they were at peace among themselves. He writes as follows:[230]

227 Dionysius of Alexandria. *Supra,* pp. 350 ff.

228 In the fifty years after Stephen, the Roman method of receiving heretics had spread so widely through the Church that to Eusebius, himself an Asiatic, it seemed the primitive one and Cyprian a leader in innovation. Yet the Council of Nicaea ordered the rebaptism of some followers of Paul of Samosata (*Canon* XIX) and Athanasius declared that baptism by Arians was vain. *Oratio contra Arium,* II, 43. Today the Greek church rebaptizes heretics. The Africans persisted in rebaptizing. *Vide infra,* pp. 466, 482.

229 Eusebius uses the name Novatus for Novatian. *Supra,* p. 382, n. 182.

230 The point of the argument here seems to be that since the churches had at last attained to peace, it would be a calamity for Stephen to introduce new causes for dissension.

5 "But I declare to you now, my brother, that all the churches throughout the East and beyond, which once were divided, are now united. And all the leaders everywhere are of one mind and rejoice greatly in the amazing peace that has come past expectation, Demetrius in Antioch, Theoctistus in Caesarea, Mazabanes in Aelia, Marinus in Tyre,—Alexander having fallen asleep,—Heliodorus in Laodicea,—Thelmydrus being dead,—Helenus in Tarsus and all the churches of Cilicia, Firmilian and all Cappadocia.[231] I have named only the more notable bishops, in order not to make my letter too long nor my words too tedious. And all Syria and Arabia, to which you send help whenever needed and whither you have just written a letter,[232] Mesopotamia, Pontus, Bithynia, in short, everyone everywhere is joyful and glorifying God in concord and brotherly love." Thus far Dionysius.

Xystus II

(257–258)

On the death of Stephen, the Roman clergy elected as his successor one who, while standing for the retention at Rome of the custom of admitting converts from heresy without rebaptism, saw no need of prolonging the struggle to force that custom upon branches of the Church that held a different opinion and was willing to return to the old policy of mutual tolerance and harmony. Dionysius and Philemon, two of the most prominent priests, who had at first supported Stephen, had received letters from Dionysius of Alexandria pleading for peace, which seem to have affected them. Other Roman Christians must have watched aghast the results of Stephen's dictatorial tactics in alienating them from staunch neighbors and brethren such as Cyprian, with

231 Some of these names we have met before. Aelia was, of course, the Roman city built by Hadrian upon the site of Jerusalem. *Supra,* p. 387.

232 One of the important testimonies to the relations maintained by the Roman church with Christian communities in the distant East. *Supra,* p. 217.

whom their relations had been so warm and close during past years of trial. Another persecution was at hand, when they all would need whatever strength they could get from one another. Whether Xystus II ever formally revoked the ban of his predecessor against the African and Asiatic churches or whether he merely resumed ordinary intercourse as if it had never been broken or as if the quarrel had been a personal affair with Stephen alone, with which he himself was not concerned, we have no way of knowing.[233]

We learn from Eusebius that Dionysius of Alexandria composed at least three letters to Xystus to explain the eastern attitude toward heretical baptism and the prime importance of peace. From two of these Eusebius gives extracts, which show Dionysius urging again that it had been useless for Stephen to expect the eastern churches to abandon, at the behest of one foreign bishop, a practice sanctioned for years by all their own bishops, both individually and in council. Having made this point courteously but firmly, Dionysius turns to topics on which he can be sure of arousing Xystus' sympathies. In the first letter he reports the appearance of the Sabellian or Monarchian heresy [234] in Egypt and the regions to the West and encloses copies of some letters he has had to write to persons affected by it. The second letter has a relieved and friendly sound, as if his worst fears of trouble with Xystus were over. In it he asks for Xystus' advice on a delicate situation that has arisen in his own congregation. A member of long standing has just realized that his baptism years before was heretical and now implores the church to baptize him anew. In the case of a fresh convert Dionysius, of course, would not have hesitated but with this man he feels that his years of faithful, eucharistic communion make a second baptism superfluous and even blasphemous. It was one instance where Roman and Egyptian could agree on a phase of the question that divided them and where Xystus was bound to be gratified by Dionysius'

[233] The life of Cyprian by his admirer Pontius says: "By this time, he had received envoys from Xystus, that good and peaceable priest and, on that account, most blessed martyr." Chap. XIV.

[234] That heresy was, of course, very familiar to a Roman. *Supra*, pp. 300, 304, 309.

attitude. It had almost the appearance of a concession, although in reality it surrendered nothing. There could have been no more diplomatic use made of such an episode. Thenceforth Rome and Alexandria appear to be on terms of cordiality and there is no further agonizing over the baptismal problem.[235] In Dionysius' account of his experiences during the subsequent persecution he mentions the fact that "one of the brethren who were present from Rome" accompanied him to his trial before the governor.[236]

Unfortunately we know less how matters stood between Rome and Africa after the resumption of communication. We possess no letter from Cyprian to or about Xystus, except the one written in August, 258, in evident haste and excitement. Brethren have come from Rome bringing the text of Valerian's rescript against the Christians, soon to be posted up in Carthage also. Already the Roman prefects are at the business of denunciation, confiscation and execution. Xystus and four deacons have been put to death in one of the cemeteries. A few days more and the Carthaginian bishop followed the Roman to martyrdom.[236a]

Eusebius, *Historia Ecclesiastica,* VII, 5, 3–6; 9, 1–5. Text. *Eusebius Werke* (*Die griechischen christlichen Schriftsteller der ersten drei Jahrhunderte*), II², 640–642, 646–648.

5 But when Stephen had filled the office for two years, he was succeeded by Xystus. To him Dionysius wrote another letter on baptism, in which he described both the views and the decisions of Stephen and of the other bishops and spoke as follows of Stephen: "He wrote earlier about Helenus and Firmilian and all the bishops in Cilicia and Cappadocia and the regions near them, to the effect that he would not commune with them for this sole reason, because, he said, they rebaptized heretics. But do you take into consideration the difficulty of the situation. For it is

235 At the council of Arles, in 314, the whole western Church voted in favor of the Roman practice.

236 Eusebius, *Historia Ecclesiastica,* VII, 11, 3.

236a Perhaps, at this time the bodies of Peter and Paul were concealed, as related *supra*, pp. 106, 108.

a fact, I know, that the largest episcopal synods have passed ordinances on this point, providing that persons converted from heresies should be instructed and then washed and purified from the filth of the old and corrupt leaven. And I wrote him of all this and entreated him."

Further on he adds: "I wrote also, at first briefly and recently at greater length, to our beloved fellow priests, Dionysius and Philemon, who originally were of the same opinion as Stephen and who wrote to me on the same subject."[237]. . .

6 In the same letter he refers also to the heretical tenets of Sabellius as becoming widely diffused in his day and says: "As for the doctrine now being disseminated in Ptolemais of the Pentapolis,[238] it is impious, rife with blasphemy against Almighty God, the Father of our Lord Jesus Christ, and with unbelief in his only begotten Son, the first born of every creature, the Word which was made man, and with misapprehension of the Holy Spirit. Inasmuch as there have come to me communications from both parties and brethren to discuss the movement, I have written letters to deal with it as wisely as, with God's help, I could. Of these I am sending you copies." . . .

9 His fifth letter[239] was written to Xystus, bishop of Rome. In it, after denouncing the heretics, he relates an incident which had occurred to him, as follows: "Truly, brother, I also am in need of counsel and desire your advice on a matter which has come before me, for fear that I may be mistaken. One of the brethren who meets with us, who has long been considered a believer and who was a member

237 Eusebius quotes later from the two letters of Dionysius to the priests, Dionysius and Philemon. *Historia Ecclesiastica,* VII, 7–8. The former succeeded Xystus in the Roman bishopric and while occupying that office had further relations with Dionysius of Alexandria. *Infra,* pp. 429 ff.

238 The Pentapolis lay well to the west of Egypt, on a tableland surrounded by desert. The region was called Cyrenaica, from Cyrene, the chief of the five towns.

239 Dionysius' fifth letter on the subject of baptism.

of our congregation before my own ordination and, I think, before the election of the blessed Heraclas,[240] was lately present at a baptism. And after hearing the questions and responses he came to me in tears and great distress and falling at my feet, confessed and insisted that the baptism with which he had been baptized among the heretics was not the same and in no way resembled this but was full of impiety and blasphemy. And he said that his soul was now convulsed with grief and he had not courage to raise his eyes to God, because he had entered the Church with those unholy words and acts. So he begged that he might have our perfect cleansing and reception and grace. But I did not dare perform the rite and told him that his long communion would suffice instead. For I should not dare to give complete renewal, for the second time, to one who has listened to the eucharistic prayers and mingled his voice in the "Amen," who has stood by the table and stretched out his hand to take the blessed food and has received it and partaken of our Lord's body and blood for many years.[241] But I urged him to be of good heart and approach the communion of saints in firm faith and strong hope. But he does not yet cease his lamentations and shudders to draw near the table and, in spite of our invitation, hardly ventures to be present at the prayers."

Cyprian, *Epistolae,* LXXX. Text. *Corpus Scriptorum Ecclesiasticorum Latinorum,* III ^{2}, 839–840.

Cyprian to his brother Successus, greeting.

. . . This is to inform you that the men have returned, whom I sent to Rome to ascertain the truth about what-

[240] Heraclas, also a pupil of Origen, was elected bishop of Alexandria about 231 or 232. He was Dionysius' immediate predecessor in the see.

[241] *I.e.,* the Spirit working through the eucharist may have purified the believer after an unwittingly heretical and invalid baptism. Dionysius lays stress on the man's own sense of the worthlessness and offensiveness of the heretical ceremony.

ever rescript has been issued regarding us and to bring us a report. For many varied and unconfirmed rumors have been going about. But the actual facts are that Valerian has sent a rescript to the Senate, to the effect that bishops, priests and deacons should be executed forthwith, senators, men of rank and Roman knights should forfeit their standing and be deprived of their property and if, after the loss of their resources, they persist in remaining Christians, should be put to death, matrons should be deprived of their property and sent into exile and all members of the imperial household who either have previously confessed or do now confess should be arrested and sent in chains, as conscripts, to the imperial estates. The emperor Valerian has also appended to the document a copy of the letter which he has sent to the governors of the provinces about us. This letter we daily expect to arrive and we stand in the strength of faith, ready to endure our passion, looking for the crown of eternal life through the goodness and mercy of the Lord. This is also to tell you that Xystus was executed in a cemetery, on August sixth, and four deacons with him. For the prefects at Rome daily push on the persecution, so that all who are denounced to them are executed and their property confiscated to the treasury. . . .

The Sermon, *On Gamblers*, by a Bishop of the Third Century at Rome

The following extracts are given to indicate the character of an ancient Latin sermon, the authorship of which has been variously attributed to Pope Victor, to Cyprian, and to an unknown Novatianist bishop of the later years of the third century. It is traditionally published among the works of Cyprian but is manifestly not his, although it seems to show traces of an acquaintanceship with Cyprian's ideas and writings. Harnack at one time thought to see in it a solitary survival of the homilies of Pope Victor, who, as Jerome tells us, wrote in Latin [242] and who, as we also know, assumed a primacy in ecclesiastical authority. Harnack's theory, however, did not meet with general acceptance and he himself has now abandoned it in favor of the view of Seeberg and others, that the preacher, evidently a person of much moral earnestness and austerity, whose name has completely disappeared, was one of the irregular bishops or antipopes whom the Novatianists and their successors continued to elect at Rome and elsewhere for over two hundred years. The opening paragraph seems to imply that the author claimed a special succession from Peter and looked upon himself as rightful head of the Roman See. If he were a Novatianist and a schismatic, he none the less held the orthodox Roman belief in the unique responsibility resting upon the bearer of Peter's keys.

For Harnack's successive discussions of this treatise, O. Gebhardt, A. Harnack, C. Schmidt (editors), *Texte und Untersuchungen zur Geschichte der altchristlichen Litteratur* (45 vols., Leipzig, 1883–1924), Vol. I, pp. 110 *sqq.*; *op. cit.* Vol. XX (1900), pp. 112 *sqq.*; A. Harnack, *Dogmengeschichte* (3 vols., Freiburg, 1898), Vol. I, p. 483, n. 4; J. Turmel, *L'Église Romaine jusqu'au Pape Victor* in *Revue Catholique des Églises* (Paris, 1905), pp. 3–21; O. Bardenhewer, *Patrology* (trans. by T. Shahan, St. Louis, 1908), pp. 199–200.

De Aleatoribus. Text. Cyprian, *Opera*, ed. by W. Hartel, *Corpus Scriptorum Ecclesiasticorum Latinorum,* III [3], 92–95.

1 . . .[243] Our concern, O faithful ones, is great for all the brotherhood, in particular over that reckless vice of every wicked man, gambling. It plunges souls into sin and the gamblers themselves into the pit of death. And whereas divine and fatherly affection has conferred upon us the leadership of the apostolate [244] and has established by divine

[242] *Supra,* p. 274, n. 87. But Victor, so far as we have evidence, does not claim unique powers for Peter nor use the passage in Matthew that singled Peter out as the rock foundation of the Church, as does the anonymous author here.

[243] The opening sentences of the sermon have been lost.

[244] The Latin phrase is: "apostolatus ducatum." It goes on: "et originem authentici apostolatus, super quem Christus fundavit ecclesiam in superiore nostro,

grace the see of the vicar of the Lord and we administer the original authoritative apostolate, upon which Christ founded his Church in the person of our great predecessor, who received at the same time the power of loosing and binding and the responsibility of forgiving sins, we are warned by the doctrine of salvation that while we are continually pardoning sinners we ourselves must not be perverted with them.

2 So for this reason we are called the salt of the earth, that by us all the brotherhood may be salted with heavenly wisdom. But when he says: "Even salt, if it hath lost its flavor, is good for nothing but to be cast out and trodden under foot of men," [245] we dread his words and are in fear, lest while living secure in the Church, because we have obtained the dignity of priesthood from the Lord, we prove negligent toward some of the delinquent brethren or by ministering false communion lose, in the Lord's wrath, by our own act, the gift which we once received, by God's grace, with honor. For the sacred Scripture says: "Woe to the shepherds!" [246] And if the shepherds themselves be negligent, how will they account to the Lord for the flock? What will they say? That they have been injured by the flock? They will not be believed. It is incredible that a shepherd can be harmed by his flock. He will be punished the more for his lie. Another Scripture says: "Do they seek thee to be their governor? Refuse to be exalted. Be unto them as one of themselves. Be careful for them and remain as thou art." [247] And again: "Regard the priest as a husbandman, furnished with every delight, and his granaries full, that from him my people may be satisfied with whatever they desire." [248] So, inasmuch as he has appointed us,

---

portamus." The word "authenticus" has the sense of original and therefore authentic and authoritative.

245 Matthew. V, 13.

246 Ezekiel, XXXIV, 2.

247 Ecclesiasticus, XXXII, 1.

248 The source of this quotation is unknown.

that is, the bishops, to be shepherds of the spiritual sheep, that is, the faithful who are placed under our care, let us see to it that no sore of vice be found among them, and let us watch carefully every day that after the heavenly medicine has been applied, their fleece may grow in beauty as they approach the radiance of the garments of heaven.

3 In the gospel, the Lord spoke to Peter. "Peter," he said, "lovest thou me?"[249] And Peter answered: "Yea, Lord, thou knowest that I love thee." And he said: "Feed my sheep." Wherefore, since we have received into our hearts this bishopric, that is, the Holy Spirit through the imposition of hands, let us show no harshness to our neighbor. The Lord admonishes us and says: "Grieve not the Holy Spirit that is within you and quench not the light that burns within you."[250] Even as the merits of martyrdom have been awarded to a bishop who has labored worthily and given saving instruction, although he has suffered no pains of the body, even so shall punishment be in store for the bishop who has been negligent and held up no examples from sacred Scripture. The apostle Paul in his lofty place exhorts us, appoints the bishops as guardians of the gospel teaching and says: "When an heir is a child, he is under guardians and administrators but when he is grown, he then receives his inheritance."[251] So we are dispensors and guardians of the gospel and it is required of dispensors and guardians that they each be found faithful and just. . . .

[The preacher proceeds to demonstrate the criminality of gambling, a device of idle, spendthrift thieves, and ends with urging the Christian not to soil his hands with dice but to lay his money on the table of the Lord and share his inheritance with the widows and the poor, thus storing up treasure in heaven and winning lands and villas in paradise.]

[249] John, XXI, 15–17. [250] Ephesians, IV, 30. [251] Galatians, IV, 1–4.

5. THE GROWTH OF JURISDICTION

Dionysius I

(259–268)

The persecution of Valerian, the most persistent and systematic effort made before the reign of Diocletian to break down the Christian Church, lasted for four years, from 257 to 261. For over eleven months, from August, 258, to July, 259, the Roman community was again without a bishop, administered surreptitiously, as in 250–251, by priests and deacons who survived in hiding. The Persian Wars, however, called Valerian to the East and in 260, he was taken captive in battle. His son, Gallienus, who stepped at once into his office, was a man of profligate habits and no resolution of purpose. For the first months of his reign, he allowed the persecution to continue intermittently, as it would, but in 261, he abruptly reversed his father's policy and issued the first formal recognition of Christianity as a *religio licita,* the practice of which could no longer be treated as criminal in itself. He added an order that houses of worship and cemeteries which had been wrested from the Christians should be returned. Eusebius cites the text of a rescript that was addressed to the bishops of the province of Egypt. "I have given command that the favor of my bounty be proclaimed throughout the world, in order that they may withdraw from places of religious worship. And for this purpose you may use this copy of my rescript, to prevent anyone from molesting you."[252] Apparently the bishops of each important province or group of provinces received some such reassuring communication.

So the latter part of Dionysius' pontificate passed in a security greater than any of his predecessors had known. As usual, after a period of stress and confusion, there was need of internal reorganization. At least, a later generation ascribed to Dionysius the institution of regular parish churches in the city, each to form an ecclesiastical center for a given urban district and to assume responsibility for the care of one of the Christian ceme-

[252] *Historia Ecclesiastica,* VII, 13.

teries outside the walls. To him also was attributed the fixation of boundaries for the suburban episcopal dioceses in the vicinity of Rome.[253] When under Gallienus' slovenly administration in the East the Scythians broke into Asiatic Cappadocia and carried off many captives, Dionysius sent a letter of encouragement to the church in the provincial capital of Caesarea and a gift of funds from Rome to be used for redeeming Christians who had been enslaved.[254]

All else that we know of his relations with the Church at large revolves about the controversy over the nature of Christ and his connection with the eternal Godhead, which was beginning to absorb the attention of teachers and laborers in the expanding field of Christian theology. We have already noted the appearance in Rome of two sects, each of which maintained a clear and consistent position on this subject, diametrically opposed to the other.[255] The Monarchians or Sabellians looked upon Christ as a temporary manifestation in flesh of the one, everlasting spirit of God, without permanent individuation distinct from the Father. The Adoptionists believed in the man Jesus, who by love and suffering had achieved divinity and fulfilled the purposes of God. The middle or orthodox view attempted to combine the advantages of these two contradictory conceptions. Christ was both as divine as the Sabellians and as human as the Adoptionists would have him. No limitations must be put upon his nature or personality in either direction. We have also heard how, in 257 or 258, the Sabellians were reported to be teaching in the Pentapolis, westward from Egypt, and how Dionysius of Alexandria wrote to the bishops in that locality, warning them against denial of Christ's humanity.[256] It now transpired that in his zeal to emphasize the difference of person between the Father and the Son, the Alexandrian had failed to guard against the danger of overstatement on so precarious a topic and had used in his letters

253 This tradition appears in the sixth century *Liber Pontificalis. Vide* L. R. Loomis, *Book of the Popes,* 32 and n. 2; A. Harnack, *The Mission and Expansion of Christianity,* Vol. II, p. 250.

254 *Infra,* p. 642.

255 *Supra,* pp. 260, n. 55, 300, 274.

256 *Supra,* p. 423. Eusebius knew four such letters. *Historia Ecclesiastica,* VII, 26.

some phrases that seemed to denote a difference of substance and to reduce the Son to the inferior level of a thing created. Some watchful brethren, scenting a lapse into Adoptionism, came travelling to Italy and informed Dionysius of Rome that his colleague in Egypt had fallen into heretical error.

The situation was certainly peculiar. A few years earlier, the Roman Dionysius as a priest had supported the efforts of his bishop, Stephen, to concentrate in his own hands a statutory and disciplinary power over the whole Church for the sake of enforcing uniformity of dogma and ritual in a matter of comparative detail.[257] But the wise and tactful expostulations of the Alexandrian Dionysius, perhaps also the spectacle of the disrupted brotherhood, had shaken his faith in methods of coercion. Now this venerable friend and peacemaker, the head of one of the great eastern sees, was himself accused of heresy on a fundamental point. Was the new successor of Peter to brandish his authority again? Dionysius acted as one conscious of a right to leadership, who yet had learned the lesson of Stephen. He issued a summary of the Christological problem, in which he indicated the pitfalls of both "the equal and opposite heresies," and then sent a letter to Alexandria telling Dionysius there what perilous thing was being said of him. He also convened a "great synod" at Rome, which agreed upon a pronunciamento to the effect, "that the Logos of God was neither a thing made nor a creature but his own inseparable and begotten Son, of the substance of the Father." The Alexandrian Dionysius responded with a treatise entitled *A Refutation and Defence,* addressed to his namesake at Rome, in which he endorsed the epithet "homoousios," *i.e.,* of the same substance or consubstantial, as applied to the Son and cleared himself of the charges of heterodoxy. The treatise itself is lost and we have only a few fragments preserved by Athanasius.[258] Neither party apparently raised at that time the question of the Roman bishop's right to call to account another metropolitan, although a century later the incident was taken as a precedent to justify Roman intrusion

[257] *Supra,* p. 423.

[258] These fragments are all collected in J. P. Migne, *Patrologia Graeca,* Vol. X, 1233 *sqq.* See also Eusebius, *Historia Ecclesiastica,* VII, 26, 1.

into the case of Athanasius.[259] As for the term "homoousios," in 325, it was introduced into the creed of Nicaea on the express ground that it had been long ago approved by the bishops of Rome and Alexandria,[260] and Athanasius wrote a pamphlet, *De Sententiis Dionysii,* to show how completely these older Fathers had in their day anticipated the Nicene position.

A few years later, another episode in the warfare of doctrines occurred at Antioch, in which the religious aspects of the case were made still more complicated by the political. After the defeat of Valerian, in 260, the Persians had held northern Syria and much of Asia Minor until expelled, in 262 and 263, by the Arab chieftain, Odenathus of Palmyra, who with his wife Zenobia proceeded to rule the Asiatic provinces as deputy of the indolent Gallienus. On their capture of Antioch, they found the bishopric in that city filled by one Paul, a priest from the Syrian town of Samosata. Paul was both an able theologian and a man of strong and dominating character. He attracted the attention of Queen Zenobia, who appointed him "ducenarius" or "procurator" in the government of the municipality. In his capacity of high civil official he assumed a state and a pomp that were hitherto unprecedented among Christian bishops, the rumors of which were shocking to the ears of his colleagues elsewhere in Asia. Moreover, Paul's theology was of the Adoptionist type. He went so far as to forbid in Antioch the singing of psalms to Christ as God and taught explicitly that the Savior had become holy through struggle and had thus attained to perpetual unity of will with the Father.[261] The Asiatic bishops, however, kept for a while the scandal of their metropolitan to themselves, appealing only to Dionysius of Alexandria for advice. They held two provincial synods, at which our old acquaintance, Firmilian of Cappadocia,[262] seems to have presided, and twice they per-

[259] When, in 341, Bishop Julius of Rome was insisting upon the right of Athanasius of Alexandria to receive a new trial, he reminded the Asiatic bishops at Antioch that it was customary, whenever suspicion rested upon an Alexandrian bishop, to send word of it at once to Rome that the case might be decided there. *Infra,* p. 515.

[260] *Infra,* p. 472.

[261] For selections illustrating Paul's doctrine see J. C. Ayer, *Source Book for Ancient Church History,* pp. 227–229.

[262] *Supra,* pp. 411, 420.

suaded Paul to promise certain amendments in his doctrine and his way of life. But the amendments were insufficient and the reports of Paul's heresies and extravagances grew and spread.

At length, in 268 or 269, a larger synod of seventy bishops, priests and deacons met at Antioch, determined to put an end to so undesirable a situation in the principal church of Asia. Dionysius of Alexandria died as the synod opened. Firmilian died upon his way from Cappadocia to attend it. Only a very few, such as Helenus of Tarsus, were left of the men who had taken part in the old struggle against Stephen for eastern independence. The assembly was bent upon removing Paul altogether, but his official position and influence with Zenobia overawed the Antiochian clergy and laity, with whom rested the right to elect a new bishop. Paul may also have been popular with the people in spite of the accusations which his opponents brought against him. The visiting synod, therefore, took the exceptional step of pronouncing him deposed for misconduct and false teaching and electing Domnus, son of Paul's predecessor Demetrianus, to fill his place.[263] But because the election was extraordinary and irregular and the see of Antioch important to the whole Church, the assembly felt it necessary to explain its action and to put Domnus on a fair footing with his colleagues at large. They drew up a letter, addressed in the first place, to Dionysius of Rome, secondly, to Maximus, who had by this time succeeded Dionysius of Alexandria, and then to all their fellow clergy and " the whole catholic Church under heaven," containing both the charges against Paul and an account of their own dealings with him. They wrote as autonomous bishops to their brethren and equals. Nevertheless, it is clear from the address whose approval was most desired and whose sanction was regarded as most valuable. Both Dionysius and Maximus seem to have accepted the explanation. At least, they made no protest

263 Compare this with Cyprian's account of the correct procedure to be followed in the treatment of an heretical bishop. Other bishops might exclude him from their synods but his provincial colleagues must elect and ordain his successor in the presence and with the consent of the local church. *Supra,* p. 401. But a century later, in the thick of the Arian dispute, irregularities like this became common enough. The most flagrant of which we happen to hear were the work of Arians. See, for example, the methods used to put an Arian bishop into the see of Alexandria. *Infra,* pp. 491, 542.

against Domnus' ordination. The eastern party of the following century contended that Dionysius' acquiescence in this exercise of power on the part of an eastern tribunal constituted a precedent sufficient to nullify the one he had set earlier by his interference with Dionysius of Alexandria.[264]

On the various movements and incidents connected with Dionysius' pontificate *vide* P. Pape, *Die Synoden von Antiochen* (Berlin, 1903), pp. 264–269; F. C. Conybeare, *Key of Truth* (Oxford, 1898); A. Harnack, *Geschichte der altchristlichen Litteratur bis Eusebius* (2 vols., Leipzig, 1893–1904), Vol. I, pp. 409–427; C. Bigg, *Origins of Christianity* (Oxford, 1909), chap. XXXV; O. Bardenhewer, *Patrology* (trans. by T. Shahan, St. Louis, 1908), § 40; B. J. Kidd, *History of the Church to A.D. 461* (3 vols., Oxford, 1922–1925), Vol. I, pp. 484–504.

Athanasius, *De Sententiis Dionysii,* 13. Text. J. P. Migne, *Patrologia Graeca,* XXV, 497–500.

13 . . . After Bishop Dionysius [of Alexandria] had heard of the events in the Pentapolis and in his zeal for religion had written, as I said, his letter to Euphranor and Ammonius against the heresy of Sabellius, some of the brethren in the church, who were orthodox themselves but who did not inquire of him in order to learn from himself what he had written, went up to Rome and spoke against him in the presence of him who had the same name, Dionysius, bishop of Rome. And the latter on hearing it wrote both against the adherents of Sabellius and against those who held the opinion for which Arius was expelled from the church.[265] And he called it an equal and opposite impiety to side with Sabellius or with those who say that the Word of God is a creature, framed and brought into being. He wrote also to Dionysius [of Alexandria] to inform him of what they had said about him. The latter

[264] They maintained that Dionysius' admission of the right of the Synod of Antioch to depose Paul deprived the Roman Julius of any authority to judge the case of Athanasius. *Infra,* p. 526. Thus both West and East cited Dionysius for their own ends.

[265] The Arianism of the fourth century was a modified offshoot of the Adoptionism of the third.

immediately replied and composed a book entitled *A Refutation and Defense.* Note here how detestable is the gang of the adversaries of Christ and how they themselves have stirred up their own disgrace. For since Dionysius, bishop of Rome, wrote against those who asserted that the Son of God was a creature and a thing made, it is obvious that not now for the first time[266] but in years past the heresy of the Arian foes of Christ has been anathematized by everyone. And since Dionysius, bishop of Alexandria, defended himself from the charge regarding the letter he had written, it is plain that he too neither thought as they say he did nor entertained the Arian error at all.[267]

Athanasius, *De Decretis Nicaenae Synodi,* 25–26. Text. J. P. Migne, *Patrologia Graeca,* XXV, 461–466.

When he [Dionysius of Alexandria] was suspected of saying that the Son was a creature and not eternal and not of the substance of the Father, he wrote to his namesake, Dionysius, bishop of Rome, and explained that this was a calumny against him. He asserted that he had never called the Son a creature and that he believed him to be of the same substance. His words are as follows: "And I have written another letter in which I have proved that their charge against me is false, namely, that I deny that Christ is of the same substance[268] as God. For although I do say that I have not found the word [homoousios] anywhere in Holy Scripture, still my argument from that point on, which they do not mention, is in harmony with the idea. . . . But this letter, as I said before, I am not able to produce

266 *I.e.,* in Athanasius' own day, the years following the Nicene Council.

267 However, Basil, the great bishop of Cappadocia, who, a few years after Athanasius, read the documents in this case, decided that the Alexandrian Dionysius had actually strayed far into Arianism. Basil, *Epistolae,* 9.

268 The word here translated "of the same substance" is ὁμοούσιος, homoousios, the same word that was introduced, through Roman influence, into the creed of Nicæa and around which the battle raged for years afterwards. *Infra,* pp. 471, 474, 492, 543 ff.

because of the state of affairs here; otherwise I should have sent you the passage as I wrote it or, rather, a copy of the whole, as I shall do, whenever I find it possible. I know and remember that I cited many instances of analogy. For I said that a plant that springs from a seed or a root is different from that whence it grew but remains absolutely of the same nature with it. And I said that a river flowing from a spring has its own name, because the spring is not called a river nor the river a spring and both are there and the river is the water from the spring."

And the great synod [269] declared that the Word of God was not a thing made nor a creature but his own inseparable and begotten Son, of the substance of the Father. There also was the bishop of Rome, Dionysius, writing against the Sabellians and voicing in the following words his indignation against those who dared to make such professions. ". . . [A denunciation, first of Sabellius, 'for saying that the Son is the Father,' and in the next place, of the 'futile' and 'diabolic' doctrine of 'the Marcionists,' which makes three gods out of the Trinity.] . . . No less should one upbraid those who teach that the Son is a creature and that the Lord was made, as if they regarded him as something really made, although the divine Scriptures bear witness that he was fittingly and rightfully begotten and was neither fashioned nor created. It is therefore a blasphemy of the gravest kind to say that the Lord was in any way moulded by a hand. For if the Son was made, there was a time when he was not. But Christ always was, if he is indeed in the Father, as he himself says, and if he is Word and Wisdom and Power. And Christ is all these according to the divine Scriptures, as you know. . . . So we must not divide into three godheads the wonderful unity of God nor diminish by creation the loftiness and surpassing greatness of the Lord, but believe in God, the Father Almighty, and in Christ

[269] Dionysius' synod at Rome.

Jesus, his Son, and in the Holy Spirit and in the unity of the Word with the God of all.[270] . . ."

Eusebius, *Historia Ecclesiastica,* VII, 30, 1–5, 17. Text. *Eusebius Werke* (*Die griechischen christlichen Schriftsteller der ersten drei Jahrhunderte*), II², 704–709; 712–713.

The pastors who had assembled to discuss the matter[271] drew up by common consent a letter addressed to Dionysius, bishop of the Romans, and to Maximus, bishop at Alexandria, and sent it around to all the provinces. In it they made clear to everyone their own fidelity and the perverted heterodoxy of Paul and the arguments and debates which they had held with him and they depicted besides the whole life and character of the man. It may be well to record here the following extracts from this report.

"Helenus, Hymenaeus, Theophilus, Theotecnus, Maximus, Proclus, Nicomas, Aelianus, Paul, Bolanus, Protogenes, Hierax, Eutychius, Theodore, Malchion and Lucius[272] and all others who dwell with us in nearby cities and nations, bishops, priests and deacons, and the churches of God, to Dionysius and Maximus and to all our fellow ministers throughout the world, bishops, priests and deacons, and to the whole catholic Church under heaven, greeting to our beloved brethren in the Lord."

A little further on they proceed: "We summoned and called upon many bishops, even from a distance, to deliver us from this baneful doctrine, such as Dionysius of Alexandria and Firmilian of Cappadocia, those blessed men.

270 The Roman Dionysius does not himself anywhere, in the passage which Athanasius quotes, use the word homoousios. Yet it is evident from the Alexandrian's letter that he demanded acceptance of it as one form of definition of the character of the unity of the Father and the Son.

271 *I.e.,* the case of Paul of Samosata, heretical bishop of Antioch and official of Queen Zenobia. *Supra,* pp. 432–433

272 This list of sixteeen names includes bishops from Tarsus, Jerusalem, Caesarea in Palestine, Bostra in Arabia, Iconium, Egypt and others of whose dioceses we are ignorant.

The former sent a letter to Antioch, for he did not regard the leader of this error as himself deserving of address and he wrote not to him but to the parish as a whole. Of his letter we give a copy below. Firmilian twice visited us and condemned his innovations, as we who were present know and testify and many others know as well. But when Paul promised to modify his tenets, Firmilian believed him and hoped that the trouble might be adjusted without any reproach to the Word. So he delayed proceedings, for he was deceived by him who denied even his own God and Lord and abandoned the faith which he once held. At length, Firmilian set out again upon his way to Antioch and came as far as Tarsus, having now had full experience of Paul's atheistic perfidy. But just then, while we who had met here were inquiring for him and waiting for his arrival, he died." . . .[273]

Then at the end of the letter, they add these words: "Therefore we have been obliged to excommunicate him, since he sets himself up against God and refuses to yield and appoint another bishop in his place for the catholic Church. Guided by God, as we believe, we have appointed Domnus, who is adorned with all the virtues becoming to a bishop and is a son of the blessed Demetrianus, who formerly presided with distinction over the same parish.[274] We have notified you of this step, that you may write to him and accept letters of communion from him. But let Paul write to Artemas [275] and let those who think as Artemas does hold communion with him."

273 The portion of the letter omitted here accuses Paul of illgotten wealth, arrogant appearances in public, surrounded by a bodyguard and seated on a high tribune, suspicious relations with women and heretical teaching as to the nature of Christ. It also mentions the fear with which the Antiochene people regarded him. It is the first account in church history of a bishop who was also a royal official, a phenomenon that ceased to be remarkable during the next two centuries.

274 Demetrianus had been Paul's predecessor. *Supra*, p. 387.

275 This may be a reference to the Artemon who professed Adoptionist theories at Rome at the beginning of the century, although it seems unlikely that he was still alive. *Supra*, pp. 275, 278. In one of the omitted passages in the letter, Paul is said to have shared "the abominable heresy of Artemas."

Felix I

(268–274)

The case of Paul of Samosata, bishop of Antioch, had, as we have said, been complicated from the outset by the fact that he exercised civil as well as spiritual authority. It was not then after all to be settled by a purely ecclesiastical agency, such as a council of priests and bishops. For Paul refused to admit the validity of the council's sentence of deposition or to surrender the church edifice. He defiantly continued to act as if still in secure possession of both his offices. Domnus and his supporters had no material resources comparable to his and were obliged to establish themselves as unostentatiously as they could about the city. In this fashion the deadlock began and lasted for several years, one party professing the orthodox doctrine and maintaining communion with the catholic churches abroad, the other consisting of Adoptionists and Paul's personal adherents, backed by the power of Queen Zenobia, who had become, since the death of Odenathus, sole sovereign in the provinces of Asia.

But in 270, the government of the world passed once more into the hands of an energetic soldier emperor, Aurelian, who set vigorously about repairing the imperial system where it had fallen into desuetude. In 272, he defeated the haughty Zenobia in battle, dispatched her to Rome to grace his triumph and restored the provincial system of administration in Roman Asia. On the taking of Antioch by the imperial legions, Paul lost his position in civil affairs, although he still held the church buildings and his episcopal title. But now the orthodox party in Antioch saw an opportunity to undermine him with his own weapons and for the first time on record, Christians at odds with one another competed for the aid of Caesar. The orthodox petitioned Aurelian to compel Paul, the favorite of the vanquished Zenobia, to withdraw from the church and to permit Domnus, the rightful bishop, to enter it. The friends of Paul, on the other hand, also addressed the emperor, urging that he was the legitimate choice of the people of Antioch, who had never concurred in his deposition.

Aurelian's patience was unequal to fathoming the intricacies of ecclesiastical argumentation. In Rome, on one occasion, he reproved the Senate for spending too long a time over a discussion, as though, he said, they were "arguing in a Christian meeting and not in the temple of all the gods." [276] His own aim was to recreate an efficient empire under a well-knit government, centralized at Rome. The Church, as a widespread organization of his subjects, might advisably be taught to defer to Italy in its religious disputes. Also it was convenient and simple for the emperor to treat the bishop of the capital city and his associates as responsible for the whole body. His answer to the petitioners, accordingly, was a command that the decision between Paul and Domnus should be submitted to the judgment of the bishops of Italy and Rome. Thus, as a result of their appeal, the Christians of Antioch forfeited for the nonce their cherished eastern independence and the primacy, for which Victor and Stephen had contended on religious grounds, came in part, for a moment, as a gift from the pagan State to Felix.

In what form the verdict was delivered to the Antiochene church, whether as the joint resolution of an Italian synod under Felix's presidency or as the judgment of Felix himself, speaking as head of the church of Italy, Eusebius does not say. He tells us merely that Paul was forced to evacuate his church. Nor do we hear that anyone anywhere raised a note of protest against the resort to the emperor. The Romans had gained too much by it to make it likely that they would object and the Asiatics were perhaps after all relieved to have the tedious quarrel ended and the see of Antioch at peace under an orthodox bishop.

In 451, at the Council of Chalcedon, in the thick of more efforts to reach a satisfactory definition of the nature of Christ, an extract was read and entered in the records from a letter that Felix wrote to Maximus and the clergy of Alexandria, in which he contrasted the Adoptionist and the orthodox views on the subject. From it we gather that he, like his predecessor, Dionysius, felt it his duty to carry on the work of formulating dogma and

[276] Flavius Vopiscus, *Aurelian*, c. XX. Quoted by A. Harnack, *The Mission and Expansion of Christianity*, Vol. II, p. 247, n. 3.

that he too presented his conclusions to other churches for their guidance.

For references see under Dionysius, *supra, p.* DCD.

Eusebius, *Historia Ecclesiastica,* VII, 30, 18–19. Text. *Eusebius Werke (Die griechischen christlichen Schriftsteller der ersten drei Jahrhunderte),* II², 715.

So after Paul had fallen from the episcopate as well as from the orthodox faith, Domnus, as we have said, was appointed to the ministry of the church at Antioch. But since Paul refused to surrender the church house,[277] a petition was sent to the emperor Aurelian and he decided the question with great justice, ordering that the building should be given to that party to whom the bishops of Italy and the city of Rome should award it. In this way, the man was exposed and driven from the church in utter disgrace by the worldly power.

Felix I, *Fragment of a letter to Bishop Maximus and the clergy of Alexandria.* Text. G. D. Mansi, *Amplissima Collectio,* I, 1114.[278]

As regards the incarnation of the Word and our faith, we believe in our Lord Jesus Christ, born of the Virgin Mary, that he is himself the eternal Son and Word of God and not man adopted by God to be another beside him. Nor did the Son of God adopt a man to be another beside himself, but being perfect God, he became at the same time also perfect man, incarnate from the Virgin.

277 The word used by Eusebius for the church edifice is *οἶκος,* the Greek counterpart to the Latin *domus* or house. The building included, probably, a house in which the bishop lived and a large hall in which religious services were celebrated. At this period, such a structure might have been the ecclesiastical centre of the city.

278 This same fragment was cited also by Cyril of Alexandria in his *Apologia.* Compare with the statements of Paul's doctrine, as in J. C. Ayer, *Source Book for Ancient Church History,* pp. 227–229.

6. THE OBSCURE PERIOD

From Eutychianus to Eusebius

(275–310)

The thirty-seven years that elapsed between the decision in the affair of Paul of Samosata and the legalization of Christianity by Constantine are, strange to say, almost a blank in papal history. Eusebius, our guide and mainstay hitherto, who found numerous letters from Roman bishops as far as Felix laid up in the library at Caesarea, whose chronology, as well as it can now be tested, seems to be accurate for Roman pontificates to that point and who, indeed, knew considerably more about the Roman See for the first two centuries after its foundation than he did about any other, not even excluding his venerable neighbor, the patriarchate of Antioch, knows suddenly nothing more. His references to the popes after Felix, the men who were his own contemporaries,[279] are of the briefest description. He can give their names and order of succession but not always the length of their terms and nothing whatever of their policies or careers. Such dates as he can muster are often confused and contradictory, with the consulates badly jumbled. For papal chronology in this period one must turn, therefore, to the *Liberian Catalogue,* drawn up at Rome under Liberius, some twenty-five or thirty years after Eusebius' death.[280] That, however, becomes at this same juncture curiously bare. In the earlier part, a few concise notices of events were inserted under the names of such bishops as Pontianus, Fabianus, Cornelius and Lucius, but now these too cease and we are left again with nothing but names and dates. Just as we have followed the Roman bishopric to the place where its claims to predominance have become defined to itself and widely asserted abroad and have even received the passing support of a tolerant emperor, the whole office recedes into

279 Eusebius, speaking earlier of Xystus II, says that he is now recording events that have happened within his own lifetime. *Historia Ecclesiastica,* VII, 27.

280 *Infra,* p. 710.

obscurity both for us and for the men who tried to learn about it a little later.[281]

The first twenty-eight years of this period were a time of unexampled prosperity for the Church. It was countenanced and indulged by the rulers of the State as never before. Its membership is said to have doubled between the reign of Gallienus and the opening of the fourth century. Halls for worship were built without concealment in many parts of Rome. Christians appeared in every rank of society, even within the circle of the imperial family. Eusebius, writing during the reign of Constantine, says of Maxentius that he "at first feigned our faith in order to please and flatter the Roman people." [282] Why at such a time did the Roman bishops stop communication with the brethren of the East or why were their letters, if they sent any, no longer preserved? Eutychianus and Gaius, whose pontificates taken together cover the years from 275 to 296, may have been men of no marked personal initiative. The eastern churches may have tacitly drawn off from Rome in dread of more interference. The emperors' prolonged absences from Italy, followed by the decisive removal of Diocletian to Nicomedia in 286, deprived the Roman bishops temporarily of imperial sanction for any efforts they might then think of making to bring the Christians of the Empire under a Roman head. But in our present ignorance we can frame no explanation that is not inadequate as well as futile.

After 303, the bitter edicts against Christianity and the growing disorder in the government, culminating in the series of civil wars between the various rivals for the throne, undoubtedly did much to hinder intercourse between churches in different provinces. The sole surviving tradition regarding the Roman See at this time which bears any trace of authenticity, is the story that Marcellinus, bishop from 296 to 304, turned apostate under the

281 During the fourth century disputes between the Roman bishop and the eastern churches, both parties searched the past for any precedents that might confirm their particular contentions but neither made any allusion that we can recognize to any event later than the time of Felix.

282 Eusebius, *Historia Ecclesiastica*, VIII, 14, 1. But Eusebius' knowledge of the whole Roman situation is obviously quite hazy. The city was still far more pagan than Christian.

persecution. In Constantine's reign, his name was in fact omitted from the Roman calendar of papal and other anniversaries. Anything as appalling, however, as the lapse of a bishop of Rome we should surely expect Eusebius to know and remark upon, for the rumor of it must infallibly have spread. But writing, as he does, while the memory of those terrible days was still vivid in his mind, he says explicitly that he intends to relate only incidents of heroism and triumph and will not mention those "who were shaken by the persecution nor those who were shipwrecked of salvation and sank by their own choice in the depths of the flood."[283] He gives a roll of honor of bishops who faced martyrdom unflinchingly and he does not include in it the bishop of Rome. In another connection entirely he speaks of Marcellinus and adds that he was "overtaken by the persecution."[284] The reader may make of it what he can. From Augustine, a century later, we hear that the sect of the Donatists, who denied the validity of sacraments performed by heretical or profane hands, regarded the Roman church as polluted on the ground that Marcellinus and three priests, Melchiades, Marcellus and Silvester, all of whom in turn subsequently became Roman bishops, had delivered up the sacred books to the pagan magistrates and had offered incense to the pagan gods. Augustine admits that he is in darkness as to the facts but declares that the Donatists have no proofs to support their accusation and that therefore he prefers to disbelieve it.[285]

After Marcellinus, came an interregnum of seven years, during which, because of the intensity of persecution, no bishop was ordained at Rome. With the advent, however, of the tyrant Maxentius in Italy religious persecution ceased as such but the government was capricious and the situation remained unstable. Marcellus, who is listed in the *Liberian Catalogue* next to

283 Eusebius, *op. cit.*, VIII, 2, 3. On Marcellinus see L. Duchesne, *Early History of the Christian Church*, Vol. II, pp. 72–74.

284 Eusebius, *op. cit.*, VII, 32, 1. The phrase is singularly ambiguous. It implies disaster of some kind and lacks the tone of eulogy with which Eusebius invariably refers to martyrs or confessors.

285 The Donatists were undoubtedly exaggerating when they included the three priests in their accusation. On them and their schism *vide infra*, pp. 450 ff., 464 ff. In the fifth century, there was a pathetic legend of Marcellinus' fall and remorseful recantation. L. R. Loomis, *Book of the Popes*, 36 and n. 2.

Marcellinus, is not mentioned at all by Eusebius. Perhaps, as Mommsen suggests, he was only a chief priest who undertook for a while the duties of bishop during the long vacancy.[286] Popular legend, a century or two later, described his condemnation by Maxentius to menial labor in the palace stables.[287] More trustworthy is his epitaph, erected some sixty years after his death by Bishop Damasus, that bears witness to his struggle with the inevitable problem of the lapsed, his insistence on strict discipline in the teeth of stormy and violent opposition and his final banishment by Maxentius, who did not punish Christians for their Christianity but for what he looked upon as pertinacious breaches of the peace. Under Eusebius, Marcellus' successor, the faction that stood for leniency in church discipline seems to have swelled to formidable proportions and to have elected a rival bishop, Heraclius, with the result that Maxentius was again provoked by their tumults to the point of deporting both Eusebius and his adversary. The comparative fullness of our information about similar crises in the Church of fifty years earlier makes it possible to read more meaning than we otherwise could into Damasus' terse lines. After Eusebius' disappearance, the Roman See once more was vacant for a year or two.

Augustine, *De Unico Baptismo; contra Petilianum,* I, 16.
Text. J. P. Migne, *Patrologia Latina,* XLIII, 610.

Now what need is there of our clearing the bishops of the Roman church from the accusations and incredible slanders that he[288] brings against them? Marcellinus and his priests, Melchiades,[289] Marcellus and Silvester, are charged by him with surrender of the sacred Scriptures and offerings of incense. But are they on that account convicted of it or are they convicted only through some palpable distortion of the documents? He says that they

286 Introduction to Mommsen's edition of the *Liber Pontificalis, Monumenta Germaniae, Regesta Pontificum Romanorum,* I.
287 L. R. Loomis, *op. cit.,* 38–39.
288 *I.e.,* Petilianus, an African Donatist.
289 Miltiades is another form of the same name.

were wicked and profane; I reply that they were innocent. Why should I take pains to prove my defense, when he has made not the slightest effort to prove his accusation? If there is any humanity in the world, I think we are more deserving of blame if we believe that persons unknown to us, against whom their enemies bring a charge which they never support by any evidence, are guilty rather than innocent. For if by chance the truth turns out to be other than we supposed, at least one is doing one's duty to humanity when, as a man, one suspects no evil of another man lightly nor gives easy credit to an accuser, since he who brings an accusation without a witness or any written proof may himself be shown to be a liar rather than a truthful plaintiff.

Damasus, *Inscription over the tomb of Marcellus.*[290] Text. L. Duchesne, *Liber Pontificalis,* I, 166, n. 10.

A venerable pastor, for he bade the apostates mourn their guilt
And was a bitter enemy to all wretches.
Thence arose anger, hatred, discord, strife,
Mutiny, bloodshed; the bonds of peace were loosed.
Accused by one who in peace denied Christ,
He was driven by the cruel tyrant[291] from his own country.
This in brief has Damasus ascertained and recorded,
That the people might know the virtue of Marcellus.

Damasus, *Inscription over the tomb of Eusebius.*[292] Text. L. Duchesne, *op. cit.,* I, 167, n. 5.

DAMASUS, THE BISHOP, ERECTED THIS

Heraclius forbade the apostates to grieve for their sins.
Eusebius taught the wretched to mourn their guilt.

290 Marcellus was buried in the cemetery of Priscilla. Damasus set up his tablet in the church of Silvester, which had been built meantime over the cemetery.

291 Maxentius.

292 The tomb of Eusebius was in a chamber of the cemetery of Callistus.

The people were rent in factions and anger mounted,
Mutiny, bloodshed, war, discord, strife.
Both were driven alike from the temple by the cruel tyrant,[293]
Though the pastor was keeping unbroken the bonds of peace.
Gladly he suffered exile under the Lord's judgment;
On the Sicilian shore he departed from earth and life.

To Eusebius, Bishop and Martyr.

[293] *I.e.*, both Eusebius and Heraclius, leader of the party of laxity, were banished by Maxentius. Eusebius seems to have held office only four months. For the dates of these bishops see the *Liberian Catalogue, infra*, p. 714.

PART III

THE SUPREME BISHOPRIC OF THE UNIVERSAL CHURCH

MILTIADES

(311–314)

Miltiades had been bishop for something over a year when Constantine, in October, 312, defeated Maxentius and set up in "the most public place" in Rome his own statue bearing the sign of Christ; yet of Miltiades we hear singularly little. Eusebius relates how Constantine was met on his memorable entry into the city by "all the members of the Senate and the other notables, with the whole Roman people and the women and children," [1] but says not a word of the Roman Christians, whose rejoicing must have been the greatest of all and with whom Eusebius would naturally have felt the deepest sympathy. Whatever his sources of information as to this thrilling event, they evidently did not include a letter from the Roman church. The rescript that issued presently from Constantine's palace, providing for state grants of aid to the churches, named Hosius, a Spaniard, bishop of Cordova, not Miltiades, as the emperor's minister and councillor in ecclesiastical affairs.

Miltiades, however, has several achievements to his credit. Before the victory at the Milvian Bridge, the churches of the city, under his direction, had returned to something approaching harmony and order and had secured from Maxentius a writ for the restitution of the property confiscated during the persecution. Armed with this document and with another from the praetorian prefect, the deacons had gone to the city prefect and had received from him their lands and buildings.[2] Upon the installation

[1] *Historia Ecclesiastica,* IX, 9, 9. It is hardly necessary to state here that the legend that attributed Constantine's conversion to Bishop Silvester is altogether fictitious, an invention, perhaps, of the fifth century. On this legend see C. B. Coleman, *Constantine the Great and Christianity* (New York, 1914), Pt. II, chaps. I and V.

[2] Augustine, *Breviculus Collationis cum Donatistis,* III, 34–36.

of the new régime, Miltiades must have made some kind of meritorious impression upon some member of the imperial family to obtain, as he did soon, the gift of the stately old palace of the Laterani on the Coelian Hill, the property of Constantine's wife Fausta, to be used henceforth as an episcopal residence. In the autumn of 313, he held a synod in this "house of the church," as we shall see. Either he or his successor, Silvester, seems to have begun the construction of a baptistery and a basilica adjacent to the palace, the originals of the present Lateran cathedral.[3] No wonder that a new and appropriate note of grandeur crept into Roman tradition, when her bishop held his court in princely halls.[4]

Other spectacular gifts came to the church from its imperial benefactors. Either in 312 or, more probably, on his second visit to Rome in 315, Constantine ordered the erection of a large and imposing basilica over the tomb of the apostle Peter in the Vatican district [5] and of two smaller structures over the tombs of Paul and Lawrence respectively, outside the walls.[6] Helena, the emperor's mother, made her home at intervals in the Sessorian Palace, not far from the Lateran, where she turned one of the halls into a basilica to receive the relics of the True Cross and other treasures from Jerusalem.[7] Thereafter it was no longer necessary to travel to Syria to find objects sanctified by the touch of the Lord. Helena had also a villa on the Via Labicana, three miles from the city, near a cemetery where lay the bodies of two martyrs who had suffered in the recent persecution. She built a small basilica over their graves and arranged that at her own death her body should be transported from the East to be interred in a mausoleum on the same spot.[8] Two of Constantine's daughters took up their abode for a while in a villa on the Via

[3] For a description of the fourth century basilica and its furniture see L. R. Loomis, *The Book of the Popes*, 47–53.

[4] *Supra*, pp. 105, 111, 117.

[5] *Supra*, p. 104. L. R. Loomis, *op. cit.*, 53–57.

[6] L. R. Loomis, *op. cit.*, 57–58, 61–63. Laurentius was the name of one of the four deacons who were executed with Xystus II, in 258. *Supra*, p. 425. He had by this time become the hero of a popular legend.

[7] This basilica was itself called "Jerusalem." L. R. Loomis, *op. cit.*, 58–60. It is now Santa Croce in Gerusalemme. On the legend of Helena see C. B. Coleman, *op. cit.*, Pt. II, chap. II, 2.

[8] L. R. Loomis, *op. cit.*, 63–65. Eusebius, *Vita Constantini*, III, 47.

Nomentana and were buried in the baptistery now called Santa Constanza.[9]

But all was not instantly peace and affluence throughout the West, because an emperor had turned Christian and there was prosperity in the church at Rome. Neither the material nor the spiritual damages of the persecution could be everywhere so speedily undone. Constantine, to be sure, arranged for grants from the state treasury to assist bishops in every city under his sway to defray the expenses of repairs and of the resumption of religious services on a large scale.[10] Eusebius preserves his letter of instruction to Caecilian, bishop of Carthage, metropolitan of the three provinces of northwestern Africa.[11] But one result of this well-meant letter was to confront the emperor with his first ecclesiastical dilemma, namely the necessity of deciding between two rival church organizations in the same city as to which was to be the proper recipient for his bounties.

The situation in Africa was not altogether unlike that created sixty years earlier by the persecution of Decius. Mensurius, bishop of Carthage at the beginning of the century, had himself evaded or compromised with the edicts of 303 and 304 that required the surrender of all copies of the Scriptures and the offering of pagan sacrifices of incense, and had tried to suppress the confessors and others of his flock who in their enthusiasm for martyrdom were provoking the magistrates to greater severity and bringing down extreme penalties upon their own heads. As a consequence, he and several other bishops like him in the vicinity, particularly one Felix of Aptonga, who was said to have given over the Scriptures without resistance or protest, had been denounced as traitors, "traditores," by the zealous party in the Carthaginian church and by many bishops outside, including a large group in Numidia. On the death of Mensurius, Caecilian,

[9] L. R. Loomis, *op. cit.*, 60–61. Ammianus Marcellinus, XXI, 1. Constantina built the basilica of Sant' Agnese.

[10] From this time on, the Church begins to rely for support more and more upon income from its lands and other forms of endowment, bestowed upon it by state officials or private individuals. The old system of dependence on the collection of a multitude of small contributions drops slowly into abeyance. E. Hatch, *The Organization of the Early Christian Churches* (London, 1918), pp. 150 *sqq.*

[11] *Infra*, pp. 454–455. An example of the similar letters, sent by Constantine to the bishops of the East after his victory over Licinius, is furnished by Eusebius, *Vita Constantini*, II, 46.

who had been a deacon under him and who was also branded by the strict opposition, was elected bishop by the majority of the congregation and regularly ordained by Felix of Aptonga and two other bishops from the neighborhood. Thereupon some seventy bishops from Numidia and other outlying regions had hastened to Carthage, joined with the disaffected clergy in the city and constituted themselves a synod. Acting in that capacity, they had pronounced Caecilian's ordination void, on the ground that the rite had been performed by the polluted hands of the "traditor" Felix, had condemned him and all his adherents, and elected one Majorinus, a reader, as bishop of Carthage in Caecilian's stead.[12] Now, at the news of Constantine's conversion to Christianity and of the stream of imperial largess that had begun to flow in the direction of the Church, this same party started to agitate for the recognition of Majorinus rather than Caecilian by the State. As long as the State had been indifferent or hostile, it had classed all Christians, heretical, schismatic or orthodox together, as equally criminal before the law. Now that it had chosen to become an interested benefactor, it at once found itself obliged to discriminate. It could not conceivably support two sects or two bishops at the same time in the same place.

Constantine seems to have heard early, perhaps from Hosius or Miltiades, that there was trouble in the African church, for in his letter to Caecilian, already mentioned, he invited him to call on the local proconsul, Anulinus, for aid against any corrupt persons who might be fomenting disturbance. He had already, apparently, instructed Anulinus to do his best by argument and persuasion to bring the discordant factions back to unity. But the party of Majorinus was not to be appeased or silenced. Anulinus wrote to the emperor that a deputation had waited on him, bringing two petitions which they had asked him to forward directly to Constantine. In other words, like the Christians of Antioch forty years previously, with property at stake, they had appealed to the government to distinguish between varieties of religious belief and morals.[13] In this instance, however, the

[12] This, of course, was not a regular method of electing a bishop. *Supra*, p. 401 and n. 208.

[13] *Supra*, pp. 439, 441.

complainants requested the appointment of ecclesiastical judges from Gaul to hear their arguments. Constantine was himself in Gaul when the petitions reached him. The writers may have intended to suggest for his convenience a choice of men in his own vicinity. But it is also not impossible that they hoped to prevent the sending of their case to Rome, where, they may have felt, a decision would tend to go against schismatics and a bishop whose election had been irregular.

Constantine is said to have been annoyed by the appeal.[14] He saw the Church of the Supreme Being not united in love and thankfulness for its mercies but stubborn and fractious and full of recriminations and bitterness. However, he named three Gallic bishops to sit as judges and summoned Caecilian and ten African bishops from each party in the dispute to appear for the proceedings. But he appointed Rome as the place of trial and wrote to Miltiades, sending him copies of the documents received and committing the further conduct of the case entirely into his hands, only advising that the affair be given a thorough investigation and settled in such a way as to put an end to divisions in the Church catholic. Whether Constantine was consciously following the precedent set by Aurelian in 274 or whether Hosius had simply advised him to submit a controversy involving another metropolitan to the Roman See, it is impossible to tell. The tribunal met on October second, 313, in a hall of the Lateran palace. By a later arrangement with the emperor, Miltiades added fifteen Italian bishops to his board of judges, thus changing completely the complexion of the court. The accusers of Caecilian were headed by Bishop Donatus of Casae Nigrae in Numidia. Majorinus, who had not been cited, did not attend.

From the accounts of Optatus of Mileve and Augustine of Hippo, the two famous Africans who years afterward engaged in written debate with the Donatists of their generation and who, in the course of their polemics, reviewed in some detail the history of the whole quarrel, we can reconstruct in outline the events of the so-called Synod of 313. It held three sessions on

14 But the remark which Optatus attributes to him seems scarcely in character, at least at this period of his reign. *Infra*, p. 459.

three different days. On the first, the Donatists [15] seem to have given vent to loud, excited talking and confused, group accusations. They were not prepared to plead in due, legal form, with one spokesman assuming the rôle of plaintiff on behalf of the rest. They presented no official records or witnesses. Their leader, Donatus, was himself at once charged by the Caecilianists with personal transgression of orthodox rules. The fact that he had undeniably performed second baptisms meant nothing in Africa, where such baptisms had been common ever since the time of Cyprian,[16] but it must have helped to prejudice the Italians against him. The Donatists finally declared that they had not their plaintiff, witnesses, etc., with them and that they would produce them another day. But when, on the second day, the court assembled, they did not appear. The third day, the judges proceeded to vote in turn, Miltiades last of all, in favor of continuing communion with Caecilian as lawful bishop of Carthage. Miltiades went on further to condemn Donatus as the leading spirit in the schism and to propose, as a mode of bringing peace to the African provinces, the recognition in every other contested city but Carthage of the bishop who had been first ordained there and the speedy transference to another see of whoever found himself by this measure dispossessed.[17] He then sent a report of the verdict to Constantine.

The emperor was not, apparently, wholly satisfied. The synod had confirmed the regular organization at Carthage but it had done nothing to pacify the serious opposition in that city and had disposed in too summary a fashion of their charges against Caecilian. He ordered both Caecilian and Donatus to wait a while longer in Italy, until two other bishops, who had not been at the synod, could visit Carthage and sound out the chances of having a new bishop elected whom every "catholic" Christian would accept. All attempt at conciliation, however, proved futile. The visiting bishops grew indignant at the uproar the Donatists were making over the treatment of their case at

[15] We use this name here for brevity. The party did not actually receive the appellation of Donatists until after the death of Majorinus and the election of another Donatus as bishop of Carthage.

[16] *Supra*, pp. 395, 410–411.

[17] This, of course, was in contrast to the Donatists' position, that they could recognize no ordination as valid which was not conferred by unstained and

Rome and concluded that the Caecilianists, who were at least on good terms with the brethren abroad, should be considered "catholic," took communion with them and sailed for home.[18] Caecilian and Donatus slipped back to Africa and the schism grew hotter than ever. The Donatists sent a second, fervid protestation to the emperor, to the effect that the trial at Rome had been the hurried work of a few men and that they had not yet received a fair hearing.[19] Constantine seems to have felt that they had some justification for their complaints. At all events, so far as our records show, he never again employed a Roman bishop in the execution of any of his ecclesiastical enterprises.

On Constantine and his church policy see all histories of the Church and the period and such special studies as G. Boissier, *La Fin du Paganisme* (3 vols., 3rd ed., Paris, 1898), Vol. I; M. A. Huttmann, *Toleration under Constantine* (New York, 1914); C. B. Coleman, *Constantine the Great and Christianity* (New York, 1914); on the Donatists, C. J. Hefele, *Histoire des Conciles* (8 vols., Paris, 1907–1921), Vol. I, Pt. I; L. Duchesne, *Le Dossier du Donatisme* in *Mélanges d'Archéologie et d'Histoire* (Paris, 1890), Vol. X, pp. 589–650; L. Duchesne, *Early History of the Christian Church* (trans. from the 4th ed. by C. Jenkins, 3 vols., London, 1910–1924), Vol. II, pp. 79–97; F. Martroye, *Une Tentative de Révolution Sociale en Afrique* in *Revue des Questions Historiques* (Paris, 1904), Vol. LXXVI (Nouvelle Serie, Vol. XXXII), pp. 353–416.

The Donatist Trial at Rome

Constantine, *Letter to Caecilian,* quoted by Eusebius, *Historia Ecclesiastica,* X, 6. Text. *Eusebius Werke* (*Die griechischen christlichen Schriftsteller*), II[2], 890.

Constantine Augustus to Caecilian, bishop of Carthage. Whereas it is our pleasure that grants should be made

authoritative hands. The Roman position was, as it had been earlier during the contest over heretical baptism, that a sacrament rightly performed was efficacious by its own virtue. Cyprian himself had insisted that once a bishop was ordained in any city it was impossible to set up another. *Supra,* pp. 359, 372.

[18] On the previous use and significance of the word "catholic," *vide supra,* p. 286.

[19] For this, see Constantine's letters of summons to the Council of Arles, *infra,* pp. 477–480.

in all the provinces of Africa and Numidia and Mauretania to ministers of the lawful and most holy catholic religion, in order to defray their expenses, I have sent word to Ursus, the illustrious head of finance in Africa, and have directed him to arrange to pay to your excellency three thousand folles.[20] Do you, therefore, when you have received this sum of money, give orders that it be distributed among all the persons I have mentioned, in accordance with the instructions sent to you by Hosius.[21] If you should find that anything more is needed to fulfil this my purpose for them all, do you without hesitation demand whatever else you discover to be necessary from Heracleides, the treasurer of our funds. For I charged him, when he was with me, that if your excellency should ask him for money, he should see that it was paid without delay. And, inasmuch as I have heard that some persons of disorderly character are plotting to turn the people from the most holy and catholic Church by methods of base corruption,[22] you are hereby informed that I commanded Anulinus, the proconsul, and also Patricius, vicar of the prefects, when they were here, to give due attention especially to this matter among all their other business, and not to ignore such a situation whenever it occurred. Wherefore, if you should observe any such persons persisting in this folly, do you go straightway to the aforesaid judges and report it to them, that they may correct them, as I commanded them when they were here. The divinity of the great God preserve you for many years.

20 A *folle* was, perhaps, 208 *denarii,* in which case the amount here mentioned would be equivalent to more than ninety thousand dollars at the present day. It is not, however, certain that this was the value.

21 *Supra,* p. 448. Hosius, bishop of Cordova, was Constantine's most intimate religious adviser from the early days of his conversion to the end of his life. How the two men first came into contact we do not know. Hosius lived, however, to deny the right of any emperor to meddle with the Church. *Infra,* p. 579.

22 The reference is, in all likelihood, to the Donatists.

Anulinus, *Letter to Constantine,* quoted by Augustine, *Epistolae,* LXXXVIII, 2. Text. Ed. by A. Goldbacher, *Corpus Scriptorum Ecclesiasticorum Latinorum,* XXXIV, 2, 408.

Anulinus, consularis, proconsul of Africa, to Constantine Augustus.[23]

The welcome and adored, celestial communication of your Majesty to Caecilian and to those who obey his leadership and are called his clergy has been by my care engrossed among my own poor records. I have urged these parties to reach an agreement by mutual consent and, inasmuch as they are now, by your Majesty's clemency, exempt from every public burden,[24] to guard the sanctity of catholic law and to uphold a right sense of reverence and the divine ordinances. But a few days since, there came to me among a crowd of people some persons who think that action ought to be taken against Caecilian and they presented to me a sealed packet, wrapped in leather, and a paper without a seal and earnestly entreated me to forward them to your Majesty's sacred and august court, as your Majesty's humble servant has hereby done, Caecilian meanwhile continuing as he was. The documents from these persons are here enclosed, that your Majesty may be able to frame a judgment regarding the whole affair. I have sent both documents, the one in a leather case with the label: "An account by the catholic Church of the charges against Caecilian, presented by the party of Majorinus," the other without a seal, attached to the same leather case.

Sent from Carthage, April 15, in the third consulship of our lord Constantine Augustus.

[23] The name of the person addressed is omitted in Augustine's text.

[24] Constantine had already begun the policy of exempting the Christian clergy from onerous civil duties, such as service as curiales.

Constantine, *Letter to Miltiades,* quoted by Eusebius, *Historia Ecclesiastica,* X, 5, 18–20. Text. *Eusebius Werke* (*Die griechischen christlichen Schriftsteller der ersten drei Jahrhunderte*), II [2], 887–888.

Constantine Augustus to Miltiades, bishop of the Romans, and to Marcus.[25]

Whereas many communications have been sent me by Anulinus, the illustrious proconsul of Africa, in which he reports that Caecilian, bishop of the city of Carthage, has been accused on numerous grounds by some of his colleagues in Africa, and whereas it seems to me a very grave matter that in those provinces which Divine Providence has chosen to entrust to my devotion and in which there is a vast multitude of people, the masses are evidently pursuing ways of error and dividing, so to speak, into two hosts, with their bishops likewise at variance, I have determined that Caecilian himself, with ten of the bishops who seem to be his accusers and ten others whom he may choose as needful for his defense, should take ship to Rome, in order that there in the presence of yourselves and of Reticius and Maternus and Marinus,[26] your colleagues, whom I have commanded to go at once to Rome for this purpose, he may be heard in whatever way you deem compatible with the most holy law.

And, in order that you may have the fullest comprehension of all this business, I have appended to this letter copies of the documents sent to me by Anulinus and have also sent them to your colleagues aforesaid. On reading them, your excellency will consider how the case may be most thoroughly investigated and justly decided.[27] For it

25 This may be some prominent priest, perhaps the man who became bishop of Rome for a few months in 336.

26 Bishops of Autun, Cologne and Arles respectively. These were the judges from Gaul, for whom the accusers of Caecilian had asked. *Supra,* p. 452.

27 It seems clear from this letter that the charges against Caecilian had struck Constantine as sufficiently serious to demand, as he says, thorough investigation. His tone toward the whole situation has changed since his letter to Anulinus.

has not escaped your attention that I have such reverence for the lawful catholic Church that I wish you to leave no schism or division whatever anywhere. May the divinity of the great God preserve you, most honored Sir, for many years.

Optatus of Mileve,[28] *De Schismate Donatistarum*, I, 22–24. Text. *Corpus Scriptorum Ecclesiasticorum Latinorum*, XXVI, 25–27.

But, inasmuch as I hear that members of your association [Donatists] have some kind of records for use in their litigations, we must inquire which of these are to be accepted as reliable, which are consistent with reason and which harmonize with the truth. Perhaps, whatever you have may prove to be mingled with lies. Our records are supported by lawsuits on both sides, by the conflicting arguments of the parties, by the final verdicts and by the letters of Constantine. As for your comment upon us: "What have Christians to do with kings? Or what have bishops in common with the palace?" if it is wrong to make acquaintance with kings, the whole blame sweeps down upon you. For your predecessors, Lucian, Dignus, Nasutius, Capito, Fidentius and others offered their petition to the emperor Constantine, who hitherto had known nothing of such matters. I have written here a copy of it. "We beseech you, Constantine, noblest of emperors, son of a just house, whose father alone among the emperors did not press on the persecution and saved Gaul from that outrage,[29] seeing that in Africa there are disputes between us

[28] On Optatus *vide supra*, p. 110. The following description of the synod held by Miltiades, with the two passages we give subsequently from Augustine, covers most of the information we have about it. There are references to it, however, in many other places. L. Duchesne, *Early History of the Christian Church*, Vol. II, pp. 79–80, notes.

[29] Constantinus Chlorus, the father of Constantine, restrained the persecution of Christians in Gaul and Britain.

and the other bishops, we beg your reverence to command that judges be appointed for us from Gaul. Sent from Lucian, Dignus, Nasutius, Capito, Fidentius and other bishops of the party of Donatus."[30]

When Constantine read this, he replied in great indignation. In his reply, he granted their request but he said: "You ask of me a judgment in this world, while I myself am awaiting the judgment of Christ."[31] However, the judges were appointed, Maternus of Cologne, Reticius of Autun and Marinus of Arles. The three Gauls and fifteen more, who were Italians, came to the city of Rome and met in the palace of Fausta in the Lateran,[32] in the fourth consulship of Constantine and the third of Licinius, on the second of October, the sixth day of the week. When they had assembled, there were present Miltiades, bishop of the city of Rome, and Reticius, Maternus and Marinus, the bishops from Gaul, and Merocles from Milan, Florianus from Sinna,[33] Zoticus from Quintianum,[34] Stennius from Rimini, Felix from Florence of the Tuscans, Gaudentius from Pisa, Constantius from Faenza, Proterius from Capua, Theophilus from Beneventum, Sabinus from Terracina, Secundus from Praeneste, Felix from Three Taverns,[35] Maximus from Ostia, Evander from Ursinum,[36] and Donatian from Forum Claudii.[37]

When these nineteen bishops had taken their seats, the case of Donatus and Caecilian was brought before them. Each of them concurred in the judgment against Donatus, who confessed to administering second baptism[38] and

30 This may be the unsealed petition mentioned by Anulinus, *supra*, p. 456.

31 This sounds as if Optatus had inserted here for effect a remark ascribed to Constantine, perhaps, but on some different and later occasion.

32 *Supra*, p. 449.

33 Probably Siena.

34 A town in Rhaetia, now become the country village, Küntzen.

35 Probably the modern Cisterna, near Rome.

36 Perhaps Urbino.

37 Unknown.

38 On this point *vide supra*, p, 453.

to laying his hands upon bishops who had lapsed,[39] a practice unknown in the Church. Witnesses introduced by Donatus admitted that they had nothing to say against Caecilian.[40] Caecilian was declared innocent by the verdict of all the bishops just enumerated, in particular by the verdict of Miltiades, with which the trial closed, in the following words: "Whereas it is evident from their own statement that Caecilian is not accused by these persons who came hither with Donatus and it is also evident that Donatus himself does not prove any charges against him, I vote that he be restored to ecclesiastical communion, with standing unimpaired, as he deserves."

Augustine, *Breviculus Collationis cum Donatistis,* XII. Text. J. P. Migne, *Patrologia Latina,* XLIII, 637.

Then in due order began to be read the report of the episcopal trial held by Melchiades, bishop of Rome, and the other Gallic and Italian bishops with him, in the city of Rome. At the opening of the report, that is, in the account of the proceedings of the first day, when the accusers of Caecilian, who had been sent there, declared that they had nothing to say against him and when Donatus of Casae Nigrae was convicted to his face of having created a schism at Carthage while Caecilian was still but a deacon,[41] — for from the schism at Carthage arose the Donatist party in opposition to the catholic Church, — these same enemies of Caecilian promised that on another day they would bring

[39] This may mean that Donatus had either admitted to penance or had re-ordained bishops who had apostatized. A bishop who had lapsed was not at this time absolved. Compare Cyprian (*supra*, p. 402) on the apostate bishop of Spain.

[40] The Donatists may have said that their charges were not against Caecilian's personal character but against the circumstances of his election or that they had not yet formulated them as they would do. Compare Augustine's account, on this same page.

[41] This also sounds as if the Donatist charges were not aimed against Caecilian in person so much as against the policies and party which he represented.

forward the persons necessary for the trial, whom they were accused of having withdrawn.[42] And after they had uttered this falsehood, they refused to appear again at the trial.

Augustine, *Epistolae,* XLIII, v, 16. Text. *Corpus Scriptorum Ecclesiasticorum Latinorum,* XXXIV, 2, 98.

Then how fine a sentence was at the last pronounced by the blessed Melchiades himself! How gentle, how upright, how wise and pacific! He did not attempt by it to exclude from his fellowship his colleagues in whom no guilt had been proved, but after putting the heavy blame solely on Donatus, whom he had discovered to be the leader of the whole mischief, he gave the rest a free opportunity to recover their sound minds and was ready to open communication even with those who were known to have been ordained by Majorinus. He proposed that wherever there were two bishops, as the result of the schism, the one first ordained should be confirmed and that another flock should be found to be governed by the second.

Optatus of Mileve, *op. cit.,* I, 26. Text. *Op. cit.,* 28.

[The emperor is informed of this decision.[43] He orders both Donatus and Caecilian to remain for a while in Italy, dispatching Caecilian to Brescia.] Then two bishops, Eunomius and Olympius, were sent to Africa so that now

[42] In the letter from which we next quote, *Epistolae,* XLIII, v and vi, Augustine gives first a longer but not much more definite description of the behavior of the Donatists on the first day of the trial. He says, however, that they were asked which one of them was Caecilian's accuser and that they replied that no one person but all the people of Majorinus' party accused him. They were then told that in a suit the accusation could not come from a crowd but must be made in the name of some person or persons, that they must produce their plaintiffs, witnesses, etc., in proper form. It was also said that there had been persons present ready to take such parts but that Donatus had withdrawn them. Donatus promised to produce them another day but he did not keep his promise or reappear himself in court.

[43] Optatus does not say that Miltiades reported it to the emperor but Augustine does.

that the two heads had been removed, they might ordain one. And they came and abode in Carthage for forty days, in order to determine where was the catholic Church.[44] But the insurgent party of Donatus would not allow them to do this and every day there were tumults stirred up by partisan zeal. The final sentence of these same bishops, Eunomius and Olympius, may be read as follows: they said that the catholic Church was the one that was spread through all the world and that the verdict delivered some time earlier by the nineteen bishops could not be annulled. So they held communion with Caecilian's clergy and returned home. We have a volume of records of these events and whoever wishes may read this toward the end. Then, first, Donatus of his own accord went back to Carthage. When Caecilian heard of it, he hastened to join his people. In this way the struggle of the parties began over again.

SILVESTER I

(314–335)

Our ignorance regarding Silvester, who succeeded Miltiades and was bishop at Rome for more than twenty eventful years, is so dense that popular fancy in later times has tried to compensate for it by weaving a wonderful mass of legends about his name. " A Roman bishop must have had some part in such rare deeds," the legends seem to say. " What existing writers failed to relate we shall supply by the power of faith and imagination." Unfortunately these picturesque fables were the work of men who knew too little history to make them plausible. Much as one might like to believe that Silvester healed the great Constantine of leprosy and baptized him in the Lateran font, one is compelled to incredulity upon learning from contemporary sources

[44] *I.e.*, the envoys were instructed to make an impartial effort to reëstablish the Carthaginian church on the broad foundations of the catholic faith and fellowship and to bring about the election of a new bishop, who had not been involved in the disputes arising out of the persecution. After forty days, they gave up their task in despair and sided with the party already recognized by the orthodox organization elsewhere. On the use of the word " catholic," *vide supra*, pp. 240, n. 11, 286.

that Constantine's conversion had taken place before he set foot in Rome and before Silvester became bishop and that his baptism occurred after Silvester's death and just before his own in far-away Nicomedia.[45] As late as the eighth century, however, the legendary tendency was still working on Silvester, producing the audacious forgery of the *Donation of Constantine,* in which Constantine's choice of his new capital was explained by his pious desire to leave Silvester in unrivalled majesty at Rome.[46]

As a matter of fact, the dazzling emperor, whose figure looms so large in all the authentic histories of his reign as to leave little space for any other,[47] seems, after his one unsatisfactory experiment with Miltiades, to have paid scant attention to the bishop of the old capital. We know from an allusion in a later document that Silvester was once " accused by sacrilegious men " and that he " carried his cause " for judgment to Constantine.[48] It is possible that this accusation originated with the Donatists, who, it may be remembered, charged all Roman bishops with pollution who were either associates or successors of the " traditor " Marcellinus.[49] If this supposition be correct, the case may have been

[45] Eusebius gives us the fullest account of these occurrences. *Supra,* p. 97. See reference to C. B. Coleman's *Constantine the Great, supra,* p. 448, n. 1. The modern *Breviarium Romanum,* in the office for December 31, St. Silvester's anniversary, still preserves an attenuated remnant of the old legend. " He zealously wrought upon Constantine . . . to protect and extend the Christian religion. He, as the ancient tradition of the Roman church attests, had Constantine recognize the images of the apostles, washed him in holy baptism and cleansed him from the leprosy of unbelief. . . . While Silvester was pope, the first Council of Nicaea was held, where in the presence of his legates, who presided, and of Constantine and of three hundred and eighteen bishops, the holy and catholic faith was expounded and Arius and his followers were condemned. At the request of the Fathers, Silvester confirmed this council in a synod which he held at Rome." The text goes on to enumerate some apocryphal decrees issued by Silvester and his imaginary synod.

[46] The latest text and translation of the *Donation* are contained in Coleman's edition of the treatise of Lorenzo Valla upon it, published recently by the Yale Press. Platina, the Vatican librarian, who in 1479 produced what was long considered an authoritative set of *Lives of the Popes* and who knew the histories of Socrates and Sozomen, as well as Valla's devastating criticisms, maintained the truth of the *Donation* and quoted largely from it. See his *Silvester.* The question of the genuineness or falsity of the document was seriously debated as late as the eighteenth century.

[47] Eusebius, Socrates, Sozomen, all see Constantine in the forefront everywhere and the story of his reign is the story of his acts, except in the matter of the Arian controversy.

[48] *Infra,* p. 671. This act was cited as ground for the claim later in the century that the Roman bishop should be subject to trial by no other bishop but only by the emperor.

[49] *Supra,* p. 444.

tried between 315 and 321, when Constantine was still making spasmodic efforts to settle the Donatist disturbances. But this is pure conjecture. We are told nothing whatever as to the circumstances or the outcome.

Immediately after Silvester's accession, in January, 314, a council of bishops from all the West was convoked at Arles by the emperor to review the decision reached a few months earlier at Rome by Silvester's predecessor, Miltiades, with regard to the Donatist revolt against Caecilian of Carthage.[50] The letters sent out by Constantine to the bishops from Britain to Pannonia and Africa are represented for us by the one addressed to Chrestus, bishop of Syracuse. We have also the letter which he despatched to the vicar or civil governor of the disordered region of Africa. The phraseology of these letters is suggestive as to Constantine's state of mind. He is irritated by the refusal of the Donatists to accept the verdict of Rome and acutely sensitive to the fact that persons who ought to be considering " their own salvation and the reverence due to our most holy doctrine " and living " in brotherly and harmonious accord " are making themselves ridiculous to the observant pagans by spiteful wranglings. None the less, he states fairly the Donatist grounds for dissatisfaction with the trial at Rome and proposes to give the complaints against Caecilian a more thorough airing before " a large number " and so to put a stop to the disgrace. It seems likely that in his eyes the Roman bishop and his court had actually failed to do full justice. Hereafter, during his whole life, he referred his ecclesiastical difficulties not to the See of Rome but to representative gatherings of the episcopate, the larger the better. His own lack of interest in the city of Rome and his own ambition to promote a sense of organic unity in the Empire may, of course, have had something to do with his preference for general councils, which might be called anywhere and which brought men from great distances together, over synods of Italians sitting at the Lateran. Whatever his motive, his powerful adherence went thenceforth to the federal rather than to the monarchical theory of the episcopate.

[50] *Supra*, pp. 459–461.

The gathering of bishops at Arles was the first that had yet been held representative of more than a local, provincial branch of the Church. It included three bishops from Britain, six from Spain, one from Dalmatia, nine from the greater churches of Italy and Sicily, such as Ostia, Portus, Capua, Syracuse, Milan and Aquileia, sixteen from Gaul and delegates from nine cities in Africa.[51] Silvester himself chose not to be present. He seems to have explained in excuse that it was impossible for him to leave the holy seats of the apostles.[52] He sent, however, two priests and two deacons to speak for him. We have no information as to the council's proceedings more than the little conveyed in the letter which, at the close of its sessions, it addressed to Silvester. But it was, as we have seen, an assemblage of western men, accustomed from of old to defer to the opinion of the one apostolic church in their midst. Silvester need not have feared any criticism, tacit or expressed, of Miltiades' conduct nor the Donatists have hoped for any sympathy. They were now branded as dangerous to law and tradition. Caecilian was again exonerated and his party recognized as the catholic church of Africa. A canon was enacted to provide that clergy could not be deposed as " traditores " without the evidence of official documents from the magistrates, and that clergy who had been consecrated by " traditores " should be regarded as truly ordained, if they were themselves worthy to hold office.

Then, with encouragement, perhaps, from Constantine, the council seized the advantage offered by the unusual assembly to reach an understanding on various other mooted points that had been the seeds of difference in the past. It resolved, for example, that the churches everywhere should all take care in the future to observe Easter on the same day and that notice of the

51 For a list of churches represented at Arles, see the signatures appended to the canons of the council as given in G. D. Mansi, *Amplissima Collectio,* Vol. II, pp. 470–477. The three Gallic bishops and two, at least, out of the fifteen Italian bishops who had sat in Miltiades' tribunal went also to Arles. There was a bishop of Ostia at both places but his name is different on the two occasions. The first may have died in the interval.

52 The language of the council's letter appears to imply this. Thus, from the outset, it became understood that a Roman bishop sent deputies to general councils held elsewhere but did not himself leave Rome. Whoever desired his presence must come to him. Italian synods under the presidency of the Roman See met always, as a matter of course, at the capital and continued to do so.

proper date should be sent out beforehand to all, "according to custom," from the Roman See.[53] It agreed that the African church, in return, no doubt, for the support it was receiving against the Donatists, should at last abandon its custom of re-baptizing converts from heresy and should admit whoever had already been baptized in the name of the Trinity with the simple laying on of hands, as the Romans did.[54] It also expressed the wish that bishops from the provinces, who visited Rome, might be assigned to city churches in which they might offer their eucharistic sacrifices. Finally, after drawing up these and other articles, the council enclosed them all in a profoundly respectful, almost apologetic letter to Silvester, signifying its regret that he had been unable to join and assist it in passing a severe verdict upon the schismatics and committing to him, as "the holder of the greater dioceses," the responsibility of communicating its conclusions to the remainder of the Church. The Western episcopate knew where its leadership lay.

The further vicissitudes of the Donatists do not much concern us. Silvester, being human, derived, perhaps, some little consolation from the fact that they spurned the sentence of the Council of Arles as vehemently as they had the sentence of Miltiades and his associates. They appealed once more to Constantine, repeating their former asseverations, that they could not recognize as bishop a man who had been consecrated by "traditores." After interviews with both Caecilian and Donatus at Milan, the emperor himself decided in favor of Caecilian. Then, as the Donatists, uniting with the Novatianists and other heretical and revolutionary parties, persisted in agitation up and down the African countryside and steadily increased in numbers, he gave orders to the provincial authorities to eject them forcibly from their churches and even threatened them, as rebels, with exile and confiscation of property.[55] But the movement had now taken on

[53] The variation as to the date of Easter was, of course, an old cause for dissension. *Supra*, pp. 246, 279.

[54] This resolution meant, it will be remembered, the surrender of a local practice that went back to the time of Cyprian and earlier. *Supra*, pp. 402, 403, 410. The Asiatic church had, apparently, already given in. *Supra*, p. 411, n. 228.

[55] A number of interesting documents, reports of government investigations, testimonies of witnesses, imperial rescripts, *etc.*, are published in the appendix to Optatus' work on the Donatists, *Corpus Scriptorum Ecclesiasticorum Latinorum*, Vol. XXVI, pp. 185 *sqq.*

a social as well as a religious character and was not to be suppressed. In 321, Constantine concluded that since no instrumentality that he could devise was capable of restoring peace, he would best leave the church in Africa to fend for itself. Between 340 and 348, his son Constans again endeavored in vain to restore the country to orthodoxy.[56] The Donatists held their own until the pagan Vandals in 428 made havoc of all Christians together.

In 323, Constantine's victory over Licinius and his assumption of rulership in the eastern half of the Empire brought him face to face with a second and still more disheartening rent in the unity of his Christian subjects, the Arian controversy at Alexandria. Arius, a priest of that city, gentle and ascetic in mien, had during his youth studied in the school of one Lucian at Antioch. Lucian's theology had felt the influence of the ideas of Paul of Samosata[57] and of others like him and put heavy emphasis upon the humanity of the redeeming Christ. Later, in his church at Alexandria, Arius had preached his own somewhat modified theory of the Godhead, namely, one eternal and supreme Father, who had created first of all creatures his Son and Word to become the Creator and Savior of mankind. The Father alone was absolute and everlasting God. The Son, who had come to earth in the flesh, was of another and inferior essence or substance, though divine above men with the divinity of the indwelling Word.[58] In course of time, Alexander, bishop of the city, had begun discussing in meetings of his clergy the peculiarities of Arius' teaching and had shown their incompatibility with catholic doctrine. He had then urged and finally commanded Arius and his friends to change their mode of speech and they had refused. A synod of Egyptian bishops under Alexander's presidency had accordingly met and deposed Arius and five other priests and six deacons of Alexandria, together with two bishops from the vicinity who had adopted similar views. Arius and his

[56] *Vide* J. C. Ayer, *Source Book for Ancient Church History*, pp. 322–325.

[57] *Supra*, pp. 432, 437. The Nestorian heresy of the fifth century, which was also regarded as underestimating Christ's divinity, centred from the first at Antioch.

[58] For a statement by Arius of his own belief see J. C. Ayer, *op. cit.*, pp. 302–303.

band had left Egypt, even as Origen had done under somewhat comparable circumstances a century before,[59] and had settled for a while in Caesarea. There our friend, the historian Eusebius, bishop of the city, had received them warmly and other bishops in Syria had shown their sympathy. A second Eusebius, bishop of Nicomedia, close to the imperial court, who had also studied in his youth at Antioch, had grown interested in the affair and had started a concerted movement among the bishops of the Orient to prevail upon their colleague at Alexandria to reconsider his action and reinstate Arius. Alexander, meanwhile, had sent letters justifying his course and exposing the depth of Arius' heresy to Silvester of Rome,[60] the bishop of Antioch and other important prelates in the East. What response he had received we do not hear.

Arius and his company, however, having obtained the endorsement of a considerable number of the bishops of Asia and sure of some support within the church at Alexandria, now ventured to return home and to resume their religious vocations. The result was, of course, a strained situation and ceaseless friction in the streets and the churches of the city. The report of it dampened Constantine's elation over his new conquests. He had hoped that helpful influences from Egypt might emanate westward to heal the miserable discord in Africa and here was Egypt itself in need of healing! And all over such unnecessary folly! As a soldier and a governor, Constantine could in part appreciate the Donatists' scruples against officers who had once betrayed their trust to the enemy but nothing in his career qualified him to grasp the finer, theological distinctions that underlay the Arian dispute. He sent his valued Hosius of Cordova to Alexandria, with a letter addressed to both Alexander and Arius together,[61] in which he solemnly protested against the rash discussion in public meetings of topics "suggested by a combative spirit," fostered "by misused leisure," which ought never to be approached but "in the seclusion of our own

[59] *Supra*, pp. 89, 312.

[60] A reference to this letter is contained in one written long afterward by Pope Liberius. *Infra*, p. 562.

[61] Eusebius, *Vita Constantini*, II, 63–73.

thoughts." Should brothers quarrel over such "trifling and silly verbal differences," "points so petty and absolutely unessential," as to which no man can ever reach certainty? The emperor, in his earnestness, condescended almost to entreaty.

The quarrel, however, had by this time spread beyond Alexandria and rival bishops were heading hostile churches in one Egyptian town after another. Hosius returned to Nicomedia with serious accounts of the situation and Constantine decided on one strenuous effort to avert the threatening schism. He would summon another council, a council of East and West together, representative of the Church of the whole, consolidated Empire, the greatest council that had ever met. There was still no uniform Easter date accepted by all the East. As in the days of Victor, the Asiatics fixed their Easter by the Jewish Passover, while the Egyptians made their own calculations for the Sunday after the first full moon of the spring equinox.[62] In consequence, the Easters of Asia and of Egypt might fall a lunar month apart. The divergency had long been regarded with indifference but now, for some unknown reason, it was arousing comment and acrimony. The Council of Arles had, indeed, ruled that all churches must hereafter take the date from Rome but its rulings had no effect upon the East. Constantine resolved that his greater council should settle that matter also, as well as the foolish business of Arius.

The Council of Nicaea, the first ecumenical council of the Church, marked, as everyone knows, an epoch in the development of ecclesiastical institutions. Provincial synods had, of course, been held in plenty, especially during the previous third century. Adjacent provinces had frequently sent representatives to larger synods, convened at one of the leading metropolitan sees. Bishops from Syria and Eastern Asia Minor had met at Antioch, from Egypt, Libya, and the Pentapolis at Alexandria, from Africa, Numidia and Mauretania at Carthage. But until Constantine brought the whole West together at Arles, these groups of provinces had not combined. At Nicaea, for the first time, bishops came from Persia, the Caucasus, the Asiatic and the Egyptian

62 *Supra*, pp. 279, 285.

provinces, Pannonia, Carthage, Spain and Gaul, to deliberate in one body for the common welfare. The Church of the Empire was personified by the throng who streamed in from all quarters of the compass to the little town on the coast of Marmora. Most Catholic writers, looking back upon this event, have felt positive that no such assembly could have taken place without the instigation or coöperation of Silvester.[63] Yet all such contemporary evidence as we have concurs in making Constantine alone the author and promoter of the huge enterprise, even as he had been of the Council of Arles. Eusebius gives him the sole credit, as do the letters issued by the council itself, and he himself, both then and afterwards, spoke of it as the synod which he had summoned. He had hoped that "a great number" of bishops at Arles might remedy the difficulties stirred up by the Donatists but they had been too stubborn. He now tried the same method on a large scale, in a spot where the influence of no one see would be likely to preponderate, trusting that with firm and dexterous management the new dissidents might be induced to submit to the will of this imposing multitude of the brethren.

As to who presided over the sessions of the council our reports are too vague and meager to be decisive. Eusebius, the only eyewitness to leave us any description, tells us that "the bishop of the imperial city failed to attend because of his advanced age but that his priests were there and filled his place."[64] So we infer that Silvester again chose to be represented by envoys. The first meeting was graced by the emperor in a purple robe,

[63] See, for instance, the *Breviarium,* quoted *supra,* p. 463, n. 45, and the modern Catholic authors, listed *infra,* p. 477.

[64] *Vita Constantini,* III, 7. There has been some attempt to argue that by the term "imperial city" Eusebius here means Constantinople rather than Rome. He uses, however, the same phrase in passages where there can be no doubt as to his meaning, *e.g.*, when giving the place of Helena's burial, III, 47 (*supra,* p. 449), and when referring to an act of the Roman Senate, IV, 69. His usual form of allusion to Constantinople is "the city that bore his [Constantine's] name"; III, 48; IV, 46, 58, 66, 70. He says once that Constantine gave annual donations "to the Roman inhabitants of *his* imperial city." In connection with Constantine's death, he says that the Roman people and Senate wanted his body brought to "the imperial city" but that it was interred in "the city that bears his name." IV, 69–70. The historian Sozomen, writing early in the following century, is more specific. "Julius [an obvious error for Silvester], bishop of Rome, failed to attend on account of his advanced age, but Vito and Vincent, priests of the same church, were present in his stead." Sozomen, *Historia Ecclesiastica,* I, 17. The historian Socrates merely repeats the phraseology of Eusebius. Socrates, *Historia Ecclesiastica,* I, 8.

who took his seat at the head of the hall. The bishop who stood next upon his right hand made an opening address of thanks and congratulation, to which Constantine replied with a speech on the eminent desirability of peace. "As soon," Eusebius says, "as he had spoken these words in the Roman tongue, which some one else interpreted, he delivered the discussion to those who presided over the council."[65] Eusebius never names the man who presided. The fifth century historian Theodoret believes that it was Eustathius, bishop of Antioch, and probabilities seem to favor his suggestion.[66] Antioch and Alexandria were the most venerated sees of the East and the bishop of Alexandria, being himself involved in the case under trial, could hardly preside over the assembly that was to try it.

But although the bishop of Rome had no direct share in the conduct of the great council, the authority of Rome was not for that reason entirely absent. The statement of catholic belief in the essential equality of the Father and the Son, drawn up after fierce debate and signed by all but six of the bishops present under pain of the imperial displeasure, was so worded as to exclude from communion henceforth any one who would question the perfect divinity of Christ. Alexander of Alexandria, his young deacon and spokesman, Athanasius, Eustathius of Antioch and Hosius of Cordova, the most influential men present, were determined to leave no loophole for future outcroppings of Adoptionism, Arianism or any kindred heresy. Their search for some conclusive and unequivocal term to express the full participation of the Son in the Father's Godhead ended in their acceptance of a word proposed by Constantine, prompted apparently by Hosius, who had himself undoubtedly been reared on Roman doctrine. This word was the famous "homoousios," consubstan-

[65] *Vita Constantini,* III, 11–13. Constantine used Latin for his letters and decrees.

[66] *Historia Ecclesiastica,* I, 6. H. Leclercq, in his notes to C. J. Hefele, *Histoire des Conciles,* Vol. I, Pt. I, p. 425 and n. 2, and L. Rivington, *The Primitive Church and the See of Peter,* pp. 161–166, attempt to make out that Hosius of Cordova presided as Silvester's representative. Eusebius, however, mentions him as "one who took his seat among the multitude." *Vita Constantini,* III, 7. Pope Julius, sixteen years later, cites the testimony of "our priests who attended the Nicene Synod" but says nothing of Hosius. Athanasius, *Apologia contra Arianos,* 32. Gelasius of Cyzicus, who toward the end of the fifth century compiled a history of the council, is the first to hazard the idea.

tial, one or equal in substance or essence, that is, in no way inferior or different.[67] When many eastern bishops, not only the Arians but others as well, demurred or vigorously objected to the adoption of an epithet not found in the Scriptures, they were referred to Origen and to another noted Alexandrian scholar who had used it, but most especially to " the bishops of old times . . . both he of the great city of Rome and he of our own city [Alexandria], who condemned those who taught that the Son is a creature and not of one substance with the Father." [68] In the East, indeed, the word " homoousios " had never come into circulation and had been actually disapproved by the synod at Antioch in the days of Paul of Samosata. It struck discordantly now on many eastern ears and savored to them clearly of Sabellianism.[69] Was no distinction then to be drawn between the Father and the Son? In the less critical West, terms equivalent in purport had been employed with entire satisfaction ever since the times of Tertullian and Callistus and the word " homoousios " itself or its Latin substitute, " consubstantialis," had been officially endorsed by Bishop Dionysius and his Roman synod in or about 265. No wonder that the creed which contained it met with instant and staunch recognition and approval at Rome and proved but a starting point for worse troubles in the East.

In the matter of the Easter date, the council attempted a compromise between Rome and Alexandria. The Asiatic bishops were first persuaded to abandon altogether their ancient habit of fixing Easter by the Jewish Passover and to agree to follow henceforth the Alexandrian rule of computation by the vernal equinox. In principle, the Alexandrian method was the same as the Roman but it was based upon a slightly different and more accurate set of astronomical calculations as to the moment when the equinox occurred. It used a nineteen-year instead of the Roman sixteen-year cycle. In consequence, the Roman and the Alexandrian

[67] *Vide* Athanasius, *Historia Arianorum,* 42, and Socrates, *Historia Ecclesiastica,* I, 8, 41. A good translation of the creed of Nicaea is in J. C. Ayer, *Source Book for Ancient Church History,* p. 306.

[68] Athanasius, quoted by Theodoret, *Historia Ecclesiastica,* I, 7. The allusion is to the two Dionysii. *Supra,* pp. 430–431, 435.

[69] For the Sabellians, who saw in the Son a phase or aspect of the eternal Father, *vide supra,* p. 300.

Easters, although often falling together, came occasionally a month apart. The council voted to retain the Alexandrian cycle but endeavored to propitiate the Romans by decreeing that the Alexandrian see " should every year inform the Roman by letter . . . of the day when Easter should be celebrated " and that " apostolic authority " should then notify the remainder of the Church.[70] The Romans, however, tenacious as ever of their own customs, did not for a long time consent to accept this arrangement. They naturally preferred the legislation of Arles on this subject to that of Nicaea and continued to set the date for the West by their own astronomical tables as before. Eighteen years later, the Council of Sardica tried again in vain to bring about coöperation between Rome and Alexandria. Between 444 and 455, Pope Leo I chose more than once of his own accord to observe the Alexandrian date rather than the Roman. But the point was not finally and positively conceded until Dionysius Exiguus, in 525, compiled his Paschal lists for the use of the Roman See on the foundation, as he frankly said, of the nineteen-year cycle of Alexandria, approved by the Fathers at Nicaea.[71]

The extant canons of Nicaea deal for the most part with questions of discipline and procedure arising from the recent government persecutions or from the survival of a few persistent heresies. Several of these canons were intended to strengthen the control of metropolitans over their provincial bishops and to ensure unanimity between bishops in carrying out sentences of excommunication. The sixth reaffirmed in particular the jurisdiction, by old custom, of the bishop of Alexandria over the churches of Egypt, Libya and the Pentapolis, on the ground that

[70] The Council of Nicaea did not embody its Easter decisions in a canon, at least not in any that has survived. The quotation above is from the *Prologus Paschalis* of Cyril of Alexandria, composed in the early fifth century. Cited by C. J. Hefele, *Histoire des Conciles,* Vol. I, Pt. I, p. 465. Pope Leo I described this resolution of the council in similar terms in his *Epistolae,* CXXI. (J. P. Migne, *Patrologia Latina,* Vol. LIV, p. 1055.) Constantine's general letter, " To the churches," which he sent out at the conclusion of the deliberations at Nicaea, joyfully announcing the solution of all difficulties, said simply that all churches, East and West, Roman, African, Egyptian, Asiatic, etc., were now keeping the same Easter. Eusebius, *Vita Constantini,* III, 19. The letter of the council to the churches of Egypt is slightly more specific. *Infra,* p. 486.

[71] Letter to Petronius, bishop of Bologna, J. P. Migne, *op. cit.,* Vol. LXVII, pp. 21–22.

the bishop of Rome possessed similar metropolitan authority. It added the proviso that the church of Antioch should also retain its customary position.[72] Canon VII ordained that the bishop of Jerusalem should have only such special honor as could be rendered him without prejudice to Antioch. The particular purpose of this legislation was, of course, to support the Alexandrian bishop in his efforts to root out Arianism in Egypt and Libya. It amounted to putting Rome as a metropolitan diocese in a class with the two most eminent eastern metropolitans, although it did not preclude further distinctions of rank within that class. An assemblage where the East was in so large a majority could scarcely at that time have done more.

Before disbanding, the council, as also the emperor, sent out jubilant letters to declare the good tidings of peace. We quote extracts from the two that went to the church of Alexandria, where the Arian contingent was still fomenting opposition, although Constantine had already taken the precaution to banish their leader, Arius.[73] In his letter, Constantine expressed his firm assurance that "that which had commended itself to three hundred bishops could be no other than the doctrine of God." But once back at home, out from under the compulsion of the imperial eye, the three hundred bishops felt freer to voice their genuine opinion of the formula they had just signed. Many who aimed to be orthodox could not reconcile themselves to the strange word, "homoousios." Conflicts began here and there over problems of interpretation and a reaction gradually set in. No one dared to dispute openly the authority of the great council, but tacitly and surreptitiously its influence was undermined and its leaders overthrown on one pretext or another. First, Eustathius of Antioch was deposed by a synod of Asiatic bishops on a charge of Sabellianism and Constantine was induced to exile him, as a heretic, to Illyricum. His successor was avowedly hos-

[72] For later emendations and interpretations of this famous canon, *vide infra,* p. 485, n. 92.

[73] Beside banishing the Arians, Constantine issued an edict in his own name ordering the burning of all Arian literature, on penalty of death. Socrates, *Historia Ecclesiastica,* I, 9, 30. In this case, he wasted no time on halfway measures, as he may have felt that he had done with the Donatists. He also devoted much energy, after the dissolution of the council, to hearing appeals and attempting to reconcile individual disputants. Eusebius, *Vita Constantini,* III, 23.

tile to the Nicene platform. Then, Eusebius of Nicomedia, who had been temporarily banished along with Arius for resistance to the orthodox viewpoint, was allowed to return and gained imperceptibly considerable ascendency over the emperor, who was too obtuse a theologian to notice how he was being manipulated. In 328, Alexander of Alexandria died and Athanasius was elected by popular acclaim to fill his place but he soon found himself hampered at every turn by the Arians and accused by his enemies to Constantine on charges varying from the smashing of a priest's chalice in Mareotis to the murder of an irregular bishop and the embezzlement of the public grain supply. The atmosphere grew thick with suspicion and intrigue.

At length, in 332 or 333, Constantine aroused himself for one more effort to allay the smouldering disquiet that he perceived about him. He called Arius, as the original ringleader, from the exile to which he and his closest adherents had been condemned after Nicaea and, in a personal interview, procured from him a vague and indefinite profession of faith, not necessarily inconsistent with the Nicene creed.[74] Constantine himself was fully satisfied with this avowal and, as the next step to a general appeasement, required Athanasius, as Alexander's successor, to restore Arius to the catholic communion in Alexandria and thus to heal the breach where it had arisen. On Athanasius' unqualified refusal, the emperor reverted once more to his favorite idea of a council, to judge this time the new situation that had sprung up between the Arians and the Alexandrian bishop. In 335, this council met at Tyre. It was in the hands of Athanasius' enemies, Arians, semi-Arians and all who for any cause disliked the formula of Nicaea, of which he was now the foremost eastern champion. No western bishop was invited. Athanasius was tried, ostensibly not so much for his doctrine as for a list of criminal enormities of which he was declared to have been guilty. Sensational evidence was hastily trumped up against him and he was sentenced to deposition from office and banishment from Egypt. The synod then moved its sittings to Jerusalem, where its members attended the dedication ceremonies of the church of the

[74] It is given in J. C. Ayer, *Source Book for Ancient Church History*, pp. 307–308.

Holy Sepulchre, and finally voted to readmit Arius and his followers to full communion. Athanasius fruitlessly tried to obtain a fair audience with the emperor. His accusers poisoned Constantine's ear. The whole blame for the prolongation of trouble and discord was put upon him and the emperor was persuaded to agree to his removal and imprisonment at Trier, on the distant borders of Gaul.[75]

In that same year, Silvester died at Rome. His seat in Italy had remained apparently tranquil, undisturbed by doctrinal controversy at home or by the change of events in the East. So far as we can discover, after the return of his priests from Nicaea, he had not intervened in anything that went on beyond Italy. Nor do we hear of any special religious activity, beside church-building, at Rome.[76] It is not hard to understand how Eusebius, recalling Constantine's tireless interest in ecclesiastical affairs everywhere, might say with enthusiasm: "He [the emperor] exercised a special care over God's Church and . . . like a general bishop, appointed by God, convoked councils of his ministers." "It was not without reason that he once, while entertaining a company of bishops, let fall the remark that he too was a bishop, speaking to them in my hearing as follows: 'You are bishops, whose jurisdiction lies within the Church. I also am a bishop, ordained by God to oversee the external business of the Church.'"[77] Certainly, if anyone performed the function of a "bishop of the bishops" during those twenty years, it was monarch rather than Roman pontiff. But neither Eusebius nor Silvester nor any of their colleagues, who dubiously or gratefully watched the widening scope of secular interference in religious affairs, such as the calling of episcopal councils, the trial of ecclesiastical disputes, the imposition of creeds and the punishment of nonconformists, showed any sign that we can now detect of realizing the portentous nature of the control that the emperor

[75] It seems superfluous to furnish references for these events. Authorities will be found conveniently indicated in the footnotes to L. Duchesne's *Early History of the Christian Church,* Vol. II, Chap. V. Constantine justified his banishment of Athanasius on the ground that so numerous a gathering of wise and enlightened bishops as the Council of Tyre could not have condemned an innocent man. *Letter to Anthony.*

[76] Silvester built a basilica on the site of the modern San Martino ai Monti.

[77] *Vita Constantini,* I, 44; IV, 24.

had in truth set over the Christian Church or the fact that in exchange for his paternal care and benevolence it had forfeited its independence. Spiritually, at least, it had been freer under the pagans.

On Constantine and the Donatists see references, *supra*, p. 454. For the Arians and the Council of Nicaea see C. J. Hefele, *Histoire des Conciles* (8 vols., Paris, 1907–1921), Vol. I, Pt. I, pp. 335 *sqq.*; Pt. II, pp. 1193 *sqq.*; J. F. Turmel, *Constantine et la Papauté* in *Revue Catholique des Églises* (Paris, 1906), Vol. III, pp. 212–216; W. Bright, *The Roman See in the Early Church* (London, 1896), pp. 75 *sqq.*; F. Loofs, *Arianismus* in J. J. Herzog and A. Hauck, *Realencyklopädie für protestantische Theologie und Kirche* (24 vols., Leipzig, 1896–1913), Vol. II; F. Loofs, *Dogmengeschichte* (Marburg, 1899), sect. 32; H. M. Gwatkin, *Studies of Arianism* (2nd ed., Cambridge, 1900); A. Harnack, *History of Dogma* (trans. by N. Buchanan, 7 vols., Boston, 1897–1901), Vol. IV, chap. I; L. Duchesne, *Early History of the Christian Church* (trans. from the 4th ed. by C. Jenkins, 3 vols., London, 1910–1924), Vol. II, chaps. III–V; H. Le Bachelet, *St. Athanase* in A. Vacant and E. Mangeneot, *Dictionnaire de Théologie Catholique* (7 vols., Paris, 1909–1922), Vol. I; J. C. Ayer, *Source Book for Ancient Church History* (New York, 1913), pp. 287–309, 360–362; B. J. Kidd, *History of the Church to A.D. 461* (3 vols., Oxford, 1922–1924), Vol. II, chaps. II and III.

1. The Donatists and the Council of Arles

Constantine, *Letter to Chrestus of Syracuse,* quoted by Eusebius, *Historia Ecclesiastica,* X, 5, 21–24. Text. *Eusebius Werke* (*Die griechischen christlichen Schriftsteller der ersten drei Jahrhunderte*), II², 888–890.

Constantine Augustus to Chrestus, bishop of the people of Syracuse.

Whereas certain persons some time ago began a wicked and perverse dispute over holy religion and heavenly power and the catholic doctrine and I wished to put an end to this strife among them, I gave command that several bishops should be sent from Gaul and that the belligerent parties, who were stubbornly and incessantly wrangling with one another, should be summoned from Africa and that the bishop of Rome should be present, so that, when all were met together, the question that seemed to be at the bottom of the disturbance might be examined and decided with every care. But since it now appears that some of these persons, oblivious both of their own salvation and of the reverence due to most holy doctrine, are not even yet refraining from private hostilities and are refusing to submit to the judgment that was then delivered and are insisting that the men who pronounced those opinions and decisions were far too few in number and too hasty and precipitate in declaring sentence before they had inquired into all the points which needed thorough investigation, therefore it is still the case that men who ought to be living in brotherly and harmonious accord are disgracefully, even outrageously, divided among themselves and are furnishing ground for derision to people whose souls are strangers to this most holy religion. Accordingly, I consider it essential to arrange that this dissension, which should have been ended by voluntary understanding when once the judgment had been pronounced, should now, if possible, be brought to a close by the participation of a large number.

Inasmuch, then, as we have ordered a great company of bishops from many different places to assemble in the city of Arles by the first of August, we have thought fit to write to you also, to bid you procure from the illustrious Latronianus, corrector [78] of Sicily, a public carriage and to bring with you two other clergy, of the second order,[79] whomever you yourself may choose, as well as three servants to attend you on the way, and to reach the place aforesaid by the appointed day; . . .

[78] A title meaning, at first, a land bailiff, at this later time, a provincial governor.

[79] The priests were sometimes, at this period, called "clergy of the second order," in contrast with "clergy of the first order," *i.e.*, the bishops.

Constantine, *Epistola ad Aelafium*. Text. *Sylloge Optatiana, Corpus Scriptorum Ecclesiasticorum Latinorum*, XXVI, 204–206.

Constantine Augustus to Aelafius.[80]

[An account of his previous effort to put a stop to the quarrel in Africa by summoning Caecilian and representatives of both parties to be tried in Rome.] And they [the judges] reported for my information, with the records which they kept, all that took place before them, affirming besides that their sentence was delivered in accordance with justice and adding that the men who had expected to injure Caecilian were so unruly during the proceedings that they were forbidding them to return to Africa after the close of the trial. From all of which I hoped, according to my estimate of the probable situation, that the rebellions and disputes which these men had so suddenly stirred up would soon be brought to a proper termination. But when I read the report which your excellency sent to Nicasius and the others about the disturbances, I perceived plainly that these people are unwilling to keep before their eyes either any consideration of their own salvation or, what is more important, the reverence due to Almighty God, and are persisting in conduct which not only brings down shame and obloquy upon themselves but which also gives ground for contempt to such persons as we know are averse to our most holy religion. You must understand also that some of these same men have come to me and asserted that this Caecilian is not worthy to perform an act of worship in our most holy religion. And when I replied to them that they were continuing a useless agitation, because the affair had been settled in the city of Rome by competent and highly approved bishops, they protested obstinately and tenaciously that the whole case had not been heard there but that these

80 Vicar of Africa.

bishops had, instead, shut themselves up in one spot and had passed the verdict which they thought expedient. . . . [Instructions to Aelafius to send Caecilian and bishops of his own and the opposite party from different provinces by public post via Spain to Arles.]

Council of Arles, *Synodical Letter to Silvester, bishop of Rome.* Text. *Sylloge Optatiana, Corpus Scriptorum Ecclesiasticorum Latinorum,* XXVI, 206–208.

Marinus, Acratius, Natalis, . . .[81] Victor and Epictetus to our most dearly beloved pope Silvester, greeting forever in the Lord.

Bound together by the common links of love and by the chain of the unity of our mother, the catholic Church, and brought to the city of Arles by the will of our devout emperor, we salute you hence with due reverence, most glorious pope. We have borne with the grave and perilous breach of our law and tradition and with the men of unruly disposition, whom the manifest will of our God and the tradition and ordinance of truth have so completely repudiated that there is no power of speech left in them and no capacity to accuse and to furnish adequate proof. So, by the judgment of God and of Mother Church, who knows and approves her own, they have been condemned and expelled. Would, O dearly beloved brother, that you had thought it wise to attend this great assemblage! We firmly believe that a more severe verdict would then have been passed against them and if you had been judging here with us, we should all have rejoiced with deeper joy. But inasmuch as you were not able to leave the place where the apostles to this day have their seats and where their blood

[81] Thirty-three bishops are named as the senders of this letter, including Marinus, Reticius and Maternus, the three from Gaul who had assisted in the trial at Rome. Marinus of Arles, whose name stands first in this and the following document, probably presided.

without ceasing witnesses to the glory of God, we did, notwithstanding, think it best, dearest brother, not only to deal with those questions which we were summoned here to decide but also to hold conferences with one another, because the provinces from which we have come are various and divergencies arise, which we think should be regulated. We accordingly resolved, in the sight of the Holy Spirit and his angels, to proceed during this present peace to judgment with regard to those problems which have been disturbing individuals everywhere. And we resolved to write first of all to you, who hold the greater dioceses,[82] that through you preferably our resolutions should be made known to everyone. And what our conclusions were we have appended to this our poor letter.

In the first place, for the sake of our own lives and salvation, we deemed it necessary to decide that the season of him who died and rose again alone for many should be observed by us all with so religious a mind that no divisions or controversies could arise from the deep worship of our devotion. So we decreed that the Lord's Easter should be celebrated by the whole world on the same day. . . . [Summary of other legislation.]

Then, being weary, he [the emperor] commanded every man to return to his see. Amen.

Council of Arles, *Canons,* I, VIII, XIII, XIX. Text. C. J. Hefele, *Histoire des Conciles,* I. Pt. I, 280 *sqq.*

Marinus and the assembly of bishops gathered in the city of Arles to their most holy lord and brother, Silvester.

What we in common council have decreed we report to

[82] The Latin is "qui maiores dioceses tenes." By the term "dioceses" may be meant the suburbicarian districts subject to the vicar of Rome. *Infra,* p. 485, n. 92.

your charity, so that everyone may know what ought to be observed in the future.

Canon I

In the first place, as regards the observance of the Lord's Easter, it was resolved that we should observe it on the same day and at the same time throughout the world and that you should send out letters, according to custom, to everyone.[83]

Canon VIII

As for the Africans, because they follow their own law and give second baptism, it was resolved that if anyone should be converted from heresy to the Church he should be asked for his creed. And if it is clear that he has been already baptised in the name of the Father, Son and Holy Spirit, hands merely should be laid upon him, that he may receive the Holy Spirit. But if, when he is questioned, he does not acknowledge the Trinity, let him be baptized.[84]

Canon XIII

It was resolved that persons who are said to have surrendered the Holy Scriptures or the sacred vessels or the names of their brethren, provided they are convicted by public records and not by unsupported rumors, should be deposed from the rank of clergy. If, however, these same persons have ordained others and the men ordained by them are worthy and fit to receive holy orders, there should be no prejudice against their ordination.[85]

[83] "Iuxta consuetudinem litteras ad omnes tu dirigas." If this canon had been ratified at Nicaea, it would have established the right for which Victor contended at the end of the second century. *Supra*, pp. 275, 279.

[84] This marks the abandonment of the principle for which the African church under Cyprian struggled against the Roman Stephen. *Supra*, pp. 394, 402 ff., 419.

[85] This canon disposes of the Donatist complaints.

Canon XIX

It was resolved that places for offering sacrifice should be assigned to the foreign bishops who are accustomed to visit the City.[86]

Augustine, *Epistolae,* CV, 8. Text. *Corpus Scriptorum Ecclesiasticorum Latinorum,* XXXIV, 600–601.

Augustine, catholic bishop, to the Donatists.

. . . .

8 Hear this: your ancestors,[87] first of all, carried the case of Caecilian to the emperor Constantine. Ask us to prove it to you and if we fail to prove it, do with us whatever you can! Then, because Constantine did not dare to judge the case of a bishop, he committed the examination and decision of it to other bishops. The trial took place in the city of Rome under the presidency of Melchiades, bishop of that church, in company with many colleagues. But after they had pronounced Caecilian innocent and given verdict against Donatus, who had precipitated the schism at Carthage, your people went a second time to the emperor and complained of the judgment of the bishops, by which they had been vanquished. For when could a wicked suitor praise the judges by whose judgment he was defeated? However, once more the kindly emperor appointed other bishops to be their judges at Arles, a city of Gaul. But from them your ancestors appealed to the emperor himself, until he himself investigated the case and declared Caecilian innocent and them scandalmongers.[88] But not even

[86] "Urbem," *i.e.,* Rome. This is the one request or suggestion proffered to Silvester.

[87] Augustine wrote this letter at the beginning of the fifth century.

[88] In another letter, XLIII, vii, 20, Augustine tells how Constantine ordered Caecilian and the Donatists to meet him at Rome (probably in 315, at the time of his second visit to the city). Caecilian, however, did not put in his appearance. Constantine was much irritated and threatened to go himself to Africa and teach them all "how the Divinity ought to be worshipped." Letter of Constantine in

after so many defeats did they keep quiet but they made themselves irksome to the emperor by their daily protests against Felix of Aptonga, by whom Caecilian had been ordained, for they insisted that he was a "traditor"[89] and for that reason Caecilian could not be a bishop, because he had been ordained by a "traditor." Then the case of Felix also was, by the emperor's order, investigated by the proconsul Aelianus and he too was proved to be innocent.

2. The Arian Question and the Council of Nicaea

Eusebius, *Vita Constantini,* III, 5, 6. Text. *Eusebius Werke (Die griechischen christlichen Schriftsteller der ersten drei Jahrhunderte)*, I, 79.

[Account of the Arian dissension in Egypt and of the long continued disagreement between different branches of the Church over the date of Easter, so that "some were afflicting themselves with fasting and austerity, while others were spending the time in festive rejoicing."] 5. . . . Of all upon earth Constantine appeared to be the only instrument of God for this good end [of general reconciliation]. When he perceived the facts I have described and saw that the letter which he had sent to the Alexandrians had produced no effect, he then aroused the energy of his mind and declared that he must engage in this one more war against the invisible adversary who was harrying the Church.

6. Thereupon, as if to bring the phalanx of God into the field against the enemy, he convoked a universal council and with respectful letters summoned the bishops to gather at once from all quarters.[90] Nor did the emperor merely

---

Corpus Scriptorum Ecclesiasticorum Latinorum, XXVI, 211. He finally, however, commanded the litigants to follow him to Milan, where Caecilian presently joined them and the last trial was held.

89 For the significance of this word *vide supra,* p. 450.

90 In Eusebius' report of Constantine's speech at the opening of the council, he represents him as saying: "With the earnest desire that a remedy for this evil

issue a bare command but by his generosity he contributed much to its accomplishment. He allowed some bishops the use of the public post and others an ample supply of horses for transportation. He selected also a propitious city for the council, Nicaea, named for victory,[91] in Bithynia. Thus, as the injunction sped everywhere, all with the utmost alacrity hastened thither.

Council of Nicaea, *Canons* VI and VII. Text. C. J. Hefele, *Histoire des Conciles,* I, Pt. I, 552–553, 569.

Canon VI

Let the ancient customs in Egypt, Libya and the Pentapolis prevail, that the bishop of Alexandria shall have jurisdiction in all these provinces, since the like is customary for the bishop of Rome also. Similarly in Antioch and the other provinces let the churches retain their privileges.[92]

[internal strife] also might be found through my aid, I immediately sent to require your presence." *Vita Constantine,* III, 12. See, in addition, the letter of the council, *infra,* p. 487. The historian Socrates, writing at the opening of the next century, gives the whole credit for the assembly to " the emperor, who saw that the church was kept in disturbance . . . [and] convened an ecumenical council, summoning by letter the bishops from everywhere." Socrates, *Historia Ecclesiastica,* I, 8. Rufinus, however, says about the same time that Constantine collected the council at the advice of the clergy, " ex sacerdotum sententia." Rufinus, *Historia Ecclesiastica,* X, 1. The *Liber Pontificalis* of the sixth or seventh century states that the council was convoked " with the approval of Silvester." L. R. Loomis, *The Book of the Popes,* 44. At the Council of Constantinople, in 682, it was declared that Constantine and Silvester assembled the Council of Nicaea, G. D. Mansi, *Sacrorum Conciliorum Nova et Amplissima Collectio* (50 vols., Venice, Florence, Paris, 1759–1924), Vol. XI, p. 662.

[91] The Greek word νίκη, niké, means victory.

[92] This translation is taken from the earliest extant Greek text. H. Leclercq has compared all the surviving early versions of this canon, Greek, Latin, Arabic, Syriac and Coptic, and gives the following rendering of the version which he believes to have been prevalent in Egypt: " Let the ancient laws be observed, especially such as concern Egypt, Libya and Pentapolis, that the bishop of Alexandria shall have jurisdiction over all these provinces, since it is a rule established by the bishops of Rome (like that which deals with Antioch and the other provinces), that precedences should be observed in the church." By this wording, the supremacy of the bishop of Alexandria over his colleagues in the surrounding provinces is not compared to that of the bishop of Rome but is sanctioned by the traditions of the Roman bishopric. H. Leclercq, notes to C. J. Hefele, *op. cit.* p. 553. Rufinus gives a Latin abridgment of the Greek, containing what he evidently took to be its gist. " Let the ancient custom prevail both at Alexandria and in the

And this is to be generally understood, that if any man be made bishop without the approbation of his metropolitan, the great council has declared that he ought not to be a bishop.[93] If, moreover, two or three bishops from natural love of contradiction oppose the general vote of the rest, when that is reasonable and in harmony with the law of the Church, then let the will of the majority prevail.

Canon VII

Inasmuch as custom and ancient tradition have required that the bishop of Aelia [94] should be treated with honor, let him, without prejudice, however, to the dignity due the metropolis, have the next position of honor.[95]

Council of Nicaea, *Synodical Letter to the Alexandrians,* quoted by Socrates, *Historia Ecclesiastica,* I, 9. Text. J. P. Migne, *Patrologia Graeca,* LXVII, 77–84.

The bishops assembled at Nicaea, composing the great and holy council, to the church of the Alexandrians, great and holy by the grace of God, and to our beloved brethren

---

city of Rome, that the Alexandrian bishop shall have oversight over Egypt and the Roman over the suburban churches [suburbicariarum ecclesiarum]." *Historia Ecclesiastica,* X, 6. A similar version was current at Carthage. The term "suburban districts" (suburbicariae regiones) was offiically applied, from Diocletian's reign onward, to the provinces governed by the "Vicarius Urbis," namely, the ten which made up central Italy, southern Italy, Sicily, Corsica and Sardinia. An introductory clause was afterwards added to the canon in the West. "The Roman church has always held the primacy." In this form the Roman legates read the canon at the Council of Chalcedon in 451 but they were promptly corrected by the eastern members, who protested against the offensive and unwarranted interpolation. But in this enlarged form the canon was thenceforward preserved and cited at Rome and in this form it still appears in the *Corpus Juris Canonici,* Dist. LXV, c. I.

93 The rights of the three patriarchs being guaranteed, the rights of the ordinary metropolitan to confirm the election of bishops within his province are next protected.

94 The name of the Roman city built upon the site of old Jerusalem. The gentile church which arose there was never regarded as possessing quite the same claim to reverence as that of the original apostolic church of the Jews.

95 *I.e.,* the bishop of Aelia or Roman Jerusalem is to rank after the bishop of Antioch.

throughout Egypt, Libya and Pentapolis, greeting in the Lord.

Whereas, by the grace of God and the summons of our most pious sovereign Constantine, who gathered us from divers cities and provinces, a great and holy council has been convened at Nicaea, it has appeared to us essential above all else to send a letter to you from the holy council, that you might know what matters have been taken into consideration and examined and what has been eventually resolved and decreed. First of all, an inquiry was made into the sacrilege and wrongdoing of Arius, in the presence of the most pious emperor Constantine. . . . [An exposition of the Arian heresy and the conclusions finally reached concerning it and its author.]

We also announce to you the good news of our agreement as to the holy feast of Easter, that through your prayers it has been adjusted in this way, that all the brethren in the East who have hitherto kept the feast with the Jews will henceforth conform to the Romans and to us and to all who from ancient times have observed Easter with us. . . . [A prayer that peace may now be established.]

Constantine, *Letter to the church of Alexandria,* quoted by Socrates, *Historia Ecclesiastica,* I, 9. Text. J. P. Migne, *Patrologia Graeca,* LXVII, 84.

Constantine Augustus to the catholic church of the Alexandrians, greeting, beloved brethren.

. . . At the command of God, the splendor of truth has dissipated and overwhelmed those dissensions, schisms, tumults and, so to speak, fatal poisons of discord. Now we all worship by name the one God and believe that he is. But in order that this might come to pass, I assembled, by God's direction, at the city of Nicaea a great number of bishops, in company with whom I myself also, who am but one of you and who rejoice exceedingly to be your fellowservant, undertook to investigate the truth. So all points which seemed by their ambiguity to furnish excuse for disputation we have discussed and clearly explained. . . . When, then, more than three hundred bishops, renowned for their wisdom and acumen, had confirmed one and the same faith, which according to the true and unerring law of God is the faith, it was discovered that Arius alone[96] was deceived by the machination of the devil and was the disseminator of mischief by his impious opinions, first among you and later among others also. . . . Now that which has proved itself acceptable to the three hundred bishops is no other than the doctrine of God, for of a certainty the Holy Spirit, dwelling in the minds of so many great men, has enlightened for them the divine will. Therefore, let no one vacillate or hesitate but let all return heartily to the way of perfect truth, so that when, as soon as possible, I arrive among you, I may offer fit thanks with you to the all-seeing God for having revealed the pure faith and restored to you the love for which you prayed. May God protect you, beloved brethren.

JULIUS I

(337–352)

After the death of Silvester comes the short pontificate of Marcus (336–337). He may have been prominent earlier as a priest and for that reason named by Constantine in his letter to Miltiades about the Donatists.[97] But about Marcus as bishop we know nothing whatever, except that he, like Silvester and like Julius also afterwards, left behind him a basilica that bore his name.[98] With Julius, the successor of Marcus, however, the See

[96] Six bishops, beside Arius, refused to sign the creed of Nicaea and were condemned with him to exile. Eleven others signed reluctantly, after expressing their disapprobation. Rufinus, *Historia Ecclesiastica,* X, 5.

[97] *Supra,* p. 457.

[98] The basilica of Marcus stood on the foundation of the present church of San Marco, not far from the Piazza Venezia. Julius is said to have built two churches in the city, one on the site now occupied by the church of Santi Apostoli;

of Rome resumes the prominence that it seems to have lacked for many years. Nor is there any apparent sign of weakened prestige or of diminished dignity. Julius steps without hesitation into the position of ecclesiastical authority on doctrine and discipline and of judge of appeals from the whole Church to which the Roman bishops of the third century had, with varying results, aspired. The West concedes it to him wholeheartedly, even though the western bishops at Sardica undertake to prescribe for him the machinery of his appellate courts. The orthodox bishops of the East, outraged by the injustice of their Arian countrymen, bring their cases to him with gratitude. Even the pro-Arian party entertains for a while the idea of a joint revision with him of the trials it has already held independently, until it falls back defiantly upon its right, as a branch of the coördinate episcopate, to pass final sentence upon its own offenders and to have its sentences respected in the West. But at this crisis the secular, imperial power behind Julius intervenes and compels the East to submission. The eastern verdicts are nullified and the orthodox beneficiaries of Rome are reinstated in their original offices. The policy of Julius appears as a triumphant continuation of that of Stephen and Dionysius.

Circumstances which seem to have prevented the immediate forerunners of Julius from making much of their claim to predominance suddenly altered and recombined in such a way as to favor him. Three months after his ordination, Constantine, whose figure, as we have said, had so long engrossed the center of the world's stage, died in Nicomedia, leaving three sons who proceeded to divide the Empire between them. Constans, the youngest, was allotted the middle territory, Italy, Africa and the Balkan peninsula as far as Thrace. Like his brothers, he had been educated as a Christian and, unlike his father, he had come under nothing but orthodox influence. Throughout his reign, he lent an attentive ear to the wishes and opinions of the one great bishop of his dominions, Julius of Rome.

---

the other, which was called "the basilica of Julius," was across the Tiber, on or near the spot covered by the hall of worship constructed by Callistus, more than a century earlier. *Supra*, p. 300. For Julius' churches outside the walls, *vide infra*, p. 715.

At first, all three brothers agreed upon the advisability of a pacific and unifying policy in church affairs. Constantine II, who was master of Gaul, Spain and Britain, at once gave orders for the release of Athanasius from detention at Trier [99] and sent word to the catholic church of Alexandria of the exile's approaching return. A general edict soon afterwards went out for the liberation of all clergy in banishment everywhere. In some instances, however, the reappearance of these men, judicially deposed, for whom successors had been provided, caused new outbreaks of resentment and antagonism. At Alexandria, the announcement of the return of Athanasius proved the signal for a concerted movement of resistance on the part of his Arian enemies in the city. Arius himself was dead but his followers were no less determined to escape from the orthodox yoke. They now elected one Pistus as their bishop in place of Athanasius and made rapid efforts to secure his recognition by other bishops abroad. In particular, they wrote to Julius at Rome and sent a priest, Macarius, and two deacons, Hesychius and Martyrius, with the letter and other documents to show that Athanasius had been rightfully deposed by the Council of Tyre and could, therefore, no longer be properly regarded as a bishop at all.

Athanasius reached Alexandria in November, 337, and took prompt measures to cope with this new project to unseat him. He assembled a synod of Egyptian bishops, who acquitted him of all charges of misconduct, repudiated the verdict of the Council of Tyre and brought countercharges in their turn against the Arians of unscrupulous brutality in their labors to manufacture evidence against Athanasius. A priest was dispatched to Rome with a synodical letter to this effect and other documents that exposed the crimes of which the Arians had been guilty. Macarius, their chief envoy at Rome, realizing perhaps that the Athanasian material rendered his own accusations worthless, did not wait to face it but slipped away from the city and went back to the East. The two deacons, Hesychius and Martyrius, whom he left behind, flustered and baffled, suggested in desperation that Julius hold his own trial of Athanasius and find out the truth for

[99] For the previous story of Athanasius *vide supra,* pp. 471, 475.

himself. Meanwhile, however, the pro-Arian Eusebius of Nicomedia had lost no time in winning an influence over the young eastern emperor, Constantius. He had also arranged for his own transference from the see of Nicomedia to that of Constantinople and for the banishment of Paul, the orthodox bishop of the capital. He was now regarded as the head of the eastern opposition to Athanasius and to the criterion of faith erected at Nicaea. In 338, he and his associates wrote to Julius, denouncing Athanasius in the blackest terms and politely inviting Julius to call another council of the interested parties and to judge the case again, if he liked. If the bishop of Rome could be induced to side against Athanasius, the latter and all others of his stamp in the East would be left isolated indeed. Julius accepted the invitation and in May or June of 339, sent out his letters of summons, not only to the Italian bishops who would compose the body of an ordinary Roman synod, but also to Athanasius at Alexandria, to Eusebius and to other prelates who had been connected with the doings at Tyre. For the first time on record, one bishop, single-handed, called in his own name a council of high metropolitans and bishops from distant parts of the Empire.

Eusebius, however, was not disposed to wait idly for the slow gathering of a council, while Athanasius was entrenching himself and strengthening the orthodox organization in Alexandria. With others of his way of thinking he had already betaken himself to the court of Constantius at Antioch to devise some method of more speedy interference. There, in a synod of Asiatic clergy, it was decided to eliminate Pistus, who had proved a poor makeshift for a bishop, and to elect some more forceful personage to take the post which, to their eyes, had been vacant ever since the deposition of Athanasius at Tyre. Their choice fell on one Gregory of Cappadocia, whom they ordained and dispatched, early in March, 339, with a military escort supplied by Constantius, to eject Athanasius by armed violence, if necessary.[100] In vain, the great mass of Alexandrian Christians refused to have anything to do with Gregory and clung to their original bishop.

[100] Of course it was scandalously illegal for a body of foreign bishops, not even sitting in Egypt, to elect and ordain a bishop for Alexandria. *Supra*, p. 401, n. 208.

The churches were stormed and one burned to the ground. Over the bodies of the wounded and slain they were delivered to the partisans of Gregory. Athanasius remained long enough to send out a solemn letter of expostulation to the whole episcopate of the Church and then withdrew to Rome, whither he had just been summoned by Julius. He was not the only refugee in distress. Paul, the bishop whom Eusebius had driven from Constantinople, Marcellus of Ancyra, a stout advocate of "homoousios" at Nicaea, and various other eastern bishops and priests, newly expelled from their places by the zeal of Eusebius and his friends, were all assembling at Rome as their only shelter. And one by one, as they arrived with their tales of Arian cruelty and injustice, Julius received them into his hospitable communion.

Julius' letter of invitation to the Eusebians, in which he had named a day toward the close of the year 339 for the gathering of his council and to which he had added some words of rebuke for their illegal transferences of bishops, contrary to the rule of Nicaea, had been carried to Antioch by two priests, Elpidius and Philoxenus. But, instead of being allowed to return promptly with their answer, the messengers were detained on one pretext or another through the late months of 339, until January, 340. By that time, the day set for the opening of the council had passed. When the two at last appeared again in Rome, they bore a missive from the Eusebians, containing not only a refusal to come to Julius at all, couched in language that was felt to be sarcastically ceremonious, but also certain other disagreeable and provocative remarks. Although not so fortunate, they wrote, as the Roman bishop in the size and resources of their churches, they still preferred to regard all bishops as equal in authority and the acts of one synod as worthy of consideration by another branch of the Church. After all, the Romans, though, no doubt, very famous for their orthodoxy, had in the first place received their teachers and their doctrines from the East. Why should the East now be expected to take second rank? Their forefathers had accepted as decisive the Roman sentence against Novatian.[101] Why, then, should not the Romans accept the sentence of Tyre

101 *Supra,* pp. 382, 386–387, 420.

against Athanasius? Julius might choose between them and the men whom they had excommunicated. He certainly could not continue in communion with every one. Let him acknowledge their right to be their own governors and judges in their own territory and they would be pleased to return to harmonious and cordial relations.[102] The Eusebians were confident by now of Constantius and in secure possession of Alexandria. They felt that they could afford to stand up to the Roman See. They had also, undoubtedly, lost their hope of ousting Athanasius by judicial means from his support in western quarters.

In the summer or autumn of 340, the deferred Roman synod met, not in the Lateran but in the church of Vito, one of the priests who had been at Nicaea.[103] Since the Eusebian bishops refused to participate, it was hardly more than a gathering of Italians to hear and pass upon the appeals of the refugees whom the Eusebians had expelled. One after another, the cases of Athanasius, Marcellus, Paul, Lucius of Adrianople, Asclepas of Gaza and other exiles were investigated and, one after another, the defendants were acquitted of heresy or misdemeanor and pronounced rightfully entitled to their ecclesiastical offices. When the sessions were over, Julius wrote a long and serious letter to the Eusebian prelates at Antioch, from which we quote largely below. It was a creditable letter, dignified yet not arrogant, betraying no personal pique but only anxiety for the state of the Church and concern that justice should be done to its ministers. He reminded the Eusebians that they themselves had revised or ignored the verdict of the Nicene Council by readmitting Arius, that Athanasius had been exculpated by the testimony of some eighty bishops of his diocese of Egypt and that their own delegates had been the first to suggest that Julius call a council at Rome for the purpose of a new trial. He assured them that they had been at fault in neglecting to send him their proofs of Athanasius' guilt and that he was still willing to convoke another council and reopen the matter, whenever they chose to appear.

102 The tenor of this letter may be compared with that of the letter written by the Asiatic Firmilian in the previous century and that of the encyclical of the eastern bishops at Sardica and of some passages in the letters of Basil and in the poem of Gregory Nazianzen on the Council of 381. *Supra*, p. 411; *infra*, pp. 522, 650, 683.

103 *Supra*, p. 470, n. 64.

He ended by informing them that a case of so grave a nature, involving so old an apostolic church as that of Alexandria, should not have been tried at all without his participation and that by ancient custom complaints against the Alexandrian bishop should be referred in the first instance to Rome for a just sentence to be issued there.[104] He sent his letter not, this time, by priests but by one of Constans' high officials, Count Gabianus.

During this same summer, the two western emperors, Constans and Constantine II, fell out with each other. Constantine was defeated and killed and Constans, the patron of Julius, became by annexation of his brother's territory master of more than two-thirds of the whole Empire, from Britain to the Black Sea and the borders of Egypt.

We hear of no reply from the Eusebians to Julius. He may have expected none, but a change of mood showed itself in their next meeting, a synod of some ninety or a hundred bishops, called at Antioch, in 341, to celebrate the dedication of the magnificent, new basilica, begun by the emperors' father, Constantine I Rumors from Alexandria of the ruthless persecution applied there in order to crush the demonstrations of loyalty to Athanasius had an ugly sound that could not quite be glossed over or explained away. Athanasius' ally, Julius, was proving unexpectedly formidable, now that the domain of his emperor Constans so far excelled that of the eastern emperor Constantius. Under these circumstances, the Synod of Antioch assumed a mild and defensive tone, issued letters protesting that its members were not really Arian at heart and drafted four different, conciliatory forms of creed, in which the most disputatious points were dexterously avoided and the most controversial terms quietly omitted.[105] Almost any type of Christian might sign any one of them with a clear conscience. The one object of the assembly's outspoken attack was Marcellus of Ancyra, who, as a matter of fact, had drifted in his later writings perilously near to Sabel-

[104] He seems to have been recalling the precedents set by Dionysius and Felix I. *Supra*, pp. 434, 441.

[105] A translation of two of the four creeds of Antioch is given in J. C. Ayer, *Source Book for Ancient Church History*, pp. 313–315. A selection from the council's canons on discipline is in *ibid.*, pp. 362–364, 369–370. These canons were approved by the western churches, although the creeds were not.

lianism in his horrified reaction against Arianism. Before dispersing, the synod, at Constantius' request, appointed a deputation of eastern bishops, Narcissus of Neronias,[106] Theodore of Heraclea and Marcus of Arethusa, to wait upon Constans in the West, explain their attitude toward Athanasius, assure him of their pacific intentions and fidelity to the true faith and present to him a creed which explicitly repudiated several of the old Arian phrases, though still leaving somewhat indefinite the origin and character of the divine Son.

Late in that year, Eusebius himself died but the praetorian prefect at Constantinople received Constantius' instructions to see that another of the same party was installed as his successor. The unfortunate Paul, who hastened from Rome, hoping to recover his see, was removed in chains to the Persian border and finally strangled. Constantius by now was a more uncompromising Arian than his teachers. Bishops and theologians might feel obliged to modify their views or the expression of them as the winds veered, but an emperor, once thoroughly convinced, saw no need of temporizing.

At this point, however, Constans, remembering perhaps his father's mode of dealing with church difficulties, proposed to his brother that the clergy of their respective dominions hold a joint council at some midway spot to see if the status of Athanasius and all other questions under dispute could not be settled by mutual discussion. The place selected by the two rulers was Sardica, the modern Sofia, a town just over the boundary of Thrace, on the edge of the territory of Constantius. Athanasius received orders from Constans to present himself there for a new trial and obeyed, after two interviews with the emperor, in Milan and in Gaul. Julius waived his previous demand that the Easterners come to the See of Rome and selected two priests and a deacon to act as his representatives at Sardica. Hosius, the veteran bishop of Cordova, who, in all likelihood, had been largely responsible for the imposition of the shibboleth " homoousios " upon the Church at Nicaea,[107] was deputed by Constans to lead the western party now and to preside over the whole assembly.

106 Narcissus had been a personal friend of Arius. He had also been at Nicaea.

107 *Supra*, p. 471.

The Council of Sardica gathered in the autumn of either 342 or 343. About eighty western bishops madc the journey, some forty of whom came from Illyricum and the neighboring provinces, the rest from farther West. At least ten crossed from Italy and six from Spain. Approximately the same number arrived from the East. They were headed by Stephen, the new bishop of Antioch, and escorted by two of Constantius' counts and an armed guard. Many from farther Asia Minor and other outlying districts were scarcely acquainted with the problems at issue and came indifferently or reluctantly. Two had the audacity to join the camp of Hosius.[108] But the leaders of the eastern contingent were strenuous Eusebians [109] or semi-Arians of the type who had been at Tyre. They hated Athanasius personally for his relentless insistence upon the Nicene standard of orthodoxy and were also determined to maintain at all costs the right of the eastern church to try and depose one of its own bishops without hindrance or criticism from the West.

On their arrival in Sardica, they refused to meet with the western party as long as it persisted in associating with Athanasius, Marcellus and Asclepas of Gaza as if they were still lawful bishops. In vain Hosius urged them to present their evidence against the three men before the council or even before himself alone, promising that if they failed to substantiate their charges and yet were unwilling to reinstate Athanasius, he himself would find a place for him in the church of Spain.[110] The Eusebians would not be placated with anything short of a preliminary recognition by the Westerners of the sentence of Tyre. Once that was granted and Athanasius and his companions treated as veritably excommunicate, they would coöperate in a new trial and consent to abide by the result. The Westerners as stubbornly refused to regard Athanasius as an outcast even for a moment. The Eusebians then held a meeting apart, in which they drew up an encyclical letter, addressed to all the clergy and faithful every-

108 They were a bishop from Petra in Palestine and one from Arabia.

109 The name Eusebian is still applicable to these men, although Eusebius was dead. They are also sometimes known as semi-Arians, for they did not hold the tenets of Arius in the original, strict sense. They merely contended that some distinction should be drawn between the divinity of the Father and that of the Son.

110 Hosius himself relates this in his letter to Constantius. *Infra*, p. 577.

where, setting forth their view of the situation. They declared that it was impossible for the western bishops at their distance to appreciate the confusion that had been created in the East by the temporary return of Athanasius, Marcellus and the rest to their old sees or for themselves to permit the western clergy to quash the decisions of an eastern tribunal. They said that on their arrival in Sardica they had been affronted by the spectacle of the very persons whom they had once solemnly condemned sitting in the midst of the western brethren as if nothing had happened. No notice had been taken of their own proposition to send new commissioners from each party to Egypt to collect more evidence there on the subject of Athanasius' alleged misdeeds. They could not acquiesce in such an infringement of their just rights and had therefore withdrawn from the assembly and now threw the responsibility of schism upon the others. They reaffirmed all their previous sentences of excommunication and deposition, including under them henceforth not only the persons already condemned at Tyre but also Julius of Rome, Hosius of Cordova and Maximin of Trier, who had been hospitable to Athanasius in his exile. They then departed in a body to Philippopolis in the heart of Thrace.

The western bishops took up the gauntlet. They first disposed formally of the cases of the three accused men before them. Athanasius, they said, needed no further vindication than the testimony of the Egyptian bishops to Julius and the notorious character of the assaults upon him at Tyre. Marcellus and Asclepas they examined and tested and found innocent. They then took up the numerous accusations which came pouring in against the Eusebians and their agents and inspected the witnesses, victims, records and implements of cruelty that were transported in quantities to Sardica from Egypt and Asia. They ended by deposing and excommunicating for crime and heresy Stephen of Antioch, Acacius of Caesarea in Palestine, Narcissus and Theodore, who had gone on the mission to Constans, Ursacius and Valens, two Pannonian bishops, and several others prominent in Eusebian activities. Theodore, Ursacius and Valens had served on the infamous commission for the Council of Tyre that had worked up the scandalous evidence against Athanasius. Valens had been newly detected in fomenting a sedition in Aquileia, in order to get himself elected bishop there and so engineer his transference from his less distinguished see in the Balkans. There was some talk in the council of another western creed and a tentative draft was actually composed, with a letter recommending it to the consideration of Julius. But Athanasius, after some exertion, prevailed upon the members to be content with the creed of Nicaea and not to follow the heretics' example and have a new creed every year.[111]

The council, however, did not disband without passing certain disciplinary canons that seemed demanded by the situation. Canons I and II prohibited again the translation of a bishop from one see to another. Others restricted the visits of bishops to the imperial court or lengthy sojourns anywhere outside their own dioceses. Three novel canons provided that bishops accused for any cause must first be tried by their fellow bishops of the same province, sitting alone, a rule that would hereafter exclude Asiatics from the first trial of an Alexandrian. If either a condemned bishop or his judges were dissatisfied, they might " honor the memory of Peter, the apostle," and appeal to the bishop of Rome, who, if he thought there had been miscarriage of justice, might appoint judges to review the case and be represented himself by a legate on the second tribunal. In the present instance, of course, the council might be regarded as such a tribunal. These canons and other documents and records were enclosed in a letter from the council to Julius at Rome, a loyal and respectful report of the whole proceeding " to their head, that is, to the See of Peter, the apostle." Two passages only in this letter might, one would imagine, have sounded ominously to a sensitive bishop's ear. " The devout emperors themselves gave us permission to debate everything." Julius will read also the letter we have written to " the most blessed Augusti " and see that we have indeed covered every question under dispute. The monarch is there, unforgettable, in the background. The coun-

[111] This tentative creed and the letter to Julius, which was never sent, are preserved in the so-called *Collection of the Deacon Theodosius*, J. P. Migne, *Patrologia Latina*, Vol. LVI, pp. 839 *sqq*.

cil convoked by him must needs have his consent for a free discussion and must render him an account of what it has done. The West was beginning its experience with Christian princes.

Julius, however, appears to have been on the whole quite satisfied, for he ordered the canons of Sardica engrossed on the registers of the Roman church, below the canons of Nicaea.[111a] The machinery devised by the council for the exercise of his privilege of creating a court of appeal was not allowed to hamper him or any of his successors. They continued, as before, to decide in person at Rome most cases that came before them. But it meant something that the appellate jurisdiction of Rome had been expressly confirmed by the episcopate of the West and by the head of the see of Alexandria.

The Council of Sardica, which was primarily intended to bring peace and a better understanding to East and West, merely intensified their hostility. Each party had now seemingly committed itself to war by its anathemas against the leaders of the other. Bishops of Rome had never, so far as we know, been so openly defied. The emperor Constantius straightway took up the cudgels for his Eusebians and forbade the three eastern bishops who had been a second time condemned, to show themselves in their old sees on pain of death. But the Westerners could also produce an imperial ally. In 344, Vincent, bishop of Capua, and Euphratas, bishop of Cologne, landed in Antioch under the protection of Constans' general Sabianus, bringing with them a letter from Constans to his brother, sternly expostulating with him for his attitude toward Athanasius and threatening to go himself in force to Alexandria and set things right there. A vile and petty plot, hatched by Stephen of Antioch to blast the reputation of Euphratas, proved a fiasco and the news of it reaching Constantius' ears so startled him that he gave unexpected attention to the western envoys and sent a dispatch to the prefect of Egypt to leave the Athanasian Christians in peace. The Eusebians, in some alarm, retaliated by sending four bishops to Constans at

111a In 419, Pope Zosimus quoted Canon V of the Council of Sardica to his legate at the Council of Carthage as one of the canons of Nicaea. The Africans sent to Constantinople, Alexandria and Antioch to inquire if that were correct.

Milan. In his presence, they refrained from mentioning Athanasius, who, they knew, had by this time Constans' unshakable, personal support, but they insisted again upon their own amicable dispositions, pointing out merely the impossibility of uniting with Marcellus, who, as we have said, had in fact shown undeniable traces of Sabellianism and whose pupil, Photinus, bishop of Sirmium, was now plainly denying the separate personality of the divine Word.

By Constans' wish, a number of western bishops were summoned to Milan to meet these eastern deputies and make one more effort to adjust their grievances.[112] The Roman bishop, as usual, sent two legates. In the atmosphere of the court, both sides ignored or forgot the resounding anathemas of Sardica and appeared willing for some concession. The case of Athanasius was still shelved. The Westerners agreed to condemn Photinus but asked, as the next step, that the Easterners abjure Arianism. This demand apparently revived too keenly the memories of old battle. The Easterners refused to disavow their past to such an extent and left Milan in anger. Two bishops, however, Ursacius and Valens, who until now had belonged to their party but whose sees lay within the dominion of Constans, decided that it was imprudent to risk his disapproval any longer, and before the assembly broke up, made public renunciation of their own Arian beliefs.

The following year, 345, Constans took a more decisive stand in behalf of the catholic cause. Gregory, the Eusebian bishop of Alexandria, died and Constans sent a peremptory note to his brother, bidding him to forestall any attempt on the part of the Eusebians to ordain a successor, and to recall Athanasius. Constantius, on the advice of his counsellors, bowed to the inevitable and sent three letters to Athanasius, urging his immediate return and guaranteeing his safety against all assault. For almost a year Athanasius hesitated. The record of Constantius and his officials in Egypt was not such as to inspire confidence and he

[112] We have no record of this meeting at Milan, only such brief references as that in Liberius' letter, *infra*, p. 561, and Hilary's allusion to Photinus, "who two years ago was condemned as a heretic by the Synod of Milan." Hilary, *Fragmenta Historica*, Series B, II, 5, 4, and II, 9, 1–2.

dreaded becoming the occasion of fresh torments for his people. He finally concluded that Constans might be trusted to provide for their protection and wrote that he would go back. He went first to see Constans and then to bid farewell to Julius and his other friends in Rome. Julius gave him a warm letter of friendship and congratulation to carry to the long-suffering church of Alexandria. His return assumed somewhat the aspect of a triumphal journey. Everywhere, even in the East, he was received by rejoicing friends. Sixteen bishops of Palestine dared to meet him at Jerusalem to do him honor. In October, 346, he was once more at home.

That same year, Ursacius, and Valens, who, in spite of their recantation at Milan, had not yet been recognized by Julius and were still technically under the ban of the excommunication at Sardica, came down to Rome and made their full submission "to the most blessed pope." They wrote and signed a humble confession of the worthlessness of the charges that had been fabricated against Athanasius, of their own earnest desire to be in communion with him and of their utter abhorrence of the heresy of Arius. They were thereupon forgiven and taken back into fellowship. The See of Rome stood outwardly loftier than it had ever been before. Yet the power that had enabled it to override the will of the East was not its own inherent virtue but the extraneous, material power of the State.

For four more years, the orthodox church organization preserved its unquestioned dominance in the West and met with no overt resistance in the East. But, in 350, the tables were abruptly turned with the assassination of Constans by a band of military conspirators at the foot of the Pyrenees. On receipt of this intelligence, his sister Eutropia, living at Rome, proclaimed her son Nepotianus as western emperor in his uncle's stead. But Count Magnentius, the choice of the legions, sent a general to Rome to deal with his young rival and Nepotianus was killed in the fighting around the city. Eutropia herself was then executed and many noble Romans suspected of fidelity to the house of Constantine were slain or banished. Constantius, however, did not let the deaths of his brother and sister wait for vengeance. In

351, he began moving slowly westward, Magnentius slowly falling back as he advanced. In 352, he crossed the passes of the Alps and descended into Italy. A year later, Magnentius committed suicide in Gaul and the world was at Constantius' feet. Already the bishops Ursacius and Valens, perceiving the new complexion which these events put upon their personal affairs, had made haste to rejoin the Eusebians, protesting that they had recanted in Italy only under compulsion. But in April, 352, before Constantius entered Rome, Julius died. He had played, on the whole, an able and honorable part as bishop, starting no quarrels and using his influence to the best of his lights in the interests of justice and unity. He was taken from the troubles to come.

The source material for Julius and his immediate successors is more abundant than the sum of what we have had hitherto for all their predecessors. The *History* of Eusebius, for example, is now carried on by three different Greek writers of the early fifth century, Socrates, Sozomen, and Theodoret, each of whom often incorporates contemporary documents entire. The works of Athanasius, Hilary of Poitiers, Optatus, Jerome, Rufinus and Augustine, all contain, in one form or another, much of historical importance for this period. In 353, the year after Julius' death, begin the extant books of the pagan *History* of Ammianus Marcellinus. The canons and encyclicals of councils and other miscellaneous matter are preserved in various collections. We have not space any longer to give every available extract on the topic in hand and can select only what seem the most significant and illuminating.

On Julius himself and the appellate jurisdiction of the Papacy, see among modern works, J. Langen, *Geschichte der römischen Kirche* (4 vols., Bonn, 1881–1893), Vol. I, pp. 424 *sqq.*; F. Loofs, *Studien und Kritiken* (Gotha, 1908–1911), p. 293; M. Friedberg, *Appelationem an den Papst,* in J. J. Herzog and A. Hauck, *Realencyklopädie für protestantische Theologie und Kirche* (24 vols., Leipzig, 1896–1913), Vol. I; C. H. Turner, *The Genuineness of the Sardican Canons,* in *Journal of Theological Studies* (London, 1902), Vol. III, pp. 370–397; C. J. Hefele, *Histoire des Conciles* (8 vols., Paris, 1907–1921), Vol. I, pp. 771 *sqq.;* P. Bernardakis, *Les Appels au Pape dans l'Église Grecque jusqu'à Photius,* in *Echos d'Orient* (Paris, 1903), Vol. VI, pp. 30–42, 118–125, 249–257; L. Duchesne, *Early History of the Christian Church* (trans. from the 4th ed. by C. Jenkins, 3 vols., London, 1910–1924), Vol. II, chap. VI; B. J. Kidd, *History of the Church to A.D. 461* (3 vols., Oxford, 1922-1924). Vol. II, chap. IV.

1. The Appeal of Athanasius to Rome

Athanasius, *Apologia contra Arianos,* 20. Text. J. P. Migne, *Patrologia Graeca,* XXV, 279–282.

[The preceding sections contain a long letter, put out by a synod of Egyptian bishops in defence of Athanasius, in which they state that an effort is being made to induce Julius of Rome to recognize the Arian pseudo-bishop Pistus and that an Arian deputation has been sent to him, consisting of a priest, Macarius, and two deacons.]

20. This letter the Egyptians sent to everyone and to Julius, bishop of Rome. And the Eusebians wrote also to Julius and thinking to frighten me,[113] requested him to call a council and to be himself the judge, if he so pleased. So, after I went up to Rome, Julius wrote a suitable reply to the Eusebians and sent them two of his own priests, Elpidius and Philoxenus. But when the Eusebians heard about me they were thrown into confusion, for they had not expected that I would go there of my own accord, and they declined the invitation of Julius, offering unsatisfactory excuses but in fact afraid that they would be convicted of the malpractices to which Valens and Ursacius later confessed.[114]

[113] *I.e.,* Athanasius. His *Apologia* is written in the first person.

[114] Ursacius and Valens were bishops of Singidunum, the modern Belgrade, and of Mursa, the modern Eszeq, respectively. They had come under the influence of Arius and, as far as they were ever sincere in their beliefs, appear to have been Arians. They had taken part in the Council of Tyre, that first condemned Athanasius in 335. Their confession and recantation, to which Athanasius here refers, occurred in 346, when for a few years the Athanasian party was in the ascendant. *Supra,* pp. 501, 502; *infra,* pp. 531–533. In his *Historia Arianorum,* 11, Athanasius gives a slightly fuller description of the Eusebians' state of mind at this time. "And Julius wrote and sent the priests Elpidius and Philoxenus and fixed a day for meeting, when they either might come or know that they were altogether suspect. But as soon as the Eusebians heard that the trial would be ecclesiastical and that no count would appear at it, no soldiers would stand before the doors, and that the findings of the synod would depend upon no imperial commandment (for by such means they have always fortified themselves against the bishops and without them they have not courage to open their lips), they were so alarmed that they detained the priests even after the day set and invented a preposterous excuse, that they were unable to go then, because of the war which was being started by the Persians."

However, more than fifty bishops came together in the place where the priest Vito held his congregation [115] and they accepted my defense and admitted me to their communion and their love. And they were indignant against the Eusebians and asked Julius to write to that effect to those who had written to him.[116] This he did and sent his letter by the hand of Count Gabianus.

Sozomen, *Historia Ecclesiastica,* III, 7–8. Text. J. P. Migne, *Patrologia Graeca,* LXVII, 1049–1056.

7. [The opponents of the Nicene creed had by this time taken possession of all the noblest sees in the East, including Alexandria, Antioch and Constantinople, and all the eastern bishops who upheld the Nicene settlement had been deposed.] But the head of the Roman church and all the clergy of the West looked upon this as a personal insult. For from the beginning they had approved the creed of the assembly of Nicaea in every point and to the present day they have not ceased to agree with it. So when Athanasius came to them they received him warmly and took upon themselves the judgment of his cause. But Eusebius was vexed at this and wrote to Julius that he might act as judge of the sentence passed on Athanasius at Tyre. But before he learned the opinion of Julius, shortly after the meeting of the synod at Antioch, he died. . . .

8. But Athanasius fled from Alexandria and came to Rome. And it happened that Paul, the bishop of Constantinople, and Marcellus of Ancyra were together there also, and Asclepas of Gaza,[117] who had resisted the Arians and

[115] This is the Roman synod of 340. *Supra,* p. 493.

[116] *I.e.,* the Eusebian bishops at Antioch, who had written a discourteous answer to Julius, refusing to attend his council. This letter is described in our next extract.

[117] Paul and Asclepas were orthodox supporters of the Nicene theology, like Athanasius. Marcellus had been a prominent antagonist of Arius at Nicaea and had afterward written a book to expose his errors at greater length. This book,

had been accused by some heterodox persons of overturning the altar and on this count had been deposed. In his place, Quintianus was ruling the church of Gaza. And Lucius, bishop of Adrianople, who had been accused on another charge and for that reason deprived of his church, was also staying at Rome. The Roman bishop investigated the case of each man and when he discovered that they all agreed upon the creed of the Council of Nicaea, he received them as of one mind into communion. And inasmuch as the oversight of everyone belongs to him, through the merit of his see,[118] he restored to each of them his proper church. And he wrote to the bishops of the East, reproving them for their wrong judgment of these men and for the disturbance they had created in the Church by not upholding the decrees of Nicaea. And he bade a few of them all come to him by a certain day [119] to show that they had now arrived at a right decision. Otherwise, he said threateningly, he would not endure it in the future if they did not cease from innovations. Such was his letter. And Athanasius and Paul, with their followers, each regained his own see [120] and they sent the letters of Julius around among the eastern bishops. But

---

however, went too far in the direction of Sabellianism, a danger to which opponents of Arianism were often liable. Marcellus had been condemned by the council of bishops at Jerusalem in 335. Even the Romans were a little uncertain of Marcellus and Julius asked him for his profession of faith. *Infra*, p. 513.

118 Socrates in this same connection uses a similar phrase. "And they explained their situation to Julius, bishop of Rome. And he, inasmuch as the church of Rome has the prerogative, armed them with forcible letters and sent them back to the East." *Historia Ecclesiastica*, II, 15. Sozomen's word, which we translate "oversight," is *κηδεμονία*. Socrates' word, translated "prerogative," is *προνομία*. The fact that these two Greek historians use different words here but preserve the same turn of idea suggests that they both were basing this part of their narrative on some common Roman or Latin source. It would hardly have occurred to them both to make just this comment of their own accord, although their general attitude of vague veneration for the Roman See allows them to transcribe it without objection. The first Roman trial of these dispossessed eastern bishops was held by Julius alone, the second by the synod under Julius, after the Eusebians had refused to coöperate.

119 The day appointed was probably toward the end of 339. Julius appears to have sent out his priests with the letter the last of May or the first of June of that year.

120 It is uncertain whether Athanasius did or did not go back to Alexandria at this time.

the latter were angered by them and met at Antioch [121] and composed a reply to Julius, a letter in very elegant and suave language but full of hostility and even dangerous menace. For they acknowledged in it that the Roman church was honored by everyone, as a church that had been from the first the school of the apostles and the mother seat [122] of true piety, even though the teachers of her doctrine had come to her from the East. But they did not propose on that account to take the second place, because their church was not first in size and numbers, as long as it did excel in virtue and understanding. And they brought charges against Julius for communing with the party of Athanasius and were indignant with him for disdaining their synod [123] and annulling their verdict. And they denounced his action as unjust and as contrary to ecclesiastical law. Then, after upbraiding him in such style and declaring that he had done them grave injury, they offered Julius peace and communion if he would recognize the deposition of those whom they had expelled and the ordination of those whom they had elected instead, and they threatened him with the contrary, if he overrode their decisions. For, they argued, the priests of the East before them had made no objection when Novatian was expelled from the church of Rome.[124] As for their infractions of the decrees of Nicaea, they made no reply to him there, explaining that they had many arguments to prove the necessity of what they had done, but that it was futile to justify themselves now on that score, when they were being blamed for trangressions in every direction at once.

121 They gathered at Antioch late in 339 or in the first weeks of 340.

122 The word is actually "metropolis."

123 *I.e.*, the Council of Tyre, which had deposed Athanasius, in 335. This is the technical grievance of the eastern bishops against Julius all through, that he failed to recognize the sentence which they had passed against one of their own number.

124 *Supra*, pp. 355, 382, 386, 420.

Julius, *Letter to the Eusebian bishops at Antioch,* quoted by Athanasius, *Apologia contra Arianos,* 21–35. Text. J. P. Migne, *Patrologia Graeca,* XXV, 281 *sqq.*

Julius to Danius, Flaccillus, Narcissus, Eusebius, Maris, Macedonius, Theodore [125] and their friends who have written to us from Antioch, our beloved brethren, greeting in the Lord.

I have read the letter which you sent back to me by my priests, Elpidius and Philoxenus, and was surprised that, whereas we had written to you in love and sincerity of truth, you should answer us in so hostile and unsuitable a manner. For the pride and arrogance of the writers were conspicuous throughout their writing. Such conduct does not belong to faith in Christ. A letter written in love should receive a response of equal love and not one of enmity. Was it not a sign of love to send you priests to sympathize with those who are in difficulty and to invite those who wrote to me to come hither, so that all questions might quickly be solved and adjusted and our brethren be no longer in trouble and no further opprobrium rest upon you? But, for some reason, my intention has so affected you as to make us feel that you are uttering mockingly, with a sort of malice, the very words with which you ostensibly pay us honor. The priests also, whom I sent you, who should have come back in happiness, have, on the contrary, returned in distress for what they saw going on among you. For my part, when I had read your letter and pondered it carefully, I kept it to myself, thinking that, in spite of all, some of you would come and I should not need to produce it and it might not be made public and vex many of the people here. But when no one came and it grew necessary to bring it out, everyone

[125] Bishops respectively of Caesarea in Cappadocia, Antioch, Neronias in Cilicia, Constantinople, Chalcedon, Mopsuestia in Cilicia and Heraclea in Thrace. What significance there may be in the order of the names we do not know.

was astonished, I assure you, and almost unable to believe that such a letter had really been written by you, for it was one of animosity far more than of love. And if the composer of it wrote out of ambition to display his eloquence, then his enterprise should find vent in other fields. For in the conduct of churches, shows of eloquence are not required, but the rules of the apostles and some care that none of the little ones in the Church be offended. . . .

Now, what cause was there for irritation or what was there in our letter to make you angry? Was it because we invited you to come here for a synod? But this proposal you should rather have accepted with joy. For men who have confidence in what they have done or, as they say, in the decisions they have made, are not annoyed when their decision is reviewed by others but are bold, because their own just decision can never become unjust. On this account, the bishops who met in the great Council of Nicaea, by the will of God, decreed that the acts of one synod should be reviewed by a later synod, so that the men who pass judgment may have before their eyes the second judgment that is to come and may take great precautions to investigate thoroughly, and those who are judged may be certain that they have not been judged by their first judges out of hostility but with uprightness.[126] But, if you are refusing to maintain among you this ancient custom, which was recorded and endorsed by the great council, your refusal is wrong, for a custom that has once prevailed in the Church and has been confirmed by councils is not properly to be rejected by a few individuals.

Apart from this, you have no right to be vexed. For when the men who were sent from you Eusebians with your letter, — I mean Macarius, the priest, and Marty-

[126] There is no such article as this among the extant canons of Nicaea, but the council passed ordinances which were not incorporated with the rest, such as the rule for Easter observance. *Supra,* p. 487. It has been suggested, however, that Julius was here freely interpreting Canon V. The reading may be corrupt.

rius and Hesychius, the deacons,—after their arrival here proved unable to hold their ground against the priests who came from Athanasius and were being confuted and exposed on every point, they then asked us to summon a synod and to invite both the bishop Athanasius of Alexandria and the Eusebians, so that in the presence of all parties a just conclusion might be reached. And then, they assured us, they would establish all the charges against Athanasius. For in our own congregation, Martyrius and Hesychius had been contradicted and the priests of Bishop Athanasius had convincingly withstood them. Martyrius, to tell the truth, was refuted in every detail and on that account he asked for the synod. Now, even if neither Martyrius nor Hesychius had asked for a synod and if I of my own will had summoned one, in order to confound the writers of your letter and to relieve our own brethren who were complaining of injustice, even so the summons would have been proper and right and ecclesiastical and good in the sight of God. But when the very men whom you Eusebians consider trustworthy have themselves asked us to call one, then you who are summoned should not be vexed but come with alacrity. . . . If, as you write, every synod has final authority and a judge is dishonored if his verdict is reviewed by others, reflect, beloved, who are dishonoring a synod and who are undoing the judgments of the past. . . .

The Arians, who were expelled for their impiety by Alexander of blessed memory, at that time bishop of Alexandria,[127] were not only banned by the people of every city but were also anathematized by all who assembled in the great Council of Nicaea. Nor was theirs a negligible offense nor a sin against a man but against our Lord Jesus Christ himself, the Son of the living God. Nevertheless, they who were once proscribed by all the world and branded by the whole Church, are now said to be accepted again, a report

[127] *Supra*, p. 467.

which, I think, should arouse even your indignation when you hear it. Who then are the dishonorers of a council? Are they not those who are setting at naught the votes of the three hundred [128] and preferring impiety to piety? For the heresy of the Ariomaniacs was detected and condemned by all the bishops from everywhere, but the bishops Athanasius and Marcellus have many adherents who speak and write on their behalf. We have had testimony that Marcellus resisted the Arians in the Council of Nicaea. As for Athanasius, we have evidence that he was not proved guilty at Tyre and was not present at all in Mareotis, where the documents against him are said to have been produced. Now you know, beloved, that examinations conducted by one party alone have no validity and are regarded as suspect. In spite of this, we, to be correct, have shown no partiality either to you or to those who have written to us for the others, but we have invited you who wrote to us to come here and also the many who have written in the others' defense, so that the whole matter might be sifted out in a synod and an innocent man might not be called guilty nor a culprit treated as spotless. So not by us is a council dishonored but by those who have so soon, contrary to a judicial decision, received back the Arians, whom everyone condemned. Of the men who once judged them the greater part are now departed to be with Christ, but some are still in this life of trial and indignant that their judgment has been reversed.

[He describes how, before the arrival of the Athanasian priests from Alexandria, Macarius, Martyrius and Hesychius had tried to persuade him to send letters to Pistus, who had been elected bishop by the Arians in Alexandria, and how Macarius had fled in the night from Rome when he knew that the Athanasians were on their way thither.]

If, as you write, the decrees of councils ought to be enforced and the precedents set by the cases of Novatian

128 The traditional number of bishops at Nicaea was three hundred or over.

and Paul of Samosata[129] ought to be followed, all the more ought the ordinances of the three hundred bishops not to be reversed nor a catholic council dishonored by a few individuals. . . . For not only have the Arians been received but also bishops have made a practice of moving from one place to another.[130] Now, if you truly believe that all bishops have the same and equal dignity, and if you do not, as you write, esteem them in proportion to the size of their cities, then he that is entrusted with a small city ought to abide in the city entrusted to him and not despise his trust nor move to another that was not committed to him, scorning that which was bestowed on him by God and loving the empty glory of men. . . .

But, perhaps, the date set was a stumbling-block, since in your letter you blamed us, because we had allowed too short a time for the gathering of the synod. But this also, beloved, is a mere pretext. For if the day had overtaken any of you on the journey, the interval before the date appointed would then have been proved too short. But when persons did not choose to set out and kept back our priests until the month of January, their pretext was due to lack of confidence. For, as I have already said, they would have come, if they had had confidence, and they would not have heeded the length of the journey nor regarded the shortness of the interval but would have been sure of just and reasonable treatment. But, perhaps, the critical situation prevented them from coming. For in your letter, you made likewise the point that we should have considered the critical situation in the East and should not have summoned you to come away. But if this situation was so critical that you could not come, as you say, you should have considered the situation before this and have refrained from creating schism and mourning and lamentation in the churches. . . .

129 *Supra,* pp. 354–355, 433–434.
130 This was a violation of Canons XV and XVI of Nicaea.

Furthermore, I must inform you that although I alone wrote the letter to you, the sentiment was not mine only but was shared by all the bishops in Italy and throughout these regions. I myself was not willing to have them all write, for fear that by their sheer number they would have excessive weight with you. None the less, the bishops met here at the season appointed and expressed the opinion which I now, in this my second letter, report to you and so, beloved, although I alone am writing, be assured that this is the feeling of us all. . . .

[The accusations against Athanasius are conflicting; many have been disproved altogether. His trial was grossly unfair. The witnesses brought against him were persons of shady character. The evidence indicates a concerted conspiracy.]

Now, when all this had been told us and so many witnesses were appearing on his behalf and so much was being presented by him in his own vindication, what ought we to have done? What does the rule of the Church require of us, if not our refusal to condemn the man, nay, rather, our reception and treatment of him like a bishop, as indeed we have treated him? Moreover, he has waited here a year and six months, expecting the arrival of you and of whoever wished to come, and by his presence he has put you all to shame, for he would not be here if he were not confident. He came, furthermore, not of his own volition but because he had received a letter of summons from us, like that which we wrote to you. Nevertheless, you have reproached us for transgression of the rules. Observe now, who have transgressed the rules, we who received a man upon such abundant testimony or those who in Antioch, thirty-six days distant from Alexandria, nominated an outsider as bishop and sent him down there with a military force![131] . . .

[It was unlawful to thrust Gregory, a total stranger,

131 *Supra*, p. 491.

upon the Alexandrian church. Terrible violence and brutality have followed his entrance there.]

As for Marcellus, since you have written of him also as an unbeliever in Christ, I am eager to inform you that he is here and has positively affirmed that your accusations against him are false. Moreover, when we asked him to state his faith, he made answer directly with boldness, so that we recognized that he professed nothing but the truth. For he professed as devout a belief in our Lord and Savior Jesus Christ as the catholic Church itself holds and he declared that he had not recently come to this belief but had reached it long ago. Indeed, our own priests who attended the Council of Nicaea, bore witness to his orthodoxy. . . . As long, then, as his faith was orthodox and he had witnesses to his orthodoxy, what again should we have done with him but treat him as a bishop, as we did, and not exclude him from communion? I have written you all this, not in order to defend them but to convince you that we have acted fairly and regularly in receiving these men and that you have no ground for resentment. . . .

Not only have the bishops Athanasius and Marcellus come to us, complaining of the injustice done them, but many other bishops as well, from Thrace, from Coele-Syria,[131a] from Phoenicia and Palestine. And many priests and persons from Alexandria and other districts met at the synod here and before all the assembled bishops made their statements and then lamented the violence and injury which their churches were enduring and asserted that still other churches were experiencing outrages, both in word and deed, like those perpetrated at Alexandria and in their own congregations. And priests have but now arrived with letters from Egypt and Alexandria, reporting that many bishops and priests who desired to come to our synod were prevented. And since the departure of Athanasius

131a *Vide supra*, p. 79, n. 43.

up to now, they say, bishops who were once confessors[132] have been beaten with stripes and others are being kept in prison, and some old men, who have been very long in the episcopate, are put to labor in the public works and almost all the clergy and the laity of the catholic Church are subject to plot and persecution. . . . In addition, those who came to the synod made accusations so horrible against some of you, — to mention no names, — that I refused to write them down. You yourselves have probably heard them from others. On that account especially, I have written to urge you to come, so that you might be present and hear and every wrong might be set right and corrected. . . .

Wherefore, as God the Father of our Lord Jesus Christ knoweth, I have thought it needful to write this to you out of care for your reputation, praying that the churches might not fall into disorder but continue as they were ordained by the apostles, that you might even now abash those who, out of mutual hatred to one another, are bringing the churches to this pass. For I have heard that some few persons are the authors of all this calamity. Make haste with your bowels of mercy to correct, as I said before, transgressions of the rule, so that whatever harm has already been done may be set right through your earnestness.

And do not write: "You have preferred the communion of Marcellus and Athanasius to ours," for such words tend not to peace but to bitterness and hatred among brethren. . . . If you think you can prove some of the charges against them and can convict them to their faces, then let whoever will come to us. For they have promised that they themselves would be ready to prove and establish what they have said to us.

So give us notice of your coming, beloved, that we may

[132] *I.e.*, confessors during the last pagan persecutions. It would seem a crowning sin for any Christians to maltreat confessors. Athanasius mentions one Potammon, who had also been at Nicaea, who was beaten to death during the Arian disturbances in Egypt. *Historia Arianorum*, 12.

write both to them and to the bishops who again will have to assemble, that the culprits may be condemned in the presence of us all and there be no more confusion in the churches. What has already happened is enough! It is enough that bishops are being sentenced to banishment in the presence of bishops![133] But I must not say much of that, lest I appear to press too hard on those who were present on those occasions. But to speak candidly, things should not have gone so far. Petty spites should not have reached the present pitch. Granted the removal, as you write, of Athanasius and Marcellus from their sees, what then is to be said of the other bishops and priests, who, as I have told you, have come here from divers places? They also said that they had been driven out and had suffered similar abuses. O beloved, the judgments of the Church are no longer patterned upon the gospel but aim only at banishment and death. Suppose, as you insist, that some guilt had lain upon them, their cases should have been tried according to the rule of the Church, not in this way. You should have written to us all, that a just sentence might be issued by us all. For the sufferers were bishops and churches of no ordinary sort but those which the apostles themselves once governed in their own persons.[134]

And why was no word sent to us particularly concerning the church of the Alexandrians? Are you ignorant that the custom has been for word to be sent to us first and then for a just decision to be proclaimed from this spot?[135] So if

[133] Orthodox bishops had apparently been sentenced by Constantius or his officials in the presence of Eusebian or Arian bishops.

[134] Julius may be referring to the tradition that Mark founded the church of Alexandria. Paul may have preached at Ancyra, the city of Marcellus. Tertullian, *Contra Marcionem,* IV, 5.

[135] Julius actually claims here for himself only the right to hear and try any charge against the bishop of Alexandria. But the sentence was later given an exaggerated interpretation. *E.g.,* "Julius wrote . . . that they had transgressed the canons of the Church, because they had not called him to their council, for, he said, it was an ecclesiastical law that whatever ordinances were made without the consent of the bishop of Rome were counted void." Sozomen, *Historia Ecclesiastica,* III, 10. See also Socrates, *Historia Ecclesiastica,* II, 17.

any grave suspicion rested upon the bishop there, notice of it should have been dispatched to the church here. As it is, they failed to inform us and acted by themselves, as they saw fit, and now wish to obtain our sanction, although we do not condemn him. Not like this were the instructions of Paul, not like this the traditions of the Fathers. This is another mode of procedure, a novel practice. I beseech you, bear with me patiently. What I write is for our common good. What we have learned from blessed Peter, the apostle, this I declare to you and I should not have written it, for I supposed you all understood it, had not these events so distressed us. . . . I ask you that such things shall not occur again, and, further, that you will write to condemn the persons who are the cause of them, that the churches may no longer suffer such hurt nor any bishop or priest be insolently abused nor any one be compelled to act contrary to his belief, as they have told us they were, nor we become a laughing stock to the pagans and, above all, that we arouse not the wrath of God. For each of us shall render an account in the day of judgment for the deeds he has done here. May we all hold the true faith of God, so that the churches may recover their own bishops and may rejoice always in Christ Jesus our Lord, through whom be glory to the Father forever and ever! Amen. I pray that you may be strong in the Lord, brethren beloved and greatly desired.

2. The Council of Sardica and the Schism Over the Jurisdiction of Rome

Sozomen, *Historia Ecclesiastica,* III, 10–12. Text. J. P. Migne, *Patrologia Graeca,* LXVII, 1057 *sqq.*

10 . . . And when Julius achieved nothing by the letter he had written on behalf of them [the exiled eastern

bishops] to the clergy of the East, he reported their misfortunes to Constans, the emperor. Then the latter wrote to his brother Constantius to send him some of the eastern bishops to justify their action. And three were selected for this errand, Narcissus, bishop of Irenopolis in Cilicia, Theodore of Heraclea in Thrace and Marcus of Arethusa in Syria. And when they had arrived in Italy, they defended their conduct and attempted to persuade the emperor that the sentence of the eastern council had been just. And when they were asked for their faith, they made no mention of that which they had defined at Antioch[136] but presented another creed in writing and even this was inconsistent with the confession of Nicaea. [Constans perceives that they had basely conspired against Athanasius and Paul and sends them back to the East.]

11 Then, at the end of three years, the eastern bishops again sent another confession to the western bishops, which is known as " the long-drawn creed," because it is composed of more words and names than its predecessors. . . . And the western clergy would not accept it, for they said that they were satisfied with the confession of Nicaea and beyond that they thought there was no need of troubling further. But when Constans asked of his brother as a favor that the partisans of Athanasius be restored to their proper sees and even wrote of it, he accomplished nothing, for the men of the heretical faction were working against it. . . . [Athanasius and Paul finally ask Constans for a council to settle on an acceptable creed for the whole Church. Both emperors then agree that bishops from East and West should meet for the purpose at Sardica.]

And the eastern bishops met first at Philippopolis in Thrace and wrote to the western bishops, who had already gathered at Sardica, to expel the Athanasians from their sessions and from communion, on the ground that they had

136 *Supra*, p. 494.

been deposed. Otherwise, they said, they would not join them. Afterwards, they came to Sardica and insisted that they would not enter the church while the men whom they had deposed were there.[137] To this the western bishops replied that they had never excluded these men from communion nor would they exclude them now, especially as Julius, bishop of the Romans, had examined their case and had not condemned them;[138] also, that the men were there and ready for trial and would refute at once the charges against them. But they achieved nothing by these communications, and when the appointed day had passed, on which they were required to decide the business for which they had been assembled, they wrote finally to each other in such terms that they ended by becoming more bitter than they had been before. Then each party met by itself and cast opposing votes.[139] For the eastern bishops confirmed their previous sentences on Athanasius and Paul and Marcellus and Asclepas and they deposed Julius, bishop of Rome, because he had been the first to commune with them, and Hosius, the confessor, for the same reason and also because he was a friend of Paulinus and of Eustathius who had been heads of the church of Antioch,[140] and Maximin, bishop of Trier, because he first communed with Paul and then brought about his return to Constantinople.[141] In addition, they deposed Protogenes, bishop of Sardica, and Gaudentius.[142] . . . And after passing these resolutions, they notified the bishops

137 Athanasius says that the eastern bishops brought two counts, imperial officers, with them to Sardica to overawe the others, but that the council met without counts and permitted no soldiers to enter. *Apologia contra Arianos*, 36; *Historia Arianorum*, 15.

138 The council, in its letter to the church of Alexandria, says that Julius, " after cautious deliberation and inquiry, decided that there should be no hesitation whatever over communion with our brother Athanasius. For he had eighty bishops as his truthful witnesses." *Apologia contra Arianos*, 37; 41.

139 Socrates says that the eastern bishops went back to Philippopolis to hold their separate meetings. *Historia Ecclesiastica*, II, 20. Athanasius agrees with him that there were seventy-six of them. *Epistolae*, XLVI.

140 On these men *vide supra*, pp. 471, 474.

141 *Supra*, pp. 491, 492, 495.

142 Protogenes, the local bishop, had taken sides with the western contingent. Gaudentius, bishop of Naisi (Nisch) in Dacia, had tried to defend Paul.

everywhere not to admit these persons to communion nor to write to them nor to receive letters from them. . . .

12 On the other hand, the party of Hosius[143] assembled and acquitted Athanasius, on the ground that he had been unjustifiably attacked by the assembly at Tyre, and Marcellus, because he declared he did not believe as they accused him of believing, and Asclepas, . . . and Lucius. . . . And they wrote to their parishes[144] to regard these men as their bishops and to expect their arrival and not to look upon Gregory in Alexandria nor Basil in Ancyra nor Quintianus in Gaza as bishops nor to have any communion with them nor even to consider them Christians. And they deposed from the bishopric Theodore, the Thracian, and Narcissus, bishop of Irenopolis, and Acacius of Caesarea in Palestine, and Menophantus of Ephesus and Ursacius of Singidunum in Moesia, and Valens of Mursae in Pannonia, and George of Laodicea, even though he was not at this council with the bishops of the East. [These were all deposed as Arians, who separate the Son from the substance of the Father, and letters were sent to all bishops to inform them of the sentence of condemnation.] . . . And they also adopted another confession of faith, longer than that of Nicaea, but preserving the same meaning and not differing much from it in words. Then Hosius and Protogenes, who presided over the western bishops at Sardica, fearing, probably, that they might be thought to have disparaged the confession of the Council of Nicaea, wrote to Julius and declared that they held the latter to be binding but that for the sake of clarity they had expressed the same meaning more at length.[145] . . . This done, both parties broke up their assemblies and every man returned to his home.

143 Hosius was evidently the most venerated person at the council. Athanasius says that he was the father of the bishops there (*Historia Arianorum*, 15), and again that "the great Hosius" presided at the sessions. *Ibid.*, 16.

144 On the use of this word in the sense of the modern "diocese," *vide supra*, p. 279, n. 99.

145 On the draft of this creed and the letter to Julius *vide supra*, p. 498.

Council of Sardica, *Canons,* III, IV, V, X. Text. C. J. Hefele, *Histoire des Conciles,* I, Pt. II, 762 *sqq.*

Canon III [146]

The bishop Hosius said: "This provision also must be added, that no bishop may go from his own province into another province where there are bishops, unless he be invited by his brethren, so that we may not seem to close the gates of charity.[147]

And this rule likewise must be observed, that if in any province one bishop has a dispute with a brother and fellow bishop, neither one of them shall summon bishops from another province as judges. But if any bishop has had sentence passed against him in any instance and believes that he is not guilty but that his cause is right, so that the judgment should be given again, if it seem good to your charity, let us honor the memory of Peter, the apostle, and let the men who judged him write to Julius, bishop of Rome, that if he think best he may have the case reviewed by the bishops of the neighboring provinces and he may constitute them as judges. And if it cannot be shown that the case is such as to warrant a reversal of sentence, the previous judgment shall not be altered but shall remain in force." [148]

Canon IV

The bishop Gaudentius said: "If it please you, there shall be added to the sincere and charitable ordinance which

146 One hundred and twenty-one bishops finally signed these canons. They included men from Spain, Gaul, Italy, Africa, Sardinia, Pannonia, Moesia and both Dacias. See the notes on the signatures in *Nicene and Post-Nicene Fathers,* Vol. IV, pp. 147–148.

147 *I.e.,* bishops are not forbidden to perform friendly services for others outside their own provinces, if they are explicitly invited to do so.

148 This canon was included by Gratian in the *Corpus Juris Canonici,* Causa VI, quaest. iv, can. 7. He gives it in the Latin version of Dionysius Exiguus, which varies slightly from the Greek in the last clauses: "and if he [the Roman bishop] decide that judgment should be rendered again, let it be so rendered and let him name the judges. But if he find that the case is such that the trial should not be repeated, the sentence shall be confirmed."

you have enacted a provision that if any bishop be deposed by the judgment of the bishops in his vicinity and claim another opportunity for defense, no other man shall be installed in his see until the bishop of Rome has judged and rendered decision in the matter." [149]

Canon V

The bishop Hosius said: "It is resolved that if any bishop be accused and the bishops of his neighborhood in assembly remove him from his rank and if he appeal to and take refuge with the blessed bishop of the church of Rome and request him to hear him and if the bishop of Rome find it just that the case should be reviewed, he may write to those bishops who live in adjoining provinces to investigate the whole matter diligently and accurately and pass sentence upon it in accordance with their conviction of the truth. And if any one ask that his case be heard a second time and if, at his request, the Roman bishop be willing to send priests from his own staff, it shall be within the bishop's powers to send such priests as he may deem expedient and right, to sit as judges with the bishops and to possess the authority of the bishop who sent them; and this is to be ordained. But if the bishop of Rome consider the other bishops sufficient for the examination and decision of the case, he shall act as in his most prudent judgment he sees best." The bishops answered: "The resolution is approved." [150]

[149] The purpose of this canon is obviously to prohibit action like that of the eastern bishops, who ordained Gregory of Cappadocia as bishop of Alexandria, while Athanasius was appealing to Julius against their sentence of deposition.

[150] It will be realized that Canon V adds to the provisions for an appeal to the pope contained in Canon III, another by which the condemned bishop, as well as his judges, may make the appeal and the pope may at his discretion send legates to represent him on the second tribunal. The Synod of Sardica might at a stretch consider itself an appellate court under this heading, as well as under the first, for both Athanasius and his eastern judges had asked Julius for a new trial and he had approved of the meeting at Sardica, although he had not summoned it. That the synod did so consider itself seems indicated by a passage in the encyclical of the eastern party, *infra*, p. 526.

[Canons VIII and IX and the first part of X contain prohibitions against the frequenting of the imperial court by bishops aspiring for benefits of one kind or another. Bishops are forbidden to appear at all at court, unless brought by summons from the emperor or by some urgent errand of charity. Even such errands are, as far as possible, to be transacted through the medium of the metropolitan bishop resident at the capital.]

Canon X

The bishop Hosius said: ". . . And those who come to Rome, as I have said, shall commit to our beloved brother and fellow bishop, Julius, the petitions which they have to present, that he may first scrutinize them to see that none of them are improper and then may give them his patronage and care and forward them to the court." All the bishops answered that they agreed and that the measure was suitable.

The Eastern Bishops at Sardica, *Encyclical Letter,* contained in Hilary, *Fragmenta Historica,* Series A, IV. Text. *Corpus Scriptorum Ecclesiasticorum Latinorum,* LXV, 49–78.

We, the bishops from divers provinces of the East, namely, the province of the Thebaid, the province of Palestine, Arabia, Phoenicia, Syria, . . .[151] and the islands of the Cyclades, Lydia, Asia, Europe, the Hellespont, Thrace, and Emimontus, who have met and held a council in the city of Sardica, to Gregory, bishop of Alexandria, the bishop of Nicomedia, the bishop of Carthage, the bishop of Campania, . . .[152] and to all our fellow bishops throughout the world

[151] The names of twelve provinces in Asia Minor and eastward are here omitted.

[152] The names or titles of eleven bishops are omitted. Julius is not included.

and to the priests and deacons and all who under heaven are members of the holy catholic Church, greeting forever in the Lord.

[A long rehearsal of the heretical tenets of Marcellus, the crimes of Athanasius and the events of the trial at Tyre.]

10 Then afterwards, Athanasius wandered through various parts of the world, seducing persons and by his specious reasoning and baleful flattery deceiving innocent bishops who did not know of his crimes, even some Egyptians who were ignorant of his behavior, and by begging letters from all of them he disturbed peaceful churches, or else he himself made fresh forgeries for his own convenience. All this, however, availed nothing against the judgment long before solemnly delivered by holy and illustrious bishops. For the recommendation of persons who had not been judges at the council and had never received the sentence of the council and are known not to have been there when the aforesaid Athanasius was heard could be of no value or assistance to him. At length, when he realized that this was all in vain, he went to Julius at Rome and to some of the bishops of his party in Italy and imposed upon them by false letters and was too readily admitted by them to communion. Thenceforward, they began to defend not so much him as their own conduct, because they had believed and communed with him too hastily. For even if his letters had come from somebody, they did not come from men who either had been his judges or had attended the council. And even if they were written by somebody, the bishops never should have hastily believed him, pleading as he was in his own behalf. But all credit was refused to the judges who had righteously passed sentence on him.

[Asclepas, Paul and Lucius have joined Athanasius and Marcellus at Rome.] . . . They did not defend themselves in the places where they had sinned nor in that vicinity nor where their accusers were, but went among strangers, who lived far from their country and were unacquainted with the truth of what had occurred, and they endeavored to undo a just sentence by referring their conduct to men who knew nothing whatever about them. It was a shrewd course. For they were aware that many of their judges and accusers and witnesses were dead, so they thought that in spite of so many serious condemnations in the past they could obtain a new trial. And they wanted to plead their case before us, who have neither extenuated nor judged them. For the men who once judged them have now departed to the Lord.

12 They wished to compel the eastern bishops to come to them, not as judges but as defendants, not as defendants but as culprits, and that at a time when their own defense was worthless, although in the past they could put up no defense at all when their accusers confuted them face to face. They planned to introduce a new law, that eastern bishops should be tried by western bishops. And they maintained that the judgment of the Church could be delivered by men who were distressed not so much over them as over their own conduct. . . .

14 Thus Athanasius, travelling into Italy and Gaul, arranged a trial for himself, several of his accusers, witnesses and judges being dead, and he believed that he could procure a second hearing, because the long passage of time was dimming the memory of his outrages. And Julius, bishop of the city of Rome, Maximin and Hosius and many others of their party gave him their iniquitous support and secured from the benevolent emperor the convocation of a council at Sardica. We ourselves went to Sardica at the emperor's letter of summons. And when we arrived there, we discovered Athanasius, Marcellus and all those evildoers, who had been excommunicated by sentence of the council and deservedly condemned every man for his crimes, sitting in the midst of the church with Hosius and Protogenes and

conversing with them and — what was worse, — celebrating the divine mysteries. . . .

15 But we, who uphold the discipline of the rule of the Church and desire to give a little aid to the unfortunate,[153] bade the adherents of Protogenes and Hosius expel the condemned men from their company and not hold communion with sinners, but join with us and listen to the sentence that had been passed by our fathers against them aforetime. For the book of Marcellus did not require an accusation and he made himself out openly a heretic. And we urged them to put no trust in these men's false assertions, for they were each one concealing his own depravity, in order to regain his office of bishop. But they resented our words, on what ground we do not know. And they would not withdraw from communion with these men but approved the sect of the heretic Marcellus and set the criminal Athanasius and the other transgressors above the faith and peace of the Church.

16 On hearing and seeing this, we eighty bishops, who had come by long journeying and much hardship to Sardica from divers remote provinces, in order to establish the peace of the Church, could not bear it without tears. For it was not a light matter that they absolutely refused to exclude from their number men whom our fathers had justly condemned in the past for their offenses We considered it wicked to commune with them nor would we share the Lord's holy sacraments with profane persons, for we guard and keep the rule of ecclesiastical discipline. . . .

17 However, we again and again besought them not to shatter what had been firmly established, nor to overturn the law, nor to break the divine mandates, nor to throw everything into confusion, nor to make the Church's tradition of no effect in even a small particular, nor to introduce

153 The text is obscure. If the rendering here is correct, the eastern bishops seem to mean that they considered the adherents of Protogenes and Hosius as unfortunates, who needed aid.

a new sect, nor to set men from the West in any way above the bishops of the East and above the holy councils. . . . But . . . they proposed to erect a court of so great authority that they might call themselves judges of the judges and might reverse, if that is allowable, the verdict of them who are now with God. . . .

18 [The eastern bishops have suggested sending commissioners from both sides to gather evidence on Athanasius in Egypt, whichever side is proved thereby to have been in error to accept its defeat without making a complaint "to emperor or council or any bishop." But the Westerners have refused. Meanwhile all kinds of miscreants are pouring into Sardica, and Hosius and Protogenes are taking them into their "conventicle."] We have refused absolutely to commune with them until they expel the men whom we have condemned and pay due respect to the council of the East. [Since then, the western bishops have tried to throw the blame of the schism on the eastern party but on themselves it certainly belongs. The eastern bishops condemn again Athanasius, Marcellus and their associates.]

26 . . . So they attempted to introduce this novelty, abhorrent to the ancient practice of the Church, that whatever eastern bishops chance to decree in council may be reversed by western bishops and, similarly, whatever the bishops of the West ordain may be annulled by those of the East. But this notion they derived from their own depraved minds. The proceedings of our ancestors show that the decrees of every council that is justly and legally conducted should be approved. For the council that was held in the city of Rome in the days of the heretics Novatus and Sabellius and Valentine [154] was confirmed by the eastern church and, again, the decision of the East in the time of Paul of Samosata was ratified by everyone. . . .

[154] Note the anachronism. On the periods of these men *vide supra*, pp. 258, 305, 382.

27 . . . Wherefore, our whole council has condemned Julius of the city of Rome, Hosius and Protogenes and Gaudentius and Maximin of Trier, in accordance with ancient law, . . . Julius, of the city of Rome, as the chief and leader of evildoers, because he was the first to open the door of communion to condemned criminals and led the way for others to overthrow the divine laws and defended Athanasius presumptuously and audaciously, without knowing either the man's witnesses or his accusers. . . . [End with a creed and the signatures of seventy-three bishops.]

Council of Sardica, *Letter to Julius of Rome*, contained in Hilary, *Fragmenta Historica*, Series B, II, 2–4. Text. *Corpus Scriptorum Ecclesiasticorum Latinorum*, LXV, 126–139.[155]

1 (Address wanting.) What we have always believed that we now know, for experience is proving and confirming for each of us what he has heard with his ears. It is true what the Apostle Paul, the most blessed teacher of the Gentiles, said of himself: "Do ye seek a proof of him who speaks in me, even Christ?"[156] For, since the Lord Christ dwelt in him, there could be no doubt that the Spirit spoke through his soul and animated the instrument of his body. And thus you, dearly beloved brother, though distant in body, have been with us in unison of mind and will. The reason for your absence was both honorable and imperative, that the schismatic wolves might not rob and plunder by stealth nor the heretical dogs bark wildly in rabid fury nor the very serpent, the devil, discharge his blasphemous venom. So it seems to us right and altogether fitting that

155 The authenticity of this letter has been sometimes questioned. See the discussion in C. J. Hefele, *Histoire des Conciles*, Vol. I, Pt. II, p. 810, n. 2. It, like the preceding, was undoubtedly written originally in Greek. We have only the Latin translations.

156 II Corinthians, XIII, 3.

the priests of the Lord from each and every province should report to their head, that is, to the See of Peter, the apostle.[157]

2 But inasmuch as our written reports contain every event and transaction and resolution of ours and as the voices of our dear brothers and fellow priests, Archydamus and Philoxenus, and of our dear son Leo, the deacon,[158] can describe them to you accurately and faithfully, it seems almost superfluous to rehearse these same things in this letter. It has been clear to everyone that those who came here from the East, who call themselves bishops, although some of their leaders have impious minds, tainted by the baleful poison of the heresy of Arius, have long been raising cowardly objections and out of distrust refusing to appear for trial and abjuring communion with you and us, although our communion is blameless, for we have believed in the testimony of more than eighty bishops together as to the innocence of Athanasius.[159] But when these others were summoned by your priests and your letter to the council which was to be held at Rome, they would not come. And it was exceedingly unjust for them to condemn Marcellus and Athanasius and to deny them fellowship in the face of the testimony of so many bishops.

3 There were three subjects for us to discuss. For our devout emperors themselves gave us permission to debate thoroughly everything under dispute and first of all, the holy faith and sound truth, which are being assailed. . . . [We have examined the charges brought by the eastern bishops against the deposed men and also the charges and

[157] The Latin of this letter is unusually crabbed and clumsy. The text of the foregoing sentence runs as follows: " Hoc enim optimum et valde congruentissimum esse videbitur, si ad caput, id est ad Petri apostoli sedem, de singulis quibusque provinciis Domini referant sacerdotes."

[158] These are the three delegates whom Julius sent to Sardica to represent him. It will be noticed that Philoxenus was one of the two priests who had earlier gone to Antioch with the summons to Rome. *Supra,* p. 503.

[159] Julius evidently sent to Sardica the letter from the Egyptian bishops, vindicating Athanasius, which had previously come to him. *Supra,* p. 503.

complaints against the eastern bishops themselves. Ursacius and Valens are especially culpable.] When you read our report to the most blessed Augusti, you will easily see that we have covered everything to the best of our ability. And, not to make the narrative long and tedious, we have indicated who were the perpetrators and what were their acts.

5 You, then, in your excellent wisdom, should provide that our brethren in Sicily, Sardinia and Italy may learn by a communication from you[160] what has been done and decreed, that they may not accept in ignorance letters of communion or certificates from men who have been degraded by a just verdict. Let Marcellus, Athanasius and Asclepas also continue in communion with us, for no one could hold against them their unrighteous trial nor the flight and cowardly behavior of the men who have refused to come to trial before the congregation of us bishops who have assembled here. Everything else, as we have said, your sympathy will learn from the full descriptions of the brethren whom you sent to us in your earnestness and love. We have appended here the names of those whom we have deposed for their crimes, that your high excellency may know who are to be debarred from communion. Do you, as we have already requested, deign to warn by letter all our brethren and fellow bishops not to receive their certificates, that is, their letters of communion. . . .

[The names of the excommunicated and, following them, of fifty-nine signatory bishops, headed by " Hosius, the Cordovan, from Spain."]

[160] This seems to contemplate that Julius should write only to the churches within his metropolitan jurisdiction. *Supra*, p. 485, n. 92. Compare this with the corresponding request made by the Council of Arles, *supra*, p. 481.

3. The Triumph of Rome

Socrates, *Historia Ecclesiastica*, II, 23. Text. J. P. Migne, *Patrologia Graeca*, LXVII, 249–256.

[Constans, on hearing what had happened at Sardica, sent word to his brother Constantius to restore Athanasius to his see on pain of war. Constantius took counsel with his own bishops, who said it was better to restore Athanasius than to have civil war. Constantius then summoned Athanasius in three letters to return.] Athanasius received these letters in Aquileia, where he was stopping on his return from Sardica, and hurried straightway to Rome.[161] And he showed the letters to the bishop Julius and brought great joy to the church of the Romans. For they thought that the emperor of the East was approving of their faith, because he was summoning Athanasius to him.

And Julius sent the following letter concerning Athanasius to the clergy and people of Alexandria.

" Julius, the bishop, to his beloved brethren, the priests and deacons and people of Alexandria, greeting in the Lord.[162]

I congratulate you, brethren beloved, because you behold now before your eyes the fruit of your faith. For, indeed, anyone may see that this has appeared in the person of Athanasius, my brother and fellow bishop, whom God is giving back to you for the purity of his own life and your prayers. . . . There is no need that I should write to you at length, for your own faith has anticipated all that I might have said to you and, by the grace of Christ, the one common desire of all your prayers has been fulfilled. Therefore,

[161] Athanasius, in his *Apologia*, 51, says: " When I received these letters, I went to Rome, to bid farewell to the church and the bishop." He seems, however, to have gone first to see Constans. The meeting of eastern and western bishops at Milan is omitted from these accounts. *Supra*, p. 500 and n. 112.

[162] This letter is also given by Athanasius, *Apologia*, 52–53. The opening salutation there is simply, " Julius, to the priests and deacons and people of Alexandria."

I congratulate you and again I repeat it, because you have kept your souls invincible in the faith. And my brother Athanasius I congratulate no less, because, although he has suffered much hardship, he has never for an hour forgotten your love and your longing for him. Although he has seemed for a time divided from you in the body, still in the spirit he has always lived as if present in your company. And I, beloved, believe that all the trials which he has undergone have not been inglorious. For both your own and his faith have become known and admired by everyone. . . .

Receive, therefore, beloved brethren, with all glory to God and rejoicing, your bishop Athanasius and those who have been his comrades in his tribulations. And be glad for the satisfaction of your prayers, you who by your saving letters have furnished meat and drink to your shepherd, who, so to speak, has hungered and thirsted for your devotion. . . .

It is right to close my letter with a prayer. May Almighty God and his Son, our Lord and Savior Jesus Christ, grant you his grace forever in recompense for your marvellous faith, which you displayed in glorious testimony for your bishop, that for you and those who come after you, here and hereafter, the better things may abide which eye hath not seen nor ear heard nor have they entered into the heart of man, which God hath prepared for them who love him, through our Lord Jesus Christ, in whom to God Almighty be glory forever and ever. Amen. I bid you, beloved brethren, farewell."

Athanasius, *Apologia contra Arianos,* 58. Text. J. P. Migne, *Patrologia Graeca,* XXV, 353–354.

[Through the influence of Julius and the emperor Constans, Athanasius returned in safety to his church at Alexandria.] On learning this, Ursacius and Valens condemned themselves for their past behavior and came to Rome and made their confession contritely and entreated pardon and wrote to Julius, the bishop of old Rome, and to me [Athanasius] as follows. The copies of their letters were sent to me by Paulinus, bishop of Trier.[163]

Ursacius and Valens, *Confession,* contained in Hilary, *Fragmenta Historica,* Series B, II, 6, 8. Text. *Corpus Scriptorum Ecclesiasticorum Latinorum,* LXV, 143–145.

A copy of the letter which, after the eastern bishops [at Jerusalem][164] had declared that Athanasius was not guilty, Valens wrote in the city of Rome with his own hand and to which Ursacius added his signature.

" Ursacius and Valens to their lord, the most blessed pope Julius.

Whereas it is well known that we have in time past brought many heinous charges by letter against the name of Bishop Athanasius, and whereas when we were summoned to an assembly by letters from your holiness, we presented no ground for the accusations we had made, we do now confess before your holiness, in the presence of all the priests, our brethren, that all the reports that have in the past come to your ears regarding the aforesaid Athanasius are falsehoods of our own fabrication and devoid of all foundation, and that we, therefore, eagerly desire to have communion with the aforesaid Athanasius, especially now that your holiness with your characteristic clemency has seen fit to pardon our wrongdoing. We declare also that if ever the eastern bishops or Athanasius himself attempts in vengeance to bring us to trial, we will not go to them without your knowledge. And with this our hand with which we have

[163] Athanasius' text of the following letters is translated from the Latin into Greek. Our text is taken from the original Latin, as found in Hilary's collection of *Fragmenta.*

[164] *Supra,* p. 501.

written, we do affirm that we have anathematized now and forever the heretic Arius and his satellites, who say: " There was a time when the Son was not," and who say that the Son was created out of nothing and who deny that the Son of God existed before all ages, as also we have stated in our former declaration which we presented at Milan. And we repeat that we have, as we said, condemned the heresy of Arius and its authors to eternity."

Then, in the hand of Ursacius: " I, Bishop Ursacius, have signed this our confession." . . .

" Ursacius and Valens to their lord and brother, Athanasius.

An opportunity has arisen of sending to you through our brother and fellow priest, Moyses, who is going to your charity, brother beloved. Through him we salute you most heartily from Aquileia and hope that you are in good health and will read our letter. You will give us a pledge of confidence also, if you will return us some reply in writing. For by this letter we notify you that we are at peace with you and in communion with the Church. The mercy of God preserve you, brother." [165]

Athanasius, *Historia Arianorum,* 29. Text. J. P. Migne, *Patrologia Graeca,* XXV, 725.

[After an interval of acquiescence and the death of Constans, the Arians began agitation again.] First of all, they persuaded Ursacius and Valens to change once more and like dogs to return to their vomit and like swine to wallow again in the former mire of their impiety. So they invented a reason for their previous repentance, that they had done it in dread of the godfearing Constans. . . . But not a soldier was present [at their recantation in Rome],

[165] To appreciate the prestige of Julius at this time, the reader should mark the contrast in tone between these two letters, the humble, abject apology to him, the perfunctory, almost nonchalant note to the injured bishop of Alexandria.

no palatine nor notary had been sent, as they are now, nor was the emperor himself there nor had they been summoned by any one, when they indited their confession. But they went voluntarily to Rome, of their own accord, and in the church, where there was no fear from without and the only fear was of God and every man had freedom of choice, they spontaneously repented and wrote their confession.

LIBERIUS

(352–366)

We have already drawn attention to the fact that Constantine, after announcing his decision to elevate Christianity to the level of a legitimate cult, approved by the State, had assumed at once, ex officio, as a matter of course, the position of chief arbiter in the conduct of the Christian organization and had treated its officials, the bishops, as members of a new branch of his state department of religions, accountable from now on to him as well as to God. It was not so much, indeed, that the Church itself changed character or became secularized, although with Constantine's gifts it did begin a rapid accumulation of lands and wealth, as that the government now ranged itself around and behind the Church and acted as a strong arm for enforcing the policies of its leaders. In addition, the emperor took on himself the functions of supreme ecclesiastical executive and judge, vigorously applying the Church's laws in the way that seemed best to him and furnishing willy-nilly to the scattered episcopate the political impetus and unifying energy which until now it had mostly lacked, in spite of earlier, ambitious efforts on the part of the Roman See to set up a centralised administration. Eusebius undoubtedly had something of this change in mind when he called Constantine a "general bishop."[166] Constans, his father's successor in the countries of Europe and West Africa, mixed far less in church business, preferring that the bishops should manage alone all ordinary religious concerns and work out their dogmatic disputes without his assistance. But at a time of crisis, an unusual enter-

[166] *Supra*, p. 476.

prise, such as a general council, might be instigated by him and must have his sanction before it could meet or hold free discussion. In the heresy-ridden provinces of Africa, he sent troops against the Donatists. And when it appeared that the integrity of the orthodox communion was menaced by flagrant injustice in the East, he threatened his brother's dominions with invasion if they persisted in violating the plain rules of ecclesiastical tradition. When he died, the church of the West had known only the advantages of a state connection, the strength, the wealth and the prestige to be derived from it.

Under Constantius, however, the brother of Constans and the last surviving son of Constantine, the West was to learn what could happen under such a system when an emperor professed an alien brand of Christianity and felt called upon to vindicate it in high places. Constantius, as we have said, had been a convinced Arian since the first years of his reign in the East. The superior might of his brother Constans had compelled him to accept, for the time being, the reversal of the sentence of his bishops against Athanasius, the eastern personification of Nicene orthodoxy, and to permit, even to urge Athanasius to return to Alexandria. But one of the first uses that he made of his conquest of Gaul, after Magnentius' death, was to require its church to ratify the verdict of the Council of Tyre by which Athanasius had been first deposed.[167]

The winter of 353–354 he spent at Arles and sent out summons to the Gallic bishops to attend him there. The Pannonian Valens, who had so promptly made his peace with the eastern Eusebians, was conspicuous in his train. The bishops of Trier, Cologne and Lyons, who had been employed by Julius in his negotiations with the Eusebians and who would have understood the gravity of the situation now, were either dead or too infirm to appear. The mass of their colleagues knew little or nothing of the deeper dogmatic issues that underlay the specific proposition made to them. Hilary of Poitiers, an eager student of whatever church literature could be found in his province, had never heard the creed of Nicaea before that winter. The older, simpler baptismal for-

[167] *Supra*, p. 475.

mulas still sufficed for the needs of the western provincial churches. Under such circumstances, these unsophisticated prelates were told of an enigmatical and obnoxious troublemaker, whom their emperor, the son of the great Constantine, asked them to condemn, as their eastern brethren apparently had already done. What Athanasius stood for was quite unintelligible. Why should they not testify to their loyalty to Constantius and their desire for peace in all the churches by signifying their disapprobation of discord?

At Rome, however, the new bishop Liberius was fully awake to the larger implications of the question at stake. During his first year of office, 352–353, while Constantius' attention was still absorbed by his campaign against Magnentius, Liberius had received certain test letters from the eastern bishops, inquiring whether, in view of the altered situation, he would now revoke the acts of his predecessor, Julius, and assent to their condemnation of Athanasius. But he was nobly resolved to be neither beguiled nor intimidated. He read the letters to a synod of his local bishops and wrote in reply that he could not accept accusations that had since been so thoroughly disproved. Soon afterward, he welcomed a deputation of Egyptian bishops who brought copies of a formal appeal of the Egyptian episcopate against any further persecution of their metropolitan. Late in the year, as reports began to come in of the doings in Gaul, he selected two Italians, Vincent, bishop of Capua, who as a priest had been at Nicaea, and one Marcellus of Campania, to carry a letter to Constantius, asking him to call a general council of the Church at some point in Italy and allow it to decide all religious problems that still lay in dispute. A council was the best possible approach to a genuine organ of ecclesiastical opinion and no emperor had as yet refused to summon one upon request. But when Vincent and Marcellus arrived at Arles, they found that the wishes of the Roman bishop counted for nothing in the general flood of enthusiasm for the son of Constantine and harmony. They were themselves before long swept off their feet and signed the document confirming Athanasius' excommunication. In vain, they feebly stipulated that the Easterners present should join the West in condemning Arius. No one heeded them. Of all the bishops who came together that year, only Paulinus, the successor of Maximin of Trier, who had perhaps himself known Athanasius during his exile, persisted in refusal to disown him and was sent by Constantius into banishment.

Liberius at Rome heard of the defalcation of his envoys but received no answer from his letter to the emperor. Instead, an imperial proclamation was posted up in the city in which he was named as an obstinate and ambitious promoter of dissension. He perceived that the turn of himself and Italy would not be long delayed and spent the interval in anxious endeavors to fortify his clergy to meet the trial that impended.[167a] To Hosius of Cordova he wrote, describing his disappointment at the lapse of Vincent and Marcellus and his own solemn determination to die rather than prove traitor. Finally, in the spring of 355, as Constantius moved eastward and established himself at Milan and it was clear that Italy's day of reckoning had arrived, Liberius sent a second letter to the emperor, explaining in moving terms his own position and the obligation that rested on him to guard unstained the faith of the apostles that had passed down through the long line of his predecessors and pleading again for a council to uphold the doctrine approved at Nicaea in the presence of Constantius' father "of holy memory." He picked his messengers this time with special care, Lucifer, bishop of Cagliari in Sardinia, who had himself offered to expostulate with the emperor, a priest, Pancratius, and a deacon, Hilary, men who, he believed, might be trusted to resist both blandishments and threats. Events proved that he chose well. He wrote also three letters to Eusebius, bishop of Vercellae in Piedmont, asking that he would stand beside them when they came into the imperial presence.

Soon after their arrival in Milan, the bishops of all Italy were convened there by Constantius' order to act upon the state of the Church. This was not, however, the general council for which Liberius had asked, that was to meet without constraint, away from the seat of government,[167b] but a synod of Italians only,

[167a] We possess a sentence from his letter to the bishop of Spoleto. "I trust that Vincent's act will not deter you from your good resolution, dearest brother." Hilary, *Fragmenta Historica,* Series B, VI, 3–4.

[167b] *Infra,* p. 570.

collected uneasily in the chancel of a church close to the palace. Eusebius himself was slow to appear and special envoys were sent by the synod and the emperor to summon him to join in the movement for unity and ecclesiastical discipline against "the sacrilegious Athanasius."[168] The Roman delegates also wrote, begging him to come as the blessed apostles did to destroy Simon Magus. But for ten days after his arrival in Milan he and the Romans were excluded from the assembly. When finally they were admitted, they proposed that every bishop present sign, first of all, the creed of Nicaea as a safeguard against heresy. But Valens snatched up the paper on which the creed was inscribed, the discussion grew stormy and the laity gathered in the church nave cried out against the Arians. At length, a proclamation from the emperor transferred the place of meeting from the church to a hall inside the palace. There Constantius himself, with his hand on his sword, sternly tendered them all their choice between signing the condemnation of Athanasius and exile. To their pleas on behalf of the canons he retorted that they should take his will for a canon, as the Syrian bishops did, and refused to listen to their protest against a government that overthrew the rules of the Church. One by one they capitulated, as the Gauls had done, persuading themselves, perhaps, that they were merely consenting to the removal of a perennial source of difficulties and doing nothing that impaired their own orthodoxy. Only a few, including Lucifer, Eusebius and Dionysius of Milan, denounced to the emperor's face the injustice of condemning an absent bishop on the bare word of an accuser, even though that accuser were the emperor himself. These men were dispatched instantly into exile and one Auxentius, a Cappadocian priest in Constantius' retinue, ignorant of Latin,[169] was brought forward and ordained bishop of Milan in Dionysius' place.[170]

168 Letters of the Council of Milan and of Constantius to Eusebius of Vercellae. J. Harduin, *Acta Conciliorum et Epistolae Decretales* (12 vols., Paris, 1714–1715), Vol. I, pp. 697–700.

169 Athanasius, *Historia Arianorum,* 75.

170 Maximus, bishop of Naples, died in exile. Rufinianus, another Italian bishop, was compelled by the Arian Epictetus to run before his chariot until he burst a blood vessel and fell dead. Drops of his blood were used afterwards to sprinkle persons possessed by devils. *Faustini et Marcellini Preces,* 26. Hilary, the Roman deacon, was scourged before he was exiled, as an extra penalty for carrying Liberius' letter. Athanasius, *Historia Arianorum,* 41.

Thus the episcopate of Italy was prevailed upon to forsake its old comrade in arms in Egypt. There still remained the head of that episcopate, the bishop of the Apostolic See, whose representatives had all preferred banishment to betrayal of the man or the cause of which he was the emblem. When the news of their fate reached Liberius, he sent them an excited letter of praise, regretting only that he had not been before them in the glory of confession and asking their prayers that the Lord might yet deign to make him their equal. What was Constantius to do with this arch-rebel? The position of the See of Rome, its hold upon the people of the city and of Italy, was such by this time that even the emperor realized he must act circumspectly and avoid provoking a riot that might assume alarming proportions. The selections which we give below recount the various vain attempts of imperial officers to bribe, cajole and terrify Liberius and the final furtive kidnapping of him by night that the populace might not be aroused. We have also a memorandum of an interview that is said to have taken place between Constantius and Liberius upon the latter's appearance in Milan, with courage and spirit still unshaken. The point to which he held fast as regarded Athanasius was the judicial one, that it was impossible without a proper trial to condemn a man who had once been acquitted on conclusive evidence and that if Constantius wished to bring fresh accusations, a fresh court must be constituted to hear and investigate them. Another general council, he repeated, would be the agency best fitted to handle the matter. Such a council was also needed to consult on the state of the faith and maintain all Christians in fidelity to the Fathers of Nicaea, and the exiled bishops should be permitted to return and take part in it. Liberius' plea was, in short, for a revival of the policy of Constans. The outcome was his own departure into exile, to the town of Beroea in Thrace, to reside under the spiritual supervision of Demophilus, the local bishop, a pronounced Arian. A deacon from Rome, named Damasus, went part of the way with him but turned back home again before reaching the destination.

At Rome, the news of Liberius' brave stand against Constantius was received with proud exultation and the city clergy in a public assembly took oath to accept no other man as bishop as long as Liberius lived. Among the most vociferous in the demonstration were the archdeacon Felix and the deacon Damasus, who was present with a description of what he had seen and heard. But the emperor had no intention of leaving so important an office untenanted nor, on the other hand, did he think it prudent to aggravate the people's resentment by imposing upon them an uncomprehending alien, as he had done at Milan. The archdeacon Felix was summoned to court and offered the seat in the Lateran. He succumbed to the splendid bait and became Constantius' nominee for the Roman bishopric. Epictetus, another of Constantius' Arian attendants, who had previously been made bishop of Civita Vecchia, performed the ordination ceremony inside the Lateran walls for fear of a tumult if it were held in a church. Three other bishops, whom Athanasius calls "ill-favored spies," assisted at the rite and three palace eunuchs represented the Christian laity.[171] After his installation, Felix gradually procured the outward submission of the majority of the city priesthood. The government addressed an edict to him on the immunities of the inferior clergy.[172] But the lay population forgot neither the heroism of Liberius nor what it considered the apostasy of Felix. When, in 357, two years after these events, Constantius himself visited Rome, he was beset by noble ladies at the palace and by crowds in the streets and the circus asking for Liberius back again. To some of these petitioners he replied sardonically that they should have their bishop and that they would find him better than when they lost him. For by that time he knew, as they did not, that exile and homesickness and the assiduous labors of Demophilus had been too much for Liberius' morale, that he had by now signed the condemnation of Athanasius and was only waiting for imperial permission to return home.

Even without Liberius, Constantius had obtained what was practically the unanimous consent of the active episcopate of the Empire to the execution of the verdict of Tyre. One more mem-

171 *Infra*, p. 576.
172 *Codex Theodosianus*, XVI, 2, 14.

ber of distinction held out, the man who represented in person the Fathers of Nicaea to the West as Athanasius did to the East, Hosius of Cordova. Immediately after the banishment of Liberius, he too had been called to face Constantius at Milan. We have no account of the interview, simply the statement that Hosius refused to abandon his old friend. Constantius, momentarily impressed, did not punish him but allowed him to return to Spain. The tenor of Hosius' defense may be gathered from the letter which he wrote after his return to the emperor to remonstrate against the abusive and threatening communications that still followed him. This venerable statesman, who in his own lifetime had seen so many varieties of relationship between the civil power and the Church, persecution under Maximin, close, paternal guardianship under Constantine, non-interfering benevolence under Constans, high-handed coercion under Constantius, now addressed to the monarch a plain and positive warning against intervention in any guise whatever in religious affairs.[173] In Hosius' younger days, he himself had helped Constantine to compel the Church to an appearance of peace. In his old age, he preferred to cite the example of Constans, who, at least, had forced no man to subscribe to anything against his will and had never

[173] That same year, 355, or early in 356, Hilary of Poitiers expressed the same idea more briefly in the introduction to his collection of documents intended to expose the evils of Arianism. "I refrain from saying that although the profoundest reverence should be paid to a king, because his kingdom is from God, nevertheless his judgment should not calmly be accepted in episcopal trials, for to Caesar the things of Caesar but to God must be rendered the things that are God's." *Fragmenta Historica,* Series B, I, 5. Hilary may well have seen a copy of Hosius' letter, as Athanasius did who preserves it for us. Athanasius, in his *Arian History,* written during his stay in the Libyan desert between 356 and 362, approached the same position. "For what concern has the emperor with any decision of the bishops? . . . When did an ordinance of the Church derive its force from an emperor or when was his ordinance ever recognized by the Church? There have been many councils held before now and many decrees passed by the Church but our fathers never sought the emperor's approval for them nor did the emperor concern himself with church affairs." *Historia Arianorum,* 52. The argument for church independence based upon historical precedent was, however, certainly more vulnerable than that based upon the principles of Scripture. Athanasius seems to be overlooking certain episodes at Nicaea. *Supra,* pp. 470, 474. The persecuted Donatists were also beginning to say: "What has an emperor to do with the Church?" Optatus, *De Schismate,* III, 3; J. C. Ayer, *Source Book for Ancient Church History,* p. 322. They may even have anticipated Hosius but we know little of their line of argument. Ambrose's famous declaration of ecclesiastical independence did not come until thirty years later. The third century Syrian *Didascalia* had drawn a line of difference between the spheres of civil and religious authority, quoting the text Hosius and Hilary used: "Render unto Caesar," etc. *Supra,* p. 157.

set himself up to judge ecclesiastical doctrine. "God has placed in your hands the Empire," he went on. "To us he has entrusted the administration of his Church. And even as he who would steal the government from you opposes the ordinance of God, so do you fear lest by taking on yourself the conduct of the Church you make yourself guilty of a grave sin." In years to come, a bishop of Rome would write such words as these but Liberius certainly had not dreamed of going so far. He had asked for ecclesiastical autonomy under a friendlier and less arbitrary master. The Spaniard was first to deny that Caesar was master of the Church at all.

But although Constantius had not secured the consent of Hosius, he felt that he had sufficient ecclesiastical warrant to evict Athanasius. In 356, the church in which the latter was celebrating a night vigil was broken into by officers and soldiers, with blasts of trumpets and drawn swords. Many of the worshippers were wounded or killed in the scuffle. Athanasius himself was quickly surrounded by a devoted band of monks and laymen, who smuggled him out into the darkness. For six years, he lived as a vagabond, hiding in the deserts and country places of Egypt. There was no longer at Rome or elsewhere anyone who dared offer him a refuge. The church buildings of Alexandria were handed back to the Arians and a council of about thirty eastern bishops at Antioch ordained one George of Cappadocia to fill Athanasius' place, as seventeen years before, they had ordained Gregory.[174] By means of Constantius, the eastern church had at last vindicated its right to do what it would with its own and the western bishops who had affronted it by reversing its decisions were either cowed or paying the penalty of exile. The year that Athanasius was driven out, a council was called at Béziers by Saturninus, the Arian bishop of Arles, to try two Gallic bishops, Hilary of Poitiers and Rhodanius of Toulouse, who had not come before Constantius and who were now working earnestly to arouse the Gallican church to a sense of what it had done. They were both deposed and banished. Hilary was sent to Asia Minor, where, however, he seized the opportunity to study

[174] *Supra,* p. 491.

the writings of the Greek Fathers, compose his book, *De Trinitate,* and agitate inconspicuously in Phrygia for the faith of Nicaea. The creed in general circulation in the East was one of those drawn up by the Council of Antioch in 341, a vague creed which omitted anything offensive to either party.[175]

In 357, the eastern cause gained its victory over Liberius.[175a] Early in that year, he admitted that the Council of Tyre had been right in condemning Athanasius and formally withdrew from communion with him. He also signed a creed similar to the one of Antioch, which avoided all reference to " substance " and left the position of the Son entirely indefinite. He then wrote to Constantius, to tell him of his submission and request that he and his fellows in exile be now allowed to go back to Italy. He wrote also to Lucifer and Eusebius, to inform them of the step he was taking, and, a few weeks later, to the bishops of the East, to notify them of his adherence to their communion and to beg them to exert their influence at court to bring about his liberation. But for another year, Constantius kept him lingering in suspense, growing more and more nervous as the months passed without bringing the release for which he was paying so dear a price. In late 357 or 358, he wrote two more letters, one to the notorious time-servers, Ursacius and Valens, the other to Vincent of Capua, the bishop whom he had once blamed so severely for failure to endure. These letters betray all too openly the intensity of the strain upon his mind. Those to the Arian bishops are painfully abject, explaining that, after all, peace and concord are preferable to martyrdom, that he has never himself defended Athanasius but has merely not wished to seem disloyal to Julius, that he is now one with them and looks to them to help restore him to the Roman church. The last contains the vague statement, sufficient for Italian consumption, that he has decided to struggle no more over Athanasius and has written to the eastern bishops, and asks Vincent to call an assembly of the bishops of Campania to

[175] *Supra,* p. 494.

[175a] Jerome wrote in after years: "Fortunatianus, an African by nationality, bishop of Aquileia, in the reign of Constantius, . . . has an odious reputation, because he was the first to tempt and break the resolution of Liberius, bishop of Rome, on his way to exile for the faith, and to bring him to subscribe to heresy." *De Viris Illustribus,* 97.

entreat the emperor to let him return. "If you wish me to die in exile, you will see; God will be judge between me and you!" These last words are added abruptly in a postscript, the irascible, suspicious outcry of a man in mental torment.

But while Liberius was being thus fast reduced to a state of spiritual collapse, Constantius decided to make one more assault upon Hosius. In the autumn of 357, the old man, nearly a centenarian, was ordered to come from Spain, in company with other western bishops, to Sirmium in Thrace, where the emperor was holding court and Liberius was waiting in misery. Pressure, more or less heavy, was applied to Hosius. He is said even to have been tortured, until his mind was dazed. At length, he yielded far enough to sign a creed, the boldest which the extreme wing of the Arians had yet formulated, repudiating explicitly the Nicene standard, forbidding future mention of "substance," and declaring in so many words that the Son was subordinate to the Father.[176] Yet, although Hosius in his weakness recanted on a matter of dogma, nothing could make him put his signature to the paper condemning Athanasius. He might perforce be counted hereafter among the Arians but not among Athanasius' enemies. He was set free when it was plain that nothing more could be wrung from him and went back to Cordova to die a year or two later.

Then, at last, in the summer of 358, Liberius was asked by the eastern bishops at Sirmium to sign one more creed, similar in tone to the one he had signed a year earlier and less heterodox than that which had been foisted upon Hosius. This done, he was set at liberty with a letter from the bishops to Felix and the Roman clergy, asking them to receive him again and bury all dissension. Not without reason was the charge inserted to keep the peace. For Liberius was returning to a see already occupied for nearly three years by the imperially nominated usurper Felix and to a church divided between those who had drifted with the Arian tide and those who had scorned and held aloof from it. The problem of which man had actually the right to the bishopric appeared puzzling. The government directed

176 A translation of this creed is in J. C. Ayer, *Source Book for Ancient Church History*, pp. 316–318. It is known as the Second of Sirmium.

them both to act as bishops in concert, regardless of the fundamental rule of catholic organization, that there could not be two heads of the Church in the same city, and of the insuperable, practical obstacles to harmony that were sure to arise between two parties, one of which felt that the other had bought safety at the price of cowardice and treachery.[177]

The accounts of the situation are somewhat confused but make sufficiently clear the fact that the city as a whole welcomed enthusiastically the news of Liberius' return, hardly realizing that he no longer deserved to be hailed as a hero, and that it hooted the idea of a dual bishopric. "A bishop for each party in the circus!" the crowds shouted in derision. Liberius seems to have hesitated a while before entering the gates, not knowing, perhaps, where to go as long as Felix occupied the Lateran. But the people solved the dilemma for him by driving Felix out and away in humiliation. Liberius made a triumphal entry and thenceforth held the post of bishop alone to all intents and purposes. Felix, after one futile effort to recover at least the basilica of Julius, resigned himself to living in innocuous retirement on an estate between Rome and Portus, although he retained his episcopal title and a group of adherents who preferred him to Liberius. Outside of Rome, neither one for the time being had much moral influence. Felix was known to be Constantius' creature. Liberius' apostasy in Thrace was not widely noised abroad but it was, of course, obvious that he could not have returned without some compromise with the imperial party. For several years to come there is no further mention of him in history.

But although Athanasius was gone and the church in the West was manned with bishops who, on that point, had yielded to the emperor, there was still no unanimity about the creed. Many had condemned the unknown Alexandrian without once suspecting his connection with their own traditional orthodoxy. In the East meanwhile, among those who disapproved of the "homoousios" a cleavage was growing up. On the one hand were those

[177] It is noteworthy that even the papal historians seem to have felt that Felix had a certain excuse for his position that other early antipopes did not have. He is the only one to be given a place in the official, papal lists. He appears there always as Felix II. The *Liber Pontificalis* makes a hero and martyr out of him. L. R. Loomis, *The Book of the Popes,* 75–79.

cautious conservatives who had always disliked the Nicene phrase as implying a Sabellian failure to distinguish between the Father and the Son but who were satisfied to substitute the word "homoiousios," "like in substance," and intended no disparagement of the Son's divinity. On the other hand was appearing, as at Sirmium, a later and more extreme type of Arian, who insisted that the Son could not even be called "like the Father" but that he was both unlike and unequal, in all respects upon a lower plane. Within the party of these Anomoeans, the "Unlikers," were soon the ubiquitous Ursacius and Valens, who began working upon Constantius to bring about the formal and general repudiation of the Nicene Creed and the adoption, instead, of a creed as radical as the one which they had forced upon Hosius. Certain of the conservatives or so-called semi-Arians began thereupon to suspect that in essentials they were, after all, nearer to the Nicene West than to this disturbing form of Arianism and that "same in substance" and "like in substance" were not so far apart as "unlike" and "like." The small orthodox or Nicene party in the East, including the exiles, Hilary of Poitiers in Asia Minor and Athanasius in Egypt, saw the immense advantage that would accrue from a rapprochement between these sober-minded semi-Arians and the church of the West and began publicly teaching the practical equivalence of "homoousios" and "homoiousios."[178] One of the semi-Arians, Basil, bishop of Ancyra, was able to secure the consent of Constantius, in an unguarded moment, to the summons of a general council to discuss the creed, expecting that in such a gathering the western bishops would join with the eastern "Homoiousians" and that together they could overwhelmingly defeat the Anomoeans.

The latter, however, were not to be trapped so easily. They quickly sent two of their own bishops to Constantius and convinced him that it would be too difficult and expensive to transport

[178] See, for example, Hilary, *De Synodis*, 11. "Men who accept everything that was endorsed at Nicaea but yet have scruples over the word 'homoousios' should not be treated as foes. I do not resist them as wild Arians nor as enemies of the faith of the Fathers. I discuss questions with them, as a brother with brothers who think as we do and disagree upon only one word." This and more are translated in J. C. Ayer, *Source Book for Ancient Church History*, pp. 319–320. See also Athanasius, *De Synodis*, 41.

so many men from the West to the East, that the difference in language would inevitably be a bar to satisfactory discussion, and that for these reasons it would be wiser to split the council and hold the western section by itself in Rimini and the eastern in Seleucia, in southern Asia Minor. They did not, however, prevent the appointment of Marcus of Arethusa, who occupied a vacillating position between the opposing factions, to draw up a formula for the emperor to present to the two assemblages to sign. Neither set of bishops was to have any say as to the creed it would endorse. They were both to be instructed to sign what was offered them, transact any other business they might have and then send each a delegation of ten out of their number to meet Constantius at Constantinople and sign together their final profession of obedience to him and agreement with one another. The creed, hereafter known as that of Rimini, displeased the Anomoeans, for it contained twice over the phrase likening the Son to the Father; but it also offended the consciences of the two wings of the eastern and western churches that we may here classify roughly together as orthodox, by its condemnation of any reference to "substance," as a cause of scandal to the people.[179]

In July, 359, nearly four hundred western bishops met, as commanded, at Rimini. No one appeared to represent the divided See of Rome.[180] Restitutus, bishop of Carthage, was the outstanding figure at the head of the great majority who wished to be loyal to the orthodox doctrine of the past. They promptly protested against the imperial formula as well as against any other criticism of the creed of Nicaea, excommunicated Ursacius and Valens and two others, who came as bearers of Constantius' instructions, and sent a deputation to the emperor to explain the impossibility of fulfilling his demands. But at court, the envoys were caught in the usual iron pressure, until one by one they rescinded in their

[179] J. C. Ayer, *Source Book for Ancient Church History*, pp. 318–319.

[180] The first letter which the council sent by its ten deputies to the emperor contained an allusion to the confusion which the policy of the Arians had produced in the church at Rome. Hilary, *Fragmenta Historica*, Series A, V, 1, 2. A synod of Damasus writing in after years to the bishops of Illyria, who were inclined to stand by the creed of Rimini, made a point of the absence of Rome. "Nor can any weight be attached to the size of the meeting at Rimini, since it is well known that neither the Roman bishop, whose judgment should have been consulted first of all, nor Vincent [of Capua], . . . nor the rest had agreed to it." Theodoret, *Historia Ecclesiastica*, II, 17; *infra*, p. 635.

own names the acts of the body which had sent them. Thereupon, they were sent back to Rimini with directions to the praetorian prefect to allow no bishop to leave the city until all had signed the formula that had been presented them.[181] Weeks passed in dull confinement. Some of the more ignorant prelates were deluded into thinking that to deny "homoousios" was different from denying Christ. At last, for utter weariness the rest also signed in order to go free.[182] Ten delegates, led by Ursacius and Valens, were dispatched to Constantinople, carrying their submission. They met there the envoys just arrived from the eastern orthodox sympathizers at Seleucia, looking eagerly for western reinforcement in the resistance they planned to make against coercion. To the dismay of these Easterners and to Hilary's total consternation, the western bishops kept sullenly to themselves and merely displayed the proofs of their debasement. Nothing seemed left for anyone but to join the synod that was called at the capital in January, 360, under the eye of Constantius, and sign the same creed. Not only Athanasius but also the council and faith of the Fathers had been abandoned by the entire Church. As Jerome said regarding the outcome of these gatherings, which had been started with so different an aim, "The whole world groaned and was amazed to find itself Arian." [183] Not only were the bishops at Constantinople required to sign the new creed but copies of it were sent about from see to see and a man who refused to sign ran the risk of deposition and exile. Never had the spirit of the Church seemed more thoroughly quelled.

A few indomitable individuals could not be silenced. Hilary of Poitiers, at the request of the Arians themselves, was commanded, as "a sower of discord and a disturber of the East," [184]

[181] Constantius himself sent a peremptory letter to the assembly, telling them it was no business of theirs to pass judgment on eastern bishops. They had only to decide their own faith. Hilary, *Fragmenta Historica,* Series A, VIII, 1–2.

[182] See the dreary tone of the letter sent by the council to Constantius, when they had obeyed and foresworn the "substance" or "ousia" and now only longed to go home. Hilary, *op. cit.,* Series A, VI, 1.

[183] *Contra Luciferianos,* 19.

[184] Sulpicius Severus, *Chronica,* II, 45, 4. Hilary could be audacious. See his second address to Constantius, composed before he left Constantinople, which contained passages like the following: "What transformations has faith passed through, even in the past year? First, a creed that permits no mention of

to leave his exile in Asia Minor and go home to Gaul, where at least he would be less in evidence. On his reappearance in the West, he set once more unostentatiously to work, preaching, writing, arguing for the faith of the Nicene Fathers and of the apostle Peter. From the occupant of the Roman See personally he seems to have expected and received no assistance. But, as he pointed out, all who had compromised with Arianism had been untrue to the faith of that disciple who, by confessing Christ as the Son of the living God, had won the power to bind and loose in earth and heaven. They had strayed from the sacred leadership of Peter and Paul, and had bowed to the strength of the world and of error. Without a mention of the contemporary bishop of Rome, he revived the memory of the great founder of the Roman See and made his confession synonymous with the doctrine to which Rome had so long been conspicuously loyal. He summoned the church of the West in effect to return not only to Nicaea but also to ideal and apostolic Rome. Bishops who had signed at Rimini in weakness or lack of comprehension were stirred to remorse.

The election of Julian as emperor, that same year, by the Gallic troops, mitigated, of course, a little the dread of Constantius' anger. While Julian was marshalling his armies to lead against the East, a council of Gallic bishops met at Paris which reaffirmed the creed of Nicaea, deposed the stubborn Arian Saturninus and ordained that all who at Rimini had denied the rightful faith under constraint, might continue in office upon a repudiation of their signatures to that heterodox formula and a declaration of allegiance to Nicaea.

In November, 361, Constantius died on his way to do battle with Julian and by his death the situation in the Church was again completely transformed. Julian at once issued an edict permitting the return of all bishops whom Constantius had banished and the worship of God by any mode whatever. The

---

'homoousios'; following that again, one that acknowledges and proclaims 'homoousios'; then, a third that indulgently concedes the simple 'substance' (ousia) as assumed by the fathers; finally, a fourth that does not concede but condemns it. And where then have we arrived? Where nothing of our own nor of anyone else before us remains for the future sacred and inviolable." *Liber ad Constantium Imperatorem,* II, 5.

measure may have been dictated by his philosophic breadth of mind, or, as Ammianus says, by a malevolent notion that the Christians, if let loose from restrictions, would extirpate one another, " no savage beasts " being " more ferocious than Christians to each other." [185] At all events, it released the Church in many places from a hated situation and allowed it to spring back into a more normal way of life. In Alexandria, the people rose spontaneously against George of Cappadocia, whom they had endured as bishop since 356, threw him into prison and then killed him and Athanasius returned, for the third time, to his see. A council, held by him at Alexandria soon afterward, arranged for the rehabilitation of all bishops who had lapsed upon a simple affirmation of allegiance to Nicaea, and for the reconciliation of the old, orthodox " Homoousians " with the conservative wing of the " Homoiousians " on the understanding that the two terms should be interpreted as equivalent and that, to guard against Sabellianism, the Godhead might be henceforth described as a Trinity within a Unity, three " persons " in one eternal " substance." [186]

In the parts of Asia where Arian theology had always had its chief following there was still some bitter division. At Antioch, four parties claimed the see and maintained a bishop, the extreme Anomoeans, the old style Arians or Eusebians, who saw no objection to the creed of Rimini and who composed the official church in possession of the great, new cathedral, and two sections of orthodox, the one headed by Paulinus, who disapproved of Athanasius' concessions to the " Homoiousians " and preferred the pure, unalloyed, Nicene " homoousios " with no strange, new qualifications as to persons, the other by Meletius, who had been himself a " Homoiousian " and now championed the creed of Nicaea with interpretations like those added at Alexandria.

In the West, Liberius broke the silence of four years and resumed the old, dignified tone of leadership as if there had been

185 Ammianus Marcellinus, *Res Gestae,* XXII, 5.

186 Extracts from the synodal letter of Athanasius' council of 362, addressed to the Meletian party at Antioch, are in J. C. Ayer, *Source Book for Ancient Church History,* pp. 349–352. Western theologians of the third century, Tertullian and Novatian, had spoken of the three persons as " tres personae." The Easterners had used the term " hypostasis " in two senses, of the persons of the Trinity and of the essence in which they were one. For the confusion which this caused later, *vide infra,* pp. 659 and n. 350k, 660 ff.

no miserable intermission. The death of Constantius had, of course, reduced his rival Felix to even greater insignificance than before. Liberius now sent to Alexandria his approval of the pacific policy adopted there.[187] Athanasius had expressed no rancor, only a scornful commiseration for the Roman's desertion of him and intercourse between the sees was restored, at least formally and outwardly. Liberius also issued, either with or without the sanction of a synod, a general letter of instructions for the guidance of western churches in the reëstablishment of orthodoxy and discipline, the first, perhaps, of all the so-called "decretal letters" of the popes. The letter itself is lost but he repeated certain articles of it in one which he wrote shortly afterward to the bishops of Italy. All who have sinned, unaware of the full extent of their guilt, may be forgiven on profession of "the apostolic and catholic faith," "especially now that all the Egyptians and the Achaeans have unanimously accepted this judgment." It is both insolent and cruel to contend that such persons can never be reinstated. He provides also for the admission, without second baptism, of Arians and other heretics who might desire to join the orthodox communion.[188]

Liberius might well take pains to champion the cause of the delinquent clergy and talk of moderation and forgiveness. For Lucifer of Cagliari and Eusebius of Vercellae, his lieutenants at the Synod of Milan in 355, to whom he had written of his own impatience to share their glory and their exile and who had remained ever since in unfaltering durance in the Thebaid, were on their way home, Lucifer, at least, in a mood of lofty severity. On his arrival in Italy, he refused to commune with any who had succumbed at Rimini and with any who had accepted their repentance. He made no specific allegations against his old chief. It is possible that he did not know exactly how Liberius had obtained his release from Thrace. He simply retired austerely to his diocese in Sardinia, "contenting himself with his own communion." At Rome, the deacon Hilary, also

[187] Athanasius, *Letter to Rufinianus,* read during the Second Council of Nicaea. G. D. Mansi, *Sacrorum Conciliorum Nova et Amplissima Collectio,* Vol. XII, p. 1029.

[188] See the allusion to Liberius' letter in the *Decretal* of Bishop Siricius, *infra, Appendix* I, p. 699.

back after his long banishment, formed the head of a party of rigor, that went the length of demanding that the signers of Rimini and those who received them must be baptized anew, if they were to be saved. But these and the one or two Arian appointees of Constantius who survived, such as Auxentius in Milan, made small discord in the harmony that spread rapidly over the West. Only the Danubian provinces, from which Ursacius and Valens had come, were inclined still to hold apart and the church of Carthage under Restitutus hesitated. Any rumors derogatory to the Roman bishop which may have circulated after 358 died down and were willingly forgotten. Few men cared to look back to the reign of Constantius or to stir up its ugly ghosts. Rufinus of Aquileia, who ten years later began a long ecclesiastical career that brought him into frequent connection with Rome and who utilized every chance to inform himself on matters of church history, wrote in his *Chronicle* that he had never been able to discover why Liberius came back so soon from exile, whether he actually did yield to Constantius or whether the emperor merely relented and let him go. So completely was the sad business hushed up and lived down! [189]

The eleven years of Constantius passed then for the West like a bad dream, leaving few traces, apparently, but a small group of dissidents here and there. There followed a long period of religious peace and growing prosperity. In the East, the abortive attempt of Julian to revive paganism caused keen uneasiness and some disturbances, which, however, were relieved by his death, in 363, and the accession of the tolerant Jovian, who tried to treat all sects fairly and countenanced no persecutions. But early in 364, Jovian also died and was succeeded by Valentinian I, who named his brother Valens as his coadjutor. The Empire was again divided and remained so thereafter with a few brief interruptions. Valentinian, who held the West and the Central Mediterranean regions, as Constans had done, was like Constans, an able administrator, interested principally in the preservation of internal order and the fortification of the

[189] Rufinus, *Historia Ecclesiastica,* I, 27. The historian Theodoret, who wrote in the following century, gives us a circumstantial story of Liberius' return to Rome without a hint of his apostasy. *Infra,* p. 582.

frontiers against the restless hordes of barbarians. As far as his own convictions were concerned, he believed sincerely in the Nicene Creed and the orthodox Church, of which Rome, in his own dominion certainly, was the undisputed head, but he preferred not to be drawn into religious questions and to leave the bishops to regulate their own affairs.[189a] Valens, on the other hand, had barely established himself at Constantinople when he fell under the spell of Eudoxius, the Arian bishop of the city, a survivor of the entourage of Constantius, determined to reassert the authority of the Councils of Rimini and Seleucia. The West, of course, was now out of reach of any eastern interference but the unfortunate East, after its short reprieve, awoke to find itself again under an emperor who was both intolerant and Arian.

In the spring of 365, the edict went out that all bishops deposed by Constantius and restored under Julian should once more withdraw from their sees. The churches were again invaded by prefects and armed men. Even the aged and much tried Athanasius was again obliged to depart, although a year later, an exception was made in his favor and he was permitted to return and govern his people until his death. Meletius was driven from Antioch. A group of moderate bishops in or near Asia Minor, including a number called Macedonians after their leader Macedonius, a former bishop of Constantinople who had been deposed by the pro-Arian assembly of 360, had recently met at Lampsacus on the Hellespont and condemned the creed of Rimini and proclaimed their firm loyalty to " homoiousios " and the near-orthodox creed of Antioch. These men now appealed to Valens for a hearing but were rebuffed. Everywhere about them they saw portents betokening a return to Constantius' policy of bigoted persecution. In their anxiety, they decided to call for sympathy and support from the West, as the orthodox eastern bishops had done twenty years before. They chose three delegates, Eustathius of Sebaste in Roman Armenia, Silvanus of Tarsus and Theophilus of Castabala in Cilicia and gave them

[189a] When the eastern bishops, in 364, sent one of their number to ask permission to hold a synod, he answered: " My place is among the laymen. I have no right to meddle in these matters. Since it is the bishops' business, let them meet where they choose." Sozomen, *Historia Ecclesiastica,* VI, 7, 2. It was not the kind of reply the East was accustomed to receive.

letters signed by sixty-four names, with instructions to see both Valentinian and Liberius, and, if necessary, to go to the length of subscribing to the Nicene Creed and "homoousios" in order to win western interest.

On their arrival in Italy, the envoys learned that the emperor was absent, fighting the Sarmatians in Gaul. They concluded not to pursue him but to concentrate their efforts on obtaining the support of the Church, beginning, of course, at Rome. So, in the last year of his life, Liberius found himself in a position comparable to that of Julius, judge of catholic doctrine and authority for East as well as for West. It is said that at first he declined to receive the "Homoiousians," insisting that they were Arians, the old enemies of his faith,[190] but that they finally convinced him of their essential accord and removed his last doubts by a written statement to the effect that they and their constituents accepted the creed of Nicaea and promised to submit any disputes that might arise to judges whom he approved. Thus satisfied, Liberius gave them a letter to the sixty-four whom they represented and to all the orthodox or "homoousian" bishops in the East, assuring them encouragingly of his own union with them in the catholic and apostolic faith and of the recovery of "almost all" the bishops of the West "from the darkness of heresy."

Armed with this credential, the three delegates halted in Sicily on their homeward voyage and received a fraternal welcome and letters from the bishops there and from others in Gaul and Africa. Upon their return home, they promptly made overtures to the scattered groups of "Homoousians" still existing in parts of Asia Minor and Syria. A joint preliminary synod of both the closely related parties was held at Tyana, the letter of Liberius was read aloud and copies circulated widely. Enthusiasm spread for a coalition of all eastern anti-Arian elements with the western church under the auspices of the one apostolic bishop who seemed competent to lead them. Plans were made for a much larger

190 Eustathius had been one of the "Homoiousians" who had taken part in Liberius' humiliation at Sirmium. The tables were turned now, the apostate prisoner become the leader of orthodoxy with a group of his old opponents suing for reconciliation. So far as our documents show, no one now mentioned Sirmium.

council at Tarsus to accomplish this step and to create a new and greater Nicene church in the East. But the consent of Valens was required for the calling of such an assembly and Valens refused.

Negotiations, thus suspended, were further impeded by the intrusion at this juncture of a new phase of the old dogmatic problem. What were the nature and position of the third person of the Trinity, the Holy Spirit? Athanasius at Alexandria was arguing that the Nicene formula must be followed to its logical conclusion and that the Spirit must be regarded as equal or "homoousios" with the Son and the Father. Many "Homoiousians" and almost all the "Homoousians" accepted this corollary to their previous thesis, but the wing which retained the name of Macedonians protested that it could not see its way to granting the additional proposition. The unity of the catholic East was broken just as it was about to crystallize. With things still in this unsettled state, Liberius died, in September, 366. His rival Felix had died in the preceding year and his followers, who had returned to Rome, had been received by Liberius in a forgiving spirit and admitted to their old standing in the church.[191]

On Liberius and his times see L. Duchesne, *Early History of the Christian Church* (trans. from the 4th ed. by C. Jenkins, 3 vols., London, 1910–1924), Vol. II, chaps. VII–X; H. M. Gwatkin, *Studies of Arianism* (2nd ed., Cambridge, 1900); A. Harnack, *History of Dogma* (trans. by N. Buchanan, 7 vols., Boston, 1897–1901), Vol. IV, chap. I; R. W. Bush, *St. Athanasius, his Life and Times* (London, 1888); G. Krüger, *Die Bedeutung des Athanasius,* in *Jahrbücher für protestantische Theologie* (Brunswick, 1890), Vol. XVI, pp. 337–356; O. Bardenhewer, *Patrology* (trans. by T. Shahan, St. Louis, 1908), § 61; B. J. Kidd, *History of the Church to A.D. 461* (3 vols., Oxford, 1922–1925), Vol. II, chaps. V–VIII.

191 During his latter years as bishop, Liberius built the magnificent basilica on the Esquiline Hill, now known as Santa Maria Maggiore. The columns, wall structure and mosaics of the nave are still substantially as he left them.

1. The Coming of Persecution

Liberius, *Letter to Hosius*, extract, quoted by Hilary, *Fragmenta Historica*, Series B, VII, 5–6. Text. *Corpus Scriptorum Ecclesiasticorum Latinorum*, LXV, 167.

And he [Liberius] wrote the following letter to Ossius regarding the downfall of Vincent. " In this connection, because I ought not to fail to notify you of everything, I do inform your holiness that many of my fellow bishops of Italy assembled here and joined with me in a petition to the most devout emperor Constantius, that he would give command, as he resolved to do some time since, for the holding of a council at Aquileia; also that Vincent of Capua, together with Marcellus, another bishop from Campania, undertook the embassy for us. Of the former I hoped much, because he thoroughly comprehended the case and had sat often as a judge in the same matter with your excellency,[192] and I believed that he would observe the rule of the gospels and of an embassy. Not only did he achieve nothing but he himself was induced to take part in the treachery there. Since his act I have been plunged into double sorrow and have determined to die for God's sake rather than become a traitor at the last or give my consent to deeds contrary to the gospel."

Liberius, *Epistolae*, III. Text. C. T. G. Schoenemann, *Pontificum Romanorum Epistolae Genuinae*, 266–267.

Bishop Liberius to his most beloved brother, Eusebius.

Your indomitable faith, dearest brother, is my support and comfort in this present life, for through it you have

[192] Vincent, in his youth, had been one of the two Roman priests at Nicaea. *Supra*, p. 470, n. 64. He had also been at Sardica with Hosius and was sent as an envoy to Constantius after that meeting. He was undoubtedly a member of the Roman synod that heard Athanasius' defense in 340.

followed the precepts of the gospels and departed no whit from the company of the Apostolic See. Through the guidance of God, I believe, who keeps those who are worthy in his priesthood, you out of your good purpose have achieved this.

Now Vincent upon his embassy was lured into treachery and the other bishops of Italy were compelled in a public assembly to submit to the verdicts of the Easterners. But then, by God's grace, our brother and fellow bishop, Lucifer, arrived from Sardinia, who, upon hearing of the snares concealed in the situation and realizing what the heretics were attempting to do under pretext of the name of Athanasius, undertook in his devotion to the faith a righteous enterprise and is going to the court of our religious prince to explain the whole case in order and to request that all the questions which have come to the general notice may be settled in an assembly of the priests of God.

So, because I know that the holy fervor of your faith is in harmony with his, I am asking you in your wisdom, if, by God's favor, he finds you at court, to put forth your earnest effort through whatever agency you can to bring all the demands of our catholic faith to the attention of the most clement emperor, that he may at last forget his anger and do what may tend wholly to our peace and to his own salvation. I think it would be superfluous to describe the entire case in detail by letter to your honor, since the aforesaid brother of mine and his companions can tell you everything by word of mouth on their arrival.

God keep you safe, dearest lord and brother.[192a]

[192a] Liberius wrote soon afterwards a second letter to Eusebius, to announce the starting of Lucifer with a priest, Pancratius, and a deacon Hilary, "to assail the enemies of the Church." *Epistolae*, V.

Liberius, *Epistolae,* VI. Text. C. T. G. Schoenemann, *op. cit.,* 273–274.

Bishop Liberius to his most beloved brother, Eusebius.[192b]

I knew, dearest lord and brother, that you who were ardent in the Spirit of God would deign to give faithful comfort in a cause of that faith that can commend us to the Lord, to our brother and fellow bishop, Lucifer, and to our fellow priest, Pancratius, who went to you with my son, the deacon Hilary, and that you could not refuse them who, you knew, had undertaken so arduous a journey out of devotion to their faith. My mind, however, was much relieved by the reading of your letter. Nay, now indeed I am confident that the affair may turn out successfully, with God's aid, because you would not forsake our brothers. Strive then as a good soldier, who expects reward from the everlasting Emperor, and endeavor to show the strength of your mind, by which I know you have despised the allurements of this world, against those who are without the light of the Church. As you hold this life in contempt, prove yourself a priest indeed, that through your labors on behalf of the Church a council may be convened and all the harm which strangers have craftily plotted to the prejudice of the faith may be converted to good. Eternal rewards wait upon your labors, as your excellent faith well understands. We must encourage you as we can, even though our exhortation be cold, that the fervent Holy Spirit, who is in you, may for the unity of the holy Church awaken your mind each moment to greater consolations.

I dispatched a letter also to our brother and fellow bishop, Fortunatianus,[192c] who, I knew, feared not the persons of men and thought rather of the recompense to

192b This is Liberius' third letter to Eusebius. It was written obviously in the same year as the previous two, *i.e.,* 354.

192c Liberius was mistaken in this man. Fortunatianus, bishop of Aquileia, joined the Arianizers at Milan and did his best to make Liberius do the same when he met him in exile. *Vide supra,* p. 543, n. 175a, and *infra,* p. 583.

come, asking him too to deign now to stand guard with you for the sincerity of his heart and the faith which he knows he has defended even at the risk of his life. I know that he will unhesitatingly support your wisdom with his counsel in the holiness of his heart and that he will not refuse you his company, if you wish it, beloved, on any occasion.

God keep you safe, dearest lord and brother.

Liberius, *Letter to Constantius,*[193] Hilary, *Fragmenta Historica,* Series A, VII. Text. *Corpus Scriptorum Ecclesiasticorum Latinorum,* LXV, 89–93.

Bishop Liberius to the most glorious Constantius Augustus.

I beseech you, most serene emperor, in your clemency to lend me your gracious ear, that the thought of my heart may be made known to your mercy. From a Christian emperor, indeed, and the son of Constantine of holy memory I ought to receive this boon without delay. Yet I know that I am struggling against difficulty, for although I have asked before for satisfaction, I cannot bring your mind, so lenient to the guilty, to favor me. The proclamation that your reverence sent some time ago to the people is exceedingly painful to me, who must bear all things with patience.[194] I marvel that your heart, that always has room for kindness, that never, as the Scripture says, keeps its wrath unto the setting of the sun, still harbors toward me its indignation. For I, most religious emperor, seek after true peace with you, which shall not be compounded of words with an inner intention of deceit but shall be reasonable and fortified by the precepts of the gospel. Not only the business of Athanasius but many other questions have

[193] This letter is also found appended, in several manuscripts, to the writings of Lucifer of Cagliari, who was the bearer of it to Constantius. *Corpus Scriptorum Ecclesiasticorum Latinorum,* Vol. LXV, preface by A. Feder, p. xl.

[194] The proclamation described *supra,* p. 537.

come up which have caused me to beg your clemency for a council, so that, first of all, in accordance with the desire of your own spirit of sincere devotion to God, the state of the faith, in which is our prime hope toward God, might be carefully discussed and then the cases of those persons who ought to observe our fidelity to God might be settled. It would have been worthy of a worshipper of God and worthy of your Empire, which is governed and increased by Christ's goodness, and particularly conducive to reverence for the holy religion, over which you keep sagacious watch, if you had granted us this request.

But there are many persons bent upon injuring the members of the Church, and they have fabricated a story that I have suppressed letters, in order that the sins of the man whom they say they have condemned might not become universally known, letters, namely, from eastern and Egyptian bishops, in all of which the same charges against Athanasius were contained.[195] But it is well known to everyone and no one denies it that we did report the letters from the East and read them to the church, read them to the council and replied to that effect to the Easterners. But we did not give them our faith and approbation, because, at the same time, the judgment of eighty other Egyptian bishops on Athanasius was the opposite of theirs and we read and communicated that also to the Italian bishops. It seemed a violation of divine law to give our support to either party, when the majority of the bishops sided with Athanasius. Eusebius, who was acting as envoy, left these letters with us, as one faithful to God, when he went in haste to Africa, but afterwards Vincent, who was our legate with the others, carried all the documents to Arles, in case he perhaps might need them in obtaining permission for a council.

[195] These were the letters sent to Liberius after his accession, in which the eastern bishops attempted to prejudice the new Roman bishop against Athanasius and impress upon him the desirability of acquiescing in the campaign against him.

So your wisdom may perceive that no thought has entered my mind unworthy of the consideration of the servants of God. God is my witness, the whole Church with its members is witness, that I am walking and have walked in all the affairs of this world in the faith and fear of my God, by the precepts and principles of the gospel and the apostles. In no rash disposition but in the maintenance and observance of divine law, I have lived in the Church, even while I performed another ministry, and have done nothing out of arrogance and nothing out of avarice for glory but only that which belonged to the law. And God is my witness that I undertook this office against my will and that my aim is to continue in it without offense to God, as long as I am in the world. The decrees that I have carried out have never been my own but the apostles', that they might be forever confirmed and upheld. I have followed the custom and rule of my predecessors and have suffered nothing to be added to the bishopric of the city of Rome and nothing to be detracted from it. And I desire always to preserve and guard unstained that faith which has come down through so long a succession of bishops, among whom have been many martyrs.

Finally, my solicitude for the Church and my piety are now prevailing upon me to unfold my cause to your reverence. The Easterners are sending word that they are willing to unite with us in peace. But what is peace, most merciful emperor, when in their party are the four bishops, Demophilus, Macedonius, Eudoxius and Martyrius, who eight years ago refused at Milan to condemn the heretical tenets of Arius and left the council in anger? [196] You, in your justice and clemency, can decide whether it is right to assent to their judgment, no matter what it means nor what peril it implies. It is no new thing which they are now craftily attempting, under the cover afforded by the case

196 *Supra*, p. 500 and n. 112.

of Athanasius. We have here a letter sent long ago by Bishop Alexander to Silvester of holy memory, in which, before the ordination of Athanasius, he reported that he had expelled from the church eleven priests and deacons, because they were espousing the heresy of Arius.[197] Some of these men are said to be living now outside the catholic Church and to have set up miniature councils for themselves, and George of Alexandria is said to be in communion with them. So what peace can there be, most serene emperor, if bishops are to be taken and forced, as is now being done in Italy, to submit to the judgments of such persons?

Hear another thing, by permission of your long-suffering benignity! We have a letter recently arrived from the envoys which we sent to your clemency.[198] In it they inform us that because of the disturbed condition of all the churches, they some time earlier agreed to yield to the judgments of the Easterners but that they made a condition, namely, that if the eastern bishops would condemn the heresy of Arius, they themselves would yield and submit to their judgments. This understanding, they say, was confirmed by writing. They then went to the council and received, after deliberation, the answer that the Easterners could not condemn the doctrine of Arius but that Athanasius must be excluded from communion and that this was all they demanded. From this let your clemency consider how the laws of the catholic religion may be duly observed and the case of this man be diligently and completely investigated.

So, once and again, we entreat your gracious and devout spirit, by that virtue which proved its power before all humankind in your defense,[199] to keep before your eyes the favor of him who controls your Empire in all things and to have these matters examined thoroughly, with full de-

[197] *Supra,* pp. 467–468.
[198] Vincent of Capua and Marcellus, who went to Arles.
[199] Against Magnentius, after the death of Constans.

liberation, in an assemblage of bishops, so that, by God's grace, our time may be at peace through you and everything may be discussed with the consent of your serenity, and the decisions which were approved by the judgment of the priests of God and to which everyone agreed in the statement of faith confirmed by so many bishops at Nicaea, in the presence of your father of holy memory, may be preserved for a pattern to posterity. The Savior himself, who from on high beholds the thought of your heart, may rejoice that in so important an undertaking you have meritoriously set the cause of faith and peace above even the needs of the State. And I have deputed my brother and fellow bishop, the holy Lucifer, with the priest Pancratius and the deacon Hilary, to go to you to entreat your clemency to deign to listen favorably to our representations. We believe that they will be able without difficulty to procure from your grace a council for the peace of all catholic churches. The mercy of almighty God preserve you to us, most merciful and devout Augustus!

Lucifer, Pancratius and Hilary, *Letter to Eusebius*. Text. J. Harduin, *Acta Conciliorum et Epistolae Decretales*, I, 698.

Bishop Lucifer, the priest Pancratius, and Hilary to their most honorific lord, Bishop Eusebius.[199a]

The head of the devil is bruised with its wicked inventions, holy lord, but we ask you for the grace granted you by our Lord; do not forget us. Deign now to hasten, that at your speedy coming the doctrine of the Arians may be overthrown. For the Lord and his Christ know that just as the name of God was glorified in the destruction of Simon by the arrival of the most blessed apostles,[199b] so Valens

[199a] Eusebius, bishop of Vercellae. This letter was evidently written from Milan, whither the Roman delegation had preceded Eusebius.

[199b] The allusion is to the downfall of Simon Magus. *Supra*, p. 176.

[the turncoat bishop from Pannonia] will be routed by your appearance and the machinations of the blaspheming Arians will be undone and wholly ruined. We, most holy lord, from the first day when we came to Vercellae even to today have longed for your piety and beseech the Lord that all the saints in this church may praise its lasting restoration and duly acclaim the valor of your spirit. We believe that this will come to pass, because we are confident that the passion of the Savior cannot be defeated.

Christ the Lord keep you glorious, most holy and most blessed.

Hilary, *Ad Constantium*, I, 3. Text. *Corpus Scriptorum Ecclesiasticorum Latinorum*, LXV, 186–187.

Eusebius, bishop of Vercellae, is one who all his life has served God. After the council at Arles, where Bishop Paulinus opposed the criminal behavior of the other party, he [Eusebius] was ordered to come to Milan. But although the synagogue of evildoers was in session there for ten days, he was forbidden to enter the church, while their perverse spite was venting itself against the holy man. Finally, when their plans were all perfected, he was summoned at the time it suited them. He appeared in company with the clergy from Rome and Lucifer, bishop of Sardinia. And when he was directed to sign the condemnation of Athanasius, he said that it was necessary first to agree upon the faith of the Church and that he knew that some of those present were polluted by the stain of heresy. And he displayed before them all the creed that was made at Nicaea, of which we have already spoken, and promised to do everything they asked of him, if they would sign that profession of faith. Dionysius, bishop of Milan, was the first to take up the paper. But when he began to write his profession, Valens snatched the pen and the paper violently from his hands, crying that nothing could be done in that way. After considerable tumult, the incident came to the knowledge of the people and everyone was deeply indignant that the bishops were attacking the faith. So, in fear of the people's judgment, the synod moved from the church to the palace.

Athanasius, *Historia Arianorum,* 33, 34, 76. Text. J. P. Migne, *Patrologia Graeca,* XXV, 731, 785.

33 . . . So it is clear to all that their [the Arians'] wisdom is not of God but of man and that the followers of Arius have in truth no king but Caesar. For through his power the enemies of Christ accomplish all their purposes. But they imagine that through him they are bringing harm upon many and do not perceive that they are making many confessors. Of which number are the godly and upright bishops who have recently made a glorious confession, Paulinus, bishop of Trier, the metropolis of Gaul, and Lucifer, bishop of the metropolis of Sardinia, Eusebius of Vercellae in Italy and Dionysius of Milan, which is also a metropolis of Italy. These men were summoned by the emperor and commanded to subscribe against Athanasius and to communicate with the heretics. And when they in astonishment at this strange order said that there was no ecclesiastical canon for it, he instantly retorted: " Take my will for a canon! The bishops of Syria have to hear speech like this! So either obey or go yourselves into exile! "

34 When the bishops heard this, they were all amazed and stretched out their hands to God and tried to reason with the emperor and persuade him, telling him that the Empire belonged not to him but to God, who had given it to him, and bidding him beware lest God might suddenly take it away. They warned him of the day of judgment and counselled him not to derange the ecclesiastical organ-

ization and not to use the Roman government to annul the rules of the Church and not to introduce the Arian heresy into the Church of God. But the emperor would not heed them nor allow them to go on speaking but threatened them more fiercely and drew his sword against them. He gave orders that some of them should be executed but afterwards, like Pharaoh, he changed his mind. . . .

76 When he [Constantius] saw the boldness of the bishops Paulinus, Lucifer, Eusebius and Dionysius and how they confuted those who spoke against the bishop [Athanasius] by citing the recantation of Ursacius and Valens and arguing that no further trust should be put in Valens, since he had once retracted what he was now asserting,[200] he suddenly stood up and said: " I am now the accuser of Athanasius; on my account, you must believe what these men say." And then, when they replied: " But how can you be an accuser, when the accused man is not here? And granted that you are his accuser, still he is not here and therefore cannot be tried. This is not a Roman court, where you, as emperor, must be believed, but it is the trial of a bishop. This trial must be fair both to the accuser and to the defendant. And how will you accuse him? For you cannot have been in the company of one who lives so far from you. And if you speak from what you have heard from these men here, you must in justice believe also what he says of himself. But if you refuse to believe him and believe these men, then it is plain that they are instigated by you to say what they do and are accusing Athanasius in order to gratify you." On hearing this and considering an honest speech as an insult, he sent them into exile.[201]

200 *Supra*, pp. 531–533.

201 Other accounts of Constantius' synod at Milan are given by Rufinus, *Historia Ecclesiastica*, X, 20–23. Sulpicius Severus, *Chronica*, II, 39; Lucifer, *Moriendum*, 1–4.

Liberius, *Letter to the exiled bishops,* Hilary, *Fragmenta Historica,* Series B, VII, 1–2. Text. *Corpus Scriptorum Ecclesiasticorum Latinorum,* LXV, 164–166.

Liberius, before he went into exile, wrote this uniform letter to the confessors, that is, to Eusebius, Dionysius and Lucifer, who were in exile:

" The enemy of the human race seems to have oppressed still more violently under the guise of peace the members of the Church. Nevertheless, your wonderful and rare faith, priests acceptable to God, has shown you here approved by God and marked you now for future glory as martyrs. I can find no words with which to proclaim your praise or to publish exultantly the merits of your valor, torn as I am between grief for your loss and joy at your glory, save that I know that this sure comfort I could give you, an assurance that I too had been driven into exile with you. I am indeed in deep sadness that dire necessity for a while detains me from your company, while I am yet in this state of suspense and expectation. For I had hoped, my devoted brethren, to be spent first for you all, so that your love might have an example of glory to follow in me. But this will be the palm of your deserts, that you were the first to pass from perseverance in faith to the illustrious glory of confession. . . . [Their trial is even worse than that of the martyrs of old and they are certain of celestial reward.]

Because you are now become very near to God, do you by your prayers lift me, your fellow priest and servant of God, to the Lord, so that when the onslaught comes, which from day to day is reported to be at hand and inflicting grievous wounds, I may be able to bear it steadfastly. May the Lord deign to make me equal to you, with faith inviolate and the state of the catholic Church unharmed! Also I wish to know more fully what happened during your audience. I beg your holiness to send me complete and accurate word by letter, so that my mind, now tortured by varying rumors, and my bodily strength, now much diminished, may feel themselves enlarged by your encouragement."

And, in another hand, " God keep you safe, my lords and brothers."

2. The Banishment of Liberius

Ammianus Marcellinus, *Res Gestae,* XV, 7, 6.[202] Text. Ed. by C. U. Clark, I, 57.

While this Leontius was governor [prefect at Rome], he received orders from Constantius to send Liberius, chief priest of the Christian law, to his court, on the ground that he was resisting the emperor's commands and the decisions of many of his own colleagues in a matter which I shall briefly explain. An assembly of worshippers of this same law, a synod, as they call it, had removed from his sacred office Athanasius, bishop at that time in Alexandria, who was too arrogant for his profession and attempted to meddle in affairs outside his sphere, as rumor constantly testified. For he was said to be extraordinarily wise in fortune-tellers' lore and in the interpretation of augural flights of birds and to have on several occasions predicted future events. Beside which, other things were attributed to him, abhorrent to the nature of the law which he administered. And Liberius, at the emperor's direction, was told to agree with the rest and confirm by his signature Athanasius' deposition from his priestly seat. But he obstinately refused and repeatedly declared that to condemn a man unseen and unheard was the ultimate crime, thus openly contradicting the emperor's will. For the latter had always hated Athanasius and, al-

202 This extract gives us the point of view of the pagan man in the street.

though he knew that his deposition was now accomplished, he still felt an ardent desire to have it confirmed by the more potent authority [203] of the bishop of the eternal city. And when this could not be obtained, Liberius was, with great difficulty, carried off in the middle of the night stealthily for fear of the people, who loved him fervently.

Athanasius, *Historia Arianorum*, 35–38. Text. J. P. Migne, *Patrologia Graeca*, XXV, 733–737.

So from the beginning they spared not even Liberius, bishop of Rome, but extended their fury until it covered even his territory.[204] They had no reverence for his see, because it is apostolic, nor respect for Rome, because she is the metropolis of the Roman Empire, nor recollection of the letters in which they had once addressed him as successor of the apostles. But they confounded everything together and forgot everything completely and thought only of satisfying their ardor for impiety. For when these ungodly men perceived that Liberius stood orthodox and disdained the Arian heresy and endeavored to prevail upon everyone to renounce and abandon it, they reasoned as follows: " If we can persuade Liberius, we shall soon overcome all the rest." And they slandered him to the emperor. Then Constantius, expecting that through Liberius he could bring over everyone to his side, wrote at once and sent a eunuch, called Eusebius, with his letter and gifts, to wheedle Liberius with the gifts and threaten him with the letter. Then the eunuch went to Rome and, first, he summoned Liberius to subscribe to the condemnation of Athanasius, saying: " This

203 The Latin is " auctoritate quoque potiore."

204 In a later passage, Athanasius says that Liberius had sent a priest, Eutropius, with a second letter to the emperor, to join the deacon Hilary, at the time that sentence was being pronounced against Lucifer, Dionysius and Eusebius, and that Eutropius was banished immediately and Hilary after a scourging. *Historia Arianorum*, 41.

is the emperor's will and command; do it!" Then he produced the gifts and pressed him, grasping him by the hand and saying: "Obey the emperor and accept these gifts."

But the bishop attempted to argue and explain to him. "How is it possible to pass this sentence on Athanasius? When not only one but two synods, assembled from everywhere, have magnificently acquitted him and the church of the Romans has dismissed him in peace, how can we condemn him? Who will approve of us, if we repudiate in absence one whom we loved when present and with whom we were in communion? This is not the rule of the Church; no such tradition have we ever received from the Fathers, who themselves derived theirs from the blessed and great apostle Peter. If the emperor is indeed concerned for the Church's peace and if he is ordering the abrogation of our letters regarding Athanasius, then let him abrogate also their proceedings against him, let him abrogate also those against everyone else and let him summon speedily a council of the Church far away from the palace, at which the emperor shall not be present nor any count appear nor any magistrate threaten us, but only the fear of God constrain us and the constitution of the apostles, that so, first of all, the faith of the Church may be kept safe, as the Fathers defined it at the Council of Nicaea, and the Arians may be expelled and, finally, heresy may be anathematized. Then, soon afterwards, let a trial be held to hear the charges which are being brought against Athanasius and anyone else as well, and also those which are being brought against the opposite party, and let the culprits be expelled and the innocent approved. For it is not possible to keep in a council men who are sacrilegious in their faith nor is it fitting that an examination into conduct should precede the examination into faith. We must first remove all discord in faith and then make our investigation into conduct. For our Lord Jesus Christ did not heal sufferers until they had expressed and declared what faith they had in him. This was the lesson we have from the Fathers and this do you report to the emperor, for it is both profitable to him and fortifying to the Church. Let him pay no heed to Ursacius and Valens, for they have retracted their former assertions and now, when they speak, are not to be trusted."

Thus spoke Bishop Liberius. And the eunuch, who was vexed not so much because he would not subscribe as because he was openly hostile to heresy, forgot that he was in the presence of a bishop and threatened him fiercely and departed with the gifts. And he committed an offense which is unknown to Christians and too audacious for eunuchs. For he imitated the transgression of Saul [205] and went to the martyr's shrine of the apostle Peter and there offered the gifts. But when Liberius heard of it, he was very displeased with the keeper of the place, because he had not prevented it, and he cast the gifts outside as an unhallowed sacrifice, and so stirred the eunuch to greater anger. Then the eunuch aroused the wrath of the emperor, saying: "We have not now to consider a method of inducing Liberius to subscribe but the fact that he is so set against heresy that he anathematizes Arians by name." He also incited the other eunuchs to say the same, for there are many or, rather, they are all eunuchs around Constantius and they can do anything with him and without them nothing can be accomplished. Then the emperor wrote to Rome and again sent off palace officials and notaries and counts with letters to the prefect either to inveigle Liberius away from Rome by a trick and send him to the emperor at court or else to persecute him with violence.

Such being the tenor of the letters, fear and treachery soon held sway throughout the city. How many houses were

205 Saul, king of Israel, committed his first transgression by offering sacrifices which he should have waited for the priest Samuel to offer. I Kings, XIII, 5–14 (Douay Version); I Samuel, XIII, 5–14 (King James Version).

menaced! How many persons were offered great bribes to turn them against Liberius! How many bishops, beholding it, went into hiding! How many free women retired to the country because of the insults of the foes of Christ! How many ascetics suffered from plots! How many sojourners and denizens in the city felt the persecution! How often and how closely was the harbor guarded and the entrance gates, that no orthodox person might come to visit Liberius! Then Rome had her experience of the enemies of Christ and knew at last what she had hardly believed before upon report, how other churches and cities had been devastated by them. . . .

[One Epictetus, an eastern adventurer, was elected through court influence bishop of Centumcellae,[205a] near Rome, and instructed to keep a watch on Liberius.]

Theodoret, *Historia Ecclesiastica,* II, 13. Text. J. P. Migne, *Patrologia Graeca,* LXXXII, 1033–1040.

The emperor Constantius said:[205b] "We have thought fit, since you are a Christian and bishop of our city, to send for you and admonish you to abjure communion with that unspeakable madman, the impious Athanasius. For the whole world has decided that this is right and by vote of a council has pronounced him debarred from the Church's communion."

Bishop Liberius said: "O Emperor, the sentence of the Church should be given with strict justice. So, if it please your piety, command that a court be assembled and it be seen if Athanasius is worthy of condemnation. Then the decision against him may be delivered according to the rule

205a The modern Civita Vecchia.

205b Athanasius gives a brief account of Liberius' interview with Constantius in his *Historia Arianorum,* 39.

of ecclesiastical procedure. For it is impossible to condemn a man whom we have not tried."

The emperor Constantius said: "All the world has condemned him for his impiety and he, as he has done from the beginning, mocks at his own danger."

Bishop Liberius said: "The men who have signed his sentence were not witnesses of the events but were actuated by greed for glory or by fear or by dread of disgrace from you."

The emperor: "What glory or fear or disgrace?"

Liberius: "Men who love not the glory of God and prefer instead their gifts from you, have condemned one whom they have neither looked upon nor judged, a deed which is iniquitous for Christians."

The emperor: "Indeed, he has been tried in person at the synod that was held in Tyre and all the bishops of the world condemned him at that synod."

Liberius: "He has never been judged in person. The men who were then assembled condemned Athanasius after he had left the tribunal."

The eunuch Eusebius said foolishly: "At the Council of Nicaea he was convicted of divergence from the catholic faith."[206]

Liberius: "Only five of those who journeyed to Mareotis and who were sent to collect evidence against him when he was accused gave sentence against him. Of these, two are now dead, Theognis and Theodore, but the other three are still living, Maris and Valens and Ursacius.[207] They were condemned at Sardica because of their part in this mission and they petitioned the council for pardon for having gathered evidence dishonestly against Athanasius in Mareotis from one side only. These petitions we have now at

[206] This remark shows, of course, the utter ignorance of the eunuch. Liberius, it will be noticed, ignores the interruption.

[207] *Supra*, pp. 475, 529, 532.

hand. Which of these men, O Emperor, ought we to believe and commune with, the three who once condemned Athanasius and later asked pardon for it or those who then condemned these three?"

The bishop Epictetus said: "O Emperor, not for the sake of his faith nor to defend the judgments of the Church is Liberius making his speech today but so that he may brag to the senators in Rome that he defeated the emperor in argument."

The emperor said to Liberius: "How large a portion of the world are you, that you take sides alone with an impious man and disturb the peace of the earth and all the universe?"

Liberius: "Even if I am alone, the word of faith is not weakened for that. Of old, three alone were found to resist the decree."[208]

The eunuch Eusebius said: "You have called our emperor a Nebuchadnezzar!"

Liberius: "By no means! But you are acting as rashly as he, when you condemn a man whom we have not tried. So I ask, first of all, that a general confession be prepared that shall confirm the faith propounded at Nicaea and then that our brothers be recalled from exile and reinstated in their proper places. If then it becomes plain that those who are now stirring up tumults in the churches will subscribe to the apostolic faith, then let them everyone meet at Alexandria, where the accused and his accusers and their defenders are, and let us examine the case and pass judgment upon it."

The bishop Epictetus said: "But the public post will not stand the strain of transporting the bishops."

Liberius: "The business of the Church will put no strain on the public post, for the churches are able to provide for the transportation of their own bishops as far as the sea."

208 The allusion is to Daniel, III.

The emperor: " It is impossible to undo what has already been formally ratified. For the will of the majority of the bishops ought to prevail. You are the only one who insists upon friendship with that impious man."

Liberius said: " O Emperor, never have we heard of a judge, in the absence of the accused, denouncing his impiety, as if he bore a personal grudge against him."

The emperor: " He has done harm to us all together but to no one so much as myself. He was not satisfied with the destruction of my older brother [209] but constantly provoked the irritation of the blessed Constans against us, although we endured with great forbearance the vehemence of both the provoker and the provoked. So no victory will be so grand for me, neither the one over Magnentius nor the one over Silvanus, as when I root out this pest from the government of the Church."

Liberius: " Use not the bishops to avenge your private enmity, O Emperor! For the hands of the Church should be raised for consecration and blessing. Therefore, if it please you, command the recall of the bishops to their own places and after it is seen that they are in accord with him who today maintains the orthodox faith as promulgated at Nicaea, then let them assemble in one spot and provide for the peace of the world, that a man who has done no wrong may not bear the reproach of a troublemaker."

The emperor: " There is but one thing wanted. I wish you to enter into communion with the churches and then I shall send you back to Rome. Consent, therefore, to the peace and subscribe and return to Rome."

Liberius: " I have taken leave already of the brethren in Rome. For the laws of the Church are of greater moment to me than a residence in Rome."

209 Constantine II had ordered the release of Athanasius from his detention at Trier and shown himself, in general, pacific in policy, but Athanasius had had no direct, personal relation with him and no connection whatever with his quarrel with Constans, which ended in his death.

The emperor: "You have an interim of three days for consideration whether you prefer to subscribe and return to Rome or to select the place of your banishment."

Liberius: "Three days or three months interim will not change my mind. Send me wherever you wish."

Then, after two days, the emperor examined Liberius and finding that he had not changed his determination, he ordered him to be banished to Beroea, in Thrace. And after Liberius had left him, the emperor sent him five hundred gold pieces for his expenses. But Liberius said to the messengers: "Take them back to the emperor, for he needs them for the payment of his soldiers. And if the emperor does not need them, give them to Auxentius and Epictetus, for they need them." Since he refused to receive money from them, the eunuch Eusebius offered him some and Liberius said to him: "You have laid waste the churches of the world and do you offer me alms, as if I were a criminal? Go! First become Christian!" After three days, having accepted nothing, he was sent into exile.

Athanasius, *Historia Arianorum*, 75. Text. J. P. Migne, *Patrologia Graeca*, XXV, 784.

Then he [Constantius] found one Epictetus, a neophyte and young adventurer, and liked him, for he saw that he was ready for mischief, and he employed him thereafter in conspiracies against any bishops he chose. For the fellow was ready to do everything that the emperor wished. Using him as his agent, Constantius carried out a shocking performance at Rome, resembling, in truth, the malignity of Antichrist. He had the palace prepared instead of the church and ordered some three of his eunuchs to attend in place of the people. Then he compelled three ill-favored [210] spies, — for

[210] The Greek word here translated "ill-favored" is κακάσκοποι. A play is doubtless intended upon its resemblance to the word ἐπίσκοποι, bishops.

no one would call them bishops, — to ordain there as bishop in the palace Felix, a man worthy of them. For all the people understood the illegality of these heretics and would not allow them to enter the church but held far aloof from them.

3. The Protest against Imperial Interference in the Church

Hosius, *Letter to Constantius,* Athanasius, *Historia Arianorum,* 44. Text. J. P. Migne, *Patrologia Graeca,* XXV, 743–748.

Hosius to the emperor Constantius, greeting in the Lord.

I was first a confessor during the persecution under your grandfather, Maximian. If you, too, persecute me, I am ready even yet to suffer everything rather than shed innocent blood and betray the truth. But I do not approve of these threatening letters from you. Cease writing them! Do not become an Arian nor listen to the eastern party nor put confidence in Ursacius and Valens! For whatever they say they are saying not because of Athanasius but because of their own heresy. Believe me, Constantius, who am your grandfather in years!

I was myself at the Council of Sardica, when you and your blessed brother Constans assembled us all together.[211] And on my own account I challenged the enemies of Athanasius, when they came to the church where I was, to bring forward whatever they had against him. I bade them have courage and not expect anything but a righteous judgment in every respect. I did this not once but twice, urging them, if they were unwilling to speak before the whole council, still to do so before me alone. I also assured them that if he were proved culpable, he would certainly be rejected by

[211] *Supra,* pp. 517 ff.

us too, but that if he were found innocent and could prove them to be false talebearers and if they then refused to receive him, I would persuade him to go with me to Spain. And Athanasius was induced to agree to these terms and made no objection, but they, without confidence in anything, still refused. On another occasion, Athanasius went to your court, when you wrote for him, and asked that his enemies, who were then in Antioch, be summoned either as a body or individually, in order that they might either convict him or be convicted, either prove him to his face to be what they asserted he was or cease slandering him in his absence. But you did not favor his proposal and they also spurned it.

Why then do you still pay heed to those who malign him? How can you endure Valens and Ursacius, who have once repented and made written confession of their calumnies? They have confessed that they were not coerced, as they pretend they were, that there were no soldiers around them and that your brother had no knowledge of it. Such things were not done under his government as are done now. God forbid! But they of their own will went up to Rome and indited their recantation in the presence of the bishop and the priests, after having previously sent to Athanasius a friendly and peaceable letter.[212] But if they pretend there was coercion and appreciate that it was wrong and if you too disapprove of it, then do you yourself refrain from coercion and write no letters and send no counts, but release those whom you have banished, lest, while you blame us for coercion, they use coercion still more violent upon us.

What wrong like this was ever done by Constans? What bishop was sent into exile? When did he act as arbiter of an ecclesiastical tribunal? Which of his palatines forced men to subscribe against anyone, as Valens and his fellows declare? Cease, I entreat you, and remember that you are

[212] *Supra*, pp. 531–534.

a mortal. Fear the day of judgment and keep yourself pure against it. Intrude not yourself into the business of the Church and give no commandment to us regarding it but learn it instead from us. God has placed in your hands the Empire: to us he has committed the administration of his Church. And as he who would steal the government from you opposes the ordinance of God, even so do you fear lest by taking upon yourself the conduct of the Church, you make yourself guilty of a grave sin. It is written: "Render unto Caesar the things that are Caesar's and unto God the things that are God's."[213] Therefore it is not permitted to us to bear rule on earth nor have you the right to burn incense. I write this out of anxiety for your salvation.

As for the purport of your letters, this is my resolution. I assuredly will not ally myself with the Arians and I anathematize their heresy. Nor will I subscribe to the condemnation of Athanasius, whom we and the church of the Romans and the entire council have pronounced guiltless. You too yourself, when at one time you comprehended this, sent for him and allowed him to return with honor to his country and his church.[214] What excuse is there for this great change? The same men who were his enemies then are so now and the calumnies they whisper now, — for they do not mention them in his presence, — are the same they were mouthing about him before you sent for him and the same that they circulated about him when they met at the council. But when I invited them to appear, as I have just said, they were unable to produce their evidence, for if they had possessed any, they would not have fled so disgracefully. Who then has prevailed upon you, after so long a time, to forget your own letters and assurances? Beware and yield not to the words of evil men, lest to gain some common advantage you make yourself guilty. Here you are serving

[213] Mark, XII, 17. [214] *Supra*, p. 530.

their advantage but in the day of judgment, you alone will have to answer for it. By your aid, they intend to injure their personal enemy and propose to make you the minister of their wickedness and, through your help, to sow the seeds of their accursed heresy in the Church. It is not prudent for the gratification of others to cast oneself into open jeopardy. Refrain, I beseech you, Constantius, and listen to me! It is incumbent upon me to write this and upon you not to despise it.

4. The Apostasy of Liberius

Quae Gesta Sunt inter Liberium et Felicem Episcopos, Collectio Avellana,[215] I. Text. Ed. by O. Gunther, *Corpus Scriptorum Ecclesiasticorum Latinorum,* XXXV, 1–5.

In the time of Emperor Constantius, son of Constantine, there was a severe persecution of the Christians on the part of the impious Arian heretics, with the connivance of Constantius, who both persecuted Bishop Athanasius for resisting the heretics and ordered all other bishops to condemn him. And all the prelates everywhere, in dread of their sovereign, agreed to do it and they condemned an innocent man without a hearing. But Liberius, bishop of Rome, and Eusebius of Vercellae and Lucifer of Cagliari and Hilary of Poitiers refused to endorse the sentence. So these men were sent into exile for preserving the faith. Damasus, a deacon of Liberius, made a pretense of accompanying him but on the journey he took flight and returned to Rome, enticed by his

[215] The *Collectio Avellana* is a sixth century assortment of documents, gathered apparently by some one who expected to use them in the composition of a church history. They cover a period of a century, beginning with the one from which we take the extract above, and include narratives, letters, imperial edicts, and other miscellaneous matter. The account here cited and the petition of Faustinus and Marcellinus, from which we quote later, are both productions of men who belonged to the Roman party of uncompromising orthodoxy, led at first by Deacon Hilary. They were scornful of Liberius for his weakness and broke into open revolt against Damasus.

ambition. However, on the day that Liberius set out into exile, all the clergy, that is, the priests and the archdeacon Felix and this deacon Damasus and all the officials of the church, all in company, in the presence of the Roman people, bound themselves by an oath that during Liberius' lifetime they would have no other bishop.[216] But the clergy did a wicked and improper thing and committed the heinous crime of perjury, for they accepted the archdeacon Felix as their bishop, after he was ordained to take the place of Liberius. This deed displeased all the people and they held aloof from his train.

After two years, the emperor Constantius came to Rome and the people asked him for Liberius and he promptly granted their request, with the words: "You shall have Liberius and he will return better than when he left you." In this way he indicated Liberius' submission, by which he had joined hands with perfidy. In the third year, Liberius returned and the Roman people went out with joy to meet him; Felix was branded by the Senate and the people and was driven from the city. But a short time later, with the support of the clergy who had perjured themselves, he broke into the city and undertook to establish himself in the basilica of Julius, beyond the Tiber.[217] But the whole multitude of the faithful and the nobles of the city drove him out again in deep disgrace.

After eight years, in the consulship of Valentinian and Valens, on November 22, Felix died and Liberius had compassion on the clergy who had perjured themselves and received them back in their own offices. Then, on September 24, in the consulship of Gratian and Dagalaifus, Liberius put off mortality.

[216] Jerome, *Chronicon*, also mentions this oath under the year of Christ 354, the thirteenth year of Constantius.

[217] *Supra*, p. 488, n. 98.

Theodoret, *Historia Ecclesiastica,* II, 14. Text. J. P. Migne, *Patrologia Graeca,* LXXXII, 1040–1041.

So the victorious champion of truth went to Thrace, as he was commanded. And when two years had elapsed, Constantius came to Rome. Then the wives of the men of rank and distinction begged their husbands to request Constantius to give the shepherd back to his flock, declaring that if the men failed to persuade him, they themselves would desert them and run away to their great shepherd. But the husbands said that they feared the emperor's resentment. " For we are men and he will perhaps think it unpardonable. But if you ask him, he will at any rate spare you and one of two things will happen. Either he will grant your petition or, if you fail to persuade him, he will dismiss you unharmed." The noble women took this suggestion and appeared before the monarch in their habitual, splendid raiment, so that he might recognize their high station from their dress and respect and spare them. In this way, they approached and entreated him to have pity on a great city, deprived of its shepherd and left a prey to the attacks of wolves. But he said that the city needed no other shepherd, for it possessed a shepherd capable of caring for it. For after the great Liberius, one of his loyal deacons had been ordained. Felix was his name. He himself maintained unsullied the faith proclaimed at Nicaea but he communed readily with those who corrupted it. No one of the inhabitants of Rome would enter a house of prayer while he was there. And these women told this to the emperor. Then he was moved by it and commanded that the best of men should be recalled and that both bishops together should rule the church.[218] But when this edict was read in the circus, the mob cried out that the emperor's decision was

[218] It seems clear from this that Theodoret did not know of Liberius' recantation.

just, — for the spectators were divided into two parties, with names from their colors, — and one bishop should lead one party and the other the other. So they turned into ridicule the emperor's edict and then gave one shout: "One God, one Christ, one bishop!" I have thought best to repeat their exact words. After these pious and righteous outcries from this Christian people, the godly Liberius returned. And Felix withdrew and dwelt in another city.

Liberius, *Letters in Exile*,[219] Hilary, *Fragmenta Historica*, Series B, VII, 8, 10, 11. Text. *Corpus Scriptorum Ecclesiasticorum Latinorum*, LXV, 168–173.

"Liberius to his dearly beloved brethren, priests and fellow bishops of the East, greeting.

For godly fear your holy faith is known to God and to men of good will. Inasmuch as the law says: "Judge righteous judgments, ye sons of men,"[220] I did not defend Athanasius but, because my predecessor, Bishop Julius of honorable memory, had received him, I was afraid that I might be considered a traitor in some sort. But when, by God's will, I realized that you had been right in condemning him, I straightway gave my assent to your judgment. And I delivered a letter concerning him to our brother Fortunatianus to carry to the emperor Constantius. So now that Athanasius has been excluded from communion with all of us and his official letters are no longer to be accepted by me, I assert that I am in peace and harmony with you everyone

[219] The following three letters have often been marked as of doubtful authenticity. The style is crude and involved and the text evidently faulty. They may have been sent out first in Greek and translated for Hilary's use into Latin. They were among the documents collected by Hilary at Constantinople in 359 and seem to bear internal marks of genuineness. One other letter attributed to Liberius in Hilary's collection is unmistakably an Arian forgery, Series B, III, 1. It was apparently composed to prove that Liberius had broken with Athanasius at the beginning of his pontificate, before leaving Rome. But it is not to be reconciled with the letters quoted here nor with the rest of our testimony.

[220] Psalms, LVII, 2.

and with all the bishops of the East and throughout the provinces.

Moreover, you may be sure that I am professing the true faith in this letter, for our common lord and brother, Demophilus, has deigned in his charity to expound to me your catholic faith, which was also discussed and expounded at Sirmium by many of our brethren and fellow bishops and adopted by all who were present. This I have gladly accepted and in no particular have I gainsaid it and to it I have declared my assent. This I follow and this I uphold. I confidently believe that I may entreat your holinesses, now that you behold me in hearty agreement with you, to put forth your efforts graciously in common council and zeal, that I may be released from banishment and return to the see which was once divinely entrusted to me."

. . . .

"Liberius in exile to Ursacius, Valens and Germinius.[221]

Whereas I know you are sons of peace and love the concord and harmony of the catholic Church, therefore, under no compulsion whatever, — as I call God to witness, — but for the sake of the blessing of peace and concord, which is preferable to martyrdom, I approach you with this letter, my lords and dearest brethren. I hereby inform your wisdom that I had condemned Athanasius, who was bishop of the Alexandrian church, before I wrote to the court of the holy emperor that I was sending a letter to the eastern bishops. And he has been cut off from the communion of the Roman church, as all the priesthood of the Roman church is witness. And my sole reason for delaying to send the letter with regard to him to our eastern brethren and fellow bishops was that my envoys whom I sent earlier from Rome to the court and the bishops who had been deported, both the former and the latter, might, if possible, be recalled from their exile.

[221] Bishop of Sirmium.

I wish you also to know that I have asked brother Fortunatianus to carry to the most clement emperor my letter which I wrote to the eastern bishops, that he too might know that I, like them, had withdrawn from communion with Athanasius. I believe that his reverence will receive it thankfully for the blessing of peace. A copy of it I addressed also to Hilary, the emperor's faithful eunuch. You, in your charity, will observe that I have acted in a friendly and innocent spirit. Wherefore, I approach you with this letter and adjure you, by almighty God and Christ Jesus his Son, our God and Lord, to go graciously to our most clement emperor Constantius and ask that for the blessing of peace and concord, in which his reverence always finds delight, he may order me to return to the church divinely committed to me, so that in his time the Roman church may not endure tribulation. By this letter you are to understand fairly and honestly, dearest brothers, that I am at peace with all you bishops of the catholic Church. Great will be the consolation that you will receive in the day of vengeance, if through you peace be restored to the Roman church. I wish also that through you our brothers and fellow bishops, Epictetus and Auxentius,[222] may learn that I am in peace and ecclesiastical communion with them. I believe that they will receive the tidings thankfully. And whoever dissents from our peace and concord, which by God's will have been established through all the world, may understand hereby that he is cut off from our communion."

Again: " Liberius in exile to Vincent.

. . . The plots of evil men, through which I have come to this pass, are well known to you. [Pray that the Lord will grant me endurance. They have taken from me my comfort, my beloved son, the deacon Urbicus.] . . .

I have thought best to notify your holiness that I have

222 These, it will be remembered, were the eastern Arians nominated by Constantius to be bishops in Milan and Civita Vecchia.

retired from the struggle over Athanasius and have sent letters regarding him to our brethren and fellow bishops of the East. Will you, accordingly, because by God's will you are everywhere at peace, assemble all the bishops of Campania and inform them of this. Send a letter from the meeting as a whole and one from yourself to the most clement emperor on the subject of our harmony and peace, so that I too may be released from my wretchedness."

And in his own hand: "God preserve you safe, my brother!" Also in his hand and written on the same page: "We are at peace with all the eastern bishops and with you. I have absolved myself to God. If you wish me to die in exile, you will see. God will be judge between me and you."

Athanasius, *Historia Arianorum,* 41. Text. J. P. Migne, *Patrologia Graeca,* XXV, 741.

But Liberius gave way, after he had been two years in exile, and subscribed for fear of threatened death. Yet this shows only their violence and Liberius' hatred of heresy and support of Athanasius as long as he had a free choice. For that which men do under torture, against their original intention, ought not to be considered the will of these terrified persons but rather that of their tormentors.[223]

Sozomen, *Historia Ecclesiastica,* IV, 15. Text. J. P. Migne, *Patrologia Graeca,* LXVII, 1149–1154.

Not long afterward, the emperor came from Rome to Sirmium and the bishops of the West sent a deputation and he summoned Liberius from Beroea. And in the presence of the eastern delegates, with the clergy also who were in

[223] This short excerpt is given to show Athanasius' attitude toward Liberius' desertion. He speaks of it again in his *Apologia,* 89.

attendance at court, he compelled Liberius to confess that the Son is not of the substance of the Father. Basil and Eustathius and Eleusius [224] were there influencing the monarch to do this, for they had great weight with him. They combined at that time in one statement the decrees that had been passed at Sirmium against Paul of Samosata and against Photinus and the creed that was drawn up at the dedication ceremonies of the church at Antioch, on the ground that some persons were attempting under cover of the word "homoousios" to prove that they were heretics. They made Liberius sign this and Athanasius and Alexander and Severianus and Crescens, who were bishops of Africa. Likewise Ursacius and Germinius, bishop of Sirmium, and Valens, bishop of Myrsae, and all the rest who were there from the East subscribed to it.

In addition, they procured from Liberius a confession in which he denounced those who do not say that the Son is like the Father in substance and everything else. For when Eudoxius and his party in Antioch, who were championing the heresy of Aetius,[225] had received the letter of Hosius, they started a report that Liberius also had disowned the "homoiousios" and was confessing that the Son was unlike the Father.

Then when this had been accomplished by the eastern delegation, the emperor permitted Liberius to return to Rome. And the bishops in Sirmium wrote to Felix, who was then at the head of the Roman church, and to the clergy there that they should receive Liberius and that both men

224 Basil was the successor of Marcellus at Ancyra, Eustathius and Eleusius, bishops of Sebaste and Cyzicus respectively. They were hardly more than semi-Arians, "Homoiousians," opposed at this time to the upholders of the Nicene "homoousios," like Liberius, and to the Sabellian Photinus (*supra*, p. 500), as well as to Paul who belittled Christ's divinity (*supra*, p. 432). The extreme Arian faction, which was to drive them later into coöperation with the "Homoousians," was not yet in control.

225 These men were the nucleus of the new, radical development of Arianism, the Anomoean party, whose creed Hosius had recently signed and who now tried to claim Liberius. Ursacius and Valens joined them.

should administer the Apostolic See and be bishops together in harmony and sink the unhappy events of Felix's ordination and the departure of Liberius in oblivion. For the people of Rome loved Liberius, as a good and generous man and one who had stoutly withstood the emperor for the faith, and a serious riot had broken out and reached the pitch of bloodshed. Felix lived but a short time afterward [226] and then Liberius alone was bishop of the church. This indeed was the dispensation of God, that the See of Peter might not be dishonored by a government of two heads, which is a symbol of discord and contrary to the laws of the Church.

5. The Orthodox Faith of Peter

Hilary of Poitiers, *Commentarius in Matthaeum,* XVI, 7. Text. J. P. Migne, *Patrologia Latina,* IX, 1009–1010.

[Comment on the confession of Peter, "Thou art the Christ, the Son of the Living God."] It is clear that the confession of Peter deserved a reward, because he discerned in a man the Son of God. Blessed is he who was praised for understanding and sight beyond mortal eyes, who looked not for that which was of flesh and blood but beheld the Son of God through revelation of the Father in heaven. Worthy was he to receive his commendation, since he was the first to recognize that which was in the Christ of God. O thou who wert called by thy new name to be the happy foundation of the Church, worthy stone of that building, to loose the jaws of hell and the gates of Tartarus and all the bonds of death! O blessed doorkeeper of heaven, to whose power are committed the keys of the eternal entrance, whose judgment upon earth is prejudged as authoritative in heaven, so that whatever is bound or loosed by it on earth assumes the same status under edict of heaven!

[226] Felix lived seven years after Liberius' return and died only a year before him.

Ibid., *De Trinitate*,[227] VI, 37. Text. J. P. Migne, *Patrologia Latina*, X, 187–188.

This faith [Peter's confession] is the foundation of the Church; through this faith the gates of hell are impotent against it. This faith holds the keys of the kingdom of heaven. Whatever this faith looses or binds on earth is bound or loosed in heaven. This faith is a gift by revelation from the Father, no false invention of Christ as a creature made from nothing, but a confession of the Son of God in his proper nature. O wretched stupidity and impious folly, that fail to recognize the witness of blessed age [228] and faith, that witness being Peter, for whom prayer was offered to the Father that his faith fail not in temptation,[229] who when he had repeated on request his profession of love for God, was grieved at the third inquiry that he was so tested, as if he were doubtful and wavering, but who was thereby thrice accounted worthy, after his three trials by the Lord to cleanse him of infirmity, to hear the words: "Feed my sheep";[230] who, when all the other apostles were silent, knew the Son of God by revelation of the Father and by his confession, surpassing the bounds of human weakness, won the superlative glory of his blessed faith! How are we now compelled to interpret his words? He confessed Christ as Son of God but you, lying priests of a novel apostolate, offer me today Christ, a creature, made out of nothing. What violence do you put upon his glorious words! He confessed the Son of God and for that was blessed. This is the revelation of the Father, this is the foundation of the Church, this is the security of eternity. For this he holds the keys of the kingdom of heaven, for this his judgments on earth are judgments of heaven. He by revelation dis-

227 This was the work composed between 356 and 359, during Hilary's exile in Asia Minor. Its original title was *De Fide adversus Arianos*.

228 "Beatae senectutis." Hilary seems to have been thinking of Peter as already an old man.

229 Luke, XXII, 31, 32.

230 John, XXI, 15–17.

closed the sacrament hidden from the ages; he voiced the faith, he declared its nature, he confessed God's Son. He who denies it and confesses instead a creature must, first, deny the apostolate of Peter, his faith, his blessedness, his priesthood, his martyrdom,[231] and next, he must realize that he is estranged from Christ, inasmuch as Peter by confessing him as the Son won all these rewards.

6. The Return of Liberius to Orthodox Leadership

Liberius, *Letter to the bishops in Italy,* Hilary, *Fragmenta Historica,* Series B, IV, 1. Text. *Corpus Scriptorum Ecclesiasticorum Latinorum,* LXV, 156–157.

Liberius to the catholic bishops in Italy, greeting forever in the Lord.

Repentance wipes out the guilt of ignorance. This we may learn also from the holy Scriptures. We read that godliness is profitable for all things and that discipline of the body is inferior to it, although that too has its profitable fruits. The nature of the present situation requires us to practice godliness. So whoever there may be who carry their zeal to the point of destroying by arrogant and cruel censure the effect of our reasonable provisions, let them consider this, that they are contradicting what apostolic authority once affirmed regarding godliness, when they say that the men who erred in ignorance at Rimini should not be forgiven.[232] They ought by rights to know that a captive falls into error and for that reason severity should not be thought of. But I, on whom it is incumbent to weigh everything in moderation, have decided, especially now that all

231 "Martyrium." The word seems here to have the sense of "martyrdom," although above, in the same paragraph, "martyr" is certainly "witness." *Supra,* p. 269, n. 71.

232 Liberius is, of course, referring to the austere party of Lucifer and Hilary, the deacon.

the Egyptians and the Achaeans have adopted the same opinion and reinstated many, that the persons of whom we have just spoken should be forgiven,[233] but that the leaders should be condemned, since they with equivocal and malicious subtlety and craft made innocent souls offend by drawing a veil before them over the truth and representing darkness as light and light as darkness.

So whoever has felt within him that wily and secret pestilential virus of the Arian doctrine but repents of his captivity to ignorance at the merciful appeal of our words and knows himself profoundly renewed, let him condemn and assail vigorously the leaders of it, whose violence he has experienced against himself, and let him commit himself totally and unreservedly to the apostolic and catholic faith, even to the consensus of the synod of Nicaea.[234] By that profession, even though to some it appears slight and inadequate, he will recover that integrity which he lost by guile. But if there is anyone of so callous a mind, — as I hardly believe there is, — that he not only denies that one who receives the medicine of health is cured but even asserts that he is taking poison and virus instead, let him be overruled by reason and counted among the leaders of deadly falsehood and punished by the spiritual might of the catholic Church.

Socrates, *Historia Ecclesiastica,* IV, 12. Text. J. P. Migne, *Patrologia Graeca,* LXVII, 483–496.

But when the Homoousians had been forcibly driven out [from positions in the eastern church], then the persecutors turned against the Macedonians. And they, in the dis-

233 Thus far the letter is almost unintelligible, as it stands in the extant Latin text. We follow a conjectural, emended text, suggested in J. P. Migne, *Patrologia Latina,* X, 714–716.

234 Liberius' literary style is never simple. Note the profusion of metaphors in this sentence.

comfort of fear rather than of actual violence, sent envoys to one another throughout the cities, to explain that they must look for shelter to the brother of their emperor and to Liberius, bishop of Rome, and that it was better to adopt their faith than to commune with Eudoxius. So they sent Eustathius of Sebaste, who had been condemned many times, and Silvanus of Tarsus in Cilicia and Theophilus of Castabala, which is a city of Cilicia. And they instructed them not to disagree with the faith of Liberius but to commune with the Roman church and to subscribe to the faith of "homoousios."[235] So these men brought letters from the dissenters at Seleucia and came to old Rome. They did not find the emperor, for he was in Gaul, engaged in the war there against the Sarmatians. But they delivered their letters to Liberius, who was very unwilling to receive them. For he said they belonged to the Arian party and could not be received by the Church, because they had overthrown the faith of Nicaea.[236] And they replied that they had repented and recognized the truth and had already abjured the faith of the Anomoeans and confessed that the Son was in all respects like the Father, and that there was no difference between likeness and "homoousios" [*i.e.* sameness of substance]. When they said this, Liberius required of them a written confession of their belief. And they offered him a document in which the very words of the creed of Nicaea had been inserted.

The letters which they had written after holding synods in Smyrna in Asia and in Pisidia and Isauria and Pamphylia

[235] Sozomen says that they "wrote to Liberius, bishop of Rome, and to the bishops of the West, on the ground that they had the right and sure faith from the apostles and ought above all others to superintend religion, and they asked them to assist their delegates with all their power and to advise with them as to what must be done in any way they thought best to restore the state of the Church." *Historia Ecclesiastica,* VI, 10. He gives the text of the profession of faith presented to Liberius. *Ibid.,* VI, 11. Compare these accounts with that given by Basil, *infra,* p. 655.

[236] It is not strange that Liberius hesitated. He had last seen Eustathius among the victorious court party at Sirmium. The creed which he had been required to sign there had been a variation of their "homoiousian" semi-Arianism.

and Lycia I have not copied here because of their length. But the document which Eustathius and the other envoys presented to Liberius runs as follows:

"Eustathius, Theophilus and Silvanus to their lord and brother and fellow minister Liberius, greeting in the Lord.

[Statement of complete adherence to the Nicene Creed.] . . . And if any one after this exposition of our faith, attempts to bring any accusation against us or against those who sent us, let him come with a letter from your holiness before the orthodox bishops whom your holiness approves and in their presence let him be tried along with us. Then if any part of the accusation be substantiated, let the guilty be punished." So with this document Liberius tied the hands of the delegates and then he received them into communion and dismissed them with the following letter.

The letter of Liberius, bishop of Rome, to the bishops of the Macedonians:

"Bishop Liberius and the bishops of Italy and the West to their beloved brethren and fellow ministers, Euethius,[237] Cyril, . . . Lucius and all the orthodox bishops in the East, greeting forever in the Lord.

The long desired joy of peace and concord, illumined by the light of faith, beloved brethren, was brought to us by your letter, which you sent us by our honored brethren, the bishops Eustathius, Silvanus and Theophilus, especially now that they have assured and proved to us that your belief and your teaching are in harmony and unison with those of my poor self and of all the bishops in Italy and the West. This we know to be the catholic and apostolic faith, which remained pure and unspotted down to the Council of Nicaea. This same faith they have professed to hold and in fullness of rejoicing they have dispelled every trace and taint of suspicion, for not only by word but also in writing they have

237 The names of the sixty-four bishops who had written to Liberius.

made a declaration to this effect. We have decided that we should append a copy of it to this our letter, so as to leave no ground for the heretics to conspire again and stir up again the sparks of their malice and set the fierce fires of discord to blazing.

Our honored brethren, Eustathius and Silvanus and Theophilus, have now affirmed that you also have always held this faith in love and will defend it to the end, namely, that faith which was professed by the three hundred and eighteen orthodox bishops at Nicaea.

And even though all the bishops of the West, assembled at Rimini, were outdone by the malignant Arians, until through over-persuasion or, to be more exact, imperial compulsion, they condemned or indirectly denied that which is the firm foundation of our faith, even so, this piece of wickedness has availed the other party nothing. For almost all the bishops who were at Rimini and were ensnared or deceived on that occasion have now returned to their senses and anathematized the profession of the convention of Rimini and have subscribed to the catholic and apostolic faith which was promulgated at Nicaea. They have come into communion with us and are bitterly indignant against the doctrine of Arius and against his adherents. And when the envoys of your love understood the meaning of that performance, they subscribed, in your names as well as in their own, to the anathema against Arius and against the transactions at Rimini, which were contrary to the faith promulgated at Nicaea and to which false testimony had led you to subscribe. So it has seemed to me fitting to write to you in support of those who ask for justice, especially since I have learned from the declaration of your envoys that the Easterners have returned to their right minds and are in accord with the orthodox in the West. . . .

[The doctrines of Rimini are now generally repudiated and men are emerging ' from the darkness of heresy into the divine light of catholic freedom.' Arians, Sabellians and Patripassians are all excommunicate.] . . ."

With this letter, Eustathius and his companions travelled first to Sicily. And there they arranged for the holding of a council of the Sicilian bishops and in their presence they professed the faith of " homoousios " and endorsed the Creed of Nicaea and after obtaining from them also a letter of similar tenor, they returned to those who had sent them. These latter, on receiving the letter of Liberius, sent messengers to the bishops of the faith of " homoousios " throughout the cities, summoning them to meet with one accord in Tarsus of Cilicia, in order to reaffirm the faith of Nicaea and to repudiate all the contentiousness that had arisen since. This would probably have come to pass, had not the man who had then most influence with the emperor prevented it. I mean Eudoxius, who was a bishop of the Arian sect and who was much displeased at the news of the council and did these men great harm. But Sabinus, in his *History of Councils,*[238] has told how the Macedonians, through the envoys whom they sent, did commune with Liberius and confirm the faith of Nicaea.

DAMASUS

(366–384)

Damasus, whose pontificate brings us to the end of this chronicle, has been called the greatest of the early Roman bishops. He was a man of much practical shrewdness and self-assertive energy. He had time and interest to spare for enterprises in more than one unusual field, such as archaeology, epigraphy and Biblical text revision, in which we cannot follow him.[239] Yet he quite as clearly lacked that greatness of spirit

238 A work long since lost.

239 On some of these enterprises, *vide supra,* pp. 108, 113. See also Jerome's preface of 383 to his version of the New Testament, contained in every edition of the Vulgate. Extracts from this are in J. C. Ayer, *Source Book for Ancient Church History,* pp. 485–486.

that shows so strikingly in his contemporaries, Athanasius, Basil, Gregory Nazianzen and Ambrose. His acts, his letters, his metrical inscriptions, all betray the same dry, cold temperament and are all singularly devoid of any spontaneous generosity of feeling, magnanimity of judgment or breadth of vision. His two letters to Jerome which we give below, the most personal pieces of writing which we have from him, contain some of the questions which his reading of the Old Testament suggested to him and show his magisterial way of checking up the sacred narrative and his impatience with such authors as spent time in discussing irrelevant subjects, like geography or philosophy.

Scholars and refugees, who could be patronized or made useful to him, works by which his name might be perpetuated in monuments about the city, these appealed to him. Great causes, that required disinterested, patient effort and far-reaching imagination and sympathy fared badly with him. Circumstances gave him an unprecedented opportunity to make the See of Rome what his forerunners had contended it should be, the head of a united Christendom. The principal bishops of the East entreated him to assume the leadership in the reconstruction of their shattered churches. An imperial decree confirmed to him the appellate jurisdiction over the entire episcopate. But he proved incapable of rising to the heights of charity or of understanding demanded of one who would make himself indeed " bishop of the bishops." Before his death, the door in the East, which had been held open for him to enter, was definitively closed. The emperors seem to have grown less whole-hearted in their support. There had always been a stubborn party of distrust and disaffection in Italy. In spite of his ostentatious activity and splendor, when measured by the standard of what he might have been and done, Damasus appears as one of those ambitious but short-sighted men who never in all their busy lives discover where greatness really lies.

As bishop, he had to meet two searching tests. The first was in the West, where the church, when he took it over, was already divided on the issues created by the devious career of his predecessor, Liberius. A clash of some kind may have been inevitable, no matter what policy Damasus represented. Our first three or four extracts reveal the pent-up indignation that burst into explosion as soon as occasion offered.[240] They reveal also the methods which Damasus and his cohorts took to deal with it. By force and bloodshed, legal and illegal, he crushed the Ursinians at Rome and drove them into exile or hiding. By vigorous demonstrations of authority he overawed the Italian bishops. In 378, twelve years after his accession, one of his episcopal synods drew up a petition to the emperors, in which it reviewed the western situation, reported the remnants of opposition that persisted here and there, and asked for the confirmation to Damasus of final jurisdiction over all bishops and metropolitans everywhere and the aid of the State in bringing to justice any who refused to submit.[241] The emperors obligingly consented and the coercive process went on. Three years later, an imperial statute conferred upon Damasus the position of supreme exponent of the true faith of the holy apostle Peter and ordered every subject of the Empire to follow his doctrine.[242] Yet, the year before his death, a petition presented by two western priests to the emperors proves the horror that some who were most orthodox in creed still felt for his ruthlessness and violence.[243] He had not convinced them nor won them over to him with all his power. By this time, indeed, the struggle had become almost altogether personal. No one then seems to have wanted to undo the restoration of the old apostates of Liberius' day, over which the controversy had first been waged. When at length a bishop of cleaner record and more pacific temper succeeded Damasus, the rebels gradually laid down their arms and harmony became possible once more.

In the East, on the other hand, Damasus inherited no handicap from his predecessor and his failure to respond to the needs of the churches there was for that reason less excusable and even more serious in its results. The letters of Basil, as also the extracts we give from other contemporary eastern writers, show how self-depreciatory had become by this time the spirit of many earnest leaders of eastern Christianity and how sincere was the deference they were prepared to pay to him of Rome.[244] In every

240 *Infra*, pp. 629, 630, 632.
241 *Infra*, p. 666.
242 *Infra*, p. 675.
243 *Infra*, p. 689.
244 See particularly *infra*, pp. 645, 652, 666.

essential of faith they felt that they were now one. They asked only that the Roman stretch out a hand of fellowship to them in their dire straits, intercede for them with the emperor, send commissioners to hear and arbitrate their ecclesiastical disputes, and assume, in general, the responsibility incumbent on one to whom God had granted the divine gifts of peace and an unerring perception of the truth. But ten years of pleading and negotiation produced no more fruitful results than the dogmatic championing by Damasus of one eastern minority party and his lofty refusal to coöperate with any others, except at the price of complete and literal submission in every detail.[245]

As late as 381, however, Gregory of Nazianzus could still dream of bringing music out of the discord of the two great choruses, seeing that nothing fundamental separated them, merely the jealousies stirred up by rival claimants for the bishoprics. His narrative poem, describing the council called at Constantinople after the accession of Theodosius and the end of government persecution, breathes the pure passion for reconciliation in the name of Christ that had burned in the souls of Basil and his friends.[246] But again the acrimonious influence of Damasus worked against it. His delegates arrived late at the council and haughtily took it to task for certain technical irregularities in eastern procedure. The bishops of Asia, already antagonized by Damasus' arrogant and dilatory treatment of their necessities, now broke into angry counter-accusations. Gregory fled home in despair. When, a year later, Damasus invited the Easterners to reopen the question of the see of Constantinople before him and his council at Rome, they replied with a letter which shows how their hearts had hardened against him. They were grateful for this sudden access of concern for their affairs but they could hardly transport themselves all the distance to Italy. Besides, their worst trials were now over.[247] About the same time, Theodosius published a list of prominent eastern bishops, whose faith might be taken as a standard of orthodoxy as well as that of Damasus. The supreme opportunity to bring East and West together under the presidency of Rome was gone. Yet the East

[245] *Infra*, pp. 646, 647, 674.

[246] *Infra*, p. 679.

[247] *Infra*, p. 686.

was still willing to acknowledge in theory the Roman primacy, as it did in the fourth canon of the Council of 381. But the same canon created a new local head for all the eastern churches, the see of "New Rome."[248]

We have summarized in the foregoing sentences a few of the conspicuous features and incidents of Damasus' administration and have called attention to a few of the more notable documents from which we quote below. The full story of his acts and policies is rather peculiarly complicated, owing to the shifting state of parties and of creeds, western as well as eastern, during the eighteen years that he occupied the Lateran. For those readers who will follow it more closely and who need to get more exactly the relationship and bearing of all our material we give our customary, amplified discussion in the ensuing pages. To make it somewhat clearer we have disposed it under three headings, the first covering Damasus' relations with the churches and clergy in Rome and Italy, the second those with the bishops of the western provinces outside Italy, and the third those with the churches of the East.

i. Damasus and the Clergy of Rome and Italy

Damasus' part in the Roman crisis caused by the banishment of Liberius has already been described.[249] He owed his election as bishop to that uncritical majority which had applauded Liberius on his return from exile and had later acquiesced in his lenient policy toward the signers of the Rimini creed, the partisans of Felix and the delegates from the eastern Homoiousians. That the Roman clergy had themselves meanwhile been growing lax and worldly in their habits is proved by the edict which the emperors ordered read in the Roman churches in the year 370, forbidding any monk or other ecclesiastic to visit the house of a widow or an heiress, or to receive gifts from a woman, even by bequest. That Damasus himself was not altogether free from personal reproach is proved by the epithet his enemies applied to him, "the ladies' ear-tickler." But on the day of his election,

[248] *Infra*, p. 686. [249] *Supra*, pp. 580–581.

a party of conscientious objectors, including seven priests and three deacons, who found the others too easy-going for their more sensitive scruples, met apart in the basilica of Julius (Santa Maria in Trastevere), chose the deacon Ursinus for their bishop and ordained him on the spot, with the aid of a bishop from Tivoli. The ordination of Damasus had been postponed until the next Sunday.

Our excerpts describe, from different standpoints, the bloody fracas that ensued. A crowd of Damasus' adherents marched across the Tiber and attacked the church of Julius, killing or wounding several Ursinians. They then proceeded with a great display of arms to fortify the Lateran against a counter-attack and to hold the consecration of Damasus. Riotous bands from both sides fought in the streets. The prefect Viventius, after some hesitation, determined to recognize Damasus and banished Ursinus and the two deacons. But the Ursinian contingent refused to come to terms and obstructed the processions of Damasus, when he and his train went in parade through the city. Damasus appealed to the prefect against their violations of order and the seven priests were arrested. Their followers thereupon rescued them from the guards and bore them off to the massive, new basilica of Liberius (Santa Maria Maggiore) on the Esquiline, which they barricaded and converted into a fortress. Damasus' men laid siege at once with axes and fire. Ammianus Marcellinus, the pagan historian, says that when the building was finally stormed, one hundred and thirty-seven corpses were counted on the floor and that the people remained for a long time in an ugly mood.

Through a series of imperial edicts, the text of which we omit for brevity's sake, we may trace the later steps in the story of this disturbance.[250] The first of these edicts, issued in the summer of 367 to the new prefect, Praetextatus, illustrates Valentinian's favorite tactics of conciliatory "laissez faire." Ursinus and his companions are to be released from banishment on the sole condition that they do not again break the peace. The

[250] These texts are contained in the so-called *Collectio Avellana*, 5–12, *Corpus Scriptorum Ecclesiasticorum Latinorum*, Vol. XXXV, pp. 48–54. *Supra*, p. 580, n. 215. Their contents are summarized briefly here.

second, a response to a complaint from Damasus that the Ursinians still occupy the basilica of Liberius, orders Praetextatus to restore the edifice to Damasus "for peace's sake." The third edict, dated January 12, 368, is obviously a reply to a discouraging report from Praetextatus and empowers him to expel Ursinus and his ministers from Rome "for the sake of the peace of the eternal city." They may live hereafter anywhere they please except in Rome. Late in the same year, an edict to Olybrius, the successor of Praetextatus, mentions tumults occasioned by the meetings of dissenters just outside the walls. Such meetings, we learn elsewhere, had been taking place in the basilica of St. Agnes on the Via Nomentana. All such assemblies are now forbidden within twenty miles of the city. A similar rescript to the vicar of the suburban diocese of Rome directs him to coöperate with the prefect in enforcing the new regulation. Ursinus himself is to be removed into confinement in Gaul. By these firm measures quiet seems to have been restored, at least outwardly. Two or three years later, Valentinian once more releases Ursinus and eight companions from their imprisonment, stipulating merely that they shall none of them set foot again in Rome or in its vicinity or stir up further agitation, and warning them that if they disobey, they will not be treated any longer as Christians but as legal outcasts, "obstreperous disturbers of the public tranquillity and enemies of law and religion."

Ursinus, however, was a man of resource and implacable resolution. By one means or another he contrived to keep Damasus on tenterhooks for some time longer. Once his party petitioned the emperor to summon a council to investigate the fitness of "a murderer" to hold the chair of Peter. In 376 or 377, a Jew called Isaac, a temporary convert to Christianity, prompted, it was generally believed, by the Ursinians, brought a criminal accusation of a grave sort against Damasus.[251] The city prefect, in whose court the case came up for trial, was unimpressed by the episcopal majesty. It suddenly looked as if

[251] The *Liber Pontificalis* says that the charge was adultery but this is probably an error. Damasus was by this time over seventy years of age. It was more likely one of excessive cruelty in the treatment of schismatics, such as the other complaints against him of which we hear. L. R. Loomis, *The Book of the Popes,* 82.

degradation, if not death, might be in store for the defendant, when the young emperor Gratian was prevailed upon to intervene and transfer the suit to his own tribunal at Milan. There Ambrose and other loyal Catholics procured an acquittal. Isaac was deported to Spain as a penalty for libel and Ursinus to prison, this time in far-away Cologne. But his followers still continued their agitation. In 381, they secured the ear of an influential eunuch, Paschasius, and then of the prefect, who in his report of that year to the emperors raised again the question of Damasus' standing and conduct. But Ambrose and the council of northern bishops at Aquileia, of which he was the leading spirit, presented a memorial in protest and once more the unpleasantness was hushed up.

One member of Ursinus' party was a bishop Aurelius, who held communion with representatives of similar austere groups abroad, such as Gregory, bishop of Granada. An ascetic priest, Macarius, met his congregation secretly at night, but was seized and so brutally mauled that he died at Ostia on the road to exile. After the death of Ursinus, in 382 or 383, his adherents elected another bishop, Ephesius by name, whom Damasus cited before the prefect Bassus as a Luciferian heretic,[252] but whom Bassus declined to punish on the ground that his schism implied no heterodoxy of doctrine.[253] It may have been this episode that inspired Jerome, then on a close and friendly footing with Damasus, to compose his dialogue against the Luciferians, setting forth in dark colors all the errors of which they were presumably guilty. In the year 383, the last of Damasus' life, two priests, Faustinus and Marcellinus, presented a lengthy petition to the emperors Valentinian, Theodosius and Arcadius, in which they rehearsed the iniquities of their various persecutors, in especial of " that extraordinary archbishop " Damasus, charging him with usurpation of regal authority and corruption of the magistrates for the purpose of driving good Christians out of Rome.

252 On Lucifer of Cagliari, *vide supra*, pp. 537, 538, 551.

253 Beside the edicts directed specifically against Ursinus and his party, there were others in existence, prohibiting heretics from meeting, owning houses of assembly, etc. The earliest of which we hear was issued by Constantine. Eusebius, *Vita Constantini*, III, 64–66. There is reference to another in *Codex Theodosianus*, XVI, 5, 4, and a reënactment in *ibid.*, 55.

There was opposition to Damasus also among the bishops of Italy. The synod which he called at Rome in 367, upon the anniversary of his ordination, agreed with him to condemn Liberius, on what score we are not told.[254] But when he proposed to the same assembly to condemn his rival Ursinus, they loudly refused, insisting that they could not condemn any man without a fair trial. When the Ursinian priest Macarius, the victim of Damasus' rough-handed followers, died in Ostia, the local bishop gave his body reverent sepulchre in the basilica of a martyr. When, after the banishment of Ursinus, Damasus himself tried and deposed certain bishops who had notoriously sympathized with the schismatics, some others denied his right to adjudicate; and two of the deposed culprits, the bishops of Parma and Pozzuoli, returned to their churches in bold defiance of his sentence, even after one of them, who had appealed to the emperor, had received answer that the Roman's verdict must be obeyed. It is doubtful whether this hostile group had been entirely eliminated by the time of Damasus' death.

Heretics also flourished and made converts in spite of all that could be done to suppress them. The Novatianists still preserved their separate organization under their own bishop[255] and the African Donatists maintained a church in connection with the parent body at Carthage.[256] Their bishop, Claudian, could not be evicted from Rome, even by an emperor's ordinance. It was, in fact, difficult to establish satisfactory relations with Africa at all, for Restitutus, bishop of the regular community at Carthage, who had been so conspicuous at Rimini,[257] refused to abjure the Rimini creed or to participate in the general retreat to the platform of Nicaea. Damasus sent instructions to have him tried by a synod, but neither he nor the African church paid any attention to this communication nor would the emperor Valentinian risk the dangers of civil interference.

[254] *Chronicle* of Prosper of Aquitaine. P. Jaffé, *Regesta Pontificum Romanorum,* (1885), Vol. I, p. 37.

[255] *Supra,* pp. 382, 426. Socrates says that until the time of Celestine I (422–432) " the Novatianists flourished exceedingly in Rome, having many churches there and collecting large congregations." *Historia Ecclesiastica,* VII, 11.

[256] *Supra,* pp. 450, 466.

[257] *Supra,* p. 547.

However, these domestic trials could be overridden after a fashion. Damasus could neither soften nor appease his adversaries nor was he quite strong enough to root them out of Rome and Italy by force. But with the help of his brawny agents and the city magistrates he could break up their illegal congregations and compel them to go more or less into hiding. The Italian bishops might mutter restive criticisms behind his back but gradually he got the majority well in hand. He called them more often to synods than any one in his position had done before. At least, there are more records of synods under him than under any of his predecessors. Jaffé lists seven to which allusions are made by contemporary writers. The first, which at one moment threatened to become mutinous, has already been mentioned. For some years afterwards, Damasus does not seem to have raised the subject of Ursinus. But in his second synod, in 368 or 369, he did procure the condemnation of that pair of veteran mischief-makers and turncoats, Ursacius and Valens,[258] a popular measure one would certainly suppose.

In his third synod, a gathering of ninety bishops from Gaul as well as Italy, held in or about 370, he expounded the dogma of the Trinity for the benefit of those who might be hazy as to the exact orthodox position, and carried through the condemnation of Auxentius, the elderly Arian, whom Constantius had installed at Milan some twenty-five years before.[259] Valentinian had already ruled that for peace's sake Auxentius should be left undisturbed as long as he lived. It required, therefore, some daring to denounce the bishop of the northern capital, under the imperial protection. Damasus, however, did not take this step until after some bold, local bishops of Venetia and Gaul had drawn up a protest against Auxentius' continuance in office. He referred, indeed, to their action by way of justifying his own. Athanasius too had been pressing him to make a definite stand against the Arians who still remained in the western provinces. The letter which went out from this synod to the East denied also the

[258] *Supra,* pp. 529, 531, 533, 564. Athanasius, *Epistola ad Afros,* 10.

[259] *Supra,* p. 538. The letter from the synod to the eastern bishops is quoted *infra,* pp. 634–636. For the "tomus" or statement of dogma, see C. J. Hefele, *Histoire des Conciles,* Vol. I, pt. II, pp. 980 *sq.;* Sozomen, *Historia Ecclesiastica,* VI, 23; Theodoret, *Historia Ecclesiastica,* II, 17.

validity of the proceedings of the apostate Council of Rimini on the ground that they had never been ratified by the Roman bishop, "whose judgment should have been asked first of all."

The fourth, fifth and seventh synods of Damasus were occupied chiefly or altogether, for anything we know to the contrary, with questions arising out of the condition of the eastern churches and the heterodox tendencies in eastern theology. But the sixth, convoked in 378, soon after Damasus' deliverance from the menace of Isaac, bore striking witness to the ascendancy which he had by that time established over his colleagues in the peninsula. It addressed a long petition to the emperors on behalf of "our holy brother Damasus," reviewing first the perils to which he had been exposed from the Ursinians and other antagonists and going on to request that all bishops who refused to submit to the judgment of his or any other similar catholic court should be compelled by the local prefect to appear and undergo sentence. All Italians should be remanded to Rome; more distant bishops to their metropolitans. Any metropolitan under accusation should be referred immediately to Rome or to judges approved by Rome. An appeal to Rome should also be allowed from any metropolitan suspected of prejudice. In short, the Roman bishop should be granted direct jurisdiction over other metropolitans and an appellate jurisdiction over the entire episcopate. A judicial hierarchy should be erected with the aid and countenance of the State.[260] As for the Roman bishop himself, he should surely never be put in a position inferior to those "whom he excels in the prerogative of his apostolic See and who are subject to the public courts from which your edict removed him." If he should ever again be involved in a suit, not strictly ecclesiastical by nature, he should be entitled to carry it straightway to the court of the emperor. In other words, he should be

260 Note the difference between the method of application of the appellate power as proposed here and by the Council of Sardica. *Supra,* pp. 520–521. Constantine had given bishops in general the right to hear all kinds of suits and had ordered state officials to assist in the execution of their verdicts. In 367, Valentinian I had published a rescript which conferred upon the Roman bishop an extended jurisdiction of some kind over other bishops. But the text of this rescript has been lost. Its existence is indicated by the wording of the petition of 378 and of the emperors' answer. Ambrose also alludes to it. *Epistolae,* XXI, 12 and 15. It was evidently less definite and far-reaching than the edict of 378.

exempt from the jurisdiction of the city prefect. Nothing less than the highest civil tribunal should be competent to try him.

The reply of the emperors was conveyed in a rescript of the same year to the vicar Aquilinus. It was favorable in tone but cautious. They sanctioned the use of state officials to enforce the centralized, judicial control of Damasus over the Church, provided only that he did not exercise it too harshly or inflict penalties worse than exclusion from the city in which the offender had held office, and also that he did not reopen cases once settled in his court. They tacitly, however, declined to remove him personally from the authority of the city magistrates, who were merely directed to refuse in the future to entertain accusations brought against him by persons of notoriously low character.

The ablest of all the younger generation of Italian churchmen lent his growing influence on principle to support the dignity of the See of Rome. Ambrose, elected bishop of Milan when Auxentius died in 374, was a son of one of the prominent Roman, Christian families. In his childhood, he had watched the ladies of his household wait upon the bishop Liberius and kiss his hand and had mimicked the bishop's stately bearing and tried to make his young sister kiss his own hand.[261] As bishop of Milan, he regarded it as his unquestionable duty to champion Roman prestige against all attacks. "They have not the inheritance of Peter," he wrote of the Ursinians, "who have not Peter's seat but rend it by wicked schism and who, furthermore, deny in their rebelliousness that sins can be forgiven in the Church, even though it was said to Peter: 'I will give unto thee the keys of the kingdom of heaven.'"[262]

His own impressive personality and strategic post at the courts of Gratian and Valentinian II made Ambrose often, to be sure, a factor of greater importance in the affairs of Italy at large than the more remote and less prepossessing Damasus could be. Occasionally also he took the initiative in ecclesiastical business as none but a Roman bishop or an emperor had ever yet done.

261 Paulinus, *Aurelius Ambrosius,* the biography of Ambrose by his secretary. On Ambrose, see also *supra,* p. 183.

262 *De Pœnitentia,* I, 7, 33. The sin here referred to especially is the sin of apostasy at Rimini.

Through his instrumentality, apparently, a council of bishops from Upper Italy,[263] Africa, Gaul and the Balkan Peninsula was called at Aquileia, in 381, to settle the status of Arianism in the Illyrian and Danubian provinces, to which Damasus had, it seems, given insufficient attention. The prelates of the East were invited to this council but they were then in the midst of their own at Constantinople and sent their regrets. Damasus neither deputed any representative from Rome nor encouraged the bishops of his vicinity to take part. Yet even this assembly did not fail to express its respect and concern for the Roman bishop. Beside deposing two Danubian bishops, it sent a protest to Gratian on Damasus' behalf against Ursinus, who, it declared, should not be allowed to continue harassing "the Roman church, the head of the whole Roman world, and the sacred faith of the apostles, whence issue the laws of our venerable communion for everyone."[263a] It sent also a letter to the eastern sovereign, Theodosius, asking him to summon a general council to discuss the disputed sees in his dominion.

A few months later, a synod held at Milan under Ambrose's own presidency sent a vigorous appeal to Theodosius against the action of the eastern bishops, who at their council in Constantinople had rejected one would-be head of the church in that city and ordained another. "It was the rule and custom of the Fathers to do as Athanasius of holy memory and later Peter, both bishops of the Alexandrian church, and many other Easterners did, that is, to fly to the judgment of the church of Rome, Italy and all the West. . . . Either he who was first ordained should return to Constantinople or else a council of us and the Easterners should be held in the city of Rome to consider the two ordinations."[264] In the spring of 382, Ambrose wrote once more to Theodosius in the name of a local synod to insist that the West had a right to ascertain with whom it ought to be in communion.[264a] Damasus perhaps wrote soon afterward to the same

[263] Upper Italy or "the diocese of Italy" was not considered part of the ordinary metropolitan jurisdiction of the Roman bishop, which included, as we have seen, only "suburbicarian" or Central and Southern Italy. With Ambrose, the bishops of Milan begin to assume a metropolitan responsibility for the North.

[263a] This and the next letter are included among the *Epistolae* of Ambrose, nos. XI and XII.

[264] Ambrose, *Epistolae,* XIII.

[264a] Ambrose, *Epistolae,* XIV

effect[265] and Gratian may have added his endorsement. At all events, Theodosius presently agreed to call the eastern bishops to meet with the western at Rome in 382, to debate again the problem of the see of Constantinople.

This council went through the form of meeting, although it had no effect upon the eastern situation, as we shall see. But, at least, it brought Damasus and Ambrose together in person and gave Damasus a confidence in Ambrose's loyalty and integrity which he seems not to have felt before. When, in that same year, the pagan members of the Roman Senate began their agitation for the repeal of Gratian's edict ordering the removal of the statue and altar of Victory from the Senate House, "holy Damasus, bishop of the Roman church, a priest elected by the will of God, sent to me [Ambrose] the memorial which the great band of Christian senators drew up, declaring that they had not authorized any such enterprise," and Ambrose assumed the rôle of spokesman for the church of Rome to Valentinian II.[266]

ii. Damasus and the Western Churches outside Italy

We know less of Damasus' relations with the western bishops beyond Italy. Of Restitutus, bishop of Carthage, we have already spoken. Acholius of Thessalonica was appointed by Damasus as his vicar in East Illyricum[266a] and acted on more than one occasion as the trusty informant and lieutenant of Rome. In Gaul, Hilary of Poitiers died in the year of Damasus' accession. His friend Martin, however, became bishop of Tours in 374, and although no such theologian and writer as Hilary, threw the weight of his wide reputation for saintliness on the side of orthodox obedience.

From Spain came, at the outset, reports of a temporary schism of the Luciferians, headed by Gregory, bishop of Granada,[267] which annoyed Damasus for a few years but which ap-

265 G. D. Mansi, *Sacrorum Conciliorum Nova et Amplissima Collectio,* III, 427.

266 Ambrose, *Epistolae,* XVII, 10. Ambrose's famous addresses to Valentinian on this subject are printed among his *Epistolae,* nos. XVII and XVIII.

266a B. J. Kidd, *History of the Church to A.D. 461,* Vol. II, p. 328, n. 5.

267 *Infra,* p. 689 and n. 396.

peared to die out after Gregory's death. Yet not long afterward, a more serious movement toward extreme asceticism in Christian life arose in the western provinces under the inspiration of a gifted preacher, Priscillian.[268] Hydatius, metropolitan of Lusitania, sent an account of it to Damasus. The latter replied in rather vague and discreet terms, laying down simply a few general principles to be adopted in dealing with zealots. If they were accused before a Spanish synod, they should not be proscribed on hearsay evidence alone but should be allowed a chance to explain and defend themselves.

In 380, such a synod met at Saragossa under the presidency of Hydatius and passed canons prohibiting the kind of excesses of which the Priscillianists were reputed to be guilty but specifying no offender by name. The Priscillianists, undeterred, continued to make proselytes and within a short time secured the election of Priscillian himself to the bishopric of Avila. Two other Spanish bishops also became members of the sect. These three now attempted to rid themselves of the hostile Hydatius by denouncing him on several scandalous counts to the episcopal body of Spain. Hydatius appealed for assistance to Italy, but this time to the emperor Gratian. Thanks to the help of Ambrose, he obtained an edict against "the false bishops and the Manicheans"[269] in Spain. Priscillian and his two associates next went in person to Milan with testimonials from their people, clearing them from the aspersions of error in doctrine, and displayed these to the quaestor. They then journeyed down to Rome to ask Damasus, "the senior and first over all," to summon Hydatius to be tried before him, as he was fully empowered to do by the legislation of 378. Damasus, however, not daring perhaps to assert his appellate authority where the emperor had become involved and ignoring the very principles he had pre-

[268] On the early Priscillianists, see Sulpicius Severus, *Chronica,* II, 46–51; also the letter from Priscillian to Damasus, from which we quote a passage below. L. Duchesne, *Early History of the Christian Church,* Vol. II, pp. 418–435, gives further bibliography.

[269] The Manichean faith, a late form of Oriental dualism, had been introduced into the Empire toward the end of the third century. Diocletian proscribed it on pain of death, and the Christian emperors made occasional efforts to suppress it. The Priscillianists were accused of a bent toward Manicheanism. *Vide* J. C. Ayer, *Source Book for Ancient Church History,* pp. 375–385.

viously preached to Hydatius, refused to receive or hear them. One of the three Spaniards died at Rome; the other two returned with their appeal to Milan, where they finally obtained a permit from a master of offices to go back unmolested to their sees in Spain. For the time being they were safe. When, a little later, another bishop, Ithacius, endeavored to bring suit against them before the praetorian prefect of Gaul, they procured a new order from Milan to the effect that they should not be tried outside Spain. Not until after the death of Gratian, were the Priscillianist leaders haled before the bishops of Gaul, whence they made their disastrous appeal to the new emperor Maximus, at Trier.

An emperor might and did upon occasion, as we have seen, contravene Damasus' authority but no other western dignitary, lay or ecclesiastical, outdid him in grandeur. Contemporary references to him, such as those scattered through our selections below, lay constant stress upon his magnificence. The prefect Praetextatus, when urged by him to become a Christian, answered in meaning jest: "With pleasure, if you will make me bishop of Rome." [270] The pagan Ammianus Marcellinus thought it quite natural that men who cared for pomp and splendor should fight with every weapon at command for the post of the Roman bishop, who exceeded even royalty in his sumptuous extravagance. The letters of Basil, of which we shall speak again later, contain more than one ironical comment on him "who is lofty and arrogant and high enthroned and for that reason unable to hearken to people on earth who tell him the truth," who, as he says, reminds one of the words of Diomed concerning Achilles:

> "Thou shouldest not entreat the lofty son of Peleus
> Nor offer countless gifts; he's proud enough."

The gulf was widening between the bishop of Rome and the ordinary bishops of the provinces, a gulf filled high with stateliness and power.

[270] Jerome, *Contra Iohannem Hieros,* 8. Quoted by L. Duchesne, *Early History of the Christian Church,* Vol. II, p. 364.

iii. Damasus and the Churches of the East

In the eyes of the eastern Christians, the position of Damasus stood for everything that was strong, free and enviable. For the first twelve years of his pontificate, 366 to 378, they themselves were enduring the oppressive persecution of the Arian emperor Valens, while the West was basking in the favors of the orthodox Valentinian I and of his son Gratian. Athanasius of Alexandria, the aged ally of the Roman bishops, who, for reasons that we know, had held but scant intercourse with Liberius, promptly opened correspondence with Liberius' successor, with the aim of impressing upon him his duty, as the new standard-bearer of the Nicene faith, to cleanse his flock from the last remnants of Arianism. When, at length, Damasus and his bishops had passed their sentences upon Ursacius, Valens and Auxentius, the most conspicuous survivors of the Arian invasion of the West, and their churches seemed, as a whole, stabilized on the right foundation, the patient exponents of the same faith in the East allowed themselves to hope that Damasus now would imitate the example of Julius and exert himself to succor his brothers everywhere in the Empire.

Within the eastern church, the doctrinal situation was somewhat less problematical than it had been in Julius' day, thirty years before. The strength of the Arian movement was obviously dwindling, even while yet it enjoyed the support of Valens, the emperor. Slowly, of its own accord, the East was habituating itself to the Nicene view of the divinity of Christ and the unity of the Triune God. The chief new development in doctrine of these years was Sabellian, the opposite of Arian, in tendency. Apollinarius, bishop of Laodicea, convinced of the necessity of preserving the unity of Jesus as an individual, began to teach that he had not two minds but one, a divine one, even while he dwelt within a human body and spirit.[271]

In 370, a valiant leader for the Trinitarians appeared in the person of Basil, called the Great, bishop of Caesarea, the capital

271 *Vide* J. Dräseke, *Apollinarios von Laodicea* (*Texte und Untersuchungen zur Geschichte der altchristlichen Literatur,* Vol. VII).

of the province of Cappadocia in Eastern Asia Minor. By birth and education Basil came of the old, mild wing of the Homoiousian party, that had by now drawn distinctly away from the pronounced Arians and was professing its acceptance of the dogma of Nicaea with merely the addition of a qualifying clause regarding the three Persons or Hypostases. His personal reputation for holiness and learning was so high that even Valens did not venture to disturb him but bestowed upon him a tract of land as a site for his hospital and other institutions of charity. Elsewhere, however, the Catholics and those who like Basil might be called Neo-Catholics, all of whom were unwilling to sign the creed of Rimini-Seleucia, were still ruthlessly excluded from their sees. Meletius of Antioch, who had also come originally from the Homoiousians and toward whom Basil felt as a brother, had been forced to flee and the churches in his city were in the hands of the Arianizers. Basil himself, surveying the scene from his outpost in Cappadocia, saw but a single channel through which help might come to the unhappy Christians of the East, where heretics and persecutors were still outwardly triumphant and even those who aimed at orthodoxy were held apart from one another by shades of past differences and memories of old grievances. Could the East be brought again into closer relationship with the West, it might not only reap immediate benefits of spiritual and material aid but it might also in the process forget its own sharp divisions and learn how better to be at peace within itself.

Basil had no near acquaintance with western circles but he knew one Easterner to whom the West was familiar ground, namely Athanasius. In 371, the year after his own ordination, he wrote to the Alexandrian to suggest that he stir up Damasus to take a more lively interest in the fate of his eastern brethren and, as a first step in the programme of pacification, recognize Meletius as bishop of Antioch in preference to either the bigoted Paulinus or his heterodox rivals.[272] A little later, a deacon, Dorotheus, of the congregation of Meletius, came to Basil with messages from his chief and a western letter-bearer arrived with news of the condemnation of the Arian bishops at Rome. The

272 *Supra*, p. 550.

result was a more positive determination on Basil's part to start a concerted appeal to the church of the West. He wrote eagerly to Meletius and Athanasius, begging them to coöperate. Dorotheus, who seemed well qualified for the enterprise, might, he thought, go by way of Antioch and Alexandria to Rome with letters from all the orthodox-minded prelates of Asia and Egypt, in which they should ask for a western commission of wise and peaceable men to meet the eastern bishops in council, ascertain on the spot who were the rightful heads of the churches and renew the old brotherly connections that had lapsed. In particular, the commission should provide for the recognition of one man as catholic bishop of Antioch. Antioch, once healed, would, like a sound head, do much to restore the eastern body. He himself gave Dorotheus a letter to Damasus, reminding him of the benevolence of Roman bishops in the past toward the East in seasons of distress and requesting him to send them envoys on his own authority, if there were difficulty in persuading a western synod to act.

The first hitch in these negotiations occurred at Alexandria. Athanasius, while on hearty terms of communion and friendship with Basil and, like him, profoundly anxious for harmony, had selected Paulinus as his candidate for the bishopric of Antioch. Naturally, therefore, he did not wish to see Dorotheus, one of Meletius' deacons, sent as the common representative to Rome. Dorotheus got no farther than Alexandria and presently returned to Cappadocia. Meanwhile, however, one Sabinus, a deacon from Milan, had appeared in Egypt with a letter from the Roman synod of 370, containing among other things the Roman statement of faith, in which the unity of Father, Son and Holy Spirit in deity, image and substance was emphatically declared. This letter and its bearer Athanasius forwarded to Basil, as if to show him what was the drift of sentiment in western quarters. Basil sent back by Sabinus two letters, one to the brethren and bishops of the West and one to Valerian of Aquileia, metropolitan of Illyria, repeating his entreaties for aid. A third letter was drawn up by a synod of thirty-two bishops, headed by Meletius, more reproachful and less tactful and conciliatory than Basil's but no less earnest in pointing out the crying necessity for western assistance. "Do not permit the faith to be extinguished in the regions where first it shone!" The West has received from the Lord the admirable gift of discernment between falsehood and truth. Let it guide the East now out of its gloom!

With these letters Sabinus returned to Italy. A year passed without a word of response. Meanwhile Athanasius died and the church of Alexandria elected his brother Peter to fill his place. Basil promptly recognized him, as also did Damasus. But the emperor Valens did not see fit to extend to him the immunity he had granted to Athanasius in his last years. The troops and the Arians burst once more into the churches and amid violence and outrage set up an Arian bishop. The clergy who refused to acknowledge him were deported to prison or the desert or the mines. Among them went also the Roman deacon sent by Damasus to congratulate Peter on his accession. Peter himself took ship to Rome, as his brother had done in the days of Julius, and met a hospitable reception from Damasus, who seems to have welcomed the opportunity to play protecting host in his turn to a distinguished exile.[273] He listened also to Peter's views on eastern affairs and learned from him to prefer the irreconcilable Paulinus to the more tolerant Meletius at Antioch and to look with a tinge of suspicion at all the ex-Homoiousians, even at Basil himself.[274]

In the summer of that year, he at last despatched a messenger to Asia, one Evagrius, a native of Antioch, who had accompanied the stalwart Eusebius of Vercellae to Italy eleven years before.[275] Evagrius brought back with him as unsatisfactory all the letters which Basil and the Asiatics had sent by Sabinus the previous

[273] Theodoret, *Historia Ecclesiastica,* V, 22. See also, Socrates, *Historia Ecclesiastica,* IV, 37.

[274] There are various allusions to Peter's presence at Rome, one of which is made by Basil below. Jerome's is interesting. "It was from some priests of Alexandria, from Pope Athanasius and later from Peter, who fled for refuge to Rome, as the safest haven for their communion, to escape the persecution of the Arian heretics, that she [Marcella] heard of the life of the blessed Anthony, then still alive, and of the monasteries in the Thebaid, founded by Pachomius, and of the discipline of virgins and widows." *Epistolae,* 127, *Ad Principiam.* Socrates, *op. cit.,* IV, 22. Sozomen, *Historia Ecclesiastica,* VI, 19. Jerome, in another place, accuses Basil of pride. He may have heard that accusation at Rome. *Chronica.*

[275] *Supra,* p. 551.

year, and a draft of a creed which must be signed without the alteration of a single word by everyone who desired communion with Rome; also a message to the effect that a deputation of eastern bishops must first appear at Rome before any western commissioners could be expected to visit the East. At Antioch, Evagrius joined the Paulinians, refused to commune with the Meletians and evaded Dorotheus, who tried to get an interview with him. Basil heard this news in the midst of correspondence with Meletius on the subject of another letter, which he had thought of sending to the West by a priest, Sanctissimus, who had been travelling about to collect the signatures of clergy of the orthodox camps. It was a cruel disappointment. Basil never hoped for humanity from Damasus again, although he did not yet relinquish the idea of arousing the sympathies of other bishops in the West.

Soon after this, a priest Vitalis, who as a Meletian had gone to Rome from Antioch but who at Rome had identified himself with the Paulinians, returned to the East with a letter to Paulinus from Damasus of formal recognition and confidence.[276] Almost immediately, however, a rumor reached Damasus that led him to fear that Vitalis' orthodoxy was not all that it should be. He sent Paulinus a hurried note of warning by a second messenger, following it quickly by a third letter, in which he enclosed a formula for Paulinus to present to Vitalis and to men like him before admitting them to his communion. The dictatorial tone of these dispatches gave no offense to Paulinus and his adherents, who were, on the contrary, enormously elated over their recognition. Basil himself acknowledged that they had received "an august and impressive testimony in their favor." Yet not on that account would he abandon Meletius. "I have never taken communion," he wrote to Epiphanius, "with any one of those who have since been introduced into that see, not because I look on them as unworthy but because I see no reason for condemning Meletius," who has been a brave defender of the faith since the days of Constantine.[277]

276 The text of Damasus' first letter to Paulinus has not been preserved. A creed which he sent to Paulinus is in Theodoret's *Historia Ecclesiastica*, V, 11.

277 Basil, *Epistolae*, CCLVIII.

He and his party now searched about for a representative to send to Rome with Sanctissimus. At first they considered Basil's brother, the gentle and scholarly Gregory of Nyssa, but Basil was sure that a more practical and sophisticated person would be better fitted to cope with a man like Damasus. In the end, they settled again upon the deacon Dorotheus and gave him letters to the western church at large and to the bishops of Italy and Gaul, in particular, and also a creed upon which they had by this time agreed among themselves. In the letters they explained that they could not forsake their persecuted flocks to go to the West, drew once more a picture of their unhappy plight and begged for a delegation to come and see for itself, speak the word of compassion and fellowship they were longing to hear and intercede with Valens for their relief.

This time the rebuff was at least less frigid. The Roman synod of 375 gave Dorotheus an audience and sent back a speedy reply.[278] In it they reviewed again all the vexed points of current theology and condemned strictly everything that leaned toward Arianism, Sabellianism or Apollinarianism.[279] It was evident that they considered the eastern creed not explicit enough on these momentous matters. They also went on to say that no one who had transgressed the canonical rules for ordination of a bishop could be readily taken into communion. This was clearly a move to bar out Meletius, who had once been elected bishop of Sebaste, although he had not retained the office. "As for relieving the injustices from which you suffer," the letter wound up, "our brother Dorotheus will undoubtedly explain everything to you by word of mouth. We have not been failing in effort, as he himself is witness." But the influence of Damasus and Peter was plain enough. No Westerners were to come to the East and no intercourse would be held with Meletius. On Dorotheus' reappearance in Cappadocia, he told Basil that Peter had thor-

278 We have not the full text of this letter, only a fragment, printed in J. P. Migne, *Patrologia Latina*, Vol. XIII, pp. 352–354.

279 Rufinus says, in speaking of Apollinarius: "His theory was first rejected in the city of Rome by a council convened by Damasus and by Peter, bishop of Alexandria, with the verdict that whoever declared that the Son of God, who was both very God and very man, was lacking in either humanity or divinity should be adjudged an alien from the Church." *Historia Ecclesiastica*, II, 20.

oughly convinced Damasus that both Meletius and Eusebius, another of the old Homoiousians banished by Valens, still belonged among the Arians and that he himself had been so exasperated by Peter's baseless insinuations that he had used unbecoming language to the Egyptian archbishop.

Basil, however, found some slight encouragement in the fact that his party and the Roman assembly were at any rate on speaking terms. In 377, he sent Dorotheus again to Rome with a letter addressed, "To the Westerners," containing a warm acknowledgment of their communication and a full and painstaking analysis of the conditions as they actually existed in the eastern churches. The cause of the Arians, he said, was already lost, although in many places they were momentarily held in power by Valens. There was really no need of repeating the old objurgations against them. The men who now constituted the true menace to the Church were those who remained in it and kept it in ferment, whose tenets were not yet generally branded as erroneous but were everywhere a disrupting element, fatal to concord. Such men were, first, Eustathius of Sebaste,[280] whom Liberius had helped to reinstate in his see and who consorted with the extreme Homoiousians who rejected the Nicene creed; second, Apollinarius, who denied the humanity of the mind of Christ; and, third, Paulinus of Antioch, whose rigid addiction to the letter of Nicaea had led him to compromise with the Sabellian Marcellus.[281] If the West would only employ its great authority to demand an unequivocal and uniform standard of faith impartially from everyone as the price of its communion and would repudiate all recusants, whatever their pretenses, the scattered multitude of eastern Catholics would rally to it with one accord. Even without a council, much might be accomplished by correspondence and messengers. Once more Dorotheus came before a Roman synod with his letter and explanations. But the Westerners, controlled by Damasus, were still cool and distrustful. They would not, they declared, pass sentence on individuals. None of the three whom Basil accused had ever been tried and

[280] On Eustathius, *vide supra,* pp. 587, 592 ff.

[281] Marcellus himself had died about 375, so there was no longer any need of bringing up his personal case. *Supra,* pp. 504, n. 117, 525.

the Apostolic See could not condemn them unheard. It would and did only repeat its general anathemas on notorious heresies.

The reply sounded final, yet within another year a Roman synod, startled, perhaps, by reports of the rapid spread of Apollinarianism, met and denounced by name both Apollinarius and his most prominent disciple, Timothy, bishop of Berytus. It was the last event of importance at Rome at which Peter of Alexandria officiated. For in August, 378, the emperor Valens was killed in battle with the Visigoths and Gratian, the western Augustus, the friend and pupil of Ambrose, became sole sovereign of the entire Empire. One of his first acts in this capacity was to order the recall of all the banished clergy. The Arian appointees of Valens fled in many places before spontaneous uprisings of the populace and left the churches to the returning Catholics. Peter hurried back to Egypt and Meletius to Antioch, albeit in that city the Arians were still sufficiently strong to keep possession of the cathedral edifice. Basil lived just long enough to see the end of tyranny, though not the union of the churches. On January 1, 379, he died, worn out prematurely with anxiety and labor.[282]

A little before his death, he had joined in a third request to Rome, to beg again that some decisive action might be taken against the party of Apollinarius. We have the answer of Damasus, addressed a few months later to the bishops of the East, more superior and condescending in tone than anything he had yet sent them. Twice he called them his "honored sons," as if to impress upon them the fact that they were not his equals.[283] He and Peter, he said, had already condemned Apollinarius and Timothy. There was no occasion for troubling further over that heretic. He would soon inevitably perish. As for themselves, they should discourage all "vain reasoning and idle speculation." They had received from himself the pattern of a sound faith. Whoever wished to be a Christian had only to observe it. It was clear that a more complete submission was

[282] Basil's name was placed at once on the calendar of eastern saints but it does not appear in any extant western martyrology earlier than that of Usuard of the time of Charles the Bald. His anniversary is observed at Rome on June 14.

[283] Until now no bishop had addressed another by any other title than that of "brother," as may be seen in all our previous documents.

expected. In September, 379, one hundred and fifty-three bishops from Syria and Asia Minor met at Antioch and subscribed unconditionally to the formulae which had come from Rome.[284]

They acted in the nick of time. Gratian had already proclaimed as fellow Augustus his Spanish general, Theodosius, and had committed to him the administration of the East. After a summer of beating back the barbarians along the Danube, Theodosius now pitched his winter-quarters at Thessalonica and proceeded to take stock of his new dominion. For a while, however, he was laid up by an illness and during his prostration he received baptism from the orthodox Acholius, bishop of the city.[285] Through him and others he heard dreary reports of the eastern church, leaderless and disunited, in woeful contrast to the prosperous and compact organization of the West. Theodosius decided, the historian Sozomen tells us, to announce at once definitely to his subjects his own views as to doctrine, "so as not to seem to coerce them by suddenly commanding them to accept a religion contrary to their belief."[286] His edict, issued in the names of himself, of Gratian and of Gratian's younger brother, Valentinian II, required of all subjects that they should follow "that religion which the holy Peter delivered to the Romans . . . and which the pontiff Damasus manifestly observes, as does also Peter, bishop of Alexandria," to wit, the faith "in the deity of Father, Son and Holy Spirit, of equal majesty in sacred Trinity." All dissenters would henceforth be liable to the penalties inflicted upon heretics. Thus the standard of Rome was imposed by ordinance of the State upon the whole Church, even as Arianism had been imposed in the East during the reigns preceding.

Theodosius, however, was not immediately free to enforce his edict everywhere. Through the season of 380, the Gothic marauders kept him away from Constantinople. But even in his

284 On the statements contained in these formulae, see L. Duchesne, *Early History of the Christian Church*, Vol. II, p. 336, n. 2.

285 Thessalonica, it must be remembered, lay in territory hitherto regarded as belonging to the sphere of the western emperor. Its bishop, therefore, was still included in the western church. Acholius acted as the vicar and instrument of Damasus in that region.

286 Sozomen, *Historia Ecclesiastica*, VII, 4.

absence, steps were taken to set up an orthodox bishop in place of Demophilus, the old Arian, who had once been mentor to Liberius[287] and who now presided in the great cathedral of Hagia Sophia. Gregory of Nazianzus, the intimate friend of Basil and, like him and Meletius, a devoted Trinitarian of the neo-orthodox wing of the Homoiousians, was chosen and ordained by the catholic groups in the city that had emerged into sight upon the death of Valens. Gregory's poetic and scholarly preaching drew crowds to the little church of the Anastasis (Resurrection). Only the arrival of Theodosius was awaited to eject Demophilus and set the new bishop in his stead.

But before that could take place, interference came from an unexpected source. Peter of Alexandria, ensconced securely in his own see and distinguished together with Damasus by the recent imperial statute, heard with chagrin that an ex-Homoiousian and a friend of Basil and Meletius was stepping into the see of the eastern capital. These offshoots of the Arians, against whom orthodox Alexandria had from the beginning waged so bitter a war, were after all, it seemed, to inherit the land. Nowhere in the East beyond Egypt would the original and uncontaminated Nicenes remain in real control.

In his vexation, Peter sponsored a reckless scheme to substitute for Gregory a Cynic philosopher, called Maximus, a bizarre sort of person, who had made a profession of Christianity while wearing the long hair and abbreviated cloak that marked the Cynic school. This Maximus now went with letters of introduction from Peter to the faithful of Constantinople and received a cordial welcome and entertainment from the unsuspecting Gregory. Instructions were meanwhile circulated surreptitiously among the Alexandrian sailors and travellers in the harbor. One night, when everyone was asleep, a mob of these Alexandrians, escorting a deputation of Egyptian clergy, stole quietly to the church of the Anastasis, elected Maximus bishop of Constantinople, sheared his flowing locks and proceeded to the ceremony of ordination. The first worshippers, coming to the church at dawn, found the rites still going on. Gregory, appalled and dis-

[287] *Supra*, p. 584.

gusted, offered to retire in Maximus' favor but his people, infuriated both at the intruder and at the Alexandrians who had connived with him, held their own bishop fast. Theodosius, informed of this dishonorable stratagem, refused to listen to Maximus' appeal for support. He returned in ignominy to Alexandria to take refuge with Peter.

But the latter now repented of his meddlesome indiscretion, seeing that he had by it displeased the emperor and seriously offended his friend Damasus. For Damasus had heard accounts of the performance at Constantinople from Acholius of Thessalonica and other bishops in the vicinity and had promptly expressed his scandalized amazement that any Christians could so far forget themselves as to propose a pagan philosopher for bishop, adding a scathing reference to interfering busybodies who did not know where to stop. Peter too, therefore, turned a cold shoulder to Maximus, who in revenge stirred up riotous scenes in the streets and had to be banished by the city prefect.

The entry of Theodosius into Constantinople on November 24, 380, put a temporary quietus on all imbroglios. Two days later, Demophilus, the Arian bishop, left the city, and the emperor himself with a gorgeous array of troops escorted Gregory to the throne of Hagia Sophia. The next step was the summons of the eastern episcopate to a general council, to give formal sanction to Gregory's installation and to take measures for the future government of the eastern church. Damasus in Italy had already heard talk of such a gathering. In the spring of 381, the assembly met. It was for the most part composed of neo-orthodox bishops from Asia Minor, Syria and the European regions about the Marmora, men whose antecedents and attitudes were like those of Basil and who now rallied around Gregory and Meletius of Antioch. Paulinus of Antioch did not appear. Peter of Alexandria died just before the council opened. His brother Timothy, who succeeded him, did not arrive until toward the end.

Meletius, as the generally accredited bishop of Antioch, presided at first over the sessions. Gregory was again solemnly installed in the cathedral, cherishing, as he says in the narrative poem from which we quote, the fond dream that in that high place he might bring back peace within the eastern church and harmony and understanding between it and the West. But scarcely was the triumphant ceremony accomplished when Meletius sickened and died. What now was to be done with the see of Antioch?

According to the story told by the historian Theodoret in the next century, the general Sapor had, the previous winter, appeared in Antioch, expelled the Arians from the principal church edifices and delivered them to Meletius, who had at that time satisfactorily demonstrated his orthodoxy by the Roman standards and had then of his own accord attempted to put an end to the schism of Paulinus by offering to share with him the rights of bishop as long as they both lived, on the condition that whoever survived should be accepted as sole head by both parties. Paulinus had proudly rejected the friendly overture but Meletius' proposition was now revived by some of his fellow comrades, notably by Gregory, who assumed the post of president of the council. Let every Catholic, he eagerly urged, now recognize Paulinus as bishop of Antioch and let the long division be healed! Why keep at enmity those for whom Christ died? Unfortunately, to the rank and file of Orientals, Paulinus stood as the candidate of the implacable Damasus and of his intimate, the unpopular Peter of Alexandria. Because of Paulinus, Peter and Damasus and their obstinacy, the peace of the brethren of Asia had been all these years delayed. Why should Asia still make all the concessions? The old, rancorous comparisons between East and West came to men's lips. "Was it not in the East that Christ was born?" "Yes," replied Gregory, "and it was in the East that he was slain." The early, happy concord of the assembly was destroyed and half obliterated scores and grudges cropped up on every side.[288]

In the midst of this turbulent discussion, Timothy arrived

[288] The fullest report of these events is given by Gregory himself in his *Carmen de Vita Sua,* from which we quote extracts. See also Sozomen, *Historia Ecclesiastica,* VII, 7. Compare this anti-western feeling with that expressed by the Council of Antioch. *Supra,* p. 506.

from Alexandria and Acholius from Thessalonica. They too advocated the recognition of Paulinus but not like Gregory with moving pleas for charity and brotherhood in the name of Christ. Instead, they blew "with the harsh wind of the West" and brandished the authority of Rome. They even, in order to cast discredit upon eastern methods, raised objections to Gregory's ordination on the ground that he had formerly been ordained to other bishoprics, although he had never occupied them. Gregory, now utterly despairing, seized upon the excuse thus presented to insist upon his own resignation. In a last fervent address, he bade farewell to the city of Constantine, to the great cathedral, to the council, to the East and to the West, for which and through which he had suffered persecution. The assembly was faced with a second empty episcopal chair. The problem of Antioch was dropped. A list of possible candidates for the vacancy in Constantinople was hastily submitted to Theodosius, who selected from it one Nectarius, an elderly and respectable government official, untroubled by passionate convictions in theology or by memories of sore ecclesiastical experience. He was at once consecrated in Gregory's place.

During its various meetings the council drew up four canons, each testifying to some one of the successive gusts of feeling that swayed it. The first declared again the faith of Nicaea and anathematized all heretics, the heterogeneous survivors of the Arian party as well as the Sabellians and the Apollinarians. The second repeated in expanded form the decree of Nicaea requiring bishops of one locality to confine their activities to that locality.[289] The bishop of Alexandria, for example, should attend only to the church in Egypt, the bishops of the East or Syria to the Syrian church, with due regard to the prerogative of Antioch, and so on. The third canon in a few terse words altered the entire framework of eastern ecclesiastical organization. "The bishop of Constantinople," it ran, "shall have the preëminence in honor after the bishop of Rome, for Constantinople is New Rome." It was a blow directly at Alexandria, which at Nicaea had ranked next to Rome. It implied also, of course, that Antioch would henceforth

289 *Supra*, p. 473.

take third place instead of second, although that see had been for a generation so torn with discord and oppression that it had almost ceased to count as an authority at all.

But even more serious to western eyes than the establishment of a new patriarchate second only to Rome, so serious indeed as quite to outweigh the value of the first definite acknowledgment by an eastern council of the Roman primacy, was the introduction of the new principle of patriarchal prerogative. If Constantinople were to stand next to Rome because it was the new capital of the Empire, then it followed that Rome was first because it was the old capital. Religious leadership, that is, belonged where the civil government fixed its seat. As the historian Sozomen said in explanation: "For already not only did the city have this title [New Rome] and a senate and ranks of population and magistracies like the Roman but also contracts were adjudicated there according to the custom of the Romans in Italy and its laws and privileges were in every respect equal to those of the other city." [290] Thus, while on the surface paying all due deference to the Roman bishop, the canon inferentially raised the whole question of the nature of his supremacy and of the rights traditionally accorded to apostolic sees. Damasus made no public protest, so far as we hear. But neither he nor his successors for some centuries would confirm any of this legislation or allow the Council of 381 to be called "ecumenical" and "second to the Council of Nicaea," as the Easterners called it.[291] Leo I, in a letter of the year 452 to the emperor Marcian and the patriarch Anatolius, gave the Roman reason for rejecting it. "The basis of things secular is one and the basis of things divine is another and there can be no sure building save on the rock which the Lord laid as foundation." [292] Not until 869, when Alexandria and Antioch had been for two centuries engulfed in the Moslem Empire, did the Roman legates at another council

290 Sozomen, *Historia Ecclesiastica,* VII, 9. Compare also Canon 28 of the Council of Chalcedon. J. C. Ayer, *Source Book for Ancient Church History,* p. 521.

291 The letter of the council to Theodosius is contained in J. C. Ayer, *op. cit.,* p. 369.

292 *Epistolae,* CIV, 3, and CVI, 2 and 5. J. C. Ayer, *op. cit.,* pp. 478–480. Compare also Gregory I, *Epistolae,* Bk. VII, 34.

in Constantinople put their names to a resolution which recognized the see of that city as second to Rome.[293]

Beside passing these canons, the council issued a statement of belief, unimpeachably Roman and orthodox. At its dissolution, the last of July, Theodosius published an edict in which he named eleven prominent eastern bishops, communion with any one of whom would hereafter constitute a sufficient guarantee of orthodoxy, and ordered that the churches everywhere should now be turned over to men of their persuasion.[294] In Antioch, the adherents of Meletius elected a priest, Flavian, as their new bishop in open contempt of Paulinus. But the West made one more effort to be heard. Letters arrived for Theodosius from the council which was being held under Ambrose at Aquileia and from the bishops of North Italy, commending him for restoring the churches to the Catholics but deploring the fact that Catholics themselves were divided and referring to the just grievances of Timothy of Alexandria and of Paulinus of Antioch against men whose faith had been shaken in times past, a thrust, of course, at the ex-Homoiousians. They did not, as they might conceivably have done, quote the edict of 378 and the right conferred by it on Damasus to judge any case involving other metropolitans. They did, however, assert the right of Rome and the western episcopacy to participate in the settlement of affairs of such wide importance and asked Theodosius to convoke a greater council of both East and West before accepting as decided the situation in Constantinople.[295] Damasus may have sent expostulations on his own account. Eventually Theodosius agreed to request his eastern bishops to attend the synod that was being called at Rome for the summer of 382.

The Roman synod of that year was an exceptionally large one, comprising many prominent heads of western churches, such as Ambrose of Milan, Acholius of Thessalonica and Valerian of Aquileia. Paulinus of Antioch and Epiphanius of Cyprus[295a]

[293] Canon XXI. On the capture of Constantinople by the freebooters of the Fourth Crusade, a Latin patriarchate was erected there which was formally styled second to Rome. At the reunion of the Greek and Latin churches in 1439, the Greek patriarch was recognized as next to the pope.

[294] *Codex Theodosianus*, XVI, 1, 3. J. C. Ayer, *op. cit.*, p. 368.

[295] Two of these letters are included in the *Epistolae* of Ambrose, XII and XIII.

[295a] On Epiphanius, *vide supra*, p. 185.

were also present. Timothy of Alexandria seems to have sent a representative. But the bishops of Constantinople, Asia and Syria, those who had made up the bulk of the Council of 381, had already planned a second council of their own at "New Rome." Some of them did not receive their summons to the West until after their arrival on the Bosphorus. They were fully satisfied with the achievements of the year before and with Nectarius and Flavian. Their creed was as orthodox as anyone's. They had kept the canonical rules of procedure. What more should anyone demand of them? Why carry the details of their personal and local arrangements before a distant and carping tribunal? They wrote a polite letter of regret and explanation to Damasus "and the other holy bishops . . . in the great city of Rome," in which they recalled once more their own past sufferings and thanked the western brethren gravely for their present courtesy in inviting them to council, "for although in the past we were once condemned to endure buffeting alone, now that our rulers are agreed with us in religion, you will not reign without us but we are to reign with you." Unhappily, they said, they had made no preparations for the long journey to the West and had received no authorization from the clergy at home to go so far. They reported their own concord in the faith and the ordination of Nectarius in Theodosius' presence. The letter was carried to Rome by three eastern delegates. The West could do nothing further. Theodosius himself apparently felt that there had been delay and interference enough, for he now sent a commission of high officials and clergy to Damasus, asking him to recognize Nectarius. There was nothing for it but to yield with as much dignity as possible.[296]

There are many signs during Damasus' pontificate that the Roman creed and the Roman primacy were being accepted in principle by the churches abroad as never before, even while his personal influence was resisted when it invaded what were regarded as local liberties of election or administration. To the generality of Christians it is plain that the faith of Rome was

[296] The letter of Damasus to Nectarius is mentioned by Pope Boniface I in the year 422. G. D. Mansi, *Sacrorum Conciliorum Nova et Amplissima Collectio*, VIII, 758.

coming to mean the right faith, the faith of the apostles, and that the See of Rome was par excellence "the Apostolic See." The letters of Basil, in spite of their hurt indignation against Damasus individually, and the autobiographic poem of Gregory Nazianzen reveal the reverence of the best eastern minds for the unswerving steadfastness of Roman leadership and doctrine and their sense of its contrast with the flounderings and errors of the East. The two letters from Jerome to Damasus, written from Syria, express the same feeling with greater ardor and frankness and no reservations. "You are the light of the world, you are the salt of the earth, you are the vessels of gold and of silver; here are the vessels of earth and of wood, the iron rod and the eternal fire. . . . Upon that rock [the See of Peter] I know the Church is built. Whoever eats the lamb outside that house is profane."

Jerome, of course, was born a Westerner but we give below a few extracts from eastern writers of the same period, which illustrate in still more picturesque style the current idealization of Peter and his see. Our first two are from an apocryphal gospel, composed in Egypt shortly before the death of Athanasius. Peter is there ordained archbishop by Jesus himself amid the applauding hosts of heaven. "No man shall be exalted above thee and thy throne and whoever has not the consecration of thy throne, his hand shall be thrust down." One perceives from a passage like this what it might mean to an Alexandrian to know that his church had the approbation of Damasus. Our last two extracts, less hyperbolic and flowery in phrasing, are not less comprehensive in significance. They come from the works of the Syrian Ephraim, who wrote at Edessa in the reign of Valens.[297] Like Hilary of Poitiers, he sees in the confession of Peter the archetype of all later proclamations of the Son of the living God, the mortal weapon against heretics and the rock foundation for true believers. "Thou art the overseer [or bishop]," says Jesus to Peter, "of those who build for me my Church on earth; if they desire at any point to build it wrongfully, do thou, the foundation, prevent them; thou art the

[297] On the quotation by Ephraim of the verses in Matthew in which Peter is given the power of the keys, *vide supra*, p. 287, n. 5.

head of the fountain from which my doctrine is drawn; thou art the head of my disciples; through thee I shall give drink to all nations."

If Damasus had but known how to be less crabbed and less narrowly literal and partisan, if he had made but one gesture of compassionate friendliness, had evinced any sign of the generous spirit of peace, the eastern churches were ready, it would seem, to fall at his feet in gratitude and relief. Basil himself said that the people everywhere would have followed him unhesitatingly. As it was, he consistently chilled and disappointed them, haggled over minutiae of phraseology and etiquette, emphasized his own superiority, took the petty or reactionary view of their disputes and shut his ears to their efforts to enlighten him, made no effectual move to help them when they needed it, intervened injudiciously when the need was past, above all displayed no pity or concern for them as brothers in want, as sheep whom he was charged to feed. In consequence, they admitted formally or, as one may say, ideally the agelong preëminence of the Roman metropolitan over their own less fortunate episcopates but they fought their way through their troubles and solved their difficulties without him. The bonds that might have riveted them to him in life were never forged. The greatest opportunity that had come to a Roman bishop beneath the government of the Empire came to Damasus and he let it slip. In another century, when the Empire had begun to crumble, other opportunities, great also but different, were to arise and Leo was to show, as Damasus had failed to do, the fullness of that authority which by long, slow stages had been gathering about the Roman See.

For references on the pontificate of Damasus, *vide supra,* p. 109; also G. Boissier, *La Fin du Paganisme* (3 vols., 3rd ed., Paris, 1898), pp. 267 *sqq.*; P. Allard, *S. Basile* (Paris, 1899); P. Allard, *Basile,* in A Vacant and E. Mangenot, *Dictionnaire de Théologie Catholique* (7 vols., Paris, 1909–1922), Vol. II; W. Bright, *The Canons of the First Four General Councils* (Oxford, 1882), pp. 90–123; H. Leclercq, *L'Espagne Chrètienne* (Paris, 1906), Chap. III; L. Duchesne, *Early History of the Christian Church* (trans. from the 4th ed. by C. Jenkins, 3 vols., London, 1910–1924), Vol. II, chaps. XI–XIII, XV; C. H. Turner, *Latin Lists of the Canonical Books: The Roman Council under Damasus, A.D. 382,* in *Journal of Theological Studies* (London, 1900), Vol. I, pp. 556 *sqq.*; B. J. Kidd, *History of the Church to A.D. 461* (3 vols. Oxford, 1922–1925), Vol. II, pp. 231–327.

1. The Dispute over Liberius' Successor

Socrates, *Historia Ecclesiastica,* IV, 29. Text. J. P. Migne, *Patrologia Graeca,* LXVII, 541–544.

When the emperor Valentinian was reigning in quiet and giving no encouragement to heresy, Damasus, successor of Liberius, obtained the priestly office of bishop at Rome. In his day, there was great disturbance in the church at Rome for the following reason. Ursinus, a deacon of the same church, was nominated when the election of bishop was being held. Then when Damasus was elected, Ursinus could not bear the disappointment of his hope and hastened to form a party in rivalry to the church. And he persuaded some obscure bishops to ordain him in secret. For he was ordained not in a church but in a concealed spot of the basilica which is called Sicinian.[298] After this had happened, dissension took possession of the people. They fought with one another not over any question of faith or of heresy but simply as to which man ought to be given charge of the episcopal see. Then street fights broke out among the mob and many were killed in battle and many laymen and clergy were punished for it by Maximin, who was prefect at that time in the city. And so Ursinus finally abandoned his attempt and those who had been his followers subsided.

298 The location of this basilica is still a matter of some dispute. The name implies that it was a private basilica or hall in the palace of the Sicinian family. It has been suggested that Liberius had used the walls and foundation of this hall in the construction of his church and that the old name still clung to his new building. But archaeologists disagree. Socrates is mistaken in saying that Ursinus was ordained there. It was the scene of the battles after Ursinus' banishment.

Quae gesta sunt inter Liberium et Felicem Episcopos, 2–3. Text. *Corpus Scriptorum Ecclesiasticorum Latinorum,* XXXV, 2–4.

Then [after the death of Liberius] the priests and the deacons, Ursinus, Amantius and Lupus, with the holy people who had kept faith with Liberius while he was in exile, began to gather in the basilica of Julius [299] and demanded that the deacon Ursinus be ordained bishop in Liberius' place. But the perjurers in Lucina [300] called for Damasus as their bishop in place of Felix. Paul, the bishop of Tibur, consecrated Ursinus. And when Damasus, who had always schemed for the bishopric, heard of it, he stirred up all the charioteers and the ignorant multitude with money until, armed with clubs, they burst into the basilica of Julius, slaughtered many of the faithful and held an orgy for three days. After seven days, with all the perjurers and the gladiators whom he had bribed with huge sums, he took possession of the Lateran basilica and was ordained bishop there and he seduced Viventius, the city judge, and Julian, prefect of the treasury, and arranged that Ursinus, a man highly revered, who had been ordained bishop before him, should be sent into exile, with the deacons Amantius and Lupus. This accomplished, Damasus began with blows and bloodshed to coerce the Roman people who opposed his processions. And he attempted to expel from the city seven priests whom he had arrested by an official. But the faithful people met those priests and snatched them away and brought them directly to the basilica of Liberius.[301]

Then Damasus and the perjurers collected the gladiators, charioteers and grave-diggers and all the clergy, with axes,

299 *Supra,* p. 488, n. 98.

300 The modern basilica is known as San Lorenzo in Lucina.

301 *Supra,* p. 555, n. 191. The new basilica of Liberius was probably the largest at this time in the city, with the exception of the basilica built by Constantine over the tomb of Peter in the Vatican district, and the basilica at the Lateran.

swords and clubs, and besieged the basilica at the second hour of the day, October 26, in the consulship of Gratian and Dagalaifus, and started a fierce battle. For they crashed down doors and laid fires and searched for an entrance, in order to break in. Some of Damasus' followers tore up the roof of the basilica as well and killed the faithful people with the tiles. Then all the forces of Damasus poured into the basilica and slew one hundred and sixty of the people, both men and women, and wounded a very large number, many of whom died. But no one died of the party of Damasus. Then, three days later, the holy people gathered together and began to repeat against him the commandment of the Lord, who said: "Fear not them who kill the body and cannot kill the soul."[302] And they sang psalms of praise and said: "The dead bodies of thy servants have they given to be meat unto the fowls of heaven, the flesh of thy saints unto the beasts of the earth; their blood have they shed like water round about Jerusalem and there was none to bury them."[303] Also the people met often in the basilica of Liberius and cried aloud, saying: "O Christian Emperor, nothing is hidden from you! Let all the bishops come to Rome and the case be tried! Damasus has now made five wars. Away with murderers from the See of Peter!" For the people of God prayed constantly for an assembly of bishops to overthrow, with a just verdict, this man who was stained with such impiety and whom the ladies loved so much that he was called the ladies' ear-tickler.

Then the voices of the people were reported to the monarch Valentinian and he was animated by godly devotion and gave permission to the exiles to return. So Ursinus and the deacons Amantius and Jovinus came back, and the holy people went joyfully out to meet them. But Damasus,

302 Matthew, X, 28.

303 Psalms, LXXVIII, 2, 3 (Douay Version); Psalms, LXXIX, 2, 3 (King James Version).

who was conscious of his many crimes, was shaken with great fear and he bribed the whole palace not to reveal his deeds to the emperor. Accordingly, the emperor, who did not know what Damasus had perpetrated, issued an edict that Ursinus should be sent back to exile, so that no further strife might break out among the people. Then Bishop Ursinus, who was a holy man and who without sin took thought for the people, delivered himself into the hands of the evildoers and on November 16, by the emperor's bidding, went willingly into exile. But the people, who feared God and were weary with much persecution, did not fear the emperor nor the judge nor Damasus himself, the criminal and murderer, but held services without clergy in the cemeteries of the martyrs. When, therefore, many of the faithful had met at St. Agnes,[304] Damasus with his creatures fell upon them and cut down many in their savage onslaught. But this brutal act displeased severely the bishops of Italy. And when he had pompously invited them to his anniversary and some of them had assembled with him,[305] he tried with entreaty and bribery to prevail upon them to pass sentence against the holy Ursinus. But they answered: "We have met here for an anniversary, not to condemn a man unheard." So his base purpose failed to achieve the result at which it aimed.

Ammianus Marcellinus, *Res Gestae,* XXVII, 3, 12–15. Text. Ed. by C. U. Clark, II, 1, 424–425.

Damasus and Ursinus were consumed with desire more than human to obtain the episcopal see and fought in bitterest rivalry to the point of death and wounds, with belligerent forces on each side, and when Viventius [the prefect] was powerless either to quell or to abate the tumult but

[304] The basilica of Sant' Agnese outside the walls.

[305] This was probably the synod of 367, held a year after Damasus' ordination.

was overwhelmed by its superior violence, he withdrew to a suburb. And Damasus was victorious in the conflict, with the aid of his partisans. It is well known that in the basilica Sicinini, which is a meeting place of the Christian sect, one hundred and thirty-seven corpses were found of persons who had been killed on one day and the people were for a long time in a ferocious mood and were quieted afterward with difficulty.

Nor, when I behold the pomp of city life, do I deny that men who covet this office in order to fulfil their ambitions may well struggle for it with every resource at their disposal. For when they have once obtained it they are ever after so secure, enriched with offerings from the ladies, riding abroad seated in their carriages, splendidly arrayed, giving banquets so lavish that they surpass the tables of royalty. They might in more truth be blessed if they disdained the greatness of the city, with which they compete in vice, and lived in imitation of some of the provincial bishops, who eat and drink plainly and sparingly, wear poor clothing and keep their faces bent upon the ground and so commend themselves continually to the divinity and his true worshippers as pure and godfearing men.

Valens, Valentinian I and Gratian, *Rescript to Damasus, Codex Theodosianus*, XVI, 2, 20. Text. C. T. G. Schoenemann, *Pontificum Romanorum Epistolae Genuinae*, 310–311.

The emperors Valens, Valentinian and Gratian Augusti to Damasus, bishop of the city of Rome.

Ecclesiastics or members of ecclesiastical bodies or those who wish to be called by the name of continent [305a] shall not visit the houses of widows and heiresses in ward but shall be excluded by the public magistrates, if hereafter the

[305a] *I.e.*, monks.

relatives or friends of the women desire to have them removed. We also ordain that the men above mentioned may receive nothing from the liberality of any woman with whom they have had private interviews under guise of religion, even by will, and that every bequest that the women leave to any of them shall be void. Not even through the medium of a third person may they obtain a gift or a legacy. Moreover, if the women attempt after our edict of warning to make them any gift or bequest, it will be confiscated to the treasury of the State. If, however, any ecclesiastics receive legacies from women to whose inheritance or property they have some title by civil law or the provisions of an edict, they may keep them on the ground of relationship.

Read in the Roman churches, July 29, in the third consulship of Valens and Valentinian Augusti.[305b]

2. The Eastern Appeal for Western Help

Roman Synod of c. 370, *Letter to the Eastern Bishops*, printed under Damasus, *Epistolae*, I. Text. J. P. Migne, *Patrologia Latina*, XIII, 347–349.

Damasus, Valerian, Vitalian, Aufidius, Pacianus, Victor, Priscus, Innocent, Abundius, Theodulus and the others who have met in the city of Rome to try the case of Auxentius and expound the faith, to the catholic bishops of the East, greeting in the Lord.

We trust that your holiness, grounded upon the teaching of the apostles, is holding fast and imparting to the people

[305b] A.D. 370. We have no Roman comment on this edict. Ambrose, writing later to Valentinian II, remarked: " Recent laws have deprived us of the right of receiving emoluments by private bequest and no one complains, for we do not consider it a hardship, since we grieve not for riches." But it is strange that " the legacy of a Christian widow to the priests of a temple is valid, to the ministers of God invalid." *Epistolae*, XVIII. Jerome said of it in 394: " I do not complain of the law; I only regret that we should have deserved it. The prohibition was a sagacious measure, designed to strengthen discipline, but after all it has not checked the avarice of the clergy or the religious." *Epistolae*, LII, 6. The law was repealed by the emperor Marcian. *Novella*, 3.

that faith which varies no whit from the beliefs of our ancestors. For no other doctrine is right for the priests of God, who have the duty of teaching others. We have learned from the report of the brothers from Gaul and Venetia that some men, not in favor of heresy, for such evil cannot befall the priests of God, but in ignorance or simple-mindedness, excited by wrong representations, are not sufficiently appreciating how the doctrine of our fathers should be upheld, while their ears are beset by varying counsels. In consequence, our brothers have resolved, on this ground particularly, to condemn Auxentius of Milan.[306]

It is right that all the masters of the law in the Roman world should have the same understanding of the law and should not violate the Lord's faith in their respective magistracies. The venom of the heretics appeared long ago, just as now again it has begun to creep out. But when the blasphemous Arians began especially to increase, our predecessors, three hundred and eighteen bishops and the envoys from the city of the holy bishop of Rome, held a council at Nicaea and erected this bulwark against the arms of the devil and provided this remedy for mortal poisons, namely, that all must believe that Father, Son and Holy Spirit are one Deity, one form and one substance; and they ruled out from our fellowship anyone who thought otherwise. This creed of salvation some men have tried since to corrupt and distort by various interpretations. But in our opening session, the men who were compelled at Rimini [307] to reject this creed made their amends as follows: they confessed that they had been entangled in discussion and for that reason had not understood that the doctrine of the Fathers, promulgated at Nicaea, was opposed to them. Nor can any weight be attached to the size of the assemblage at Rimini,

306 The wording here is somewhat obscure, but Damasus and his synod are evidently citing with approbation the action of the bishops of Gaul and Venetia. For Auxentius, *vide supra*, pp. 538, 604.

307 *Supra*, p. 547.

inasmuch as it is well known that neither the Roman bishop, whose judgment should have been asked first of all, nor Vincent,[308] who had served unstained as priest for so many years, nor any others of like standing ratified its decisions and especially since, as we have said, the very men who are known to have succumbed to pressure there have now with better counsel declared their remorse.

So you see clearly that this one faith, which was founded at Nicaea upon the authority of the apostles, must be maintained with steadfastness forever and that in it the people of the East who consider themselves catholic find their glory, as do those of the West. Nor do we believe that any other measure is possible but to deprive men of contrary opinion of their communion with us and of the title of bishop, so that their flocks may breathe freely upon liberation from their errors. For how can they correct the misdeeds of the people when possessed by error themselves? Let then your loving faith be in harmony with all the priests of God! We are sure that you are fixed and confirmed in it and so also should you be certain that we are in righteous agreement with you. Do you testify to your holy approbation in your letters in reply.

I, the deacon Sabinus, delegate from Milan, present this authentic copy.

Basil, *Epistolae,* LXVI. Text. J. P. Migne, *Patrologia Graeca,* XXXII, 424–425.

To Athanasius, bishop of Alexandria.[309]

No one, I believe, is so distressed at the present position or, to be more exact, confusion of the churches as your honor, for you compare the present with the past and understand how far this has fallen from that. . . . But the more deeply

[308] Vincent of Capua, *supra,* pp. 470, n. 64, 499, 536.
[309] Written in 371.

your excellency feels this distress, the more determined we think you must be to exert your wisdom on the churches' behalf. I, for my part, have long been convinced, as far as my mediocre intelligence can judge of current affairs, that the one way of assisting our churches lies in securing the sympathy of the western bishops. For if they were willing to display the same energy for the sake of the flock in our countries which they have put forth over one or two men convicted of heterodoxy in the West, our whole situation would assuredly be benefited. Our sovereign [310] would treat with respect that imposing body of men and the laity everywhere would follow them unhesitatingly.

Who then is more competent to bring this about than your wise self? Who is keener to perceive what must be done? Who is more experienced in the execution of beneficent plans? Who suffers more profoundly in the affliction of the brethren? What is more revered in all the West than your august, grey hairs? . . . Send men well versed in sound doctrine from the holy church under your care to the bishops of the West. Recount to them the troubles which weigh us down. Suggest a method of relief. . . . I know that letters are weak to arouse men in a matter of such moment. You yourself, however, need no exhortation from others, any more than heroic athletes need the children's cheers. We are not offering instruction to an ignorant person but giving fresh impetus to one who has already put forth his strength.

To settle the affairs of the whole East you must, perhaps, have the support of others and wait for the men of the West. But the restoration to order of the church at Antioch is a matter, obviously, for your reverence. . . . If Antioch could be set right, it would, like a healthy head, supply soundness to the entire body. . . .

[310] The Arian Valens.

Ibid., LXVII. Text. *Op. cit.*, 425–428.

To Athanasius.[311]

[At the request of Deacon Dorotheus I will repeat more explicitly what I said in my earlier letter, viz., that all the East and I myself desire to see Meletius recognized as the head of the church of Antioch.] And your watchful wisdom has not failed to observe that the Westerners who are in agreement with you are now also of the same mind, as their letters show which were brought to us by the blessed Silvanus.[312]

Ibid., LXVIII. Text. *Op. cit.*, 428–429.

To Meletius, bishop of Antioch.[311]

[I am sending Deacon Dorotheus back to confer with you.] In brief, I have reached the conclusion that this same brother, Dorotheus, should go to Rome to stir up some of the Italians to visit us by way of the sea, in order to avoid persons who would hinder them. [I think they might have influence with Valens.] If then the idea seems feasible to you, will you kindly prepare letters and draw up memoranda as to what he ought to say there and to whom. And in order that your letters may carry weight, do you add the names of all who are of your party, even if they are not at Antioch. . . .

311 Written later in 371.

312 Silvanus, of whom we do not hear elsewhere, may have been the bearer of a letter describing the condemnation of Ursacius and Valens at the synod of 368 or perhaps that of Auxentius by the bishops of Venetia and Gaul and the determination of the West to uphold orthodoxy. From that Basil erroneously inferred that the West would support Meletius.

Ibid., LXIX. Text. *Op. cit.*, 429–433.

To Athanasius, bishop of Alexandria.

As time passes it steadily confirms the opinion which I have long had of your holiness; nay, rather, the course of events day by day enhances it. . . . I have, therefore, sent to your reverence our brother Dorotheus, a deacon in the church of the honorable bishop Meletius, a man of good zeal for the orthodox faith and desirous also of seeing peace among the churches. . . . You will welcome him, I know, and regard him with friendly eyes. You will strengthen him by the aid of your prayers and forward him on his way with letters. In addition, you will send with him some of the earnest men of your city and so speed him on his road to whatever lies ahead.

It has seemed to me wise to send a letter to the bishop of Rome, to ask him to look into the situation here and give us advice and, since it is difficult to obtain men from the West by general order from a synod, to urge him to exercise his personal authority in the matter and appoint men able to endure the hardships of a journey, able too, by gentleness and firmness of character, to correct the unruly among us here and speak with propriety and moderation, thoroughly acquainted with all that has occurred since Rimini, in order to undo the measures forcibly enacted on that occasion. They should travel here without anyone's knowledge, without ostentation and by sea, so as to escape the notice of the enemies of peace.

Another request is made by some of the men here, an inevitable one it appears to me too, namely, that the western bishops denounce the heresy of Marcellus [313] as grievous and pernicious and contrary to sound faith. For hitherto in all the letters they write, they never fail to anathematize up

[313] *Supra*, pp. 492, 493, 500, 504, n. 117, 513.

and down the ill-famed Arius and to exclude him from the churches. But apparently they attach no blame to Marcellus, who propounded an impious doctrine, diametrically opposed to that of Arius, and sacrilegiously attacked the very existence of the only-begotten Godhead and misinterpreted the term "word." . . . Nevertheless they seem never to have condemned him and are therefore culpable, because at the beginning, during their ignorance of the truth about him, they received him into communion with the Church. The present state of affairs makes it especially needful that attention should be called to him, in order that persons seeking an opportunity for mischief may be prevented from finding it by the union of all sound believers with your holiness and that all who lack true faith may be sharply distinguished and we may know who are on our side and not struggle as in a night battle, unable to tell friends from foes.

Only, I do beseech you to dispatch the deacon I spoke of by the first boat, that some of the objects for which we pray may be accomplished, at least during the coming year. One thing you comprehend even before I mention it, and will provide for, I know, which is, that when, God willing, the commissioners come, they are not to precipitate schisms between the churches but are to use every means to bring together men of the same beliefs, even though they find some who cherish personal grounds for dissension, so that the orthodox laity may not split apart into many factions, seceding in company with their bishops. . . .

Ibid., LXX. Text. *Op. cit.*, 433–436.

[Letter to Damasus.] [314]

To revive the ancient laws of love and restore again to vigorous life the peace of the Fathers, that heavenly and saving gift of Christ, which in the passage of time has withered away, is both essential and salutary for us and will be, I know, a delight to your Christian heart. For what could give more joy than the sight of those who are separated by so vast a distance bound together by the ties of love into one harmonious membership in the body of Christ? The entire East, almost, — I call East the lands from Illyricum to Egypt, — is now ravaged, honored father, by heavy storm and tempest. The heresy planted long ago by Arius, enemy of the truth, is now flaunting again. Like some bitter root it is bearing deadly fruit and overtopping us, for in every parish the champions of right doctrine have been driven by calumny and outrage from their churches and the control of affairs has been put into the hands of men who lead captive the souls of the simpler folk. We look for but one solution of our troubles, a visit from your clemency.

Always in the past your extraordinary affection toward us has been a consolation to us and for a short time we were cheered in heart by the glowing report that we were to receive a visit from you. So, when we were disappointed in that hope and could endure it no longer, we decided to entreat you by letter to take some course to help us and to send some men who are like-minded with us, either to reconcile our disputants and bring into friendship again the churches of God or, at least, to discover for you who are responsible for our disorder, that you may understand in future with whom you should be in communion.

[314] This letter, as we have it, bears no address or superscription but there can be no doubt for whom it was intended. It is presumably the letter to which Basil refers above.

We are proposing nothing novel whatever but something that was customary among those men of the past who were blessed and dear to God, particularly among you. For we remember hearing from our fathers, when we questioned them, and reading in documents still preserved among us, that the most blessed bishop Dionysius,[315] who is famous among you for his orthodox faith and other virtues, visited by a letter our church of Caesarea and admonished by letter our fathers and sent men to ransom our brethren from captivity. Our condition now is harder and more painful and more in need of succor. We are mourning not the destruction of material buildings but the loss of churches. We see about us not the enslavement of bodies but the captivity of souls, achieved every day by the champions of heresy. So if you be not now inclined to help us, you will soon find no one to whom to stretch out a hand, for we shall have fallen under the dominion of heresy.

Ibid., LXXXIX. Text. *Op. cit.*, 469–472.

To Meletius, bishop of Antioch.[316]

[I am sending Dorotheus to you.] And if you have any ground for writing to the Westerners, because it is quite necessary that letters should go to them from some of us, do you prepare your letters. We have received the deacon Sabinus, whom they sent to us,[317] and we have written to the Illyrians and to the bishops of Italy and Gaul and to some who have written privately to us. It would be desirable to have a man sent, as if from the synod as a body, to carry a second letter. Do you have one written. . . .

[315] *Supra*, p. 429. [316] Written in 372. [317] *Supra*, p. 636.

Ibid., XC. Text. *Op. cit.*, 472–476.

To the holy brethren and bishops in the West.[317a]

The good God, who ever mingles comfort with affliction, has granted us even now, in the midst of many distresses, some partial consolation in the letter which our honored father, Bishop Athanasius, has received from you and forwarded to us. For it is evidence of your sound faith and proof of your unshaken harmony and concord, testifying that the shepherds are following in the footsteps of the Fathers and feeding the Lord's people with knowledge. . . . The Lord has also given me encouragement through my son, the godly deacon Sabinus, who has nourished my heart by his good reports of you. He will give you an exact account of us with information from his own experience, that you may, first of all, aid us in our struggle by earnest and persistent prayer to the Lord and may, secondly, not refuse to extend such solace as lies in your power to our oppressed churches. . . .

[Description of the demoralization of the churches.] Let there be freely repeated among us that good proclamation of the Fathers, whereby they overwhelmed the infamous heresy of Arius and built up the churches in sound doctrine, . . . so that, even as the Lord has given you liberty for the truth, and glory in the confession of the divine and saving Trinity, he may, through your prayers and your aid, grant the same boons to gladden us. The deacon of whom I spoke will report everything to you in love. We assent to all that your honors have canonically done and approve your apostolic zeal for orthodoxy.

317a Written in 372.

Ibid., XCI. Text. *Op. cit.*, 476.

To Valerian, bishop of the Illyrians.[318]

[A letter to be delivered by Sabinus on his way West, commending him to Valerian's hospitality and explaining the eastern need of help.]

Ibid., XCII. Text. *Op. cit.*, 477–484.

Meletius, Eusebius, Basil, . . . Gregory and Daphnus,[319] to their godly and holy brothers and fellow ministers, the bishops in harmony with us in Italy and Gaul, greeting in the Lord.

. . . We are heartened by the reasonable hope that perhaps, if we relate our troubles to you, we may induce you to give us that assistance which we have not yet received. . . . For you have not been ignorant of our state, honored brethren, since the report of it has spread to the ends of the earth. Nor have you been without sympathy for brethren of like faith with you, for you are disciples of the apostle who teaches that love for our neighbor is the fulfilling of the law.[320] But, as we have said, the judgment of God, which has ordained that we must pay in full the penalty laid upon us for our sins, has held you back. But now, at last, we beseech you to show your ardor for the truth and your compassion for us and to hear all, especially what has heretofore escaped your ears, from our pious brother, the deacon Sabinus, who can himself tell you what our letter omits. We implore you now to put on bowels of

318 Written in 372. Valerian's see was at Aquileia.

319 The list of the senders of this letter contains thirty-two names of bishops from Syria and Central and Southern Asia Minor. The first four that we give were bishops of Antioch, Samosata, Caesarea in Cappadocia, and Nyssa respectively. The see of Daphnus is unknown.

320 Romans, XIII, 10.

mercy, discard all timidity and undertake the labor of love, counting neither length of journey, interests at home nor any other human consideration. . . .

[Description of disorders in the church from Illyricum to the Thebaid, spread of heresy, bitterness, doubt and moral laxity.] Do not allow half the world to be engulfed in error! Do not permit the faith to be extinguished in the regions where first it shone! . . .

Unquestionably there is need of haste, if the survivors are to be rescued, and many brethren must come, so that the visitors with ourselves may make up a full synod and have influence to effect a reform, not merely through the dignity of those who send them but also through the weight of their own numbers. And they shall restore the creed promulgated by our fathers at Nicaea and outlaw heresy and speak peace to the churches, bringing into unison all who are of one mind. . . . For assuredly the gift bestowed by the Lord upon your piety is worthy of the highest admiration, namely, your power to discern between the false and the true and pure, and to teach the faith of the Fathers without any equivocation.

Ibid., CXX. Text. *Op. cit.*, 537–540.

To Meletius, bishop of Antioch.[321]

I have received a letter from the godly bishop Eusebius [of Samosata], in which he urges us to write again to the Westerners about the state of the Church. . . . [I send you herewith a memorandum and ask you to draw up the letter.] We are ready to subscribe to it and to see that it is conveyed promptly to those who are in communion with us, so that when it has received all their signatures, it may go to the messenger who is soon to set out to the bishops of the West.

321 Written in 373 and sent by the priest Sanctissimus.

Ibid., CXXIX. Text. *Op. cit.*, 557–561.

To Meletius, bishop of Antioch.[322]

[I know that Sanctissimus must have reached you by now with my letter. If it seems best to you to write again to the West, will you have the letter drawn up and I will have a list of the names of the men in my locality made out to be appended to it, when finished. I, for my part, did not know what more to say to the Westerners, for I have already told them the essentials.] One point, however, has occurred to me as hitherto unmentioned and as furnishing an excuse for another letter and that is a request to them not to accept indiscriminately communion with men who come from the East but, after they have once chosen to support one side, to receive persons only on the recommendation of their fellow communicants and not to take in everyone who writes a creed with some pretense of orthodoxy.

Ibid., CXXXVIII. Text. *Op. cit.*, 577–581.

To Eusebius, bishop of Samosata.[323]

. . . The priest Evagrius, son of Pompeianus of Antioch, who went some time ago to the West with the blessed Eusebius,[324] has now returned from Rome. He asks of us a letter containing certain statements dictated by the men there. Our own letters he has brought back to us as unsatisfactory to their precise minds. He also asks us to send at once a deputation of men of high repute, in order to give their people a plausible reason for visiting us. . . . What attitude I am to take toward Evagrius' proposals I was

322 Written in 373.
323 Written in 373 or 374.
324 Evagrius of Antioch had accompanied Eusebius of Vercellae to Italy on his return from exile after the death of Constantius. *Supra*, p. 551.

anxious to learn myself in a personal conversation with you but in my present state of ill health I am cut off from everything. [Will you write to me and offer prayer, both privately and publicly in your synod, that I may decide rightly?]

Ibid., CLVI. Text. *Op. cit.*, 613–617.

To the priest Evagrius.[325]

[I hope you will be able to promote peace in the church at Antioch. I myself cannot cross the Armenian mountains in winter. I am sorry to hear from Dorotheus that you avoided being in his company.] As for my sending anyone to the West, it is wholly out of the question. I have no one fit for such an errand.

Damasus, *Epistolae,* III. Text. J. P. Migne, *Patrologia Latina,* XIII, 356–357.

Damasus to his dearly beloved brother Paulinus.[326]

I have already sent you a letter by my son Vitalis, in which I left everything to your decision and judgment. Then I wrote you a note by the priest Petronius, at the very moment of his departure, to say that some things had made me uneasy. Now, in order that you may have no lingering scruples and may not in your praiseworthy spirit of caution debar some perhaps who are eager to unite with the Church, we are sending a formula of faith, not so much to you, who are already joined to the communion of this same faith, as to those who may wish by subscribing to it to be joined to you, that is, to us through you.

325 Written soon after the preceding.

326 Written in 375 to Paulinus, head of the uncompromising orthodox party at Antioch, opposed to Meletius and Basil. *Supra,* pp. 550, 614.

So, if my son Vitalis, of whom I spoke, and those who are with him desire to unite with you, they should first sign the creed which was confirmed at Nicaea by the pious will of the Fathers. Then, since no one can apply a remedy to future wounds and the heresy which after that time, as report says, spread over the East has now to be rooted out,[327] they should confess that the Wisdom, the Word, the Son of God took on human body, spirit and mind, that is, the whole Adam, or, to speak more plainly, all our ancient humanity without sin. For just as by confessing that he assumed a human body, we do not thereby ascribe to him human passions and vices as well, so too by declaring that he assumed the spirit and mind of a man, we do not thereby assert that he suffered the sinfulness of human thoughts. . . .

Whoever then subscribes to this letter, provided he has previously subscribed to the canons of the Church and to the faith of Nicaea, you should receive without hesitation. Not that you may not present our statement to converts also on their reception but that we prefer to give you liberty in receiving them.

Basil, *Epistolae,* CCXIV. Text. J. P. Migne, *Patrologia Graeca,* XXXII, 785–789.

To Count Terentius.[328]

[I hear that you have returned to public life and are now in Antioch.] And in addition to this, I have heard a rumor that the brothers of the party of Paulinus are beginning to discuss with your excellency the question of union with us. By " us " I mean the party of Bishop Meletius, the man of God. I hear also that these Paulinians

327 The heresy of Apollinarius. *Supra,* p. 611.

328 Written in 375. Terentius was an orthodox Christian. Ammianus Marcellinus, XXVII, 12, and XXXI. In 372, he had been in command of twelve legions in Georgia and Basil had written to him regarding the provision to be made for bishops for the church in Armenia.

are now carrying around a letter from the Westerners, which assigns to them the bishopric of the Antiochene church and misrepresents Meletius, the admirable bishop of the true Church of God. I am not surprised at it. The Westerners are totally ignorant of affairs here. Those who pretend to understand describe things to them in a spirit of combativeness rather than of truth. . . . But your excellency has on the spot men who can tell you accurately what passed between the bishops during the reign of Jovian and from them I beg you to get information.

Nevertheless, I accuse no one; I pray that I may have love to all and "especially unto them who are of the household of faith."[329] I congratulate those who have secured the letter from Rome. Because it is an august and impressive testimony in their favor, I hope it is genuine and corroborated by their own conduct. But I can never, on account of it, persuade myself either to ignore Meletius or to forget the church under him or to treat as trivial and immaterial to true religion the questions which caused the division. I shall never consent to yield merely because some man has received a letter from other men and is enormously elated over it. Even if it came from heaven itself, if it were not in accord with the sound doctrine of faith, I could not regard the writer as a member of the communion of saints. . . .

Ibid., CCXV. Text. *Op. cit.*, 789–792.

To the priest Dorotheus.[330]

[I have been writing to Count Terentius and am sending the letter by the state treasurer, who is travelling by the imperial post, with instructions to show it to you before delivering it.] I do not understand why no one has told

[329] Galatians, VI, 10.

[330] Written in 375.

you that the land road to Rome is quite impassable in winter, since the country between Constantinople and our own district is full of enemies. If you take the sea route, the season is open, if indeed my good brother Gregory [331] will agree to go by ship and will undertake the commission for this business. I myself do not see who are to accompany him and I know that he is altogether inexperienced in ecclesiastical negotiations. A man of gracious disposition would meet him with respect and every consideration but what benefit could result to our cause from an interview between one who is lofty and arrogant and high enthroned and for that reason unable to listen to people on the earth who tell him the truth and one like my brother, in whose character there is no room for abject servility?

Ibid., CCXXXIX. Text. *Op. cit.*, 889–893.

To Eusebius, bishop of Samosata.[332]

. . . The news from the West you have heard already, for our brother Dorotheus has told you everything. What sort of letters should be given to him when he goes there? Perhaps he will share his journey with the noble Sanctissimus, who is evincing much enthusiasm, travelling around the East and collecting signatures and letters from every man of note. What kind of letters they should be writing or how I am to sympathize with the writers I do not know. If you find anyone soon coming our way, be so good as to inform me. For there come to my mind the words of Diomed:

"Thou shouldest not entreat the lofty son of Peleus
Nor offer countless gifts; he's proud enough." [333]

Natures that are inherently arrogant grow more insolent still when they are courted. And if the Lord be gracious to

[331] Gregory of Nyssa. [332] Written in 375. [333] *Iliad*, IX, 698–699.

us, what other bulwark do we need? But if the wrath of God continue, what help can come to us from the supercilious West? For they neither know the truth nor try to learn it but are taken up with false suspicions and are acting now as they did before in the case of Marcellus, when they quarrelled with those who told them the facts and by their own course confirmed him in his heresy. Along with the general communication, I have wanted myself to write to their Coryphaeus,[334] — nothing indeed about the situation of the Church but only to suggest mildly that they do not know the truth about events here and are not selecting the road by which they might learn it, that, as a rule, they ought not to attack men who are crushed by tribulation, that they must not take hauteur for dignity and that injustice ends simply in arousing bitterness against God. . . .

Ibid., CCXLII. Text. *Op. cit.*, 900–901.

To the Westerners.[335]

[The eastern church has struggled through terrible storms, supported only by its faith in God. It has looked for help from the West but has failed to obtain it.]

How does it happen that we have received no letter of consolation, no visit from our brothers, nothing of what you owe us by the law of love? This is now the thirteenth year since the war of the heretics burst upon us.[336] During it, the churches have suffered more affliction than all that has been recorded since the gospel of Christ was first preached.[337] . . . We implore you, now at least, to stretch

334 The leader of the chorus in Attic drama. The allusion, of course, is to Damasus.

335 Written in 375. This and the following letter were apparently carried by Dorotheus on his first mission to the West.

336 The Arian emperor Valens began his reign in 363.

337 This is rhetorical exaggeration, intended to catch the attention of the West. In his *Epistolae,* CCXC, Basil reminds the church of Nicopolis that their pains are light in comparison with those endured by the Fathers, that they are not tortured in body, imprisoned, etc.

out your hand to the churches of the East, who are at present stricken to their knees, and to send messengers to remind us of the prizes laid up in store for those who suffer for Christ. A familiar voice has always less power over us than a strange one which brings us comfort, especially one that comes from men famed, by God's grace, everywhere among the noblest. For the report is spread among all men how you have remained inviolate in your faith and have preserved unstained the tradition of the apostles. . . . Do you, whom we love and long for, behave as physicians for the wounded and trainers for the sound in body. Heal whatever is diseased and anoint whatever is strong for true piety. . . .

Ibid., CCXLIII. Text. *Op. cit.*, 901–912.

Basil, bishop of Caesarea in Cappadocia, to his most pious and dear brothers and fellow ministers in concord, the bishops of Gaul and Italy.[338]

Our Lord Jesus Christ, who deigned to call the whole Church of God his body and who has made us severally members one of another, has likewise ordained that we should all live near to one another as befits harmonious members. . . . We have already at other times appealed to your love to send us help and sympathy but because our punishment was not complete, you were not permitted to be disposed to aid us. We beg now especially that our calamities may be brought, through your good agency, to the attention of the emperor of your portion of the world,[339] but, if this be too difficult, that you send envoys to visit and encourage us in our trouble and to behold with their own eyes the suffering of the East. For it cannot be appreciated

[338] Written at the same time as the preceding.
[339] Gratian, who had just succeeded Valentinian I.

by hearsay, because no words can be found to give an adequate picture of our condition.

[For our loyalty to the Church's tradition we are suffering hardships, such as exile, prohibition of assembly, etc., and heresy is fast increasing. It may soon reach the West. You are not to think yourselves safe. The East is fighting your battle as well as its own.]

On this account it would have been desirable if many of us could have taken the journey to your reverences and could each have described his own case. But let this be an indication to you of the oppression under which we live, that we are not free to travel. For if any man leaves his church for even the briefest interval, he abandons his people to the mercy of the conspirators. But, by God's grace, we have sent you one to represent the many, our revered and beloved brother and fellow priest, Dorotheus. He is competent to supply by his own information whatever facts our letter has omitted, for he has followed everything carefully and is zealous for the true faith. Receive him in peace and send him speedily back to us to bring us good news of your eagerness to succor the brotherhood.

Ibid., CCLIII. Text. *Op. cit.*, 940.

To the priests of Antioch.[340]

[Sanctissimus will partly relieve your anxiety by assuring you of the love and interest of the West. He will also tell you things that require serious consideration. We have heard only half reports hitherto. Now Sanctissimus comes, able to explain clearly and reliably the whole position of the West and to offer sound advice.]

340 Written in 376, after the return of Sanctissimus and Dorotheus. *Epistolae*, CCLIV–CCLVI, are letters of introduction for Sanctissimus to the churches of Laodicea, Carrhi, etc.

Ibid., CCLXIII. Text. *Op. cit.*, 976–981.

To the Westerners.[341]

May the Lord God in whom we have trusted grant to each of you grace to realize your hopes in measure equal to the joy wherewith you have filled our hearts, for the letter which you sent us by our beloved fellow priests[342] and for the sympathy which you felt for us in our distresses, as if, indeed, you had put on bowels of mercy, as these priests have told us. For even if our wounds remain the same, still it is a solace to us to have our physicians ready and able, if they find opportunity, to apply quick balm to our hurts. Wherefore I salute you in reply by our beloved friends and beg you, if the Lord enables you to come to us, not to hesitate to visit us. . . . At least, send us such letters as you should write to encourage the afflicted and raise up the downtrodden.

[Our church is not now so much disturbed by out and out Arians, who have been publicly expelled and denounced for impiety, as by men clad in sheep's clothing, harmless in aspect, who have "come out from us" and still distract the simpleminded.] These men we implore you to denounce plainly and openly to all the churches of the East, so that they may either turn back to the right path and join honestly with us or, if they persist in error, may confine their mischief to themselves and be hindered from introducing their plague, by means of unguarded communion, among their neighbors. I must name these persons to you so that you may yourselves appreciate who are brewing disturbance among us and may indicate them clearly to our churches. For a statement from us is suspected by many people, who imagine that we probably bear illwill to these men for some personal grudge.

[341] Written in 377 and given to Dorotheus on his second mission to the West.
[342] For the surviving fragment of this letter *vide supra*, p. 616 and n. 278.

But you, because you live so far away from them, have great weight with our people and, besides, the grace of God has chosen you to care for those in tribulation. And if many of you combine to issue this decree, then the great number of its authors will certainly bring about its unquestioning acceptance by everybody.

One of the men who has caused me much anxiety is Eustathius of Sebaste in Lesser Armenia. He was originally a disciple and pupil of Arius during the period when the latter was influential in Alexandria and was concocting his notorious blasphemies against the only-begotten Son. Eustathius was reckoned one of his most devoted adherents. On his return to his own country, he made profession of the orthodox faith before Hermogenes, the blessed bishop of Caesarea, who had been on the point of condemning him for false doctrine. Under such circumstances, he was ordained by Hermogenes but at Hermogenes' death he went immediately to Eusebius of Constantinople, who was one of the chief supporters of the impious teachings of Arius.[343] For some reason or another he was expelled from Constantinople and coming back to his own country, he defended himself a second time, endeavoring to conceal his erroneous opinions under a cloak of verbal orthodoxy.

But no sooner had he attained to the rank of bishop than he openly wrote an anathema on the " homoousios " in the Arian synod at Ancyra.[344] Thence he went to Seleucia and took part in the infamous acts of his fellow heretics.[345] Again, at Constantinople, he expressed his assent to the heretics' creed. Then, when he had been expelled from his bishopric because of his condemnation at Melitine,[346] he conceived of a way to secure his reinstatement, namely, to

343 This was Eusebius of Nicomedia, later of Constantinople. *Supra,* p. 491.

344 In 358, when the "homoiousian" formula was endorsed and twelve anathemas issued against all who rejected it.

345 Council of Rimini-Seleucia. *Supra,* pp. 546–548.

346 An orthodox gathering in 358.

go to you. I do not know what sort of instructions the blessed bishop Liberius gave him nor what agreement he made with him, save that Eustathius brought back a letter reinstating him, which he displayed to the synod at Tyana, and obtained his restoration to his see.[347] He is now denouncing the very creed upon which he was accepted. He consorts with those who anathematize the " homoousios " and is head of the heresy of the Pneumatomachi.[348] But as it is from the West that he derives his authority to molest the churches and through the power bestowed on him by you that he subjugates many, it is essential that his correction come from the same source and that you send a letter to the churches, stating the terms on which he was once received and the extent to which he has since altered his position and forfeited the favor shown by the Fathers at that time.

[Account of the heretical activities of Apollinarius and of Paulinus of Antioch, who has accepted followers of Marcellus of Ancyra.] . . .

We entreat you to show some concern for these things. You would show it, if you would write to all the churches of the East that you will continue in communion with those who have so perverted the doctrine, provided they repent, but that if they prefer to abide contentiously by their innovations, you will separate yourselves from them. We are aware that we ought to sit in council with you and discuss these questions in common deliberation. But the times do not permit it and procrastination is perilous, for the mischief these men have introduced has taken root. Hence I am obliged to send these brethren to you, that you may procure from them all the information which my letter has omitted and they may prevail upon your reverences to send to the churches of God that aid for which they pray.

347 *Supra,* pp. 553-554.

348 The party of ultra conservatives who refused to admit the equality of the Holy Spirit with the Father and the Son. *Supra,* p. 555.

Ibid., CCLXV. Text. *Op. cit.*, 989–992.

[To three Egyptian bishops in exile.[349] A warning not to receive the followers of Marcellus into communion. You yourselves are not alone but have many fellow believers left in the East " and in the West they are all in harmony with you and us. We have received the ' tome ' of their faith and keep it with us and follow their sound doctrine." The disciples of Marcellus should not be received until they have been restored to communion by the West and the faithful in the East.]

Ibid., CCLXVI. Text. *Op. cit.*, 992–996.

To Peter, bishop of Alexandria.[350]

[I am glad of your sympathy and of your stand on behalf of church discipline. I am sorry to hear that Dorotheus has been discourteous in speaking to you.] On his return, he told me of the conversation he had had with your excellency in the presence of the august bishop Damasus and grieved me by saying that our most godly brothers and fellow ministers, Meletius and Eusebius, had been grouped with the Ariomaniacs. Even if there were no other evidence of their orthodoxy, certainly the war waged against them by the Arians is a strong indication for all fairminded persons of their right belief. [I give you my earnest assurance of their orthodoxy. I have myself heard them testify to it. Now above all things we want peace, in order to unite the churches of the East.]

349 Written in 377. On the state of the Egyptian church *vide supra*, p. 553.

350 Written sometime between 375 and 377. Peter II succeeded Athanasius as bishop of Alexandria in May, 373. Within a few months, he was forced by Arian persecution to flee to Damasus at Rome.

3. The Eastern Faith in Peter

Jerome, *Epistolae,* XV, To Damasus.[350a] Text. C. T. G. Schoenemann, *Pontificum Romanorum Epistolae Genuinae,* 374–378.

Because the East is shattered by the ancient, fierce antagonisms of its peoples and is rending into tiny fragments the undivided and woven tunic of the Lord and the wolves are destroying Christ's vineyard, so that amid these dry pools that hold no water it is difficult to know where is the fountain sealed and the garden enclosed,[350b] therefore I have thought best to turn to the See of Peter and to the faith that was praised by the apostle's lips, to ask now food for my soul from the source where once I received the raiment of Christ.[350c] Nor can the vast stretches of the watery element nor the breadth of lands that lie between us prevent my search for the precious pearl. "Where the body is, there will the eagles be gathered together."[350d] An evil posterity has squandered its patrimony. You alone preserve unspoiled the heritage of the Fathers. Yonder the good soil of your earth is bringing forth the pure seed of the Lord a hundred fold; here the grain is buried in the furrows and degenerating into tares and wild oats. In the West, the sun of justice is now rising; in the East, Lucifer, he who fell from heaven, has set his throne above the stars. You are the light of the world, you are the salt of the earth, you are the vessels of gold and of silver; here are the vessels of earth and of wood, the iron rod and the eternal fire.

For this reason your [350e] greatness terrifies me, yet mercy

350a The internal evidence shows that Jerome wrote this letter from Syria, about 377 A.D. *Vide supra,* p. 112.

350b Canticles, II, 15, and IV, 12; Jeremias, II, 13.

350c Jerome had been received into the church at Rome before his departure for the East.

350d Luke XVII, 37.

350e To this point Jerome has been using the pronoun of the second person in the plural number. From here on he most often uses the singular.

invites me to you. A victim I implore the priest for salvation, a sheep the shepherd for protection. Away with jealousy of the Roman preëminence, away with ambition! I speak to the successor of the fisherman and to the disciple of the cross. I follow no one as chief save Christ but I am joined in communion with your blessedness, that is, with the See of Peter. Upon that rock I know the Church is built. Whoever eats the lamb outside that house is profane.[350f] He who is not in Noah's ark will perish when the flood overwhelms all. And I, who for my sins have journeyed to this solitude which lies between Syria and the bounds of barbarism, and cannot look to receive the Lord's holy thing from your holiness over the wide spaces that separate us, am for this reason adhering to your colleagues here, the confessors of Egypt,[350g] and am hiding my little barque behind their great ships. I do not know Vitalis, I repudiate Meletius, I am ignorant of Paulinus.[350h] He who gathers not with you scatters; that is, he who is not of Christ is of Antichrist.

Now, alas! after the creed of Nicaea, after the decision at Alexandria,[350i] in which the West took an equal share, the bishops of the Arians and the Donatists [350j] are demanding of me, a Roman, a new phrase, " three hypostases." [350k]

[350f] Exodus, XII, 22.

[350g] The orthodox clergy from Egypt in exile. *Vide supra,* pp. 553, 657.

[350h] The rival bishops in the see of Antioch. Vitalis had been consecrated by Apollinarius in 376. *Vide supra,* pp. 550, 611, 615.

[350i] The council which met at Alexandria in 362, the year after the death of Constantius, under the presidency of Athanasius, and at which Eusebius of Vercellae was present and Lucifer of Cagliari was represented, before the return of these two exiles to the West. *Vide supra,* p. 550.

[350j] The word Jerome uses for Donatists is " Campenses " or " countryfolk." The Donatists were said to draw their support mainly from the country districts.

[350k] The Greek word, " hypostasis," was now being used by the neo-orthodox Homoiousians in the sense in which the Westerners used the Latin " persona," to indicate the personal subsistence of Father, Son and Spirit respectively in the Trinity. The same party used the word, " ousia," to signify the substance or essence in which the Three were One. " Hypostasis," however, had been also employed by the older Arians in the sense of substance and in that sense the three hypostases had been condemned at Nicaea. Jerome, like many other Westerners, was suspicious of the word and felt that " three hypostases " might still be interpreted as " three substances " or tritheism. *Supra,* p. 550 and n. 186.

What apostles, I ask them, gave us that? What new Paul, teacher of the gentiles, taught us that? We inquire what they suppose we can understand by "three hypostases"; they reply, "three persons subsisting." We answer that we believe in that, but the sense is not enough; they demand the actual phrase, for some sort of poison lurks in the syllables. We cry: "If any man confess not the three hypostases or three inhypostatized, that is, the three persons subsisting, let him be anathema!" and because we do not repeat their very words, they pronounce us heretics. Yet if anyone who understands "hypostasis" as "ousia"[350l] does not say there is one hypostasis in three persons, he is an alien from Christ; but at that declaration we are blasted along with you under the brand of Sabellianism.[350m]

Issue your commandment, I beg, if you please, and then I shall not fear to speak of the three hypostases. At your bidding, a new creed shall be set up after the Nicene and we orthodox shall confess in words like the Arians'. All schools of secular learning take "hypostasis" to be nothing but "ousia" [substance] and will anyone, I ask, with blasphemous lips preach three substances? The nature of God is one only, which is true. . . . But since that one nature is perfect and one Deity exists in three persons, which is true, and is one nature, whoever says that there are three objects, that is, three hypostases, meaning "ousias," is trying under the name of piety to declare that there are three natures. And if this is so, why do we separate ourselves from the Arians, seeing that we are united with them in perfidy? Let Ursinus join with your blessedness, let Auxentius associate with Ambrose![350n] Far be this from the faith of Rome; may the devout hearts of its people never imbibe such sacrilege! Let us be satisfied to speak of one

[350l] *I.e.*, as what the Latins meant by "substance."

[350m] The Homoiousians felt that the western hesitation to accept "hypostasis" in their sense was due to a taint of Sabellianism. *Supra*, p. 550.

[350n] For Ursinus and Auxentius *vide supra*, pp. 600, 538.

substance and three persons subsisting, perfect, equal, coeternal! Let us, if you please, not mention the three hypostases but keep to one only! It tends to bad feeling when the meaning is the same but the words differ. Let us be satisfied with the creed we have learned! Or if you think that we ought to admit the three hypostases under their interpretation, we will not refuse, but, believe me, poison lurks beneath the honey. The angel of Satan has transformed himself into an angel of light. They explain "hypostasis" correctly but when I say that I hold the belief which they themselves are expounding, they call me heretic. Why do they cling so strenuously to that one word? What are they hiding beneath their ambiguous speech? If they believe in accordance with their interpretation, I do not condemn their views. If I believe as they themselves pretend to do, they should permit me too to express their meaning in my words.

Therefore I implore your blessedness, by the crucified Savior of the world, by the Trinity of one substance, to authorize me by letter either to speak or to refuse to speak of the hypostases. And since perhaps the letter-carriers may be unable to find the obscure spot where I live, graciously address your communication to the priest Evagrius, whom you know well. Will you at the same time inform me with whom I should hold communion at Antioch, for the Donatists, who are uniting with the heretics of Tarsus,[350o] boast that they have the authority of your communion in preaching the three hypostases with the old meaning.

Ibid., XVI, To Damasus. Text. C. T. G. Schoenemann, *op. cit.*, 379–380.

The importunate woman in the gospel at last deserved to be heard.[350p] Even though the door had been shut and

350o The Arians were in possession at Tarsus. 350p Luke, XVIII, 2–5.

barred and it was midnight, the friend received bread from his friend.[350q] God himself, whom no resistant power can bend, was overcome by the publican's prayers.[350r] The city of Nineveh, which was doomed for its sin, survived by its mourning.[350s] Why these repeated instances and this long preliminary? In order that you, who are great, may cast your eyes upon one who is small, that the rich shepherd may not despise the puny sheep. . . .

[A brief account of his troubles.] I meanwhile cry out: "Whoever is joined to the See of Peter, is mine!" Meletius, Vitalis and Paulinus say they belong to you. I might believe it if one of them declared it. As it is, either two of them are lying or else all. So I implore your blessedness, by the cross of the Lord, by the passion of Christ, the necessary glory of our faith, to follow the apostles in merit as you follow them in honor. So may you sit with the Twelve upon the judgment-seat, so may another gird you with Peter in your old age,[350t] so may you obtain the citizenship of heaven with Paul, as you notify me by letter with whom I should hold communion in Syria! Do not scorn the soul for whom Christ died!

Evangelium Duodecim Apostolorum.[351] Extracts translated into German and quoted by F. Haase, *Apostel und Evangelisten in den orientalischen Überlieferungen* (*Neutestamentliche Abhandlungen,* IX, pt. 1–3), 126–129.

I

When the days of his exaltation were fulfilled, he called the apostles and said unto them: "Lo, the days of my departure from this world are nigh to be fulfilled. What my

350q Luke, XI, 5–8.
350r Luke, XVIII, 13–14.
350s Jonas, III, 5–10.
350t John, XXI, 18.
351 A Coptic apocryphal work of the middle or latter part of the fourth century.

Father has given me, that have I given you. I have not left you without imparting to you all that you desire.

Peter, thou art the beginning of the calling of thy brethren. Come to me on this rock, that I may bless thee and make thee known before all the world. Never shall thy head feel pain nor thine eyes lack light at thy going hence. Thy nails shall not wither. Thy hair shall not fall. The festering grave shall not corrupt thy body forever. No wrinkle shall appear upon thy skin forever. Incline thy head to me, O Peter! The right hand of my Father is laid upon thee, wherefore I ordain thee archbishop. . . . Let the four and twenty elders fill their vials with sweet odors and pour them over thee today,[352] O Peter, to ordain thee archbishop. Let the four beasts praise me and my Father today and sing the ' Thrice holy,' for today my chosen Peter shall be ordained archbishop. Ye seven aeons of light, open one upon another, for the power of my Father shall descend from you and rest upon the mouth of my chosen Peter. Ye treasuries of heaven and ye dwelling-places of my kingdom, rejoice today, for your keys shall be given to my chosen Peter. Ye dominions and powers of heaven, rejoice, for we shall give unchangeable power forever to the tongue of Peter. Ye thrones and princes, rejoice today, for I shall give to my chosen Peter fatherhood over tens of thousands forever. O all thou earth, rejoice today, for I have given to one who is compassionate the power to bind and loose. O Paradise, rejoice today, and shed forth a sweet odor, for I will put an incorruptible robe upon Peter forever. O Hell, be sorrowful today with thy powers, for I have pledged to my chosen Peter a covenant forever; for I will build my Church and the gates of Hell shall not prevail against it."

And when Jesus had said this to Peter on the mount, he said unto him: " Simon Peter, tell me. Who am I? " And Peter straightway looked up into heaven and saw the seven

352 Revelation, V, 8.

heavens opened one upon another; he saw the glory of the Father and all the hosts of heaven descending upon the mount for the ordination of the bishop; he saw the right hand of the good Father descending, his head of the same aspect as the Son,[353] filled with the Holy Spirit. And when he saw him, he fell down prostrate and cried out as he lay there and said: "Thou art the Christ, the Son of the living God!" Jesus said unto him: "Blessed art thou, Simon Bariona, for flesh and blood have not revealed this to thee but my Father who is in heaven. Now go hence, that I may give thy tongue the power of my tongue to loose and to bind." Then he laid his hand upon his head and all the heavenly hosts sang the Trisagion, so that the stones which were on the mount cried out with them: "Worthy, worthy, worthy is the father, the archbishop Peter!" When Peter had received this great honor, his countenance shone. He shone before the apostles like the sun, like Moses of old time. . . .

II[354]

Then [after the Ascension] the Father with the Son and the Holy Spirit stretched forth his hand over the head of Peter and he ordained him archbishop of the whole world. And he blessed him and said: "Thou shalt be the head of the leaders in my kingdom and thou shalt be it likewise in the whole world. For I, my well-beloved Son and the Holy Spirit have laid our hands upon thee. And whatever thou shalt bind on earth shall be bound also in heaven and whatever thou shalt loose on earth shall be loosed in heaven. No man shall be exalted above thee and thy throne and whoever has not the consecration of thy throne, his hand shall be thrust down. Thy breath shall be filled with the breath of

353 An expression, of course, of the Nicene orthodox doctrine of the unity of the Son and the Father.

354 This extract is from a slightly later version of the same apocryphal *Evangelium.*

the Holy Spirit, so that he whom thou shalt baptize shall verily receive the Holy Spirit." All the hosts of heaven cried: "Amen! Alleluja!"

Ephraim the Syrian, *Comments on Peter*. Text. *Evangelii concordantis expositio facta a S. Ephraemo in Lat., transl.*, J. B. Aucher and G. Moesinger, 51 and 231–232. (Quoted by F. Haase, *op. cit.*, 168–169.)

He [Simon] was a timid man, because he was overcome by fear at the voice of a maid.[355] He was poor, because he could not even pay the tribute for himself, that was half a stater,[356] and he said: "Silver and gold have I none." [357] And he was foolish, because after he had begun to deny the Lord, he knew not how to escape by any pretext. . . .

And thus Simon, who was terrified by a maid, felt no terror at all at the Romans but with a stout heart adjured them to crucify him with his head downward toward the earth.[358] By night Simon denied, by day he confessed. By the burning coals he denied, by the burning coals he confessed. When he denied, the earth was witness; when he confessed, the earth and sea, each according to its nature, were present to witness.

Ibid. Text. *S. Ephraemi Syri Hymni et Sermones*, ed. and trans. into Latin by T. J. Lamy, I, 411–412, *Prolegomena*, LXXV.

Our Lord chose Simon Peter and appointed him chief of the apostles, foundation of the holy Church and guardian of his establishment. He appointed him head of the apostles

355 Mark, XIV, 66–70.

356 Matthew, XVII, 23–26 (Douay Version); 24–27 (King James Version).

357 Acts, III, 6.

358 *Supra*, p. 152.

and commanded him to feed his flock and teach it laws for preserving the purity of its beliefs. . . .

" Simon, my disciple, I have appointed thee as foundation of the holy Church; I have called thee ere this Peter, because thou shalt support all my building; thou art the overseer [359] of those who build for me my Church on earth; if they desire to build it in any way wrongly, do thou, the foundation, prevent them; thou art the head of the fountain from which my doctrine is drawn, thou art the head of my disciples; through thee I shall give drink to all nations; thine is that life-giving sweetness which I bestow; I have chosen thee to be as the first-born in my society and to become heir of my treasures; I have given thee the keys of my kingdom. Lo, I have made thee chief over all my treasures." [360]

4. The Imperial Confirmation of Roman Jurisdiction

The Roman Synod of 378, *Address to the Emperors Gratian and Valentinian II.* Text. G. D. Mansi, *Sacrorum Conciliorum Nova et Amplissima Collectio,* III, 624.

It is an extraordinary testimony to your glorious piety, most clement princes, that when we, an almost innumerable multitude, had gathered from the divers regions of Italy at the sublime altar of the Apostolic See and were considering what requests to make of you on behalf of the churches, we were not able to think of anything better than what you out of your spontaneous interest have already granted. We saw also that we should feel no shame at asking, that your

[359] Lamy's Latin rendering for this word is " inspector." It is, however, in Syriac the same which is used for " bishop."

[360] A Syrian hymn of this century derives from Peter the power of the priest to consecrate and ordain, as follows: " Simon took the fish which he had caught and offered them to the Lord. Our priest, through the power he has received from Peter, has taken virgins and innocents and offered them in the feast to the Lord of the feast." Quoted by F. Haase, *Apostel und Evangelisten in den orientalischen Überlieferungen,* p. 173.

bounties were not dependent upon petitions and that a series of imperial decrees stands already in our favor. As for the justice of this present petition, we succeeded long ago in obtaining the things we are now requesting but we still need to repeat our requests, for we have so entirely failed to secure the execution of the promises given to us that we now beg to have them given afresh. And while wicked miscreants, most clement emperors, are demonstrating their mad folly, may your righteousness feel increasing obligation to bestow your mercies often upon the Church!

For at first, filled with the divine spirit and, by the Lord's grace, pursuant to the commandment of the holy apostles, whose approval you hold in high esteem, you decided to restore the body of the Church, which the reckless Ursinus had torn asunder by his efforts to usurp honor beyond his merits. Then when he, the prime mover, had been condemned and the others who had joined him for love of disorder had been duly removed from that dangerous conspiracy, you agreed that the bishop of Rome should conduct the trial of the other bishops of the churches, so that the high priest of religion and his associates might judge concerning religion, for fear that disparagement might be done to the priestly office, if, as might frequently happen, a priest could anywhere be lightly subjected to the frivolous sentence of a profane judge.

. . . [The standards and methods of episcopal courts are different from those of secular courts and the former are better fitted to deal with questions of religion. They do not resort to torture.]

But Ursinus, although long since banished by your clemency's edict, is trying in secrecy, by means of those men whom he sacrilegiously and illegally ordained, to win over all the evil-minded. Some bishops, who unfortunately are still in the churches, have been incited by his example, to form a conspiracy of wicked insolence and argue lawlessly that they should not accept the judgment of the Roman bishop, even as men argue who know that by their deserts they should be condemned or as those who have been condemned appeal to a mob of the common populace and threaten their judges with terror of death. . . .

The bishop of Parma, deposed by our verdict, impudently retains his church. And Florentius of Pozzuoli, condemned and deposed, who then troubled your serene ears and procured a rescript to the effect that if he had been deposed by sentence of the priesthood of the city of Rome, there must be no resistance to the sentence, crept back after six years to his city, seized a church and by his audacity excited wild riots in the very town of Pozzuoli from which he had been driven out.

In Africa, your clemency ordered that the case of Restitutus [361] should be tried by the bishops. He should have submitted but instead he defiantly evaded the requirement of pleading his case.

In Africa also, you commanded that the sacrilegious second baptizers [362] should be expelled. After their expulsion, they ordained Claudian, who then came as a pseudo-bishop to create disturbance in the city of Rome. Contrary to the teachings of the Holy Scriptures, contrary to gospel law, he declares that all the bishops of past and present times have possessed no mysteries [363] but have been, as we might say, pagans. Your serenity has indeed ordered that he should be removed from Rome and returned to his own country. But disregarding this decree, he still remains, though often arrested, and does not hesitate to administer second baptism frequently to poor persons and freedmen, whom he bribes with money. He does harm rather through

[361] On Restitutus of Carthage, *vide supra,* p. 603.

[362] The descendants of the Donatists of Constantine's reign. *Supra,* pp. 450–453, 463 ff.

[363] *I.e.,* have had no valid sacraments.

his following than by his claim to a power which manifestly no man can bestow twice.

To crown all, the faction of Ursinus stirred up a few men, who had profaned the sacred mysteries by rejoining the synagogue, and caused them to aim at the life of our holy brother Damasus. The blood of innocents was shed and frauds were concocted which your pious oversight detected by an intuition almost divine. The church was despoiled of nearly all her ministers. It is easy to see how, by their stratagems, when he who has the office of judge in all disputes [364] heard the suit, there was no one competent to pass sentence on the lapsed nor on the seditious invaders of the episcopacy.

But since, by your serene judgment, the innocence of our honored brother Damasus has been proven, the truth has become plain and the fellow Isaac [365] has received his merited fate for his inability to substantiate his accusations. So now we beseech your clemency that we be not again harassed by numerous lawsuits. May your piety deign to enact that anyone who is condemned either by this court or by any of our catholic courts and who attempts illegally to retain his church or who, when summoned by sacerdotal authority, contemptuously refuses to appear, shall be summoned by officials of the State, the prefects of the prefecture of Italy or the vicar of the city of Rome, and come to Rome. If a situation of the kind occurs in a remote region, let the case be referred through the local tribunal to the metropolitan. If the offender is a metropolitan, he shall perforce come to Rome or else be directed to appear without delay before those whom the Roman bishop names as judges. In this way, men who have been deposed will be removed from

[364] *I.e.*, the city prefect, from whose court the case of Damasus was carried to the emperor Gratian.

[365] Isaac was the author of several theological treatises during his stay in the Church. J. P. Migne, *Patrologia Graeca*, Vol. XXXIII, p. 1541; G. Morin, *Revue d'Histoire et de Littérature Réligieuse* (Paris, 1899), Vol. IV, pp. 97 *sqq.*; L. Duchesne, *Early History of the Christian Church*, Vol. II, p. 371, n. 2.

the places in which they were priests and not usurp again impudently the post of which they have been rightfully deprived. However, if the metropolitan or any of the bishops are suspected of partiality or prejudice, let an appeal be granted either to the bishop of Rome or to a council of fifteen bishops of the vicinity. Whoever is sentenced to exclusion, let him be still and submit. But if he does not respect the judgment of God, then let him be coerced, so that we may live in peace and concord with due thankfulness to our Lord and ascribe the safety of the people to your serenity.

Our honored brother Damasus, whose case furnishes proof of your judgment, should not be put in a position inferior to those to whom he is officially equal, whom he excels in the prerogative of his Apostolic See and who are subject to the public courts from which your edict has removed him, our priestly head. After your decision in his case, he did not refuse your judgment but seeks to keep the honor you conferred upon him. For in the realm of civil laws, what life can be better protected than that which depends upon the judgment of your clemency? In any matter also affecting the exalted person of a bishop, provision should be made by strict ecclesiastical ordinances that not names only but characters should be taken into consideration and a scandalmonger who endeavors to asperse a high dignitary should be prevented from injuring one of impregnable innocence. An attack upon religion should be left to its ministers.

Hear then this request, which the holy Damasus desires to refer to your piety rather than to execute himself and which is intended not to disparage anyone but to confer upon the emperors what is in idea nothing new and accords with the example of the ancients, namely, that a Roman bishop, if his case is not within the competence of an assembly of his fellow bishops, may defend himself before the court of the emperor. Bishop Silvester, when accused by sacrilegious men, carried his case to your predecessor Constantine. Similar instances are mentioned in the Scriptures. When the holy apostle was imprisoned by a servant, he appealed unto Caesar and was sent to Caesar.[366] Your majesty should look into the case in advance and if there is any doubt, determine what points need investigation, that the judge may be required to follow the procedure you have deemed best and not allowed to act according to his arbitrary will. . . .

Gratian and Valentinian II, *Rescript of 378, Collectio Avellana,* 13. Text. *Corpus Scriptorum Ecclesiasticorum Latinorum,* XXXV, 54–58.

Gratian and Valentinian, Augusti, to the vicar Aquilinus.

[We wish to have our previous edicts enforced. The adherents of Ursinus have been ordered to withdraw to a distance of one hundred miles from Rome. You are to look up our letter of instructions with regard to them which we sent to your predecessor Simplicius.[367] Ursinus himself is now in prison at Cologne. Isaac has been dispatched to Spain, under pain of death if he makes more trouble. But we hear now from the council of bishops that Florentius of Pozzuoli, after a sentence of deposition, is still trying to stir up the Church and is holding unlawful meetings, relying on the indifference of the pagan magistrates for his immunity. Claudian from Africa is at Rome corrupting the faithful, in spite of our orders that he be returned. The schismatics have attacked " the most holy See " with shocking slanders and disturbed the people for whom the bishop " is hostage to the Deity." [368] Hereafter you will banish everyone guilty

[366] Acts, XXV, 11.

[367] This letter was perhaps the edict of 374, part of which is contained in *Codex Theodosianus,* IX, 29, 1.

[368] " Pro quo ille divinitati obses est."

of such abominable conduct to a distance of one hundred miles from Rome and see too that they are expelled from the towns where they are damaging the churches.]

11 It is furthermore our will that whoever is condemned by the judgment of Damasus, delivered with the counsel of five or seven bishops, or by judgment and counsel of the Catholics and attempts unlawfully to retain his church, or who when summoned to the ecclesiastical tribunal contumaciously refuses to appear, shall be arrested by the authority of the illustrious prefects of the prefectures of Gaul and Italy and sent to the episcopal court or remanded by the proconsuls and vicars to the city of Rome under escort. Or if any such case of insolent misbehavior occurs in regions at a distance, the entire conduct of that case shall be reserved for examination by the metropolitan bishop of the province. Or if the offender himself is a metropolitan, then perforce he shall go without delay to Rome or to such men as the Roman bishop appoints as judges, with the understanding, however, that whoever are deposed shall be excluded only from the confines of that city in which they were priests. For we punish leniently those who deserve severity and we requite their sacrilegious disobedience more mercifully than it merits. And if a metropolitan bishop or any other prelate is suspected of partiality or prejudice, the accused may appeal to the bishop of Rome or to a council of fifteen bishops of the vicinity, provided that after the trial has been concluded what was settled shall not be opened again. We desire also that the principle which natural justice has dictated to our minds in the conduct of minor business and the hearing of trivial cases should be applied much more thoroughly in cases of gravity, so that it may not be easy for a miscreant, notorious for depravity, to assume by foul slanders the rôle of plaintiff against a person of distinction or to offer testimony as witness in the accusation of a bishop.

5. The Faith of Rome Prescribed as the Standard for the East

Damasus, *Letter to the Eastern Bishops,* quoted by Theodoret, *Historia Ecclesiastica,* V, 10. Text. J. P. Migne, *Patrologia Graeca,* LXXXII, 1219–1222.

And when the renowned Damasus heard of the rise of this [Apollinarian] heresy, he announced the expulsion not only of Apollinarius but also of Timothy, his follower. And he informed the eastern bishops of it by a letter which I have thought valuable to insert in my history.

The letter of Damasus, bishop of Rome.[369]

" Since your love renders to the Apostolic See the reverence which is its due, do you, most honored sons, accept much for yourselves.

Even though we are within that holy church in which the holy apostle sat and taught us how we ought to guide the rudder which we have received, we confess nevertheless that we are unworthy of our honor. But for this very reason we strive with all our might, if perchance we may attain to the glory of his blessedness. Be then hereby informed that we have sometime since condemned Timothy, the unhallowed disciple of the heretic Apollinarius, with his impious doctrine, and we believe that what remains of him will obtain no consideration whatever henceforth. But if that old serpent, who has once and again been smitten, revives for his own undoing and continues without the Church, ceaselessly endeavoring to overthrow the faithless with his deadly poisons, do you still avoid him like a pestilence and be mindful of the faith of the apostles, that is, of that which was set down in writing by the Fathers at Nicaea. Do you abide on firm ground, strong in the faith and immovable, and permit hereafter neither your clergy nor your laity to listen

369 Written in 378.

to vain reasonings and idle speculations. For we have once for all furnished a pattern and he who knows himself a Christian may keep it. It was committed to us by the apostles, for the holy Paul says: "If any man bring you another gospel than that ye have received, let him be anathema."[370] Christ, the Son of God, our Lord, gave by his own passion abundant salvation to the race of man, that he might free from every sin the whole man beset by sins. Whoever says that he had less of humanity or less of divinity is inspired by the spirit of the devil and reveals himself as a son of Gehenna.

Why then do you ask me again for my condemnation of Timothy? Here, by judgment of the Apostolic See, in the presence of Peter, bishop of the city of Alexandria, he has been condemned, along with his teacher Apollinarius, who also in the day of judgment will undergo his merited punishments and torments. And if, acting like a man with hope, he is still deluding some unstable persons, although by demolishing his creed he has demolished his true hope in Christ, then there will perish with him in similar manner whoever wills to withstand the rule of the Church. God keep you in health, most honored sons!"

And the bishops who were assembled in great Rome wrote other letters against various heresies, which I have thought necessary to insert in my history. [There follows a series of anathemas against a long list of theological errors, said by Theodoret to have been sent by Damasus "to Bishop Paulinus[371] in Macedonia, when he was at Thessalonica."]

370 Galatians, I, 8.

371 Paulinus is probably Paulinus of Antioch. The communication may have been sent to him when he was on his way home from Rome, after the council of 382.

Gratian, Valentinian II and Theodosius, *Edict of February 27, 380, Codex Theodosianus,* XVI, 1, 2. Text. C. Mirbt, *Quellen zur Geschichte des Papsttums,* 4th ed., 134.

It is our will that all the peoples subject to the government of our clemency shall follow that religion which the holy Peter delivered to the Romans, as pious tradition from him to the present times declares it, and as the pontiff Damasus manifestly observes it, as also does Peter, bishop of Alexandria, a man of apostolic sanctity; that is, that in accordance with the apostolic teaching and gospel doctrine, we should believe in the deity of the Father and the Son and the Holy Spirit, of equal majesty, in sacred Trinity. Those who follow this law we order shall be included under the name of catholic Christians. All others we pronounce mad and insane and require that they bear the ignominy of teachers of heresy; their conventicles shall not receive the title of churches; they shall be chastised first by divine vengeance and then by the punishment of our indignation, with divine approval.

Theodoret, *Historia Ecclesiastica,* V, 2–3. Text. J. P. Migne, *Patrologia Graeca,* LXXXII, 1197–1201.

He [Gratian, on his accession to complete empire in 378] at once displayed the piety which he felt and offered the first fruits of his empire to the King of all. For he drew up an edict to the effect that the shepherds who had been driven out should be recalled and restored to their flocks and that the houses of God should be delivered to those who were in communion with Damasus. This Damasus was bishop of Rome, noted for his praiseworthy life, who aimed to speak and act always in defense of the doctrine of the apostles. After Liberius, he had succeeded to the administration of the church. And Gratian sent out with this edict Sapor, a general, a famous man of the time, and he instructed him to expel the preachers of the blasphemy of Arius, like wild beasts, from the sacred folds and to restore the good shepherds to God's flocks. And in every nation this was accomplished without dissension but in Antioch, the chief city of the East, a contest took place, as follows.

. . . [Account of the three parties that still existed in the churches of Antioch, led by Paulinus, Meletius and Apollinarius respectively.] . . . Then when the general Sapor arrived and published the imperial edict, Paulinus insisted that he was of the party of Damasus and Apollinarius made the same claim, concealing his heterodoxy. But the godly Meletius remained silent, allowing them to wrangle.[372] Then the sagacious Flavian, who was still at that time in the ranks of the priests,[372a] spoke first to Paulinus in the hearing of the general. "If, my friend, you receive the communion of Damasus, explain to us clearly how your doctrines agree. For although he acknowledges one substance in the Trinity, he unquestionably preaches three persons.[373] But you, on the contrary, deny the Trinity of the persons. Show us then how your doctrines are in unison and take the churches in accordance with the edict." So, having shut the mouth of Paulinus with this challenge, he turned to Apollinarius. "I am astonished that you, my friend, fight so viciously against the truth, when you know perfectly that the admirable Damasus declares that our nature was assumed in its entirety by God, the Word. But you persistently assert the opposite, for you deprive our intelligence of its salvation. If this charge against you is false, abjure now the strange doctrine you have invented,

372 Compare this with Jerome's picture of the situation, *supra*, p. 662.

372a Flavian succeeded Meletius as bishop in 381.

373 The Greek word is "hypostases." Paulinus was one of those conservative Nicenes who was unwilling to add to the unity of substance the Trinity of persons. *Supra*, p. 550.

profess the doctrine of Damasus and take the sacred buildings." Thus the wise Flavian with his truthful arguments silenced their flow of words.

Then Meletius, gentlest of all men, said in mild friendliness to Paulinus: "Seeing that the Lord of the sheep has committed to me the care of these sheep and you have received the charge of the rest and our little ones are in devout communion with one another, let us, my friend, unite our flocks and have done with the contest for the leadership. Let us feed our sheep together and minister to them together! And if there is jealousy over the central chair,[374] I will undertake to dispel that too. For I will lay the Gospel in that chair and let us seat ourselves on either side of it. If I am the first to reach the end of life, then you, my friend, alone shall hold the chief place. And if the end comes first to you, I in my turn, to the best of my power, will care for the sheep." So mild and friendly were the words of the godly Meletius. But Paulinus would not accept this proposal. And the general, who was judge of their conversation, delivered the churches to the great Meletius.

6. The Council of Constantinople and the Revival of Eastern Separatism

Damasus, *Epistolae,* V. Text. J. P. Migne, *Patrologia Latina,* XIII, 365–369.

Damasus to his dearly beloved brothers, Acholius, Eurydicus, Severus, Uranius, Philip and John.[375]

The reading of your loving letter, dearest brothers, has plunged me into deep sorrow, that at the very time when

[374] *I.e.,* the chair of the bishop in the center of the apse or chief place in the church.

[375] Acholius was bishop of Thessalonica. Eurydicus and the other four to whom this letter is addressed were probably also Macedonian bishops. The year is 380.

the heretics have been trodden down by the might of God, a deputation should come from Egypt with a demand contrary to the rule of church discipline, and endeavor to appoint a Cynic, an alien to our faith, to the bishopric of the city of Constantinople. What insanity, what astounding presumption, passing our comprehension! It makes clear how busybodies, who presume to do too much, fail to understand what they ought to do. They had not read the words of the apostle: "If a man have long hair, it is a shame to him."[376] They did not realize that the philosopher's habit does not become the appearance of a Christian. They had not heard the apostle's warning not to be spoiled of the robe of a sound faith by philosophy and vain deceits, in which they had long ago believed.[377] . . . Philosophy is the friend of the wisdom of the world but the enemy of faith, the poison of hope and the bitterest foe of love. What harmony is there between the temple of God and idols? What part has Christ in Belial?

But some will say perhaps: "He was a Christian." Never should the name of Christian be bestowed on one who wears the dress of an idol; it is not possible for one who aims thus to ingratiate himself with the heathen to have any fellowship with us in perfect faith. So it was fitting that the Egyptians should be denounced by everyone when they departed, condemning their own mistake, and that he then, with hair shorn and without any proper ordination, should both suffer the loss to his pate and fail to achieve his ambition. It was right that a wrong enterprise should be foiled by general authority.

For the next step, I hear that it has been decided to hold a council at Constantinople[378] and I urge you to put forth

376 I Corinthians, XI, 14. The Cynics let their hair and beards grow long. Their garb was a small pallium or cloak over a short tunic, somewhat less than ordinary clothing.

377 Colossians, II, 8.

378 The council of Constantinople of 381.

sincere efforts to have a bishop elected for that city who has nothing reprehensible about him, so that, by God's favor, the peace of the catholic priesthood may be confirmed unbroken and no controversies arise hereafter in the Church. . . . [I admonish you also not to allow your bishops to move from one city to another, contrary to the statutes of the Fathers.][379]

Damasus, *Epistolae,* VI. Text. J. P. Migne, *Patrologia Latina,* XIII, 369–370.

[To Acholius, bishop of Thessalonica. A short note added to the above to introduce Rusticus, the "silentiarius"[380] of the emperor Gratian, who had received baptism at Rome and was now going on a mission to Macedonia.]

Gregory of Nazianzus, *Poemata,* II, 2, xi, *Carmen de Vita Sua* (381), II, 562, *passim ad fin.* Text. J. P. Migne, *Patrologia Graeca,* XXXVII, 1067–1166.[381]

562. Nature hath not bestowed on us two suns
But she hath made two Romes, to be the lights
For all the world, an old power and a new,
Differing from one another, inasmuch
As one illumes the East and one the West,
But beauty matching beauty equally.

[379] Gregory of Nazianzus, whom the Catholics of Constantinople had already chosen as their bishop and who was of the party of Basil and Meletius, had been some time previously ordained bishop in the Asiatic town of Sasima and again at Nazianzus, although he had never served.

[380] The "silentiarius" of this period was a sort of privy councillor, one of the high court officials.

[381] This long, narrative poem, a sort of apologia for his career in Constantinople, was composed by Gregory upon his abdication from the see of that city and his withdrawal from the Council of 381. *Vide supra,* pp. 620–623.

The faith of her who hath been from of old
Even yet is steady, holding all the West
Firm in the doctrine of salvation;
So rightly she, who sitteth above all,
Adoreth all the harmony of God.[382]
But the new city, that once stood so fair,
(She I call mine, although no longer mine,)
Now lieth fallen in the depths of ruin.
For since that light town, brimming o'er with sins,
Alexandria, fever heat of folly,
Sent forth the abominable desolation,
Arius, . . .
We have walked divided over many roads. . . .

[Description of the dissensions in the eastern church over the dogma of the Trinity. The fiasco of the Cynic Maximus, the Alexandrian candidate for the see of Constantinople.]

856. Sages, unfold the event! To me it seems
Past comprehending, if no sage explain,
How Peter,[383] he the arbiter of bishops,
Who first acknowledged me with letters fit,
Free manifestly from duplicity,
As his own letters to me testify,
And honored me with tokens of my see,
Now sent to us a hart in place of maid.[384]
'Tis dark to me, it needs interpreter. . . .

[End of the affair of Maximus. Gregory's own work and preaching in the city. The arrival of Theodosius and

382 The Greek of these two lines, 571–572, is as follows:

Καθὼς δίκαιον τὴν πρόεδρον τῶν ὅλων
Ὅλην σέβουσαν τὴν Θεοῦ συμφωνίαν.

I.e., it is just that she who presides over all adores all the harmony of God. The allusion in the last phrase is, of course, to the orthodox doctrine of the Trinity.

383 Peter, metropolitan of Alexandria. *Supra*, p. 614.

384 The figure is taken from Agamemnon's substitution of a hart at Aulis for his daughter Iphigenia, whom he had sworn to sacrifice.

Gregory's installation, first by him and then by a council, on the episcopal throne.]

1514. Here [between Egypt and Constantinople] there presided a most holy man,
Simple in habit, artless, full of God,
Calm-eyed, a sign of courage and devotion
To all beholders, the Spirit's handiwork.
Who knows not him whom these my words depict,
The head over the church of Antioch, . . .
Who much hath suffered for God's Holy Ghost,
E'en if once led by alien hands brief while
Astray, now lit with grace of shining victories? [385]
These men ordained me in the sacred seat
Despite my cries and groans; yet one sole thought
Made me not quite refuse. Bear witness, Word!
What was it? It is wrong to hide the truth.
I thought in the vain fancying of my heart . . .
If I possessed the power of this seat
(For outward state adds much authority),
Like a conductor with two choruses,
Bringing both near together to himself,
One thus, one so, as is the chorus law,
I might make music out of foul discord. . . .
The bishops and the teachers of the people,
The givers of the Spirit, they who speak
From their high seats the words that save the world,
Who preach to all forever only peace
With voices that resound throughout the churches,
Against each other rage in bitterness,
Vociferating, marshalling their allies,
Blackening each other with fierce accusation,
Attacking, being vanquished in attack,

[385] Meletius. *Supra*, pp. 550, 553, 612.

Contending to be foremost to destroy,
And all for lust of dominance and rule,[386]
(How shall I cry these things aloud? What words?)
Till they have laid our universe in ruins,
As I said, when I first began my speech.
This schism between East and West is plain
A rift in thought more than in space and clime,
For they are joined midway, if not at ends.
But there is nought to join men split apart,
Not by their piety (though their pride pretends it,
Quick to deceive,) but by disputes for sees.[387] . . .

[Death of Meletius. Proposal in the council to elect another bishop to continue the opposition to Paulinus, the candidate at Antioch favored by the West. Gregory addresses the assembly, urging it to take this chance for peace, recognize Paulinus and at his death let the reunited people choose one bishop for them all.]

1635. ". . . And thus might come relief from many ills.
By this we win the stranger to our side,
A great thing (for the West seems now to me
A stranger), and by trying a new way,
Appease the city, that great, weary flock.
Oh end at last, oh end the world's long storm
And pity those now sorely rent asunder,
Those who are near their pain, those who come after!
Let no man hope to show what may befall,
If strife like this prevail for many years.
Our holy and most venerable faith
Hangs in suspense, whether it will be saved
Or perish in the wreckage of our wars. . . .

[386] The Greek for this line, 1556, is *Λύσσῃ φιλαρχίας τε καὶ μοναρχίας*.
[387] E.g., the quarrel as to who should be recognized as orthodox bishop of Antioch, Meletius or Paulinus.

Let us but yield a little and so reap
A greater victory, and be saved by God
And save the world now miserably destroyed!
To conquer is not glory in all fields.
A noble loss is better than base winning. . . ."

[Outcries follow Gregory's speech, and wrangling confusion.]

1690. Behold how marvellous their reasoning!
"Our practice must be guided by the sun.
Our leader must be taken from that land
Where God shone on us, clad in robe of flesh."
"So then, shall we be tied to circumstance
Nor know our leader is the flesh of Christ,
Firstfruit of all our race? What if he here
Was born," says one, "here likewise was the sin
By which he here so speedily was slain,
Whence came his rising and our own redemption!"
"Should not these disputants submit," I said,
"To those instructed ones who know the right?
We see hereby their arrogance throughout.
What is it that they need? Our sweet and fair
Wellspring of ancient faith, that joined in one
The nature worshipful of Triune God,
Of which Nicaea once became the school.
'Tis this I see disturbed and dark defiled
By surging floods of men of shifty minds. . . ."

[Sickened by the spectacle of insincerity, vulgar spite and selfishness, Gregory changes his dwelling-place to one farther from the church and plans to resign his office. His people entreat him to stay.]

1796. Thus they lamented but I still withstood.
And soon God sent the way for my release.

For lo! there came on hasty summons thither
The Macedonians and men of Egypt, framers
Of laws and of the mysteries of God,
Pelting us with the harsh wind of the West.
Then rose against them all the eastern throng,
Baring fierce teeth, like wild boars, for the fray
(If I may like it to some tragedy).
Looks full of fury, eyes aflame with fire,
They met in battle. In the thick of strife,
With passion more than reason in control,
They cast some sharp aspersions e'en on me,
Recalling rules now long ago outworn,[388]
Which chiefly meant that I, no doubt, was free.
Not that they wished me ill or aimed to take
My see for another; no, they sought to harm
Those who had given me the see, as plain
They told me in some secret messages.
They meant not to endure that lawless pride
Which showed itself in old and recent days.
I meanwhile, like a horse in tether fast,
Even while weak with suffering and disease,
Ceased not in mind to lash out with my feet
And neigh against my bondage and my reins,
Wild to escape to fields and solitude.
And when these men made charges, as I said,
I broke my bonds and joyous snatched the excuse. . . .

[Gregory begs the council to let him go. He has been their Jonah and if they keep him, there will be new trouble. From them he goes to Theodosius and asks permission to leave the office and the assembly.]

388 They recalled, apparently, the canons of previous councils, forbidding the translation of bishops from one see to another. *Supra*, pp. 498, 511 and n. 130. Gregory had been twice ordained before, to the sees of Sasima and Nazianzus, although he had never occupied the office in either place.

1893. ". . . Do thou impose on them concord and peace;
Bid them lay down their arms, e'en for thy sake,
If neither fear of God or hell suffice.
Erect a trophy for this bloodless fight,
Thou who hast quelled barbarians' dauntless might.
Demand of me," — I showed him my grey hairs
And drops of sweat that I had shed for God, —
" To endure and suffer in the whole world's stead.
Thou knowest my misery when they set me here." . . .

[Theodosius gives reluctant consent. Gregory tries before his departure to placate and reconcile everyone to his going.]

1945. What give I to the churches? All my tears.
For God has brought me to this, turned my life
And twisted it through many changing rounds.
What will befall them? Tell me, Word of God!
I pray they come to that serene abode
Where dwells my Trinity, that single flame,
In whose dim shadows we now rise and soar.

Council of Constantinople of 381, *Canons,* II and III. Text. C. J. Hefele, *Histoire des Conciles,* II, Pt. I, 21–27.

II. The bishops in charge of a diocese[389] are not to go to churches outside their own boundaries nor bring confusion into the churches but, as the canons prescribe,[390] let the bishop of Alexandria alone control the administration in Egypt and the bishops of the East govern the East alone, having regard for the privileges of the church of Antioch, which are mentioned in the canons of Nicaea; and let the

[389] The " diocese " here is the civil division of the Empire of the fourth century. There were five in the East, the diocese of Egypt, of which Alexandria was the capital, the diocese of the East with Antioch as chief city, the diocese of Asia with Ephesus, of Pontus with Caesarea in Cappadocia and of Thrace with at first Heraclea, then Constantinople.

[390] The sixth canon of Nicaea. *Supra,* p. 485.

bishops of the diocese of Asia have the management alone of affairs in Asia and the bishop of Pontus of affairs in Pontus and those of Thrace of affairs in Thrace. And let no bishops leave their diocese for ordinations or any other ecclesiastical functions, unless they be invited. If this canon concerning the diocese be observed, it is obvious that the synod of each province should regulate the business of that province in accordance with the decrees of Nicaea.[391] But the churches of God among heathen nations should be governed according to the practice which has prevailed since the Fathers.

III. Notwithstanding, the bishop of Constantinople shall have the preëminence in honor after the bishop of Rome, for Constantinople is New Rome.[392]

Theodoret, *Historia Ecclesiastica,* V, 8–9. Text. J. P. Migne, *Patrologia Graeca,* LXXXII, 1212–1217.

And the following summer [382], the majority of them [the eastern clergy] met again in that city [Constantinople], for the needs of the Church brought them together once more, and they received a synodical letter from the bishops of the West, inviting them to go to Rome, because a great council was being assembled there. But they excused themselves from the long journey on the ground that nothing would be gained by it. And they sent a letter describing the storm that had overtaken their churches and hinting that the Westerners had been indifferent to it. And they inserted in their letter a summary of the apostolic faith. The letter itself will demonstrate plainly the fortitude and wisdom of the writers.

391 The fifth canon of Nicaea defined the rights of provincial synods. There were several provinces in each diocese.

392 This canon was included by Gratian in his *Concordantia,* dist. XXII, c. 3, but to it was added the note: "This canon is one of those which the Apostolic See of Rome at first and for a long time afterwards refused to accept." The phrase here translated "the preëminence in honor" is, in the Greek, τὰ πρεσβεῖα τῆς τιμῆς. For comment on it *vide supra,* p. 624 and n. 290.

"The holy synod of the orthodox bishops who have assembled in the great city of Constantinople, to their honored lords and most reverend brothers and fellow ministers, Damasus, Ambrose, Britton, Valerian, Acholius, Anemius, Basil[393] and the other holy bishops who have assembled in the great city of Rome, greeting in the Lord.

It is probably superfluous to offer information to your reverences, as if you were ignorant, or to rehearse to you the multitude of the sufferings inflicted upon us by the power of the Arians. For we do not believe that your piety regards what befalls us as so trivial a matter that you need to be told of the sorrows with which you must be sympathizing; nor were the tempests that engulfed us so light as to escape your notice. The time of our persecutions is still recent, so that their memory is fresh not only for those who suffered but also for those who in love made the sufferers' pain their own. . . . [A brief reminder of their tribulations in the past and of the persistent activity of heretics in the churches.]

You have, however, shown your brotherly love toward us and have invited us by the letters of our most devout emperor, as if we were your own members, to the synod which, by God's will, you are convening at Rome, for although we were once condemned to endure buffeting alone, now that our rulers are agreed with us in religion, you will not reign without us but we are to reign with you, as the apostle says. Our desire was, if it had been possible, for us all as a body to leave our churches and gratify our longing for you instead of attending to their necessities. But who will give us the wings of a dove that we may fly away and be at rest with you? Such a proceeding would leave the churches totally unprotected, just as they are beginning

393 Valerian was bishop of Aquileia and Anemius of Sirmium, Acholius, as we know, of Thessalonica. The sees of Britton and Basil are unknown.

to recover, and the journey would be quite unfeasible for most of us. For we have come as far as Constantinople in compliance with the letter sent last year from your honors to the most religious emperor Theodosius, after the council at Aquileia. We prepared ourselves only to come as far as Constantinople and we have brought the endorsement of the bishops who remained in the provinces for this council only. We neither foresaw the need of any longer journey nor did we hear anything of it before we met at Constantinople. Beside all this, the shortness of the interval allowed has given us no time to prepare for a longer expedition or to send word to all the bishops of our communion in the provinces and obtain their endorsements.

Since then these considerations and many more besides have prevented most of us from coming, we have taken the next best step to further the general reconstruction and prove our love to you by urging our revered and honored fellow ministers and brothers, bishops Cyriacus, Eusebius and Priscian, to undertake happily the journey to you. Through them we shall make clear to you that our purpose is for peace and bent upon unity and that our zeal is for the right faith. . . . [A statement of loyalty to the creed of Nicaea, followed by a condemnation of Sabellians, Arians and other heretics.]

This then in brief is our faith, which is preached by us without dissimulation. And you may be yet further satisfied regarding it, if you will deign to read the tome drawn up at Antioch by the synod which met there [394] and the one issued last year at Constantinople by the ecumenical council, in which we confessed our faith at greater length and to which we added a statement anathematizing the heresies which have been lately devised. . . . [In accordance with the rule of Nicaea, we have recently filled the places of several important bishops, ordained Nectarius at Constan-

394 The synod of 379, which accepted the Roman formula.

tinople in the presence of Theodosius, etc.] We request your reverences to rejoice with us over what we have lawfully and canonically accomplished. . . .

7. The Rule of Damasus in the West

Marcellinus and Faustinus, *De Confessione Verae Fidei . . . Preces Valentiniano, Theodosio et Arcadio,* 77–85, *Collectio Avellana,* II. Text. *Corpus Scriptorum Ecclesiasticorum Latinorum,* XXXV, 28–30.[395]

. . . Moreover, even in the city of Rome, what bitter persecutions have been directed against the faithful! There the blessed bishop Aurelius, who held communion with the most blessed Gregory,[396] was several times assaulted; yet this holy man, though often mistreated, died a natural death. But the priest Macarius suffered worse injury at wicked hands. He was a priest in this same city of Rome, a man of extraordinary abstinence, who never cheered his stomach with wine nor invigorated his body with a dish of meat but softened his harsh diet only with oil and spent himself in fastings and prayers. By the merits of his faith and austerity, indeed, he won the grace of the Holy Spirit, so that he cast out demons from the bodies of persons possessed. We have said this much of his life and character that it may be plain how impious they are who do not allow such men to live within the Roman Empire.

At this time, a cruel persecution was raging against us, instigated by that extraordinary archbishop, Damasus, and faithful priests were forbidden to gather freely by day the holy congregations of the people to worship Christ as God. So, because under these circumstances the sacraments of our

[395] This petition was presented to the emperors at Constantinople in 383 or 384.

[396] Gregory of Granada in Spain, who belonged to the Luciferian or austere party.

salvation had to be administered at unusual hours or else stealthily, this holy priest Macarius was keeping vigils in a certain house, gathering the brotherhood together, so that the holy people might confirm their faith by divine lessons, at least at night. But the devil, who favors the wicked because the wicked favor the devil, would not endure to have the divine sacraments celebrated even in concealment. The clergy of Damasus ere long set a trap and when they discovered that the priest Macarius was keeping sacred vigils with his people, they burst into the house with officers and scattered the unresisting people and seized the priest and would not lead him away but dragged him over the stones in such a manner as to inflict a fearful wound on his head and the next day they haled him before the judge as one guilty of a grave crime. Then the judge, on the strength of an imperial rescript, attempted to compel and browbeat him to come to an agreement with Damasus. But the priest remembered the judgment of God and feared not the judge before him and spurned the communion of the perfidious Damasus and was therefore ordered into exile.

But when he was at Ostia, he died from the brutality of his wound. Such was his holiness that even the bishop of that town, Florentius by name, who was in communion with Damasus, held him in reverence. For when the brothers had buried him in a certain ancient tomb, Florentius would not allow him to lie there, in what seemed an unbecoming sepulchre, but transferred him from that place and buried him in the basilica of the martyr Asterius, where he lies in the presbytery, in a fitting tomb. So by this service Florentius strove to separate himself as far as he could from the crime of Damasus.

Let your serenity consider this! If you are willing that such offenses should be committed within the Roman Empire by men who are prevaricators against the holy and the faithful, have you no dread that the flood of the faithful will weigh down the Roman Empire? This same Damasus has assumed royal authority and attacked other catholic priests and laymen and sent them into exile, conducting his suits through pagan lawyers, with the judges showing him partiality, although your edicts were issued against heretics, not against Catholics, and Catholics who did not desert the true faith even under heretical emperors but suffered much oppression. Even of late he has tried to persecute cruelly the blessed bishop Ephesius, the fervent disciple of the holy faith, who was ordained for the unpolluted people of Rome by the steadfast bishop Taorgius, himself a man of unspotted faith. Through his lawyers he cited them before the judge Bassus,[397] invidiously describing them by a false name, accusing them under the title of Luciferians. But Bassus, who once revered the catholic faith, knew that there was no heretical corruption in Lucifer; was well aware, in fact, that he had endured ten years of exile for the catholic faith. And in his firm uprightness he overruled the accusations of Damasus, refusing to take steps to persecute men who were catholic and sound in faith and stating positively that the edicts of the emperors were plainly directed against heretics only, not against those who kept the holy faith without concern for the world. Then, for the first time, Damasus blushed, because one judge had been found who righteously interpreted and executed the imperial edicts.[398]

Priscillian, *Liber ad Damasum Episcopum.* Text. Ed. by G. Schepss, *Corpus Scriptorum Ecclesiasticorum Latinorum,* XVIII, 34–43.

Although the catholic faith, that possesses the way of a creed given by God, aims rather at the glory of belief than

[397] This Bassus was city prefect in 382.

[398] The text of this petition is followed by an imperial order to one Cynegus, that the petitioners, who are evidently catholic, should be permitted to worship in peace. *Corpus Scriptorum Ecclesiasticorum Latinorum,* Vol. XXXV, pp. 45–46.

of speech, because things that rely upon their own truth require no skill in interpretation, as the apostle says: "Avoid contentions of the law,"[399] nevertheless we are overborne by the necessity which the injustice of Bishop Hydatius has imposed upon us, even though we have always followed the course of patience and have endeavored to endure rather than resort to action. And we are glad that the situation has reached the point where we must state our belief to you, who are the senior of us all and who after acquiring experience of life have arrived, by aid of blessed Peter, to the glory of the Apostolic See, and that we must fulfil before you the faithful words of the apostle, who says: "With the heart we believe to justification and with the mouth confession is made unto salvation."[400] . . . [A description of the author's whole life as peaceloving, quiet and faithful.]

Then, in the episcopal council which was held at Saragossa, not one of our number was held guilty, not one was accused, not one condemned, no charge of wrong thought or life was brought against us, no one, I will not say felt bound, but even cared to produce any complaint. Some admonition was given there by Hydatius, as if he were instituting a rule for the conduct of life. No one of us was reprimanded by that, for your letter against evildoers had great authority with us, in which you had bidden us by the gospel precepts to pass no sentence on men in their absence and without a hearing. . . . [Statement of creed, followed by an account of the trouble created through and over Hydatius.]

But we, who do not fail in a matter of faith to prefer the judgment of saints to that of the world,[401] have come to Rome with resentment against no man but asking this one thing, that we might come to you first, so that our silence

399 Titus, III, 9.

400 II Corinthians, IV, 13.

401 Hydatius had shortly before this appealed to the emperor Gratian for support in his conflict with the Priscillianists. *Supra,* p. 609.

might not be interpreted as fears of conscience, and that we might present a statement setting forth what has occurred and, more important than all else, the catholic faith in which we live. . . .

Therefore, we entreat your reverence, if the faith which we profess is clear before God and in harmony with that which you transmit as a bequest to you from the apostles, if the testimonies of our churches, written in letters of peace, are in your possession, if we neither can nor should believe differently regarding the Scriptures, if no one, not even as a layman,[402] has been condemned on the proof of any charge brought against him, — although the priesthood is no cover for crime and a priest may be deposed who, as a layman, already deserves condemnation, — we implore you to give us audience, — because you are senior and first over all, — and to summon Hydatius to confront us. And if he believes he can prove something against us, he will not lose the crown of eternal priesthood, if he pursues the zeal of the Lord to the end.[403] Or if in your innate benevolence you wish to threaten no one with the injustice which he has inflicted upon us, we beg you to send letters to your brothers, the bishops of Spain. For we all ask, in order to prevent any injustice, that a council should be convened and Hydatius summoned, so as to decide upon the guilty to their faces and try no one unheard. . . . [We desire no harm to anyone and are willing to forgive Hydatius. We ask only an investigation.]

402 *I.e.*, no member of the clergy has been convicted of any offense for which a layman would be punished by the civil law.

403 I Esdras, IX, 7.

Damasus, *Epistolae,* VIII. Text. C. T. G. Schoenemann, *Pontificum Romanorum Epistolae Genuinae,* 402.

Bishop Damasus to his most beloved son, Jerome, greeting in the Lord.[404]

I have been reading the commentaries in Greek and Latin on the interpretation of the gospels, which have been written both in the past and recently by our own, that is, orthodox scholars, and find that they offer not only different but actually contrary explanations of the phrase: "Osanna to the Son of David!" It is your duty, beloved, to clear away conjectures and expose ambiguities with your ardent and strenuous intelligence and write us the genuine meaning, — what it is in Hebrew, — so that for this as for many other services we may give you earnest thanks in Christ Jesus.

Damasus, *Epistolae,* IX. Text. *Op. cit.,* 403–404.

Damasus to his most beloved son, Jerome.

You are drowsy and have been reading for a long time now rather than writing, so I have decided to send you some small questions to arouse you, — not because you ought not to read, for reading is the daily food on which speech lives and waxes fat, but because the fruit of your reading is your writing. Yesterday, when you sent my messenger back, you said you had no letters ready but those which you composed some time ago in your hermitage[405] and which I have read and pondered with utmost attention. But you sent word besides that you might write letters by working secretly at

404 This and the following letter were written during the years 383–384, after Jerome's return to Rome in the train of Paulinus to attend the Synod of 382. The answers are found in Jerome's *Epistolae,* XX and XXXVI.

405 *I.e.,* during his stay in the Syrian desert. Jerome had sent Damasus from Constantinople his treatise on the Seraphim.

night, if I wished. I gladly accept your offer of what I had determined to request, even if you refused it. Nor do I think that any kind of conversation or discussion would be more fitting for us than talk about the Scriptures, that is, that I should ask questions and you should answer. No other life, in my opinion, would be happier under the sun; such food of the soul is sweeter than all honey. "How sweet," says the prophet, "are thy words unto my taste! sweeter than honey to my mouth!"[406] For since, as our chief orator says, we men differ from beasts in that we can speak,[407] how praiseworthy is he who outdoes other men in that gift by which mankind excels the beasts!

So gird up your loins and resolve for me the problems I here set you, observing moderation in both directions, that my questions may not lack solutions nor your letters brevity. I must admit to you that I do not enjoy the books of Lactantius which you gave me a while ago, because many of his letters run on to a thousand lines and they seldom deal with our doctrine. In consequence, their length begets weariness in the reader. Those that are short are of more interest to schoolmen than to us, for they treat of metres and the situation of countries and philosophers.[408]

1 What means the line in Genesis: "Whosoever slayeth Cain, shall suffer vengeance sevenfold?"[409]

2 If God made everything very good, why did he lay on Noah the command for the clean and the unclean beasts,[410] when nothing good can be unclean? And in the New Testament, after the vision had been shown to Peter and he said: "Far be it from me, Lord; for nothing common or unclean has ever entered into my mouth," the voice from heaven answered: "What God hath cleansed, that call not thou common."[411]

406 Psalms, CXVIII (King James' Version, CXIX), 103.
407 Cicero, *De Oratore,* I, 8.
408 For Damasus' opinion of philosophy, *vide supra,* p. 678.
409 Genesis, IV, 15. 410 Genesis, VII, 2. 411 Acts, X, 14, 15.

3 Why does God say to Abraham that in the fourth generation the children of Israel shall return out of Egypt[412] and Moses later write: "Now in the fifth generation the children of Israel went out of the land of Egypt."[413] This, certainly, unless it may be explained, seems like a contradiction.

4 Why did Abraham receive circumcision as a sign of his faith?[414]

5 Why was Isaac, a just man, dear to God, deceived so that in error he blessed not the son he chose but the son he did not choose?[415]

412 Genesis, XV, 16.
413 Exodus, XIII, 18.
414 Genesis, XVII, 10–14, 23–27.
415 Genesis, XXVII, 21–35.

APPENDIX I

The Decretal of Siricius to Himerius of Tarragona

Two months after the death of Damasus, on February 10, 385, his successor, Siricius, wrote a letter to Himerius, bishop of Tarragona in Spain, in reply to one which Himerius had sent to Damasus, reporting certain abuses and scandals in the churches of his province. This was not the first of the series of papal executive orders to go out in the form of letters, addressed to this or that bishop or group of bishops, prescribing regulations for the conduct of their flocks. Siricius himself refers to one issued by Liberius to expedite the general recovery from the effects of the Council of Rimini.[1] But it is the earliest of these so-called decretals, *epistolae decretales,* which has come down to our time.

For that reason it seems appropriate to append it to the documents in this book, not because of the information it contains as to monasticism and the clerical orders in the fourth century, but because it illustrates, perhaps, the type of letter that Liberius may have written and in certain of its phrases foreshadows the development of papal executive and legislative power in the stage next beyond that to which we have traced it. Whether this development had in point of fact been anticipated by Liberius or Damasus we cannot be sure. We see only that Siricius, in taking up, as he says, the responsibilities of Damasus, assumes the right to make ordinances for the metropolitans and clergy of the West and classes the statutes of the Apostolic See and the venerable canons of the councils together as laws of which no priest of the Lord may be ignorant. He is writing, one must note, for western churches only, as far as his explicit directions

[1] *Supra,* p. 551. Both Liberius and Damasus had sent instructions to individual communities in the East as well as in the West.

go,[2] but his West includes Spaniards and Gauls and Carthaginians in provinces far beyond Italy.

The decretal itself is more than the instructions of a senior bishop to his junior colleagues on ways to remedy evils in congregations under their authority. In several of its provisions it goes behind the local bishop and metropolitan altogether and establishes relations by its own authority directly with the lesser clergy, monks and laity of these distant regions. The local bishop is for the moment merely the organ of communication between the chief shepherd and the sheep. All priests are to keep the rules or be "plucked from the solid, apostolic rock upon which Christ built the universal Church." Offenders are "deposed by authority of the Apostolic See from every ecclesiastical position which they have abused."

The source of Siricius' authority is Peter, although he likes, whenever possible, to find further support for it in Paul. But it is Peter, mystically present in his heirs, the bishops of Rome, who protects and watches over them in their care of his ministry. In a later letter, to the bishops of Africa, Siricius mentions a gathering of prelates held in the Vatican, "by the relics of the holy apostle Peter, through whom both the apostolate and the episcopate had their beginning in Christ."[3] All bishops then have a share in Peter's powers. In another letter, to the bishop of Thessalonica, he declines to interfere in a case which could be competently handled by the local, episcopal tribunal.[4] But to a unique extent the spirit of Peter is in that see which beyond all others is "apostolic," to which "belong the daily supervision and unceasing care of all the churches." When other authorities weaken or fail it is there as the church's rock foundation.

[2] One of Siricius' later letters is addressed "to the orthodox in divers provinces." *Epistolae*, VI.

[3] *Epistolae*, V.

[4] *Epistolae*, IX.

Siricius, *Epistolae,* I. Text. C. T. G. Schoenemann, *Pontificum Romanorum Epistolae Genuinae,* 408–416.

Siricius to Himerius, bishop of Tarragona.

1 The report, my brother, which you sent to our predecessor, Damasus of holy memory, found me already installed in his seat, for so the Lord has ordained. On reading it carefully in the assembly of the brethren, we discovered as many points in it that deserved rebuke and correction as we hoped to find worthy of praise. And since we must assume the labors and responsibilities of him whose honor we have assumed, by God's grace, now that the requisite notice has first been given of our elevation, we will not deny you a full reply to each detail of your inquiry, as the Lord deigns to inspire us. For in view of our office we have no right to dissemble and none to keep silence, since it is our duty more than anyone's to be zealous for the Christian faith.[5] We bear the burdens of all who are heavy laden; nay, rather, the blessed apostle Peter bears them in us and protects and watches over us, his heirs, as we trust, in all the care of his ministry.

2 Now, on your front page you wrote that many who had been baptized by the impious Arians were eager to join the catholic faith and that some of our brothers proposed to baptize them a second time. This is not permissible, for the apostle forbids the practice,[6] the canons prohibit it [7] and the decrees that were sent out to the provinces by Liberius, my predecessor of venerable memory, after the nullification of the Council of Rimini condemn it. Such persons, along with the Novatians and other heretics, we receive into the con-

[5] In a later letter "to the orthodox in divers provinces," Siricius says: "And I, upon whom rests the care of all the churches, if I dissemble, shall hear the Lord saying:" etc. *Epistolae,* VI.

[6] Ephesians, IV, 5.

[7] For the canon of Arles, *vide supra,* p. 482.

gregation of Catholics, as it was prescribed in the synod, by simply the invocation of the sevenfold Spirit, with the imposition of the bishop's hand. All the East and the West keep this custom. You too henceforth ought not to deviate from this path, if you do not wish to be cut off from our college by sentence of our synod.

3 Next, you mention the reprehensible confusion, demanding correction, that exists among your candidates, who are baptized just as each one pleases. Our fellow priests, — we say this with indignation, — are presuming to act in this way not on the ground of any authority but solely out of carelessness. Uncounted multitudes, you state, everywhere and freely, at the season of Christ's Nativity and Epiphany and also on the festivals of the apostles and martyrs, receive the mystery of baptism, although both with us and with all the churches this privilege is confined particularly to the Lord's days of Easter and of Pentecost. On these days only, throughout the year, should the sacrament of baptism in general be administered to persons coming into the faith and only those should be selected who have presented their names forty days or more beforehand and have purified themselves by exorcisms and daily prayers and fastings, so that the precept of the apostle may be fulfilled, that the old leaven be purged out and then the new lump begun.[8] Yet although we say that the reverence due to holy Easter should be nowise diminished, we also desire that babes who for their youth are not yet able to speak and persons in any extremity who need the sacred wave of baptism should be succored with all speed, lest we risk the destruction of our own souls by denying the font of salvation to those who seek it and someone may depart from this world and lose the kingdom and life. If then any persons are involved in the peril of shipwreck, the raid of an enemy, the dangers of a siege or any desperate

[8] I Corinthians, V, 7.

state of bodily illness and ask for solace by the one aid of faith, let them receive the reward of regeneration for which they beg at the very moment they wish it. Let your errors hitherto in this respect be sufficient! Now let all your priests observe the rule here given, unless they wish to be plucked from the solid, apostolic rock upon which Christ built the universal Church.

4 You add also that some Christians have strayed into apostasy, — the mention of which is sin, — and have polluted themselves by the worship of idols and the contamination of sacrifices. We command you to cut them off from the body and blood of Christ, by which they were once redeemed in the new birth. If ever by chance they repent and turn to mourning, they shall do penance [9] as long as they live and at their last end obtain the grace of reconciliation, for, as the Lord teaches us, we desire not the death of the sinner but that he should be converted and live.[10]

5 As regards the marriage ceremony, you inquire if a man may take in wedlock a girl betrothed to another. We forbid this absolutely, for the blessing which the priest bestows upon her before her marriage is like a sacrilege among the faithful, if it is marred by any such dishonor.

6 You also thought proper, beloved, to consult the Apostolic See over those persons who, after doing penance, have returned like dogs and swine to their former vomit and wallow and have hungered again for the soldier's belt, the pleasures of the games, new marriages and forbidden adulteries, whose admitted incontinence is betrayed by the children begotten after their absolution. For such persons, who no longer possess the remedy of penance, we have thought best to decree that they may join in church with the faithful in prayer only, but that they may be present at the holy celebration of the mysteries, even though they are not worthy. They shall, however, be excluded from

[9] Agenda poenitentia est.

[10] Ezechiel, XVIII, 23.

the feast of the Lord's table, so that while suffering at least from this restriction, they may chasten themselves for their sins and furnish an example to others to deter them from wanton desires. Yet, inasmuch as they fell through frailty of the flesh, we bid you succor them with the gift of the viaticum, through the grace of communion, when they start on their way to the Lord. We think you should follow this rule with women also, who after penance have yielded to similar pollution.

7 Furthermore, you state that there are monks and nuns who have cast aside their resolution to be holy and are sunk so deep in licentiousness that after first meeting stealthily under cover of the monasteries in illicit and sacrilegious passion, they have then on a sudden through despair of conscience begotten children freely in these illicit relations, a thing condemned both by civil law and by the rules of the Church. We direct you to expel these shameless and abominable persons from the company of the monasteries and the congregations of the churches, that they may be thrown into the jails and mourn their terrible crime with constant lamentation and burn with the purifying fire of repentance, so that mercy may help them, at least in death, out of pure compassion, with the grace of communion.

8 Let us now proceed to the most holy orders of the clergy, who, we learn upon your information, beloved, are so oppressed and demoralized throughout your provinces, to the injury of our venerable religion, that in the words of Jeremiah we might say: "Who will give water to my head or a fountain of tears to my eyes? And I will weep day and night for this people."[11] If the blessed prophet says that his tears cannot suffice to bewail the sins of the people, how great must be the grief that smites us when we are forced to deplore the crimes of those who are a part of our body, especially since, as blessed Paul says, to us belong the

[11] Jeremias, IX, 1.

daily supervision and unceasing care of all the churches! "For who is weak and I am not weak? Who is offended and I do not burn?"[12] For we are told that many priests and Levites of Christ, after long years of consecration, have begotten offspring from their wives as well as in disgraceful adultery and that they are defending their sin on the ground that we read in the Old Testament that priests and ministers were allowed the privilege of begetting children.

9 Now let any man who is addicted to lust and inculcates vice explain to me why, if he thinks that in the law of Moses the Lord relaxed occasionally the reins on loose living for the priestly orders, the Lord also instructed those to whom he was committing the holy of holies, saying: "Be ye holy, even as I, your Lord God, am holy."[13] Why were the priests bidden to take up their dwelling in the temple, far from their homes, during their year of service? Why but for the purpose that they might have no carnal intercourse even with their wives but in the radiance of an upright conscience offer an acceptable gift unto God? When their time of service was fulfilled, they were permitted association with their wives but solely for the sake of progeny, because it had been commanded that no man from any tribe but that of Levi should be allowed in the ministry of God.

10 Now the Lord Jesus, when he illumined us by his appearing, declared in the gospel that he was come to fulfil the law, not to destroy it.[14] And so he desired that the Church, whose bridegroom he is, should have her visage shining with the splendor of chastity, that in the day of judgment, when he comes again, he might find her without spot or blemish, as he ordained by his apostle.[15] Hence all we priests and Levites are bound by the unbreakable law of those instructions to subdue our hearts and bodies to soberness and modesty from the day of our ordination, that

[12] II Corinthians, XI, 29.
[13] Leviticus, XX, 7.
[14] Matthew, V, 17.
[15] Ephesians, V, 27.

we may be wholly pleasing to our God in the sacrifices which we daily offer. " They that are in the flesh," says the vessel of election, " cannot please God. But ye are now not in the flesh but in the Spirit, if so be that the Spirit of God dwelleth in you." [16] And where but in holy bodies, as we read, can the Spirit of God have a dwelling-place?

11 Inasmuch as some of the men of whom we speak protest sorrowfully, as your holiness reports, that they fell in ignorance, we direct you not to refuse them mercy, on condition that they remain as long as they live, without any advancement in honor, in the office in which their guilt was detected, provided, however, that they undertake to live in continence hereafter. As for those who unwarrantably rely upon the excuse of the privilege which they maintain was granted them by the old law, let them understand that they are deposed by authority of the Apostolic See from every ecclesiastical position which they have abused and that never again may they handle the venerable mysteries, of which they deprived themselves by clinging to their obscene passions. And inasmuch as present warnings teach us to be on our guard in the future, if any bishop, priest or deacon is hereafter discovered in such crime, as we trust there will not be, let him now and at once understand that every way to leniency through us is barred, for wounds that do not heal by fomentation must be cut out by the knife.

12 We learn, furthermore, that men of untrammelled and unknown lives, who have had many wives, are aspiring to the aforesaid offices in the Church, just as they fancy For this we do not blame so much those who obtain these positions through immoderate ambition as the metropolitan bishops in particular, who connive at unlawful aims and despise the commandments of our God, as far as in them is. We pass in silence over our deeper suspicions but where is that ordinance of our God, established when he gave the

[16] Romans, VIII, 8–9.

law through Moses, saying: " My priests shall marry but once "? And in another place: " A priest shall take a virgin to wife, not a widow, nor one that was put away, nor a harlot." [17] Following this, the apostle who changed from persecutor to preacher charged both the priest and the deacon that they should be the husbands of one wife.[18] But all these precepts are scorned by the bishops of your districts, as if they rather meant the opposite. Now we must not overlook transgressions of this kind, lest we be smitten by the just voice of the indignant Lord, saying: " Thou sawest the thief and wentest with him and wast a partaker with adulterers." [19] Therefore we here by general announcement decree what must henceforth be observed by all the churches and what must be avoided.

13 Whoever then vows himself to the service of the Church from his infancy should be baptized before the years of puberty and given a share in the ministry of the readers. If he lives honorably from the period of adolescence to his thirtieth year and is content with one wife, one whom he receives as a virgin through the priest with the general benediction, he should be made an acolyte and a subdeacon. If thereafter he maintains the level of his previous continence, he should receive the rank of deacon. If then he performs his ministry commendably for more than five years, he should appropriately be granted the priesthood. Finally, after ten more years, he may rise to the episcopal chair, if through all this time he is approved for uprightness of life and faith.

14 He who is already of adult years when his change to a better mind prompts him to leave the laity for the sacred army, shall attain the fruit of his desire only upon condition that immediately after his baptism he join the band of readers or exorcists, provided also that he be known to have had

[17] Leviticus, XXI, 13–14; Ezechiel, XLIV, 22.
[18] I Timothy, III, 2.
[19] Psalms, XLIX, 18 (King James' Version, L, 18).

or to have but one wife and to have taken her as a virgin. When such a man has been initiated and has served for two years, he shall for the next five years be acolyte and subdeacon and thus be promoted to the diaconate, if during this period he is judged worthy. Then, in the course of time, he may for his deserts win the priesthood and the bishopric, if the choice of the clergy and the people lights upon him.

15 If any member of the clergy marries a widow or else a second wife, he shall at once be stripped of every privilege of ecclesiastical rank and admitted to lay communion only. This he may still receive on condition that he commit no offense later for which he should lose it.

16 We do not allow women to be in the houses of clergy, save only those whom the Council of Nicaea permitted to dwell with them for bare purposes of necessity.

17 We expect and desire that monks of high reputation for the soberness of their characters and the holy manner of their lives and faith should join the ranks of the clergy. Those under thirty years of age should be promoted through the lower orders, step by step, as time passes, and thus reach the distinction of the diaconate or the priesthood with the consecration of their maturer years. They should not at one bound rise to the height of the episcopate until they have served out the terms which we have just prescribed for each office.

18 It is right also that we should rule that even as no member of the clergy is admitted to penance, so too no layman after penance and reconciliation may obtain the honor of clerical office. For although such men have been cleansed from the stain of all their sins, yet they ought not to take up the implements for administering the sacraments, after having once themselves been the vessels of vice.

19 And forasmuch as the one excuse of ignorance is offered for all these offenses which have come to us for re-

buke and we on our part must in clemency forgive that out of sheer piety, every penitent, every twice-married, every husband of a widow, who has undeservedly and wrongfully forced his way into the sacred army, shall understand that we grant him pardon on this condition, that he reckon it a great boon to lose all hope of promotion but to remain in perpetual security in the rank in which he now is. But the chief bishops of all the provinces shall know henceforth that if they undertake again to raise any such person to the sacred ranks, a fitting sentence will needs be pronounced both on them and on those whom they promote contrary to the canons and to our prohibition.

20 We have, I think, dearest brother, disposed of all the questions which were contained in your letter of inquiry and have, I believe, returned adequate answers to each of the cases which you reported by our son, the priest Bassianus, to the Roman church as to the head of your body. Now we do once and again urge you, brother, to bend your mind to observing the canons and keeping the decretals that have been ordained. Do you bring these decisions we are sending you to the knowledge of all our fellow bishops and not only of those who are stationed within your diocese. Send our salutary instructions to all the Carthaginians and Baeticians,[20] Lusitanians [21] and Gallicians also and to those who live in the provinces bordering yours on either side, with an accompanying letter from you. And whereas no priest of the Lord is free to be ignorant of the statutes of the Apostolic See and the venerable provisions of the canons, it may be even more expedient and a very glorious distinction for you, beloved, and for your ancient bishopric, if the general letter which I have written to you individually is brought to the attention of all our brothers through your earnest

20 Baetica was a province of southern Spain, including the present Andalusia and a part of Granada.

21 Lusitania was western Spain, including the modern Portugal and parts of the Spanish provinces of Estremadura and Toledo.

diligence. In this way the salutary ordinances we have made, not inadvisedly but prudently, with utmost care and deliberation, may continue unviolated and all opportunity for excuses, which we can no longer admit from anyone, may be closed in the future.

Dated the eleventh of February, in the consulship of Arcadius and Bauto.[22]

22 A.D. 385.

APPENDIX II

The Liberian Catalogue

It seems advisable to insert in a Second Appendix the list of Roman bishops from Peter to Liberius contained in the Compendium of 354,[1] thereby completing as far as possible our collection of all the important documentary material bearing on the rise of the See through the age of Damasus. This list, commonly known as the Liberian Catalogue from the name of the bishop under whom it was produced, is of little or no value as a record until it reaches the third century. The names of the first bishops are unquestionably derived from earlier, second century lists, such as those of Irenaeus and Hegesippus. One of these lists gave the name of the predecessor of Clement as Anacletus, another as Cletus. The compiler who drew upon them, seeing the two forms, mistook them for the names of two men and thus inserted an extra bishop. He also moved them both to places after Clement, with the idea apparently of bringing Clement nearer to Peter to accord better with the Clementine legend.[2] In the third century, the construction of chronological tables to include the terms of Roman bishops together with the consular Fasti and the reigns of emperors seems definitely to have begun. It was possible at that time to ascertain the years of most of the bishops of that century. But one of these chronographers, unwilling to have his pontifical list precise only toward the end, went back and added years and dates for all the previous episcopates, of which the names solely had survived. The confusion obvious in our text in the dates given for the pontificates of the period of persecution in the middle of this century is probably due, in part, at least, to the blunders of a later copyist, who entered under one name the date that belonged under another. For the latter part of the third century and the opening of the

[1] *Supra*, pp. 104–105.

[2] *Supra*, pp. 85, n. 63, 159, 164. *Vide* Lightfoot, *Apostolic Fathers*, Pt. 2, Vol. I, pp. 261 ff.; Kidd, *History of the Church to A.D. 461*, Vol. I, pp. 125 ff.

fourth these figures are the most trustworthy that we have.[3] The whole catalogue went through more than one process of re-editing at the hands of its continuators before its final emergence as we have it, during one of which processes the months and days were suffixed to the years of the bishops from first to last. It was probably not much before 354 that Peter himself was given the title of bishop and set definitely in the position of head of the episcopal line.[3a]

Text. Ed. by Th. Mommsen, *Monumenta Germaniae Historica, Auctores Antiquissimi,* IX, *Chronica Minora,* I, 73 *sqq*.

In the reign of Tiberius Caesar, our Lord Jesus Christ suffered under the constellation of the Gemini, March 25, and after his ascension the blessed Peter undertook the episcopate. From his time, in due order of succession, we give everyone who has been bishop, how many years he was in office and under what emperor.

Peter, 25 years,[4] 1 month, 9 days, was bishop in the time of Tiberius Caesar and of Gaius and of Tiberius Claudius and of Nero, from the consulship of Minucius and Longinus (A.D. 30) to that of Nero and Verus (55). He suffered together with Paul, June 29, under the aforesaid consuls, in the reign of Nero.

Linus, 12 years, 4 months, 12 days, was bishop in the time of Nero, from the consulship of Saturninus and Scipio (56) to that of Capito and Rufus (67).

Clement, 9 years, 11 months, 12 days, was bishop in the time of Galba and of Vespasian, from the consulship of Tracalus and Italicus (68) to the sixth of Vespasian and first of Titus (76).

3 On this obscure period, *vide supra,* p. 442.

3a On the significance of this *vide supra,* pp. 65–66.

4 On the twenty-five year episcopate of Peter *vide supra,* p. 105.

Cletus,[5] 6 years, 2 months, 10 days, was bishop in the time of Titus and at the commencement of Domitian, from the eighth consulship of Vespasian and fifth of Domitian (77) to the ninth of Domitian and first of Rufus (83).

Anaclitus,[6] 12 years, 10 months, 3 days, was bishop in the time of Domitian, from the tenth consulship of Domitian and first of Sabinus (84) to the seventeenth of Domitian and first of Clement (95).

Aristus,[7] 13 years, 7 months, 2 days, was bishop at the end of Domitian and in the time of Nerva and of Trajan, from the consulship of Valens and Verus (96) to that of Gallus and Bradua (108).

Alexander, 7 years, 2 months, 1 day, was bishop in the time of Trajan, from the consulship of Palma and Tullius (109) to that of Velianus and Vetus (116).

Sixtus, 10 years, 3 months, 21 days, was bishop in the time of Adrian, from the consulship of Niger and Apronianus (117) to the third of Verus and first of Ambibulus (126).

Telesforus, 11 years, 3 months, 3 days, was bishop in the time of Antoninus Macrinus, from the consulship of Titianus and Gallicanus (127) to that of Caesar and Balbinus (137).

Higinus, 12 years, 3 months, 6 days, was bishop in the time of Verus . . . from the consulship of Gallicanus and Vetus (150) to that of Presens and Rufinus (153).

Pius, 20 years, 4 months, 21 days, was bishop in the time of Antoninus Pius, from the consulship of Clarus and Severus (146) to that of the two Augusti (161). While he was bishop, his brother Ermes wrote a book,[8] in which is contained the message that an angel gave him, when he came to him in the guise of a shepherd.[9]

[5] In the oldest lists Cletus succeeds Linus. *Supra*, pp. 249, 268.

[6] Another form of the name Cletus. Two bishops have been made out of one. *Supra*, p. 709.

[7] Or Evaristus.

[8] On Hermas and his book, *The Shepherd*, *vide supra*, p. 242.

[9] The name of Anicetus is lacking here. He should follow Pius.

Soter, 9 years, . . .[10] 3 months, 2 days, was bishop in the time of Antoninus and of Commodus, from the consulship of Verus and Herenianus (171) to that of Paternus and Bradua (185).

Victor, 9 years, 2 months, 10 days, was bishop in the time . . .[11] of Antoninus, from the consulship of Saturninus and Gallus (198) to that of Presens and Extricatus (217).

Calixtus, 5 years, 2 months, 10 days, was bishop in the time of Macrinus and of Eliogabalus, from the consulship of Antoninus and Adventus (218) to the third of Antoninus and first of Alexander (222).

Urbanus, 8 years, 11 months, 12 days, was bishop in the time of Alexander, from the consulship of Maximus and Elianus (223) to that of Agricola and Clementinus (230).

Pontianus, 5 years, 2 months, 7 days, was bishop in the time of Alexander, from the consulship of Pompeianus and Pelignianus (231). At that time, the bishop Pontianus and the priest Ypollitus were transported into exile to Sardinia, to the island Vocina, in the consulship of Severus and Quintianus (235), and in the same island he died, September 28,[11a] and in his place Antheros was ordained, November 21, in the aforesaid consulship (235).

Antheros, one month, 10 days. He fell asleep, January 3, in the consulship of Maximus and Africanus (236).

Fabius, 14 years, 1 month, 10 days, was bishop in the time of Maximin and of Gordianus and of Philip, from the consulship of Maximin and Africanus (236) to the second of Decius and first of Gratus (250). He suffered, January 21.[11b] He divided the regions among the deacons and ordered many buildings to be erected in the cemeteries. After

[10] Only the first three words in this paragraph belong to the notice of Soter's episcopate. After the lacuna, it continues with the notice of Eleutherus, whose name is omitted.

[11] The latter part of Victor's notice and the first of Zephyrinus' have disappeared.

[11a] On Hippolytus and Pontianus, *vide supra*, pp. 297, 299.

[11b] On Fabianus, *vide supra*, p. 313.

his passion, Moses and Maximus, the priests, and Nicostratus, the deacon, were seized and thrown into prison. At that time, Novatus arrived from Africa and drew away Novatian and certain confessors from the Church;[12] afterwards Moses died in prison, where he had continued 11 months and 11 days.

Cornelius, 2 years, 3 months, 10 days, from the fourth consulship of Decius and second of Decius (251) to that of Gallus and Volusianus (252). While he was bishop, Novatus ordained Novatian outside the church in the city of Rome and Nicostratus in Africa. Thereupon the confessors, who had withdrawn from Cornelius with Maximus the priest, who was with Moses, returned into the church. After this, they were banished to Centumcellae. In that place, he fell asleep with glory.

Lucius, 3 years, 8 months, 10 days, was bishop in the time of Gallus and of Volusianus until the third consulship of Valerian and second of Gallienus (255). He was an exile and afterwards, by the will of God, he returned in safety to the church,[12a] . . . March 5, in the aforesaid consulship.

Steffanus, 4 years, 2 months, 21 days, was bishop in the time of Valerian and Gallienus, from the consulship of Volusianus and Maximus (253) to the third of Valerian and second of Gallienus (255).[13]

Xystus, 2 years, 11 months, 6 days, began his bishopric in the consulship of Maximus and Glabrio (256) to that of Tuscus and Bassus (258) and he suffered August 6 [13a] . . . from the consulship of Tuscus and Bassus (258) to July 21, in the consulship of Aemilianus and Bassus (259).

12 This and the references in the next paragraph are to the Novatianist schism. *Supra*, pp. 340–341, 348 ff.

12a On Lucius *vide supra*, p. 389.

13 A comparison of the consular dates given for Stephen with those given for Lucius, Xystus and Dionysius shows much confusion in reckoning. The text may be corrupt.

13a On Xystus II and his martyrdom, *vide supra*, p. 420.

Dionisius, 8 years, 2 months, 4 days, was bishop in the time of Gallienus, from July 22, in the consulship of Aemilianus and Bassus (259), to December 26, in the consulship of Claudius and Paternus (269).

Felix, 5 years, 11 months, 25 days, was bishop in the time of Claudius and of Aurelian, from the consulship of Claudius and Paternus (269) to the second consulship of Aurelian and first of Capitolinus (274).

Eutycianus, 8 years, 11 months, 3 days, was bishop in the time of Aurelian, from the third consulship of Aurelian and first of Marcellinus (275) to December 7 in the second consulship of Carus and first of Carinus (283).

Gaius, 12 years, 4 months, 7 days, was bishop in the time of Carus and Carinus, from December 17, in the second consulship of Carus and first of Carinus (283), to April 22, in the sixth of Diocletian and second of Constantius (296).

Marcellinus,[14] 8 years, 3 months, 25 days, was bishop in the time of Maxentius, from his tenth consulship and the first sixth consulship of Diocletian and second of Constantius (296), to the ninth consulship of Diocletian and eighth of Maximian (304). At that time, there was a persecution and the bishopric was empty 7 years, 6 months, and 25 days.

Marcellus, one year, 6 months, 20 days, was bishop in the time of Maxentius, from his tenth consulship and the first of Maximian until after the tenth consulship and seventh (309).

Eusebius, 4 months, 16 days, from April 18 to August 17.

Miltiades, 3 years, 6 months, 8 days, from July 2, in the eighth consulship of Maximian alone, that was in the month of September, in the consulship of Volusianus and Rufinus (311), to January 11, in that of Volusianus and Annianus (314).

Silvester, 21 years, 11 months, was bishop in the time of Constantine, from the consulship of Volusianus and

[14] On the problem of Marcellinus and Marcellus, *vide supra*, pp. 443–445.

Annianus (314), January 31, until January 1, in the consulship of Constantius and Albinus (335).

Marcus, 8 months, 20 days, and he was bishop in the time of Constantine, in the consulship of Nepotianus and Facundus (336), from January 18 to October 7 in the aforesaid consulship.

Julius, 15 years, 1 month, 11 days, was bishop in the time of Constantine, from the consulship of Felicianus and Titianus (337), February 6, to April 12, in the fifth of Constantius and first of Constantius Caesar (352). He erected many buildings: the basilica on the Via Portuese, at the third milestone; the basilica on the Via Flaminia, which is called the basilica of Valentinus, at the second milestone; the basilica Julia, which is in the seventh region, near the forum of the divine Trajan; the basilica across the Tiber, in the fourteenth region, near (the basilica of) Callistus; the basilica on the Via Aurelia, at the third milestone, near (the cemetery of) Callistus.[15]

Liberius, . . . was bishop in the time of Constantius and Constantius, from May 22 to . . . , from the fifth consulship of Constantius and first of Constantius Caesar (352).

15 On Julius *vide supra*, p. 488 and n. 98.

THE POPES OF THE FIRST FOUR CENTURIES

Chronological List of Popes

I.	Peter	XXI.	Fabianus (236–250)
II.	Linus	XXII.	Cornelius (251–253)
III.	Cletus	XXIII.	Lucius (253–254)
IV.	Clement I	XXIV.	Stephen I (254–257)
V.	Anencletus	XXV.	Xystus II (257–258)
VI.	Evaristus	XXVI.	Dionysius (259–268)
VII.	Alexander	XXVII.	Felix I (269–274)
VIII.	Xystus I	XXVIII.	Eutychianus (275–283)
IX.	Telesphorus	XXIX.	Gaius (283–296)
X.	Hyginus	XXX.	Marcellinus (296–304)
XI.	Pius I	XXXI.	Marcellus (308–309)
XII.	Anicetus	XXXII.	Eusebius (309 *or* 310)
XIII.	Soter	XXXIII.	Miltiades (311–314)
XIV.	Eleutherus	XXXIV.	Silvester (314–335)
XV.	Victor	XXXV.	Marcus (336)
XVI.	Zephyrinus	XXXVI.	Julius I (337–352)
XVII.	Callistus I	XXXVII.	Liberius (352–366)
XVIII.	Urbanus I	XXXVIII.	Felix II (355–358)
XIX.	Pontianus (230–235)	XXXIX.	Damasus (366–384)
XX.	Anteros (235–236)	XL.	Siricius (384–399)

INDEX

DATE DUE

DEMCO 38-297